John Ogdoni.

22. Wymondley Road.
            Hitchin   Herts.   SG4 9PN.

GW00542189

TRACE ELEMENT METABOLISM IN ANIMALS

Assistant Editors

I. BREMNER
J. K. CHESTERS
J. QUARTERMAN

Trace Element Unit,
Nutritional Biochemistry Department,
Rowett Research Institute, Bucksburn, Aberdeen

TRACE ELEMENT METABOLISM IN ANIMALS

Proceedings of
WAAP/IBP International Symposium
Aberdeen, Scotland, July 1969

General Editor

C. F. MILLS

Head of Department of Nutritional Biochemistry
Rowett Research Institute, Bucksburn, Aberdeen

E. & S. LIVINGSTONE

EDINBURGH AND LONDON

1970

ISBN 0 443 00713 6

PREFACE

THE study of trace element metabolism and function and the nature of disorders arising from trace element deficiency and excess in man and other animals is a field of scientific endeavour which cuts right across the conventionally accepted boundaries of biochemistry, physiology, nutrition and human and veterinary medicine. At the early meetings, during which the ideas for this Symposium first took shape, it was agreed that one of the most important factors responsible for the slow application of knowledge of the importance of the trace elements in the nutrition of domesticated animals and man was the inadequacy of existing opportunities to discuss recent research findings and to consider the limitations of existing knowledge. It was agreed that steps should be taken to promote an interdisciplinary meeting at which the opportunity would be provided for discussion of these topics. It rapidly became apparent that this proposal to hold a Symposium on Trace Element Metabolism in Animals had generated widespread interest and it became obvious that the objectives of the meeting would best be served by making it truly international in character. In recognition of this international character the co-sponsors of the Symposium thus became the International Biological Programme and the World Association for Animal Production.

The meeting had two main objectives; firstly, to provide a forum in which recent progress in studies of the metabolism and functional roles of the trace elements could be discussed, and secondly, to provide the opportunity for an interchange of ideas between workers investigating these fundamental aspects of the biological function of the trace elements and those whose task it is to apply their findings in the fields of nutrition and human or veterinary medicine. These aims were chosen because of the belief of the organizers that from a meeting of this nature could come a concentration of effort on those problems which today so often prevent us from clearly recognizing the existence of disorders arising from trace element deficiency or excess and prevent us from making a clear quantitative assessment of the requirements of animals for many of the trace elements.

This International Symposium was held in Aberdeen in July 1969. The proceedings of this conference, including the discussions following many of the scientific contributions, have been edited and are collected in this volume. Most of the 154 invited participants were active workers in the field under review and as a result the Symposium was vigorous and the discussions concise.

Due to circumstances beyond the Organizing Committee's control it is regrettable that coverage of recent work on chromium and cobalt is incomplete but, with these exceptions, this volume presents a picture of the state of existing knowledge and emphasizes points of growth and conflict in the study of trace element metabolism and utilization.

To assist rapid publication the proofs of papers and records of the discussions were not generally circulated to participants for correction and the General Editor therefore accepts full responsibility for any errors or omissions.

The preparation of this volume would have been a much more difficult task without the help of Drs I. Bremner, J. Quarterman and J. K. Chesters who acted as assistant editors and without the advice of Mr R. B. Williams who acted as Symposium treasurer. We are indebted to Mr W. Morton for his meticulous work in preparing tape recordings of all discussions, to Miss E. S. Davidson and Mrs J. Webster who bore the immense task of transcribing the proceedings and to Mr T. D. Bell who prepared the index. Finally we are pleased to acknowledge the help of the staff of the School of Agriculture, University of Aberdeen who acted as hosts for the meeting and to thank the staff of Messrs E. and S. Livingstone for their help and encouragement during the preparation of this volume for publication.

To Beryl and Caroline I would like to add a personal apology for those occasions during the past two years when I have been found thinking abstractedly of Symposium affairs at times when my thoughts should have been elsewhere. To a wife and to a daughter I express sincere thanks for the patience and encouragement which did so much to make my own participation in this meeting so enjoyable.

C. F. MILLS

Aberdeen, 1970   General Editor

Local Organizing Committee

Dr C. F. MILLS (Chairman)
Dr J. QUARTERMAN (Secretary)
Mr R. B. WILLIAMS (Treasurer)
Dr K. L. BLAXTER
Dr R. L. MITCHELL

Secretariat: WAAP/IBP Trace Element Symposium,
c/o The Rowett Research Institute,
Bucksburn, Aberdeen, Scotland,
AB2 9SB.

Parent Committee

Dr C. F. MILLS (Chairman)	U.K.
Dr J. VAN DER GRIFT	Holland
Dr G. N. HAVRE	Norway
Professor M. KIRCHGESSNER	West Germany
Professor A. SPÄIS	Greece

LIST OF PARTICIPANTS

AMMERMAN, C. B., Department of Animal Science, Nutrition Laboratory, University of Florida, Gainesville, Florida, 32601, U.S.A.

ANDREW, C. S., (CSIRO), Cunningham Laboratory, Mill Road, St Lucia, Queensland, Australia.

ANKE, M., Institut für Tierernährung der Friedrich-Schiller-Universität, Jena, Dornburger Strasse 24, Jena, G.D.R.

ARCHER, F. C., Soil Science Department, National Agricultural Advisory Service, Ministry of Agriculture Fisheries and Food, Kenton Bar, Newcastle-on-Tyne, U.K.

ASTRUP, H. N., Animal Nutrition Department, Agricultural College of Norway, Vollebekk, Norway.

BAALSRUD, N.-L., Veterinaer, Vormsund, Norway.

BELL, M. C., University of Tennessee, AEC Agricultural Research Laboratory, 1299 Bethel Valley Road, Oak Ridge, Tennessee, U.S.A.

BERROW, M., Macaulay Institute for Soil Research, Craigiebuckler, Aberdeen, AB9 2QJ, U.K.

BIENFET, V., Faculté de Médecine Vétérinaire de l'État, Cureghem-Bruxelles 7, 45, Rue des Vétérinaires, Belgium.

BINOT, H., Faculté de Médecine Vétérinaire de l'État, Cureghem-Bruxelles 7, 45, Rue des Vétérinaires, Belgium.

BLAXTER, K. L., Rowett Research Institute, Bucksburn, Aberdeen, AB2 9SB, U.K.

BLOKHINA, Rosalia I., Vernadsky Institute of Geochemistry and Analytical Chemistry, USSR Acadaemy of Sciences, 47, Vorobyevskoe Shosse, Moscow, U.S.S.R.

BREMNER, I., Rowett Research Institute, Bucksburn, Aberdeen, AB2 9SB, U.K.

BURNS, K. N., Agricultural Research Council, 160 Great Portland Street, London, W.1., U.K.

BURRIDGE, J. G., Macaulay Institute for Soil Research, Craigiebuckler, Aberdeen, AB9 2QJ, U.K.

CAMBEROS, H. R., Division of Biological Sciences, University of Florida, 220 William Bartram Hall, Gainesville, 32601, Florida, U.S.A.

CHESTERS, J. K., Rowett Research Institute, Bucksburn, Aberdeen, AB2 9SB, U.K.

CREHAN, M. P., Colborn Vitafeeds Ltd, 54/56 Garmoyle Street, Belfast, N. Ireland, U.K.

CUTHBERTSON, Sir David, Department of Pathology, Glasgow University and Royal Infirmary, Castle Street, Glasgow, C.4, U.K.

DALGARNO, A. C., Rowett Research Institute, Bucksburn, Aberdeen, AB2 9SB, U.K.

DEÁN-GUELBENZU, M., Facultad de Farmacia, Departamento de Bioquimica, University of Madrid, Spain.

DE KOCK, P. C., Macaulay Institute for Soil Research, Craigiebuckler, Aberdeen, AB9 2QJ, U.K.

DESAI, I. D., Division of Human Nutrition, University of British Columbia, Vancouver, Canada.

DEWAR, W. A., Agricultural Research Council, Poultry Research Centre, West Mains Road, Edinburgh 9, U.K.

DIPLOCK, A. T., Royal Free Hospital School of Medicine, Department of Biochemistry, 8 Hunter Street, London, W.C.1, U.K.

ELLISON, H., Croda Agricultural Ltd., Berkshire House, 168–173 High Holborn, London, W.C.1, U.K.

LIST OF PARTICIPANTS

ELMES, Margaret E., Physiology Department, Medical Biology Centre, The Queen's University of Belfast, BT9 7BL, N. Ireland, U.K.

EVERSON, Gladys J., Department of Home Economics, The University of Texas at Austin, Austin, Texas 78712, U.S.A.

VAN DER FEIJST, TH., Agricultural Bureau for Trace Elements, Arnhem, Steenstraat 44, Holland.

FELL, G. S., Pathological Biochemistry Department, Royal Infirmary, Glasgow, C.4, U.K.

FERNANDEZ, D., North of Scotland College of Agriculture, University of Aberdeen, 581 King Street, Aberdeen, AB9 IUD, U.K.

FIGUEROA, Vilda, Instituto de Ciencia Animal, Calle 30 No. 761, Nuevo Vedado, La Habana, Cuba.

FLEMING, G. A., Irish Agricultural Institute, Soils Division, Johnstown Castle Agricultural College, Wexford, Eire.

FLODH, H., Institut für farmakologi, Veterinärhögskolan, S-104 05 Stockholm 50, Sweden.

FLORENCE, E., Rowett Research Institute, Bucksburn, Aberdeen, AB2 95B, U.K.

FORTH, W., Institut für Pharmakologie und Toxikologie des Universität des Saarlandes, 665 Homburg/Saar, W. Germany.

GANTHER, H., Department of Biochemistry, School of Medicine, Reynolds Building, Belknap Campus, University of Louisville, Kentucky 40208, U.S.A.

GARCÍA-AMO, Carmen, Departamento de Bioquimica, Facultad de Farmacia, University of Madrid, Spain.

GARTNER, R. J., Animal Research Institute, Yeerongpilly, 4105, Queensland, Australia.

GODWIN, K. O., Division of Nutritional Biochemistry, CSIRO, Kintore Avenue, University of Adelaide, South Australia.

GRASSMANN, E., Institut für Tierernaährung, 8050 Friesing-Weihenstephan, München, W. Germany.

HADJIMARKOS, D. M., University of Oregon Dental School, Portland, Oregon 97201, U.S.A.

HALL, G. A., Department of Veterinary Pathology, P.O. Box 147, Liverpool L69 3BX, U.K.

HALL, T., Cavendish Laboratory, Free School Lane, Cambridge, CB3 9JF, U.K.

HANNAN, J., Department of Veterinary Medicine, University College, Dublin, Veterinary College of Ireland, Dublin 4, Eire.

HANSARD, S. L., University of Tennessee, Department of Animal Husbandry-Veterinary Science, P.O. Box 1071, Knoxville, Tennessee 37901, U.S.A.

HARTLEY, W. J., Department of Veterinary Medicine, Sydney University, P.B. Camden, N.S.W., Australia.

HARTMANS, J., Instituut voor Biologisch en Scheikundig Onderzoek van Landbouwgewassen, Wageningen, Bornsesteeg 65/67, Postbus 14, Holland.

HAVRE, G. N., Institutt for Biokjemi, Norgesveterinaerhøgskole, Oslo 4, Norway.

HEATON, F. W., Department of Biological Sciences, University of Lancaster, St Leonard's House, Lancaster, U.K.

HEMINGWAY, R. G., Glasgow University Veterinary School, Bearsden, Glasgow, U.K.

HEMPHILL, D. D., 1–43 Agriculture Building, University of Missouri, Columbia, Missouri 65201, U.S.A.

HEWITT, G. C., International Nickel Ltd., Thames House, Millbank, London, S.W.1, U.K.

HIDIROGLOU, M., Canadian Department of Agriculture, Animal Research Institute, Central Experiment Farm, Ottawa, Canada.

x

HILL, R., Department of Animal Husbandry and Hygiene, The Royal Veterinary College, University of London, Bolton's Park, Potters Bar, Hertfordshire, U.K.
HOEKSTRA, W. G., Department of Biochemistry, University of Wisconsin, Madison, Wisconsin 53706, U.S.A.
HORVATH, D. J., College of Agriculture and Forestry, Department of Animal Industry and Veterinary Science, Morgantown, West Virginia 26506, U.S.A.
HORVATH, Z., Allatorvostudományi Egyetem, Belgyógyászati Klinika, Budapest, VII, Landler Jenő u. 2, Hungary.
HOWELL, J. McC., Department of Veterinary Pathology, The University, Chatham Street, P.O. Box 147, Liverpool L69 3BX, U.K.
HSU, J. M., Veterans Administration Hospital, 3900 Loch Raven Boulevard, Baltimore, Maryland 21218, U.S.A.
HUSAIN, S. L., Department of Dermatology, Royal Infirmary, Glasgow, C.4, U.K.
IGLESIAS, A., Apdo, 24, San Jose de las Lajas, La Habana, Cuba.
ISHMAEL, J., Department of Veterinary Pathology, University of Liverpool, Chatham Street, P.O. Box 147, Liverpool L69 3BX, U.K.
JENKINS, G. N., Department of Oral Physiology, University of Newcastle Dental School, Markham Laboratories, Upper Claremont Street, Newcastle-on-Tyne NE2 4AJ, U.K.
JENKINS, K. J., Canada Department of Agriculture, Research Branch, Biochemistry Section, Animal Research Institute, Central Experimental Farm, Ottawa 3, Ontario, Canada.
JEPPERSEN, C., Department of Physiology, Bülawsvej 13, 1870 Copenhagen, Denmark.
JONES, D. I. H., Welsh Plant Breeding Station, Aberystwyth, Cardiganshire, U.K.
JONES, L. H. P., Grassland Research Institute, Hurley, nr. Maidenhead, Berks, U.K.
KAY, H. D., 2 Christchurch Gardens, Reading, Berks, U.K.
KEITH, M. C., Unilever Ltd., Greyhope Road, Aberdeen, U.K.
KENNEDY, Patricia M., Moredun Research Institute, 408 Gilmerton Road, Edinburgh EH17 7JH, U.K.
KERR, R. H. P., Colborn Vitafeeds Ltd., Barton Mills, Canterbury, Kent, U.K.
KIRCHGESSNER, M., Institut für Tierernährung, 8050 Friesing-Weihenstephan, München, W. Germany.
KNIGHT, A. H., Macaulay Institute for Soil Research, Craigiebuckler, Aberdeen AB9 2QJ, U.K.
KRATZER, F. H., Department of Poultry Husbandry, University of California, Davis, California 95616, U.S.A.
LAMOND, M., Centre de Recherches Zoot. et Vét., Theix, par Saint-Genès-Champanelle (63–Puy-de-Dôme), France.
LANNEK, N., Department of Medicine I, Royal Veterinary College, S–104 05 Stockholm 50, Sweden.
LANTZSCH, H.-J., Institut für Tierernährung, 7000 Stuttgart-Hohenheim, Postfach 62, W. Germany.
LASSITER, J. W., Department of Animal Science, University of Georgia, College of Agriculture, Athens, Georgia 30601, U.S.A.
VAN LEEUWEN, J. M., Institut voor Veevoedingsonderzoek, Keern 33, Hoorn, Holland.
LEKAREV, V., Vernadsky Institute of Geochemistry and Analytical Chemistry, U.S.S.R. Academy of Sciences, 47, Vorobyevskoe Shosse, Moscow, U.S.S.R.
LETUNOVA, Svetlana V., Vernadsky Institute of Geochemistry and Analytical Chemistry, U.S.S.R. Academy of Sciences, 47, Vorobyevskoe Shosse, Moscow, U.S.S.R.

LIST OF PARTICIPANTS

LEWIS, Gwyneth, Ministry of Agriculture, Fisheries and Food Central Veterinary Laboratory, New Haw, Weybridge, Surrey, U.K.

LLOYD, M. K., Ministry of Agriculture, Fisheries and Food Central Veterinary Laboratory, New Haw, Weybridge, Surrey, U.K.

LÖRCHER, K., Institut für Tierzucht und Tierernährung, der Freien Universität Berlin, 1 Berlin 33 (Dahlem), Brümmerstrasse 34, W. Berlin, W. Germany.

LOW, G., National Institute for Research in Dairying, Shinfield, Reading, U.K.

LUECKE, R. W., Department of Biochemistry, Michigan State University, East Lansing, Michigan 48823, U.S.A.

MACPHERSON, A., Chemistry Department, West of Scotland Agricultural College, Auchincruive, U.K.

MARIMON, B., Department of Biological Sciences, University of Lancaster, St Leonardgate, Lancaster, U.K.

MATRONE, G., Biochemistry Department, North Carolina State University, Raleigh, North Carolina 27607, U.S.A.

MCCONNELL, K. P., Department of Biochemistry, University of Louisville, School of Medicine, Luoisville, Kentucky 40202, U.S.A.

MCDONALD, D., North of Scotland College of Agriculture, University of Aberdeen, 581 King Street, Aberdeen AB9 1UD, U.K.

MILLER, E. R., Animal Husbandry Department, Michigan State University, East Lansing, Michigan 48823, U.S.A.

MILLER, W. J., University of Georgia, Dairy Science Department, L-P Building, Athens, Georgia 30601, U.S.A.

MILLS, C. F., Rowett Research Institute, Bucksburn, Aberdeen AB2 9SB, U.K.

MITCHELL, R. L., Macaulay Institute for Soil Research, Craigiebuckler, Aberdeen AB9 2QJ, U.K.

MOORE, D. R., Croda Agricultural Ltd., Berkshire House, 168–173 High Holborn, London, W.C.1, U.K.

MURRAY, J., University of Minnesota, Department of Medicine, Mayo Memorial Building, Minneapolis, Minnesota 55455, U.S.A.

OBERLEAS, D., Department of Medicine, Wayne State University, Detroit, Michigan Veterans Administration Hospital, Allen Park, Michigan 48101, U.S.A.

PALLAUF, J., Institut für Tierernährung, 8050 Friesing-Weihenstephan, München, W. Germany.

PANIĆ, B. R., Institute for the Application of Nuclear Energy in Agriculture, Veterinary Medicine and Forestry, Zemyn, Baranjska 15, P.O. Box 46, Yugoslavia.

PAVLOTSKAYA, F., Vernadsky Institute of Geochemistry and Analytical Chemistry, U.S.S.R. Academy of Sciences, 47, Vorobyevskoe Shosse, Moscow, U.S.S.R.

PEARCE, G. R., School of Agriculture, University of Melbourne, Parkville, Victoria 3052, Australia.

PERIGAUD, S., Centre de Recherches Zoot. et Vét., Theix, par Saint-Genès-Champanelle (63–Puy-de-Dôme), France.

POOLE, D. B. R., The Irish Agricultural Institute, Dunsinea, Castleknock, Co. Dublin, Eire.

PORIES, W. J., University of Rochester, Department of Surgery, 260 Crittenden Boulevard, Rochester, N.Y. 14620, U.S.A.

PORTER, H., New England Medical Center Hospital, 171 Harrison Avenue, Boston, Massachusetts 02111, U.S.A.

QUARTERMAN, J., Rowett Research Institute, Bucksburn, Aberdeen AB2 9SB, U.K.

RAETSKAYA, U., All-Union Research Institute in Animal Breeding, Dubrovitsky, Podolsk, Moscow region, U.S.S.R.

xii

LIST OF PARTICIPANTS

REINHOLD, J. G., Biochemistry Department, American University of Beirut, Lebanon.

REITH, J. W. S., Macaulay Institute for Soil Research, Craigiebuckler, Aberdeen AB9 2QJ, U.K.

RISH, M., 15, Maxim Gorky Boulevard, Samarkand State University, Samarkand, U.S.S.R.

SADIKOVA, I., Institute of Helminthology, 90, St. Novo-Cheremuskhinskaya, Moscow-259, U.S.S.R.

SAMOKHIN, V., All-Union Research Institute in Animal Breeding, Dubrovitsky, Podolsk, Moscow region, U.S.S.R.

SANTOS-RUIZ, A., Departamento de Bioquimica, Facultad de Farmacia, Universidad de Madrid, Spain.

SCHLEGEL, H., Deutsches Amt für Materiel- und Warenprüfung, 4201 Grossgräfendorf 75, Kreis Merseburg, G.D.R.

SCHÜRCH, A., Institut für Tierernährung, Eidg. Technische Hochschule, Universitätstrasse 2, 8006 Zürich, Switzerland.

SCHWARZ, K., Veterans Administration Hospital, 5901 East Seventh Street, Long Beach, California 90801, U.S.A.

SCOTT, R., Urological Department, Royal Infirmary, Glasgow, C.4, U.K.

SCOTT, R. O., Macaulay Institute for Soil Research, Craigiebuckler, Aberdeen AB9 2QJ, U.K.

SHARMAN, G. A. M., Rowett Research Institute, Bucksburn, Aberdeen AB2 9SB, U.K.

SINA, Mebrure, Bacteriology Institute, FAO, Sheep and Goat Diseases Laboratory, Pendik, Stanbul, Turkey.

SMITH, B. S. W., Moredun Research Institute, 408 Gilmerton Road, Edinburgh EH17 7JH, U.K.

SMITH, H., Department of Forensic Medicine, The University of Glasgow, Glasgow, W.2, U.K.

SOURKES, T. L., Department of Psychiatry, McGill University, 1033 Pine Avenue, Montreal, Canada.

SPENCER, Herta, Metabolic Section, Veterans Administration, Edward Hines Jr., Hospital, Hines, Illinois 60141, U.S.A.

STRAIN, W. H., University of Rochester, School of Medicine and Dentistry, 260 Crittenden Boulevard, Rochester, N.Y. 14620, U.S.A.

SURÁNYI, E., Department of Animal Nutrition, University of Veterinary Medicine, VII Rottenbiller U.50, Budapest, Hungary.

SUTTIE, J. W., Department of Biochemistry, College of Agricultural and Life Sciences, University of Wisconsin, Madison, Wisconsin 53706, U.S.A.

SUTTLE, N. F., Moredun Research Institute, 408 Gilmerton Road, Edinburgh EH17 7JH, U.K.

TELFER, S. B., North of Scotland College of Agriculture, University of Aberdeen, 581 King Street, Aberdeen AB9 1UD, U.K.

TERLECKI, S., Ministry of Agriculture Fisheries and Food, Central Veterinary Laboratory, New Haw, Weybridge, Surrey, U.K.

THOMPSON, J. K., North of Scotland College of Agriculture, University of Aberdeen, 581 King Street, Aberdeen AB9 1UD, U.K.

THORNTON, I., Imperial College of Science and Technology, Royal School of Mines, Prince Consort Road, London, S.W.7, U.K.

TODD, J. R., Ministry of Agriculture for Northern Ireland, Veterinary Laboratories, The Farm, Stormont, N. Ireland, U.K.

TÖLGYESI, G., Department of Animal Nutrition, University of Veterinary Medicine, Budapest VII, Rottenbiller U.50, Hungary.

xiii

LIST OF PARTICIPANTS

TOPPS, J. H., North of Scotland College of Agriculture, University of Aberdeen, 581 King Street, Aberdeen AB9 1UD, U.K.

TOUROUKANOVA, E., Vernadsky Institute of Geochemistry and Analytical Chemistry, U.S.S.R. Academy of Sciences, 47, Vorobyevskoe Shosse, Moscow, U.S.S.R.

TRINDER, N., National Agricultural Advisory Service, Government Buildings, Newton Bar, Newcastle-on-Tyne, U.K.

ULLREY, D. E., Animal Husbandry Department, Michigan State University, East Lansing, Michigan 48823, U.S.A.

UNDERWOOD, E. J., Institute of Agriculture, University of Western Australia, Nedlands, W. Australia 6009, Australia.

UVAROV, Olga, Veterinary Advisory Department, Glaxo Laboratories Ltd., Greenford, Middlesex, U.K.

VAN CAMPEN, D., U.S. Department of Agriculture, Plant, Soil and Nutrition Laboratory, Towet Road, Ithaca, New York 14850, U.S.A.

VOROTNITSKAYA, I. E., Vernadsky Institute of Geochemistry and Analytical Chemistry, U.S.S.R. Academy of Sciences, 47, Vorobyevskoe Shosse, Moscow, U.S.S.R.

WADDINGTON, J., The British Aluminium Co. Ltd., Chalfont Park, Gerrards Cross, Bucks, U.K.

WALKER, H. F., North of Scotland College of Agriculture, University of Aberdeen, 581 King Street, Aberdeen AB9 1UD, U.K.

WARD, G., Animal Production Section, International Atomic Energy Agency, Kärntner Ring 11, 1010 Vienna, Austria.

WARD, P. F. V., The Institute for Animal Physiology, Babraham, Cambridge, U.K.

WHITEHEAD, D. C., Grassland Research Institute, Hurley, nr. Maidenhead, Berks, U.K.

WIENER, G., Animal Breeding Research Organisation, West Mains Road, Edinburgh EH17 7JH, U.K.

WILLIAMS, R. B., Rowett Research Institute, Bucksburn, Aberdeen AB2 9SB, U.K.

WILLS, E. D., Department of Biochemistry, The Medical College of St. Barhtolomew's Hospital, Charterhouse Square, London, E.C.1, U.K.

ZELENSKAYA, A., Moscow Veterinary Academy, Laboratory of Metabolism and Pathology, 23 Kuzminky, Moscow, U.S.S.R.

ZIMINA, R., Department of Biogeography, Institute of Geography, Academy of Sciences, 29, Staromonetny Pereulok, Moscow G-17, U.S.S.R.

ACKNOWLEDGEMENTS

THE organization of this Symposium would not have been possible without the help of many industrial companies who gave their support by making generous financial contributions. These were as follows:

Imperial Chemical & Scottish Agricultural Industries Ltd
Spillers Ltd
Colborn Vitafeeds Ltd
Shell International Petroleum Company Ltd
British Oil and Cake Mills Ltd
International Nickel Ltd
Beecham Group Ltd
British Society for Animal Production
Cooper Nutrition Products Ltd
Ranks Hovis McDougall Ltd
Rio Tinto Zinc Corporation Ltd
Roche Products Ltd
Silcock & Lever Feeds Ltd
Isaac Spencer & Co. (Abdn.) Ltd
Boots Pure Drug Company Ltd
British Aluminium Company Ltd
Cerebos (Agriculture) Ltd
Farm Feed Formulators
Croda Agricultural Ltd

The Organizers particularly wish to acknowledge the assistance of The Royal Society, London, and the Wellcome Trust for their financial support during the very early stages of the organization of this meeting.

The help of the following who gave generously of their time to further the work of the Symposium is very gratefully acknowledged:

Social Activities: Margaret I. Chalmers, Alice E. Jaffrey, Shirley McGregor, D. Beryl Mills, Winifred E. Quarterman.

Symposium Organization: J. A. Bell, I. Bremner, J. K. Chesters, A. C. Dalgarno, Margaret Elrick, E. Florence, Marion Fraser, I. Grant, Penelope Herford, Irene Hird, A. D. Hughes, Carole McDougall, Isabel McKenzie, Susan Malloch, R. B. Marshall, G. Milne, J. Mathieson, Marie Nicol, G. C. Smith.

CONTENTS

Section 1—EXPERIMENTAL TECHNIQUES IN THE STUDY OF TRACE ELEMENT METABOLISM IN ANIMALS

President: K. O. GODWIN *Vice President:* I. BREMNER

xvii

Section 3—METABOLIC CONSEQUENCES OF
TRACE ELEMENT DEFICIENCY AND EXCESS

Presidents: M. KIRCHGESSNER and K. J. JENKINS
Vice Presidents: N. F. SUTTLE and J. K. CHESTERS

CONTENTS

Section 7—SOIL/PLANT/ANIMAL RELATIONSHIPS IN THE
AETIOLOGY OF DISORDERS ARISING FROM TRACE
ELEMENT DEFICIENCY AND EXCESS
President: J. HARTMANS *Vice President:* J. H. TOPPS

xxiii

Section 8—PROBLEMS IN THE DETECTION OF TRACE ELEMENT DEFICIENCY AND EXCESS: AN EVALUATION OF SURVEY TECHNIQUES

President: G. N. HAVRE *Vice President:* G. A. HALL

PAGE

Section 9—AN APPRAISAL OF ANALYTICAL TECHNIQUES FOR THE DETERMINATION OF THE TRACE ELEMENTS

President: R. L. MITCHELL   *Vice President:* C. F. MILLS

Concluding Plenary Session

OPENING ADDRESS

BY SYMPOSIUM PRESIDENT: SIR DAVID CUTHBERTSON

C.B.E., M.D., D.Sc., LL.D., F.R.C.P.E., F.R.C.S.E., F.R.S.E.

Immediate Past President, International Union of Nutritional Sciences
Formerly, Director, Rowett Research Institute,
Hon. Research Fellow, Glasgow University

GOOD morning to you all and welcome to this city of Aberdeen and to this meeting in its University.

This is a very ancient University instituted in 1495 in this old part of Aberdeen. Interest in trace elements in this area developed rather more recently in departments of the nearby Rowett and Macaulay Institutes but perhaps some of the earliest studies on trace elements in Scotland took place in a Glasgow laboratory I had during the nineteen-twenties where we became interested in serum copper in the days before I became so closely concerned with the physiology and nutrition of animals of agricultural importance. My main role in the development of studies of the trace elements has, however, been to act as a sort of catalyst from time to time and, in connection with this present meeting, to help to promote the liaison between the International Biological Programme (IBP) and the World Association for Animal Production (WAAP) that has supported the organization of this meeting. The initial stimulus that ultimately led to the promotion of this Symposium came during a visit of Professor Breirem of Norway to the Rowett Institute some years ago, when he and Dr Mills were discussing what the European Association for Animal Production (now a member of WAAP) could do to promote the development of trace element studies. A sub-commission of EAAP was formed to consider proposals arising from this meeting and this group decided to promote the present Symposium as a part of its future activities. The union with IBP did much to help with the financial problems of organising this meeting through a grant kindly provided by the Royal Society, London, and further support was generously provided by British industry.

These were the beginnings and since then our local committee has done valiant work preparing the ground for this meeting. There are about 160 people here representing some 23 nations and I think this is very satisfying to our Aberdeen colleagues. The meetings have largely been arranged so that they will reveal the newer aspects of fundamental work going on in this field, as well as assisting those who have to apply this knowledge to work out

1

means of identification and rectification of problems arising from excess or a deficiency of a particular trace element.

In opening this meeting it gives me very great pleasure indeed to welcome as first speaker, Professor Underwood, who is known to you all through his masterly book on trace element metabolism in humans and animals; he is now busy on his third edition! He and Professor Filmer were the first to reveal the nutritional significance of cobalt and thereby initiated something which has grown and reached tremendous economic proportions. Indeed, I think about 12 years ago I wrote to Sir Ian Clunies Ross asking his opinion on the contribution of trace element research to the wealth and economic wellbeing of Australia and he put it that in years to come it may well rise to £50 million per annum. I wrote similarly to Dr Cunningham of New Zealand and he stressed that it might be of the order of £18 to 20 millions for New Zealand at that time. Now with all the additional interest that has developed in this field and the revelation of further trace element deficiencies and excesses and also of substances which affect their utilisation, such as cadmium, I would think, and perhaps Professor Underwood would agree, that the scale of their economic importance must be about £500 million per annum. This economic assessment does not take into account the benefits arising directly from a greater understanding of the role of trace elements in man—a field upon which much interest is now being focused.

I have very great pleasure in declaring this Symposium open. It is 'open' in the widest sense of the word; not only in the formal sessions but also in the corridors, lounges, the cafeteria and even in the open air for, as you all know, much of the useful work of this meeting will inevitably be done during your informal discussions in these pleasant surroundings.

PLENARY SESSION

INTRODUCTORY LECTURE
by
PROFESSOR E. J. UNDERWOOD

TRACE ELEMENT PROBLEMS IN HUMAN HEALTH AND NUTRITION

Earlier in this address I cast some doubt on the rather comforting assumption of the past that human dietaries well-balanced in other respects will inevitably provide an abundance of all the trace elements with little chance of deleterious excess. Let us examine these doubts in respect to the five elements, iron, fluorine, zinc, chromium and cadmium.

Iron. Iron deficiency is the most widespread and frequently encountered, clinically-manifest, mineral deficiency disease in man. It appears to be as common today as it was 50 years ago. In adult men the condition is rare and usually associated with chronic blood loss from infections, malignancy, ulcers, hookworm infestation or schistosomiasis. Iron deficiency anemia is much more common in women during the fertile period because of additional iron losses in menstruation, pregnancy and lactation. Its incidence in such women has been reported to be as high as 20 to 25 per cent. in recent Swedish (Rybo, 1966), English (Jacobs *et al.*, 1965) and U.S. studies (Bothwell and Finch, 1962). In economically underprivileged groups, in both the developed and underdeveloped countries, the incidence is even higher, especially during the childbearing years. In fact, surveys carried out in some underdeveloped tropical countries have revealed moderate to severe anaemia, responsive to iron therapy, in more than 50 per cent. of the women examined. Such a high incidence is usually aggravated by blood loss from intestinal and other parasites but it is basically a reflection of inadequate intakes of available iron to meet the replacement needs of repeated child-bearing and of high dermal losses of iron from excessive sweating. The dietary iron deficit is further aggravated by a heavy dependence on cereal grains from which iron is very poorly absorbed. In this connection Hussain and coworkers (1965) have recently made an extremely important observation. They showed that the iron in wheat is only 4 per cent. absorbed in normal subjects and only 7 per cent. in iron-deficient subjects. In other words, not only are high cereal diets poor sources of available iron but the well-established ability of the body to increase iron absorption in response to increased iron need is much more limited with these sources of iron than it is with iron salts or even with haemoglobin or myoglobin iron from muscle and organ meats.

The precarious position of women in respect to iron is further revealed by the studies of Monsen, Kuhn and Finch (1967) carried out in U.S.A. only two years ago. These workers showed that to provide the iron needs of 95 per cent. of normal, menstruating women, enough iron must be consumed to permit the absorption of approximately 2·0 mg. iron per day. If we assume that the diets consumed are good mixed diets, and place the overall iron absorption generally at 14 per cent., the total dietary iron requirement will be 14 mg./day. Many otherwise-adequate diets do not supply this amount of iron daily. Furthermore, there is reason to suspect that food iron consumption may be declining among calorie-conscious women due to (1) decreased total calorie intake and (2) reduced opportunities for iron contamination as a result of improved cleanliness in commercial handling of foods and a declining domestic use of iron cooking vessels.

The evidence just presented conspires to suggest that a significant segment of the human population may be suffering from a mild deficiency of at least one trace element, namely iron. This situation has been recognized for several years in several countries by the enactment of legislation for the iron-enrichment of white flour. Unfortunately the most common form of iron used for this purpose is finely divided metallic iron or ferrum redactum. Two separate investigations have recently shown that this form of iron is very poorly absorbed and is therefore not an efficient means of improving the iron status of women (Elwood, 1963; Fritz, 1969).

Fluorine. I would now like to turn to an entirely different trace element, fluorine, which has achieved both fame and notoriety over the last 20 years as a result of its use in municipal water supplies as a means of reducing the incidence of human dental caries. I do not want to discuss this aspect of fluorine and will assume that an audience as intelligent, as objective and as informed as the one I am now addressing accepts the overwhelming evidence that controlled fluoridation of the water supply is a safe and effective means of reducing dental caries by some 60 per cent., provided that such water is consumed by children during the years of tooth formation. However, I would remind you that acceptance of this proposition carries the further implication that dietary intakes of fluorine by children not consuming such treated water are inadequate, if relative freedom from caries is taken as a criterion of adequacy.

Additional evidence is now accumulating that fluoride intakes are also commonly inadequate for the maintenance of a normal skeleton in the adult population. I am not referring to the several studies that have appeared demonstrating the benefits of fluoride therapy in cases of osteoporosis and other demineralizing bone diseases. These lie outside the scope of this address. I refer particularly to the work of Bernstein and coworkers (1966) in two areas of North Dakota. Over 1000 X-rays of the lower lumbar spine were obtained from adults over age 45 in an area where the water supply provided 0·15 to 0·30 p.p.m. F and in another area where the water contained 4 to 6 p.p.m. F. As expected, the incidence of decreased bone density increased with age in both communities but at all ages there was substantially less osteoporosis in the high fluoride area, the differences being highly significant in women. The difference in the incidence of collapsed or distorted vertebrae in women was even greater. For example, in the 55 to 65 year age group, seven times as many women in the low fluoride area demonstrated collapsed vertebrae as in those from the high fluoride area. A surprising and remarkable further observation made in this study was that calcification of the aorta was substantially and significantly less in the men from the high than from the low-fluoride area.

These findings raise a number of important questions. If we extrapolate from the data of Smith and Frame (1965), obtained from a study of 2063 women living in Detroit, there are approximately 14 million women in the United States with a significant degree of osteoporosis of which they are unaware. This figure excludes those with obvious clinical disabilities associated with osteoporosis. There is every reason to expect a similar incidence of osteoporosis in women in other countries with similar dietary habits and fluoride intakes, although it must be remembered that tea-drinking communities ingest far more fluorine, other things being equal, than coffee-drinking communities. Since the consumption of water containing 4 to 6 p.p.m. F significantly reduces the incidence of this widespread osteoporosis and collapsed vertebrae in women, and since the maintenance of a normal skeleton can reasonably be regarded as a criterion of dietary adequacy, it can be urged that millions of women are suffering from inadequate fluoride intakes—in other words from fluorine deficiency.

It is easier to accept this radical concept than to suggest a workable solution. Fluoridation of the water-supply to 4 p.p.m. F is impossible because 2 p.p.m. is the maximum that can be tolerated by children without a significant and unsightly degree of mottled enamel and 1 p.p.m. F is considered the level of 'maximum health with maximum safety' for children. As it is equally impossible to visualize one level in the water-supply for children and another for adults, it is clear that these findings with fluorine pose formidable public health problems.

Zinc. Most normal human dietaries supply about 9 to 12 mg.

11

Zn per day. Intakes of this magnitude can be considered adequate in the sense that none of the typical stigmata of zinc deficiency, as they appear in experimental animals, have been observed in man. An exception is provided by the male dwarfs living in parts of the Middle East, studied so revealingly by Prasad and his associates (Prasad *et al.*, 1961; 1963). The dwarfism and hypogonadism of these individuals arise from a zinc deficiency, 'conditioned' by a combination of factors adversely affecting zinc utilization operating throughout the growing period when zinc needs are at their highest. The diets consumed by the dwarfs consist mainly of wheat and corn bread and supply approximately the same amounts of total zinc as ordinary 'western' diets. These intakes of zinc appear to be inadequate because: (1) absorption is abnormally low, due to the high levels of dietary phytates and possibly to the practice of clay-eating and (2) losses of zinc are abnormally high, due to excessive sweating and to faecal and urinary blood losses from hookworm infestation and schistosomiasis in many instances. In any case a spectacular improvement in growth and a dramatic development of the external genitalia and secondary sex character- istics occur following transfer of the dwarfs to an improved diet plus supplementary zinc.

An analogous situation appears to exist with cattle in certain parts of the world. Manifestation of zinc deficiency, responsive to zinc therapy, have been observed in growing and mature cattle in Guyana (Legg and Sears, 1960) and in Scandinavia (Haaranen, 1963; Dynna and Havre, 1963), where the pasture or fodder zinc concentrations were reported to range from 18 to as high as 80 p.p.m. Since these levels of zinc are comparable with those of other areas where no signs of zinc deficiency appear in cattle and since these levels are also substantially higher than those found necessary for cattle under experimental conditions with semi- synthetic diets, it seems that we are dealing with a zinc deficiency 'conditioned' by some factor or factors in the herbage or the environment of the affected areas which have yet to be incriminated. It is clear that further studies of the factors affecting the zinc requirements of man and grazing ruminants constitute an attractive and a fruitful field for future research.

The whole question of zinc requirements and the criteria of adequacy to be applied in assessing these requirements has been raised to a new plane of significance by the discovery of Pories and Strain (1966) that zinc supplementation, at the rate of 150 mg. Zn/ day, of the normal diets of normal young men, significantly increases the rate of wound healing and can induce marked clinical improvement in sufferers from atherosclerosis. I do not propose to go into details of these exciting findings, especially as we are to hear from Dr Pories later in this Symposium, but it seems clear that there is an intensive demand for zinc in the rapid cell growth of wound healing from incisions or from burns or bone fractures which cannot adequately be met by absorption from normal diets or by mobilization from the limited body zinc stores. On these criteria, therefore, all ordinary diets are deficient in zinc, despite the fact that they appear perfectly adequate for growth and sexual development, the functions most seriously affected in zinc-deficient animals.

In view of these facts and the possibility of widespread marginal zinc deficiency in man, it is pertinent to look at the factors determining zinc intakes. As was suggested earlier in respect to iron and for the same reasons, zinc intakes may be declining because of a tendency towards lower calorie intakes as a result of calorie-consciousness and reduced physical activity and as a consequence of reduced opportunity for zinc contamination of foods and water supplies due to a declining use of galvanised pipes and vessels. Already Kubota, Lazar and Losee (1966) have demonstrated significant regional differences in plasma zinc levels in human adults in U.S.A., which presumably reflect differences in dietary zinc levels. Whether this, in turn, is due to differences in dietary habits, which seems unlikely, or to local differences in the zinc contents of the foods and water supplies, is unknown. However, there is ample evidence that the zinc contents of pastures, fodders and grains are affected by soil conditions and fertilizer practices so there is every reason to expect that many human foods would be similarly affected. Indeed, in a small study carried out by me a few years ago the zinc content of wheat grain was found to be profoundly influenced by the treatment accorded to the growing plant (Underwood, 1962). Grain samples from zinc-low soils averaged only 18 p.p.m. Zn, compared with 35 p.p.m. for samples from the same soils fertilized with zinc oxide at the rate of 3 lb/acre. These findings point strongly to the importance of a further field for further research, namely the effects of changing living conditions and agronomic practices upon zinc intakes by man and by animals.

Chromium. Evidence is steadily accumulating that mild or marginal deficiencies of chormium, the most recent of the essential trace elements, may occur in man. In 1959 Schwarz and Mertz showed that Cr^{+++} is required by the rat for the maintenance of normal glucose utilization. Subsequently these workers (Mertz, 1967 and Schroeder, 1966) developed a more severely chromium-

13

deficient state in rats which resulted in a further worsening of the glucose tolerance and in hyperglycemia and glycosuria, increased lipid deposition in the aorta and decreased growth and longevity. The hypothesis was advanced that chromium acts as a cofactor with insulin.

Chromium is less securely involved in human health and nutrition, although the combined evidence from several independent studies certainly points to such an involvement. The impaired glucose tolerance which is common in old people can in some cases, where the impairment is mild, be restored to normal by oral supplementation with 150 μg. chromium as $CrCl_3$, thus raising their chromium intakes from an average of 50 to 200 μg./day (Levine et al., 1968). It is perhaps significant in this connection that human tissue chromium levels decline with age in most organs, other than the lungs (Schroeder et al., 1962). In a further carefully controlled clinical trial, three of six patients with mild diabetes showed a significant improvement of glucose tolerance when their chromium intakes were similarly raised from 50 to 200 μg./day (Glinsmann and Mertz, 1966). Finally, mention should be made of the significant improvement or complete normalization of glucose tolerance that can be achieved overnight in some areas by chromium supplementation of the milk powder treatment of infants suffering from protein-calorie malnutrition, or marasmus and kwashiokor, as demonstrated by Hopkins and Majaj (Hopkins and Majaj, 1966; Majaj and Hopkins, 1966).

All these findings taken together can be interpreted as strong evidence that chromium is essential to the well-being of man, as it is to the rat, and that many human dietaries are sub-optimal in chromium. Large-scale surveys and much further study of the factors affecting chromium intakes and utilization will be necessary to provide unequivocal proof. In addition, it is essential that concurrent investigations be undertaken of the effects of changes in dietary habits upon chromium intakes and of changes in agricultural and industrial practices upon the chromium content of foods. Virtually nothing is now known in any of these areas, although there is limited evidence that low chromium intakes are associated with diets high in sugar and refined cereals and that high or more satisfactory chromium intakes are provided by diets high in animal protein (Schroeder et al., 1962).

I am tempted to continue this consideration of trace elements in human health and nutrition and particularly to turn from the effects of marginal deficiencies and of criteria of adequacy to the potential ill-effects of marginal chronic toxicities and of criteria of safety or tolerance. Evidence is growing that certain elements, notably cadmium, lead and mercury, are entering the urban environment in increasing quantities, so imposing an increasing burden upon industrialized man through both ingestion and inhalation. Effective health regulations and control procedures have minimized the chances of acute industrial health hazards from these and other elements but the biological consequences of long-term exposure to the lesser concentrations present in the average urban environment have only just begun to be realized. With cadmium the position is already highly suspect, to say the least, if one extrapolates from the disturbingly indicative studies of Schroeder (1965) and Perry (1968) on the relation of cadmium to hypertension in rats and in man. Very little is yet known of the factors affecting dietary and other sources of cadmium or of the levels of this element in foods, water supplies and air which may or may not constitute a potential health hazard to man. Again I must emphasize that such studies, with the effects of changing living habits as the motivating force, are just as necessary for cadmium as a potentially toxic trace element, as was suggested earlier for iron, zinc and chromium in relation to possible deficiencies of those elements in man.

MODE OF ACTION OF THE TRACE ELEMENTS

In a paper presented to the Sixth International Congress of Nutrition in 1963 I made the following statement: 'embarrassingly little is yet known of the precise metabolic roles of the trace elements or of their specific functional relationship to the clinical and pathological disturbances which accompany deficiencies and toxicoses. In fact, at the present state of knowledge it is rare indeed to be able to relate any significant change in enzymic activity in the tissues to the clinical or pathological picture presented by the trace element-deficient animal'. I then went on to say 'the bridging of the gap between the findings of the nutritionist and those of the enzymologist is the most urgent, and at the same time the most hopeful, need of the future if the physiological functions of the trace elements are to be fully understood'. In the six years since those words were written the gap has been bridged at several points but it is still possible to be 'embarrassed' by numerous examples of failure to identify and relate many of the basic biochemical lesions of deficiency and toxicity to the gross manifestations in the animal.

In this respect let me mention the severe epithelial lesions so characteristic of the zinc-deficient animal. We have still virtually

15

no understanding of the precise mode of action of zinc in its special relation to the structure and function of the integument. Nor can we yet pinpoint the locus of action of zinc in bone formation or explain why skeletal abnormalities are so much more obvious and severe in zinc deficiency in birds than they are in mammals. The activity of alkaline phosphatase, a zinc metalloenzyme, is invariably reduced in the normal bones. This is apparently not the significant defect since the ash content of such bones is not necessarily subnormal. Zinc therefore appears to act at some earlier, unidentified step in the metabolic pathways of cartilage or bone matrix formation.

Skeletal abnormalities are similarly characteristic of manganese deficiency in birds and mammals but the site of action of manganese is better understood than that of zinc, largely due to the researches of Leach (1967) with chicks and of Hurley (1968) and Tsai and Everson (1967) with rats and guinea-pigs. Calcification does not itself seem to be greatly impaired but there is a severe reduction in the chondroitin sulphate content of epiphyseal cartilage and this defect appears to be specific for manganese deficiency. Manganese has thus been shown to play a vital role in the synthesis of acid mucopolysaccharide, substances important to the maintenance of the rigidity of connective tissue. Impairment in the production of these substances could therefore explain the skeletal abnormalities observed and a defect in matrix formation rather than in calcification can be incriminated as their cause. Substantial and encouraging progress has obviously been made with this element in relating a biochemical defect to a clinical and pathological manifestation of the deficiency, although the particular step in the metabolic pathways of mucopolysaccharide synthesis at which manganese operates has yet to be identified.

In copper deficiency a relationship between a biochemical defect involving the copper metalloenzyme, amine oxidase, and a pathological disturbance in the animal, manifested by ruptures of the major blood vessels, has been even more impressively and precisely demonstrated. In 1961, O'Dell and associates and Carnes and associates reported independently that the high mortality of copper-deficient chicks and pigs, respectively, resulted from internal haemorrhage due to rupture of the large blood vessels. Subsequently, aortic rupture, with degeneration of the elastic membrane, was demonstrated by others in copper-deficient chicks (Carlton and Henderson, 1963; Simpson and Harms, 1964) and extensive internal haemorrhages with a high incidence of aortic aneurisms were also observed in young copper-deficient guinea-pigs by Everson and coworkers (1967). A series of studies in several laboratories in England and U.S.A. then combined to elucidate the role of copper in elastin biosynthesis. This can briefly be stated in the words of Hill, Starcher and Kim (1968) who themselves made notable contributions to the solution of this problem. They put the position as follows: 'The primary biochemical lesion is a reduction in amine oxidase activity of the aorta. This reduction in enzymatic activity results, in turn, in a reduced capacity for oxidatively deaminating the epsilon amino group of the lysine residues in elastin. The reduction in oxidative deamination results, in turn, in less lysine being converted to desmosine. The reduction in desmosine, which is the cross-linkage group of elastin, results in fewer cross-linkages in this protein, which, in turn, results in less elasticity of the aorta'.

Unfortunately, few success stories comparable to that linking copper with elastin formation, pinpointing its mode of action and relating this to a major pathological disturbance in the animal, can be cited for other trace elements. In fact, the other great success story in this area of trace element research relates also to copper. Following the original demonstration of a significant lowering of copper and cytochrome oxidase in the brain of 'swayback' lambs by Howell and Davidson (1959), Mills and coworkers (Mills and Williams, 1962; Fell et al., 1965) and Barlow (1963) have shown that the groups of nerve cells showing the morphological lesions of the disease, the large motor neurones of the red nucleus and of the ventral horns of the grey matter in the spinal cord, also show the most severe biochemical lesion, a deficiency in cytochrome oxidase. The condition of ataxia in swayback can thus be related to a low copper content in the brain, leading to a deficiency of cytochrome oxidase in the motor neurones.

There is no lack of evidence of changes in enzyme activities in other trace element deficiencies and toxicoses but few of them have been related so convincingly to functional or structural changes in the animal, as just described for the cardiovascular and central nervous system disorders of copper deficiency. Reduced concentrations of several dehydrogenases, but not of others, have been demonstrated in the tissues of zinc-deficient rats (Prasad et al., 1967) and pancreatic carboxypeptidase activity has similarly been shown to be significantly reduced in such animals (Hsu et al., 1966; Mills et al., 1967). The differences in susceptibility of different zinc-dependent enzymes are probably related to differences in the firmness of the binding of the zinc to the apoenzyme but the relevance of the changes in enzyme activity to the various

17

manifestations of zinc deficiency in the animal is not clear. Nor are the precise mechanisms involved in the new well-documented impairment of RNA synthesis, and hence DNA and protein synthesis, in zinc deficiency at all understood. In fact, my colleague Dr Somers and I have recently shown that ribonuclease activity is significantly *increased* in the testes of zinc-deficient rats and that this increase is accompanied by higher non-protein-nitrogen and lower RNA, DNA and protein concentrations in this tissue (Somers and Underwood, 1969). These findings suggest that zinc is not only concerned with nucleic acid and protein anabolism, as just mentioned, but also with nucleic acid and protein catabolism, through its controlling effect upon ribonuclease activity.

CONCLUDING COMMENTS

I had hoped in this introductory lecture to refer to some recent work in my own laboratory by Drs Somers and Gawthorne on the biochemical defects in cobalt/vitamin B_{12} deficiency in sheep and also to comment on the increasing range and importance of trace element interaction in animals. The latter are of interest primarily because of their impact upon standards of adequacy and of safety of a wide range of trace elements, most notably zinc, copper, manganese, iron, cadmium and selenium. I believe that further studies of such interactions, with a view to understanding and quantitating their effects, constitute one of the most significant areas of future trace element research, especially in the light of growing evidence that trace metal antagonisms frequently arise from competition for protein-binding sites in the intestinal mucosa and elsewhere in the tissues.

Reluctantly I must leave this intriguing area to later speakers and turn my attention to a wider and, happily, a concluding, sphere. When considering trace elements in human health and nutrition I stressed the importance of man-made changes in the environment and of new criteria of adequacy which are raising the nutritional importance of the trace elements to a new plane of significance and are adding a new dimension to nutritional physiology. Man-made environmental changes are likely to be equally important in the future to the trace element nutrition of livestock.

Over large areas of the earth's surface, particularly but not exclusively in the developing countries, animal productivity is at present limited by serious shortages of available protein and energy which could easily mask trace element inadequacies except where they are severe. In addition there are generally genetic limitations upon individual animal productivity, coupled with the presence of infections and parasitic diseases which are usually well-controlled in technically advanced countries. As these limitations upon production are increasingly recognized and rectified, local trace element deficiencies, which are now obscured, will almost certainly arise. These will not be the easily recognizable acute conditions with well-marked stigmata but mild or marginal deficiencies, difficult to diagnose and expressed mostly as a vague unthriftiness or sub-optimal productivity. This has been the recent history of many countries as their animal industries become more intensified and plant productivity from the land is increased. In Australia, for instance, mild or marginal cobalt, copper and selenium deficiencies have only become apparent over large areas in recent years as farming practices have changed in those areas. Indeed, even in U.S.A. certain types of natural fattening rations for steers have quite recently been shown to be deficient in cobalt and possibly in zinc (Raun et al., 1968).

Finally, we should consider the role of the plant breeder concerned almost exclusively with the production of ever higher-yielding varieties and strains of crop and pasture plants, which could lead to changes in their trace element composition, partly from an increased draw upon possibly limited supplies of the elements in the soil and partly as a reflection of inherent changes in their genetic constitution. We should not forget the experience of the New Zealanders with their short-rotation, high-yielding rye grass which turned out to contain only one-fifth to one-tenth of the iodine concentrations of its perennial rye grass parent, irrespective of soil iodine status. At the present time the world is witnessing an agricultural revolution in the developing countries through the advent of the new 'miracle' wheats and rice emerging initially from the Rockefeller Mexican programme and the International Rice Research Institute in the Phillipines. With the proper treatment these new varieties of grain yield two to three times that of their local predecessors but there is no guarantee that such phenomenal yield increases are not obtained at some expense of trace element content or that treatment with nitrogen and phosphate alone is sufficient to supply the plants' needs for various trace elements. These elements are so important to the nutrition of man and animals and subtle deficiencies or imbalance can so easily arise by man-made changes in the environment, as I have tried to show in this introductory address, that problems will almost certainly arise in the future unless these possibilities are recognized now and appropriate steps taken to anticipate and avoid them. This is a further area for useful trace element research with a deep significance for the survival of man himself in a changing and challenging world.

In attempting to survey progress in trace element research, as a prelude to the more detailed presentations to follow, I was reminded of a story told of Sir Winston Churchill at the height of his fame. A deputation from the Women's Christian Temperance Union, concerned at the harm that his reputation as a brandy drinker was doing to their cause, waited upon Sir Winston at No. 10 Downing Street. They stood before him and said, 'Mr Prime Minister we have calculated that if all the brandy you had drunk was poured into this room it would come right up to our necks'. Gazing at these formidable women, Sir Winston is said to have replied, 'So much accomplished, so much still to be done'. This is how I felt towards the end of this address and I suspect that many of us will be echoing the words 'So much accomplished, so much still to be done' as this Symposium concludes.

REFERENCES

BARLOW, R. M. (1963). *J. comp. Path. Ther.* **73**, 51, 61.
BERNSTEIN, D. S., SADOWSKY, N., HEGSTED, D. M., GURI, C. D. & STARE, F. J. (1966). *J. Am. med. Ass.* **198**, 499.
BOLING, E. A. (1966). *Spectrochim. Acta*, **22**, 425.
BOTHWELL, T. H. & FINCH, C. A. (1962). In *Iron Metabolism*, Boston: Little Brown.
BRECH, F. & CROSS, L. (1962). *Appl. Spectrosc.* **16**, 59.
CARLTON, W. W. & HENDERSON, W. (1963). *J. Nutr.* **81**, 200.
CARNES, W. H., SHIELDS, G. S., CARTWRIGHT, G. E. & WINTROBE, M. M. (1961). *Fedn Proc. Fedn Am. Socs exp. Biol.* **20**, 118.
DYNNA, P. & HAVRE, G. N. (1963). *Acta vet. scand.* **4**, 197.
ELWOOD, P. C. (1963). *Br. med. J.* **1**, 224.
EVERSON, G. J., TSAI, M. C. & WANG, T. (1967). *J. Nutr.* **93**, 533.
FELL, B. F., MILLS, C. F. & BOYNE, R. (1965). *Res. vet. Sci.* **6**, 170.
FRITZ, J. C. (1969). *Int. Congr. Nutr.,* Maryland.
FOLEY, B., JOHNSON, S. A., HACKLEY, B., SMITH, J. C. & HALSTED, J. A. (1968). *Proc. Soc. exp. Biol. Med.* **128**, 265.
GLINSMANN, W. H. & MERTZ, W. (1966). *Metabolism,* **15**, 510.
HAARANEN, S. (1963). *Nord VetMed.* **15**, 536.
HACKLEY, B. M., SMITH, J. C. & HALSTED, J. A. (1968). *Clin. Chem.* **14**, 1.
HILL, C. H., STARCHER, B. & KIM, C. (1968). *Fedn Proc. Fedn Am. Socs exp. Biol.* **26**, 129.
HOPKINS, L. L. & MAJAJ, A. S. (1966). *Proc. 7th Int. Congr. Nutr.*
HOWELL, J. McC. & DAVISON, A. N. (1959). *Biochem. J.* **72**, 365.
HSU, J. M., ANILANE, J. K. & SCANLAN, D. E. (1966). *Science,* N.Y. **153**, 882.
HURLEY, L. S. (1968). In *Proceedings of the 2nd Missouri Conference on Trace Substances in Environmental Health,* p. 41. Ed. Hemphill, D.D. Univ. Missouri.
HUSSAIN, R., WALKER, R. B., LAYRISSE, M., CLARK, P. & FINCH, C. A. (1965). *Am. J. clin. Nutr.* **16**, 464.
JACOBS, A., KILPATRICK, G. S. & WHITLEY, S. (1965). *Postgrad Med.* **41**, 418.
KUBOTA, J., LAZAR, V. A. & LOSEE, F. (1966). *Archs envir. Hlth* **16**, 788.
LEACH, R. M. Jr. (1967). *Fedn Proc. Fedn Am. Socs exp. Biol.* **26**, 118.
LEGG, S. P. & SEARS, L. (1960). *Nature, Lond.* **186**, 1061.
LEVINE, R. A., STREETEN, D. H. P. & DOISY, R. J. (1968). *Metabolism,* **17**, 114.
MAJAJ, A. S. & HOPKINS, L. L. (1966). *J. méd. liban.* **19**, 177.

MERTZ, W. (1967). *Fedn Proc. Fedn Am. Socs exp. Biol.* **26**, 186.
MILLS, C. F., QUARTERMAN, J., WILLIAMS, R. B., DALGARNO, A. C. & PANIĆ, B. (1967). *Biochem. J.* **102**, 712.
MILLS, C. F. & WILLIAMS, R. B. (1962). *Biochem. J.* **85**, 629.
MONSEN, E. R., KUHN, I. R. & FINCH, C. A. (1967). *Am. J. clin. Nutr.* **20**, 842.
O'DELL, B. L., HARDWICK, B. C., REYNOLDS, G. & SAVAGE, J. E. (1961). *Proc. Soc. exp. Biol. Med.* **108**, 402.
PERRY, H. M. Jr. (1968). In *Proceedings of the 2nd Missouri Conference on Trace Substances in Environmental Health,* p. 101. Ed. Hemphill, D.D. Univ. Missouri.
PORIES, W. J. & STRAIN, W. H. (1966). In *Zinc Metabolism.* Ed. Prasad, A. S. Springfield: Thomas.
PRASAD, A. S., HALSTED, J. A. & NADIMI, M. (1961). *Am. J. Med.* **31**, 532.
PRASAD, A. S., MIALE, A., FARID, Z., SANDSTEAD, H. H., SCHULERT, A. S. & DARBY, W. J. (1963). *Arch. intern. Med.* **111**, 407.
PRASAD, A. S., OBERLEAS, D., WOLF, P. & HORWITZ, J. P. (1967). *J. clin. Invest.* **46**, 549.
RAUN, N. S., STABLES, G. L., POPE, L. S., HARPER, O. F., WALLER, G. R., RENBARGER, R. & TILLMAN, A. D. (1968). *J. Anim. Sci.* **27**, 1695.
ROSAN, C. R., HEALY, M. & MCNARY, W. (1963). *Science, N.Y.* **142**, 236.
RYBO, R. (1966). *Acta obstet. gynec. scand.* **45**, Suppl. 7.
SCHROEDER, H. A. (1965). *J. chron. Dis.* **18**, 647.
SCHROEDER, H. (1966). *J. Nutr.* **88**, 439.
SCHROEDER, H. A., BALASSA, J. J. & TIPTON, I. H. (1962). *J. chron. Dis.* **15**, 941.
SCHWARZ, K. & MERTZ, W. (1959). *Archs Biochem. Biophys.* **85**, 292.
SIMPSON, C. F. & HARMS, R. H. (1964). *Expl. molec. Path.* **3**, 390.
SMITH, R. W. Jr. & FRAME, B. (1966). *New England J. Med.* **273**, 73.
SOMERS, M. & UNDERWOOD, E. J. (1969). *Aust. J. biol. Sci.* (in press).
TSAI, H. C. C. & EVERSON, G. J. (1967). *J. Nutr.* **91**, 447.
UNDERWOOD, E. J. (1962). *Proc. 12th World's Poultry Congr.,* Sydney, Australia, p. 216.
YUNICE, A., PERRY, E. F., PERRY, H. M. Jr. & KOIRTYOHANN, R. (1968). In *Proceedings of the 2nd Missouri Conference on Trace Substances in Environmental Health,* p. 261. Ed. Hemphill, D. D. Univ. Missouri.

SECTION 1

EXPERIMENTAL TECHNIQUES IN THE STUDY OF TRACE ELEMENT METABOLISM IN ANIMALS

President: K. O. GODWIN
Vice President: I. BREMNER

CONTROL OF ENVIRONMENTAL CONDITIONS IN TRACE ELEMENT RESEARCH: AN EXPERIMENTAL APPROACH TO UNRECOGNIZED TRACE ELEMENT REQUIREMENTS*

K. SCHWARZ

Laboratory of Experimental Metabolic Diseases, Medical Research Programs, Veterans Administration Hospital, Long Beach, California, and Department of Biological Chemistry School of Medicine, University of California, Los Angeles, California, U.S.A.

RESEARCH on unidentified dietary factors has entered a new era over the past two decades. It took almost three-quarters of a century to identify the main organic constituents, primarily the amino acids and vitamins which are necessary to maintain growth and survival of the mammalian organism. Since these compounds are available in pure crystalline form one can now elucidate as yet unresolved inorganic trace factor requirements. Until approximately 1950 only six trace elements had been recognized as essential for animals: iron, iodine, copper, manganese, zinc, and cobalt (Table I). In 1953 molybdenum was added. The physiological importance of two other elements, selenium and chromium, was established in our laboratory in 1957 (Schwarz and Foltz) and 1959 (Schwarz and Mertz) respectively.

Table I. *Discovery of trace element requirements*

Iron	17th century	
Iodine	19th century	Chatin, A. (1850–1854).
Copper	1928	Hart, E. B., Steenbock, H., Waddell, J., and Elvehjem, C. A. (1928).
Manganese	1931	Kemmerer, A. R. and Todd, W. R. (1931).
Zinc	1934	Todd, W. R., Elvehjem, C. A. and Hart, E. B. (1934).
Cobalt	1935	Underwood, E. J. and Filmer, J. F. (1935). Marston, H. R. (1935). Lines, E. W. (1935).
Molybdenum	1953	de Renzo, E. C., Kaleita, E., Heytler, P., Oleson, J. J., Hutchings, B. L. and Williams, J. H. (1953). Richert, D. A. and Westerfeld, W. W. (1953).
Selenium	1957	Schwarz, K. and Foltz, C. M. (1957).
Chromium (III)	1959	Schwarz, K. and Mertz, W. (1959).

Following these discoveries we made the decision to develop a systematic, novel approach to the discovery of hitherto unidentified trace element requirements by combining the use of highly

* Supported in part by U.S. Public Health Service Research Grant AM 08669.

purified amino acid diets with recently developed ultraclean room and isolator techniques. Progress in the detection of new trace element deficiency diseases clearly depends on experimental conditions which effectively bar the animal from the agent under study. Not only the diet and the drinking water but other sources of impurities such as caging, food cups, water bottles, handling and dust from the air have to be monitored to make possible the demonstration of new trace element requirements. The dose levels at which such elements can be physiologically effective are in the microgram or submicrogram range.

After exploring several other possibilities we developed a trace element-sterile isolator system for the maintenance of rats and other small animals (Fig. 1)*. The system is based on the use of plastics for all components; there is no metal, glass, or rubber. We realize that various plastics contain significant amounts of trace

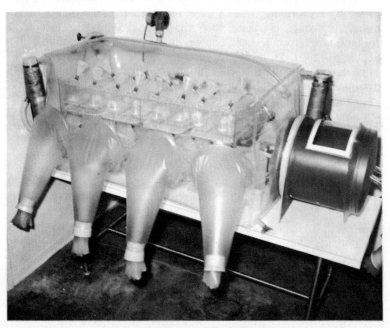

FIG. 1. Improved trace element-sterile isolator system for small laboratory animals (Schwarz *et al.*, 1969).

* Manufactured by the Standard Safety Equipment Company, Palatine, Illinois, Their assistance in technical details is acknowledged.

elements but assume that these are so tightly bound in the structural lattice of the polymer molecule that they are not leached out or available to the animal upon contact. The isolator is basically a modification of the Trexler isolator for germ-free animals. The system is composed of the following basic elements: isolator, air lock, blower, air filter assembly, cage assembly, refuse trays, food cups, water bottles and scales.

An earlier version of the system has been described (Smith and Schwarz, 1967). The basic design of the revised model and the plastic materials used in its construction are the same as before but a number of improvements have been made since then. An air lock has been added which greatly facilitates the passage of articles in and out of the trace element-sterile inner area. The new version has six working sleeves instead of two. A vinyl zipper extends over the entire top of the isolator to facilitate cleaning and setting-up operations. The new system holds a rack which accommodates 32 animals in individual plexiglass cages, while in the older system rats were kept in groups of five per cage. A new weighing device consists of a dietary scale shielded entirely in plastic. A major additional improvement in the operation of the isolator has been the introduction of calcium chloride hexahydrate ($CaCl_2.6H_2O$) in the refuse trays under the cages, primarily to keep the humidity in the isolator at a constant level of approximately 50 per cent at 21 to $22°C$. The agent also prevents microbial decomposition and the formation of undesirable odours.

The isolator system works so well as a single barrier to trace element contamination that we have found it unnecessary to use the more elaborate ultra-clean room techniques initially planned. In our more recent work, however, we have installed a laminar-flow air filter in the room which houses the isolators. This filter eliminates almost all dust down to a particle size of 0.35μ from the isolator facility. The individual air filter units on each isolator in turn remove not only dust but also all demonstrable micro-organisms such as bacteria, yeasts and moulds from the air circulating through the unit. Experiments are *not* carried out under germ-free conditions and no efforts are made to observe sterile precautions. A recent study of the microflora in animals inside such isolators has shown that it is rather normal (Hughes *et al.*, 1969) even though *E. coli* is absent from animals started on the amino acid diet inside the isolator immediately after weaning.

For animals inside the isolator the diet is the main source of trace element contamination. Impurities in inorganic and organic

27

constituents of the diet can be most damaging to this kind of experimentation. In our experience the inorganic constituents of the salt mixtures in purified diets are the most hazardous sources of impurities. Analytically pure chemicals are usually less than 99·9 per cent. pure, i.e., they contain more than 1 mg. of impurities per g. New standards of purity of dietary ingredients need to be established for trace element research. A great deal of work lies ahead of us in this particular field since special methods must be developed for the purification of inorganic as well as organic dietary constituents.

The animal itself must also be taken into account as a ' source ' of trace elements since it carries with it a given store of trace elements introduced at the beginning of the experiment. This input of any physiologically essential trace element may suffice to cover the requirement of the growing animal for quite some time. An eventual deficiency will develop when the *balance* between gains and losses reaches a critical threshhold, i.e., a level so low that it is incompatible with the maintenance of normal physiological functions and health. On the positive side of the ledger are the initial endowment of the animal and the daily traces obtained from the diet, the water and the environment, if any. On the negative side are the daily losses, as well as the ' dilution ' of the available endowment during growth. In addition it must be realized that severe losses of biologically available trace elements can occur within the animal by conversion of the element into inert, inactive forms, such as insoluble deposits, very stable coordination complexes, or stable salts. In some cases the input is so low and the daily losses so great that a deficiency results within a few days after initiation of a deficient dietary regimen. A typical example of this type is Zn. In other cases the reserves of a trace element within the organism of a weanling rat are so large that it may take months before a deficiency can be developed.

Large supplies of a trace element may be avoided in freshly weaned animals if care is taken to see that they never obtain access to laboratory chow. For some of our experiments food is removed two to three days prior to weaning and the animals are weaned as early as possible, for example 18 to 20 days after birth. This method has led to rather constant, satisfactory results in tests of biologically active selenium compounds and other experiments.

We have been able to produce a new disease in rats in the trace element-sterile isolator system, using an amino acid diet with relatively pure components of commercial origin. The new deficiency syndrome is clearly due to the lack of trace elements and we are in the process of identifying a novel, essential trace element preventing this condition. The diet initially used in these studies has been described (Smith and Schwarz, 1967). It has been improved since then (Schwarz and Vinyard, 1969).

With the amino acid diet currently in use in our laboratory rats grow well and appear perfectly normal when raised in the animal room under conventional conditions, i.e., in metal cages, with glass water bottles, rubber stoppers, etc. Animals on the same diet inside the trace element-sterile isolator develop a rather severe deficiency disease after one to three weeks. They show lack of growth (Table II), seborrhea, shaggy fur and a rather severe loss of hair (Fig. 2) which occasionally leads to complete alopecia. No gross pathology, other than the skin changes, has been discovered to date. When laboratory chow is fed inside the trace element-sterile isolator the animals perform very well and look perfectly normal.

Table II. *Effect of yeast ash on trace element deficiency in controlled environment system*

	Appearance		Daily weight gain	
	Conventional	Controlled	Conventional g./day	Controlled g./day
Basal amino acid diet	normal	alopecia seborrhea	1.7 ± 0.10	1.2 ± 0.20
Basal amino acid diet + 0.4% ash of Torula yeast	normal	normal	2.0 ± 0.11	1.7 ± 0.02
Laboratory ration	normal	excellent	3.4 ± 0.50	3.5 ± 0.08

Supplementation of a few per cent. of yeast, liver powder, or other sources of unidentified factors to the diet prevents the deficiency inside the trace element-sterile system. A similar effect is seen with 1 per cent. yeast ash, proving that the new deficiency disease is indeed largely caused by a trace element deficiency. The results do not exclude the possibility that the missing trace element is present in organically bound form before ashing.

Identification of the missing element has been under way for several years. It is possible that we are dealing with a multiple deficiency. To the uninitiated, identification of the missing trace element among the 90 elements known to occur in nature may appear to be a relatively simple task. In practice, however, this has turned out to be difficult. One reason is the fact that one rarely, if ever, finds a chemical that is absolutely pure. We know

29

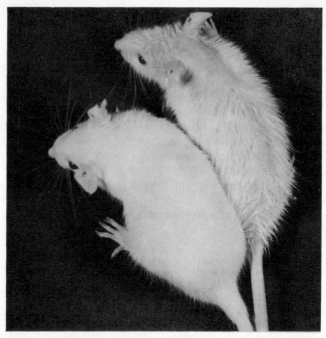

Fig. 2. Unidentified trace element deficiency. Left animal: outside control, kept under conventional conditions on purified diet. Right animal: maintained for 20 days on the same diet in the trace element-sterile environment system.

several 'analytically pure' salts which have a preventive effect on our deficiency disease when applied at unphysiologically high dose levels, i.e., at levels of approximately 0·1 per cent. in the diet. We have attempted to trace down the impurities in these salts since the active element appears to be present as a low level contaminant. It is our suspicion that the new trace element is one which is not readily 'seen' by methods such as emission spectography or atomic absorption analysis. In general our approach to the identification of the trace element lacking under our experimental conditions has consisted of systematic tests of individual elements suspected of trace element functions and the application of classical, step-by-step procedures of qualitative inorganic analysis to yeast ash.

From the physiological point of view potentially new essential trace elements should fulfil a number of postulates which distinguish them from the non-essentials. One would expect that an essential trace element is present in the newborn and excreted in milk. However, the latter does not necessarily hold true since some trace elements, for instance Fe, can be present to such an excess in the newborn that they must be eliminated after birth. An essential trace element should be normally found in the organism and tissues and it should not be accumulated to levels which are toxic, i.e., the organism should have a homeostatic mechanism for the maintenance of rather constant levels of the element in blood and tissue. This is the case for most of the trace elements known thus far to be essential. The element must also be present at physiological levels in a normal diet.

Some elements detectable in small amounts in tissues are considered to be simply 'contaminants' because of their similarity to major elemental constituents of the body. Strontium and barium, for example, are found at low levels in bone and in tissues and are regarded as impurities of calcium in the system. One could argue, however, that nothing really accompanies anything else in the organism by coincidence since effective and often highly selective mechanisms are available to prevent the accidental penetration of undesirable constituents into the tissues.

If we speak about trace dimensions purity is a relative term. One cannot categorically exclude *any* element from being essential except by stating that one has shown it to be not essential at a certain, accurately determined level. Thus, progress in this field is singularly dependent on the sensitivity and the accuracy of the analytical methods applied to the specific element in question.

A review of the periodic system of the elements (Fig. 3) from the point of view of physiological function in the mammalian organism leads to some interesting results. Only 11 of the 92 elements listed in the classical system account for the bulk of living matter. Only nine others have been established today as physiologically essential in trace amounts. There are 16 elements which are very unlikely to be essential for life. Six of them are inert gases, and two, technetium (atomic number 43) and promethium (atomic number 61) exist only in synthetic form. Eight others, polonium, astatine, francium, radium, actinium, thorium, protactinium and uranium (numbers 84, 85, and 87 to 92), may be too radioactive to be of any account in physiological systems. It is difficult, however, to make conclusive statements about radioactive elements since some of the most abundant, biologically important elements occur in nature in radioactive form, even though their level of radioactivity is so minimal that it does not appear to be of significance. A typical example is potassium.

This account of the periodic system leaves 56 elements which

31

could be considered as possible pretenders to trace element function. Twenty-four of these fulfil at least in part the postulates which have been stated above for potential essentiality; they are so marked on Figure 3. Some of the better known examples are arsenic, germanium, nickel, titanium, vanadium and fluorine. An interesting situation exists in the first series of the transition elements which contain six of the nine presently known essential trace elements. From Cr (24) to Zn (30) these elements are arranged in consecutive order, with the exception of Ni which occupies a position among these elements but has not yet been shown to be essential.

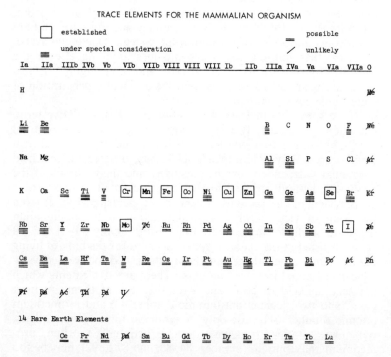

FIG. 3. Established, possible and potential trace elements for the mammalian organism (modified after Schwarz, 1968).

On the whole it is remarkable that the 11 elements which constitute the bulk of living matter are all quite small. They belong to the lowest 20 elements in the periodic system. All nine essential trace elements presently known are of slightly higher atomic weight so that there is no overlap between the main body constituents and the area of the essential trace elements in the periodic system. Most of the known essentials, in turn, have relatively low atomic numbers ranging from 24 to 34. Only two elements, Mo and I, with atomic numbers 42 and 53, are somewhat larger. It is noteworthy that none of the 39 elements with higher atomic numbers have thus far been shown to be of any physiological significance for animals.

The availability of specific, accurate and highly sensitive methods of analysis is of paramount importance in the search for new essential trace elements. With few exceptions, the problems encountered in analyzing for one or the other of the elements discussed above as potential trace elements are numerous and quite different from element to element, as well as from material to material to be analyzed. There is no universally applicable method of analysis since the sensitivities of each method for various trace elements show great differences. The field is developing rapidly

Table III. *Trace element composition of dust from isolator experiment and domestic furnace filters*

(All figures in parts per million)

Element	Dust from Domestic Furnace Filter	Air Filter Media, Clean	Air Filter Media, Used*	Dust (Difference)
Ag	5·4			
Al	**	29,000	25,000	**
B	**	2,800	2,400	**
Ca	10,000	280	350	70
Co	19			
Cr	220	130	110	**
Cu	82	3·1	41	37·9
Fe	5,300	220	360	140
K	2·6			
Mg	8,200	58	780	722
Mn	160	47	190	143
Na	**	31,000	28,000	**
Ni	160		89	89
P	trace			
Pb	7,400	380	15,000	14,620
Si	**	190,000	140,000	**
Sn	66		110	110
Sr	86		trace	trace
Ti	**	77,000	53,000	**
V	70	120	140	20
Zn	900			
Zr	26	7,600	5,900	

* Applied for four weeks in the air filter assembly of an isolator.
** Constituent of the air filter media.

Table IV. *Trace elements in dietary components as determined by semiquantitative emission spectrography*
(All figures in parts per million)

Element	Amino Acids	Sucrose	Lard	Oil	Salts	Trace Suppl.	Vits.	NaHCO$_3$	NaH$_2$PO$_4$·H$_2$O	K$_2$CO$_3$	Cellulose
Ag	0·019										
Al	1·1	0·45	0·045	0·16	71	3	1·2				0·24
B	0·17	0·026					0·65				0·020
Ba											
Bi											
Ca	4·4	1·7	0·052	0·086	13*	31	0·13*	270	18	2·6	4·1
Cd											
Co						1·3*	0·99				
Cr	1·0	0·035	0·029	0·070	<3	1·1*	0·17				0·029
Cu	0·17	0·54	0·019	0·17	29	0·15*	0·030	3·2			0·040
Fe	6·0		0·72		600	0·6*	6·2				0·41
K					5·1*		<50		<0·1*	57*	
Li											
Mg	1·5	0·36	0·043	0·060	0·85*	8·5*	44	4·8	1·3	0·58	0·63
Mn	0·26				0·25*	0·98*	0·55				0·054
Mo						0·13*	0·30				
Na	25	0·032	0·85		10*		21	28*	17*	62	4·1
Ni	0·095			0·11	19*				23*		0·40
P							0·18*				
Pb							3·2				
Sb											
Si	5·4	3·8	1·0	3·6	850	9·8	9·3	40	20		0·75
Sn			0·40		350						
Sr							1·4				
Ti	0·05	0·024		0·053	20						
V											
Zn	0·50										0·027

* In percent.

and the methods usually depend on expensive equipment such as atomic absorption spectrometers, emission spectrographs, nuclear reactors for activation analysis, X-ray emission fluorometers, mass spectrometers, etc. In many cases, one may be compelled to use the services of a laboratory specializing in one or the other method rather than carrying out analyses in one's own laboratory. We have found emission spectrographic analysis carried out by a commercial laboratory of high competence most useful in the screening of dietary ingredients, tissues and building materials for ultraclean environments. The method produces semi-quantitative values for 25 elements. Some representative examples are shown in Tables III, IV and V.

Table V. *Trace elements in casein, amino acid mixture S7 and several amino acids, as determined by semiquantitative emission spectrography*

(All figures in parts per million)

Element	Casein	Amino Acid Mixture S7	Histidine* (Source I)	Histidine* (Source II)	Lysine**	Cystine***
Ag		0·025				
Al	45	2·1	2	0·69	0·26	2·4
B	2·1	0·085	0·19	0·014		0·051
Ba				1·2		
Bi						trace
Ca	1100		2·1		0·36	1·8
Cd			0·22	0·071		
Co						
Cr	0·16		5·2		0·043	0·42
Cu	3·4		0·28		1·4	0·54
Fe	16		3·3		1·2	3
K	50					
Li	5	1				
Mg	170		0·39		0·063	0·53
Mn	9		0·38		0·025	0·12
Mo				0·044		
Na			360			
Ni	0·20	0·15	3·6	0·30	0·16	0·68
P	4400					trace
Pb	4	5·8	0·76	0·30	0·074	0·65
Sb			6·8			
Si	98	15	8·6	0·55	0·84	8·1
Sn	7·5	1·3	0·28	0·062	0·089	0·096
Sr	0·10	0·01		0·019		
Ti	1·2	0·25	0·19	0·034	trace	0·29
V						
Zn	120		5·2		trace	0·52
Zr				0·34		0·018

* L-Histidine.HC1.H$_2$O
** L-Lysine.HC1
*** L-Cystine

Animals in the ultraclean environment system described above will revert to normal within a few days if a breakthrough of dust occurs in the air filter system. Dust thus appears to be one of the main sources of unidentified trace elements for our animals kept under conventional conditions. Table III presents emission-spectrographic data obtained with dust deposited on air filter media used for four weeks on the ultraclean isolator. Data obtained with dust taken from a domestic furnace filter are also shown. The most important finding concerns excessive amounts of lead, with approximately 15000 p.p.m., i.e., 15 mg. of Pb deposited in 1 g. of air filter medium in the course of the experiment in the laboratory, located close to areas of heavy traffic. In the residential area, much further removed from traffic and located close to the Pacific Ocean, the Pb content still amounts to 7400 p.p.m. The question arises whether this Pb could originate from paints as well as from gasoline. It is seen that dust also contributes several other elements. The data indicate that relatively high amounts of Cu, Mn, Ni, Sn and V are present.

Screening of the various dietary constituents used in the preparation of the basal ration has shown that different components contribute widely different trace contaminants to the ration (Table IV). It is seen that commercial sucrose and commercial fats are actually some of the purest materials found anywhere, obviously because of the high development of the technologies used in their preparation. Such analyses have been helpful in monitoring individual trace elements. We have been able, for instance, to produce a diet which was very low in silicon and another which was exceedingly low in V. Extensive use has been made of this method in the selection of individual lots of amino acids offered by suppliers. Table V presents values obtained with casein, our standard amino acid mixture, and several individual amino acids. It is apparent that the amino acid mixture is far superior to casein in most, but not all, of the elements which were determined. Elements for which values are not listed were not detected. The data on two samples of histidine illustrate how differences in quality can be made evident by this relatively simple method.

Two different sets of data on the distribution of trace elements in the dietary amino acid mixture are shown in Tables IV and V. There are 19 individual constituents in this mixture. The values in Table IV were obtained in 1969 with a batch of commercial amino acids currently in use, whereas those in Table V represent findings made in 1967 with a mixture of specially recrystallized amino acids. In the batch of recrystallized amino acids many elements are not detectable which are present in the other lot. However, certain elements, for instance Si, are contained at higher levels in the recrystallized material. Application of different screening techniques, on the other hand, may lead to the detection of unexpected impurities in compounds which, from the emission spectrographic point of view, are absolutely pure. A highly purified sample of lithium carbonate, for instance, which showed no contamination whatsoever by emission spectrography, revealed 49 p.p.m. of tungsten, 18 p.p.m. of aluminum, and 2 p.p.m. of sodium when submitted to neutron activation analysis. The various plastics used in the construction of our isolator system produced results similar to those presented by R. O. Scott later in this Symposium.

The trace element-sterile system described here lends itself readily to definitive, critical studies on the essentiality of *any* element for which a potential physiological role has not yet been established, provided that suitable methods of analysis are available and that procedures can be developed to eliminate the element under investigation from the constituents of the diet. It is hoped that this approach will lead to new discoveries in the trace element field.

Acknowledgement. The author is greatly indebted to J. Cecil Smith, Jr., and Mrs Elizabeth Vinyard for their excellent collaboration on this project.

REFERENCES

CHATIN, A. (1850–1854). *C.r. hebd. Séanc. Acad. Sci. Paris,* **30–39.**
DERENZO, E. C., KALEITA, E., HEYTLER, P., OLESON, J. J., HUTCHINGS, B. L. & WILLIAMS, J. H. (1953). *J. Am. chem. Soc.* **75,** 753.
HART, E. B., STEENBOCK, H., WADDELL, J. & ELVEHJEM, C. A. (1928). *J. biol. Chem.* **77,** 797.
HUGHES, M. K., FUSILLO, M. H. & SMITH, J. C. (1969). In press.
KEMMERER, A. R. & TODD, W. R. (1931). *J. biol. Chem.* **94,** 317.
LINES, E. W. (1935). *J. Coun. scient. ind. Res. Aust.* **8,** 117.
MARSTON, H. R. (1935). *J. Coun. scient. ind. Res. Aust.* **8,** 111.
RICHERT, D. A. & WESTERFELD, W. W. (1953). *J. biol. Chem.* **203,** 915.
SCHWARZ, K. (1968). In *Human Ecology in Space Flight,* ed. Calloway, D. New York: Academy of Sciences.
SCHWARZ, K. & FOLTZ, C. M. (1957). *J. Am. chem. Soc.* **79,** 3292.
SCHWARZ, K. & MERTZ, W. (1959). *Archs Biochem. Biophys.* **85,** 292.
SCHWARZ, K. & VINYARD, E. (1969). To be published.
SCHWARZ, K., VINYARD, E. H. & THOMPSON, P. G. (1969). To be published.
SMITH, J. C. & SCHWARZ, K. (1967). *J. Nutr.* **93,** 182.
TODD, W. R., ELVEHJEM, C. A. & HART, E. B. (1934). *Am. J. Physiol.* **107,** 146.
UNDERWOOD, E. J. & FILMER, J. F. (1935). *Aust. vet. J.* **11,** 84.

DISCUSSION

Underwood (Perth). Has Dr Schwarz considered in his recent work the approach to identifying the apparently essential elements concerned in giving responses in his highly purified diets by going back to the old fractionation procedures in the way in which both he and others have used successfully in the past? I got the impression that having obtained a response with, say, liver or yeast ash, he is now 'spotting' the element concerned by detailed spectrographic analysis rather than by fractionation.

Schwarz (Long Beach). We do both. We are fractionating ash and this has been promising in eliminating a number of elements. The other successful approach might be to take a 'pure' chemical which gives a positive effect if used in large amounts and then track down its impurities.

Diplock (London). Could Dr Schwarz say more about the factor G he mentioned in his presentation?

Schwarz (Long Beach). At the moment I am convinced that factor G doesn't have anything to do with the trace elements; but I was similarly convinced that factor 3 wasn't when I first tried to isolate it! In preliminary work we did in 1952 we found that in rats on amino acid diets one can get growth-promoting effects from 1 or 2 per cent. of yeast or liver which cannot be explained by lack of a known vitamin or an amino acid imbalance. We started work on fractionating this substance about four and a half years ago and we now have it two- to four-thousand fold purified. It is water soluble and effective at dose levels similar to those of the water soluble vitamins, but we know little yet about its chemistry. It is relatively widely distributed in those items of food which have been considered to have a high protein value, like egg albumin and lactalbumin. It increases the efficiency of food conversion and nitrogen utilization by about 20 to 30 per cent. (Schwarz, K. 1970. *J. Nutr.* in press; Schwarz, K., Smith, J. C. & Oda, T. A. 1967. *Lancet,* **1,** 732.)

PROBLEMS IN THE EXECUTION OF NUTRITIONAL AND METABOLIC EXPERIMENTS WITH TRACE ELEMENT DEFICIENT ANIMALS

C. F. MILLS AND J. K. CHESTERS

Rowett Research Institute, Bucksburn, Aberdeen, Scotland

MUCH of the effort expended in research upon the trace elements is directed towards determining the biochemical roles of these elements, to the study of metabolic defects which give rise to clinical lesions and to the study of factors which may influence and modify trace element requirement and availability for specific physiological functions. Progress in all these fields has been intermittent and it is probably true to say that, compared with the rate at which our understanding of the metabolic role of the vitamins has grown during recent years, our understanding of the role of many of the trace elements is developing much more slowly. As in all other fields of scientific work the generality may be made that where progress becomes slow as a result of conflict between individual workers' findings this is usually a consequence of imperfect definition or imperfect appreciation of the experimental conditions under which investigations have been carried out. The field of trace element research is no exception to this rule and many examples from published literature can be quoted to illustrate the situation. Probably the most outstanding among these is the rough road along which investigations upon the essential role of Cu have travelled from the days of the conflict between Myers (Beard *et al.,* 1931; Beard and Myers, 1931; Eveleth *et al.,* 1932–33) on the one hand and Elvehjem and his co-workers on the other (Waddell *et al.,* 1928; Elvehjem, 1935) as to whether Cu was an essential nutrient or could be replaced by Fe. The dust of this controversy is only just settling from the appreciation that certain aspects of Fe and Cu metabolism are inter-related and that an interaction exists between Cu and Zn which will undoubtedly make it easier to produce Cu deficiency in a rat maintained in a galvanised cage than in a glass cage!

Regrettably, not all the examples that could be quoted are historic; some are with us at the present day and outstanding among these is the present conflict of opinion on the primary metabolic role of Zn where differences of opinion reign on the effects of Zn deficiency on RNA, DNA, pyridine nucleotides, the dehydrogenase enzymes, carboxypeptidase, alkaline phosphatase and even on the effects of deficiency upon the efficiency of conversion of food to weight gain.

In the belief that many of these differing opinions could arise from the wide variety of circumstances under which investigations are carried out we formed the opinion that our own contribution to this Symposium could usefully survey the nature of differing responses to a trace element that could arise from changes in experimental procedure. To do this we have elected to describe some of the problems and difficulties we have encountered in the studies of Zn metabolism by the Rowett Institute group of workers.

THE PROBLEM OF DEFINING EXPERIMENTAL CONDITIONS

Comparisons between the results of different investigators working in this field are only valid if clear statements are available regarding the following points:

1. The nature of the diet used to induce deficiency and, particularly, whether or not reliance has been placed upon the presence of trace element binding factors in the diet to produce deficiency rather than undertaking the more difficult task of removing the metal under study from dietary components.

2. The age or weight of the animal at the commencement of depletion.

3. A description of the dose/response curve obtained on replacement of the missing nutrient under the conditions in which subsequent investigational work is carried out.

4. Information on the method of management of control animals used in metabolic studies and particularly in situations where deficiency has an adverse effect upon food consumption.

We and our colleagues at the Rowett Institute who have been recently studying the effects of Zn deficiency in the rat and in larger animals have been particularly concerned with the problem of obtaining stable experimental conditions upon which to base investigations of the nature of metabolic lesions. Full details of these procedures will be published elsewhere (Williams and Mills, 1970; Chesters and Quarterman, 1970). Basically the procedure depends upon the preparation of a semi-synthetic diet containing purified mineral components and using a low-Zn protein source such as egg albumen or casein reprecipitated in the presence of EDTA. This diet normally contains between 0·7 and 0·8 p.p.m. Zn and when fed to newly weaned rats rapidly leads to the development of Zn deficiency. The performance of male animals on a typical experiment in which the effect of a lack of supplementary Zn upon weight gain was investigated are given in Figure 1. One of the most notable features of the use of this diet is that despite the absence of components known to reduce Zn availability the onset of deficiency as shown by a decline in the rate of growth is extremely rapid and usually occurs between four and six days after the diet is first offered. This situation makes possible the accurate assessment of the period of time for which deficiency has limited performance—the implications of this will be considered later.

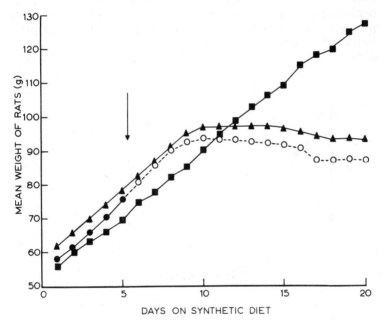

FIG. 1. Influence of dietary zinc content and restricted feeding on the growth of groups of male rats.
○ < 1 p.p.m. Zn, *ad lib.* ●, ■ 40 p.p.m. Zn, *ad lib.*; →change to deficient diet, ▲ 40 p.p.m. Zn, pair-fed.

Many factors may influence the nature of the animal's response to sub-optimal or 'borderline' levels of a limiting nutrient and in the case of the trace metals it is probably true to say that the more important of these are the existence of antagonistic interactions between the trace metals themselves and the presence of components which by virtue of their affinity for the trace element under study modify its fate during digestion, absorption and utilization. Where such factors have been identified, their content in the experimental diet can be stated but all too often during the early

41

stages of investigational work the nature of these factors is un-known. In such situations it becomes imperative to assess the nature of the dose/response curve at an early stage of the work and Figures 2A and 2B illustrate the nature of this response curve in male and female rats maintained on our basal diet supplemented with different levels of Zn and fed for an experimental period of 21 days (Williams and Mills, 1970). Such a procedure clearly illustrates the point that under our experimental conditions the requirements of the rat for normal growth are met when the diet provides 12 p.p.m. Zn; a finding which agrees closely with that of Forbes and Yohe (1960) based upon work using a similar type of diet.

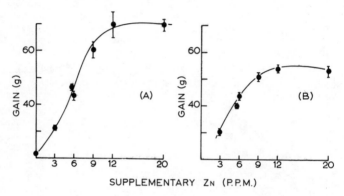

FIG. 2. Influence of dietary zinc content on 21 day weight gain. (A) male rats; (B) female rats.

The value of such response curves is again apparent from Forbes and Yohe's work (1960). They compared the response to supplementary Zn obtained when the basal diet consisted of casein or soya bean protein as nitrogen sources and the dis-similarities between these curves clearly exemplify the value of this 'calibration' procedure when faced with the task of attempting to assess the probable severity of deficiency induced by the type of diet fed. Failure to present such data on performance makes this assessment difficult or even impossible.

PRIMARY METABOLIC LESION OR SECONDARY EFFECT?
   Success or failure in the search for the primary metabolic defect arising as a consequence of deficiency of a trace metal depends greatly upon the degree of deficiency induced at the time such investigations are carried out. This in turn is a function of the

severity of the treatment as governed by the extent to which it has been possible to free the basal diet of the metal under investigation and secondly upon the period for which this diet has been fed. We are all well aware that the development of a deficiency syndrome may be regarded as a step-wise process; different organs suffer depletion of their content of individual elements at different rates and sufficient is known about differences in the affinity of physiologically important metal binding systems to suggest that we should not expect that the loss of essential elements from all active sites would proceed at the same rate. These points lend emphasis to the importance of our endeavours towards defining the degree of depletion suffered before metabolic studies are undertaken. They also emphasize that we should not necessarily expect to find the same metabolic lesions in situations where the rat has, for example, been depleted of Zn for 28 days (Theuer, 1965) as where it has been depleted for 73 to 150 days (Kfoury et al., 1968).

To illustrate the importance of attempting to define the degree of depletion in assessing the significance of metabolic effects we may cite the differences of opinion which exist as to whether deficiency of Zn in the rat influences the efficiency of conversion of ingested food into liveweight gain. The findings of Theuer (1965) on the one hand and of Prasad, Oberleas, Wolf and Horwitz (1967) and C.S.I.R.O. (1954) on the other illustrate this situation. The results presented in Figures 2A and 2B from our own work illustrate that at dietary Zn concentrations of 6 or 9 p.p.m. the supply of Zn is inadequate to support a maximum rate of growth.

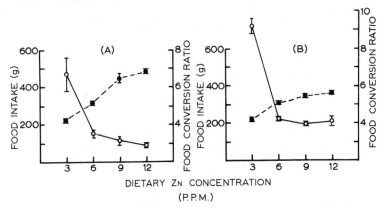

Fig. 3. Influence of dietary zinc content on food intake and food conversion ratio of the rat (39 day experimental period). (A) males; (B) females; ● food intake; ○ food conversion ratio.

Such rats would undoubtedly be deemed to be Zn-deficient and yet reference to the results presented in Figures 3A and 3B indicates that while these Zn concentrations had an adverse effect upon food consumption, no adverse effects on food conversion ratio are apparent (Williams and Mills, 1970). In contrast diets providing only 3 p.p.m. Zn have a highly significant effect on both parameters. From the above points the obvious conclusion is that the nature of the effects arising depends greatly upon the degree of depletion.

The task of differentiating between primary and secondary metabolic lesions is always difficult. Success or failure frequently depends upon the precise definition of the objective of the study. The initial approach is usually dictated by the appearance of a clinical lesion in a particular tissue and the detection of a deranged metabolic system. The assessment of whether the limiting trace element is directly involved at the site under study or whether the defect is a consequence of a deranged function at another site leading, for example, to a limitation in the supply of an essential precursor, inevitably becomes more difficult as the number of sites affected increases with progressive depletion. It has been our experience that progress is more certain if, once having detected a lesion, the immediately ensuing studies are devoted to the assessment of whether or not this defect is apparent before gross clinical changes are observed. Such considerations have dictated the approach used by ourselves and our colleagues at the Rowett Institute studying the effects of Zn deficiency on polynucleotide metabolism (Williams and Chesters, 1970; this volume p. 164) and upon the influence of Zn deficiency on alimentary muco-substances (Quarterman, Humphries and Florence, 1970; this volume. p. 167); both of these studies were carried out long before many of the characteristic clinical signs of Zn deficiency were expected to occur and in the former instance were commenced after only one day of Zn depletion.

SELECTION OF FEEDING REGIMES FOR CONTROL ANIMALS IN METABOLIC STUDIES

The declining growth rate of rats four to five days after first feeding a Zn-deficient diet (Fig. 1) is accompanied by a change in the pattern of food intake. Figure 4 drawn from data obtained from a typical animal illustrates that shortly after the introduction of a deficient diet food intake does not increase with time and becomes highly variable and cyclic in nature. These cycles appear every three to five days. To obtain an expression of the daily food intake and its variability we have analyzed data obtained from rats

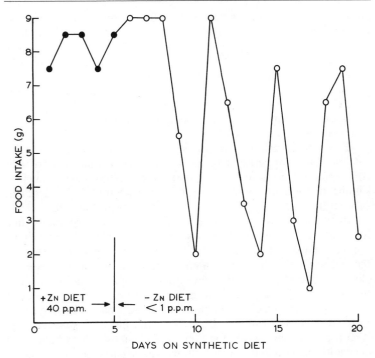

FIG. 4. Influence of dietary zinc content on daily food intake of a rat fed *ad lib*. ● 40 p.p.m. Zn diet; ○ < 1 p.p.m. Zn.

receiving Zn-supplemented diet (40 p.p.m.) *ad lib*. and deficient diet (less than 1 p.p.m.). For male animals of 80 g. the mean daily intake was 8·0 g./day and the standard deviation of daily intake ± 1·1 g./day, and for deficient animals intake was 5·5 g./day with a standard deviation of ± 2·8 g./day. Studying these effects with rats fed 3, 6, 9 or 12 p.p.m. Zn it was apparent that a more normal pattern of food consumption was only restored when the diet provided 12 p.p.m. Diets providing less than 1 and 3 p.p.m. produced very similar patterns while those providing 6 or 9 p.p.m. showed less evidence of cycles of high and low food consumption.

The reduction of food intake and the increase in its variability are highly characteristic of Zn deficiency. The magnitude of these effects and the rapidity of onset can, however, be modified by changes in dietary composition. Restricting the protein content of the deficient diet to 5 per cent. by replacement of protein by starch caused a reduced rate of growth, prolonged the period before

45

growth ceased on the deficient diet, led to an increase in food consumption after growth had ceased (mean consumption at 80 g., 6·3 g./day) and reduced the variability of intake (S.D. ± 1·3 g./day). We have found, furthermore, that if deficient rats are offered the normal (20 per cent. protein) Zn-deficient diet in a restricted daily allocation of 5·0 g./day (i.e. 0·5 g. less than the average *ad lib.* intake of deficient animals) growth failure occurs later, cycles of low food consumption are abolished and the day-to-day variation of intake becomes markedly less.

These observations naturally stimulated our curiosity as to the role of Zn in appetite regulation particularly since two of our colleagues (Humphries and Quarterman, 1968) have shown a significant increase in the rate of food consumption of deficient rats within 4 hours of the first inclusion of Zn in the diet.

In such a situation the choice of an appropriate feeding regime for control animals used in studies of the underlying metabolic lesions is particularly difficult. The data of Figure 1 illustrate that the earliest growth lesion, namely poor food consumption, is closely associated with the development of Zn deficiency. It is therefore clearly inappropriate in investigations of the function of Zn to use *ad lib.* fed control animals as the sole basis of comparison with Zn-deficient animals. In such a situation the usual recourse is to a paired-feeding regime and we and many others have used deficient and pair-fed control animals as a basis for such studies in the past. However, it is becoming increasingly apparent that such a system of management is not wholly acceptable and can lead to gross errors in metabolic studies. Our own earliest experience of this arose in the investigations of one of our colleagues (R. B. Williams, personal communication) on the influence of Zn deficiency on the summated activities of glucose-6-phosphate dehydrogenase and 6–phospho-gluconate dehydrogenase in Zn-deficient and pair-fed control rats. Following the preliminary conclusion that the activity of these enzymes in livers of deficient rats remained constant during the 35 day experimental period after weaning whereas that of Zn-supplemented rats trebled in activity, it was later found that the rise in activity in pair-fed control rats was an adaptive response induced by the pair-feeding regime and was not found in *ad lib.* fed Zn-supplemented rats. That such responses occur is hardly surprising when one considers that under such experimental situations the pair-fed control rat is consuming the greater part of its daily allocation of food within 3 to 4 hours and starving for the remainder of the day whereas the deficient rat is gradually consuming an equal amount of food spaced fairly evenly throughout the day. The recent work of Potter and his colleagues (Potter *et al.,* 1968; Baril and Potter, 1968) has clearly shown that the imposition of such a system of feeding, even when the diet is nutritionally adequate, leads to systematic oscillations in the activity of many of the enzymes involved in amino acid and carbohydrate metabolism, in the levels of corticosterone and in the rates of amino acid transport in liver. The work of Fabry and his group, reviewed by Fabry (1967), has illustrated the more long-term nature of adaptive responses in pathways of lipogenesis and in the fate of many metabolic intermediates. Our gradually dawning appreciation of the magnitude of these changes has naturally led to an extensive re-appraisal of some of our own earlier work employing conventionally pair-fed animals and details of this have been published elsewhere (Mills *et al.,* 1969).

In our view there are only two ways in which it is possible to avoid complications arising from the imposition of an abnormal pattern of food consumption in metabolic experiments. These are: (1) to restrict metabolic investigations to the period before food intake has become adversely affected by the missing nutrient, or (2) to employ more precise methods of pair feeding by the use of an automatic feeding device such that the intake of control animals more closely parallels that of the deficient animal throughout the day.

Both these approaches have been used in some of our own studies on the metabolic role of Zn. Investigations that have been conducted before appetite failure has become apparent are those on the influence of Zn deficiency upon the incorporation of ^{3}H-thymidine into tissue DNA (Williams and Chesters, 1970) and some of our earlier investigations of the effect of deficiency upon pancreatic carboxypeptidase where a reduction in activity was apparent before food intake had fallen (Mills *et al.,* 1967). In these studies we are satisfied that differences between Zn-deficient and control rats are not attributable to differences in the pattern of food intake. For longer term investigations of the later effects of deficiency upon amino acid, carbohydrate and lipid metabolism we have developed a system of automatic feeding in which the intake of control rats can be closely related to that of deficient rats throughout the day (Quarterman, Williams and Humphries, 1970). These feeders illustrated in Figure 5 consist of a rotating perspex turntable from which is cut a groove to hold the day's allocation of diet, this assembly being rotated once every 24 hours by a synchronous motor. The turntable protrudes into the cage exposing only a small segment of the disc at one time. This

47

assembly has proved satisfactory in use and is simple and in-expensive to produce. A more sophisticated automatic feeder has been developed by Suttie and further illustration of the value of this approach in studies of metabolic defects is provided by

FIG. 5. Perspex and glass cage with time-controlled feeder for use in studies of trace element deficiency. The perspex disc with dietary allocation in the groove is rotated by a 24 hour clock motor mounted below it.

reference to his paper in this volume. Using a feeding system of this nature it becomes practicable not only to ensure a uniform intake of diet by control animals fed a restricted quantity of food but also to 'profile' intake so that hourly variations in intake by experimental animals can be closely reproduced in animals fed nutritionally adequate diets. Such an approach provides the only acceptable alternative to the frequently employed procedure of starving experimental and control animals for a given period before metabolic investigations are carried out in the attempt to bring them both to a common level of metabolic activity.

48

CONCLUSIONS
It is our belief that many of the discrepancies apparent in statements concerning the possible functional roles of many of the trace elements arise from inadequate experimental control, from the failure to recognize that metabolic pathways become modified with age and with the duration and severity of depletion of tissue reserves of an essential nutrient. Furthermore, an additional problem is the failure to appreciate that the imposition of abnormal patterns of food intake upon animals fed a nutritionally adequate diet leads to a modification of metabolic processes; a situation which demands experimental control if erroneous conclusions are to be avoided in comparative studies of 'control' and deficient animals.

Progress towards the understanding of the role of the trace elements, as of other micro-nutrients, has been made from two directions; firstly from the fractionation of tissue preparations leading ultimately to the extraction, purification and identification of trace-metal bearing components often having an enzymic function, and secondly, from *in vivo* studies of the metabolic response to trace-element depletion. In this paper we have tried to illustrate that the latter approach provides many opportunities for the misinterpretation of data if adequate control of experimental animals is not exercised. Our appreciation of the importance of precise experimental control has largely arisen from work quite unrelated to studies of the trace elements and it is suggested that the application of this information in our own studies may do much to make progress more certain.

The views expressed in this paper have been derived from many stimulating discussions between ourselves and our colleagues in the Trace Element Unit at the Rowett Institute; we wish to thank them for their helpful comments and for permission to include some of their experimental data.

REFERENCES
BARIL, E. F. & POTTER, V. R. (1968). *J. Nutr.* **95,** 228.
BEARD, H. H., BAKER, R. W. & MYERS, V. C. (1931). *J. biol. Chem.* **94,** 123.
BEARD, H. H. & MYERS, V. C. (1931). *J. biol. Chem.* **94,** 71.
CHESTERS, J. K. & QUARTERMAN, J. (1970). Submitted for publication.
C.S.I.R.O. (1954). *6th Annual Report Commonwealth Scientific and Industrial Research Organisation, Australia,* p. 45.
ELVEHJEM, C. A. (1935). *Physiol. Rev.* **15,** 471.
EVELETH, M. W., BING, F. C. & MYERS, V. C. (1932–33). *Proc. Soc. exp. Biol. Med.* **30,** 852.
FABRY, P. (1967). In *Handbook of Physiology,* ed. Code, C. F. vol. 6 (1). Alimentary Canal, ch. 3. Washington: American Physiologic Society.
FORBES, R. M. & YOHE, M. (1960). *J. Nutr.* **70,** 53.

HUMPHRIES, W. R. & QUARTERMAN, J. (1968). *Proc. Nutr. Soc.* **27**, 54A.
KFOURY, G. A., REINHOLD, J. G. & SIMONIAN, S. J. (1968). *J. Nutr.* **95**, 102.
MILLS, C. F., QUARTERMAN, J., CHESTERS, J. K., WILLIAMS, R. B. & DALGARNO, A. C. (1969). *Am. J. clin. Nutr.* **22**, 1240.
MILLS, C. F., QUARTERMAN, J., WILLIAMS, R. B., DALGARNO, A. C. & PANIC, B. (1967). *Biochem. J.* **102**, 712.
POTTER, V. R., BARIL, E. F., WATANABE, M. & WHITTLE, E. D. (1968). *Fedn Proc. Fedn Am. Socs exp. Biol.* **27**, 1238.
PRASAD, A. S., OBERLEAS, D., WOLF, P. & HORWITZ, J. P. (1967). *J. clin. Invest.* **46**, 549.
QUARTERMAN, J., WILLIAMS, R. B. & HUMPHRIES, W. R. (1970). Submitted for publication.
THEUER, R. C. (1965). *A study of metabolic alterations in the zinc deficient rat.* Ph.D. Thesis: University of Wisconsin.
WADDELL, J., ELVEHJEM, C. A., STEENBOCK, H. & HART, E. B. (1928). *J. biol. Chem.* **77**, 769.
WILLIAMS, R. B. & MILLS, C. F. (1970). *Br. J. Nutr.* In press.

DISCUSSION

Kirchgessner (Munich). I would like to support the comments of Dr Mills on the care needed in carrying out experiments with the trace elements by reporting the results we have obtained in balance trials with steers maintained at different environmental temperatures. A higher faecal excretion of Zn, Mn, Co and Fe occurred at temperatures of 10° or 30° than at 20°. Cu excretion wasn't affected by environmental temperature within these limits. We have found a higher urinary excretion of Co at 10° than at 20° environmental temperature. Temperature should be taken into account when planning such experiments.

Mills (Aberdeen). I agree. There is already ample evidence that the Mg requirement of the rat is influenced by environmental temperature and Naftalin's work on dietary liver necrosis carried out before Se was discovered showed that environmental temperature was extremely important in influencing the percentage of animals affected. In view of these points it is perhaps surprising that so rarely does one find data on the environmental temperature at which work was carried out.

Suttie (Madison). I wonder if Dr Mills would comment more on the cyclic nature of the appetite repression he sees in Zn-deficient animals and has he any idea what is causing it?

Mills (Aberdeen). We can't really comment reliably on the mechanism at the moment. We are however quite confident that we can pick up a Zn-deficient rat by the characteristic pattern of eating that emerges within four to five days of feeding a diet containing less than 1 p.p.m. Zn. This observation is made in every experiment we carry out. The pattern of the cycle is constant within the limits of three and a half to four days. Dr Quarterman, tomorrow, will be describing some of his work on muco-substances in the digestive tract in relation to this phenomenon and we are also looking at amino acid patterns in tissues during Zn deficiency and their possible relationship to this effect. It seems that what may be happening is that when the Zn-deficient rat eats a substantial amount of food a metabolite is produced which suppresses appetite and until that metabolite is cleared food intake remains low. Beyond the fact that it is related apparently to the protein level of the diet and to the fact that if an upper limit is placed on food consumption the cycle doesn't appear we have not yet made a great deal of progress in elucidating the mechanism. The cycles of high and low food intake pose major problems in the design of the metabolic investigations we have to carry out. We have to be careful to compare deficient and control animals at their respective 'peaks' or 'troughs' of intake to reach valid conclusions on what Zn may be doing in metabolic terms.

Suttie (Madison). If you forcibly impose such a cycle of high and low intake upon a control rat and then offer it food *ad libitum* does the cycle continue?

Mills (Aberdeen). We haven't tried this. All I can say is that pair-fed control animals subjected to the same pattern appear to adapt after a period of about 21 days and begin to gain weight slowly although this is not a very convincing difference. Because of this all our metabolic work is now restricted to the very early days of Zn deficiency before this adaptation has taken place in control animals. We are really hunting for a cyclic process having a frequency of three and a half to four days which may underlie this effect on food consumption and which may be affected by Zn deficiency. One possibility I haven't mentioned is that during the brief periods of low intake Zn may be mobilized from the tissues. We know that the Zn-deficient animals still contain a lot of Zn; tissue catabolism during periods of low food intake may be accompanied by a liberation of Zn which then restores appetite. In connection with this the only point we can say is that if this process is taking place it is not being accompanied by any changes in plasma Zn content.

Horvath (Morgantown, W.Va.). Have you made any measurements of physical activity of animals maintained on meal eating or nibbling patterns of food concumption?

Mills (Aberdeen). We haven't measured activity quantitatively but we can see no major differences between deficient and control animals that would be sufficient to explain the differences in efficiency of food conversion to liveweight gain.

Schwarz (Long Beach). Do you see any porphyrin changes in the Zn-deficient animals and could the periodicity of the changes you have described be related to porphyrin metabolism?

Mills (Aberdeen). Yes we do. Following prolonged deprivation of Zn we see the deposition of a porphyrin-like pigment around the nose and hair and this probably first appears about three weeks after the start of depletion. This I would thus regard as a late change and we are now concentrating most of our efforts on the period from one to five days after the commencement of feeding Zn-deficient diets as will be described in the papers by Dr Quarterman and Dr Chesters later in the programme of this meeting.

Lassiter (Athens, Ga.). I would like to refer to Professor Kirchgessner's comment on the influence of temperature on trace metal excretion and to ask what measurements of water intake were made?

Kirchgessner (Munich). Water intake increased progressively from $10°$ to $30°$ C but the effects on metal excretion in faeces and urine cannot be directly related to water intake or output.

NUTRITIONAL STUDIES WITH NICKEL

R. H. WELLENREITER, D. E. ULLREY AND E. R. MILLER

Michigan State University, East Lansing, Michigan, U.S.A.

BIOLOGY is full of surprises! The discovery that chromium is as vital to life as it is to the shine on an automobile bumper, was an exciting revelation to scientists who work in Michigan. If for no other reason, the ubiquitous use of Cr on that four-wheeled product of Detroit technology may serve to protect us from the dangers of glucose intolerance. The discovery is important, nevertheless, and has led us to consider what other additions might be made to the burgeoning list of elements essential for life.

When one examines period 4 in the table of elements, and works across from Cr, with an atomic number of 24, to zinc, with an atomic number of 30, only one element stands out in its lack of definition as an essential nutrient. That element is nickel.

Its location in the periodic table, among elements with established physiological functions, leads one to wonder whether it, too, might not be vital for some unrecognized biochemical role. Nickel varies in its electronic configuration from its near neighbours, cobalt, iron and manganese, only in the number of electrons in the 3d orbital, while the 4s orbital is filled. These elements are all members of the first transition series and are characterized by multiple valency. Because electronic expansion is not in the outermost shell, these elements have a fixed ionic radius and similar chemical and physical properties. Superficially, at least, there is no obvious reason why Ni could not be physiologically important.

If one hopes to establish an essential physiological role for a trace metal, such as Ni, in a living macro-organism, the selection of that organism is very important. We chose the Japanese quail (*Coturnix coturnix japonica*) for the following reasons: (1) The possibility of depleting tissues of a trace metal by feeding purified diets is generally increased by following this practice through successive generations. The Japanese quail has a very short generation time, producing the first eggs 35 to 37 days after hatching. Incubation requires 17 to 18 days. A practical generation time is, thus, about 8 weeks. (2) This species has a very high metabolic rate which tends to exaggerate nutrient requirements. (3) The cost of highly purified diets per animal unit is less than for many other species because of comparatively low absolute food intake. (4) The bird is small enough to conveniently house in a filtered air environment. This latter point is important because, in the industrialized area in which we work, airborne Ni contaminants are a significant problem, presumably emanating from factories, automobile exhausts and tobacco smoke.

Consequently the birds were housed in isolators designed for gnotobiotic research, equipped with 'absolute' filters capable of removing particles of 0·3 nm. diameter or larger. To eliminate other environmental contamination, plastics which contained undetectable Ni levels were used for feeders and waterers. All surfaces in contact with the birds were repeatedly washed with 6N HCl and rinsed with deionized, distilled, steam condensate to reduce the chance of contamination between experiments. The floors of the growing cages were covered with un-inked newsprint to absorb excreta and this was changed each day. Adult birds were housed on plastic flooring which permitted the excreta to fall into a space below.

Studies of this type are partially dependent upon satisfactory systems of chemical analysis. The Ni content of materials in contact with the birds, and of the diets, was determined by atomic absorption spectrophotometry after digestion with nitric and perchloric acids, chelation at pH 1·8 with ammonium pyrrolidino dithiocarbamate and extraction into methyl isobutyl ketone. The sensitivity of the system, as normally used, was approximately 50 p.p.b. This could be increased, when necessary, by digesting larger samples and extracting into smaller volumes of methyl isobutyl ketone.

Six experimental trials have been conducted so far. Trials 1 and 2 were devoted to development of the basal diet and creation of the first generation of Ni-low and Ni-supplemented birds. The basal diet, which is now producing rates of gain and reproductive performance equal to a natural diet currently in use by our Poultry Science Department, is shown in Table I.

Table I. *Composition of basal diet*

BASAL DIET		MINERALS IN DIET (p.p.m)				
Glucose·H_2O	41·83%					
Casein, high protein	35·00	KCl	Ca	12000	Zn	80
L-Glutamic acid.HCl	5·74	$FeSO_4.7H_2O$	P	10880	Cu	12
Glycine.HCl	1·36	KI	K	4752	I	6
L-Arginine.HCl	1·13	Na_2SeO_3	Na	2490	Mo	3
Corn oil	5.00	$CrK(SO_4)_2.12H_2O$	Cl	1501	Cr	1
Cellulose	3·00	$NiCO_3$	Mg	1400	F	1
Mineral mix	6·68		S	114	Co	0·5
Vitamin mix	0·25		Mn	90	Se	0·1
Ethoxyquin	0·0125		Fe	88	Ni	0·08
	100·0025					

MINERAL SALTS USED

$CaCO_3$	$ZnSO_4.7H_2O$
$CaHPO_4$	$CuSO_4$
$NaHCO_3$	$NaMoO_4.2H_2O$
$4MgCO_3.Mg(OH)_2.H_2O$	$CoCO_3$
$MnSO_4.H_2O$	$KHCO_3$
	NaF

VITAMINS IN DIET (p.p.m.)

Retinyl palmitate	16·5	Pyridoxine HCl	30.0
Cholecalciferol	0·06	Folic Acid	12·0
D-α-Tocopheryl acetate	300·0	Biotin	0·33
Menadione	3·6	Cyanocobalamin	0·04
Thiamine mononitrate	30·0	Choline chloride	6000·0
Riboflavin	30·0	Ascorbic acid	240·0
D-Calcium pantothenate	90·0	Inositol	390·0
Nicotinic acid	210·0	p-Amino benzoic acid	39·0

Although all mineral salts were J. T. Baker reagent grade chemicals, it was necessary to further purify the Ca, P, Mg and Co salts, as well as the cellulose, to bring Ni concentration to acceptably low levels. The unfortified diet contained 80 p.p.b. of Ni. The water provided for drinking was redistilled, deionized, distilled, steam condensate.

Early growth of the birds in trial 1 was not normal due to an apparent vitamin deficiency which was empirically corrected by tripling the vitamin levels to those shown in Table I. Growth improved immediately, but without differences between birds receiving either 80 or 1720 p.p.b. of Ni. The reproductive performance of these birds is shown in Table II. Since they were not housed individually, no statistical analysis is possible. Eggs from these birds were incubated for production of the second generation, and the gain data for these birds are shown in Table III (trial 4).

Table II. *Egg production, fertility and hatchability of birds receiving diets providing 80 or 1720 p.p.b. of nickel (trial 1)*

Item	− Ni	+ Ni
Eggs/bird/day	·54	·65
Egg weight, g.	9·2	8·8
Cracked eggs, %	22·3	13·9
Fertility, %	82·4	79·9
Hatchability, %	56·2	48·8

Table III. *Effects of dietary treatment on bodyweight (g), gain/feed and per cent. survival (nos. in parentheses)*

TRIAL 3—BODYWEIGHT & GAIN/FEED

Diet	0 Day	14 Days	25 Days	Gain/Feed
− Arg − Ni	6·7	21·7	47·2	·43
+ Arg − Ni	6·8	41·9	76·5	·45
− Arg + Ni	6·8	22·9	48·9	·44
+ Arg + Ni	6·5	42·0	77·6	·46

TRIAL 4—BODYWEIGHT

Diet	0 Day	9 Days	16 Days	20 Days	27 Days
− Ni	6·2	24·9	45·0	53·8	76·4
+ Ni	5·8	24·2	44·6	58·4	79·3

TRIAL 5—BODYWEIGHT & GAIN/FEED

Diet	0 Day	13 Days	27 Days	Gain/Feed
− Arg − Ni	6·0	12·8	33·3(74)	·28
+ Arg − Ni	6·0	23·8	57·0(85)	·34
− Arg + Ni	6·0	12·7	30·7(67)	·28
+ Arg + Ni	6·0	22·4	55·6(90)	·35

TRIAL 6—BODYWEIGHT & GAIN/FEED

Diet	0 Day	7 Days	14 Days	21 Days	Gain/Feed
−Arg − Ni	6·8	9·1	12·9	20·2(90)	·33
+Arg − Ni	6·7	12·1	22·8	37·3(94)	·48
−Arg + Ni	6·6	9·0	13·1	21·1(74)	·34
+ Arg + Ni	6·5	11·3	21·2	38·5(81)	·47

Reproduction of the second generation birds has been underway for some time and eggs from these birds are now being incubated for the production of the third generation. To date, no differences between the Ni-low and Ni-supplemented birds in appearance have been seen, as long as the basal diet was adequate in other respects.

In this regard, it has been known for some time that the chick cannot synthesize arginine. Tamir and Ratner (1963a) were unable to find carbamyl phosphate synthetase in chick kidney or liver, which explains the chick's inability to grow on ornithine in place of arginine. In birds, as opposed to mammals, presumably 'arginine has become an indispensable amino acid as a result of the change in pattern of nitrogen excretion brought about by replacing arginine synthesis and urea excretion by purine synthesis and uric acid excretion' (Tamir and Ratner, 1963b).

A number of workers have isolated an arginase from both chick liver and kidney, although the activity in liver is quite low. The function of this enzyme in the chick is not definitely known. It is not required for ornithine synthesis since this compound can arise by transamidination. Its activity must contribute to the relatively high requirement of the bird for arginine, since only that arginine which escapes degradation is available for creatine and protein synthesis. Its activity is increased by certain conditions of amino acid imbalance, and a diet which is first-limiting in arginine and has an excess of lysine will result in slow growth of chicks and an increase in kidney arginase activity (Nesheim, 1968).

Mammalian arginase is activated by divalent metal ions, particularly Mn^{2+}, Ni^{2+} and Co^{2+} (Greenberg, 1951). While the involvement of Ni *in vitro* is not presumptive evidence for importance *in vivo*, a possible role in the activation of avian kidney arginase was considered worthy of pursuit. If, in fact, Ni does activate arginase *in vivo,* a low level of tissue Ni, and consequently a low level of arginase activity, might be beneficial to a bird with a wide lysine : arginine ratio. Thus, trial 3 was designed.

The basal diet was altered by removing the supplemental arginine for half the birds. This resulted in a lysine : arginine ratio of 2·0 for the low arginine group and of 1·1 for the arginine-supplemented group. Each of these treatment groups was then given no supplementary nickel or 2000 p.p.b.

The effect on bodyweight and gain/feed is shown in Table III. The low arginine birds were significantly (P < 0·01) lighter at all ages than the arginine-supplemented birds, but the two Ni treatments resulted in no significant differences in weight. There appeared to be a significant difference in breast-feathering of the low arginine birds in favour of those supplemented with Ni, and this subjective observation was confirmed independently by three persons without knowledge of treatments. No feathering differences were noted in the arginine-supplemented birds.

Trials 5 and 6 were designed to exaggerate the amino acid imbalance by lowering casein in all diets from 35 to 25 per cent. and by increasing tyrosine from 1·36 per cent. to 2·36 per cent. (Nesheim, 1969). This diet was then supplemented with L-arginine·HCl (1·13 per cent.) for half the birds. All birds received either no supplemental nickel or 5000 p.p.b.

The effect of treatments in trial 5 on bodyweight, gain/feed and survival is shown in Table III. There was a tendency for Ni-supplemented birds to weigh less, but the only significant (P < 0·01) difference was between those birds receiving supplemental arginine or no supplemental arginine.

Trial 6 differed from trial 5 only in the reduction of Mn in all diets from 90 to 40 p.p.m. This was done in the hope of exaggerating the effect of Ni on arginase activity. Results of this trial are shown in Table III. Once again the only effects on weight related to the presence or absence of supplemental arginine. The addition of Ni to either level of arginine appeared to result in an appreciably greater death loss.

Tissues from birds on trials 3, 5 and 6 are currently undergoing analysis for Ni concentration, arginase activity and evidence of histopathology. Certain plasma samples are also being examined for amino acid concentration.

The positive effect of Ni on breast-feathering, in birds which are relatively arginine deficient but on adequate protein intake is interesting but needs to be repeated. Our work is still in progress and firm conclusions as to the essentiality of Ni must wait for further results. At this preliminary point it would appear that requirements for Ni, on diets which are adequate in other respects, are probably below 80 p.p.b.

REFERENCES

GREENBERG, D. M. (1951). *The Enzymes,* vol. 1, part 2, p. 893. New York: Academic Press.
NESHEIM, M. C. (1968). *J. Nutr.* **99,** 79.
NESHEIM, M. C. (1969). *Fedn Proc. Fedn Am. Socs exp. Biol.* **28,** 689.
TAMIR, H. & RATNER, F. (1963a). *Archs Biochem. Biophys.* **102,** 249.
TAMIR, H. & RATNER, F. (1963b). *Archs Biochem. Biophys.* **102,** 259.

DISCUSSION

Schwarz (Long Beach). Have you fed your diet to species other than chicks? I have heard that with diets below 60 parts per billion, Sauberlich and his group have obtained a clear-cut Ni deficiency in rats.

Ullrey (E. Lansing). We have not so far tried other species.

RADIOCHEMICAL PROCEDURES FOR PARTITIONING MATERNAL-FOETAL MINERAL REQUIREMENTS AND PREGNANCY ANABOLISM IN GRAVID SWINE

S. L. HANSARD

University of Tennessee, Institute of Agriculture, Knoxville, Tennessee, U.S.A.

MATERNAL control of foetal environment and nurture has prevented a direct approach to many of the interesting and fascinating problems of foetal-placental and maternal physiology. Nevertheless progress has been continuous on the development of basic metabolic procedures for determination of rates and amounts of mineral transfer (Hansard, 1965; Widdas, 1961). Investigations have been hampered by anatomical inaccessibility and the complexity of the problems for studying foetal and maternal circulations simultaneously. However, indirect procedures for estimating body compartment size and composition, subsequent to sacrifice for organ and tissue analyses, have presented unique advantages for farm animal research (Hansard, 1963). These several methods for measuring both rate and quantity of minerals transferred from dam to foetus have been discussed by Barcroft (1946), Robinson (1957), Reynolds (1965), Hansard (1965), and range from whole body analyses of dam and foetus to use of indicators and radioactive labelled substances for predicting composition change, quantitating specific mechanisms, membrane permeability and

58

transport rates, foetal accretion, and for estimations of deposition rates and pregnancy anabolism (Hansard, 1969).

The presence of a growing foetus progressively adds an extra physiological load to the sow, and much of the maternal response is accredited to this increased body burden. There is evidence that specific metabolic adjustments occur in the pregnant sow that increase ultimate retention and utilizations of all nutrients above those of the non-gravid female (Salmon-Legagneur and Rerat, 1962). These adjustments are variable, but result in body weight increase and marked maternal accretion above that of the products of conception (Bourdel, 1957). The part maternal anabolism plays in foetal development and growth has been elucidated for only a selected number of nutrients, and little progress has been made in quantitation of immediate physiological effects upon post-natal adjustments and subsequent maternal and progeny performance. Quantitation of maternal nutrient requirements therefore, for economic foetal development and growth, must involve individual and combined nutrient accretion for both maternal and foetal utilization, allowing for adequate adjustments for post-natal performance in both dam and foetus.

Current radiochemical studies with yearling gilts have indicated wide variations in maternal absorption for selected macro- and micro-minerals. However, those minerals absorbed have been observed to pass freely from dam to foetus at all stages of gestation, with quantity and rate increasing progressively with advanced pregnancy to parturition. Augmented foetal mineral transfer has been associated directly with the increasing needs of the growing foetus, structural changes in the placenta and the expanding membrane exchange area. Foetal deposition patterns and utilization of those minerals transferred have closely paralleled those of the dam in that they are rapidly removed from foetal circulation by the several competing physiological processes. This report is concerned with the absorption and transfer of selected minerals from the sow to her foetuses and the efficiency of this partition in yearling gravid gilts.

MATERIALS AND METHODS

The experimental animals used in these studies consisted of 168 yearling Poland China, Duroc and Hampshire gilts. Following breeding they were randomly divided according to breeding dates into three groups for sacrifice at 35, 75, and 112 days gestation. All animals were maintained on a conventional corn-soybean oil meal gestation ration containing 16 per cent. protein and supplemented with adequate vitamins and minerals (Hansard *et al.*, 1966). Two weeks before sacrifice each gilt was placed in a metabolism unit equipped for the separate collection of faeces and urine (Hansard, 1951). Following oral or intravenous administration of a single tracer dose of the radioisotope, blood and balance data were collected until sacrifice, after 168 hours, for selected maternal-foetal tissue and organ samples. Placental membranes and fluids were weighed and sampled, and foetuses were immediately separated from the placenta, weighed, measured and either ashed for whole body analyses, or foetal tissues and organs were taken for radiochemical analyses. All data were standardized for dose, litter size and body weight for comparative purposes, and balance data were employed to adjust tissue radioactivity values to that retained by the dam. Procedures permitted comparison of movement and behaviour patterns of the radioisotopes, unmasked by differences due to maternal absorption.

RESULTS AND DISCUSSION

The foetus is dependant directly upon the dam for all nutrients (Robinson, 1957; Widdas, 1961). These sources are either endogenous, or maintained from the current feed intake. It is obvious, therefore, that foetal supply is dependent upon a readily available maternal source. Dams deprived of essential minerals for extended periods, or limited in current dietary intake could provoke foetal deficiencies and subsequent structural or functional abnormalities. Factors depressing maternal absorption and/or retention would likewise limit foetal availability.

Mineral Absorption. Foetal mineral source, therefore, is best defined in terms of quantity available from these mineral sources. This involves absorption into the blood, transfer across the placental barriers, the irrigation coefficient of the uterus and the velocity constants of the transplacental movement (Moustgaard, 1962). Conventional radiochemical balance procedures permit measurement of absorption values for net maternal mineral retention calculations (Hansard, 1965). The 7-day excretory pathways of the selected radiominerals used in this study are shown in Table I. Values illustrate the variations observed in urinary-faecal partition and the subsequent net absorption. It is evident that more of an intravenous than oral dose was retained and that, except for ^{35}S, the greater part of the ingested minerals were excreted via the faeces within 168 hours. Although there was a

Table I. *Excretory pathways for selected radioisotopes in gravid gilts**

Radioisotope	Excretion of Oral and I.V. Dose, % Faeces	Urine	Net Absorption
^{45}Ca	†71(13)‡	0·1(0·2)	29
^{32}P	55(18)	5·0(7·0)	40
^{35}S	15(8)	63·0(72)	22
^{59}Fe	83(6)	0·3(0·2)	17
^{65}Zn	90(4)	0·1(0·2)	10

* Seven day balance studies with yearling, gravid gilts. † Oral dose. ‡ I.V. dose.

trend toward increased absorption with gestation age, differences due to pregnancy were not significant. The unusual excretory pattern of sulfate-S was of interest in that both the ingested and injected ^{35}S had similar excretory pathways. Dietary mineral behaviour in the gastrointestinal tract of sows are reflected by these radiomineral values; and from these, maternal absorption and retention can be estimated (Hansard, 1969) to range from 10 per cent. for Zn to 40 per cent. for P.

Radiominerals in Conception Products. Retained radiominerals may either be deposited in the maternal tissue and organs or transferred to the placenta, fluids, and foetuses. These percentage composition values, 168 hours after dose administration, showing distribution patterns are demonstrated by trimesters in Figure 1 and

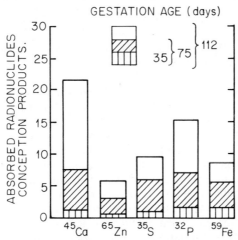

FIG. 1. Gestation age effects upon retention of selected radionuclides in total products of conception of gilts (placenta, fluids and foetuses) 168 hours after dose administration.

indicate the magnitude of difference due to gestation age for the various radioisotopes. It was of interest that during early pregnancy most of the total radioactivity in the conception products was in the placenta itself, but during the final trimesters a proportionally greater part was in the foetuses, with less in membranes and fluids. After seven days 99 per cent. of that 21·3 per cent. ^{45}Ca absorbed and transferred to the total placental complex was contained in the eight foetuses, whereas 40 per cent. of the ^{59}Fe, 46 per cent. of the ^{65}Zn, and 28 per cent. of the ^{32}P remained in the placenta itself. Contribution by placental fluids to the total conception products were small, except that ^{59}Fe and ^{35}S were significantly higher than other isotopes.

These relationships are borne out by data in Table II, showing the accumulative composition and proportional distribution of selected stable minerals deposited in the total conception products

Table II. *Mineral composition of products of conception in swine at 112 days gestation*

| Mineral* | Products of Conception | | | |
	Total Placenta	Placental Fluids†	Average Foetus	Total Products
Calcium, g.	0·59	0·62	9·9	80·4
Phosphorus, g.	0·62	8·15	5·3	43·2
Sulphur, inorg., g.	5·7	0·24	1·0	14·1
Iron, mg.	30·5	0·8	34·8	309·5
Zinc, mg.	55·8	1·4	26·8	271·6

* Minerals calculated per kg. wet weight, and total in eight foetus litter.
† All placental fluids were combined for sampling after removal of foetuses.

of the gravid third trimester gilt. Except for Fe and Zn, where 10 to 20 per cent. of the total was in the placenta, most of the minerals were contained in the foetus itself. The dynamic nature of this accretion by the foetus is reflected by accumulation of selected minerals in Figure 2, and parallel foetal development and growth rates during gestation. Early in the second trimester, growth was augmented and foetal weight increased 30 times and length 7 times, to a mass equal that of the placental membranes (Hansard and Berry, 1969). Net weight increase, however, was greatest during the final trimester, when foetal weight tripled and total length doubled. Early formation of haemoglobin caused Fe levels to increase rapidly, while Cu, Mn and S accumulated slowly with age. Increased skeletal ossification was reflected by the Ca

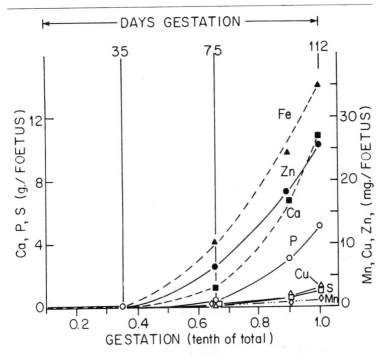

Fig. 2. Accumulative foetal accretion of selected minerals in gravid gilts during gestation.

deposition rate, which exceeded that for P and Mg during the final trimester (Manners and McCrea, 1963; Widdowson, 1968).

Maternal Anabolism of Minerals. Radiochemical procedures for calculation of true absorption of minerals (Hansard, 1956, 1965) provide an estimation of the total ingested minerals absorbed and retained by the maternal body. After standardization of animal age, weight, and dietary and nutritional histories, conventional radiochemical methods permit a quantitative comparison of the distribution of those minerals retained in various animal organs and tissues (Hansard, 1969). Gravid females sacrificed at specific periods of pregnancy permit separate analyses of the placenta, fluids, and whole foetus for the calculation of total minerals or radionuclides in these products of conception. If it is assumed that after equilibrium (seven days) the radioisotope distributes itself in tissues and organs like the absorbed stable minerals, then by difference calculated from absorption values (Table I) and the radiochemical analyses of the conception

63

products, maternal mineral stores can be estimated. The partition of ^{45}Ca in the gravid gilt at 35, 75, and 112 days gestation is shown schematically in Figure 3 and illustrates that maternal stores

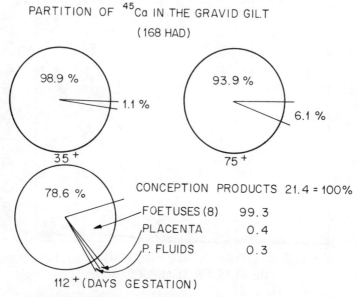

PARTITION OF ^{45}Ca IN THE GRAVID GILT

(168 HAD)

98.9 %

1.1 %

35$^+$

93.9 %

6.1 %

75$^+$

78.6 %

112$^+$(DAYS GESTATION)

CONCEPTION PRODUCTS 21.4 = 100%

FOETUSES (8)   99. 3

PLACENTA   0. 4

P. FLUIDS   0. 3

FIG. 3. Calculated partition of total absorbed ^{45}Ca in conception products and maternal body of gravid gilts at 35, 75 and 112 days gestation.

comprise the greater part of that ^{45}Ca absorbed and retained during all states of pregnancy. Maternal anabolism was greatest during early gestation, and decreased from 99 per cent. at 35 to 78·6 at 112 days when 99·3 per cent. of that ^{45}Ca retained by the conception products was in the eight foetuses. On this assumption, it can be calculated that a sow with a litter of eight pigs absorbing 9·3 g. from the 30 g. per day ingested Ca, at 75 days gestation was depositing 5·9 per cent. in the total foetuses or 0·55 g. of that Ca absorbed daily. Relative evaluation comparisons between actual chemical analyses of foetuses at 75 and 112 days and that calculated from radio-Ca values showed good agreement, and indicated deposition of foetal Ca to increase to 21·4 per cent. of 9·3 g. to equal 1·99 g. per day. This value approximated the total calculated Ca accretion value of 1·83 g. per day from the chemical analyses. Like agreement was observed for P, S, Fe and Zn. The slight but apparent discrepancy between the radioisotope and actual stable values could be accounted for by the accelerated changes with increased pregnancy, the inherent errors in balance measurements, and/or possibly to the limited Ca foetal-dam feedback observed in other species (Wilde *et al.*, 1946; MacDonald *et al.*, 1965). In that the radiomineral values reflected the actual chemical partition in the products of conception, the reciprocal of this value therefore (9·3 g. absorbed less 1·99 g. in conception products) or 7·2 g. per day would be deposited and retained in the body of the third trimester gravid gilt. Value for the partition of P, S, Zn and Fe are tabulated in Table III and suggest maternal stores for S, Fe

Table III. *Whole body partition of absorbed radioisotopes by gravid third trimester gilts*

| Radioisotopes | Absorption* | Products of Conception, % | | | | Maternal Stores‡ |
		Placenta	Fluids	Foetuses†	Total	
^{45}Ca	29	0·3	0·3	99·3	21·3	78·7
^{32}P	40	28·0	0·1	71·9	15·6	84·4
^{35}S	32	26·5	9·9	63·6	9·1	91·0
^{65}Zn	10	46·7	0·4	52·9	5·2	94·8
^{59}Fe	17	40·0	5·3	54·7	8·4	91·6

* Calculated as percentage absorbed dose retained after seven days.
† Calculated as percentage of total dose in conception products retained by placenta, fluids and foetus.
‡ Maternal stores calculated as 100 minus that retained radioisotope in conception products.

and Zn are greater than those for Ca and P. The significance of this progressive maternal retention in terms of foetal development and growth, and the subsequent effects on lactation and the productive life of the sow is generally recognized, and procedures for quantitating this foetal-maternal relationship should assist in clarification.

Efficiency Coefficients for Compartment Partition. Radio-chemical balance and subsequent composition values for the total products of conception permit further calculations of efficiency coefficients for these major compartments and provide a means for estimation of mineral utilization by the gravid gilt.

These calculated percentage values for selected minerals have been tabulated in Table IV and suggest the body of the dam itself to be the biggest competitor for absorbed minerals and the greatest barrier between those minerals ingested and the foetus. This was more evident for Fe, Zn and S than for Ca and P. Minerals absorbed and deposited in the products of conception were readily

65

Table IV. *Efficiency coefficients for compartment absorption in gravid third trimester gilts*

Radioisotopes	Compartment Transfer, %		
	G.I. Tract*	Dam to foetus, placenta and fluids†	Placenta to Foetus‡
^{45}Ca	29	21	99
^{32}P	40	16	72
^{35}S	32	9	64
^{65}Zn	10	5	53
^{59}Fe	17	8	55

* Calculated as percentage of single oral dose absorbed after seven days.
† Calculated as percentage of absorbed dose transferred to foetus, placenta and fluids.
‡ Calculated as percentage of absorbed dose in total (100 per cent.) conception products transferred to total foetus after seven days.

available to the foetus, but selective placental retention suggested a 'protective action' for the minor elements Fe, Zn and to a lesser extent S. The absorbed Ca and P, however, were readily transferred to the products of conception and the greater portion was deposited in the foetuses. The gravid third trimester gilt, for example, absorbed 29 per cent. of the ingested ^{45}Ca, but only a fifth of this (21 per cent.) was transferred to the conception products, and 99 per cent. was subsequently deposited in the foetuses. Values were lower for the micro-elements. Only one-twentieth of the 10 per cent. ^{65}Zn absorbed was transferred to the conception products and the placenta itself retained nearly 50 per cent. of this with slightly more than one-half of this being deposited in the total foetuses. These wide variations in percentage distribution of radiominerals after equilibrium (168 hours) reflect the remarkable maternal control and selective mineral deposition and partition for foetal development. These values provide an indirect approach to foetal utilization and subsequent quantitation of requirements in terms of maternal source. Nutritionally these procedures suggest a better understanding of maternal-foetal relationships and permit a feasible approach to minimizing maternal anabolism during gestation by ration formulation.

REFERENCES

BARCROFT, J. (1946). *Researches on Prenatal Life.* Oxford: Blackwell.
BOURDEL, G. (1957). *Proc. 4th Int. Congr. Nutr.* 27.
HANSARD, S. L. (1951). *Nucleonics,* **9,** 38.
HANSARD, S. L. (1956). *US-AEC TID,* **7512,** 31.

HANSARD, S. L. (1963). In *Body Composition,* Ed. Brozek, *Ann. N.Y. Acad. Sci.* 110, 229.
HANSARD, S. L., ITOH, H., GLENN, J. C. & THRASHER, D. M. (1966). *J. Nutr.* 89, 335.
HANSARD, S. L. (1965). In *Hanford Symposium on Swine in Biomedical Research.* Seattle: Frayn.
HANSARD, S. L. (1969). In *Proceedings Radiation Biology of the Foetal and Juvenile Mammals,* chap. 1. Washington: Hanford.
HANSARD, S. L. & BERRY, R. K. (1969). In *Animal Growth and Nutrition.* Ed. Hafez, E.S.E. & Dyer, I. A. chap. 2. Philadelphia: Lea and Febiger.
MACDONALD, N. S., HUTCHINSON, D. L., HELPER, M. & GLYNN, E. (1965). *Proc. Soc. exp. Biol. Med.* 119, 476.
MANNERS, J. J. & McCREA, M. R. (1963). *Br. J. Nutr.* 17, 495.
MOUSTGAARD, J. (1962). In *Nutrition of Pigs and Poultry.* Ed. Morgan, J. T. & Lewis, D. chap. 13. London: Butterworth.
REYNOLDS, S. M. R. (1965). In *Physiology of the Uterus,* chap. 29. New York: Hafner.
ROBINSON, T. J. (1957). In *Progress in Physiology of Farm Animals.* Ed. Hammond, J. London: Butterworth.
SALMON-LEGAGNEUR, E. & RERAT, A. (1962). In *Nutrition of Pigs and Poultry.* Ed. Morgan, J. T. & Lewis, D. chap. 14. London: Butterworth.
WIDDAS, W. F. (1961). *Br. med. Bull.* 17, 107.
WIDDOWSON, E. M. (1968). In *Biology of Gestation. II The Foetus and the Neonate.* Ed. Assali, N. S. chap. 1. London: Academic Press.
WILDE, W. S., COWIE, D. B. & FLEXNER, L. B. (1946). *Am. J. Physiol.* 147, 360.

DISTRIBUTION AND KINETICS OF ^{60}CoCl$_2$ AND LABELLED VITAMIN B$_{12}$ USING AUTORADIOGRAPHY AND IMPULSE COUNTING

HANS FLODH

Department of Pharmacology, Royal Veterinary College, Stockholm 50, Sweden

THE distribution of ^{60}CoCl$_2$ and labelled vitamin B$_{12}$ was studied in adult male and female pregnant and non-pregnant mice in order to increase knowledge of the fine tissue localization and placental transportation of these substances, especially of vitamin B$_{12}$. The methods used were whole body autoradiography (Ullberg, 1954, 1958), microautoradiography and impulse counting.

Vitamin B$_{12}$ showed a peculiar and characteristic distribution pattern (Flodh, 1968a, b). The placental passage and foetal accumulation of radio-B$_{12}$ were very unusual. There was a rapid and abundant uptake in the placenta immediately after the injection followed by a slow further transfer to the foetuses, which one to four days after injection had a much higher concentration of radioactivity than the maternal tissues (Fig. 1). This placental transportation of B$_{12}$ showed similarities in time sequence with

67

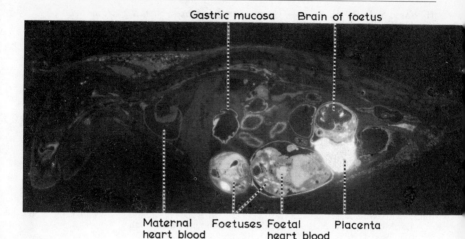

Gastric mucosa   Brain of foetus

Maternal   Foetuses Foetal   Placenta
heart blood   heart blood

FIG. 1. Autoradiogram of ^{58}Co-vit.B_{12} in a pregnant mouse 4 hours after an i.v. injection. The concentration is much higher in the foetuses than in the mother. The placentae still have the highest concentration.

the intestinal absorption of the vitamin and indicated a transportation mechanism in the placenta similar to that which is found in the intestine. Binding to a specific transportation protein might be necessary for normal placental transfer of vitamin B_{12} in the same way as binding to intrinsic factor is necessary for its normal intestinal absorption (Flodh, 1968a, b; Ullberg et al., 1967). A rapid relative decrease of foetal accumulation with increased B_{12} dose was also observed. This indicates a limit of the capacity of the transportation mechanism in the placenta, similar to that which is found for the intestinal absorption of the vitamin.

In male and female non-pregnant mice the highest concentration of radio-B_{12} was found in the kidneys, reproductive and endocrine organs, gastric mucosa and liver. The radioactivity in the testicles was selectively localized in the primary spermatocytes and interstitial cells and in the ovaries in the walls of growing follicles. These findings are in good agreement with earlier suggestions that vitamin B_{12} plays a role in spermatogenesis (Busch, 1957; Sharp and Witts, 1962; Tomaszewski, 1963; Watson, 1962) and with observations that B_{12} deficiency can cause temporary sterility in women, probably by suppressing ovulation (Smith, 1962).

In the pituitary, high concentration was observed in pars

distalis and especially in pars intermedia, which is regarded as the site of production of the melanocyte stimulating hormone, intermedin. This is interesting since both hyperpigmentation (Baker *et al.*, 1963) and vitiligo (Wintrobe, 1967) have been observed in pernicious anemia.

Larynx Lung Pancreas

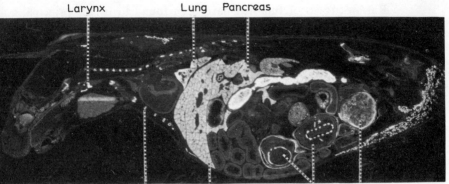

Costal cartilage Liver Foetuses Placenta

FIG. 2. Autoradiogram of ^{60}CoCl$_2$ in a pregnant mouse 24 hours after an i.v. injection. High concentration is seen in maternal cartilage and foetal bone.

The distribution of cobalt chloride was entirely different from that of vitamin B$_{12}$ (Flodh, 1968a and b). Cobalt was found after injection to be highly concentrated in maternal cartilages and foetal skeleton (Fig. 2). Within the foetuses it was almost selectively localized in the bones.

REFERENCES

BAKER, S. J., IGNATIUS, M., JOHNSON, S. & VAISH, S. K. (1963). *Br. med. J.* **1**, 1713.
BUSCH, E. (1957). *Anim. Breed. Abstr.* **25**, 147.
FLODH, H. (1968a). *Acta radiol.* **7**, 121.
FLODH, H. (1968b). *Acta radiol.* Suppl. 284.
SHARP, A. A. & WITTS, L. J. (1962). *Lancet*, **2**, 779.
SMITH, M. D. (1962). *Lancet*, **2**, 934.
TOMASZEWSKI, L., ZMUDZKA, B. & NADWORNY, J. (1963). *Lancet*, **1**, 170.
ULLBERG, S. (1954). *Acta radiol.* Suppl. 118.
ULLBERG, S. (1958). *2nd Int. Conf. peaceful Uses atom. Energy*, **24**, 248.
ULLBERG, S., KRISTOFFERSSON, H., FLODH, H. & HANNGREN, A. (1967). *Archs int. Pharmacodyn. Thér.* **167**, 431.
WATSON, A. A. (1962). *Lancet*, **2**, 644.
WINTROBE, M. M. (1967). *Clinical Hematology.* 6th ed. 502. Philadelphia: Lea & Febiger.

METABOLISM OF TUNGSTEN BY SHEEP AND SWINE

M. C. BELL AND N. N. SNEED

UT-AEC Agricultural Research Laboratory, Oak Ridge, Tennessee, U.S.A.

RADIOISOTOPES of tungsten have been found to be the principal radioactivity from many of the nuclear cratering tests (Kaye and Crossley, 1968). Essington, Nishita and Steen (1965) reported that radioisotopes of W with half-lives of 69 to 145 days contributed over 90 per cent. of the radioactivity from the Sedan cratering test. Plants grown on ejecta from cratering tests concentrate very high levels of radio-W through their roots (Romney *et al.*, 1966). Data on animal metabolism of W are limited. No physiological need has been shown for this element although it is chemically related to molybdenum. Owen and Proudfoot (1968) fed goats and cows sodium tungstate (6 g. and 20 g. respectively) and inhibited xanthine oxidase activity in milk with no effect on milk yields. Neither tungstate nor molybdate affected xanthine oxidase *in vitro*. In this paper data are presented on the effect of ration and route of administration on metabolism of ^{185}W in swine and sheep.

MATERIALS AND METHODS

For these tests a total of 16 growing barrows and 22 mature wethers were fed the experimental rations described by Bell, Sneed and Hall (1966). During the experimental periods all animals were restrained in stalls designed for separate collection of urine and faeces. After an adjustment period they were dosed with tracer levels of ^{185}W as tungstate in NH_4OH. Swine were either injected intravenously or given ^{185}W by stomach tube; sheep were dosed orally with ^{185}W in a gelatin capsule or by abomasal injection. Doses per animal averaged 1·5 mCi with a specific activity of 5 mCi/mg. of W. Ashed tissue and excreta samples were dissolved in aqua regia, dried, then placed into a thin-window gas-flow beta counter for radioactive analysis.

RESULTS AND DISCUSSION

In swine, urinary excretion was the principal route for both orally and intravenously administered ^{185}W from a 5-day collection period. Faecal excretion amounted to 25 per cent. from an oral dose but only 2 per cent. from intravenous ^{185}W, indicating little re-excretion of absorbed ^{185}W. Sheep fed the same high concentrate swine ration excreted 44 ± 6 per cent. in urine and

70

42 ± 8 per cent. in faeces from oral ^{185}W during a 7-day collection period. However, when sheep on this ration were dosed directly into the abomasum the excretion pattern of ^{185}W was more similar to swine with urinary and faecal excretion accounting for 65 ± 14 per cent. and 17 ± 6 per cent. of the ^{185}W respectively. Sheep fed a roughage ration excreted most of the radioactivity in the faeces from both routes of administration. Urinary ^{185}W excretions were 2 per cent. for oral and 13 ± 4 per cent. for abomasal doses.

Swine and sheep excrete ^{185}W at a much slower rate than laboratory animals (Wase, 1956). Most of the ^{185}W was excreted by swine in 24 hours while only 15 per cent. was excreted in 24 hours by the sheep, excluding those fed the concentrate ration and dosed into the abomasum, which excreted 35 per cent.

These data suggest that tracer levels of ^{185}W adsorb to feed particles, especially those high in cellulose. Tungsten metabolism may also be altered by the action of rumen bacteria making it less available for absorption from the gastrointestinal tract of sheep.

In six sheep sacrificed 48 hours after oral dosing, the ^{185}W-tissue concentration was greatest in kidney > liver > lymph nodes > bone > lungs > pancreas > muscle. In six swine sacrificed 48 hours after oral dosing, the ^{185}W-tissue concentration was kidney > bone > brain > lymph nodes > liver > spleen > skin > muscle. ^{185}W concentration in gastrointestinal contents averaged 10 times greater than in animal tissue with the highest concentration in the large intestine of both species. Sheep consistently had higher concentrations of ^{185}W in the intestinal contents than swine, while swine had higher tissue concentrations in kidney, bone, brain, lymph nodes, and spleen than the same sheep tissue. Swine kidney contained 0·0048 per cent. of the dose/g. while sheep kidney contained 0·0015 per cent.

These data show that ^{185}W is readily absorbed by sheep and swine and the apparent absorption and excretion is affected by species, ration and route of administration similar to ^{99}Mo as reported by Bell, Sneed and Hall (1966).

Acknowledgements. This work was completed under Contract AT–40–1–GEN–242 with the U.S. Atomic Energy Commission through the Tennessee Agricultural Experiment Station. This manuscript is published with the permission of the Dean of the University of Tennessee Agricultural Experiment Station, Knoxville.

REFERENCES

Bell, M. C., Sneed, N. N. & Hall, R. F. (1966). *Proc. 7th Int. Congr. Nutr.* **5**, 765.
Essington, E. H., Nishita, H. & Steen, A. J. (1965). *Hlth Phys.* **11**, 689.
Kaye, S. V. & Crossley, D. A. (1968). *Hlth Phys.* **14**, 162.

OWEN, E. C. & PROUDFOOT, R. (1968). *Br. J. Nutr.* **22,** 331.
ROMNEY, E. M., STEEN, A. J., WOOD, R. A. & RHOADS, W. A. (1966). In *Radioecological Concentration Processes,* p. 391. New York: Pergamon Press.
WASE, A. W. (1956). *Archs Biochem. Biophys.* **61,** 272.

DISCUSSION

Godwin (Adelaide). Have you looked at the incorporation of ^{185}W into rumen micro-organisms as it seems possible that the species differences you describe may be due to uptake by rumen microflora?

Bell (Oak Ridge). This is a possibility but we haven't investigated it.

Spencer (Hines, Illinois). You mentioned that the metabolism of W is similar to that of Mo; are the concentrations of W and Mo in the liver similar? Do you think that the high ^{185}W activity you found in the kidney is due to a high activity in the urine?

Bell (Oak Ridge). In the pig the ^{185}W activity of the liver was higher than that of bone or brain whereas in the sheep the liver activity was lower than in these other organs. The kidney activity was higher than liver in both species and this is probably due to urinary excretion. The activity in the kidney of the pig was considerably higher than that in the sheep.

Lassiter (Athens, Ga.). What is your explanation of the different patterns of excretion on ruminants fed roughage rations or concentrate rations?

Bell (Oak Ridge). We believe that during fermentation in the rumen the cellulose of the roughage ration may have adsorbed ^{185}W in a similar mechanism to that reported for molybdenum; we have however obtained this effect even when the isotope has been administered directly into the abomasum.

SECTION 2

PATHOLOGY AND CLINICAL EFFECTS OF TRACE ELEMENT DEFICIENCY AND EXCESS

Presidents: W. J. MILLER (Session 1)
D. B. R. POOLE (Session 2)

Vice Presidents: C. F. MILLS (Session 1)
R. B. WILLIAMS (Session 2)

THE FUNCTIONAL ROLE OF ZINC IN
EPIDERMAL TISSUES

WALTER J. PORIES AND WILLIAM H. STRAIN

*University of Rochester School of Medicine and Dentistry,
Rochester, New York, U.S.A.*

WE have studied the role of zinc in epidermal tissues. We chose
skin because it is rich in Zn (Underwood, 1962) and because it is
a sensitive indicator of Zn metabolism.

Zinc-deficient animals are unable to grow healthy epidermis
and epithelial appendages; poultry produce frizzy, brittle feathers
(Zeigler *et al.,* 1962), domestic animals develop dull scraggly fur
with parakeratosis (Tucker and Salmon, 1955) and humans present
scaly, vulnerable skin. Chronic sores are common. The delay in
healing associated with Zn deficiency is largely caused by the lack
of epidermal migration across the granulations. If healing finally
occurs the scar is delicate, the tensile strength is reduced and the
wound frequently breaks down. These lesions clear rapidly with
the administration of biologically available Zn salts.

We followed the Zn flux in skin with radionuclides. In our
first study (Savlov *et al.,* 1962), we measured the uptake of ^{65}Zn
by healing wounds in rats. The wounds, as well as the adjacent
non-traumatized skin, demonstrated immediate uptake of the
radioisotope, reflecting the high rate of Zn exchange within
epidermal tissues. The wound, however, preferentially concentrated the ^{65}Zn for the first seven days after injury, reflecting active
Zn tropism of healing tissues. The radio-Zn was not incorporated
into the scar tissue, suggesting that Zn plays a catalytic rather
than a structural role in wound healing.

Further studies (Strain *et al.,* 1964) indicated that Zn is also
rapidly incorporated into the epithelial appendages. Radio-Zn
can be detected in the fur of the rat within 5 minutes and continues
to accumulate at a rapid and consistent rate especially after the
sixth day. Zinc incorporated into epithelial tissues appears to be
non-exchangeable and is lost to the organism. Hair, therefore,
acts as a recording filament, permitting frequent assessment of Zn
stores without injury to the organism.

In spite of the early and rapid movement of Zn into the wound,
acceleration of healing from Zn therapy does not occur until 14 to
21 days after wounding. Sandstead and Shepard (1968) first noted
an increase in tensile strength in medicated rats after the fourteenth

day. We (Strain *et al.*, 1953) demonstrated increased rates of wound closure in rats on Zn supplementation after the twenty-first day. Similarly, in man, acceleration does not become measurable until the twentieth day after wounding (Pories *et al.*, 1967). This coincides with the period of wound epithelization when the epidermis migrates across the granulations.

The response is very different in Zn-deficient patients with delayed wound healing. In such subjects the epithelium piles up in ridges and lumps at the edge of the wound, progressing only slowly across the healing surface. If epithelization is complete the surface is scaly and vulnerable, ulcerating again with minimal trauma. Therapy with Zn sulphate, USP, ($ZnSO_4.7H_2O$), 220 mg. three times a day, produces rapid changes. Migration is apparent within 3 to 4 days and the wound closes rapidly with firm, healthy epidermis. If Zn deficiency recurs the wound may again break down and remain an open sore until Zn levels are restored.

Zinc-deficient wounds are common in the average general hospital. In a series of 17 patients with chronic indolent wounds we (Pories *et al.*, 1969) found 12 to have serum Zn levels of less than 100 μg./100 ml. All 12 progressed to rapid healing within weeks in spite of no change in local wound therapy and although most wounds had been present one to two years. Similar findings in a well-designed trial with 104 patients have recently been reported by Husain (1969).

Zinc therapy seems to be beneficial during healing in normal man. Our controlled trial with 20 young, healthy airmen with granulating wounds showed significant acceleration in the group medicated with $ZnSO_4$, USP, (48.8 ± 2.6 days vs. 80.1 ± 13.7 days; $p < 0.02$). The study suggested that even young men might have difficulty in quickly mobilizing adequate Zn stores to meet the demands of the healing wound. In contrast, Miller and his co-workers (Miller *et al.*, 1965; 1967) found no effect with the addition of extra Zn salts to calves on synthetic diets, although acceleration had been noted in Zn-deficient cattle.

These data demonstrate the dependence of epithelium on adequate Zn levels and suggest that migration, proliferation and maturation of the epidermis are partly controlled by peripatetic Zn. The failure of epithelial proliferation associated with Zn deficiency may be evidence of lack of catalyzing Zn enzymes and consequent inability to synthetize RNA and DNA. However, intracellular processes are complex and Zn probably has additional roles in controlling the movement of large molecules, unlocking or sealing reactive sites, and altering the ionic mileau of the substrate.

At these intracellular levels minute changes in concentration can produce profound metabolic alterations. Zinc metabolism is also related to that of ascorbic acid, protein synthesis, metal sulphydryl bonds, and other essential elements.

Zinc deficiency is a common cause of epidermal problems in animals and man. The recognition of epithelial abnormalities characteristic of Zn deficiency should be followed by therapy with nontoxic, biologically available Zn salts.

Acknowledgements. Aided in part by grants HE 10213 and RH 00042, U.S. Public Health Service; and by the Horatio H. Burtt and C. S. Lunt Research Funds of the University of Rochester.

REFERENCES

HUSAIN, S. L. (1969). *Lancet*, **1**, 1069.
MILLER, W. J., BLACKMON, D. M., HIERS, J. M. Jr., FOWLER, P. R., CLIFTON, C. M. & GENTRY, R. P. (1967). *J. Dairy Sci.* **50**, 715.
MILLER, W. J., MORTON, J. D., PITTS, W. J. & CLIFTON, C. M. (1965). *Proc. Soc. exp. Biol. Med.* **118**, 427.
PORIES, W. J., HENZEL, J. H., ROB, C. G. & STRAIN, W. H. (1967). *Ann. Surg.* **165**, 432.
PORIES, W. J., STRAIN, W. H., PEER, R. M. & LANDEW, M. H. (1969). *Curr. Topics surg. Res.* **1**, 315.
SANDSTEAD, H. H. & SHEPARD, G. H. (1968). *Proc. Soc. exp. Biol. Med.* **128**, 687.
SAVLOV, E. D., STRAIN, W. H. & HUEGIN, F. (1962). *J. surg. Res.* **2**, 209.
STRAIN, W. H., BERLINER, W. P., LANKAU, C. A. Jr., McEVOY, R. K., PORIES, W. J. & GREENLAW, R. H. (1964). *J. nucl. Med.* **5**, 664.
STRAIN, W. H., DUTTON, A. M., HEYER, H. B. & RAMSEY, G. H. (1953). *Experimental Studies on the Acceleration of Burn and Wound Healing.* Rochester: University of Rochester.
TUCKER, H. F. & SALMON, W. D. (1955). *Proc. Soc. exp. Biol. Med.* **88**, 613.
UNDERWOOD, E. J. (1962). *Trace Elements in Human and Animal Nutrition.* chap. 6. 2nd ed. New York: Academic Press.
ZEIGLER, T. R., SCOTT, M. L., McEVOY, R. K., GREENLAW, R. H., HUEGIN, F. & STRAIN, W. H. (1962). *Proc. Soc. exp. Biol. Med.* **109**, 239.

THE ROLE OF ZINC IN TISSUE REPAIR AFTER INJURY

WILLIAM H. STRAIN AND WALTER J. PORIES

University of Rochester School of Medicine and Dentistry, Rochester, New York, U.S.A.

IN 1967 we reported on the successful use of oral zinc sulphate, 220 mg. t.i.d., for the promotion of healing in man (Pories *et al.,* 1967a and b). There has been abundant confirmation of this therapy, with the best supporting evidence by Husain (1969). Although oral Zn therapy promotes healing in many species, the benefit of tissue repair is especially important for ageing humans.

The roles of Zn in healing are poorly understood and warrant extensive further investigation.

It is evident that Zn can play many roles in tissue repair if the metabolism of the element is considered. To be utilized, Zn must be available from the diet, be absorbed from the alimentary tract, undergo normal translocations in the metabolic pools and maintain element reservoirs such as bone and liver. All these transformations are affected by diet, age and sex. The metabolism of Zn may also be influenced by interactions with other elements like Cd, Ca, Cu, Fe and Se.

AVAILABILITY OF ZINC

All diets appear to contain adequate amounts of Zn, but very little of the metal seems to be available. Zinc may be firmly bound in raw food by chelates (O'Dell and Savage, 1960), such as calcium Zn-phytate. Presumably the phytates are broken up by cooking, but other chelating agents are doubtless present to bind the metal. The availability of Zn is a critical factor.

Studies on rats have shown that the pancreas is involved in liberating Zn from the diet. Hsu *et al* (1966) and Mills *et al*. (1967) have shown relationships between carboxypeptidase A and Zn status. More recently Hsu *et al*. (1969) have found a marked increase in the oxidation of methionine in Zn deficiency. Thus the pancreatic enzymes may both act to liberate Zn from the food and preserve methionine through the action of the metal.

We accidentally obtained evidence that the pancreas plays an important role in making Zn available. Some years ago we found that depancreatized dogs maintained on insulin could not concentrate cholecystographic agents to opacify the gallbladder. In the course of these experiments one operated dog, which had lost considerable hair and had developed cage sores, bolted a strip of metal present in its food. The metal lodged in the dog's stomach and subsequently the gallbladder could be visualized but the effect gradually diminished. We postulated from the radiographs that the metal was a strip of galvanized sheet iron and the return of visualization was from dissolution of Zn in the stomach.

This Zn hypothesis was tested by administering Zn salts to six depancreatized dogs. With the administration of Zn salts all dogs visualized their gallbladder, regrew hair on denuded parts and healed cage sores. It seems reasonable to ascribe to the pancreas and pancreatic juice the property of making Zn available from the diet, although more details are needed, especially for man.

INTESTINAL WALL

In our work (Strain *et al.*, 1953; 1954) on the promotion of healing in rats by oral administration of Zn, we found that the Zn complexes of methionine, cystine and cysteine were very satisfactory thereapeutic agents for promoting healing of excised wounds. This work began with the accidental addition of Zn to the rat diet by incorporating impure β-phenyllactic acid in the food. Thus we must also consider hydroxy-amino acids as well as sulphur-amino acids as agents for increasing the availability of Zn from the diet.

The effects of age and sex on the absorption of Zn and other essential elements are poorly documented. Accordingly the uptake and retention of ^{65}Zn and other common γ-emitting radioisotopes were measured in young (1·5 month), adult (3 month) and old

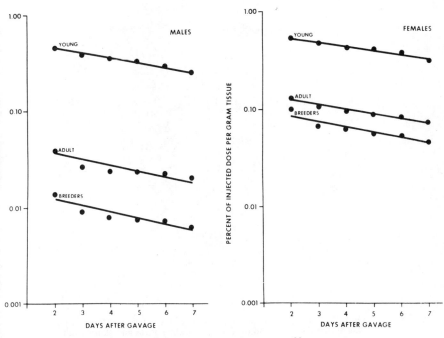

FIG. 1. Age and sex differences of body burden of ^{85}Sr in young, adult, and old breeder rats of both sexes following administration of c.5 μCi of ^{85}Sr by stomach tube. Young females absorb and retain the radioisotope slightly more than young males, adult females five times more than adult males, and old breeder females 10 times more than old breeder males. Analogous results are obtained with other radioisotopes.

(12 + month) breeder rats of both sexes to study essential element absorption. Measurements were conducted by following changes in body burdens over a period of seven days after administering c. 5 μCi of each radioelement by gavage to four rats of each age and sex. Whole body radioactivity determinations were made daily in a scintillation detector for small animals (Strain, Pories, Datillo *et al.*, 1968a).

All radioisotopes were absorbed and retained more by young than old rats, and by females more than males as illustrated in Figure 1 for ^{85}Sr. Sex effect was slight in young animals but

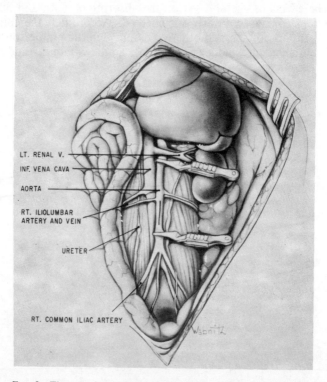

LT. RENAL V.

INF. VENA CAVA

AORTA

RT. ILIOLUMBAR
ARTERY AND VEIN

URETER

RT. COMMON ILIAC ARTERY

FIG. 2. The experimental preparation of the rat used in measuring the accumulation of radio-Zn by the healing aorta and skin. Under pentobarbital anaesthesia a laporotomy was performed, the aorta clamped with two 27 mm. serrefines and an aortotomy carried out. The aortotomy was immediately closed with 000 polyethylene. Post-operatively the rat was injected intravenously with c.5 μCi of ^{65}ZnCl$_2$ in normal saline. At the time of sacrifice the radioactivity of the healing segment of the aorta or skin was compared with that of the proximal unoperated artery or skin, respectively.

became more definite in older groups. When the radioisotopes were ranked in order of decreasing absorption and retention the following sequence was obtained: $^{85}Sr > {}^{65}Zn > {}^{59}Fe > {}^{54}Co > {}^{55}Cr$. There was more than a hundredfold difference in absorption and retention from ^{65}Zn to ^{51}Cr in this sequence. The same sequence presumably applies to the stable forms of these elements and to man as well as to rats.

TISSUE REPAIR

The accumulation of radio-Zn at the site of healing was used to study tissue repair in arteries and skin. It was postulated that accumulation of radio-Zn in healing wounds would indicate active participation of the metal in repair. In carrying out this programme, rats were subjected to 1 cm. full-thickness aortotomies as shown in Figure 2. Each rat was injected postoperatively with c. 5 μCi of $^{65}ZnCl_2$ in 1 ml. of saline. Groups of four rats were sacrificed on the first, second, fourth, sixth and tenth days after operation. After sacrifice, the aortotomy and a normal section of each aorta were removed by dissection, cleaned, and retention of radio-Zn per gram of tissue determined. Skin and skin wound were handled in similar fashion (Strain, Pories, Peer *et al.*, 1968).

There was a marked difference in the preferential accumulation of radio-Zn in the healing artery and skin. The highest relative differences were evident on the first to second day after operation for the artery as shown in Figure 3; the third day for the skin, as described earlier (p. 76). Thus additional evidence was

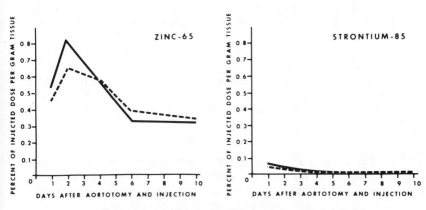

FIG. 3. Comparative retention of radioisotopes by wounded (solid line) and normal aorta. The wounded tissue retains radio-Zn much more than normal tissue but not radio-Sr.

accumulated that Zn was an important element for tissue repair after injury to arteries and skin.

BONE

Radio-Zn uptake has been used to study fracture healing experimentally (Haumont and McLean, 1966) but Zn therapy as a healing agent for bone tissue in man has not been developed. One problem is the lack of good methods of studying bone repair.

The extremely important participation of Zn in bone growth and repair has been shown by elegant studies of a number of groups. Some years ago Blamberg et al. (1960) and Kienholz et al. (1961) demonstrated that chicks hatched from Zn-deficient eggs have severe skeletal and tissue malformations. More recently, Hurley and Swenerton (1966) placed pregnant rats on Zn-deficient diets early in pregnancy and obtained foetuses at term with equally severe skeletal and soft tissue defects.

The application of Zn therapy to growth problems in animals began with Tucker and Salmon (1955) and in man with Prasad et al. (1963). In spite of the widespread application of Zn therapy in domestic and laboratory animals there is still no real understanding of the mechanisms.

INTERRELATIONSHIPS WITH OTHER ELEMENTS

The gonadal tissue damage produced by Cd salts, which leads to sterility in both sexes, is an extremely interesting phenomenon. The testicular damage can be produced also by tying off circulation to the testes or the injury can be prevented by prior administration of Se (Mason and Young, 1967), Zn (Parizek, 1957), or relatively large amounts of Co salts (Gunn et al., 1968). Despite the large amount of work that has been devoted to these problems, and to the hypertension produced experimentally by Cd (Schroeder, 1967), no answers are available for the mechanism, either for the toxicity of Cd or for the protective action of the trace elements.

SUMMARY

The roles of Zn in tissue repair after injury reflect the normal metabolism of Zn summarized in Figure 4. Utilization of Zn is dependent on liberation of the element from the diet, absorption from the alimentary tract and translocations in the metabolic pools. Adequate stores of Zn must be maintained in body reservoirs such as bone, liver and skin for optimal growth and repair. The Zn

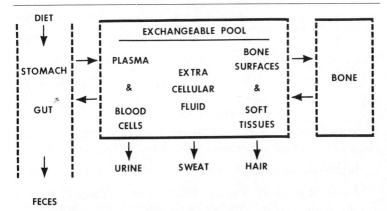

FIG. 4. Compartment model of Zn metabolism.

status may be determined for various pools by analyzing serum, plasma, blood cells, urine, sweat and hair.

Acknowledgements. Aided in part by grants HE 10213 and RH 00042, U.S. Public Health Service; and by the Horatio H. Burtt and C. S. Lunt Research Funds of the University of Rochester.

REFERENCES

BLAMBERG, D. L., BLACKWOOD, U. B., SUPPLEE, W. C. & COMBS, G. F. (1960). *Proc. Soc. exp. Biol. Med.* **104,** 217.
GUNN, S. A., GOULD, T. C. & ANDERSON, W. A. D. (1968). *Proc. Soc. exp. Biol. Med.* **128,** 591.
HAUMONT, S. & McLEAN, F. C. (1966). In *Zinc Metabolism,* ed. Prasad, A. S. p. 169. Springfield: Illinois: Thomas.
HSU, J. M., ANILANE, J. K. & SCANLAN, D. E. (1966). *Science, N.Y.* **153,** 882.
HSU, J. M., ANTHONY, W. L. & BUCHANAN, P. J. (1969). *J. Nutr.* **97,** 279.
HURLEY, L. & SWENERTON, H. (1966). *Proc. Soc. exp. Biol. Med.* **123,** 692.
HUSAIN, S. L. (1969). *Lancet,* **1,** 1069.
KIENHOLZ, E. W., TURK, D. E., SUNDE, M. L. & HOEKSTRA, W. G. (1961). *J. Nutr.* **75,** 211.
MASON, K. E. & YOUNG, J. O. (1967). In *Selenium in Biomedicine,* p. 383. Westport, Connecticut: Avi.
MILLS, C. F., QUARTERMAN, J., WILLIAMS, R. B., DALGARNO, A. C. & PANIĆ, B. (1967). *Biochem. J.* **102,** 712.
O'DELL, B. L. & SAVAGE, J. E. (1960). *Proc. Soc. exp. Biol. Med.* **103,** 304.
PARIZEK, J. (1957). *J. Endocr.* **15,** 56.
PORIES, W. J., HENZEL, J. H., ROB, C. G. & STRAIN, W. H. (1967a). *Lancet,* **1,** 121.
PORIES, W. J., HENZEL, J. H., ROB, C. G. & STRAIN, W. H. (1967b). *Ann. Surg.* **165,** 432.
PRASAD, A. S., MIALE, A. Jr., FARID, Z., SANDSTEAD, H. H., SCHULERT, A. R. & DARBY, W. J. (1963). *Archs intern. Med.* **111,** 407.
SCHROEDER, H. A. (1967). *Circulation,* **35,** 570.
STRAIN, W. H., DUTTON, A. M., HEYER, H. B., PORIES, W. J. & RAMSEY, G. H. (1954). *Experimental Studies on the Acceleration of Burn and Wound Healing.* Report, Rochester: University of Rochester.

STRAIN, W. H., DUTTON, A. M., HEYER, H. B. & RAMSEY, G. H. (1953). Report. Rochester: University of Rochester.
STRAIN, W. H., PORIES, W. J., DATTILO, E., PEER, R. M. & ZARESKY, S. A. (1968). *Trans. Amer. nucl. Soc.* **11,** 476.
STRAIN, W. H., PORIES, W. J., PEER, R. M., CHILDERS, R. C., WORLAND, R. L., ZARESKY, S. A. & ROB, C. G. (1968). *Trans. Am. nucl. Soc.* **11,** 475.
TUCKER, H. F. & SALMON, W. D. (1955). *Proc. Soc. exp. Biol. Med.* **88,** 613.

DISCUSSION

Mills (Aberdeen). Could I ask Drs Pories and Strain what they think is the primary function of Zn in the healing wound?

Strain (Rochester). We feel it is probably an organizing factor.

Pories (Rochester). I don't think there is any doubt from work on both plants and animals that Zn is essential for protein synthesis. We can therefore see effects of deficiency on growth and development in the foetus and young animal and these processes are not very much different from wound healing. The impairment of protein synthesis may be because the Zn is a metal moiety of several enzymes such as alkaline phosphatase, lactic dehydrogenase, enolase, carbonic anhydrase and many others. But this however can not be the whole story, because when one looks at Zn-deficient animals and measures the activity of these enzymes it is amazing how few times there are any changes in their activity, even in the severely deficient animal. It may be, however, that the role of Zn is in catalyzing reactions which influence relationships between several possible products of enzymic reactions and that by changing the concentration of Zn we may influence the balance between competing reactions. This, however, is speculation and we have no direct evidence for such a suggestion.

Elmes (Belfast). Can you say why your patients were Zn-deficient? Was it due to dietary deficiency, malabsorption or excessive loss?

Pories (Rochester). Some patients are from poor sociological conditions where their diets are terrible and some could be expected to be Zn-deficient. Most, however, have been in hospital for up to two years and are under treatment for poorly healing wounds. In these cases the diet is good and yet they give responses to Zn, so they must be absorbing the element poorly. We don't know why this should be. In some cases the deficiency appears to be due to an increased loss due to diarrhoea or from a fistula. But most of these situations however seem to be related to poor absorption and this does not seem to be an uncommon situation.

THE MODE OF ACTION OF FLUORIDE AND THE ROLE OF MOLYBDENUM AND OTHER TRACE ELEMENTS IN DENTAL CARIES

G. N. JENKINS

Department of Oral Physiology,
University of Newcastle Dental School, Newcastle

THE clinical data on the effect of 1 p.p.m. of fluoride in drinking water, in reducing dental caries incidence by about half, are among the best established in the whole dental field (Jenkins, 1967a). The question of its mode of action has, however, been much more controversial and many details are still confused although a general pattern is now emerging.

FLUORIDE AND ENAMEL SOLUBILITY RATE

The most widely held hypothesis suggests that F ingested during tooth formation, or immediately after eruption, reduces the solubility-rate of the enamel, thereby building up its resistance to the bacterial acids formed in the 'dental plaque' (the deposit of protein and bacteria) on the enamel surface. It is easy to demonstrate that enamel treated *in vitro* with a dilute F solution takes up F ions firmly and is reduced in solubility-rate. The question is whether the enamel can be affected sufficiently *in vivo* by the extremely low concentrations of F in tissue fluids (0·02 to 0·04 p.p.m.) to influence solubility. The concentration of F on the outer surface of enamel (say 1000 p.p.m.) is 5 to 10 times higher than that within (Brudevold *et al.*, 1956; Jenkins and Speirs, 1953) so that meaningful solubility measurements must be made on the outer (preferably intact) surface. Such tests have been carried out in three laboratories (Healy and Ludwig, 1966; Isaac *et al.*, 1958; Jenkins *et al.*, 1952) and they all agree that, on average, enamel formed under the influence of F shows a slight but consistent trend towards being less soluble than the controls (Table I). Fluoride is readily bound by the permeable enamel present in early caries where it apparently exerts an especially large effect on solubility, presumably resulting in a slowing of the development of the cavity. Needless to say these *in vitro* data do not prove the solubility hypothesis but make it more probable.

The means by which F reduces solubility is uncertain. It was originally thought that F converted some of the hydroxyapatite, the main constituent of enamel, into fluorapatite which was con-

Table I. *Effect of fluoride of drinking water on enamel solubility-rate (µg of P dissolved from teeth under standard conditions, with numbers of teeth in brackets)*

F of water	0	1	2	% difference
Deciduous teeth	10·4 (77)	9·2 (79)		11·5 (not sig.)
Deciduous teeth	12 (109)		9·5 (109)	21 (sig.)
Permanent teeth	12·7 (108)		12·1 (112)	5 (not sig.)
Permanent teeth (early caries)	8·2 (108)		6·7 (112)	18 (sig.)

(From Dowse and Jenkins, 1957; Jenkins *et al.*, 1952.)

sidered to be a more stable and less soluble crystal, although even with the highest F levels in enamel—overdoses excepted—only 1 molecule in 20 becomes fluorapatite. Doubts, still unresolved, have arisen about the lower solubility of fluorapatite and several other possibilities arise. In developing bone, F uptake is known to increase the size of the crystals and reduce the number of defects (probably in competition with carbonate which has the reverse properties) which would tend to reduce solubility-rates but this has not been well established in enamel. Caries is now thought to consist of short bursts of decalcification caused by the acid formed immediately after meals, followed by some remineralisation from the dissolved ions in the intervals between meals when the pH of the enamel surface is higher. *In vitro* work shows that F not only favours this deposition of mineral from saturated solutions, but favours its deposition in the apatite form which is less soluble than other possible crystals such as whitlockite or octa calcium phosphate. Thus the disparity between removal and reforming of mineral matter might be reduced by F leading to a slower development of a cavity.

The evidence for the solubility hypothesis has, until quite recently, overshadowed other ideas but evidence for additional contributory factors is now accumulating.

MORPHOLOGICAL EFFECTS

Clinical reports have commented on the narrower fissures and more rounded cusps of teeth formed where the water contains F (Forrest, 1956). Animal experiments have also shown that if F is injected at the time the molars are forming, their morphology is altered in such a way that the teeth would be expected to be more self-cleansing (Kruger, 1959, 1962). A survey in an artificially fluoridated area in New Zealand has confirmed that there are statistically significant differences in the size and shape of teeth compared with the controls (Table II) although these differences in size are very small (about 2 per cent.) and their practical importance is doubtful (Cooper and Ludwig, 1965).

Table II. *Effect of fluoride and molybdenum on morphology of human teeth (means in mm. with numbers of subjects in brackets)*

	Control	F	Mo	
Mesio-distal diameter	10·30 (86)	10·11 (102)	10·32 (100)	} F effect
Bucco-lingual diameter	10·31 (99)	10·18 (100)	10·28 (100)	} on size
Cusp height	2·68 (66)	2·54 (63)	2·52 (74)	} F and Mo
Buccal convexity	0·35 (98)	0·31 (92)	0·33 (93)	} effect on shape

(Cooper and Ludwig, 1965.)

INHIBITION OF PLAQUE BACTERIA

The validity of the hypothesis of bacterial inhibition depends on knowing: (1) the concentration of F necessary to inhibit bacterial acid production and (2) the concentration of F present in the plaque. Concentrations of 5 and 10 p.p.m. can inhibit quite markedly and even 1 and 2 p.p.m. have a detectable effect (Bibby and Van Kesteren, 1940; Jenkins, 1959; Wright and Jenkins, 1954) but these levels are much higher than the 0·02 to 0·04 p.p.m. of F ion now believed to be in saliva (Aasenden *et al.,* 1968). However, the plaque has the capacity for storing F so that its concentration is hundreds of times higher than that of the saliva which bathes it, and is affected by the F of the drinking water (Dawes *et al.,* 1965; Hardwick and Leach, 1962). It is clear that these concentrations could not arise unless F in the plaque was bound in some way and recent evidence suggests that it is bound in or on the bacteria and in a form which can inhibit bacterial metabolism (Jenkins *et al.,* 1969). Table III shows the F concentration within thoroughly washed streptococci isolated from the human mouth and grown on media containing various levels of F, and includes the final pH reached when they were incubated with sugar illustrating the inhibitory effect of the stored F. It will be noted that F has been taken up even from the control medium which contained only about 0·5 p.p.m. as a contaminant. Comparisons of the pH changes when plaques collected from residents of high F areas are allowed to stand with sugar have consistently shown that the change is 0·1 to 0·2 of a pH unit less than in plaques from controls. These differences are likely to influence caries because they occur at a level (about 5 to 5·5) where small pH

87

differences can tip the balance between some enamel dissolving and none at all.

Table III. *F concentration (p.p.m.) of plaque bacteria grown on medium containing F and pH change when washed bacteria were incubated with sugar*

F in media p.p.m.	F in bacteria p.p.m.	Final pH after incubation with sugar
0	56	4·72
2	130	5·00
5	259	5·16
10	273	5·43

(Seven other isolates gave similar results.)

The source of the F in plaque is not definitely known but is probably the saliva. Food and drink probably have too transient an effect to be important and the F of enamel rises with age whereas a steady fall would be expected if it were continually entering the plaque and being removed daily by tooth brushing.

CONCLUSION ON THE MODE OF ACTION OF FLUORIDE

Evidence has been presented in support of all three major hypotheses and the question seems not to be which hypothesis is right but what is the relative contribution of each? About two thirds of the effect of F depends upon the ingestion of F during tooth formation and this presumably requires F built into the enamel. The remaining third can occur with F received after tooth formation and may thus be explained by antibacterial effects in the plaque.

MOLYBDENUM AND CARIES

Epidemiological evidence from three areas suggests independently that increased Mo intake is related to reduced caries (for a detailed review, *see* Jenkins, 1967b).

In Hungary, Adler and Straub (1953) found a town with an exceptionally low caries incidence and 0·1 p.p.m. of Mo was reported in its water supply. Animal experiments by the same group of workers confirmed that 0·1 p.p.m of Mo in drinking water reduced caries (Table IVA).

During the search for a suitable control town for Hastings, New Zealand, where artificial fluoridation was planned, caries

88

incidence was found to be exceptionally low in Napier (Table IVB). Many of the vegetables eaten in this town were grown on a patch of alkaline soil raised from the sea-bed by an earthquake as recently as 1932. Analysis of these vegetables showed several differences of which 10 p.p.m. of Mo seemed the most likely to be concerned in caries. The soil was not especially high in Mo but its alkalinity favoured Mo uptake by plants. Animal experiments showed that caries was reduced by including the ash of Napier vegetables or the ash of control vegetables supplemented by an equivalent amount of Mo (Ludwig, 1963).

Table IV. *Dental caries incidence in relation to Mo intake*
(Av. No. of decayed, missing and filled teeth)

A. Hungary
(*Adler and Straub*, 1953)

	Age of subjects	Mo area	Control	% difference
	7	0·04	0·25	84
	10	0·55	1·04	47
	14	0·85	1·48	43
Evidence of increased Mo intake		Mo of water 0·1 p.p.m.	0 p.p.m.	

B. New Zealand
(*Ludwig*, 1963)

	Age of subjects	Mo area	Control	% difference
	6	0·59	1·24	52
	9	3·81	4·58	17
	12	6·88	10·1	32
Evidence of increased Mo intake		Mo of vegetables up to 10 p.p.m.	0 p.p.m.	

C. Somerset, England
(*Anderson*, 1969)

	Mo area	Control	% difference
Caries	4·59	5·71	20
Mo (μg./l) in water	3	1·8	
milk	50	30	
urine	57	33	
whole teeth	70	50	
F of water (p.p.m.)	0·09	0·10	
F of whole teeth (p.p.m.)	194	128	

The third piece of evidence was collected in the test area of Somerset (Anderson, 1969) where caries incidence was also found to be lower than in neighbouring Yeovil (Table IVC). Milk was the only locally consumed agricultural product and was found to contain a higher Mo concentration than the control. Analyses of whole teeth and of 'spot' urine samples from children in the two areas indicated a higher Mo intake.

Although each of these surveys has limitations, taken together and along with less specific evidence mentioned below, the case for an association of Mo with low caries incidence seems established. Many animal experiments have been reported but with contradictory results; the contradictions have arisen probably because of uncontrolled variations in the concentration Mo in the basal diets and of the other trace elements known (Cu, S) or thought (Mn, W) to interact with it.

It will be noted from Table IVc that the F concentrations of the teeth were higher in the Mo area although there was no difference in the water-borne F. This might suggest that the lower caries resulted from some unsuspected dietary source of F and this may indeed be the explanation. On the other hand there is some evidence from animal experiments (summarized by Jenkins, 1967b) that Mo may influence F metabolism and that its mode of action in caries might be by enhancing the effect of F.

Little is known about the possible mode of action of Mo. Physiological concentrations affect neither the solubility or crystal form of apatite nor the metabolism of oral bacteria (Jenkins, 1967b). Kruger (1959, 1962) has shown that somewhat large doses injected into very young rats influenced the morphology of the developing molars and measurements of small groups of human teeth in Napier showed slight but statistically significant differences (16 per cent.) in fissure depth and convexity (6 per cent.) of the buccal surface compared with those in a control town (Table II).

EPIDEMIOLOGICAL EVIDENCE ON OTHER TRACE ELEMENTS IN CARIES

The results of five independent surveys in widely separated parts of the world in which caries incidence has been related to trace elements in the environment (soil, water or food) have given some support to the importance of Mo and have also shown a correlation between a low caries incidence and high concentrations of boron, strontium and lithium (Table V). The nature of the link between caries and these elements is quite unknown but when elucidated it offers the promise of new methods of caries prevention at least as effective as F.

Table V. *Summary of trace elements with high concentrations in plants, soil or water associated with a low caries incidence*

New Zealand (plants)	U.S.A. (water)			New Guinea (soils)
	Ohio (1)	Ohio (2)	S. Carolina	
B	B	B	B	—
—	Li	Li	—	Li
Mo	Mo	Mo	—	—
Sr	Sr	Sr	Sr	Sr
high pH (soils)	—	—	—	high pH

(Barmes, 1969; Cadell, 1964; Losee and Adkins, 1969.)

REFERENCES

AASENDEN, R., BRUDEVOLD, F. & RICHARDSON, B. (1968). *Archs oral Biol.* **13,** 625.
ADLER, P. & STRAUB, J. (1953). *Acta med. hung.* **4,** 221.
ANDERSON, R. J. (1969). *Caries Res.* **3,** 75.
BARMES, D. E. (1969). *Caries Res.* **3,** 44.
BIBBY, B. G. & van KESTEREN, M. (1940). *J. dent. Res.* **19,** 391.
BRUDEVOLD, F., GARDNER, D. E. & SMITH, F. A. (1956). *J. dent. Res.* **35,** 420.
CADELL, P. B. (1964). *Aust. dent. J.* **9,** 32.
COOPER, V. K. & LUDWIG, T. G. (1965). *N.Z. dent. J.* **61,** 23.
DAWES, C., JENKINS, G. N., HARDWICK, J. L. & LEACH, S. A. (1965). *Br. dent. J.* **119,** 164.
DOWSE, C. M. & JENKINS, G. N. (1957). *J. dent. Res.* **36,** Abstr. 30, 816.
FORREST, J. R. (1956). *Br. dent. J.* **100,** 195.
HARDWICK, J. L. & LEACH, S. A. (1962). *Archs oral Biol. Suppl. Proceedings of the 9th ORCA Congress,* p. 151.
HEALY, W. B. & LUDWIG, T. G. (1966). *N.Z. dent. J.* **62,** 276.
ISAAC, S., BRUDEVOLD, F., SMITH, F. A. & GARDNER, D. E. (1958). *J. dent. Res.* **37,** 254.
JENKINS, G. N. (1959). *Archs oral Biol.* **1,** 33.
JENKINS, G. N. (1967a). *Wld Rev. Nutr. Diet.* **7,** 138.
JENKINS, G. N. (1967b). *Br. dent. J.* **122,** 435, 500, 545.
JENKINS, G. N., ARMSTRONG, P. A. & SPEIRS, R. L. (1952). *Proc. R. Soc. Med.* **45,** 517.
JENKINS, G. N., EDGAR, W. M. & FERGUSON, D. B. (1969). *Archs oral Biol.* **14,** 105.
JENKINS, G. N. & SPEIRS, R. L. (1953). *J. Physiol., Lond.* **121,** 21.
KRUGER, B. J. (1959). *Pap. Dep. Dent. Univ. Qd* **1,** 3.
KRUGER, B. J. (1962). *J. dent. Res.* **41,** 215.
LOSEE, F. L. & ADKINS, B. L. (1969). *Caries Res.* **3,** 23.
LUDWIG, T. G. (1963). *Aust. dent. J.* **8,** 109.
WRIGHT, D. E. & JENKINS, G. N. (1954). *Br. dent. J.* **96,** 30.

GENETIC VARIATION
IN COPPER METABOLISM OF SHEEP

G. WIENER

*A.R.C. Animal Breeding Research Organization,
West Mains Road, Edinburgh, Scotland*

AND

A. C. FIELD

Moredun Research Institute, Gilmerton, Edinburgh, Scotland

THE purpose of this paper is to review some of the evidence, which has been obtained over the past four years, suggesting that there is genetic variation in the copper metabolism of sheep.

MATERIAL

The evidence is derived from two genetically diverse flocks of sheep on two farms in Peeblesshire, Scotland. The salient feature of management in both flocks is that the different genetic classes are treated alike. Each flock was run as a unit in fields of sown pastures. Details were given by Wiener (1966) and Wiener *et al.* (1969).

Flock 1. The sheep belonged to three breeds: Scottish Blackface, Cheviot and Welsh Mountain and the crosses between them. Crossbred lambs were themselves the offspring of crossbred parents (each parent being the same cross e.g. (Blackface x Cheviot) x (Blackface x Cheviot)). Both purebred and crossbred sheep are represented at different levels of inbreeding (0, 25, 37·5, 50 and 59 per cent.). The ewes were aged from 2 to 5 years old at lambing. The flock has been closed to females since 1955 and to males since 1958. There are approximately 300 breeding ewes in the flock, with younger stock in addition.

Flock 2. About 200 four-year-old Scottish Blackface ewes and a few Blackface x Swaledale ewes were mated to each of two rams from each of five breeds: Border Leicester, Clun Forest, Dorset Horn, Finnish Landrace and Merino. Part of the evidence is derived from the offspring of these matings. Further evidence comes from the next generation obtained by mating females of each of the five crossbred types to each of two rams of each of three further breeds: Oxford Down, Southdown and Soay.

92

RESULTS AND DISCUSSION

SWAYBACK

In 1964 about 15 per cent. of the lambs born alive in flock 1, and 12 per cent. of those in flock 2, were lost from swayback, mostly of a delayed type. There were, however, considerable differences attributable to breeds (flock 1) and to sires (flock 2). In flock 1, nearly 40 per cent. of Blackface lambs showed ataxia, 11 per cent. of the Cheviots and none of the Welsh. Crossbreds had incidences approximately intermediate between those of the pure breeds contributing to the cross. Level of inbreeding had no apparent effect on the incidence. In flock 2 the offspring groups of particular sires varied in swayback incidence from 0 per cent. to 35 per cent. Details were given by Wiener (1966) and Wiener and Sampford (1969) who also showed that the effects of breed and of sire were statistically significant even after adjusting for effects of weight of ewe and of lamb which vary considerably, as a result of the choice of breeds. Probability estimates for the occurrence of swayback in relation to genetic factors varied from 0 to 80 per cent.

COPPER IN BLOOD

Flock 1. Sheep were first bled in January 1965, nine months after the outbreak of swayback. Copper levels in whole blood were found to differ markedly between the breeds. Crossbreds had concentrations of Cu in their blood approximately at the level shown by the pure breed with the higher level contributing to the cross (Wiener and Field, 1966). The adjusted breed values (derived from an analysis involving 'fitting of constants') are shown in Figure 1.

Immediately following this bleeding, the ewes were injected with 50 mg. of Cu (as CuCaEDTA, 'Coprin', Glaxo Laboratories) as a prophylactic measure against swayback. The sheep were bled again four months later and then at intervals for a year. Figure 1 shows that in spite of large changes in average levels of Cu the ranking of the three pure breeds was unaffected and the crossbreds continued to show a marked heterotic effect.

Twenty of the ewes which had produced swayback lambs in 1964 had been retained. Figure 2 shows that their blood Cu levels were indistinguishable from those of their normal contemporaries in the summer but significantly lower in winter (the sheep were from 5 to 12 weeks pregnant in January).

The greater seasonal fluctuation in Cu level of the 'swayback' group is mirrored by differences in the fluctuations of the breeds

93

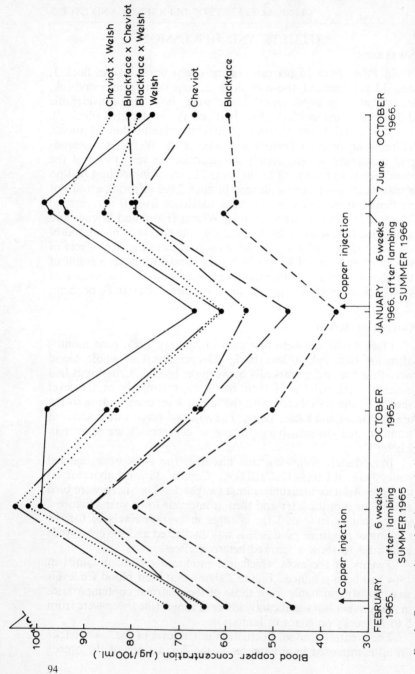

FIG. 1. Concentrations of Cu in the whole blood of six breed classes of sheep on seven occasions when other factors of variation are held constant. The adjusted mean of the flock is included in the breed values. (First and last points on the graph are based on samples of ewes drawn from the flock.) (From Wiener, Field and Wood 1969, reproduced by courtesy of the editor of the Journal of Agricultural

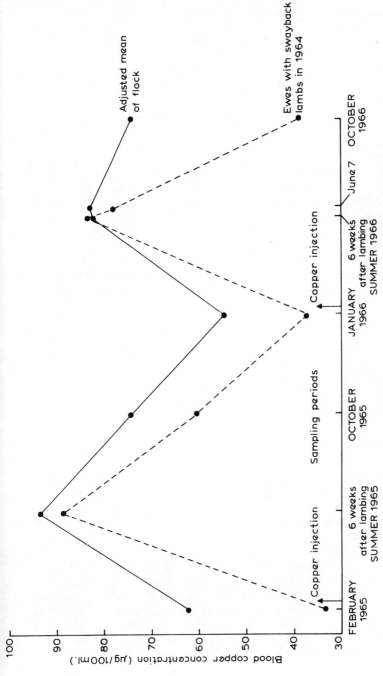

FIG. 2. Concentrations of Cu in the whole blood of adult female sheep which produced swayback lambs in 1964, in relation to the adjusted mean of the flock, at seven subsequent occasions. (From Wiener, Field and Wood, 1969, reproduced by courtesy of the editor of the Journal of Agricultural Science, Cambridge.)

95

in Figure 1. The Blackfaces declined most and the Welsh least between the summer of 1965 and January 1966. Relative to the starting point of each breed, the breed differences in the change of concentration appear more dramatic. Statistical confirmation of the significance of the breed effects on changes in concentrations has been obtained in current (unpublished) analyses.

Flock 2. Table I shows the concentrations of Cu in the blood plasma of the five crossbred classes of ewe and in that of their lambs. The figures shown are unweighted averages of sub-class means. Preliminary statistical analysis has shown that the variation among breeds of dam and variation among lambs attributable to sire breed is significant (P < 0·01). The most important feature of the breed variation shown in this table is that two of the columns show variation attributable to breed of sire only—the maternal

Table I. *Copper concentration in the blood plasma (μg/100ml.) of adult ewes and their 15 week-old lambs. (The ewes were the offspring of Scottish Blackface mothers and the breed of sire shown)*

Sire of ewes (maternal grandsire of lambs)	By breed of ewe				By breed of sire		
	Ewes		Lambs		Sire of lambs	Lambs	
	No.	Cu	No.	Cu		No.	Cu
Border Leicester	29	105	44	149			
Clun Forest	36	116	47	149	Oxford	87	130
Dorset Horn	38	114	53	137	Southdown	80	137
Finnish Landrace	42	98	83	139			
Merino	33	88	28	136	Soay	88	156
Significance of breed variation (P)	< 0·01		NS			< 0·01	

contribution, both genetic and non-genetic, being either constant (the mothers of the crossbred ewes were nearly all Blackface) or averaged out (each breed of sire was mated to each crossbreed of ewe). Non-genetic maternal transmission of blood Cu levels need not therefore be postulated as a major cause of breed differences in adult sheep.

The regression of the Cu level in the lambs on that in their mothers, within sire groups, was 0·22 (95 per cent. confidence limits 0·09 to 0·35). Twice this regression (0·44), when parent and offspring are observed at the same age, represents an estimate of heritability, that is the proportion of the total variation in the trait which would respond to selection. However since the relationship here is between the Cu level of adult ewes and that of their 15 week old lambs the heritability estimate is valid only if the trait in the lamb and the adult can be regarded as being the same. Maternal transmission of Cu from the mother to her lamb could affect the magnitude of the regression.

COPPER IN LIVER

In October 1966, a sample of 68 sheep representing all the breeds from flock 1 were slaughtered. The breed variation in liver and blood Cu levels (see Wiener and Field, 1969) is shown in Table II. The Blackfaces and their crosses were low in liver Cu whilst Cheviot, Welsh and Cheviot x Welsh values were higher and not very different from each other. The marked effect of the Blackface genotype on the liver Cu level of crosses with the Blackface contrasts with the positive heterosis shown by the blood Cu level of crosses.

Lambs in flock 1 which had died between birth and weaning (at 15 weeks old) in 1967 and 1968 had their liver Cu concentration

Table II. *Copper concentrations of liver (p.p.m. D.M.) and of whole blood (µg/100 ml.) of three breeds of female sheep and their crosses. (Fitted values obtained by least squares)*

		Cu in			
		liver		blood	
	No. of animals	Fitted value	SE	Fitted value	SE
Blackface	12	14·3	13·8	59·8	7·6
Cheviot	7	44·7	17·0	66·8	9·4
Welsh	13	49·7	13·1	75·7	7·2
Blackface x Cheviot	12	26·2	14·3	80·8	7·9
Blackface x Welsh	12	23·2	13·9	78·6	7·7
Cheviot x Welsh	12	54·9	13·6	84·4	7·5

(From Wiener and Field, 1969, reproduced by courtesy of the editor of *J. comp. Path. Ther.*)

determined as part of a detailed post-mortem examination. Deaths were attributed to a multiplicity of causes and were not associated with an outbreak of any specific disease (MacLeod and Barlow, unpublished). Results, without regard to cause of death (Table III) show variation in liver Cu concentration attributable to breed ($P < 0.002$) and to age at death ($P < 0.001$). These, along with the week of birth of the lamb, were the most important of the readily identifiable sources of variation. The ranking of the three pure breeds among the lambs agrees with that among the sample of adults shown in Table II. Crossbred lambs, however, had Cu levels which, on average, were not significantly different from the levels intermediate between those of the pure breeds represented. The depressing effect of the Blackface genotype on liver Cu noted for adults (Table II) was not observed.

The age trends are interesting in showing a decline with increasing age at death. The values for lambs dying within two days of birth (Table III) are also clearly higher than the values for adults shown in Table II. Unless lambs which died and which are from ewes injected with Cu during mid-pregnancy are atypical of lambs in general in respect of liver Cu, this finding appears to conflict with evidence quoted by Underwood (1962) that, unlike the young of most species, newborn sheep do not have markedly higher levels of liver Cu than adults. Riley *et al.* (1961) have, however, reported that the concentration of Cu in the liver of normal live lambs

Table III. *Copper concentration (p.p.m. of D.M.) in liver and brain of 166 lambs which died between birth and weaning in 1967 and 1968. (Adjusted breed values* and adjustment factors for age at death).*

	No.†	Liver Cu	Brain Cu
Breed:			
Blackface	18	128	9·1
Cheviot	24	140	9·9
Welsh	17	241	12·9
Blackface x Cheviot	50	161	10·7
Blackface x Welsh	27	161	10·8
Cheviot x Welsh	30	168	10·1
Range of SE of differences‡		±21·4−29·6	±0·9−1·2
Age at death:			
Still born	41	0	0
New born	27	14·6	−0·21
1 − 2 days	52	15·6	0·40
3 − 7 days	11	−57·6	−0·16
1 − 6 weeks	16	−46·8	0·89
6 − 15 weeks	19	−135·3	0·10
Range of SE of differences‡		±18·3−32·3	±0·7−1·3

* The breed values are for stillborn, single, 25 per cent. inbred female lambs in 1967 born to 1st parity, F_2 dams in the 1st week of lambing.
† Number of animals available for estimate.
‡ The higher SE's apply to the values with lower numbers of observations and vice versa.

within 24 hours of birth was significantly higher than that of their dams and that by 3 months old the levels in lambs had fallen. In the present study not all breeds were represented at each age of death among the lambs which died; although the linear model used for fitting constants provides an estimate for every class. It should not, however, be inferred from Table III that Blackface lambs dying between 6 and 15 weeks old had no Cu in their livers. The high standard errors allow for ample possibility of positive values. The inference to be drawn is that Blackface lambs had lower liver Cu levels than lambs of the other breeds and that lambs of the oldest age class had a lower concentration than those dying within 2 days.

COPPER IN BRAIN

Copper concentration in the brain was also determined for the lambs referred to above. Table III shows significant breed effects ($P < 0.05$) and an absence of age effects. The ranking of the three pure breeds was as for blood and liver Cu; crossbreds were intermediate in level between the levels of the pure breeds involved.

DEATHS FOLLOWING COPPER INJECTION

In February 1969, as in the four previous years, ewes were given a subcutaneous injection of 50 mg Cu (as CuCaEDTA) but only 280 out of the total of 360 ewes were treated. Ten of the 280 injected ewes died within three days of injection and an eleventh ewe died three weeks later. The clinical history, taken in conjunction with the post mortem findings (which were similar in all cases except the last sheep to die), strongly suggest that the deaths resulted from the Cu injections, the lesions being compatible with those described for 'acute' Cu poisoning (Watt and MacLeod, unpublished). The live weight of the sheep which died varied considerably and deaths were not confined to small sheep. Liver Cu concentrations ranged from 107 to 357 p.p.m. D.M. (average 196). In the present context the interesting feature of the results is that the deaths were associated with the breeding of the sheep. The 11 which died were Welsh Mountain (4) or a cross with Welsh (7). There were no Blackface, Cheviot or Blackface x Cheviot among the dead whereas five would have been expected in proportion to the numbers injected. The difference between Welsh and non-Welsh representation is significant on a χ^2 test ($P < 0.001$).

CONCLUSIONS

The evidence from the two flocks shows clearly that genetic factors influence the concentrations of Cu in blood, liver and brain of sheep. The Cu associated syndrome of swayback, and possibly the susceptibility to Cu poisoning, are also affected by genotype. Crossbred sheep have clearly more Cu in their blood than the midparental level but, on more limited evidence, crossbreds are possibly no more resistant to swayback and may not store more Cu in their livers than the average of the corresponding pure breeds. The results provide a hint therefore of some independence of the genetic mechanisms affecting Cu in blood, in liver and in the incidence of swayback. This hypothesis will require experimental verification.

The evidence for genetic variation in Cu concentrations of blood and tissues and in swayback incidence makes it seem possible that some of the susceptibility of particular farms to outbreaks of swayback should be attributed to the type of sheep kept. In many cases, with particular sheep tied to (and 'acclimatized to') particular farms, the relative contribution of each to the occurrence of swayback must be difficult, or impossible, to determine. However, a reappraisal of past reports of swayback outbreaks in the light of the genetic evidence might be worthwhile. The evidence of genetic variation in Cu concentrations also suggests that there may be more than one 'normal' range for all sheep. The levels below and above which disorders arise may not be the same for all sheep. Some evidence of this was given by Wiener et al. (1969).

Future work is aimed at elucidating the physiological mechanisms which give rise to the genetic differences. Evidence of genetic variation in mineral concentration is not, however, confined to Cu (for evidence in other minerals see Field et al., 1969). The opportunity would seem to exist therefore, for catering more precisely for the mineral requirements of genetically different groups of sheep under those conditions where nutrition is readily controllable as, for example, in housed sheep. For large areas of the world, where sheep are kept under extensive conditions, there is at least the hope that sheep can be genetically fitted to the mineral deficiencies, or occasionally the excesses, of those environments.

REFERENCES

FIELD, A. C., WIENER, G. & WOOD, J. (1969). *J. agric. Sci., Camb.* **73**, 267.
RILEY, J. W., HARVEY, J. M., WATSON, J. W. & LEVITT, M. S. (1961). *Qd J. agric. Sci.* **18**, 353.
UNDERWOOD, E. V. (1962). *Trace Elements in Human and Animal Nutrition.* London: Academic Press.

WIENER, G. (1966). *J. comp. Path. Ther.* **76**, 435.
WIENER, G. & FIELD, A. C. (1966). *Nature, Lond.* **209**, 835.
WIENER, G. & FIELD, A. C. (1969). *J. comp. Path. Ther.* **79**, 7.
WIENER, G. & SAMPFORD, M. R. (1969). *J. agric. Sci., Camb.* **73**, 25.
WIENER, G., FIELD, A. C. & WOOD, JEAN (1969). *J. agric. Sci., Camb.* **72**, 93.

DISCUSSION

Howell (Liverpool). I think that Dr Wiener agrees that some caution should be exercised in the interpretation of results for liver Cu levels of lambs that have died. If such a lamb has an area of inflammation it will have a higher liver Cu level than a lamb of the same age and genetic makeup that is healthy. You might be on much safer ground if you compare brain Cu levels if you have to use post mortem material. A further query relates to the CuCaEDTA injection experiment in which you found that the Welsh breed was particularly susceptible. Were all the groups injected on the same day or were the Welsh animals injected on one day and others on subsequent days? In the work that Dr Ishmael and I have been doing on CuCaEDTA toxicity we have found, for example, that if three groups of animals are gathered on successive days and injected, one group may suffer an appreciable proportion of losses whereas the other two groups may show none. We don't understand this. I wonder if this happened in Dr Wiener's experiment?

Wiener (Edinburgh). I agree that the liver Cu data obtained from lambs that died may not be typical of all animals; however, this is not the major point. The differences between breeds for the 170 lambs which died have the same ranking as liver Cu differences from perfectly normal adults which were surplus to requirement and were killed. Thus we have two sets of evidence illustrating breed differences, one from normal adults and one from lambs which died. In answer to your second point, the animals were derived from a genetically heterogeneous flock which was formed in 1955. They are all handled as a group and injected within a short interval.

Hidiroglou (Ottawa). Are there any breed differences in the Cu concentration of the wool?

Wiener (Edinburgh). I am afraid we did not determine this; perhaps we should have done.

Cuthbertson (Glasgow). Is there any hint of an intra-breed dispersion of Cu levels such as Evans found when examining potassium in the red cells of sheep, where he found differences in proportions of high and low red cell K values?

Wiener (Edinburgh). Unfortunately, not; this would have been very interesting and exciting.

Reinhold (Beirut). Examination of the livers of newly born rats shows Zn concentrations that are almost double those of newly weaned rats. This suggests that the high concentration of Cu described by the speaker may be a manifestation of a general tendency for metal accumulation by the foetal liver during late stages of gestation to meet requirements for the first days of postnatal life.

Rish (Samarkand). Did you correlate the Cu concentration of blood with the caeruloplasmin level or with direct reacting Cu and is there any suggestion of genetic differences in caeruloplasmin levels?

Field (Edinburgh). We have not measured either caeruloplasmin or 'direct reacting' Cu in blood. Since caeruloplasmin is the major component of Cu in the blood we have assumed that our observed genetic changes are in this fraction. There may be genetic variation in the 'direct reacting' Cu, but since in the normal animal only about 10 mg. of Cu per 100 ml. of blood is in this fraction, existing analytical methods would hardly be satisfactory to do this.

Rish (Samarkand). In newborn Karakul lambs liver Cu usually ranges between 20 and 30 p.p.m. and then gradually increases to 80 in the adult. Your results show inverse kinetics with the newborn concentration on a fresh weight basis of 60 p.p.m. decreasing thereafter. I wonder if you can explain these differences between our results?

Wiener (Edinburgh). I'm sorry but I am not competent to comment on this difference; I merely present our results as facts that we found. If I can present a further fact, the audience may like to think about the implications. We are inbreeding rapidly in our experiments and some skeletal and other deformities arise. Two years ago we had 15 cases, a large crop, and in that year the liver Cu of skeletally deformed lambs was on the average double that of other lambs of the same age which had died for reasons other than skeletal abnormalities.

THE PATHOLOGY OF SWAYBACK

J. McC. HOWELL

Department of Veterinary Pathology, University of Liverpool, U.K.

SWAYBACK is an ataxic disorder of lambs which is produced when the central nervous system (CNS) develops in conditions of copper deficiency. Lesions may be found in the cerebrum, large neurones of the brain stem and spinal cord, and in the white matter of the spinal cord.

The brain may show several macroscopic lesions. It may be swollen and compressed within the cranial cavity or shrunken and surrounded by an excess of clear cerebrospinal fluid. The cerebral white matter may contain areas of gelatinous change in which a few nerve fibres are present in a loose glial network or there may be complete destruction of white matter which produces cavities surrounded by glia (Innes and Shearer, 1940; Barlow *et al.*, 1960; Innes and Saunders, 1962). In most cases there is little effect on neurones of the cerebral cortex although Roberts, Williams and Harvard (1966a, b) have described marked cerebral oedema and extensive damage to cortical neurones. It is probable that lesions in the cerebral white matter only occur when Cu depletion is very severe. These lesions arise before myelination; they may be anoxic in origin, and are similar to changes seen in human infantile cystic encephalopathies (Howell *et al.*, 1964; Cancilla and Barlow, 1966a; Howell, 1968, 1970a and b). However, these lesions are not specific to swayback and are not constantly present (Howell, 1968).

Chromatolysis and necrosis of large neurones in the brain s em and spinal cord are seen in all swayback lambs (Barlow *et al.*, 1960; Barlow *et al.*, 1964; Howell *et al.*, 1964). Electron microscopy has shown that affected neurones increase in size, show a progressive loss of Nissl substance, alterations in the Golgi apparatus and mitochrondria and a striking increase in neurofibrils (Cancilla and Barlow, 1966b).

Changes in the white matter of the spinal cord are constantly present in swayback and are found in the lateral columns below the point of entry of the dorsal nerve root and in the ventral columns adjacent to the median fissure. They appear to be long spinal tracts and the lesion is least marked in the lumbar cord, involves much of the periphery of the thoracic cord and is well defined as tract-like areas in the cervical cord and fades out in the

103

medulla. Fewer myelinated fibres are present in these areas and the stroma appears to be more plentiful. Swollen axons and gitter cells are rare. It has been demonstrated that products of myelin degeneration are not present in the spinal cord of young lambs (Howell *et al.*, 1964). The correlated results of Sudan, OTAN (Adams, 1959) and Marchi techniques have confirmed that myelin degeneration was absent in young swayback lambs but was present in older animals (Howell *et al.*, 1969). Electron microscopic examination of this lesion in young swayback lambs revealed a degeneration of axons within apparently normal myelin sheaths (Cancilla and Barlow, 1968). The axon disintegrated and finally the myelin sheath was destroyed. The steps were regarded as being identical with those described in Wallerian degeneration following axon section in the spinal cord. They did not, however, describe any accumulation of fibrils within the axoplasm, a change which was the most prominent and consistent abnormality observed in the neurones of swayback lambs (Cancilla and Barlow, 1966b).

The tissues of swayback animals are low in Cu during the development of the CNS. A loss of cytochrome oxidase activity has been demonstrated (Howell and Davison, 1959; Mills and Williams, 1962; Barlow, 1963) and the CNS of swayback lambs has a lower content of myelin lipids than that of normal animals (Howell *et al.*, 1964; 1969). Lambs developing in this abnormal biochemical environment have lesions in myelinated structures and in large neurones of the brain stem and spinal cord. The lambs are born with fewer than normal myelinated fibres in localized areas of the spinal cord. If they survive some of the nerve fibres degenerate and this may be a primary axonal/neuronal degeneration. It is of interest that long tracts are involved and one would expect the neurones which supply and maintain these long axons to be most susceptible to metabolic insult. A better understanding of the pathology will be obtained when the development of the lesions *in utero* has been studied and when experimental studies of CNS nerve fibre degeneration, similar to those of Daniel and Strich (1969) have been performed on sheep.

REFERENCES

Adams, C. W. M. (1959). *J. Path. Bact.* **77,** 648.
Barlow, R. M. (1963). *J. comp. Path. Ther.* **73,** 61.
Barlow, R. M., Field, A. C. & Ganson, N. A. (1964). *J. comp. Path. Ther.* **74,** 530.
Barlow, R. M., Purves, D., Butler, E. J. & Macintyre, I. J. (1960). *J. comp. Path. Ther.* **70,** 411.
Cancilla, P. A. & Barlow, R. M. (1966a). *Acta Neuropath.* **6,** 260.
Cancilla, P. A. & Barlow, R. M. (1966b). *Acta Neuropath.* **6,** 251.

CANCILLA, P. A. & BARLOW, R. M. (1968). *Acta Neuropath.* **11**, 294.
DANIEL, P. M. & STRICH, S. J. (1969). *Acta Neuropath.* **12**, 314.
HOWELL, J. McC. (1968). *Proc. Nutr. Soc.* **27**, 85.
HOWELL, J. McC. (1970a). *Wld Rev. Nutr. Diet.* **12**, 377.
HOWELL, J. McC. (1970b). Diseases affecting myelination in domestic animals. In *Myelination.* (Ed. Davison, A. N. & Peters, A.) Springfield, Illinois: Thomas. In press.
HOWELL, J. McC. & DAVISON, A. N. (1959). *Biochem. J.* **72**, 365.
HOWELL, J. McC., DAVISON, A. N. & OXBERRY, J. (1964). *Res. vet. Sci.* **5**, 376.
HOWELL, J. McC., DAVISON, A. N. & OXBERRY, J. (1969). *Acta Neuropath.* **12**, 33.
INNES, J. R. M. & SAUNDERS, L. A. (1962). *Comparative Neuropathology.* New York: Academic Press.
INNES, J. R. M. & SHEARER, G. D. (1940). *J. comp. Path. Ther.* **53**, 1.
MILLS, C. F. & WILLIAMS, R. B. (1962). *Biochem. J.* **85**, 629.
ROBERTS, H. E., WILLIAMS, B. M. & HARVARD, A. (1966a). *J. comp. Path. Ther.* **76**, 279.
ROBERTS, H. E., WILLIAMS, B. M. & HARVARD, A. (1966b). *J. comp. Path. Ther.* **76**, 285.

DISCUSSION

Sourkes (Montreal). You mention specifically the changes in the red nucleus. Do you mean to imply that degenerative changes in these descending fibres were responsible for the end effects seen in swayback? Has the sequence of events leading to swayback been investigated by experimental neurologists?

Howell (Liverpool). Degenerative changes in neurones are also apparent in sites other than the red nucleus. I don't know what these tracts are but I don't think that because there is a lesion in the red nucleus there will be a lesion in these other sites because I think there are a lot of interneuronal connections within the rubro-spinal tract. I have transected the brain stems of foetuses *in utero* posterior to the red nucleus and allowed them to develop for between two and five weeks before examination. A number of these foetuses were alive, they had respiratory movements and could move their legs. They were then slaughtered. I had produced a lesion, and in some cases a large lesion in the brain stem but the spinal cords examined by H and E and by Loyez staining procedures showed that the spinal cord, although smaller than that of the twin which acted as a control, did not have lesions comparable to swayback; to all intents and purposes the procedure produced normal, but small, spinal cords.

Camberos (Gainesville). Which are the most specific lesions of swayback?

Howell (Liverpool). In the United Kingdom if we have ataxic lambs with cerebral cavities then I am happier with my diagnosis than just with ataxic lambs. Cerebral cavitation is however not a constant feature. Innes has reported it in 60 per cent. of his cases, Barlow in 40 per cent., and I have seen it in 20 per cent. of our cases. The lesions constantly present in swayback lambs are those in the white matter of the spinal cord and the neuronal degeneration. As the lambs grow older, and some of them survive well, the neurone lesions are more difficult to find but are nevertheless detectable in lambs of eight months of age. The white matter lesions are still quite prominent at this age.

Anke (Jena). What is the Cu concentration of the brains of swayback lambs?

Howell (Liverpool). Although we have determined the Cu concentration of brain I regard the brain as rather heterogeneous and most of our analyses have been carried out on thoracic spinal cord. These figures have been published but I am unable to quote them at the moment other than to say that the Cu content of the spinal cord of affected animals is significantly lower than normal. This is a better guide to the Cu status of individual cases than liver Cu.

INFERTILITY ASSOCIATED WITH EXPERIMENTAL COPPER DEFICIENCY IN SHEEP, GUINEA-PIGS AND RATS

J. McC. HOWELL AND G. A. HALL

Department of Veterinary Pathology, University of Liverpool, U.K.

OUR interest in swayback led us to investigate the effect of copper deficiency on the foetus *in utero*. Keil and Nelson (1931) and Dutt and Mills (1960) had shown that rats require Cu to produce living young. Cu deficiency has been associated with lowered fertility in cattle but the nature of the disturbance has not been determined (Underwood, 1962). We have investigated this problem in sheep, guinea-pigs and rats (Howell, 1968, 1969; Hall and Howell, 1969; Howell and Hall, 1969).

A semi-synthetic diet was fed to Welsh Mountain lambs, which were divided into a group of nine fed the deficient diet and a group of seven controls fed the diet supplemented with 10 p.p.m. of Cu. Rams were introduced to the group after they had been fed the diets for five months; ten days previous to this the mean weights and whole blood Cu levels of the deficient and control groups were 24·3 kg., and 17·5 μg./100 ml. and 23·3 kg. and 107·1 μg./100 ml. respectively. One of the controls died and was not pregnant, the remaining six each produced a single lamb of mean weight 3·5 kg. Two of the Cu-deficient group aborted small dead immature foetuses, five others died during the probable period of pregnancy and were not pregnant. Live lambs were not born to the nine deficient sheep.

Six mature female guinea-pigs were fed a synthetic diet containing less than 0·5 p.p.m. of Cu (Howell, 1969). Five, six, and seven received this diet supplemented with 10, 25 and 50 p.p.m. of Cu respectively. Males were introduced after four weeks and removed one month later, and again after 18 weeks and removed six weeks later. In the 50 p.p.m. supplemented group 14 matings were possible, evidence of conception was seen in 10, 14 live and 5 dead young were produced and 9 were dead *in utero*. In the 25 p.p.m. group 12 matings could have been made; evidence of conception was seen in 6, 10 live and 3 dead young were produced and 5 were dead *in utero*. Nine matings were possible in the 10 p.p.m. group; evidence of conception was seen in three, four live and one dead pup were produced and four were dead *in utero*. In the deficient group 11 matings could have occurred, evidence of conception was seen in 5, and was followed by foetal resorption. The mean terminal liver Cu contents in the adults were 252·4, 88·4, 34·1, and 8·6 p.p.m., in the 50, 25, 10 p.p.m. and Cu-deficient group respectively.

A number of experiments have been performed with hooded rats fed a diet of milk treated with hydrogen sulphide (Hall and Howell, 1969). Controls were given this diet supplemented with 100, 50, 20 or 10 μg. of Cu given on five days of the week, and stock rats fed commercial diet were also used. There were 32 matings in stock rats and 24 litters born. In the 100 μg. control group there were 20 matings and 15 litters born. In the 50 μg. group seven litters were produced from eight matings. There were eight matings in the 20 μg. control group producing four litters. In the 10 μg. group there were seven matings and one litter. In the deficient rats there were 40 matings but foetal resorption occurred and litters were not produced. These rats had been fed the diets for four or eight weeks before males were introduced. In other experiments eight rats were mated after being fed the deficient diet for two weeks. There were no litters and in five evidence of foetal resorption was seen. Five other rats were fed the deficient diet as soon as they were mated; 44 pups were born, 29 were dead, and all had subcutaneous haemorrhages similar to those described by O'Dell, Hardwick and Reynolds (1961). Six rats were fed the diet at the highest level of Cu supplementation as soon as they

107

were mated; 66 pups were born, nine were dead and one of these had a small area of subcutaneous haemorrhage.

Gravid uteri were examined histologically from Cu-deficient, control and stock rats. Results from the control and stock rats were similar. The first lesion was seen in deficient rats on day 13 of pregnancy and consisted of necrosis of foetal tissue, and was followed on day 15 by necrosis of the placenta (Howell and Hall, 1969).

This work has shown that Cu deficiency will induce infertility in rats, guinea-pigs and sheep. The effect of minimal Cu supplementation is now being investigated.

REFERENCES

DUTT, B. & MILLS, C. F. (1960). *J. comp. Path. Ther.* **70,** 120.
HALL, G. A. & HOWELL, J. McC. (1969). *Br. J. Nutr.* **23,** 41.
HOWELL, J. McC. (1968). *Vet. Rec.* **83,** 226.
HOWELL, J. McC. (1969). *Vet. Rec.* **84,** 517.
HOWELL, J. McC. & HALL, G. A. (1969). *Br. J. Nutr.* **23,** 47.
KEIL, H. L. & NELSON, V. E. (1931). *J. biol. Chem.* **93,** 49.
O'DELL, B. J., HARDWICK, B. C. & REYNOLDS, G. (1961). *J. Nutr.* **73,** 151.
UNDERWOOD, E. J. (1962). *Trace Elements in Human and Animal Nutrition.* New York: Academic Press.

DISCUSSION

Suttle (Edinburgh). Was the remarkable difference in liveweight gain between your supplemented and unsupplemented lambs due to differences in food consumption or to differences in food conversion efficiency? Were there also differences in food consumption between supplemented and unsupplemented rats and guinea-pigs?

Howell (Liverpool). The effect of Cu deficiency on food consumption occurs very late on in the deficiency. The effects of Cu deficiency upon appetite do not appear to be as dramatic as those of Zn deficiency.

Suttle (Edinburgh). I would be most surprised if a ewe lamb of normal Cu status but having a liveweight comparable to those of your unsupplemented animals was able to produce viable offspring.

Howell (Liverpool). The animal I illustrated was 15 months old and had been on the diet for 12 months. At the time the ram was introduced and for some time afterwards there was no great weight difference between control and treated animals. Some weight difference between control and treated animals might how-ever have been apparent at the ime of abortions.

Lewis (Weybridge). I would like to congratulate Dr Howell on his paper. When most of us went on to using a semi-purified diet for Cu work we thought we had eliminated variability asso-ciated with different diets but now that we are using similar diets we are not always getting the same results. We haven't been able to find quite the same effects on weight gain and upon fertility as Dr Howell. We have reared lambs from 3 weeks of age on a semi-purified diet containing about 1 p.p.m. Cu and have maintained them on this treatment to breeding age. Lambs on this treatment have maintained a good rate of growth and a good appetite. Blood Cu has fallen to a low level shortly after the introduction of treatment and liver Cu concentrations are usually below 5 p.p.m. We have however noted that if for any reason animals begin to deteriorate in condition they do so very rapidly when on a Cu-deficient treatment. (Miss Lewis illustrated her comments by reference to the performance of a 2 year old Cu-deficient ram and ewe which were successfully mated to produce a swayback off-spring.)

Wiener (Edinburgh) Dr Howell, I am interested in the results you have quoted for mortality and litter size in guinea-pigs main-tained on different levels of Cu. There appeared to be a steady improvement and increase in litter size with increasing level of Cu supplementation. How do you account for this and do you now revise your estimates regarding Cu requirement?

Howell (Liverpool). Much more work is required to clarify the Cu requirements of the guinea-pig. We commonly obtained litter sizes of 3 or 4 in guinea-pigs maintained on 25 or 50 p.p.m. Cu. I think that not as many young were born of animals on 25 p.p.m. as on 50 p.p.m. as the conception rate was much lower; males were introduced twice and after the first occasion copulation plugs were found but no conceptions occurred.

PRODUCTION OF SWAYBACK
BY EXPERIMENTAL COPPER DEFICIENCY

N. F. SUTTLE AND A. C. FIELD

Moredun Research Institute, Edinburgh, U.K.

THE object of our study was to find a dietary treatment to produce a consistently high incidence of swayback for studies on the pathogenesis of the condition. Diets low in copper and high in molybdenum and sulphate, either singularly or in combination, were used. In Experiment 1 groups of Scottish Blackface ewes were arranged in a 2×2 factorial design and the levels of Cu were 1·2 and 11·2 μg./g. and of Mo + SO$_4$ 0·2 μg./g. + 0·73 g./kg. DM and 25·2 μg./g. + 6·0 g./kg. dry matter respectively. The treatments were continued for 20 months from mating and throughout two gestations: viable lambs from the first and second crops were killed at birth and 10 weeks of age, respectively. The composition of the basal semi-purified diet, amounts of food offered and details of analytical and histological methods have been described elsewhere (Suttle and Field, 1968a, b). The results are summarized in Table I. Removing Cu from or adding Mo + SO$_4$ to the diet reduced brain Cu concentrations in the lamb at birth; in Group C (see Table I) these effetcs were additive, brain cytochrome oxidase activities were reduced and central nervous lesions of swayback were found in one lamb. Ewes from Group C developed achromotrichia and anaemia and after parturition became extremely emaciated; they were replaced by ewes of the same breed from another source prior to the second mating. After the second gestation three unsupplemented ewes from Group A were anaemic; of these one had aborted during late pregnancy and the others produced the only cases of delayed swayback found in that group. The replacement ewes in Group C in their first gestation developed similar clinical abnormalities to their predecessors but their offspring included 6 congenital cases and 1 subclinical delayed case of swayback with very low brain Cu concentrations and cytochrome oxidase activities. Congenital swayback had not been produced previously under experimental conditions but since there were no controls for the replacement Group C ewes it was decided to conduct a further experiment to confirm this important finding.

Groups of Blackface ewes from the replacement source were given the same diets as in Experiment 1, except for the diet contain-

Table I. *Summary of clinical and biochemical data from experimental attempts to produce Swayback in lambs*

Dietary Supplement	Group	Expt. No.	Lamb Crop	Number of Ewes	Number of Lambs Born	Mean Ewe Plasma Cu last two months of pregnancy (μg./100 ml.)	Ewe Haemoglobin at Parturition (g./100 ml.)	Lamb Brain Cu (μg./g. DM)	Lamb Brain Cytochrome Oxidase (ml.O₂/ h./mg.DM)	Cases of Swayback
None	A	1	1	8	9	30±5·8*	12·1±0·9	7·1±1·1	158±18	0
		1	2	8	9	11±2·1	9·0±1·0	4·3±0·8	98±18	2 Delayed
		2	1	13	13	26±3·6	12·6±0·8	5·8±0·7	86±10	0
Cu (10 μg./g.)	B	1	1	6	5	90±6·2	11·9±0·2	10·9±0·6	159±28	0
		1	2	6	8	104±5·5	12·7±0·4	10·5±0·6	174±15	0
		2	1	6	5	108±3·5	12·4±1·6	14·5±1·2	108±16	0
Mo + SO₄ (25 μg./g. + 5·3 g./kg.)	C	1	1	6	5	49±6·3	8·8±0·7	3·2±1·3	49±19	1 Delayed (?)
		1	1R	8	8	22±2·1	8·3±0·1	1·8±0·1	59±20	6 Congenital, 1 Delayed
		2	1	13	9	55±4·7	9·9±0·7	6·2±1·0	114±35	3 Congenital, 1 Delayed
Cu + Mo + SO₄	D	1	1	5	6	101±7·9	10·8±1·8	6·9±1·0	146±15	0
		1	2	5	9	125±3·7	10·4±0·7	7·1±0·6	138±19	0

* Standard error of mean.
1R Denotes first crop from replacement ewes

111

ing Cu and Mo + SO_4 at the higher levels which was omitted (Experiment 2). The results are summarized in Table I. Unsupplemented ewes again remained healthy during the first gestation and produced normal offspring. Of the ewes given the low Cu diet with added Mo + SO_4, however, six were barren and one aborted and the offspring included three congenital cases and one delayed case of swayback. The severity of the syndrome was not correlated with assessments of Cu status since the mean Cu concentrations in the plasma of ewes and brain of lambs were higher than those for Group C after the first gestation in Experiment 1 in which offspring were clinically normal at birth. The different response of 'replacement' ewes to Cu deficiency was emphasized in the second pregnancy of Experiment 2. Three months prior to mating six of the 11 surviving ewes on the low Cu diet were given 45 mg. Cu subcutaneously as CuCa EDTA: only one did not produce a lamb and haemoglobin levels were normal at parturition. Of the five uninjected ewes, however, two aborted in mid-pregnancy, one apparently resorbed its foetus and one was barren; all ewes became anaemic, haemoglobin values ranging from 2·3 to 8·1 g./100 ml. Anaemia and reproductive failure had not been found extensively in unsupplemented ewes in our previous experiments.

The present experiments show clearly the importance of genetic variation in the response of sheep to Cu deficiency: with the low Cu diet the response varied from a low incidence of delayed swayback to reproductive failure and severe anaemia after two gestations, and with the low Cu diet supplemented with Mo + SO_4 from anaemia only to reproductive failure, anaemia and congenital swayback after one gestation. Since the margin between reproductive failure and production of swayback offspring is narrow, it may not be practicable to use such treatments to study the pathogenesis of swayback using serial slaughter techniques.

REFERENCES

SUTTLE, N. F. & FIELD, A. C. (1968a). *J. comp. Path. Ther.* **78,** 351.
SUTTLE, N. F. & FIELD, A. C. (1968b). *J. comp. Path. Ther.* **78,** 363.

DISCUSSION

Everson (Austin, Texas). I am very interested in reports of uncomplicated Cu deficiency in the lamb. It has been our experience with the guinea-pig that if the liver Cu concentration on a dry matter basis is in the neighbourhood of 2 to 4 p.p.m. ataxia frequently results in the offspring. Dr Howell has shown that at a 0 p.p.m. Cu content in the diet no young are produced, whereas at 10 p.p.m. normal young are produced. We have found that Cu concentrations between 0·5 and 1 p.p.m. in the diet do produce brain defects in the young.

Suttle (Edinburgh). May I just add to my paper the comment that I feel that the hope of producing a dietary treatment which will yield a high proportion of swayback animals is a rather remote one because of genetic variability arising both within and between sources of sheep and also because the margin between infertility and production of swayback offspring is such a narrow one.

Porter (Boston, Mass.). In considering the relation of brain Cu and cytochrome oxidase to swayback it might be helpful to keep in mind, that, in the adult at least, cytochrome oxidase Cu makes up only a small part of total brain Cu. The critical level might reflect depletion of one of these proteins, for example cytochrome oxidase at a time after total brain Cu has been lowered by depletion of other Cu proteins. If one had the material available it might be helpful to determine, firstly, what other Cu proteins are present in the normal newborn or foetal as opposed to adult brain and, secondly, what happens to these other Cu proteins in brains suffering Cu depletion and swayback.

Suttle (Edinburgh). I would agree. We know for example that Mo alters the distribution of Cu both in the liver and in the bloodstream and I am sure it is the answer to these relatively high brain coppers that we are finding in some swayback offspring.

Thornton (London). Swayback has been artificially induced by feeding Mo to sheep on low Cu diets. Has swayback ever been associated with excess Mo in herbage under natural grazing conditions?

Suttle (Edinburgh). Molybdenum does not appear to be important as a cause of swayback in the United Kingdom. We may however have to rethink our ideas about the importance of Mo as in recent work in the U.S.A. anaemia has been induced in experimental animals by including supplements providing 2 p.p.m. Mo in a low Cu diet. It is also possible that where the dietary Cu is already of low availability very small variations in dietary Mo content may become important.

AN EXAMINATION OF THE COPPER STATUS IN 'MUERTE SÚBITA' (SUDDEN DEATH) IN CUBAN CATTLE

VILDA FIGUEROA AND T. M. SUTHERLAND

Instituto de Ciencia Animal, Habana, Cuba

'MUERTE SÚBITA' (sudden death) occurs in cattle in Cuba with appreciable frequency. It is characterized by collapse and death of apparently healthy animals when exposed to stress, usually that of being driven. Incidence is seasonal and restricted to specific areas. The condition thus simulates 'falling disease' associated with copper deficiency in Australia (Bennetts *et al.*, 1941; Bennetts *et al.*, 1942) and in Florida (Becker *et al.*, 1953; Becker *et al.*, 1965).

Preliminary studies disclosed a Cu deficiency in a pasture area, on the north east Camagüey coast, where 'muerte súbita' was prevalent. Three groups, each of 16 Brahman bulls, were studied in this area from January 1967. They were animals of three to four years old already in the area four to five months; animals of 16 to 18 months born and raised in neighbouring areas subject to the condition and animals of 16 to 18 months raised in areas free of 'muerte súbita'. Half of each group were given monthly from January to June 120 mg. Cu as copper sulphate in saline by intravenous infusion.

Mortality was high (56 per cent.). The most susceptible were the young animals brought from areas free of sudden death of which 14 died, nine during the first three months. The remaining deaths in all groups occurred with the onset of the rains in June and July. The groups entered the experiment with different serum Cu concentrations. The young pre-exposed bulls had mean serum concentrations of Cu of 27.7 ± 7.6 μg./100 ml. indicative of possible deficiency (Underwood, 1962). The young bulls not pre-exposed (6.80 ± 3.6 μg./100 ml.) and the older bulls (58.4 ± 4.7 μg./100 ml.) had values within the normal range for bulls in Cuba.

After Cu infusion began there was no increase in serum Cu in the old bulls or the young bulls from non-suspect areas, which maintained normal serum concentrations. The young bulls from the suspect area showed a considerable increase ($P < .001$) in serum levels to 66.8 ± 6.8 μg./100 ml. after one month's treatment and remained in the normal range thereafter. By May there were no significant differences between subgroups although the untreated pre-exposed bulls had the lowest levels (41.4 ± 14.3 μg./100 ml.).

No difference was found in mean serum Cu concentration

(μg./100 ml.) between the victims of 'muerte súbita' (treated 54·7; untreated 48·4 S.E.D. ± 5·98) and 19 animals surviving the experiment (treated 56·8; untreated 50·5 S.E.D. ± 6·43).

Tissue Cu analyses were made on 18 victims of 'muerte súbita' and on 12 survivors deliberately slaughtered after 10 months. Copper infusions effectively increased liver Cu concentrations. Untreated young bulls had a mean liver Cu concentration (16 p.p.m. dry matter basis) usually taken as indicative of deficiency. Young bulls drawn from the safe area had liver Cu in the normal range (80 p.p.m.) and the older bulls had values (46 p.p.m.) which were low but not deficient. Liver (X) and heart (Y) concentrations (p.p.m. dry matter basis) were negatively correlated: $Y = 17·35 - 0·0085X \pm 0·0036$; $r = 0·42 \pm 0·19$ (P < ·05).

Six samples of grass taken during the experiment showed Cu in the range 3 to 5 p.p.m., Mo 0·61 to 1·57 p.p.m. and SO_4 0·90 to 1·4 per cent. on a dry matter basis.

Two victims in a geographically separate area, Bayamo, with a similar history of 'muerte súbita' had normal liver and serum Cu concentrations of 110 and 70 p.p.m. and 43·7 and 70·6 μg./ 100 ml. Surviving animals (10) had a mean serum concentration of 66·0 ± 8·8 μg./100 ml.

This pasture contained Cu 10 p.p.m., Mo 1·18 p.p.m. and SO_4 0·66 per cent. on a dry matter basis. On autopsy oedema of the lungs was consistently found and some defects of the hearts but we did not find the degenerative fibrosis associated with 'falling disease'.

In conclusion the pasture analysis in the Camagüey experiment and the associated low levels of serum and liver Cu in the animals are indicative of a potential Cu deficiency but the ineffectiveness of Cu infusion and especially the susceptibility and rapidity of onset in the young animals brought to the pasture in good Cu status and maintained in this condition make it unlikely that Cu deficiency is the cause of 'muerte súbita'.

REFERENCES

BECKER, R. B., ARNOLD, P. T., KIRK, W. G., DAVIS, G. K. & KIDDER, R. W. (1953). *Bull. Fla agric. Exp. Stn* No. 513.
BECKER, R. B., HENDERSON, J. R. & LEIGHTY, R. G. (1965). *Bull. Fla agric. Exp. Stn* No. 699.
BENNETTS, H. W., BECK, A. B., HARLEY, R. & EVANS, S. T. (1941). *Aust. vet. J.* **17**, 85.
BENNETTS, H. W., HARLEY, R. & EVANS, S. T. (1942). *Aust vet. J.* **18**, 50.
UNDERWOOD, E. J. (1962). *Trace Elements in Human and Animal Nutrition.* New York: Academic Press.

DISCUSSION

Hartmans (Wageningen). Can you tell us something about the histological picture of this disease?

Figueroa (Havana). Macroscopically nothing is apparent but congestion and oedema in the lungs. Microscopically, oedema is apparent in the lung and heart and pericarditis in the heart. Sometimes, but not consistently, nephrosis is apparent in the kidney.

Uvarov (Greenford, Middlesex). Do any of the animals ever show clinical signs of Cu deficiency and have you examined the livers of animals by bacteriological tests under anaerobic conditions?

Figueroa (Havana). There are no clinical signs of Cu deficiency; animals appeared normal until sudden death occurred. We have considered the possibility of enterotoxaemia by examination of the liver under anaerobic conditions and have also prepared inocula for injection into the rat with negative findings.

Lewis (Weybridge). Have you determined serum Mg levels?

Figueroa (Havana). Yes; serum Mg levels are usually between 2 and 3 mg. per 100 ml. blood. There is no difference in Mg levels between victims and survivors.

Wiener (Edinburgh). Is there the possibility that genetic differences in susceptibility may be involved in this disease?

Figueroa (Havana). There could be.

Underwood (Perth). Why was the Cu administered intravenously? Is it not possible that most of the Cu was excreted rapidly so failing to improve the Cu status of the cattle? The liver Cu levels of treated animals, although higher, were not greatly so and the blood Cu levels of treated animals were still in a deficient range or close to it.

Figueroa (Havana). Intravenous injection was used to achieve a rapid increase in Cu status. Blood Cu levels of between 60 and 70 mg. per 100 ml. have been commonly found in some areas of Cuba where cattle are clinically normal, although this range might be regarded as low elsewhere. The treatment period in this experiment was of 5 months' duration; surviving animals were killed 10 months after the start of the experiment and between 5 and 10 months there was evidence for a decline in liver Cu concentration, indicating that Cu was being withdrawn from the liver subsequent to the cessation of Cu treatment.

Horvath (Morgantown, W.Va.). Are there any differences in plant species between normal and affected areas?

Figueroa (Havana). We are at present investigating the possibility of toxic weeds in these areas.

A COMBINED COPPER-ZINC DEFICIENCY IN CATTLE: CLINICAL SYMPTOMS

G. N. HAVRE

Institute of Biochemistry, The Veterinary College of Norway, Oslo, Norway

THE disease was originally observed in 1961 in a district of Norway where the Zn and Cu content in the grass were found to be lower than 40 p.p.m. and 5 p.p.m. respectively.

Since then the prevalence of the disease has been studied and it has been recognized in several parts of the country, especially in the coastal districts. In cases of reported deficiencies where administration of Cu and Zn has had a beneficial effect, the content of Zn and Cu in the feed has practically always been below the limits stated above (Dynna and Havre, 1963; Dynna and Havre, 1964; Havre and Dynna, 1967).

The clinical symptoms of the disease are quite interesting and, as there are possibilities for confusion with other diseases, it might be pertinent to give a more detailed description of the symptoms as they have been observed and studied under Norwegian conditions.

It seems appropriate to distinguish between symptoms on young calves aged from three weeks to five months, on young animals up to two years old and on lactating cows.

Calves. The disease may start with a moderate scouring. In spite of the fact that the appetite is normal, in the early stages of the disease at least, the growth of the animal is always found to be retarded and on occasions, to have ceased. As the symptoms become more severe the calves ail, become debilitated and are frequently recumbent. At this stage indications of dehydration with haemoconcentration may be observed.

117

The early symptoms are later combined with hyperkeratotic skin alterations, starting at the bridge of the nose from the muzzle and upwards, and subsequently the same alterations occur on the ears and backwards on the neck. Moreover, loss of hair occurs around the eyes, developing the, so-called, 'copper spectacles'.

Hyperkeratosis may also be seen on the extremities from the hoofs and upwards, or exclusively on the croup. In the most severe cases the whole body may be covered with hyperkeratotic incrustations. The incrustations are easily removed and if the condition is combined with strong itching, which is unusual in young animals however, bleeding lesions may develop.

Young animals. Anamnestic information always describes an animal in retarded growth, in spite of a rather good appetite. The body of the animal is, however, well proportioned and, in contrast to many other cases of deficiencies where the growth is retarded, a disproportion in size between head and body is rarely observed. As a consequence the animals have a juvenile appearance. Furthermore they are usually indolent and easy to handle compared with healthy animals of the same age.

Hyperkeratotic skin symptoms, as in calves with 'copper spectacles', are often seen but dandruff and loss of hair are equally frequent. The histological alterations which give rise to the loss of hair in the case of Cu-Zn deficiency start in the tip of the hair. In a normal animal pigment is more concentrated in the tip of the hair than in the remainder; the decolouration observed in Cu-Zn-deficient animals is not due to a depigmentation of the hair but to a loss of the most pigmented part of it. The hair-layer looks sparse but the hairs are firmly fixed and can never be removed in lumps. This is an important point to be noted. On animals which are kept in damp stalls a special skin disease, very similar to a Cu-Zn deficiency, is frequently seen. The tail itching as well as other symptoms are quite similar and the two diseases are often confused. Zinc-copper administration has, of course, no effect on this particular disorder but ventilation of the stall has. In this disease, however, the hair layer loosens and may easily be removed in handfuls.

Lactating cows. The main symptoms are the hyperkeratotic skin alterations occurring mainly on the head, the neck and the croup. Strong itching is more frequent than in young animals and calves. A folding of the skin due to oedema in the corium is typical in older animals. If the skin alterations are combined with itching, and localized to spots of the body exposed to scraping and rubbing, the animals may have a bald appearance, with bleeding lesions in extreme cases. The disease is most frequent in pregnant animals from the sixth month and until calving. Some animals seem to be more susceptible to the disease than others.

All the symptoms which are described above are typical for the combined Cu-Zn deficiency. A pure Zn deficiency has never been observed by the author, probably due to the fact that in Norway a low Zn content in grass and hay always seems to be combined with a low Cu content. This has been the case in practically all the samples examined by the author.

Acknowledgement. The author is indebted to Dr O. Dynna for valuable assistance in evaluating symptoms.

REFERENCES

DYNNA, O. & HAVRE, G. N. (1963). *Acta vet. scand.* **4**, 197.
DYNNA, O. & HAVRE, G. N. (1964). *Proc. 9th Int. Grassld Congr.* p. 717.
HAVRE, G. N. & DYNNA, O. (1967). *Foderjournalen,* **6**, 69.

DISCUSSION

Bienfet (Brussels). Do you have symptoms of Cu or Zn deficiency in horses in the same region?

Havre (Oslo). No, but there are very few horses there.

Thornton (London). Are these low concentrations of Zn and Cu in herbage associated with any particular soil type? Are they from sandy areas or are they in areas where the Zn or Cu could be complexed with organic matter in the soil and not available to the plant?

Havre (Oslo). Mostly they are from sandy areas.

Fleming (Wexford). I was interested that you found both the Zn and Cu low in herbage. We have found that as herbage matures the Cu levels fall but Zn levels remain relatively constant. Zinc accumulation appears to be able to keep pace with herbage growth. The results obtained depend very much upon time of year and stage of maturity at sampling.

Havre (Oslo). We have found the same thing. In these cases we have analysed hay as well as grass and whenever the grass contains less than 40 p.p.m. Zn, Cu is usually about 5 to 6 p.p.m.

CHRONIC COPPER POISONING IN SHEEP—
BIOCHEMICAL STUDIES OF THE HAEMOLYTIC PROCESS

R. H. THOMPSON AND J. R. TODD

Veterinary Research Laboratories, Stormont, Belfast, U.K.

THE metabolism of copper is complicated by its interactions with molybdenum and sulphate (and perhaps other factors) and it is one of the very few elements of which deficiency and toxic excess can occur under normal agricultural operations. Chronic Cu poisoning occurs under grazing conditions in parts of Australia, from accidental, or sometimes intentional spraying of pasture with Cu pesticides, from excessive Cu supplementation of rations and has recently shown up as a problem when sheep are housed for extended periods (Broughton and Hardy, 1934; Bull, 1964; Eden, 1940; Todd, 1962, 1969).

Sheep are the most susceptible animals and high Cu intake or very low Mo and SO_4 intakes lead to positive Cu balance and the accumulation of Cu in the tissues, particularly the liver. The normal concentration of Cu in liver is generally less than 50 p.p.m. in the wet tissue. Passive accumulation can take place for long periods with liver Cu increasing to 500 p.p.m. or more without clinical evidence of toxicity. The toxic phase is an acute illness referred to as the haemolytic crisis and is caused by, or at least follows, the release of Cu into the blood. The clinical symptoms include mathaemoglobinaemia, jaundice, haemoglobinuria, loss of appetite and excessive thirst. The haemolysis is very rapid, the normal PCV of 35 to 40 per cent. falling to 10 per cent. or less in two to three days.

The biochemistry of blood in chronic Cu poisoning has been extensively studied (Barden, 1962; McCosker, 1968; Todd and Thompson, 1963). Blood Cu remains normal until one to two days before clinical symptoms appear, and then increases to 5 to 20 times normal. Haemoglobin concentration falls rapidly over the next two to three days, and methaemoglobin (MHb) increases, reaching a peak in one to two days, and falls again—the pattern being similar to blood Cu. The other interesting feature is the dramatic fall in glutathione (GSH). These changes in MHb and GSH occur in other haemolytic conditions such as the drug induced haemolysis and Wilson's disease in man, and can also be produced by repeated i.v. injections of small amounts of Cu over two to four days (Todd and Thompson, 1964). Haemolysis is as severe but the animal does not become ill and haemopoiesis proceeds uneventfully. Although addition of minute amounts of copper to erythrocytes suspended in normal saline causes haemolysis, incubation of blood with added Cu does not cause these changes. Plasma proteins apparently have a protective effect and it therefore seems that haemolysis in the living animal is not the direct action of Cu ions.

Investigations showed that the changes occurring *in vivo* during the haemolytic crisis could be produced *in vitro* by incubating blood with homogenates of liver from sheep that had died of Cu poisoning. The activity was lower in homogenates made shortly after death than when stored, but liver from normal animals showed little or no activity even after storage for several months in deep freeze.

Physical fractionation of livers showed that the activities were associated with the larger particulate (nuclear) fractions of the cell and not with mitochondrial or microsomal fractions. Chemical fractionation showed that MHb formation and GSH destruction are not necessarily part of the haemolytic process. Figure 1 summarizes the results of ether extraction. Whole homogenates

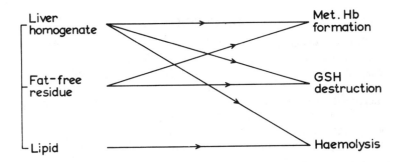

FIG. 1. Chemical fractionation of liver and biochemical activity towards erythrocytes.

caused MHb formation, GSH destruction and haemolysis. After ether extraction the residue caused MHb formation and GSH destruction but not haemolysis, and extracted lipid material caused haemolysis but had no effect on MHb or GSH. On incubating either the whole homogenate or the extracted lipid with blood there is a lag period of 10 to 15 minutes and then haemolysis is almost instantaneous. Even after one hour the fat-free residue produces no haemolysis. All the Cu is in the residue, there being none in the ether extract.

Chromatography of the lipid material on alumina columns yielded fractions of enhanced haemolytic activity. These fractions contained no phosphorus and therefore the possibility of lysolecithins being involved can be ruled out. The haemolytic activity of fractions paralleled their reactions to the thiobarbituric acid test, which suggested that oxidation of unsaturated fatty acids was involved. Whether these compounds are involved in haemolysis *in vivo* is difficult to say, since these compounds are highly reactive and the possibility of oxidation taking place after death or during extraction is very high.

REFERENCES

BARDEN, P. J. (1962). Ph.D. Thesis. University of Edinburgh.
BROUGHTON, J. B. & HARDY, W. T. (1934). *Bull. Tex. agric. Exp. Stn* No. 499.
BULL, L. B. (1964). *The Victorian Veterinary Proceedings*, p. 17.
EDEN, A. (1940). *J. comp. Path. Ther.* **53**, 90.
MCCOSKER, P. J. (1968). *Res. vet. Sci.* **9**, 103.
TODD, J. R. (1962). *Vet. Bull., Weybridge* **32**, 573.
TODD, J. R. (1969). *Proc. Nutr. Soc.* **28**, 189.
TODD, J. R. & THOMPSON, R. H. (1963). *Br. vet. J.* **119**, 161.
TODD, J. R. & THOMPSON, R. H. (1964). *J. comp. Path. Ther.* **74**, 542.

DISCUSSION

Van Leeuwen (Hoorn). Dr Van Adrichem in 1965 carried out some work at Hoorn on the effects of Cu poisoning on serum enzymes such as GOT and LDH. Before the animals showed clinical symptoms the activities of these serum enzymes were increased. At the end of his experiment poisoning was prevented in some animals by treatment with Mo compounds and recovery was complete and was accompanied by a decline in the activity of these enzymes in serum. Have you had any similar experience?

Todd (Belfast). In 1963 we found some increases in serum GOT and LDH as much as six weeks before the haemolytic crisis and dramatic rises in GOT, GPT and LDH in serum have frequently been found at the time of the haemolytic crisis. We have also investigated the effects of Mo and SO_4. In some cases animals have recovered, in other cases they have not.

Gartner (Yeerongpilly). Could Dr Todd tell us to what extent the picture of the clinical phase of acute Cu poisoning in sheep differs from that described for chronic Cu poisoning?

Todd (Belfast). The acute Cu poisoning is associated with severe gastro-enteritis; there is scouring and diarrhoea, with great damage to the mucosa of the intestinal tract. There is not really time for increases in the liver content of Cu. The blood Cu content may double but you do not get the increases to 10 to 20 times the normal blood Cu content that occurs with chronic Cu poisoning and there is, of course, no haemolysis.

ADVERSE EFFECTS FROM IRON SUPPLEMENTATION OF BROILER FEED

J. Márkus, T. Fekete and E. Surányi

Department of Animal Nutrition,
University of Veterinary Medicine, Budapest

In the last few years we have investigated the microelement requirements of Lohmann-Nichols hybrid chickens and during studies of the effects of iron supplementation we have obtained surprising results.

Compound feeds are generally supplemented with 20 to 30 mg./kg. of Fe as sulphate or carbonate. The original Fe content of the feed constituents is often several times that amount. The general view is that overdosage of Fe does not cause poisoning; the question is whether excess Fe, though non-poisonous, may not have some other disadvantage.

The compound feed of Lohmann hybrid chickens, which originally contained 192·8 p.p.m. of Fe was, between the ages of 10 to 56 days, supplemented with 0, 10, 20 and 40 p.p.m. of Fe (0, 23·7, 47·4 and 94·8 mg./kg. of Fe carbonate) and combined with four different supplementary levels of four other microelements (manganese, copper, zinc and iodine). The levels were 0, 20, 40 and 80 p.p.m. for Mn; 0, 15, 30 and 60 p.p.m. for Zn; 0, 1, 2 and 4 p.p.m. for Cu and 0, 0·2, 0·4 and 0·8 p.p.m. for I in the compound feed. Thus a total of 16 experimental groups were formed, each consisting of 15 chickens. At 8 weeks the average body weights of the chickens given 0, 10, 20 and 40 p.p.m. of Fe supplement were 1485, 1430, 1459 and 1418 g. respectively. As demonstrated by analysis of variance, Fe supplementation effected a significant (P = 5 per cent.) decrease whereas the other four microelements together caused a highly significant (P = 0·1 per cent.) increase of weight gain. No interaction was demonstrable between Fe and the other four elements.

In another experiment with groups of 15 sexed Lohmann-Nichols hybrid male chickens and with one repeat of each treatment we investigated the effect on weight gain of supplementation of the feed with 20 p.p.m. Fe in the form of carbonate and also with 30 p.p.m. Zn, 2 p.p.m. Cu and 0, 80 and 160 p.p.m. Mn. In the groups with 0, 80 and 160 p.p.m. Mn the average weight gains were 1208·0, 1225·0 and 1228·0 g. without and 1168·0, 1191·3 and 1187·0 g. with Fe supplementation. Again Fe produced an adverse effect and the differences between the Fe supplemented and unsupplemented groups were also significant.

In a third experiment with groups of 15 Lohmann-Nichols hybrid chickens we investigated whether there was any difference between the effect of Fe in the form of oxalate or carbonate. The average weight gain of chickens of the control group (not supplemented with Mn, Zn, Cu and I) and of the other two groups were as shown in Table I.

Table I. *Average weight gain in groups of chickens with 40 p.p.m. Fe supplementation in their rations*

Mn	Zn	Cu	I		FeCO$_3$		Fe oxalate	
				No.	average weight gain (g.)		No.	average weight gain (g.)
supplement (p.p.m.)								
—	—	—	—	15 + 15	1387		15 + 15	1359
40	30	30	0·4	15 + 15	1341		15 + 15	1377
80	60	40	0·8	15 + 15	1315		13 + 15	1293

There were no significant differences between the effect of the two different Fe compounds whether or not Mn, Zn, Cu or I were also added.

Up to now all our results demonstrate that the supplementation of broiler feed with Fe is disadvantageous. It can be supposed that Fe given as supplement could form a complex compound with one of the proteins of the feed and its dissimilation and absorption is prevented in the digestive tract. An alternative and perhaps more complicated supposition is that the Fe given as supplement could prevent the function of one or more enzyme systems in the organism. The solving of these questions warrants further investigations.

DISCUSSION

Ullrey (East Lansing). Were the Fe compounds used analysed for evidence of contamination which might have produced the effects you noted?

Suranyi (Budapest). No, we have only recently started this work.

THE EFFECTS OF MANGANESE DEFICIENCY DURING GESTATION OF THE OFFSPRING

GLADYS J. EVERSON

The University of Texas at Austin, Austin, Texas, U.S.A.

MY assignment is to review some of the changes which occur in animals which are deficient in manganese and to describe a series of studies which have been completed with Ruth Shrader, Margaret Tsai and Lucille Hurley which have explored Mn deficiency in the guinea-pig.

The essential nature of Mn in animal nutrition was established in 1931 by investigators at the University of Wisconsin and McCollum and his associates at John Hopkins University. In 1943 Shils and McCollum re-examined early work on this trace element and described changes generally agreed upon as associated with Mn deficiency:

1. This element is essential for optimum growth.
2. A deficiency of Mn during gestation results in poor viability of the offspring.
3. The young of severely deficient animals have skeletal abnormalities.
4. Many of the Mn-deficient offspring are ataxic at birth showing incoordination and poor equilibrium.
5. Mn deficiency causes sterility in the male.
6. There is a decrease in arginase activity of the liver in Mn-deficient animals.

Oddly, these interesting changes have attracted few investigators and today many of the deficiency signs are not fully understood. As Dr Underwood has mentioned earlier in the symposium the function of Mn is unknown.

Our interest in Mn deficiency began in 1955 when it was decided that there might be advantages in using the guinea-pig as the experimental animal since this species could provide larger amounts of tissues where these were needed, the guinea-pig undergoes a higher degree of maturation of tissues at birth than animals

125

previously investigated and possibly there would be advantages in having offspring which would consume purified rations almost immediately after birth. We were successful in developing a pelleted, semi-purified ration which supported reproduction equal to that obtained with commercial feeds. The control diet used provided 125 p.p.m. Mn while the deficient ration contained 2 to 3 p.p.m.

A high percentage of the young of mothers fed the deficient diet throughout the total gestation period were ataxic at birth and these animals continued to have abnormal head movements and some incoordination during growth and on into adult life. The incidence of stillbirths was usually high and many young failed to survive longer than three to four days.

Cleared specimens stained with Alizarin-Red S revealed several types of skeletal abnormalities in newborn Mn-deficient animals. There was a shortening of the long bones, enlargement and malformations of the joints, a shortening and doming of the skull, deformities of the ribs or missing ribs and anterior-posterior flattening of the chest. We became interested in the chemical make-up of cartilage of Mn-deficient animals since these skeletal defects suggested an early flaw in cartilage matrix. Hyaluronic acid, chondroitin sulphates and heparin of rib and epiphyseal cartilage were determined by Margaret Tsai for Mn-deficient and control animals at birth. These analyses revealed that there were statistically significant differences in the amounts of each acid mucopolysaccharide present in cartilage between the two groups of animals. The omission of Mn from the maternal diet resulted in a reduction of all acid mucopolysaccharides suggesting that Mn is involved in the normal development of cartilage.

Simultaneously, studies were undertaken to determine the nature of the abnormal head movements characteristic of Mn-deficient animals. Structural and histochemical studies were made of portions of the inner ear. Oil of wintergreen preparations of the ear made by Ruth Shrader have revealed a failure of normal otolith development in the utricle and saccule in Mn-deficient young.

In control animals the densely calcified structure of the otoliths was easily identified in such oil of wintergreen preparations while in Mn-deficient animals the otoliths were abnormal or could not be visualized. In all cases where abnormal head movements have been observed either unilateral or bilateral otolith defects have been found. Supplementation with Mn postnatally has not improved the symptoms of vestibular disorders. A smaller proportion of deficient animals also were found to have abnormal curvatures of the semi-circular canals and misshapen ampullae.

Preparations of the macular portion of the ear were stained to determine the relative concentration of acid mucopolysaccharides (AMPS) of otolithic membrane for control and Mn-deficient animals. Positive tests for AMPS were observed only when the otoliths appeared to be normal. These findings suggest that when the prenatal diet is deficient in Mn otolithic development is impaired and there appears to be a defect in cartilagenous matrix which regulates otolith development.

More recent work has dealt with the response of Mn-deficient guinea-pigs to glucose administration since a search of the literature concerned with connective tissue disorders interested us in the observation that there is an increased excretion of AMPS in the urine of diabetic subjects. After considerable preliminary testing of glucose utilization by means of oral administration of the sugar and blood sampling by nail bed clipping, a pattern of abnormal glucose tolerance was established for the Mn-deficient animals. However, frequent erratic blood sugar values were encountered which we believed were due to stress and the anaesthetic being used during a four-hour test period. Successful testing of glucose utilization was accomplished through the use of cannulated animals prepared by Ruth Shrader. A cannula of fine polyethylene tubing was inserted into the aorta via the carotid artery. The free end of the cannula was drawn out through the skin just above the fat pads at the back of the neck and was coiled tightly so as to provide ample length for frequent sampling of blood or glucose administration and to prevent the animals from tearing the cannula. After appropriate recovery time glucose utilization was tested in the relaxed unanaesthetized animals.

In young adults, congenitally deficient in Mn, there was a somewhat elevated blood glucose in the fasting state. Deficient animals showed glucose responses resembling the diabetic subject. Control animals, in contrast, always showed prompt return of the blood glucose concentration to normal. After two months of supplementation with Mn (during which time the animals received the control ration containing 125 p.p.m. Mn) previously deficient animals which had demonstrated reduced glucose utilization now responded normally. We have tested only one length of Mn supplementation which was 60 days.

Gross abnormalities of the pancreas of Mn-deficient guinea-pigs have been found in animals which were stillborn or appeared

127

to have little chance of survival. Histological examination of pancreatic tissue revealed marked hypoplasia of the pancreas and where this occurred islet population was reduced and the islet size was increased.

In young adult Mn-deficient guinea-pigs there was a decrease in the number of pancreatic islets and these were enlarged in size. The pancreatic islets of the Mn-deficient animals contained less intensely granulated beta cells and an increased number of alpha cells. Following dietary supplementation with Mn for two months, it was found that the number of islets increased and the beta cells appeared to be more heavily granulated.

The absence of adequate Mn in the maternal diet during development of the guinea-pig resulted in changes in pancreatic tissue markedly affecting both acinar tissues and islet cells. The role of Mn in connection with these changes is unknown and work is now underway to study this phase more thoroughly.

We have also attempted to identify metabolic differences in the Mn-deficient animals at birth by determining certain components of the urine. Urine was removed by syringe from the bladders of newborn animals at autopsy and specimens were compared on the basis of creatinine content. To date free sugars and sugar alcohols have been determined using paper chromatographic techniques. Both control and Mn-deficient guinea-pigs excrete detectable amounts of nine sugars at birth (arabinose, fructose, fucose, galactose, glucose, lactose, mannose, ribose and xylose). Of these we have been able to distinguish differences only in the amount of ribose present. Ribose was present in somewhat larger amounts in the urine of Mn-deficient guinea-pigs at birth. In addition the urine of Mn-deficient animals contained approximately one-third the amount of myoinositol found in the urine of control animals. We are uncertain of the significance of these differences and are attempting to study the importance of inositol during foetal development in the presence of Mn deficiency. To what extent the conversion of inositol to glucuronic acid may be of importance here is unknown.

A final effect of Mn deficiency in the guinea-pig which has interested us is the onset of tremor, digital twitching and strong regular twitching of the hind legs or all four legs. This late developing syndrome has at times been observed in approximately one-third of the congenitally deficient offspring but at other times the incidence may be as low as 5 to 10 per cent. of the young adult animals. We are not certain of the nature of this change. Tremor and twitching can be alleviated by administration of Mn and the length of supplementation required to eliminate this syndrome has varied from 11 days to as long as 55 days.

These studies clearly indicate the value of further investigation of the importance of Mn in the developing foetus and hopefully these findings will stimulate other investigators to undertake new approaches to elucidate the role of Mn in animal nutrition.

DISCUSSION

Hill (London). You mentioned that the content of mucopolysaccharides in the cartilage of newborn Mn-deficient guinea-pigs was low. Were the animals affected uniformly?

Everson (Austin, Texas). Yes. There was reduction of approximately 30 per cent. in the concentration of chondroitin sulphates, heparin and hyaluronic acid.

Spencer (Hines, Ill.). Are there any skeletal lesions in the Mn-deficient dam and do you think that the neurological lesions are due to a low content of Mn in brain tissue?

Everson (Austin, Texas). The mothers appear to be perfectly normal even when they have had several litters on the Mn-deficient diet. Recent work has shown that there are high concentrations of Mn in certain parts of the brain and I do not believe that all the abnormal movements of the Mn-deficient animals can be explained by the absence of the calcified area in the inner ear.

Lassiter (Athens, Ga.). Do you think the decrease in inositol excretion might be due to differences in lipositol metabolism?

Everson (Austin, Texas). We feel that it is possible that in the foetus inositol is a more important source of glucuronic acid than it is in the adult animal. There is however very little information on the pathways of inositol metabolism and we are ourselves intending to do some work with inositol inhibitors to see if we can produce the same sort of abnormalities.

Mills (Aberdeen). Are there circumstances known in which the reputed effects of Mn deficiency in lowering liver arginase activity lead to adverse clinical effects? Are there, for example, any adverse effects of feeding high-protein diets to Mn-deficient offspring?

Everson (Austin, Texas). I am very uncertain about these effects of Mn deficiency on arginase activity. It may be that there

129

are metabolic circumstances under which the arginase defect may be important but we have not investigated these. We have only examined the effect of diets containing 30 per cent. protein.

INFLUENCE OF MANGANESE ON SKELETAL DEVELOPMENT IN THE SHEEP AND RAT

J. W. LASSITER, J. D. MORTON AND W. J. MILLER

Department of Animal Science, University of Georgia, Athens, Georgia, U.S.A.

THE nutritional importance of manganese for the ovine has never been determined clearly, although it is believed that it functions as it does in other animals. Generally Mn deficiency has not been a practical problem so, until recently, little information has been obtained concerning the effects of Mn upon skeletal development in this species (Lassiter and Morton, 1968).

In our laboratory, early weaned lambs that received a purified diet containing less than 1 p.p.m. Mn over a five-month period exhibited bone changes that were similar to those that arise in Mn-deficient animals. The tibias from deficient lambs were lighter, had reduced volumes, were shorter and had lower breaking strength than those from controls that received the same diets supplemented with 29 p.p.m. Mn. They also were somewhat lower in ash, calcium and Mn contents. Serum alkaline phosphatase was significantly below that of control lambs but kidney alkaline phosphatase was increased.

While the biochemical mechanisms by which Mn is involved in normal osteogenesis are not yet clear, they do not appear to be related to bone calcification (Tsai and Everson, 1967). Subnormal bone alkaline phosphatase activity does not invariably occur with Mn deficiency. Rather, Mn appears to be necessary for the production and maintenance of the organic matrix and a reduction in the mucopolysaccharide and hexosamine content of epiphyseal cartilage has been shown.

An efficient homeostatic mechanism for Mn appears to operate in vertebrate animals (Britton and Cotzias, 1966; Hughes *et al.*, 1966; Papavasiliou *et al.*, 1966). The body pool is small and the body does not ordinarily accumulate Mn, so that total body excretion is continuously very nearly equal to intake. Twenty-five to 50 per cent. of the body pool is often ingested daily. Disorders due to Mn deficiency or excess thus would appear to stem from factors that result in rapid or slow rates of turnover in this pool. Discovery of factors affecting this rate of turnover would contradict some accepted concepts and explain some of the puzzling clinical cases observed, including reports of Mn deficiency symptoms when Mn intake were many times those necessary to prevent experimental Mn deficiency.

The effect of dietary Ca and phosphorus on the metabolism of [54]Mn in rats has been studied in our laboratory. Rats fed a diet containing 0·6 per cent. Ca excreted via faeces, over a 4-day period, only half as much of an intraperitoneal [54]Mn dose as those fed 0·1 per cent. Ca. Also, those given the 0·6 per cent. Ca diet retained several times as much [54]Mn in the livers as on the lower Ca diet. Dietary phosphorus caused no significant differences in [54]Mn excretion.

Turnover of parenterally administered [54]Mn is directly related to the level of stable Mn in the diet over a wide range of dietary Mn concentrations (Britton and Cotzias, 1966). Our results show that a 0·6 per cent. dietary Ca level greatly decreased excretion of parenterally administered [54]Mn, relative to a 0·1 per cent. Ca diet. This indicates that Ca plays an important role in Mn metabolism other than by affecting absorption and suggests that dietary Ca can have a great effect upon retention of absorbed Mn. The results raise valid questions about how readily and to what degree dietary factors affect tissue Mn concentrations.

In another experiment rats fed 0·6 per cent. Ca for 21 days prior to oral dosing with [54]Mn excreted significantly less [54]Mn in the faeces over a four day period and deposited twice as much in the tibia as rats fed 0·1 per cent. Ca. This indicates that, at least under some conditions, increased dietary Ca enhances Mn absorption. Also, whereas dietary P had no significant effect on retention of intraperitoneally administered [54]Mn, 0·9 per cent. P caused significantly higher retention of orally administered [54]Mn than did 0·4 per cent. P.

In our laboratory observations with sheep on the apparent absorption of stable Mn in Coastal Bermudagrass hay (*Cynodon dactylon*, horticultural variety Coastal) also suggest that P affects Mn absorption. When ground hay was mixed with 2 per cent. poultry fat and 0·6 per cent. salt, mean apparent Mn absorption was 22 per cent. When 1½ per cent. phosphoric acid was also mixed with the hay apparent absorption was only 4 per cent.

The abundant evidence of the need for Mn in skeletal development in various other species probably applies to the sheep. While Ca has long been recognized as a factor depressing Mn absorption, our results have shown that Ca can also enhance Mn absorption and play an important role in Mn metabolism other than by affecting absorption. Much yet needs to be learned about conditions and factors that influence Mn homeostasis and of conditions that affect the metabolism of absorbed Mn.

REFERENCES

BRITTON, A. A. & COTZIAS, G. C. (1966). *Am. J. Physiol.* **211**, 203.
HUGHES, E. R., MILLER, S. T. & COTZIAS, G. C. (1966). *Am. J. Physiol.* **211**, 207.
LASSITER, J. W. & MORTON, J. D. (1968). *J. Anim. Sci.* **27**, 776.
PAPAVASILIOU, P. S., MILLER, S. T. & COTZIAS, G. C. (1966). *Am. J. Physiol.* **211**, 211.
TSAI, H. C. & EVERSON, G. J. (1967). *J. Nutr.* **91**, 447.

DISCUSSION

Underwood (Perth). Early in your paper you hinted that manganese deficiency might be of greater practical importance than is generally appreciated. I am aware of some rather limited Dutch work implicating Mn deficiency in cattle under field conditions and even this seems to be a conditioned Mn deficiency rather than a direct one and there is some not entirely convincing evidence from elsewhere of Mn deficiency adversely affecting fertility in dairy cows. Do you have any additional information on such points?

Lassiter (Athens, Ga.). In making this point I was merely referring to the frequency with which one meets under practical circumstances animals born with bone abnormalities and congenital defects which are not explicable on the information we have at the moment. I realize I may be on dangerous ground suggesting that there could be a relationship between these effects and Mn deficiency, but it nevertheless seems possible in view of the observations that have been made on Mn deficiency in laboratory animals.

Hartmans (Hoorn). In reply to Professor Underwood's remark on conditioned Mn deficiency in the Netherlands, it can now be clearly stated that the symptoms described in the publications dealing with this work must be due to factors other than Mn. Following an extensive reinvestigation of these cases it has been found that there were no signs of Mn deficiency even when the rations contained as little as 25 to 30 p.p.m. in the dry matter of the ration. These earlier reports of the existence of a conditioned Mn deficiency in cattle must therefore be regarded as incorrect.

MANGANESE DEFICIENCY AND RADIOISOTOPE STUDIES ON MANGANESE METABOLISM

M. ANKE AND B. GROPPEL

Department of Animal Production, University of Jena, D.D.R.

IN the early sixties we produced manganese deficiency in calves which were fed on milk-maize rations containing 8 p.p.m. Mn. The deficiency first appeared in the form of a nervous tremor of the tongue. Later we observed a general ataxia and a trembling of muscles. Moreover, after 14 weeks we discovered a little excrescence on the front tarsal joint and a stiff and steeper position of the front legs (Anke, 1966) which hindered the movements of the animals. Rojas, Dyer and Cassalt (1965) obtained similar results when testing Mn influence on calves. During the same period research workers of our institute came to the conclusion that Mn supply possibly influences the fecundity of cows, because there are relations between the Mn supply and the number of services per conception (Pflug, 1966; Werner and Anke, 1960).

In order to examine the effect of Mn supply on reproduction, lactation and growth as well as to examine Mn deficiency, female goats were constantly tested from 1966 to 1969. One group of goats received 100 p.p.m. Mn, whereas a second got only 20 p.p.m. during the first year and 6 p.p.m. in the following. From comparisons with the control group we know (as former tests with calves had already shown) that a low Mn ration leads to no change in growth. However, the goats of the low Mn group came into oestrus later than those of the control group. The symptoms of oestrus were extremely weak; in most cases they were not noticed by the male. To become pregnant, goats of the low Mn group needed more inseminations than those of the control group. Furthermore, 23 per cent. of the low Mn goats aborted in the third to fifth month of pregnancy whereas there was no abortion in control group. Similar abortions had been noticed by Everson, Hurley and Geiger (1959) and colleagues in Mn-deficient guinea-pigs. The female goats which did not abort had the same number of kids in both groups. The proportion of female to male kids changed from 1:1·5 (control group) to 1:2·3 (low group), i.e. there were more male kids. (This result was confirmed by 498 calves of a Mn deficiency trial with cattle. The cows of the control group produced calves with a sex ratio, female to male, of 1:1, and the cows of the Mn-deficient group 1:1·3.)

Table I. *Fecundity and mortality of goats during the test with a low Mn supply*

	Control Group	Low Mn Group
Number of goats	27	28
Pregnant goats in %	100	93
Inseminations per pregnant goat	1·07	1·42
Abortions (%)	0	23
Kids per goat	1·63	1·55
Proportion of female to male kids	1:1·5	1:2·3
Birth weight of kids (g.)	3263	2642***
Mortality of dams (%)	18	43

*** = P < 0·001

The birth weights of the low Mn group kids differed greatly from those of the control group. On average the low group kids weighed 20 per cent. less. The weights of the two groups had a tendency to converge up to an age of 28 days but later the difference became bigger again. After the sixth week the first obvious signs of Mn deficiency appeared.

Many (43 per cent.) of the Mn-deficient goats died during the test period, while there was only 18 per cent. mortality in the other group. The period between the first signs of deficiency and the time of death differed from animal to animal. A small number of goats showed no obvious signs of deficiency after three years, whereas others died within two months.

Ten per cent. of the goats and lambs showed nervous disturbances as a first symptom and, later, paralysis of hind legs and ataxia generally followed. Paralysis was not reversible and led to death after different periods. Those animals which were paralysed had no skeletal deformations. Twenty per cent. of the low Mn goats, whether pregnant or milking, suffered from bony excrescences, mainly on the front tarsal joint and 30 per cent. of the kids suffered from the same condition. Front tarsal joint excrescences and other deformities were visible, at the earliest, six weeks after birth.

An analysis of various organs taken from control and Mn-deficient goats and newly born kids proved that there was a general shortage of Mn in the femur and liver of the kids as well as in their total body. In this connection it is interesting that the hair of a fully grown goat indicates the degree of Mn supply better than other parts of the body. This is not true for the hair of a newly born kid.

Such an analysis can also show the interrelations between Mn

Table II. *Manganese and ash concentration in different parts of the body of goats and their kids*

	Dams		Kids	
	Control Group	Low Mn Group	Control Group	Low Mn Group
Liver Mn p.p.m.	5·6	2·6*	12	3·2***
Femur Mn p.p.m.	3·9	3·1*	12	6·6**
Femur ash (%)	32	28*	59	55*
Total body Mn p.p.m.	—	—	5·6	3·3*
Total body ash (%)	—	—	23	20—
Hair Mn p.p.m.	11·1	3·5*	1·02	0·96—

$* = P < 0.05; ** = P < 0.01; *** = P < 0.001; — = P > 0.05$

supply and ossification. Our institute (Anke, 1966) and also Lassiter and Morton (1968) have reported that low Mn animals had a lower ash concentration in the femur and, within the ash, the Ca and P percentages were greatly reduced. This correlation between reduced Mn content and lowered ash, Ca and P concentrations in the skeleton of older animals suggests an effect of Mn on bone ossification. To investigate this, 220 human ribs were analysed. Men and women have significantly different Mn, ash, Ca and P concentrations in their bones but the concentrations always decrease with age. This decrease begins immediately after puberty. The Mn concentration of the ribs is nonlinearly correlated with the ash, P and Ca content of the rib. The correlation coefficient is 0·84 in all cases. This is true only for the elements and substances just mentioned. Though there is also a change in the Cu, Zn, Fe, Na and K concentration of the human skeleton, the latter elements follow other trends.

The metabolic effect of Mn was examined by feeding ^{52}Mn to hens and cows in a 96-hour test. The result was that most of the absorbed Mn was transported to skeleton and ovaries. A considerable amount of the ^{52}Mn also went to the liver, feathers, muscles and kidneys. However, it disappeared from these tissues after a short time and was deposited mainly in the bones but partly in the ovaries. This ^{52}Mn distribution demonstrates the importance of Mn for bone structure and for reproduction.

REFERENCES

ANKE, M. (1966). *Arch. Tierernähr.* **16,** 199.
EVERSON, G. J., HURLEY, L. S. & GEIGER, J. F. (1959). *J. Nutr.* **68,** 49.
LASSITER, J. W. & MORTON, J. D. (1968). *J. Anim. Sci.* **27,** 776.
PFLUG, D. (1966). *Jahrbuch Tierernähr. u. Fütterung* **6,** 123.
ROJAS, A. A., DYER, I. A. & CASSALT, W. A. (1965). *J. Anim. Sci.* **24,** 664.
WERNER, A. & ANKE, M. (1960). *Arch. Tierernähr.* **10,** 142.

DISCUSSION

Lassiter (Athens, Georgia). Your data on the Mn content of of human rib bones clearly illustrate a declining Mn content with increasing age. This is a relationship which exists with many other mineral elements and I have often speculated as to whether the declining content may be a cause of ageing rather than an effect of ageing.

Strain (Rochester). Are the skeletal abnormalities of your goats such that they have difficulty in rising when they have been lying on the ground?

Anke (Jena). They often have great difficulty but they can rise.

Underwood (Perth). I am not clear what were the minimum Mn levels at which you obtained the symptoms of deficiency. Do you regard 10 p.p.m. as a deficient level and 20 p.p.m. as not deficient?

Anke (Jena). There appear to be very great genetic differences in the response to Mn. We have had goats develop lesions on the front tarsal joints with 20 p.p.m. Mn but only in two cases. In later experiments using 6 p.p.m. some animals developed no lesions, others developed lesions on the front legs and others on the hind legs. In all, 28 animals have been used in these trials and there have been great differences between animals in the lesions exhibited. There must be big differences between animals in the efficiency of absorption and utilization of Mn and I am not able to state the Mn requirement with certainty.

Gartner (Yeerongpilly). What was the calcium level in these synthetic rations?

Anke (Jena). Five grams per kilogram. Phosphorus was at the same concentration.

Mills (Aberdeen). How were your experimental animals housed? I ask because we attempted to produce Mn deficiency in sheep and failed even though the synthetic diet used contained only about 1 p.p.m. Mn. We think the reason we failed was probably because the animals consumed some sawdust used as bedding which contained an appreciably higher concentration of Mn.

Anke (Jena). We have the animals in wooden cages and the ration contained cellulose (paper), wheatmeal and urea.

THE MATRIX AND URONIC ACID CONTENTS OF THIN AND THICK SHELLS PRODUCED BY PULLETS GIVEN DIETS OF VARYING MANGANESE AND PHOSPHORUS CONTENT

MARGARET LONGSTAFF AND R. HILL

The Royal Veterinary College, University of London, U.K.

LEACH and Meunster (1962) found a lower galactosamine content in bone cartilage of chicks given a low manganese diet than in similar tissue of chicks given a high Mn diet, suggesting a relationship between Mn, acid mucopolysaccharide and mineralization. This has been considered in relation to shell calcification.

Five diets based on maize meal, meat and bone meal, dried separated milk and steamed bone meal or calcium carbonate were given to groups of 11 pullets from 16 weeks of age. There were three levels of Mn, about 7, 27 and 57 mg./kg., all with a high P content, about 1·7 per cent.: they were designated A + P, B + P, C + P respectively. A high level of P was known to exaggerate the effect of a low Mn diet on shell formation, at least in the early stages of egg production (Longstaff and Hill, 1968). The low Mn diet was modified by replacing part of the meat and bone meal by steamed bone meal to give a still higher P content, about 2·3 per cent. (diet A + 2P) and the high Mn diet had meat and bone meal reduced and steamed bone meal replaced by calcium carbonate to give a low, or normal P diet, about 0·7 per cent. (diet C).

At the start of lay a large number of soft shells were produced by birds given diets A + 2P and A + P, a moderate number by those given diet B + P and very few by those given diets C + P and C. Of the first 10 eggs laid by each bird on these diets, the number of soft shells were on average 3·6, 3·7, 1·5, 0·4 and 0·1 respectively. There were also more cracked shells from low than high Mn diets. The first six whole, firm shells from each bird were taken for measurements of strength, by deformation, and thickness as weight per unit area. Strength and thickness increased significantly from diet A + 2P through A + P, B + P and C + P to C. Mean deformation values were $35·3\mu$ for diet A + 2P and $22·8\mu$ for diet C, and corresponding weight per unit area values were 64·1 and 76·0 mg./cm.^{2} Three months after the start of lay six shells were taken from each bird and the same measurements were made. For each dietary group shells had increased in strength and thickness; the increase was large and significant for diets A + 2P and

A + P but small and not significant for diets C + P and C, thus the dietary differences at three months were much smaller than at the start of lay but overall they remained significant.

Shells from birds on each of the five diets were taken for analysis, 47 at the start of lay, first/second or seventh/eighth shell, and 38 three months later. They were treated briefly with EDTA solution to permit removal of membranes and cuticle, then after drying and weighing were decalcified completely in EDTA solution. The matrix was washed, dried and weighed and samples were taken for determination of uronic acid by the method of Bitter and Muir (1962). From these measurements values were obtained for calcium weight per unit area, matrix weight per unit area, uronic acid content of matrix (per cent. of dry matter) and uronic acid weight per unit area.

Among these 85 shells the effects of treatment on strength and thickness or calcium weight per unit area were similar to those described above though in general they just failed to reach significance. The uronic acid content of matrix followed very closely the pattern of strength and calcium: at the start of lay the matrices of shells from diets A + 2P and A + P had much lower uronic acid contents, 1·35 and 1·37 per cent. respectively, than those of shells from diets C + P and C, 2·13 and 1·93 per cent. respectively. The value for diet B + P was intermediate, 1·66 per cent., and overall differences were highly significant. Uronic acid content increased in all groups between the start of lay and three months later: the increase was larger for low than high Mn diets, thus dietary differences, although still significant were considerably smaller at three months than at the start of lay.

Weights of matrix per unit area, unlike uronic acid contents, did not follow the pattern of calcium. The tendency was for an inverse relationship to occur between Ca and matrix weights: thus thin low Ca shells of diets A + 2P, A + P and B + P at the start of lay and of A + 2P at three months had slightly larger matrix weights per unit area than those of normal shells from diet C at the start of lay and A + P, B + P, C + P and C after three months of egg production. These elevated matrix weights of thin low Ca shells were not sufficiently large to erase uronic acid differences when they were calculated as weight per unit area; values for diets A + 2P and A + P and B + P at the start of lay and A + 2P after three months were lower than those for diets C + P at the start and A + P, B + P and C after three months.

The low-Mn-high-P diets did not impair the formation of shell matrix as a whole but they markedly depressed the acid mucopolysaccharide content of matrix as measured by uronic acid (Baker and Balch, 1962) and it seems probable that the thin low-Ca shells produced by birds given these diets arose from this effect on acid mucopolysaccharide.

REFERENCES

BAKER, J. R. & BALCH, D. A. (1962). *Biochem. J.* **82**, 352.
BITTER, T. & MUIR, H. M. (1962). *Analyt. Biochem.* **4**, 330.
LEACH, R. M. & MUENSTER, A. M. (1962). *J. Nutr.* **78**, 51.
LONGSTAFF, MARGARET & HILL, R. (1968). *Proc. Nutr. Soc.* **27**, 38A.

DISCUSSION

Bell (Oak Ridge). Do you believe that the improvement in shell production with time is an adaptation to the diet through changes in mucopolysaccharide production? Could such a change near the time of sexual maturity be related to hormonal changes themselves improving the shell?

Hill (London). It has been suggested to us that our improvement in shell characteristics is due to a gradual increase in the Mn content of our diets, but this has occurred too frequently in different experiments and has not been borne out by analyses of the diets. I think it is probable that there is an increase in Mn retention or utilization occurring at or near the time of sexual maturation. Bolton has suggested that there is a relationship between hormone production and Mn metabolism as he has found that oestrogen increases the level of Mn in the blood of pullets. Our analytical procedures have not been sufficiently satisfactory to produce convincing confirmatory evidence of this. We have certainly found no striking changes in blood Mn but perhaps we ought to be looking elsewhere than in blood.

SECTION 3

METABOLIC CONSEQUENCES OF TRACE ELEMENT DEFICIENCY AND EXCESS

Presidents: M. KIRCHGESSNER (*Session* 1)
K. J. JENKINS (*Session* 2)

Vice Presidents: N. F. SUTTLE (*Session* 1)
J. K. CHESTERS (*Session* 2)

ZINC CONCENTRATIONS AND ENZYME ACTIVITIES OF RAT TISSUES DURING THE INITIAL STAGES OF ZINC DEPLETION

J. G. REINHOLD, ENID PASCOE, M. ARSLANIAN and K. BITAR

Department of Biochemistry, American University of Beirut, Beirut, Lebanon

THE interest of our group in Beirut in zinc deficiency stems from the suggestion by Prasad, Halsted and Nadimi (1961) that one type of dwarfness among boys in Iran, and perhaps elsewhere, is caused by lack of sufficient Zn to support the growth and development of pubescence. We sought by study of experimentally produced Zn deficiency in rats to learn more about the biochemical disturbances associated with low intakes of Zn.

In our earlier experiments, Zn depletion was produced by diets containing 2·0 to 4·5 ppm. of Zn (Reinhold *et al.*, 1967). The diets consisted of casein 10 per cent., gelatin 5 per cent., dextrin 60 per cent., sucrose 9·4 per cent., corn oil 6 per cent., vitamins and minerals. The last included enough calcium carbonate to make the Ca concentration of the diet 1 per cent. None of the major components was capable of forming stable nonabsorbable complexes with Zn. In order to diminish as a cause of chemical changes the decreased food intake which promptly followed consumption of diets low in Zn, control rats were fed an equal weight of the same diet supplemented with enough Zn to provide a concentration of 20 to 30 p.p.m. Rats weighed 40 to 50 g. when started on the diets. Both sexes were used.

Although weight gains were less and lesions of skin and small intestines were prevalent among rats with low Zn intakes, we found, as have others, that Zn concentrations of the visceral organs of the depleted rats remained at the same concentrations as those of the controls when Zn was fed at these levels. The only significant decrease in Zn concentration was in the mucosa of the small intestine, the liver showing a decline that was not statistically significant. Zinc concentrations in serum also did not decrease significantly. On the other hand, the concentration of Zn in hair fell rapidly to about half of that in the hair of the controls. Some rats died as a result of bleeding into the upper gastrointestinal tract, and some because of pulmonary infections. However, most survived for the duration of the experiments, 70 to 150 days.

When in more recent experiments the Zn concentration of the deficient diets was decreased to approximately 1·5 p.p.m., the

143

effects were not only more severe but were evident in a much shorter time. Experiments were carried out in which pairs of rats, one having consumed the diet low in Zn, the other an equal quantity of the Zn-supplemented control diet, were killed at intervals beginning one day after the diets were started. The rats were anaesthetized with ether, the abdomen and thorax exposed, and blood collected by puncture of the heart; 0·1 ml. of 20 per cent. sodium citrate was used as anticoagulent. Blood was removed from the viscera by perfusion with cold 0·14 M-NaCl solution until the liver was light grey and blood no longer flowed from the severed vena cava. Homogenates of intestinal mucosa were made in 0·14 M-NaCl solution; those of liver in 0·32 M-sucrose. Dilutions were 1/10. These were assayed for enzyme activity and analyzed for Zn by atomic absorption spectrophotometry after being subjected to a wet-ashing procedure.

Figure 1 shows the combined results of three such experiments. It may be seen that the plasma Zn concentrations of the rats receiving the diets low in Zn remained at the level of the controls after 24 hours, but that a significant decline had occurred two days later. The downward trend persisted to a minimum concentration at 15 days, then reversed temporarily and subsequently resumed. Plasma Zn concentrations of the control rats showed no significant change.

Zinc concentrations in the livers of depleted rats followed a course similar to those in plasma except that a large decrease appears to have occurred on the first day (Fig. 1). Liver Zn concentrations were more variable than those of plasma and their significance must be interpreted accordingly. Nevertheless, a downward trend prevails both in depleted and control rats during the first two weeks, with the former having consistently lower Zn concentrations than the controls. As in plasma, minimal values occurred 10 to 15 days after the diets were started. Whether the subsequent rise is real or not must await additional studies. In the controls the declining Zn concentrations probably represent an adjustment to the intake of 30 p.p.m. of Zn provided by the control diet from the higher Zn content of the pre-experimental stock diet.

The contrast of these results with those of the earlier experiments confirms the decisive importance of the level of Zn intake upon Zn homeostasis. Intakes of 2·0 to 4·5 p.p.m. of Zn enabled maintenance of Zn concentrations that were normal or nearly so in plasma and visceral organs. Halving these intakes produced acute changes with substantial lowering of Zn concentrations. Dreosti, Tao and Hurley (1968) fed diets to pregnant rats contain-

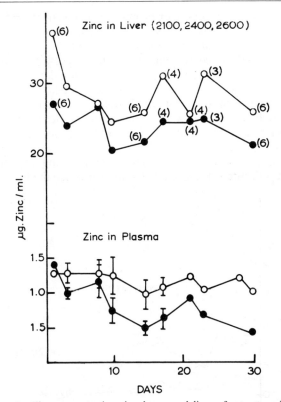

FIG. 1. Zinc concentrations in plasma and liver of rats at various intervals during the consumption of a diet low in Zn. ●——●, rats fed diets containing 1·5 p.p.m. of Zn; o——o, control rats fed equal amounts of a diet containing about 30 p.p.m. of Zn. Each point represents the average of the number of rats shown in parentheses along the upper curves. Bars show standard deviations of plasma analyses.

ing less than 1 p.p.m. of Zn. A striking decline in plasma Zn concentration followed within 24 hours.

It is clear from these findings that the rat is dependent upon Zn provided by food each day for maintenance of Zn concentrations in plasma, liver and other tissues. Mills, Dalgarno, Williams and Quarterman (1967) had reached this conclusion previously from experiments in which calves and lambs were fed diets low in Zn. Plasma Zn concentrations were lowered after 36 hours and fell to less than half of the control values within a week with diets containing < 1 p.p.m. of Zn. This decline was not prevented by

145

administration of a pre-experimental Zn supplement for several weeks before Zn deprivation was begun. They concluded that the capacity for storage of Zn in the body is limited.

The lowered concentrations of Zn in tissues adversely affect the activities of certain enzymes. Kfoury, Reinhold and Simonian (1968) showed that the activities of three Zn metallo-enzymes (liver alcohol dehydrogenase, intestinal alkaline phosphatase and kidney glutamic dehydrogenase) were depressed in Zn-deficient rats. On the other hand, four enzymes having no dependence upon Zn were unaffected.

The behaviour of Zn metallo-enzymes during the onset of depletion is of interest, especially the time at which the first changes

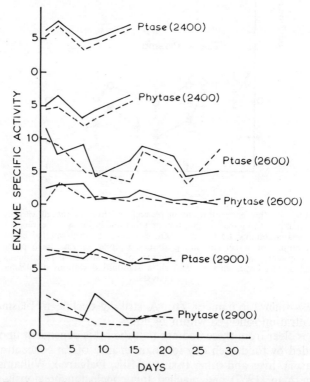

FIG. 2. Intestinal alkaline phosphatase and phytase specific activities of rats fed diets low in Zn shown at various intervals. The results of three experiments are shown each represented by two pairs of curves, one for phosphatase and one for phytase. Each point indicates the averaged results for two rats: ——— control rats: — — — — , deficient rats.

in activity are detectable. The results of such studies in which alkaline phosphatase and phytase activities in the intestinal mucose were measured are shown in Figure 2. Three separate experiments are included. Each point represents the assays of the activities of these enzymes in two depleted or two control rats. It may be seen that the Zn-depleted rats of Series 2400 and 2600 showed lower activities of phosphatase and phytase than those of their paired controls for most of the time. In Series 2900, phytase activity is initially higher in the rats fed the low Zn diet but shows a steady decline to activities less than those of the controls which fluctuate and show no similar trend.

There is a similarity between the time-activity behaviour of the intestinal enzymes and that of the plasma and liver Zn concentrations. This may be more than coincidental. Minimal enzyme activities occur at approximately the same time as the minimum for Zn concentrations, while the rising enzyme activities that follow are associated with a similar trend in Zn concentrations.

Phytate inhibits absorption of Zn and other divalent cations and probably contributes to the low plasma Zn concentrations that are observed among the rural populations of the Middle East. We were especially interested therefore in investigating the effects of Zn depletion upon intestinal phytase activity. Although we have already seen (Fig. 2) that changes in phytase activities resembled those of phosphatase activities in the course of the experiments, comparison of 69 pairs of phytase and phosphatase assays, assembled from five separate experimental series, shows that the mean phytase activity of the depleted rats is significantly lowered (Fig. 3) whereas the mean phosphatase activity is not (Fig. 4). However, after 60 to 70 days of a low Zn intake, low intestinal phosphatase activities prevail (Kfoury et al., 1968).

The lowered phytase activities associated with Zn depletion suggested that phytase was dependent upon Zn for optimal activity. This was proved to be true in experiments to be published elsewhere in detail (Bitar and Reinhold) and described here briefly. Dialysis of a partly purified phytase preparation of rat intestine against 0·01 M-disodium EDTA caused its activity to decrease by one-third. Replacement of the Zn removed by dialysis restored the activity. Further addition of Zn augmented the activities to values exceeding those of the untreated purified enzyme. Ultimately the solubility limit of Zn phytate was exceeded and no further stimulation occurred. Similar treatment of the phytase of chicken intestine resulted in complete inactivation by disodium EDTA. Addition of Zn caused only partial restoration of activity, a finding that

147

suggests that Zn has a structural role in phytase. Aders and Hill (1967) reported that the intestinal phytase of the chicken requires Zn for optimal activity.

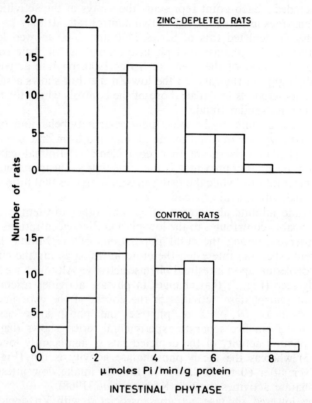

FIG. 3. Histogram showing the frequencies of the specific activities of intestinal phytase in Zn-depleted (upper) and control rats (lower) during the first 28 days of low Zn intake. See Figure 1 for Zn intakes.

Alcohol dehydrogenase activities of liver showed no changes that could be attributed to low Zn intakes of the depleted rats during the time included by the present experiments. However, lowered activities were found at a later stage by Kfoury, Reinhold and Simonian (1968). They also detected a correlation of alcohol dehydrogenase activities with Zn concentrations in liver, although it proved to be statistically significant only for the deficient and not for the control rats. The investigation of this relationship has continued and it is now clear that it exists in both control and deficient groups. Calculation of coefficients of correlation for the present series of experiments has yielded values as high as $r = 0.83$ when results for depleted and control rats are combined. Intestinal alkaline phosphatase activity also has been found to correlate significantly with Zn concentration in the mucosa ($r = 0.81$). These values are highly significant statistically ($p = <0.001$). Phytase,

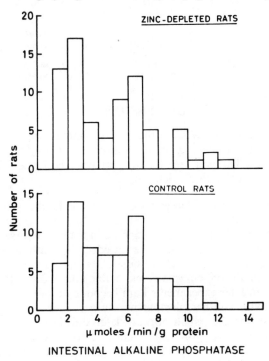

Fig. 4. Histograms of intestinal alkaline phosphatase specific activities of Zn-depleted and control rats during the first 28 days of low Zn intake.

on the other hand, is less closely correlated ($r = 0.41$) with no demonstrable correlation in some deficient groups. Each of these enzymes by itself includes less than 1 per cent. of the Zn in the liver, or 5 per cent. of that in intestinal mucosa so that variations in concentration of the enzymes examined do not explain the correlation. Although the significance of this relationship is not known, it appears to involve a mechanism which affects and possibly regulates the activities of the Zn metallo-enzymes we have studied.

Acknowledgements. This work was supported by Grant No. AM–09622 from the National Institute of Arthritis and Metabolic Diseases, Bethesda.
The authors are indebted to Miss Aznive Sabundjian for technical assistance and to Miss Madeleine Basmadjian for assistance with the manuscript.

REFERENCES

ADERS, C. E. & HILL, C. H. (1967). *Fedn Proc. Fedn Am. Socs exp. Biol.* **26**, 524.
DREOSTI, I. E., TAO, S. H. & HURLEY, L. S. (1968). *Proc. Soc. exp. Biol. Med.* **128**, 169.
KFOURY, G. A., REINHOLD, J. G. & SIMONIAN, S. J. (1968). *J. Nutr.* **95**, 102.
MILLS, C. F., DALGARNO, A. C., WILLIAMS, R. B. & QUARTERMAN, J. (1967). *Bri. J. Nutr.* **21**, 751.
PRASAD, A. S., HALSTED, J. A. & NADIMI, M. (1961). *Am. J. Med.* **31**, 532.
REINHOLD, J. G., KFOURY, G. A. & THOMAS, T. A. (1967). *J. Nutr.* **92**, 173.

DISCUSSION

Mills (Aberdeen). What is the earliest time at which you find changes in enzyme activity in the intestinal mucosa of the Zn-depleting rat? Do you feel that the mucosa is a site which is particularly sensitive to Zn deficiency?

Reinhold (Beirut). Changes are detectable in the activity of phytase in the intestinal mucosa within the first one to three days of Zn depletion. Alcohol dehydrogenase in liver, of course, shows no change in this time. It may be an effect of synthesis but my feeling is that it is more likely to be a stabilization effect; that in the absence of Zn the enzyme is less stable and is degraded more rapidly. From later experiments I am becoming quite sure that we are dealing with another phenomenon in a change of the type of alkaline phosphatase which appears later during depletion. We find differences in K_m for magnesium and for Zn, differences in chromatographic behaviour and some ambiguous differences in electrophoretic behaviour.

Sourkes (Montreal). Is Zn deficiency in the rat accompanied by any behavioural changes and are there any changes in the alcohol dehydrogenase activity of brain tissue? I ask because noradrenaline of brain is oxidized to yield the sulphate of 4-hydroxy-3-methoxy phenylglycol. Alcohol dehydrogenase presumably plays a role in reduction of the aldehyde group.

Reinhold (Beirut). Dr Pascoe in our group is working on brain, but she has not so far been able to detect in this early stage of Zn deficiency a change of Zn concentration in the brain. She is about to undertake estimations of alcohol dehydrogenase in the brain.

ZINC DEFICIENCY AND THE METABOLISM OF LABELLED CYSTINE IN RATS

J. M. Hsu, W. L. Anthony and P. J. Buchanan

*Biochemistry Research Laboratory, Veterans Administration Hospital
and the Department of Biochemistry,
The Johns Hopkins University, Baltimore, U.S.A.*

Previous reports from this laboratory indicate that zinc deficiency in rats results in an increase in the incorporation of glycine-1-^{14}C into liver glutathione (GSH) (Hsu *et al.*, 1968) and an enhancement of methionine-methyl-^{14}C oxidation (Hsu *et al.*, 1969). Since the latter is a precursor of cysteine, a component of the GSH molecule, it is desirable to determine the role of Zn in the metabolism of cysteine. Results of this study are presented here.

MATERIALS AND METHODS

Animals and diet. Zn deficiency was produced in three week-old male Sprague-Dawley rats by feeding a diet low in Zn as previously described (Hsu *et al.*, 1969). Metabolic studies were begun after 14 to 22 days of *ad libitum* feeding, by which time symptoms of Zn deficiency had appeared.

Collection and assay of expired $^{14}CO_2$. After an overnight fast, rats were injected intramuscularly with DL-cystine-1-^{14}C (5·7 mCi/mmol., 5 μCi/100g. body weight) and placed immediately in individual glass metabolism cages for one to six hours. The expired $^{14}CO_2$ was collected and the radioactivity counted according to the procedure described previously (Hsu *et al.*, 1969).

Liver GSH assay. Liver GSH concentration was determined according to the method of Patterson and Lazarow (1955). ^{14}C-labelled GSH was isolated by the method of Goldzieher *et al.*, (1958).

Preparation of tissue protein fraction. The protein fraction was prepared by the following modified procedure of Wool and Krahl (1959). Equal volumes of 10 per cent. trichloroacetic acid (TCA) were added to 5 per cent. water homogenates of tissue. The suspension was centrifuged, and the sediment washed thrice successively with 5 ml. of 5 per cent. TCA containing 3·73 mg. of unlabelled L-cysteine. The residue was then dissolved in 3 ml. of 88 per cent. formic acid and 0·6 ml. of 30 per cent. hydrogen peroxide and allowed to stand 30 minutes at 25 to 28°. Five

Table I. *Cumulative percentage of DL-cystine-1-^{14}C converted to $^{14}CO_2$ by Zn-Supplemented and Zn-deficient rats*

Type of diet	No. of rats	L-Cysteine carrier 60 μMoles/100 g.	Average body weight	Hours		
				2	4	6
			g.			
Zn-supplemented	6	—	115 ±3*	26·26 ±5·01	36·80 ±5·67‡	40·63 ±5·86†
Zn-deficient	6	—	61 ±5	31·29 ±2·61	45·80 ±2·82	51·96 ±2·85
Zn-supplemented	7	+	123 ±2	33·86 ±3·41	49·58 ±2·97	54·15 ±2·08‡
Zn-deficient	7	+	59 ±4	38·66 ±2·18	54·30 ±3·49	59·67 ±3·35

* Mean + SD.
† Difference between Zn-supplemented and Zn-deficient rats is statistically significant (P < 0·01).
‡ Difference between Zn-supplemented and Zn-deficient rats is statistically significant (P < 0·05).

Table II. *Incorporation of DL-cystine-1-^{14}C into tissue protein*

Type of diet	Days on expt. diet	Hours after injection	Average body weight	Specific activity c.p.m./mg. protein		
				Pancreas	Liver	Kidney
			g			
Zn-supplemented (6)[1]	14	2	113 ±6*†	184 ±40†	41 ±3·4†	99 ±2·0‡
Zn-deficient (6)	14	2	62 ±2	320 ±51	27 ±4·6	72 ±3·9
Zn-supplemented (6)	21	4	155 ±15†	241 ±42	30 ±3·6†	83 ±7·7‡
Zn-deficient (6)	21	4	73 ±6	206 ±33	23 ±2·7	73 ±1·6

[1] Numbers in brackets indicate the number of rats used.
* Mean + SD.
† Difference between Zn-supplemented and Zn-deficient rats is statistically significant (P < 0·01).
‡ Difference between Zn-supplemented and Zn-deficient rats is statistically significant (P < 0·05).

volumes of 10 per cent. TCA were added to the performic acid-treated solution. The resulting precipitate was collected by centrifugation, washed twice with acetone and allowed to dry for a few minutes at room temperature. The protein precipitates were digested by adding 1 ml. of Hyamine and heating in a $45°$ water bath for 30 minutes or longer until completely dissolved.

In some experiments, 0.5 ml. duplicates of 5 per cent. tissue homogenates were added to counting vials containing 1 ml. of Hyamine and the mixture heated at 55 to $60°$ for one hour or less until completely digested. The TCA soluble fractions obtained from liver homogenate were neutralized and the total volumes measured.

The radioactivity in all samples was determined by mixing with the scintillation solution, diotol (Herberg, 1960) and counting in a Packard liquid scintillation spectrometer. An internal standard was used to correct for quenching. Urinary inorganic sulphate was precipitated as benzidine sulphate according to the method of Kahn and Leiboff (1928). The precipitate was washed twice with 50 per cent. ethanol, dissolved in Hyamine and an aliquot counted in diotol.

RESULTS

The cumulative production of $^{14}CO_2$ after DL-cystine-1-^{14}C injection in Zn-supplemented and Zn-deficient rats was measured. Table I shows that Zn deficiency resulted in a greatly increased production of $^{14}CO_2$, six hours after isotope administration. Table I also shows that an intraperitoneal injection of unlabelled L-cysteine (60 μmol./100g. body weight), 10 minutes before DL-cystine-1-^{14}C injection, significantly increased the amount of $^{14}CO_2$ in expired air from Zn-supplemented rats when compared to those receiving no carrier dose. Only a slight increase was observed in the percentage expired as $^{14}CO_2$ when Zn-deficient rats were injected with the carrier dose. Therefore the increased oxidation of DL-cystine-1-^{14}C seemed to be influenced less by pool size in Zn-deficient rats than in Zn-supplemented rats.

To test whether the observed 25 per cent. increase in the oxidation of DL-cystine-1-^{14}C in Zn-deficient rats reduces its availability such that other biochemical aberrations occur, incorporation of labelled cystine into protein and GSH was studied.

Table II indicates that at both two and four hours post-injection, significantly more ^{14}C was incorporated into liver and kidney proteins of Zn-supplemented rats than those of Zn-deficient rats. However, the radioactivity of pancreatic proteins examined at the end of two hours was markedly increased in Zn-deficient rats.

153

Table III. *Distribution of radioactivity in liver[1]*

Type of diet	Average body weight g.	Liver weight g.	Total protein		Distribution of radioactivity % of absorbed ^{14}C		Specific activity of protein c.p.m./mg. protein
			mg./liver	%	Total	Acid soluble fraction	
Zn-supplemented (6)[2]	155±15*†	5·39±0·79†	1350±218†	25±1·43	4·59±1·00	3·25±0·89	30±3·61†
Zn-deficient (6)	73±6	2·42±0·31	642±99	26±1·98	4·76±0·87	4·32±1·18	23±2·65

[1] Rats were killed 4 hours after DL-Cystine-1-^{14}C injection.
[2] Numbers in brackets indicate the number of rats used.
* Mean + SD.
† Difference between Zn-supplemented and Zn-deficient rats is statistically significant (P < 0·01).

Table IV. *Incorporation of labelled cystine into liver GSH*

Type of diet	Compound used	Hours after injection	GSH μmol./100 g.	Radioactivity		% of injected ^{14}C found as GSH in 1 g. of liver
				c.p.m./mg. GSH	c.p.m./g.	
Zn-supplemented (5)[1]	DL-Cystine-1-^{14}C	4	178±29*†	28245±5971‡	15398±3801‡	0·046±0·01†
Zn-deficient (4)	DL-Cystine-1-^{14}C	4	308±59	38256±3770	36052±5808	0·189±0·030
Zn-supplemented (4)	L-Cystine-^{35}S	3	230±39†	18331±2669	13050±3754‡	0·255±·054†
Zn-deficient (3)	L-Cystine-^{35}S	3	425±9	30065±10021	38930±11817	1·105±·297
Zn-supplemented (4)	L-Cystine-^{35}S	4	179±35†	35347±9949‡	17356±5442‡	0·310±0·81†
Zn-deficient (4)	L-Cystine-^{35}S	4	293±44	57666±5003	43336±12968	1·403±·271
Zn-supplemented (5)	L-Cystine-^{35}S	20	243±42†	5655±424	4215±630†	0·068±·007†
Zn-deficient (4)	L-Cystine-^{35}S	20	410±76	6292±757	7984±1914	0·229±·043

[1] Figures in brackets indicate the number of rats used.
* Mean + SD.
† Difference between Zn-supplemented and Zn-deficient rats is statistically significant (P < 0·01).
‡ Difference between Zn-supplemented and Zn-deficient rats is statistically significant (P < 0·05).

When examined at the end of four hours this increase had disappeared. In the second experiment, the longer time on the experimental diets is not likely to explain this difference since the trends in liver and kidney remain unchanged.

Analysis of the uptake of labelled cystine was carried out four hours post-injection (Table III). The percentage of the injected radioactivity found in the whole liver was about the same in Zn-deficient rats as in Zn-supplemented rats. The percentage of the radioactivity found in the TCA soluble fraction tended to be higher in the deficient group but did not reach a statistical significance.

Biosynthesis of liver GSH was monitored using both DL-cystine-1-^{14}C and L-cystine-^{35}S (Table IV). Despite the increased radioactivity of the respiratory $^{14}CO_2$, the amount of ^{14}C incorporated into GSH (expressed as c.p.m./mg. of GSH) was about 40 per cent. higher at four hours in Zn-deficient rats as compared to Zn-supplemented rats. When the data were calculated as c.p.m./g. liver and percentage of injected dose, Zn-deficient rats had more than twice as much GSH radioactivity as Zn-supplemented rats.

In the experiments using L-cystine-^{35}S, the specific activity of liver GSH was about 64 per cent. higher at both three and four hours in Zn-deficient rats than in their respective Zn-supplemented controls. By 20 hours there was little difference between the two groups in the specific activity of liver GSH.

Table V. *Distribution of ^{35}S, 24 hours after L-cystine-^{35}S injection*

Type of diet	% of injected radioactivity	
	Zn-supplemented (6)[1]	Zn-deficient (6)
Urine	$21 \cdot 61 \pm 2 \cdot 17$* †	$33 \cdot 45 \pm 8 \cdot 90$
Faeces	Trace	Trace
Liver	$2 \cdot 28 \pm 0 \cdot 158$‡	$3 \cdot 82 \pm 1 \cdot 156$
Kidney	$1 \cdot 11 \pm 0 \cdot 160$‡	$1 \cdot 51 \pm 0 \cdot 153$
Carcass	$61 \cdot 3 \pm 3 \cdot 4$†	$45 \cdot 4 \pm 2 \cdot 6$

[1]. Numbers in brackets indicate the number of rats used.
*. Mean + SD.
†. Difference between Zn-supplemented and Zn-deficient rats is statistically significant ($P < 0 \cdot 01$).
‡. Difference between Zn-supplemented and Zn-deficient rats is statistically significant ($P < 0 \cdot 05$).

As shown in Table V, differences exist between Zn-supplemented and Zn-deficient rats in the distribution of ^{35}S after isotope injection. Urinary excretion of total ^{35}S activity was greater by 50 per cent. in Zn-deficient rats than in Zn-supplemented animals. The livers and kidneys of rats fed a Zn-deficient diet contained a greater proportion of the injected radioactivity from L-cystine-^{35}S than did those of Zn-supplemented rats. Conversely, the radioactivity in the carcasses of Zn-deficient rats was only 73 per cent. of control value.

The increased urinary excretion of radioactive sulphur prompted us to measure inorganic sulphate at 8, 16 and 24 hours. When expressed as percentage of injected dose, the mean values and standard deviations of ^{35}S in urinary inorganic sulphate for Zn-supplemented rats were: 7.84 ± 2.41, 10.61 ± 1.81, 11.76 ± 2.13 and for Zn-deficient rats 12.02 ± 1.60, 15.81 ± 1.32 and 17.95 ± 1.39 respectively. The total ^{35}S found in the urine at these time periods was also consistently higher (Fig. 1) in Zn-deficient rats.

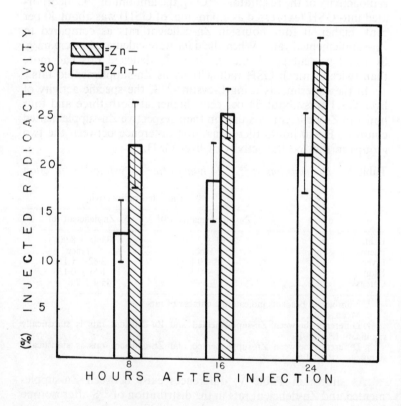

FIG. 1. Effect of zinc deficiency on urinary excretion of ^{35}S in rats following L-Cystine-^{35}S injection. The vertical lines are standard deviations.

CONCLUSIONS

The results clearly indicate that various metabolic pathways of cystine are altered in rats suffering from dietary deprivation of Zn. The increased expired $^{14}CO_2$ from injection of DL-cystine-1-^{14}C in Zn-deficient rats may be linked to a defect in the utilization of this amino acid for protein synthesis. The fact that the rate of incorporation of glycine-1-^{14}C (Hsu *et al.*, 1968) and glutamic acid-1-^{14}C (unpublished data) into tissue proteins was unaffected by Zn deficiency leads one to believe that this trace element is specifically involved with S-containing amino acids.

That the formation of liver GSH from labelled cystine is enhanced in Zn-deficient rats is not unexpected since deficiency of Zn caused an increase in the incorporation rate of glycine-1-^{14}C into the tripeptide (Hsu *et al.*, 1968). The lack of differences in the specific activity of GSH at 20 hours further suggests that its turnover rate increased in Zn-deficient rats, but the significance and cause of this alteration remains to be studied. In addition to its specific role as a co-factor for numerous enzymes, GSH plays a part in the liver in detoxication processes by formation of a variety of conjugated organic compounds that are excreted in the bile or urine or both. This process is one of the hepatic mechanisms for metabolizing or disposing of a variety of toxic substances (Combes and Stakelum, 1960). It would be of some interest to determine the relationship, if any, between toxic materials produced and the excess GSH synthesised by Zn-deficient rats.

The data in the present study show that Zn deficiency is associated with enhanced urinary excretion of inorganic sulphate. Some investigations have demonstrated that many tissues in the chick are equipped with the enzymes necessary for conversion of sulphate-^{35}S into taurine (Miraglia *et al.*, 1966). If this be true in rats an increased urinary taurine content during Zn deficiency could be derived from the excess amount of sulphate. Tests are in progress to clarify this possibility.

REFERENCES

COMBES, B. & STAKELUM, G. S. (1960). *J. clin. Invest.* **39**, 1214.
GOLDZIEHER, J. W., BESCH, P. K. & VELEZ, M. (1958). *J. biol. Chem.* **231**, 445.
HERBERG, R. J. (1960). *Analyt. Chem.* **32**, 42.
HSU, J. M., ANTHONY, W. L. & BUCHANAN, P. J. (1968). *Proc. Soc. exp. Biol. Med.* **127**, 1048.
HSU, J. M., ANTHONY, W. L. & BUCHANAN, P. J. (1969). *J. Nutr.* **97**, 279.
KAHN, B. S. & LEIBOFF, S. L. (1928). *J. biol. Chem.* **80**, 623.
MIRAGLIA, R. J., MARTIN, W. G., SPAETH, D. G. & PATRICK, H. (1966). *Proc. Soc. exp. Biol. Med.* **123**, 725.
PATTERSON, J. W. & LAZAROW, A. (1955). *Meth. biochem. Analysis*, **2**, 274.
WOOL, I. G. & KRAHL, M. E. (1959). *Am. J. Physiol.* **196**, 961.

DISCUSSION

Underwood (Perth). Dr Hsu may be interested to know that my colleague, Dr Somers, and I have obtained evidence which supports his data indicating an increased urinary excretion of sulphur in Zn deficiency. In work with Zn-deficient ram lambs we have obtained highly significant increases in urinary sulphur and nitrogen excretion compared with that from normal lambs consuming and digesting the same amounts of food. There were no changes in faecal sulphur excretion. We have interpreted this as evidence of an impairment of protein metabolism without relating this specifically as you have done to the sulphur amino acids themselves.

Pories (Rochester). I would like to compliment Dr Hsu on an excellent piece of work. Yesterday I was asked how Zn accelerates wound healing and I was unable to answer except to say that it stimulated protein synthesis. Your studies promise to give us a much better and more specific answer.

Hsu (Baltimore). I would like to add that the increased urinary excretion of sulphate in the Zn-deficient animal is reversible by giving a daily injection of 400 μg. of Zn daily for three days.

ZINC DEFICIENCY AND TISSUE NUCLEIC ACID AND PROTEIN CONCENTRATION

P. K. Ku, D. E. Ullrey and E. R. Miller

Michigan State University, East Lansing, Michigan, U.S.A.

The classification of zinc as a dietary essential for the rat was established more than 30 years ago by Todd and Elvehjem (1934) and its importance has since been repeatedly confirmed in other mammals and birds. A number of symptoms of Zn deficiency have been described but of great practical importance in the pig is the almost complete cessation of growth when the Zn deficiency is severe. There are a number of potential explanations for this cessation of growth, not the least of which is the poor food consumption.

We have been particularly interested in whether Zn deficiency is affecting growth by adversely influencing protein synthesis and/ or nucleic acid metabolism. Wacker and Vallee in 1959 reported

158

that many metals, including Zn, were consistently found in RNA and DNA, regardless of their origin. The concentration of such metals was much less in DNA than in RNA. It was suggested that certain of these metals may play a role in the maintenance of the configuration of RNA molecules, perhaps linking purine or pyrimidine bases, or both, through covalent bonds.

Fujioka and Lieberman (1964) in a study of the effect of EDTA on DNA synthesis in the partially hepatectomized rat suggested that Zn is necessary for DNA synthesis. These workers reported that the rate of protein and RNA synthesis was not influenced by Zn. However, Williams et al. (1965) showed that the rate of incorporation of ^{32}P into both liver RNA and DNA was reduced in the Zn-deficient rat. Macapinlac et al. (1968) suggested that an increase in protein and RNA catabolism occurs in Zn-deficient rat testes rather than a decrease in synthesis. Theuer and Hoekstra (1966) have found a significant increase in the amino acid oxidation rate in Zn-deficient rats, while Hsu and Anthony (1969) have found that the rate of incorporation of methionine ^{14}C into the plasma, liver and kidney proteins of Zn-deficient rats is less than in Zn-adequate rats. Perhaps C. F. Mills and his associates at the Rowett Institute will be able to provide us with a final resolution of these diverse observations through the use of their unique feeding procedures. In the hope that the following descriptive data will not confuse the issue too much, we shall proceed.

Table I. *Composition of basal diet*

	%
Glucose (monohydrate)	50·7
Isolated soy protein	30·0
DL-methionine	0·3
α-Cellulose	5·0
Lard	5·0
Mineral mix	6·0
Corn oil with fat soluble vitamins[a]	1·0
Water with water soluble vitamins[a]	2·0
	100·0

[a] Concentration identical with that used by Miller et al. (1964).

Three trials, involving 42 pigs, have been conducted and the basal diet used in all trials is shown in Table I. Trials 1 and 2 were essentially identical, with half of the pigs receiving 12 p.p.m. of Zn and the other half receiving 90 p.p.m. of Zn. They were individually pair-fed once daily. The effect on bodyweight gain and gain/feed is shown in Table II. Serum samples were taken for determination of Zn concentration and alkaline phosphatase activity upon two occasions and these values are also shown in Table II.

Table II. *Effect of Zn level on bodyweight gain, gain/feed, serum Zn and serum alkaline phosphatase activity (trial 1 and 2)*

	12 p.p.m. Zn		90 p.p.m. Zn	
Trial number	1	2	1	2
Number of pigs	6	8	6	8
Days on experiment	23	28	23	28
Initial weight, kg.	2·11	2·36	2·10	2·36
Average daily gain, g.	72*	79*	153	150
Gain/feed	0·36*	0·38*	0·72	0·70
Serum Zn, μg./100 ml.				
Trial 1–14d., trial 2–20d.	26·3*	17·4*	48·8	52·6
Trial 1–23d., trial 2–28d.	12·0*	14·0*	62·2	60·3
Alkaline phosphatase, Sigma units				
Trial 1–14d., trial 2–20d.	1·8*	2·9*	6·6	8·6
Trial 1–23d., trial 2–28d.	2·2*	0·4*	8·5	3·7

* Significantly (P < 0·01) less than like values on 90 p.p.m. Zn

After 23 (trial 1) or 28 (trial 2) days on experiment, the pigs were killed. Certain organ weights are shown in Table III.

Table III. *Effect of Zn level on organ weights (g.) or as a per cent. of bodyweight (trials 1 and 2)*

	12 p.p.m. Zn		90 p.p.m. Zn	
Trial number	1	2	1	2
Bodyweight, kg.	3·76	4·57	5·62	6·56
Liver, g.(%)	122*(3·2)	117*(2·6)	169(3·0)	173(2·6)
Thymus, g.(%)	4·1*(·10)*	4·6*(·10)*	10·1(·18)	14·4(·21)
Pancreas, g.(%)	7·4*(·19)	6·6*(·14)*	10·2(·18)	13·5(·20)
Kidneys, g.(%)	25*(·67)	32*(·70)	33(·58)	41(·62)
Spleen, g.(%)	6·1*(·16)	8·2*(·17)	9·0(·16)	11·5(·17)
Brain, g.(%)	41(1·1)*	47(1·0)*	43(0·8)	48(0·7)

* Significantly (P < 0·01) different from like values on 90 p.p.m. Zn

The effects of treatment on tissue dry matter, ether extract, protein, RNA and DNA concentration are shown in Table IV. Protein was determined by the Lowry method (Miller, 1959). RNA was determined by the orcinol method of Mejbaum (1939) as modified by Tucker and Reece (1962) using yeast RNA as a standard. DNA was determined by the diphenylamine method (Giles and Myers, 1965) using calf thymus DNA as the standard.

Trial 3 was of a somewhat different design and included a biotin treatment based on the suspicion that some of the skin lesions

Table IV. *Effect of Zn level on dry matter, ether extract, protein, RNA and DNA concentration of thymus, pancreas, liver, kidney, spleen and brain (trials 1 and 2)*[a]

	Thymus				Pancreas				Liver			
	12 p.p.m. Zn		90 p.p.m. Zn		12 p.p.m. Zn		90 p.p.m. Zn		12 p.p.m. Zn		90 p.p.m. Zn	
Experiment number	1	2	1	2	1	2	1	2	1	2	1	2
Dry matter, %	20·8	20·2	21·1	20·3	23·8	23·3	22·6	24·3	27·5	27·0	28·7*	27·3
Ether extract, %	2·6	2·3	2·1	2·2	1·8	1·9	1·9	2·0	1·6	2·0	1·4	2·0
Protein, mg./g.	121·9	120·1	126·2	128·3	165·2	150·0	156·4	158·0	170·0*	185·3	153·7	178·0
RNA, mg./g.	9·3	7·2	9·0	9·0	18·0	19·8	22·7	21·9	17·4	17·7	29·8*	20·0
DNA, mg./g.	22·0	21·3	30·2*	28·2*	0·28	0·91	1·26*	0·65	1·99	2·36	2·10	2·56
RNA/DNA	0·42*	0·37	0·31	0·32	130	170	19	103	9·0	7·7	14·4*	7·8
Protein/RNA	13·3	16·9*	14·1	14·4	9·2*	7·8	6·9	7·4	9·8	10·8	5·3	9·2
Protein/DNA	5·6*	6·3*	4·3	4·5	485*	1511	125	842	88·0	79·8	74·2	70·1

	Kidney				Spleen				Brain			
	12 p.p.m. Zn		90 p.p.m. Zn		12 p.p.m. Zn		90 p.p.m. Zn		12 p.p.m. Zn		90 p.p.m. Zn	
	1	2	1	2	1	2	1	2	1	2	1	2
Dry matter, %	20·6*	20·4	19·7	21·2	21·1	21·0	20·7	21·0	18·7	20·1	19·4	20·0
Ether extract, %	2·3	2·8	2·2	2·9	1·73	1·74	1·86	1·85	7·1	8·1	7·4	8·0
Protein, mg./g.	117·0	137·3	119·0	135·2	153·4	153·0	154·1	156·4	98·7	101·5	98·8	103·0
RNA, mg./g.	7·2	7·7	7·2	8·2	9·8	9·8	9·8	9·4	3·6	2·7	3·6	2·9
DNA, mg./g.	5·2	5·0	4·9	4·7	6·8	9·2	7·1	8·4	0·54	0·45	0·50	0·41
RNA/DNA	1·39	1·57	1·48	1·73	1·44	1·07	1·39	1·13	6·6	7·1	7·4	7·5
Protein/RNA	16·2	17·8*	16·5	16·6	16·2	15·7	15·8	16·7	27·9	37·0	27·7	36·6
Protein/DNA	22·5	27·8	24·6	28·8	23·5	15·8	21·9	18·9*	184·0	264·2	205·3	265·2

[a] Concentration expressed on a fresh basis
* Significantly (P < 0·01) different from like values on other zinc level

Table V. *Effect of Zn and biotin treatments on bodyweight gain, gain/feed and protein, RNA and DNA concentration of thymus, pancreas and liver (trial 3)*[a]

| | BODYWEIGHT GAIN AND GAIN/FEED | | | |
| | 12 p.p.m. Zn | | 90 p.p.m. Zn | |
	0 p.p.m. Biotin	1 p.p.m. Biotin	0 p.p.m. Biotin	1 p.p.m. Biotin
Number of pigs	3	3	3	3
Days on experiment	31	31	31	31
Initial weight, kg.	2·20	2·28	2·22	2·24
Average daily gain, g.	37·7	37·4	130·8*	191·2*†
Average daily feed, g.	187·0	196·0	316·7*	323·7*
Gain/feed	0·21	0·20	0·42*	0·62*

	THYMUS PROTEIN, RNA AND DNA			
Protein, mg./g.	65·0	89·0	114·4*	114·0*
RNA, mg./g.	7·9	10·5	8·0	7·9
DNA, mg./g.	5·7	4·8	17·7*	19·5*
RNA/DNA	1·72	2·25*	0·45	0·41
Protein/RNA	9·8	9·1	14·8	15·1
Protein/DNA	13·6	19·4*	6·5	5·9

	PANCREAS PROTEIN, RNA AND DNA			
Protein, mg./g.	139·0	138·0	145·3	145·7
RNA, mg./g.	20·6	20·4	25·6*	25·6*
DNA, mg./g.	1·58	1·66	4·00*	3·96
RNA/DNA	14·1	21·4	6·8	9·3
Protein/RNA	6·9	6·8	5·7	5·7
Protein/DNA	94·0*	142·4	38·0	52·2

	LIVER PROTEIN, RNA AND DNA			
Protein, mg./g.	137·3*	140·8*	111·7	104·7
RNA, mg./g.	18·0	22·5	34·7*	36·4*
DNA, mg./g.	2·70	2·09	1·95	2·21
RNA/DNA	7·2	11·0	20·1	16·5*
Protein/RNA	7·62*	6·69*	3·54	2·98
Protein/DNA	54·9	69·6	59·5	47·8

	SPLEEN PROTEIN, RNA AND DNA			
Protein, mg./g.	153·4	149·7	159·7	148·3
RNA, mg./g.	9·4	9·5	9·2	10·4
DNA, mg./g.	5·3	4·9	5·2	4·2
RNA/DNA	2·0	2·8	2·0	2·6
Protein/RNA	16·2	15·9	18·0	14·3
Protein/DNA	30·9	42·9	36·5	37·3

[a] Concentration expressed on a fresh basis
* Significantly ($P < 0·01$) different from like values on other Zn level
† Significantly ($P < 0·05$) greater than 0 p.p.m. biotin, 90 p.p.m. Zn group

which had been seen on the basal diet used previously (containing 50 p.p.b. of biotin) were related to a shortage of this vitamin. These pigs were fed *ad libitum*. The effects of Zn and biotin treatments on bodyweight gain, gain/feed and the protein, RNA and DNA concentration of thymus, pancreas and liver are shown in Table V. It is interesting that biotin supplementation increased gain and gain/feed on the high Zn level but not on the low.

In all three trials thymus DNA concentration was depressed in Zn-deficiency, pancreatic DNA in two out of three trials and liver DNA in none out of three. Pancreatic RNA concentration tended to be depressed in Zn-deficient pigs in three out of three trials (although only trial 3 was statistically significant). Liver RNA concentration was depressed in Zn deficiency in three out of three trials (although only trials 1 and 3 were significant). The protein concentration in liver was elevated in Zn deficiency in three out of three trials (trials 1 and 3 were significant) and in thymus was depressed in all three trials (only trial 3 was significant).

Based on the decline in DNA concentration in Zn-deficient thymus and pancreas it would appear that there has either been a change in predominant cell type with fewer but larger cells being present, or else the cells normally present have undergone hypertrophy. Taking into consideration the severe involution of these two organs one might speculate that either DNA synthesis in these organs is seriously interfered with or DNA catabolism is exaggerated by Zn deficiency.

The effect of Zn deficiency on liver seemed to be quite different from the effect on thymus and pancreas. Based on DNA concentration alone there seemed to be neither decreased DNA synthesis nor increased DNA catabolism. DNA turnover rates were not measured. The increase in liver protein concentration, while RNA concentration decreased, seems somewhat anomalous. However, it has been shown by Yatvin and Wannemacher (1965) that adrenocortical hormones will stimulate protein synthesis in liver and diminish it in muscle, and in the liver this increased rate of protein biosynthesis was accompanied by a decreased cellular RNA level. Thus our observation may be related to a general stress effect and not to Zn deficiency *per se*. There is no doubt that further carefully designed and conducted dynamic studies will be necessary to finally elucidate the role of Zn in protein and nucleic acid metabolism.

REFERENCES

FUJIOKA, M. & LIEBERMAN, I. (1964). *J. biol. Chem.* **239**, 1164.
GILES, K. W. & MYERS, A. (1965). *Nature, Lond.* **206**, 93.
HSU, J. M. & ANTHONY, W. L. (1969). *Fedn Proc. Fedn Am. Socs exp. Biol.* **28**, 762.

163

MACAPINLAC, M. P., PEARSON, W. N., BARNEY, G. H. & DARBY, W. J. (1968).
    J. Nutr. **95**, 569.
MEJBAUM, W. (1939). *Hoppe-Seyler's Z. physiol. Chem.* **258**, 117.
MILLER, E. R., ULLREY, D. E., ZUTAUT, C. L., BALTZER, B. V., SCHMIDT, D. A.,
    VINCENT, B. H., HOEFFER, J. A. & LUECKE, R. W. (1964). *J. Nutr.* **83**, 140.
MILLER, G. J. (1959). *Analyt. Chem.* **31**, 964.
THEUER, R. C. & HOEKSTRA, W. G. (1966). *J. Nutr.* **89**, 448.
TODD, W. R., ELVEHJEM, C. A. & HART, E. B. (1934). *Am. J. Physiol.* **107**, 146.
TUCKER, H. A. & REECE, R. P. (1962). *Proc. Soc. exp. Biol. Med.* **111**, 639.
WACKER, W. E. C. & VALLEE, B. L. (1959). *J. biol. Chem.* **234**, 3257.
WILLIAMS, R. B., MILLS, C. F., QUARTERMAN, J. & DALGARNO, A. C. (1965).
    Biochem. J. **95**, 29P.
YATVIN, M. B. & WANNEMACHER, R. W., Jr. (1965). *Endocrinology*, **76**, 418.

EFFECTS OF ZINC DEFICIENCY ON NUCLEIC ACID SYNTHESIS IN THE RAT

R. B. WILLIAMS and J. K. CHESTERS

Rowett Research Institute, Bucksburn, Aberdeen, U.K.

FUJIOKA and Lieberman in 1964 showed that Zn stimulated DNA synthesis in the livers of partially-hepatectomised rats perfused with EDTA. It is possible that this effect might not be operative in the rat eating a Zn-deficient diet since tissue Zn concentrations show only minor changes. Other investigators studying nucleic acid synthesis in Zn-deficient animals have produced conflicting results. Studies of this nature are complicated by the early cessation of growth and reduced food intakes of the Zn-deficient animal which make a controlled experiment virtually impossible. If failure of the rat to grow resulted from a reduction in the rate of nucleic acid synthesis it occurred to us that it might be possible to demonstrate a defect in nucleic acid synthesis before growth ceased and food intake declined thus eliminating the difficulty of providing control animals.

In the initial experiment groups of rats were killed two hours after injection of [^{3}H]-thymidine and at various times over a period of 11 days after transfer to the Zn-deficient diet. DNA synthesis decreased throughout the period but it was not possible to distinguish between the effect of Zn deficiency and the unexpectedly rapid decline with age. In one group where pair-fed controls were used, no difference in incorporation could be found after 11 days of deficiency.

In a second experiment thymidine incorporation was measured in groups of rats which were all of the same age but had been fed the Zn-deficient diet for 0 to 5 days. The results shown in Figure 1 indicate a progressive fall in DNA specific activity as the period of deficiency extended. In every tissue examined there was a linear trend, significant for all except testis.

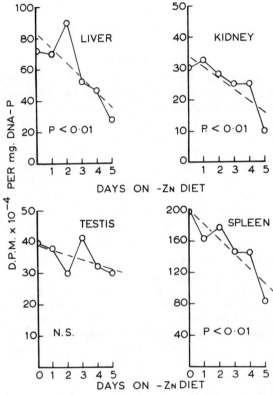

FIG. 1. Tritiated thymidine incorporation into DNA of Zn-deficient rats.

In the same experiment [^{14}C]-lysine incorporation into protein was measured after a 20-minute period. In kidney and spleen only incorporation fell by a small but significant amount as the period of Zn deficiency progressed.

These experiments would appear to confirm the original observations of Fujioka and Lieberman that Zn deficiency results in a reduction of DNA synthesis and that this effect is immediate and of greater magnitude than a fall in protein synthesis.

165

The relatively small effect of early Zn deficiency on protein synthesis is in accordance with our observation that there was no consistent effect on nuclear RNA synthesis in rat liver as measured by [^{14}C]-orotate incorporation during the early period of deficiency.

REFERENCE

FUJIOKA, M. & LIEBERMAN, I. (1964). *J. biol. Chem.* **239**, 1164.

DISCUSSION

Underwood (Perth). In contrast to the data reported by Dr Chesters we have found a significant reduction in DNA and RNA concentration in the testes of Zn-deficient rats compared with pair-fed controls. This was correlated with a significantly higher concentration of non-protein nitrogen in the testes and an increased ribonuclease activity. As far as I am aware this last finding is new for animal tissues although an increase in RNAase activity has been previously reported from work with Zn-deficient plants. I should emphasize however that the rats in our experiment had been a longer period on the deficient diet than in Dr Chester's and Mr Williams's work and they were showing clear clinical signs of deficiency.

Chesters (Aberdeen). The testis is an organ which is differentiating very rapidly in this age of animal and it is not typical of the body as a whole, as is apparent from its differential growth with respect to the rest of the body. We feel that many of the reported effects of Zn deficiency are secondary in nature, hence our emphasis upon studies very early in the deficiency state. Furthermore, many studies have been carried out using control animals that are twice the weight of deficient animals and in such situations it becomes impossible to draw valid conclusions from studies with an organ which is subject to such rapid changes in differential growth as is the testis. It is to me significant that some of the effects we have found elsewhere we have not found in testes and although the testis is undoubtedly dependent upon Zn; I regard it as a special case.

Hsu (Baltimore). You have shown a small but significant increase in the incorporation of [^{14}C]-lysine into kidney and spleen proteins in the Zn-deficient rat but on the other hand you have shown that the concentration of DNA is significantly lower in kidney but not in spleen. Do you have any comments on these points?

Chesters (Aberdeen). The concentration of DNA in the kidney fell to 97 per cent. of that in the control animals. This was statistically significant but I doubt its biological significance and more work will be required to establish this effect. A fall in lysine incorporation into protein occurred in only two of the four tissues whereas a much greater fall in thymidine incorporation into DNA occurred in all four tissues.

Hsu (Baltimore). When were the animals killed after the injection of [^{14}C]-lysine?

Chesters (Aberdeen). Twenty minutes after injection.

CHANGES IN APPETITE AND ALIMENTARY MUCO-SUBSTANCES IN ZINC DEFICIENCY

J. QUARTERMAN, W. R. HUMPHRIES and E. FLORENCE
Rowett Research Institute, Bucksburn, Aberdeen, U.K.

Loss of appetite is one of the earliest observed signs of Zn deficiency (Mills and Chesters, this volume, p. 39) and similarly recovery of appetite occurs within a few hours of giving Zn to Zn-deficient rats (Humphries & Quarterman, 1968). This increased appetite follows the ingestion of only 1 to 2 g. of food containing 6 to 12 μg. Zn which is less than 1 per cent. of the total body Zn, even in a deficient rat.

Such a rapid action of so small a quantity of Zn may be explicable if the Zn causes some changes in that part of the body where it first comes into contact, *i.e.* the gut and before it is diluted by the body pool of Zn. Preliminary experiments with barium meals showed that in many Zn-deficient rats the barium meal reached the ileo-caecal junction later than in Zn-supplemented rats. Further, in many of the Zn-deficient rats the radiographs showed mottled, semi-opaque areas in the terminal ileum and caecum whereas those of control animals were uniformly opaque. It was thought possible that the latter changes were associated with increased amounts of mucus and this has been shown to be the case.

Soluble, non-dialysable hexosamine and sialic acid were used as measures of muco-substances. Contents of parts of the alimentary tract and scrapings of the mucosa were extracted with 0·2 M-NaCl, centrifuged at 40,000 g and dialysed against 0·01 M-NaCl containing

0·001 M-tris buffer, and 0·05 M-EDTA. Sialic acid and hexosamine were estimated in hydrolyses of the resulting solution by the methods of Warren (1959) and Levvy and McAllan (1959).

Consistent effects of Zn deficiency were found in the caecum. The amount of hexosamine and sialic acid was nearly twice as great in Zn-deficient animals as in pair-fed controls, in the soluble fraction of the contents and of the mucosal scrapings in relation both to protein and to total wet weight. In the solid material precipitated by centrifugation, hexosamine but not sialic acid was increased in Zn deficiency.

The mixture of soluble muco-substances is changed qualitatively as well as quantitatively. They were subjected to gradient layer separation on a DEAE-cellulose column (Fig. 1) and it was found that the later-eluted, presumably more highly polar, components were increased relatively to the earlier-eluted components.

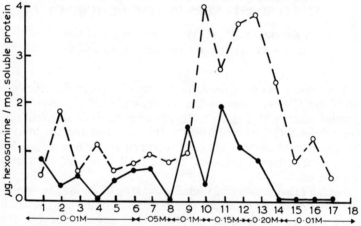

FIG. 1. Chromatography on DEAE cellulose of the soluble, non-dialysable extract of caecal mucosa from Zn-deficient (o . . . o) and Zn-supplemented (● . . . ●) rats.

Zinc-deficient rats have a very wide daily variation of food intake (Mills and Chesters, this volume, p. 39) and these changes in caecal muco-substances were observed after a day of high intake, *i.e.* 8 to 10 g. After a day of low food intake, 0 to 3 g., there was little or no change in the total, soluble, non-dialysable hexosamine in Zn deficiency although a qualitative change in the composition of the mixture, similar to that shown in Figure 1, was observed.

When Zn-deficient rats were repleted with Zn the pattern of muco-substances observed in the DEAE-cellulose column fractions had not changed in 8 hours but had returned to normal in 24 hours. Thus the observed changes in appetite on repletion are faster than the changes in the caecal muco-substances.

Histology of the caecal epithelium stained with periodic acid-Schiff showed increased numbers of goblet cells, many of which remained undischarged up to the top of the crypts of Lieberkühn, and increased amounts of mucus in the crypts and adhering to the surface of the mucosa.

The changes of chemically detectable muco-substances described in this paper may thus be due to changes in the development of goblet cells in Zn deficiency and not to a role of Zn in the biosynthesis or breakdown of muco-substances.

REFERENCES

HUMPHRIES, W. R. & QUARTERMAN, J. (1968). *Proc. Nutr. Soc.* **27**, 54A.
LEVVY, G. A. & MCALLAN, A. (1959). *Biochem. J.* **73**, 127.
WARREN, L. (1959). *J. biol. Chem.* **234**, 1971.

DISCUSSION

Hoekstra (Madison). I would like to comment on the point in which you associated mucus production with delayed development of the goblet cells in the Zn-deficient rat. We find a similar situation in the lesions of the epiphysis of the tibiotarsus of the Zn-deficient chick. Those cells furthest from the blood supply, and thus from the nutrient supply, seem to produce more matrix rather than less, more hexosamine is present in these localised areas and, like you, we have interpreted this as a delay in the maturation of these cells. Work on the oesophageal lesion of Zn deficiency by Barney and others at Vanderbilt University indicates also that here the cells may fail to differentiate properly. A role for Zn in differentiation may be one of its more general roles.

Reinhold (Beirut). Have you measured the lengths of the several segments of the intestine? We have found that the length of the oesophagus may be increased by as much as 50 per cent. in Zn-deficient rats.

Quarterman (Aberdeen). No, but we have measured total wet weight and have found no significant difference.

Husain (Glasgow). What is the difference between the skin lesion in psoriasis in the human and parakeratosis in the skin of the Zn-deficient rat? Do you get any dilation of the blood vessels?

169

Quarterman (Aberdeen). We have not made an extensive study of the skin lesion at the Rowett. Parakeratosis is a late sign of deficiency in the rat and we have been concentrating on earlier events.

Hoekstra (Madison). On that point I would like to comment that our colleague, Dr Anderson, has made an extensive histochemical study of psoriatic skin of the human and parakeratotic skin of the pig. There are many dramatic similarities and very few dissimilarities. In parakeratosis there is extensive dilation of the blood vessels but the tortuosity of the vessels is not as great as in the psoriatic human. Another colleague, Dr Cooper, has tried to treat several cases of psoriasis in man with Zn but it has not cured the disease and he maintains that it has modified the lesion in part but it is still there.

THE EFFECT OF ZINC DEFICIENCY ON GROWTH AND UTILIZATION OF PHYTATE CONTAINING PROTEINS

D. OBERLEAS and A. S. PRASAD

Wayne State University, Detroit, Michigan and Veterans Administration Hospital, Allen Park, Michigan, U.S.A.

GROWTH was first used as an index of protein quality when Osborne, Mendel and Ferry (1919) developed the protein efficiency ratio as a means of biological evaluation. Zinc was not then considered an essential element for animals and thus was not added to the diet. This methodology was developed with lactalbumin and casein which most likely were adequate in Zn. However, the failure to supplement with Zn has been customary during the last half century in the bioassy of proteins from several sources. When Todd, Elvehjem and Hart (1934) demonstrated the essentiality of Zn for the rat, growth failure was the first and most marked symptom noted. O'Dell and Savage (1957) were first to demonstrate that Zn was less available from plant seed proteins than from animal proteins. O'Dell and Savage (1960) also demonstrated that phytate, present in plant seeds, caused decreased Zn availability. The mechanism of phytate action and its accentuation by Ca was subsequently reported by Oberleas, Muhrer and O'Dell (1966). The present experiments studied the effect of Zn on growth of rats and utilization of phytate-containing soybean protein.

Weanling male rats of Holtzman strain were allotted by weight among the experimental treatments. Basal diets calculated to contain 4, 8, 12, 16 and 20 per cent. soybean assay protein (4·9, 9·1, 13·8, 18·8 and 22·7 per cent. by analysis) with 10 per cent. corn oil, 5 per cent. minerals, 2 per cent. calcium carbonate, vitamins and methionine, and the balance as glucose monohydrate. Dietary phytate was equalized at 1 per cent. in all diets by the addition of phytic acid. Control diets were prepared by adding 55 mg./kg. of Zn as $ZnCO_3$ to the basal diets. The animals were housed in stainless steel cages and given distilled water in vinyl stoppered glass bottles. The animals were weighed weekly. Trace elements were determined by atomic absorption following wet ashing with HNO_3. Enzyme activities were determined by established procedures.

Growth rates on the basal diets for a 10-week period were (gm./kg.): 0·2, 6·4, 10·6, 15·0 and 21·4 respectively, and for the Zn-supplemented groups: 2·6, 20·9, 29·3, 31·8 and 31·8 respectively. The basal groups receiving only 4 or 8 per cent. protein had a 75 per cent. mortality. With Zn supplementation mortality in these protein groups was reduced to 8 per cent. The growth rate of the 8 per cent. protein, Zn-supplemented group was similar to the 20

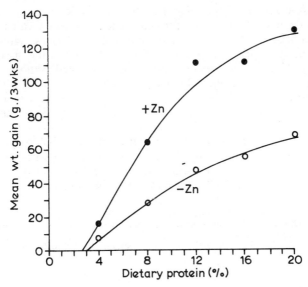

FIG. 1. The relationship between growth and level of dietary protein as affected by Zn.

per cent. basal group and no improvement in growth rate could be achieved above 12 per cent. protein with Zn-supplementation. The relationship between growth (weight gain for three weeks) and level of dietary protein as affected by Zn is shown in Figure 1 expressed according to the Slope Ratio Assay Method of Hegsted and Chang (1965). The relative potency for the basal diets (4 to 20 per cent. inclusive) was 25·2 and the Zn-supplemented diets (4 to 12 per cent. inclusive) was 81·4 using a published lactalbumin standard slope as 100 per cent. These compared favourably with the 43·3 for soy protein and 69·2 for casein reported by Hegsted and Chang (1965). These earlier values were reported on diets supplemented with neither Zn nor methionine. Also their diets contained no added phytate or Ca to accentuate a Zn deficiency. Previous data have shown that equivalent growth may be obtained from soy protein and casein diets provided the soy diet was supplemented with Zn (O'Dell and Savage, 1960). This indicates that Zn has an important role in the utilization of protein for growth.

Organ dry weight was more affected by Zn supplementation than by dietary protein level. Trace element contents have normally been expressed per unit of dry matter. Comparing content per unit of dry matter with content/organ, it was found that decidedly different conclusions would be drawn by these methods not only for tissue Zn but also for Cu, Fe and Mn. Differences in activity of Zn dependent enzymes expressed per unit of protein can also be shown between Zn-deficient and control animal tissues. However, with organ protein constituting a sizeable portion of the organ dry matter, the differences seen are not nearly as marked as those shown histochemically by Prasad, Oberleas, Wolf and Horwitz (1967) and Prasad, et al. (1969). Trace element content or enzyme activity can be expressed per organ in small animals but this becomes impractical in large animals or man. Since the ideal expression would be content or activity per cell, DNA may be the most stable component of the cell of Zn-deficient tissues which is proportional to cell numbers. Trace element content or enzyme activity per unit of DNA appears to be the best basis for expression.

Acknowledgements. This work was made possible through grants from USPHS Grant AM–08142, Detroit General Hospital Research Corporation and the Veterans Administration.

The authors acknowledge the technical assistance of Mr S. Ray Collins and Mrs Daria Koniuch.

REFERENCES

HEGSTED, D. M. & CHANG, Y. O. (1965). *J. Nutr.* **85**, 159.
OBERLEAS, D., MUHRER, M. E. & O'DELL, B. L. (1966). *J. Nutr.* **90**, 56.

O'DELL, B. L. & SAVAGE, J. E. (1957). *Fedn Proc. Fedn Am. Socs. exp. Biol.* **16**, 394.
O'DELL, B. L. & SAVAGE, J. E. (1960). *Proc. Soc. exp. Biol. Med.* **103**, 304.
OSBORNE, T. B., MENDEL, L. B. & FERRY, E. L. (1919). *J. biol. Chem.* **37**, 223.
PRASAD, A. S., OBERLEAS, D., WOLF, P. & HORWITZ, J. P. (1967). *J. clin. Invest.* **46**, 549.
PRASAD, A. S., OBERLEAS, D., WOLF, P., HORWITZ, J. P., MILLER, E. R. & LUECKE, R. W. (1969). *Am. J. clin. Nutr.* **22**, 628.
TODD, W. R., ELVEHJEM, C. A. & HART, E. B. (1934). *Am. J. Physiol.* **107**, 146.

DISCUSSION

Horvath (Morgantown, W.Va.). I have heard comments similar to yours made by specialists working on both selenium and chromium with respect to studies on kwashiorkor and I am wondering whether the problem isn't wider than you suggest.

Oberleas (Detroit). It is quite likely but I think the most important need is for Zn supplementation in these investigations.

Hill (London). Do you agree that the title phytate-containing proteins might be misleading as there is some evidence that these effects on Zn availability are not entirely accounted for by phytate?

Oberleas (Detroit). Yes, but in my experience the major effect on Zn availability is due to phytate in the protein.

INHIBITORY EFFECT OF CADMIUM ON ALKALINE PHOSPHATASE OF KIDNEY AND PROSTATE OF GUINEA-PIG

B. RIBAS-OZONAS, M. DEAN-GUELBENZU and A. SANTOS-RUIZ

Departamento de Bioquímica, Facultad de Farmacia, Madrid, Spain

CADMIUM and zinc are situated in the same group of the periodic table; the first may displace the second from its enzymatic protein compounds because it has a greater affinity with -SH groups. The lack of turnover of Cd induces it to inactivate the molecules to which it is alloyed (Cotzias *et al.,* 1961). It is toxic and dangerous for living animals and for humans, nevertheless it is a common component of the body (Hennig and Anke, 1964). It is detectable in invertebrates, in mammals, in foods (Schroder *et al.,* 1967) and in the atmosphere of industrial towns (Tabor and Warren, 1958; Carroll, 1966). Pulido, Kägi and Vallée (1966) have found Cd in the metallothioneine of the kidney. It is very possible that

173

slow contamination of the human body with Cd might take place during the animal's life-span.

We thought it would be of interest to use histochemical techniques to check the inhibitory effect of Cd on a Zn enzyme, alkaline phosphatase, and to compare this effect with that produced on other non-Zn enzymes.

MATERIALS AND METHODS

Two doses of 3 mg. of Cd per kg. were administered intraperitoneally to male guinea-pigs, which were sacrificed four days later. Another lot of animals was treated in the same way but with an injection of 4 mg. of Zn per kg. A third group of non-treated animals was used for control.

The kidney, prostate, liver, spleen and muscle were dissected. The organs which showed greatest alkaline phosphatase activity were the kidney and the prostate gland, and these interested us most.

The dissected organs were treated with alcohol and then frozen in solid carbon dioxide; sections 8 μm. thick were obtained simultaneously from experimental and control organs. The sections obtained were left to dry in a cold environment ($-20°$), placed on 'silica-gel' and then immersed in acetone for 10 minutes. They were exposed to the air for 60 seconds and immersed in substrate solution for incubating. They were then washed in distilled water for 2 seconds, immersed in 4 per cent. formol for 10 minutes, rinsed in distilled water again and, finally, left to colour in 0·1 per cent. methylgreen solution for 15 to 20 minutes. The prepared sections were mounted in glycero-gelatine.

We have used the following substrate solutions:

Alkaline phosphatase: 10 ml. of 1 per cent. sodium veronal (pH 9·2), with 5 mg. sodium naphthyl-phosphate and 10 mg. Echtblau BB (Hoecht). These were incubated at room temperature for 10 to 60 minutes, left in water for 24 hours, colour developed and mounted.

Acid phosphatase: To 5 ml. veronal-acetate buffer (Michaelis), with 0·1 ml. 1 per cent. α-naphthyl phosphate and 3 ml. distilled water was added 1·6 ml. of 'hexazonie' solution (see below). The pH was adjusted with NaOH to 6·5 and the preparation incubated and fixed as above.

Esterase: To 10 ml. disodium phosphate (0·1 M) with 0·5 ml. of hexazonie solution and 0·1 ml. of α-naphthyl acetate, 1 per cent. (w/v) in acetone was added N-NaOH to adjust the pH to 7·4.

The 'hexazonie' solution was prepared as follows:
Sol. A: Sodium nitrite 4 per cent. w/v freshly prepared aqueous solution;
Sol. B: p. fuschine 4 per cent. (w/v) in 2N-HCl;
Mix A and B drop by drop in ratio 1:1 w/v.

RESULTS AND DISCUSSION

ZINC-CONTAINING ENZYMES

Alkaline phosphatase of the kidney: This is localised in the kidney tubules. From observation of the control animal sections we noted activity in the epithelium of the kidney tubules but none in the glomeruli. In sections of the animal organs treated with Zn an increase in colour was noted in relation to the organs of the control. However, in sections of animal organs treated with Cd the colour intensity was lowered.

Alkaline phosphatase of the prostate gland: This was localized in the capillaries of the epithelial tissue. In the sections of the prostate glands of guinea-pigs treated with Zn, colour production was noted in the basal zone of the cylindrical epithelial cells, while in those treated with Cd we noted a much lower alkaline phosphatase activity.

These results indicate that Cd inhibits alkaline phosphatase activity in the kidney and prostate gland of the guinea-pig. This is in accordance with our own previous tests *in vitro* on the serum phosphatase of the guinea-pig and also with the results obtained by Piscator (1966) on rabbits.

OTHER ENZYMES

Acid phosphatase: Localisation was analogous to alkaline phosphatase in the kidney and the prostate gland but with no difference in colour intensity observed in the sections from treated and control animals.

Esterase: In the kidney sections we noted colour production in the 'tubuli cortorti' and 'distal' cells and none in the glomeruli. In the prostate gland the activity was localised in the glandular epithelium. The colour intensity was the same for organ sections from Cd and Zn treated animals and from untreated animals.

The acid phosphatase and esterase activities in the kidneys and prostate glands of guinea-pig did not change after treatment with Zn and Cd.

175

OTHER OBSERVATIONS

The sections of kidney taken from Zn and Cd treated and untreated animals were stained with Haematoxylin Eosin but showed no changes in their structure. We did not observe the specific necrotic effects of Cd on kidney which were cited by other authors (Piscator, 1966; Cameron and Foster, 1963) possibly because exposure to the dose was very short. We think that it would be possible to observe more contrasting reactions than those obtained from our tests. To do this it would be necessary to produce chronic intoxication of the animals in question in order to induce more intense reactions at the molecular level.

REFERENCES

CAMERON, E. & FOSTER, C. L. (1963). *J. Anat.* **97**, 269.
CARROLL, R. E. (1966). *J. Am. med. Ass.* **198**, 267.
COTZIAS, G. C., BORG, D. C. & SELLECK, B. (1961). *Am. J. Physiol.* **201**, 927.
HENNIG, A. & ANKE, M. (1964). *Arch. Tierernähr,* **14**, 55.
PISCATOR, M.-K. L. (1966). Bekmans Tryckerier A.B. Stockholm.
PULIDO, P., KAGI, J. H. R. & VALLEE, B. L. (1966). *Biochemistry, N.Y.* **5**, 17, 1768.
SCHROEDER, H. A., NASON, A. P., TIPTON, I. H. & BALASSA, J. J. (1967). *J. chron. Dis.* **20**, 179.
TABOR, E. C. & WARREN, W. V. (1958). *A.M.A. Archs ind. Hlth,* **17**, 145.

INDUCTION OF THE ENZYMES OF PURINE METABOLISM BY COPPER AND MOLYBDENUM

V. V. KOVALSKY and I. E. VOROTNITSKAYA

Biogeochemical Laboratory, Vernadsky Institute of Geochemistry and Analytical Chemistry, U.S.S.R. Academy of Sciences, Moscow, U.S.S.R.

THE presence of metals in the prosthetic group of xanthine oxidase of various sources has been identified by isolation and further purification of the enzymes. As has already been shown (De Renzo *et al.,* 1953; Green and Beinert, 1953; Richert and Westerfeld, 1953) there is a relation between xanthine oxidase activity and the molybdenum present in the enzyme. The presence of iron has also been demonstrated in the enzyme, the ratio Fe:Mo:FAD in xanthine oxidase preparations isolated from livers of rat, calf and chicken being respectively 8:1:2 (Richert and Westerfeld, 1954), 4:1:1 (Kielly, 1955) and 8:1:1 (Remy *et al.,* 1955). As is shown, xanthine oxidase isolated from bull small intestine contains copper, the most active preparation of this enzyme having a ratio

Fe :Cu :FAD = 17·4 :4·2 :1·0 and the contents of other metals including Mo being inconstant.

It has been demonstrated by Hart and also in our laboratory that xanthine oxidase synthesis may be induced by Mo (Kovalsky and Yarovaya, 1961; Hart and Brau, 1967).

Dependence of xanthine oxidase synthesis in liver and kidney tissues of rats upon the ratio of Mo and Cu in the diet has been studied in our laboratory. Three-week-old male rats were used for the experiment. Copper sulphate and ammonium molybdate were added to the basic diet. The rats were drenched by means of a syringe with a solution of the salts mentioned above in a constant volume of 1 ml. per day. One control and seven experimental groups of rats were used. Rats of the first four experimental groups received 400, 250, 120 and 50 μg, of Mo daily and the remaining three groups 160, 320 and 640 μg. of Cu. The Mo and Cu contents of the diet were determined by chemical techniques (Zn-dithiol [Marshall, 1964] for Mo, diphenylcarbazone for Cu [Lapin and Makarova, 1953]). The Cu to Mo ratios in the diet were 0·2, 0·32, 0·66, 1·6, 8, 16 and 32 respectively. The Cu :Mo ratio in the control group was 4. The experiment was repeated three times with individual examination of each rat. After a month of supplementation of Mo and Cu to the diet, the activity of xanthine oxidase in liver and kidney and of urate oxidase in liver was studied. Uric acid was identified (Eichhorn *et al.,* 1961; Kalckar, 1947) and the concentrations of uric acid, Mo and Cu were determined (Fig. 1).

It has been demonstrated that an increase in dietary Mo level (Cu content being constant) up to Cu/Mo = 1·6 raises xanthine oxidase activity in liver tissue from 13 to 28 and in kidney tissue from 7 to 12 relative units.* Further increase of the amount of Mo causes an inhibition of xanthine oxidase activity. An increase in dietary Cu level (Mo content being constant) to Cu/Mo = 16, also raises xanthine oxidase activity in liver tissue from 13 to 24 and in kidney tissue from 7 to 12 relative units.

Thus, two maxima in xanthine oxidase activity are observed in rat tissue: one at a high Mo level in the diet (Cu content being constant) and the other at high level of Cu (Mo content being constant). On the basis of the above we made the assumption that xanthine oxidase may be induced by an increased level either of Mo or Cu in the diet. This may be explained by the existence of two kinds of enzyme: a Mo- and a Cu-containing xanthine oxidase.

* The decolouration of a 0·1 ml. of 0·00113 M solution of methylene blue per minute in the presence of 1 mg. xanthine at 38° is referred to as a unit of activity.

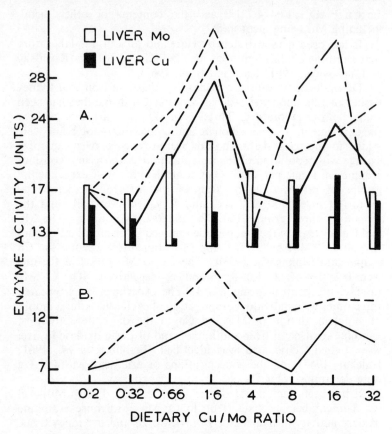

FIG. 1. The influence of the Cu/Mo ratio of the diet of rats on the synthesis of xanthine oxidase, uricase and uric acid in liver (A) and kidney (B) tissue. For definition of units of enzyme activity see text. ————— xanthine oxidase; — - — uricase; — — — uric acid.

As is seen from Figure 1, the Mo-induced xanthine oxidase produces a higher amount of uric acid than the xanthine oxidase induced by Cu. An increase of xanthine oxidase activity in bio-geochemical provinces with high Mo content is known to cause an increase in the concentration of uric acid. Since there is no urate oxidase in humans this causes a high incidence of endemic gout. Under the same conditions, endemic Mo toxicosis in animals is observed (Kovalsky and Yarovaya, 1961 and 1966). The increase of activity of Mo-induced xanthine oxidase cannot be explained by natural selection of a favourable adaptation of the human to

178

environmental conditions since it gives rise to endemic gout (Kovalsky, 1967). The fact that the maximum activity of xanthine oxidase induced by Cu does not correspond to the maximum in uric formation remains unexplained.

An increase of Mo-induced xanthine oxidase activity causes a rise in the concentration of uric acid which in its turn induces the synthesis of urate oxidase without Cu supplementation to the diet (the Cu content of tissues being normal). The induction of urate oxidase may be considered an adaptation to environment since it prevents the accumulation of uric acid in mammalian tissues. The maxima of Cu-induced xanthine oxidase and urate oxidase activity coincide in spite of a relatively low concentration of uric acid. This may be explained by an independent induction by Cu of the Cu-containing urate oxidase. In other words, when Mo is added to a rat diet (with normal Cu content) the induction of urate oxidase may be explained by the influence of uric acid, and when Cu is added (with normal Mo content in the diet) the induction of urate oxidase is caused evidently by an excess of Cu.

The induction of xanthine oxidase and urate oxidase by Mo or Cu may be considered as a model for investigation of endemic effects at the molecular level.

REFERENCES

DE RENZO, E. C., KALEITA, E., HEYTLER, P. G., OLESON, J. J., HUTCHINGS, B. L. & WILLIAMS, J. H. (1953). *Archs Biochem. Biophys.* **45**, 247.

EICHHORN, F., ZELMANOWSKI, S., LEW, E., RUTENBERG, A. & FANIAS, B. (1961). *J. clin. Path.* **14**, 450.

GREEN, D. E. & BEINERT, H. (1953). *Biochim. biophys. Acta*, **11**, 599.

HART, L. & BRAU, R. C. (1967). *Biochim. biophys. Acta*, **146**, 611.

KALCKAR, H. M. (1947). *J. biol. Chem.* **167**, 429.

KIELLEY, R. K. (1955). *J. biol. Chem.* **216**, 405.

KOVALSKY, V. V. (1967). *Dokl. Vaschnil.* 12.

KOVALSKY, V. V. & YAROVAYA, G. A. (1961). *Sh. Obshchey biologii* **22**, No. 3.

KOVALSKY, V. V. & YAROVAYA, G. A. (1966). *Agrokhimija*, 8.

LAPIN, L. N. & MAKAROVA, V. P. (1953). *Pochvovedenie*, 8.

MARSHALL, J. (1964). *Econ. Geol.* **59**, N.1.

REMY, C., RICHERT, D. A., DOISY, R. J., WELLS, I. C. & WESTERFELD, W. W. (1955). *J. biol. Chem.* **217**, 293.

RICHERT, D. A. & WESTERFELD, W. W. (1953). *J. biol. Chem.* **203**, 915.

RICHERT, D. A. & WESTERFELD, W. W. (1954). *J. biol. Chem.* **209**, 179.

METABOLIC ALTERATIONS IN A DIETARY
FLUORIDE TOXICITY

J. W. SUTTIE

Department of Biochemistry, University of Wisconsin, Madison, Wisconsin, U.S.A.

THE ingestion of excessive amounts of dietary fluoride by the laboratory rat produces a number of consistent responses which have been extensively studied and recently reviewed (Davis, 1961; Hodge and Smith, 1965; Smith, 1966). In our laboratory we have been specifically interested in the depression of food intake which is at least to some extent related to an increase in plasma F (Shearer and Suttie, 1967; Simon and Suttie, 1968). This food intake depression is most severe within the first week of F ingestion and by the end of two to three weeks has been to a considerable degree overcome. We have previously postulated (Shearer and Suttie, 1967) that the relationship between food intake and plasma F concentration is an indirect one, mediated through an effect of F on tissue enzyme activity which results in a shift in the concentration of some metabolite(s), and that this altered balance of tissue metabolites, rather than the increase in F concentration, is the signal for the depressed dietary intake. The ability of the animal to increase its dietary intake in the presence of continued plasma and tissue F could then be explained as alterations of metabolic pathways which return the critical metabolites to more normal concentrations.

Although F is a well known inhibitor of many *in vitro* enzyme systems (Hodge and Smith, 1965) there is little data to indicate what metabolic lesions might be present in the tissues of an intact animal fed high concentrations of F in the diet. One method of localizing an alteration in a metabolic pathway is to assay the products and reactants of a series of metabolic reactions and to express these data as a cross-over plot of the pathway. This method has been used extensively in establishing the control points in glycolysis and gluconeogenesis and has been recently reviewed (Newsholme and Gevers, 1967; Scutton and Utter, 1968).

In an attempt to locate points of F inhibition in carbohydrate metabolism, the liver concentration of many glycolytic and some TCA cycle intermediates were analyzed in control rats and in rats fed 450 or 600 p.p.m. F (as NaF) for three days. The data in Figure 1 indicate that in the rats fed F there were small decreases

180

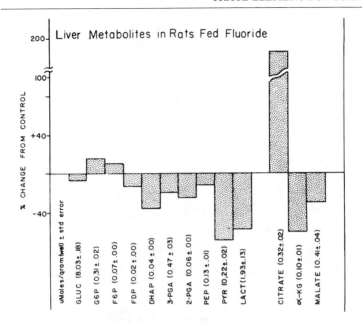

Fig. 1. Liver metabolites in rats fed 600 p.p.m. F. Female, 200 g. rats were fed a 600 p.p.m. F diet for three days and killed at 8 a.m. The values are expressed as the percentage change from the amount found in the control rats for each of the metabolites. The values at the bottom of the graph are the metabolite values for the control rats.

in a number of metabolites, rather large decreases in pyruvate and lactate and a large increase in liver citrate.

The rats fed this level of dietary F not only have a decreased food consumption but also show an altered pattern of consumption. They eat the same number of meals per day but may spend up to twice as much time eating each meal. Because of this we have developed (Suttie, 1968) a programmed pellet dispenser which can force a control rat to consume its daily ration in the identical manner to that exhibited by the F-fed rat. The data shown in Figure 2 indicate that when control rats were forced to consume their diet in the same manner as F-fed animals, the shifts in the metabolite pattern were rather similar to those previously seen as a result of F ingestion. The most pronounced change is that the large increase in liver citrate seen in rats fed F was not seen in the programme-fed animals. The data summarized in Figure 2 also indicate that, as has been previously shown for food intake, the metabolite pattern tends to return to normal values by 16 days.

181

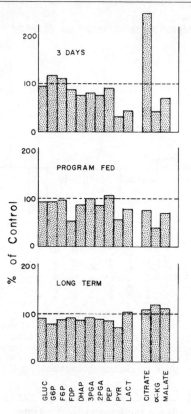

Fig. 2. Effect of fluoride and pattern of intake on rat liver metabolites. Female, 200 g. rats were fed 600 p.p.m. F for three days, or were fed the control diet with the same pattern of intake as was seen in the F-fed rats for three days (programme fed). The long-term group were 200 g. female rats fed a 450 p.p.m. F diet for 18 days. The effects of 450 or 600 p.p.m. F at three days are essentially the same. The values were all obtained at 8 a.m. and are expressed as percentages of the control values. For absolute values see Figure 1.

Although not a true cross-over point, the drop seen in pyruvate and lactate levels would suggest that there may be an effect on the activity of liver pyruvate kinase. This enzyme was found to be rather insensitive to *in vitro* addition of F. However, when rats were fed 600 p.p.m. F for three days, or 14 days, or fed the control diet from the programmed dispenser, the activity of the enzyme in the liver was found to be 67 per cent., 100 per cent. and 64 per cent. of controls.

182

A similar indirect effect of F can be seen in the area of amino acid metabolism. When rats were fed 450 p.p.m. F there was a depression of most plasma amino acids and an elevation of plasma glycine. This change in plasma amino acid pattern could be to a large extent duplicated by feeding control rats with the programmed pellet dispenser and thus forcing them to eat in the same manner as the F-fed rats (Fig. 3).

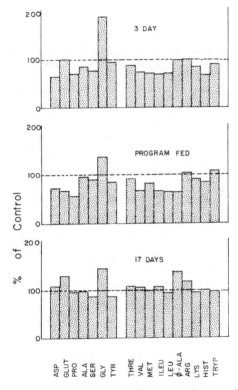

FIG. 3. Effect of fluoride and pattern of intake on plasma amino acids. Female, 150 g. rats were fed 450 p.p.m. F for three or 17 days, or were fed the control diet in the same amount and pattern as seen in F-fed rats for three days (programme fed). The amino acid analyses were performed on pooled plasma obtained at 8 a.m. from five rats in each group. The values are expressed as percentages of corresponding controls.

Thus, it is apparent that a number of metabolic alterations can be seen when rats are fed levels of F which are sufficiently high to produce a chronic toxicity. With the exception of an increase in

183

liver citrate, however, these changes appear secondary to a more direct effect on food intake. This would also appear to be true for the changes in carbohydrate metabolism (Zebrowski and Suttie, 1966) and the liver enzyme changes (Carlson and Suttie, 1966) which we have previously observed. Because of this effect on food intake, the nature of controls used in these experiments is of considerable importance. The effectiveness of the programmed pellet dispenser as an appropriate control can readily be seen from the data on liver enzyme alterations seen in Table I. If a conventional pair-fed group had been the only control included in this experiment it could have erroneously been concluded that F had a direct effect on the level of liver glucose-6-phosphate dehydrogenase.

Table I. *Effect of dietary fluoride and method of feeding on pentose cycle dehydrogenase*

			Enzyme activity	
Group	Weight change g./week	Food intake g./day	Glucose 6-phosphate dehydrogenase	6-phosphogluconate dehydrogenase
			units/mg. protein	
Control	+ 35	13·0	3·53 ± 0·24	4·73 ± 0·37
600 p.p.m. F	− 12	7·0	1·95 ± 0·10	4·24 ± 0·28
Pair fed	− 8	7·2	4·00 ± 2·10	5·21 ± 0·40
Control, fed by programmed dispenser	− 11	6·6	1·39 ± 0·17	3·94 ± 0·28

Six 140 g. rats per group were fed the control or 600 p.p.m. F diet for one week. The pair-fed group was given an amount of diet equal to that eaten by the control group the previous day. The programmed dispenser group received their diet in an intake pattern based on that previously observed for rats consuming 600 p.p.m. F (Suttie, 1968), Values are mean ± S.E.

The effect of F on citrate metabolism is further illustrated in Figure 4. Not only is there an increase in liver citrate but also a temporary increase in blood citrate. These changes occur at the same time that F is exerting an effect on food intake and during the time that the bone citrate content is decreasing. This decrease in bone citrate has been shown to be the result of an increase in the size of bone crystals (Zipkin *et al.*, 1963) which releases previously surface-bound citrate.

In an attempt to explain the increase in blood and liver citrate during F ingestion, a number of experiments were conducted. It could be calculated that about 5 mg. of citrate were removed from the skeleton each day during the first week of F ingestion. It was shown that infusing 3 or 10 mg. citrate per day into the femoral vein had no effect on tissue citrate, nor was the oxidation of an injected

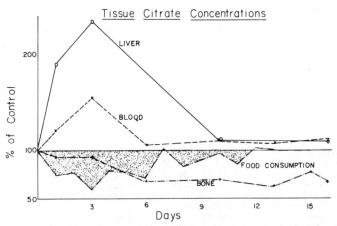

FIG. 4. Changes in tissue citrate concentration with time. Female, 150 g. rats were fed the 450 p.p.m. F diet and animals removed at varying times from one to 16 days. The values are expressed as percentages of the corresponding controls for that day and there were five to six animals/group/day. The shaded area represents the drop in food consumption. Control citrate concentrations were 0·33 μmol./g. wet liver, 0·15 μmol./ml. blood, and 32 μmol./g. dry bone.

dose of [^{14}C]-citrate impaired in F-fed animals. In an isolated perfused liver, an addition of F to the perfusate which was sufficient to cause a change in liver glycolytic intermediates indicative of an inhibition of enolase had no effect on tissue citrate levels. Hac and Freeman (1967, 1969) have also noted an effect of F on serum citrate and have suggested that it may be the result of an increased action of parathyroid hormone. We have, however, found that parathyroid-extomized rats show some increase in liver citrate content when fed F containing diets. It seems clear, therefore, that the citrate effect is not a simple one, and its cause has not been clearly established. However, as it is one of the few effects we have observed that seems to be directly due to F and is not a reflection of altered food intake, it is an observation which may be very important in understanding the basic biochemical lesions resulting from dietary F ingestion.

These studies have indicated that it is possible to observe pronounced effects on the tissue levels of many metabolic intermediates in a trace element toxicity. These changes can be of considerable value in pointing to areas where the element may be exerting its toxic action. These studies also point out that when metabolic alterations are sought in animals with various toxicities and deficiencies, the choice of appropriate controls is all important.

185

We have found that in this situation a normal pair-fed control is not appropriate and can be extremely misleading. The technique of programming the food intake of control animals to the intake of the experimental animals is a relatively simple one which could be applied to a wide variety of similar studies.

Acknowledgements. Previously unpublished data in this paper are from studies carried out in collaboration with Dr T. R. Shearer, Mr Joel LeSaouter, and Mrs Kathleen Nelson.

REFERENCES

CARLSON, J. R. & SUTTIE, J. W. (1966). *Am. J. Physiol.* **210**, 79.
DAVIS, R. K. (1961). *J. occup. Med.* **3**, 593.
HAC, L. R. & FREEMAN, S. (1967). *Am. J. Physiol.* **212**, 213.
HAC, L. R. & FREEMAN, S. (1969). *Am. J. Physiol.* **216**, 179.
HODGE, H. C. & SMITH, F. A. (1965). In *Fluorine Chemistry*, Vol. IV. Ed. Simons, J. H. New York: Academic Press.
NEWSHOLME, E. A. & GEVERS, W. (1967). *Vitams Horm.* **25**, 1.
SCRUTTON, M. C. & UTTER, M. F. (1968). *A. Rev. Biochem.* **37**, 249.
SHEARER, T. R. & SUTTIE, J. W. (1967). *Am. J. Physiol.* **212**, 1165.
SIMON, G. & SUTTIE, J. W. (1968). *J. Nutr.* **96**, 152.
SMITH, F. A. (1966). In *Handbook of Experimental Pharmacology*, Vol. XX: Metabolism of Inorganic Fluoride. Ed. Eichler, O., Farah, A., Herken, H. & Welch, A. D. New York: Springer.
SUTTIE, J. W. (1968). *J. Nutr.* **96**, 529.
ZEBROWSKI, E. J. & SUTTIE, J. W. (1966). *J. Nutr.* **88**, 267.
ZIPKIN, I. F., SCHRAER, R., SCHRAER, H. & LEE, W. A. (1963). *Archs oral Biol.* **8**, 119.

DISCUSSION

Jenkins (Newcastle). Does the level of 600 p.p.m. F affect the taste of the food and is poor appetite merely a consequence? This level of F would cause nausea in man, does it with the rat?

Suttie (Madison). These points are difficult to solve. We have shown under carefully controlled conditions that the infusion of F into the femoral vein causes appetite depression as well as F in the food. Furthermore, there is a sharp break in the effects of increasing F concentration upon food consumption. At 200 or 300 p.p.m. F there are seldom effects on appetite; with 400 p.p.m. F effects on appetite depression are marked. It is difficult to believe that the animal can distinguish between 300 and 400 p.p.m. solely on the basis of taste, although it may be possible. With regard to nausea, the animal doesn't eat because it doesn't feel well. It doesn't feel well because it is faced with an abnormal balance of metabolites but we have no idea what these are. I think this is true of many conditions in which there is poor food consumption.

Spencer (Hines, Illinois). You mentioned uncertainty about

Freeman's suggestion that F might influence parathyroid function. We have been unable to confirm that a prolonged high-F intake in man induces hyperparathyroidism. We have found a decrease in serum phosphorus but serum and urinary calcium are not indicative of this condition.

STUDIES ON AN ALTERNATIVE PATHWAY FOR THE METABOLISM OF FLUOROACETATE

P. F. V. WARD

A.R.C. Institute of Animal Physiology, Babraham, Cambridge, U.K.

WHEN an animal is given sufficient fluoroacetate the most important metabolic route followed is its 'lethal synthesis' to fluorocitrate and the blocking of the citric acid cycle with the consequent death of the animal. If animals are given sub-lethal doses of fluoroacetate much less is known about its metabolism. Reports so far indicate that trace amounts given to sheep, rats and guinea pigs cause atrophy of the testes and affect bone structure (Mazzanti *et al.,* 1964; Peters *et al.,* 1969). Recently Lovelace, Miller and Welkie (1968) isolated fluoroacetate and fluorocitrate from forage crops grown in an environment high in F, thus giving impetus to the study of alternative routes for the metabolism of organic F compounds at a level where the blocking of the citric acid cycle is not of overwhelming consequence.

Because plants can tolerate much higher levels of fluoroacetate than animals and because of the need to isolate milligram quantities of metabolites for structural studies, the lettuce was chosen for preliminary studies with ^{14}C-labelled fluoroacetate. The plants were incubated in one of three ways: (1) for 43 hours with sodium $[1-^{14}C]$-acetate (1 mg./kg. wet wt.); (2) for 21 hours with sodium fluoroacetate (50 mg./kg. wet wt.) followed by 43 hours with sodium $[1\ ^{14}C]$-fluoroacetate (50 mg./kg. wet wt,); or (3) for 43 hours with sodium $[1-^{14}C]$-fluoroacetate (50 mg./kg. wet wt.). Each plant was placed in a desiccator with its roots immersed in 300 ml. water and air was bubbled through the water at 20 to 30 ml./min. The effluent gas was dried with $CaCl_2$ and the CO_2 absorbed in δ-2-methoxyethanol-ethanolamine (2:1, v/v).

In the $[^{14}C]$-acetate treated plants, about 15 per cent. of the radioactivity was expired as CO_2 and this was unaffected by the

187

presence of fluoroacetate, but in the [^{14}C]-fluoroacetate treated plants only 0·5 per cent. of the radioactivity was expired as CO_2. This shows that fluoroacetate at this level is not noticeably blocking the citric acid cycle and that very little of it is being metabolized via the cycle. Citrate levels in the fluoroacetate treated plants were about 30 μmol./g. dry wt., around double those of untreated plants. This indicates that aconitase is being partially inhibited though the increase in citrate level is low when compared with animals where a 10 to 50 times increase is common.

The plants treated with [^{14}C]-fluoroacetate were then examined to ascertain the distribution of radioactivity. All the radioactivity could be extracted by ethanol-water mixtures (Canvin and Beevers, 1961). Aqueous solutions of this extract would pass through a cationic exchange column (Amberlite IR120) but the radioactivity was completely absorbed on an anionic exchange column (Amberlite IRA400) showing that it was entirely associated with acidic material. Continuous ethereal extraction of the acidified radioactive extract removed about half the radioactivity. This was found to be about 4 per cent. fluorocitrate and the remainder unchanged fluoroacetate. This illustrates that plants, like animals, are capable of synthesizing fluorocitrate from fluoroacctate. Either due to the localization of the newly synthesized fluorocitrate or to its relative inability to inhibit plant aconitase this synthesis is not as lethal as in animals. Whether the metabolism of fluoroacetate to fluorocitrate is a minor pathway in animals is not known because of its toxic effects but it is certainly a minor pathway in lettuce.

The remaining half of the radioactivity which is associated with the bulk of the metabolized fluoroacetate was not extractable from water by ether and was in one or more highly acidic involatile compounds that were insoluble in organic solvents and not gas-chromatographable. These compounds could not therefore be carboxylic acids or their fluoro derivatives. Attempts to isolate the radioactive components by preparing their trimethylsilyl derivatives were unsuccessful. The plant extract was first purified on a Sephadex G–25 column, the radioactivity being eluted with low molecular weight compounds. This was followed by further purification on cellulose columns (Isherwood and Barrett, 1967) from which the radioactive components eluted with the sugar phosphates. Two dimensional paper chromatography of the eluate revealed two radioactive spots, one much more intense than the other. They contained no phosphorus. The preparation of milligram quantities of both components was possible by exploiting their unusual behaviour on an Amberlite IR 120 cationic exchange column in the H^+ form. When eluted from such a column with water they emerge only after the bulk of the plant material has been eluted and are thus separated from it and also from other material tightly absorbed by the column. Both components give characteristic infra-red absorptions showing carboxyl and substituted amide groups. The major component contains 7·1 per cent. nitrogen and 2 nitrogen atoms per carboxyl group. Structural studies are proceeding.

REFERENCES

CANVIN, D. T. & BEEVERS, H. (1961). *J. biol. Chem.* **236**, 988.
ISHERWOOD, F. A. & BARRETT, F. C. (1967). *Biochem. J.* **104**, 922.
LOVELACE, J., MILLER, G. W. & WELKIE, G. W. (1968). *Atmos. Environ.* **2**, 187.
MAZZANTI, L., LOPEZ, M. & BERTI, M. G. (1964). *Experientia*, **20**, 492.
PETERS, R. A., SHORTHOUSE, M. & WARD, P. F. V. (1969). *Biochem. J.* **113**, 9P.

DISCUSSION

Suttie (Madison). Do you confirm Miller's report that there is fluoroacetate and fluorocitrate in the plant or is most of the fluorine inorganic?

Ward (Babraham). Only on one occasion have we found fluorocitrate in the plant. The total F content is greater than can be accounted for as inorganic F and thus the balance is organic.

Suttie (Madison). From Miller's report others have concluded that fluorocitrate is the most important agent causing fluorosis. The Boyce-Thompson group are, however, unable to reproduce Miller's observations. No one investigating field cases of fluorosis in cattle has ever seen anything resembling fluoroacetate or fluorocitrate poisoning. From the levels of fluoroacetate and fluorocitrate that Miller reports as being present in the plant one would expect animals to be flopping over! This kind of thing does not happen. Miller also reports an increased citrate in horses fed these compounds—we find that inorganic fluoride gives the same result. These points are important and are in doubt.

Ward (Babraham). I keep an open mind on these points at the moment and this is why I am looking for other fluorine-containing metabolites. I have quite definitely failed to find fluorocitrate in plants from a farm at Peterborough where there is severe fluorosis. A high proportion of the total fluoride is organic but it is not proving easy to identify the F-containing compounds.

Suttie (Madison). Is the organic fluoride acid-hydrolysable and could it be a peptide?

Ward (Babraham). It is only hydrolized by strong acid but it may well be a peptide or a component associated with a peptide.

Bell (Oak Ridge). Do you expect the same toxicity from feeding fluoroacetate or fluorocitrate to ruminants as you get in the rat? Will not the rumen bacteria break down these compounds?

Ward (Babraham). Bacteria are well known for the ease with which they break the C—F bond. Lindsay and Annison have however found that large doses of fluoroacetate will kill a sheep, so rumen bacteria obviously cannot completely degrade large doses.

RECENT STUDIES ON THE INTERACTIONS BETWEEN VITAMIN E AND SELENIUM

A. T. DIPLOCK

University of London, Royal Free Hospital School of Medicine, London, U.K.

WHEN vitamin E and Se are absent from the diet of weanling rats there is a rapid development of hepatic necrosis with a high incidence of mortality. This condition was studied in detail by Schwarz (1962) who described three stages in the development of the disease: (1) an initial period of 7 to 12 days, (2) a latent phase of 10 to 15 days, in which profound morphological alterations are detectable by electron microscopy and, (3) a brief terminal phase characterized by gross macroscopic liver damage. Schwarz considers that the respiratory defect that develops during the latent phase may be due to a defect in the lipoyl dehydrogenase moiety of the α-oxoglutarate dehydrogenase system, although attempts to demonstrate the presence of stoichiometric amounts of Se in the enzyme were unsuccessful. In contrast to the suggestion that Se has a specific role as a cofactor in an enzyme system, it has been suggested by several workers that the function of Se is simply that of a powerful biological antioxidant (Hamilton and Tappel, 1963; Shimazu and Tappel, 1964; Caldwell and Tappel, 1965; Tappel, 1965; Witting and Horwitt, 1964). If this is so, liver necrosis produced by witholding Se from vitamin E-deficient rats must be caused by proliferation of lipid peroxidation.

In the present communication I will first describe some experiments designed to subject the antioxidant hypothesis of vitamin E and Se action to a rigorous test, then discuss some recent work on interactions between Se and vitamin E, and finally attempt to formulate a tenative new hypothesis for the mode of action of vitamin E and Se.

THE ANTIOXIDANT HYPOTHESIS OF ACTION OF VITAMIN E AND SELENIUM

The work to be discussed formed a part of a large programme designed to test the antioxidant theory of vitamin E and Se action. This work has been published in full elsewhere (Green *et al.*, 1967a; Diplock *et al.*, 1967a; Diplock *et al.*, 1967b; Green *et al.*, 1967b) and has been reviewed recently by Green and Bunyan (1969). It is necessary to digress here to discuss the function of vitamin E, before returning to a discussion of the inter-relationships between the vitamin and Se. The concept of the possible function of vitamin E as a biological free-radical scavenger was put forward by a number of early workers to account for the exacerbating effect of polyunsaturated fatty acids in some vitamin E deficiency diseases. It was presented in its most sophisticated form by Tappel (1962) who postulated that the antioxygenic capacity of tocopherol could be greatly enhanced by the formation of a chain of redox couples involving ascorbate, glutathione reductase and NADPH (Fig. 1).

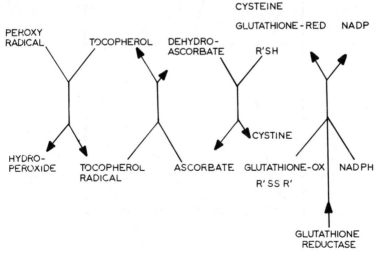

FIG. 1. Postulated *in vivo* redox couples (Tappel, 1962).

191

In this scheme it would be expected that as the amount of the initial substrate (polyunsaturated fatty acid) is increased a greater number of cycles of oxidation and reduction of tocopherol would occur. Experiment 1 was therefore designed to examine the destruction of α-tocopherol in an *in vitro* peroxidizing system and the effect of synergism with ascorbate on this system. α-Tocopherol (0·1 mg./ml.) and, where appropriate, ascorbic acid (3 mg./ml.) were dissolved together (with the aid of a drop of 80 per cent. v/v ethanol) in the substrate MOME; (MOME = methyl esters of maize oil fatty acids, stripped of unsaponifiable material and molecularly distilled). The solutions were dispersed in 1 ml. portions in micro-beakers and heated in an oven at 100°. Replicate beakers from each group were withdrawn at intervals and analysed for α-tocopherol, ascorbic acid and peroxides. The results are given in Figure 2. The significant observation in this

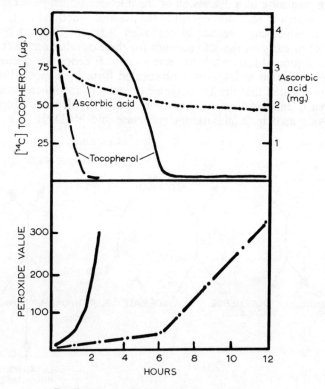

FIG. 2. Peroxidation in maize oil methyl esters.

experiment is that α-tocopherol was destroyed continuously even during the period of maximal protection by the secondary antioxidant; destruction occurred before the end of the induction period. Furthermore, whether tocopherol was present alone or with synergist, its rate of decomposition was markedly increased as the rate of peroxidation accelerated.

In Experiment 2, the peroxidation of liver homogenates from vitamin E-deficient rats given differing amounts of unsaturated fatty acids, was studied; this peroxidation is catalysed by metal ions and other factors as might be expected to occur *in vivo*. Twelve 6-month-old, vitamin E-deficient, female rats were each given orally 500 μg. ^{14}C-α-tocopherol. After 48 hours the rats were divided into two groups: one group received a vitamin E-deficient casein diet containing 10 per cent. of methyl oleate and the other the diet containing 10 per cent. of methyl esters of cod-liver oil fatty acids (CLOME) that had been stripped of unsaponifiable material and molecularly distilled. Five days later, pairs of rats from each group were killed and an homogenate (10 per cent. w/v in 0·1 M phosphate buffer, pH 7·4) was made from each pair of livers; samples were taken for determination of malondialdehyde and [^{14}C] α-tocopherol. The remainder of the homogenate was incubated in air at 37° for 2 hours and malondialdehyde and [^{14}C] α-tocopherol were measured again. The results are given in Table I and show that homogenates prepared from animals receiving unsaturated lipid peroxidized significantly more than homogenates prepared from controls and that during the process more tocopherol was destroyed.

Table I. *Peroxidation and tocopherol decomposition during the incubation of liver homogenates prepared from rats given dietary methyl oleate (OLME) or cod-liver oil methyl esters (CLOME).*
(Mean values with standard deviations)

Dietary lipid	No. of pairs of rats	α-Tocopherol*		α-Tocopherol loss on incubation (%)	Malondialdehyde (μg./g. tissue/h)
		At zero time (μg.)	After 2 hr. (μg.)		
10% OLME	3	2·72 ± 0·73	2·14 ± 0·36	21·3 ± 11·5	53·3 ± 1·2
10% CLOME	3	2·35 ± 0·76	1·16 ± 0·41†	50·5 ± 4·8†	64·7 ± 2·8‡

* [^{14}C] α-tocopherol recovered from 15 ml. of 10% (w/v) homogenate.
† Significantly different from group A (P < 0·05).
‡ Significantly different from group A (P < 0·01).

Experiment 3 was designed to study the rate of destruction of α-tocopherol in rats given either a diet containing a large amount of polyunsaturated fatty acids or a diet containing relatively saturated fat. Twenty, three-month-old, vitamin E-deficient male rats were each given 50·4 μg. [^{14}C] α-tocopherol orally on two successive days. After an interval of 24 hours the rats were divided into two groups; the rats in one group were given the vitamin E-deficient casein diet with the addition of 10 per cent. CLOME and the rats in the other group were given the diet with 10 per cent. of methyl oleate added. Rats were killed in pairs from each group, 3, 12, 18, 24 and 31 days after beginning the experimental regimen, and the entire carcasses analysed for [^{14}C] α-tocopherol. The results, given in Figure 3, show that there was no evidence for peroxidative destruction of α-tocopherol.

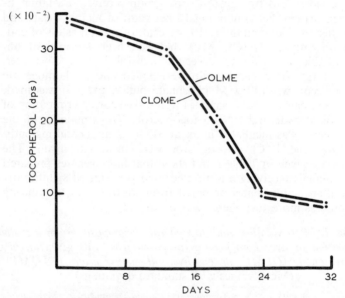

FIG. 3. Decay of total body [^{14}C] tocopherol in rats given 10% dietary OLME or CLOME.

This brief reference to work that forms a part of a large series of experiments indicates the conclusion that we reached when all the work was evaluated. Using the same basic technique we studied the metabolism of small amounts of [^{14}C] α-tocopherol in a number of situations, both those involving Se and those that do not, known to lead to pathological signs of vitamin E-deficiency disease, all of which, it has been supposed, are caused by lipid peroxidation. In all the experiments we were unable to find any

Table II. *Effect of Se deficiency on the metabolism of [^{14}C] D-α-tocopherol in weanling rats given a fat-free necrogenic casein diet, with and without supplements of methyl oleate (OLME) and maize oil fatty acid methyl esters (MOME)*

The rats used for analysis were housed individually in tube cages. There were six in each group and each rat received 52·5 μg. (6412 dps) [^{14}C] D-α-tocopherol. They were killed after 11 days on the experimental diets and combined in pairs for analysis (three such analyses per group). Results are given as means with standard deviations. The rats used for survival and necrosis studies were housed in groups in cages.

Group	Dietary supplement	Liver Wt (g.)	Liver [^{14}C]α-tocopherol (dps/g.)	Liver [^{14}C] metabolites (total dps)	Carcass Wt (g.)	Carcass [^{14}C]α-tocopherol (total dps)	Carcass [^{14}C] metabolites (total dps)	Incidence of necrosis*	Survival time (days)	No. of survivors at 78 days†
1	None	4·17 ± 0·70	9·2 ± 2·4	6·4 ± 2·9	62·4 ± 15·3	641 ± 112	418 ± 68	3‡/15	75·9 ± 7·0	13/15
2	0·05 p.p.m. Se	4·46 ± 0·61	8·1 ± 3·9	3·6 ± 1·9	65·0 ± 15·6	527 ± 121	349 ± 184	0/8	78·0 ± 0	8/8
3	2% OLME	4·16 ± 0·46	10·0 ± 2·5	3·7 ± 0·8	63·7 ± 17·7	509 ± 119	368 ± 66	0/8	—	—
4	2% OLME + 0·05 p.p.m. Se	4·17 ± 0·55	8·3 ± 2·0	4·0 ± 1·4	63·8 ± 15·7	508 ± 128	395 ± 74	—	—	10/16
5	2% MOME	3·93 ± 0·85	9·7 ± 1·9	4·6 ± 2·7	64·9 ± 15·4	594 ± 111	303 ± 49	7§/16	70·2 ± 10·8	—
6	2% MOME + 0·05 p.p.m. Se	4·47 ± 0·38	6·6 ± 1·3	3·9 ± 1·0	63·7 ± 14·1	526 ± 41	352 ± 105	0/7	78·0 ± 0	7/7

dps, disintegrations/sec.
* No. of rats in group in denominator; no. with necrosis in numerator.
† No. of rats in group in denominator; no. of survivors in numerator.
‡ Three other rats in this group had post-necrotic scarring.
§ One other rat in this group had post-necrotic scarring.

195

evidence for an increase in lipid peroxidation as judged by: (1) an increase in the rate of destruction of α-tocopherol and, (2) an increase in the level of lipid peroxides in the tissues, as measured by a sensitive iodimetric technique. Thus in nutritional hepatic necrosis, for example, we studied the metabolism of radioactive tocopherol in the pre-necrotic, 'latent' phase, as defined by Schwarz (1962). Table II shows that, when a trace amount of [14C] α-tocopherol was given to rats fed a vitamin E- and Se-deficient diet, and a similar diet supplemented with 0·05 p.p.m. Se, there was no alteration in the [14C] α-tocopherol found in the liver and remainder of the carcass after 11 days, indicating that the rate of destruction of tocopherol was not greater in those rats that would subsequently have died from liver necrosis. Furthermore, the addition of 2 per cent. of CLOME to the diet did not alter the amount of [14C] α-tocopherol recovered, although it did substantially increase the incidence of the disease.

THE POSSIBLE FUNCTION OF α-TOCOPHEROL IN RELATION TO Se AND NONHAEM-Fe PROTEINS

The doubt cast on the validity of the antioxidant hypothesis necessitates a complete re-evaluation of the role of vitamin E and Se in mammalian biochemistry. Any hypothesis that is advanced must take into consideration four relevant observations. First, the action of α-tocopherol may be mimicked *in vivo* by certain synthetic antioxidants. Secondly, certain lesions such as nutritional liver necrosis in the rat or exudative diathesis in the chick may be prevented by administration of either Se or tocopherol. Thirdly, these lesions may be partially prevented by a high dietary level of S-amino acids. Fourthly, many of the vitamin E deficiency syndromes are exacerbated by dietary polyunsaturated fatty acids.

It has been noted that Schwarz (1962) considers that liver necrosis in the rat is caused by a mitochondrial lesion that develops during the latent phase of the disease and this is confirmed by his observations of widespread mitochondrial (and endoplasmic reticulum) damage at this stage in the disease (Piccardo and Schwarz, 1958). With regard to the functioning of the endoplasmic reticulum, α-tocopherol is thought to protect against the toxicity of CCl_4 (Gallagher, 1961) which may be associated with the functioning of the microsomal cytochrome P_{450} system (McLean, 1967). Furthermore, microsomal oxidative demethylation, which involves cytochrome P450 appears to be decreased in vitamin E deficiency (Carpenter, 1967).

Consideration of these and other relevant observations has led us to speculate (Diplock *et al.*, 1968) that α-tocopherol may function as a membrane localised antioxidant, but that the protection afforded is not to unsaturated fatty acyl residues but to susceptible active centres containing S or Se. A tempting candidate for a specific class of catalytically active compounds containing such potentially sensitive active sites is the nonhaem-Fe proteins. Such proteins are known to be involved in hydroxylation and other reactions in the endoplasmic reticulum, in electron transfer in mitochondria and in nucleotide metabolism in the nucleus. However, in order to account for the effects of Se, such a hypothesis would require the existence of a new class of nonhaem-Fe proteins, containing selenide instead of sulphide at the active centre. It is known that sulphide can be replaced *in vitro* by selenide in at least one nonhaem-Fe protein (Tsibris *et al.*, 1968) and we understand (Orme-Johnson, W., personal communication) that the selenide in such modified proteins is exceptionally susceptible to autoxidation. This therefore encouraged us to determine whether or not livers of rats, maintained with Se, contain the element in the selenide form. The experiment to be described is a study of the effect of α-tocopherol *in vivo,* and of antioxidants *in vitro*, on the oxidation state of radioactive Se in rat liver.

Twenty-four weanling male Wister rats were given an 8·3 per cent casein, vitamin E-deficient diet formulated to contain the minimum of Se needed to prevent liver necrosis. Four weeks later the diet was changed to a vitamin E- and Se-deficient torula yeast diet in order to lower tissue Se levels further, and after a further week the rats were divided into two groups of 12: each rat in one group received orally 10 mg. α-tocopherol daily for three days; the rats in the other group received no α-tocopherol. The torula yeast diet was continued during this three day period in which the liver tocopherol level of the rats in the first group would be expected to rise, providing protection for any labile Se compounds formed from ^{75}Se on the second and third days when all rats received orally 18μg (equivalent to 34 μCi.) of ^{75}Se as sodium selenite. All the rats were killed on the fourth day and their livers were removed at once and placed in ice-cold 0·25M sucrose containing 5mM mercaptoethanol and 100 μg./ml. α-tocopherol. The livers of each group of rats were divided into three lots of four and two 5 g. portions were taken from each lot, one portion being homogenized in 45 ml. of 0·25M sucrose, the other portion in 0·25M sucrose containing 100 μg./ml. α-tocopherol and 5mM mercaptoethanol. Mitochondrial, microsomal and supernatant fractions were prepared and the particulate fractions resuspended

Table III. *Distribution of ^{75}Se among rat liver cell fractions*

	Vit. E-deficient Rats 158 ± 8 $8 \cdot 36 \pm 0 \cdot 21$		Vit. E-supplemented Rats 171 ± 10 $8 \cdot 57 \pm 0 \cdot 23$	
Mean Rat Weight (g.) Mean Liver Weight (g.)	Liver homogenized in 0·25 M sucrose with Antioxidants*	Liver homogenized in 0·25 M sucrose	Liver homogenized in 0·25 M sucrose with Antioxidants*	Liver homogenized in 0·25 M sucrose
Total liver ^{75}Se (dps/liver x 10⁻⁴)	13·5	14·4	13·3	12·2
% of total liver ^{75}Se in:				
(a) Mitochondrial Fraction	23·3	26·5	28·7	27·2
(b) Microsomal Fraction	14·4	13·2	15·5	13·1
(c) Supernatant Fraction	23·7	22·4	23·3	25·3
(d) Cell Debris Fraction	38·6	37·9	32·5	34·4

* Mercaptoethanol, 5 mM
α-tocopherol, 100 μg./ml.

Table IV. *Apparent oxidation state of Se in rat liver*
MITOCHONDRIAL FRACTION
(Results are expressed as % of total ^{75}Se in the fraction)

	Vit. E-deficient Rats			Vit. E-supplemented Rats		
	'Selenide'	'Selenite'	'Selenate'	'Selenide'	'Selenite'	'Selenate'
Liver homogenized in 0·25 M sucrose with Antioxidants	25·5 ± 1·6‡	25·2 ± 1·5	49·3 ± 2·9	36·1 ± 5·1§	20·0 ± 13·7	43·9 ± 9·5
Liver homogenized in 0·25 M sucrose	10·7 ± 1·8*	25·2 ± 4·9	64·1 ± 6·5	12·9 ± 1·1†	34·6 ± 6·7	52·5 ± 5·6

*, ‡ significantly different $P > 0 \cdot 01$.
†, § significantly different $P > 0 \cdot 001$.
‡, § significantly different $P > 0 \cdot 05$.

in sucrose containing the antioxidants where appropriate. ^{75}Se was counted in portions of the fractions in a 2 in. well-crystal counter. After counting, each fraction was acidified with concentrated HCl and N_2 passed for 15 minutes to drive off volatile Se; foaming was prevented by the addition of a few drops of octanol. The dilution due to the acid was without effect on the counting efficiency. When the acidified mixture had been counted, Zn dust was added, the mixture flushed with N_2 as before, and the residue recounted.

Table III shows the amount of ^{75}Se recovered from the livers and the distribution of ^{75}Se among the subcellular fractions. In this and subsequent figures the results are the means of triplicate values. Neither dietary supplementation with vitamin E nor *in vitro* addition of antioxidants affected the recovery or intracellular distribution of total ^{75}Se.

Table IV shows the apparent oxidation state of Se in the mitochondrial fractions of the livers treated in the way described. Three possible oxidation states are delineated: the portion of the total ^{75}Se which is volatile on acidification we have tentatively called 'selenide'; the portion of the total that requires reduction with Zn and acid before it is acid-volatile we have called 'selenite' and the remainder, which presumably contains Se of higher oxidation states, we have, for convenience, called 'selenate'. It will be seen that the addition *in vitro* of antioxidants significantly increased the proportion of 'selenide' recovered, and that the administration of α-tocopherol to the rats significantly increased even further the proportion of Se present as 'selenide'. This increase in 'selenide' appears to have been at the expense both of 'selenite' and 'selenate'.

Table V presents similar data for the microsomal fractions and, as in the case of the mitochondria, both antioxidants *in vitro* and α-tocopherol *in vivo* increased the proportions of 'selenide' found. Here, these increases are accompanied by a significant fall in the proportion of 'selenite'.

Table VI presents the data for the supernatant fractions. Here the *in vitro* antioxidants have caused a significant increase in the 'selenide' found, although the relative amount is still smaller than in the other two fractions. Dietary supplementation with vitamin E was without effect on the proportion of 'selenide'.

Figure 4 summarizes the data given in the previous three figures on the *in vivo* effect of vitamin E. In addition it can be seen from the Figure that, while only a small portion of the total ^{75}Se in the mitochondrial and microsomal fractions is dialysable,

Table V. *Apparent oxidation state of Se in rat liver*

MICROSOMAL FRACTION

(Results are expressed as % of total ^{75}Se in the fraction)

	Vit. E-deficient Rats			Vit. E-supplemented Rats		
	'Selenide'	'Selenite'	'Selenate'	'Selenide'	'Selenite'	'Selenate'
Liver homogenized in 0·25 M sucrose with Antioxidants	30·2 ± 1·7‡	16·1 ± 2·3	53·7 ± 3·9	43·1 ± 1·7§	3·6 ± 2·1	53·2 ± 1·4
Liver homogenized in 0·25 M sucrose	16·8 ± 5·5*	21·5 ± 2·2	61·7 ± 3·3	22·1 ± 5·8†	17·3 ± 3·9	60·6 ± 15·3

*, ‡ significantly different P   0·01
†, § significantly different P   0·05.
‡, § significantly different P   0·001.

Table VI. *Apparent oxidation state of Se in rat liver*

SUPERNATANT FRACTION

(Results are expressed as % of total ^{75}Se in the fraction)

	Vit. E-deficient Rats			Vit. E-supplemented Rats		
	'Selenide'	'Selenite'	'Selenate'	'Selenide'	'Selenite'	'Selenate'
Liver homogenized in 0·25 M sucrose with Antioxidants	14·1 ± 1·5‡	17·4 ± 3·5	68·5 ± 4·5	18·3 ± 2·4§	11·9 ± 2·9	70·3 ± 5·2
Liver homogenized in 0·25 M sucrose	8·1 ± 0·5	10·3 ± 0·9	81·7 ± 0·7†	6·1 ± 0·5†	7·6 ± 0·9	86·3 ± 0·7

*, ‡ significantly different P > 0·01.
†, § significantly different P > 0·001.
‡, § no significant difference.

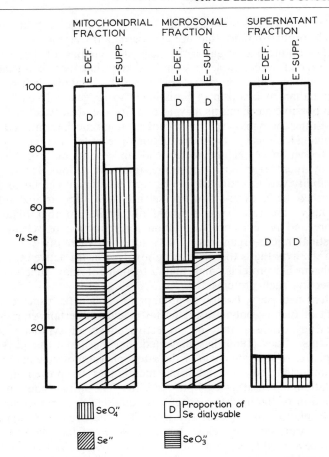

FIG. 4. Summary of experimental data showing the effect of Vitamin
E on the apparent oxidation state of Se and the dialysability of the Se.

the greater part of the Se in the supernatant fraction is dialysable.
These results indicate that the Se in the supernatant fraction is
probably not bound to protein, unlike that in the mitochondrial
and microsomal fractions.

   The results that we have presented show four main features:
first, Se has been found to be present in rat liver mitochondria and
endoplasmic reticulum in at least three oxidation states; secondly,
the amount of acid-labile Se, tentatively identified as 'selenide', is
dependent on the vitamin E status of the animal; thirdly, the
'selenide' is very susceptible to *in vitro* oxidation, and fourthly,

while the mitochondrial and microsomal 'selenide' appears to be largely protein-bound, that in the supernatant fraction is not.

The nature and origin of the 'selenide' remains for the present a matter of speculation. It seems unlikely that there is a general intracellular reduction of selenite since, by analogy with S, the mammalian metabolism of Se is likely to be generally oxidative. Two possible mechanisms may account for the presence of reduced Se. Either there may be a specific intracellular mechanism, perhaps involving tocopherol, for the reduction of selenite, or, alternatively, the reduction of selenite to an acid-labile form may be carried out by microorganisms prior to intestinal absorption. The second possibility was investigated in a further experiment similar to that described here, except that the selenite was administered intravenously: the result was substantially similar to that obtained before and no evidence was found for reduction of selenite by intestinal micro-organisms. Our results are therefore consistent with the hypothesis that Se may be involved in the active centre of nonhaem-Fe proteins, and that α-tocopherol may function by protecting such proteins.

It is necessary, finally, to attempt to explain the exacerbating effect of dietary polyunsaturated fatty acids in certain vitamin E deficiency diseases and the protective effects of synthetic antioxidants. Lucy (1966) has suggested that the liquid-like physical properties of the side-chain of the α-tocopherol molecule may play an important role in stabilising membranes by preventing the oxidation of unsaturated lipids *in vivo*. The initial stage in the oxidation of the lipid in a tocopherol-deficient membrane may be the formation of a radical by interaction between two adjacent polyunsaturated fatty acids. In the presence of tocopherol, such a process might be prevented by the physical barrier formed between the reactive species by the tocopherol side-chain. In these circumstances, the expenditure of tocopherol would not be accelerated by the addition of large amounts of dietary polyunsaturated fatty acids as would be expected if the protection afforded were by classical antioxidant means since the physical intervention of tocopherol that is envisaged would not involve its destruction. The synthetic antioxidants however could act in the classical manner by acting as proton donors to prevent the proliferation of radicals formed among the membrane lipids in the absence of vitamin E. Whether the second stage in the peroxidation process, the interaction of fatty acyl radicals with molecular oxygen, occurs, remains a matter of speculation. However, it would seem unlikely that peroxides are ever formed *in vivo* in the absence of α-tocopherol, since we were unable to find any evidence, using a sensitive microiodimetric technique, for the presence of large amounts of lipid peroxides in tissues of vitamin E-deficient animals that had been given dietary polyunsaturated fatty acids (Bunyan, Murrell *et al.*, 1967; Bunyan, Green *et al.*, 1968).

In summary, therefore, we suggest that tocopherol may be bound closely into membrane structures by its side-chain and possibly has some function in promoting membrane stability. The chromanol ring may then be able to provide a redox function toward S and Se in the manner proposed.

Acknowledgements. The work described in the first section of this paper was carried out in collaboration with Drs J. Green and J. Bunyan; that described in the second section was done in collaboration with Professor J. A. Lucy and Professor H. Baum. I am indebted to Beecham Research Laboratories Ltd for generous gifts of vitamin-deficient diets.

REFERENCES

BUNYAN, J., GREEN, J., MURRELL, E. A., DIPLOCK, A. T. & CAWTHORNE, M. A. (1968). *Br. J. Nutr.* **22**, 97.

BUNYAN, J., MURRELL, E. A., GREEN, J. & DIPLOCK, A. T. (1967). *Br. J. Nutr.* **21**, 475.

CALDWELL, K. A. & TAPPEL, A. L. (1965). *Archs Biochem. Biophys.* **112**, 196.

CARPENTER, M. P. (1967). *Fedn Proc. Fedn Am. Socs exp. Biol.* **26**, 475.

DIPLOCK, A. T., BAUM, H. & LUCY, J. A. (1968). *Proc. 5th Meet. Fedn Europ. Biochem. Socs.* p. 121.

DIPLOCK, A. T., BUNYAN, J., MCHALE, D. & GREEN, J. (1967a). *Br. J. Nutr.* **21**, 103.

DIPLOCK, A. T., GREEN, J., BUNYAN, J., MCHALE, D. & MUTHY, I. R. (1967b). *Br. J. Nutr.* **21**, 115.

GALLAGHER, C. H. (1961). *Nature, Lond.* **192**, 881.

GREEN, J. & BUNYAN, J. (1969). *Nutr. Abstr. Rev.* **39**, 321.

GREEN, J., DIPLOCK, A. T., BUNYAN, J., MCHALE, D. & MUTHY, I. R. (1967a). *Br. J. Nutr.* **21**, 69.

GREEN, J., DIPLOCK, A. T., BUNYAN, J., MUTHY, I. R. & MCHALE, D. (1967b). *Br. J. Nutr.* **21**, 497.

HAMILTON, J. W. & TAPPEL, A. L. (1963). *J. Nutr.* **79**, 493.

LUCY, J. A. (1966). *Biochem J.* **99**, 57P.

MCLEAN, A. E. M. (1967). *Biochem. J.* **103**, 13P.

PICCARDO, M. G. & SCHWARZ, K. (1958). In *Liver Function.* Ed. Braner, R. W. pp. 528–534. Washington, D.C.: American Institute of Biological Sciences.

SCHWARZ, K. (1962). *Vitams Horm.* **20**, 463.

SHIMAZU, F. & TAPPEL, A. L. (1964). *Science, N.Y.* **143**, 369.

TAPPEL, A. L. (1962). *Vitams Horm.* **20**, 493.

TAPPEL, A. L. (1965). *Fedn Proc. Fedn Am. Socs exp. Biol.* **24**, 73.

TSIBRIS, J. C. M., NAMTREDT, M. J. & GUNSALUS, I. C. (1968). *Biochem. biophys. Res. Commun.* **30**, 323.

WITTING, L. A. & HORWITT, M. K. (1964). *J. Nutr.* **82**, 19.

DISCUSSION

Fleming (Wexford). When plants are fed selenite after a while red elemental Se is found adjacent to the roots and this is attributed to microbiological reduction of the selenite. Is it possible that what you think is selenide in the rat liver may be elemental Se?

Diplock (London). This is certainly possible; it is why I have referred to 'selenide' in quotation marks throughout my paper.

Schwarz (Long Beach). I am glad that others have joined the attempts we have been making since 1943 to point out that vitamin E and Se aren't really antioxidants but they do something much more positive in intermediary metabolism. Secondly, I would like to say that the lipoyl dehydrogenase theory we postulated some nine years ago was only a suggestion but we still think that vitamin E and Se are concerned in the suture between the Krebs cycle and the electron transport chain. There is a theory that the site of binding of labile Fe in enzymes of the ferredoxin type (i.e. the sulphydryl groups) may be associated with Se in intermediary metabolism in this area between succinic acid and the cytochromes. I discussed this possibility with Dr Beinert some time ago. He had tried to find Se in some of these enzymes but in none of the naturally occurring ferredoxins had he ever found a signal which would indicate the presence of Se. This does not exclude the possibility that Se may be there *in vivo* but gets in and out easily in an exchange reaction with S.

Ganther (Louisville). Can you offer an explanation of the action of Se, vitamin E and antioxidants in protecting the rat against metal induced necrosis of the liver? This effect you have clearly demonstrated in your recent work with Ag.

Diplock (London). This is puzzling; I can only guess that Ag is complexing Se so that it is prevented from entering its normal functional sites.

BIOPOTENCY OF ORGANOSELENIUM COMPOUNDS: SOME BASIC REGULARITIES IN THE RELATIONSHIP BETWEEN STRUCTURE AND BIOPOTENCY IN SERIES OF MONOSELENO- AND DISELENO-DICARBOXYLIC ACIDS AND SELENA-MONOCARBOXYLIC ACIDS

K. SCHWARZ

Laboratory of Experimental Metabolic Diseases, Medical Research Programs, Veterans Administration Hospital, Long Beach, California, and Department of Biological Chemistry, School of Medicine, University of California, Los Angeles, California, U.S.A.

A SIGNIFICANT but frequently neglected aspect of trace element function is presented by the fact that different compounds derived from an element can have greatly different biopotencies, and pass through different metabolic pathways. Large quantitative differences are found in the effectiveness of various selenium compounds tested against dietary liver necrosis in the rat (Schwarz and Foltz, 1958; Schwarz, 1961). Purified concentrates of a natural organic form of Se (Factor 3) from kidney powder showed a 50 per cent. effective dose level (ED_{50}) of 0·72 μg. of Se in 100 g. of diet (Schwarz, 1961) while the ED_{50} for selenite-Se was 2·2 μg. per cent. Many synthetic organic Se compounds were almost completely inactive. Representative earlier findings are shown in Table I.

Table I. *Relative activities of selenium compounds against dietary necrotic liver degeneration* (Schwarz, 1961)

	ED_{50},* μg % Se
Factor 3	·7
Sodium selenite	2·2
Selenocystine	2·4
Benzeneseleninic acid	6·7
Selenouracil	ca.60
Phenylselenide	134
Selenium (grey modification)	Inactive (> 300)
4-Carboxybenzeneseleninic acid	Inactive (> 300)

* The effective dose level, in μg. per 100 g. of diet, required for 50% protection.

A sizeable effort has been made in our laboratory over the past 10 years, in collaboration with Professor Arne Fredga and his associates at the Institute of Organic Chemistry of the University of Uppsala, Sweden, to clarify the relationships between structure and biopotency of organic Se derivatives. The final aim of these investigations is the synthesis of highly effective Se compounds with low toxicity which could be useful in the treatment of diseases such as muscular dystrophy, liver necrosis, degenerative myocarditis and other clinical equivalents of Se-responsive diseases in animals.

In assessing the biopotency of series of organic Se derivatives, selenite-Se has been used as a standard. Potencies presented in Figures 1 to 4 and Table II are expressed in percentage of potency of selenite-Se (for details see Schwarz and Fredga, 1969a). Thus far the activity of over 700 substances has been determined; almost 400 of these originated in Professor Fredga's institute. The rest were largely prepared in our own laboratory.

A fragment of the accumulated results is presented here to illustrate some of the structural principles which determine the

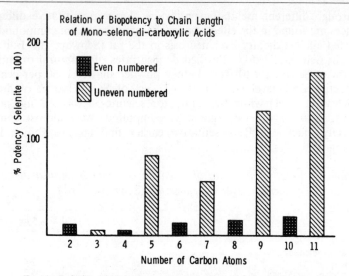

FIG. 1. Relation of biological potency to chain length of monoseleno-dicarboxylic acids, $HOOC\text{-}(CH_2)_n\text{-}Se\text{-}(CH_2)_n\text{-}COOH$ (Schwarz and Fredga, 1969a).

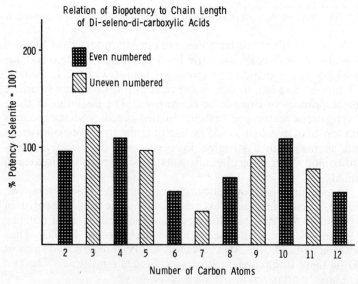

FIG. 2. Relation of biological potency to chain length of diseleno-dicarboxylic acids, $HOOC\text{-}(CH_2)_n\text{-}Se\text{-}Se\text{-}(CH_2)_n\text{-}COOH$ (Schwarz and Fredga, 1969a).

potency of organo-Se derivatives in the prevention of Se-responsive deficiency diseases. The following three types of compounds are discussed:

I. $HOOC-(CH_2)_n-Se-(CH_2)_n-COOH$
     Monoseleno-dicarboxylic acids.
II. $HOOC-(CH_2)_n-Se-Se-(CH_2)_n-COOH$
     Diseleno-dicarboxylic acids.
III. $CH_3-(CH_2)_m-Se-(CH_2)_n-COOH$
     Selena-carboxylic acids.

In the series of symmetrical monoseleno-dicarboxylic acids (formula I) the first three members (acetic to butyric acid) show very low activity (Fig. 1). From valeric to undecanoic acid a clear-cut *alternating* effect is observed; the even numbered acids are rather inactive and those with uneven numbers are potent.

Results with analogous diseleno-dicarboxylic acids,

$$HOOC-(CH_2)_n-Se-Se-(CH_2)_n-COOH,$$

are fundamentally different (Fig. 2). There is no alternating effect. The first three members are biologically active with an optimum at the C_3 level. In both the mono- and the diseleno-dicarboxylic acid series a minimum of potency is seen at chain length C_7 and a maximum at chain length C_{10} to C_{11}.

The basic regularities seen in the series of the monoseleno-dicarboxylic acids and the basic difference between mono- and diseleno compounds can be explained in simple physicochemical terms. Alternating effects between even and uneven numbered chain lengths of carboxylic acids are well-known in physical chemistry (for example, in melting points and crystal structure). They are related to the fact that in *uneven* numbered fatty acids the carboxyl group is on the *same* side of the zigzag chain of carbon atoms as the terminal methyl group, at least in the solid state. In compounds with *even* numbered chains the carboxyl group is on the *opposite* side of the terminal methyl group. In analogy the Se atom in the monoseleno-dicarboxylic acids (formula I) with an *even* number of C chains extending to both sides, is on the *same* side as the carboxyl group. With *uneven* numbered C chains the terminal carboxyl groups are on the *opposite* side of the Se atom.

The bond angle of the $-C-Se-C-$ configuration differs from that of the $-C-C-C-$ group. The latter group has an angle of $109°\ 28'$. The bond angle of the former has not been accurately determined but is likely to be in the vicinity of $100°$. The monoseleno-compounds are bent at the centre of the molecule in consequence of the smaller bond angle at the $-C-Se-C-$ bridge, while in a chain of C atoms the bond angles compensate for each other.

Because of this apex in their centre, monoseleno-dicarboxylic acids with uneven numbered C chains may be more accessible to binding on cell surfaces, protein or enzyme sites. Their carboxyl groups are opposite to the Se atom. The compounds with even numbered C chains have carboxyl groups which may be less accessible since the apex produced by the Se atom in the centre of the molecule interferes.

These considerations do not pertain to the dicarboxylic acids (formula II) which contain two adjacent Se atoms at the centre. They have a basically different spatial configuration since their two C chains are not situated in the same plane. In analogy to disulphides, the diselenide group (–C–Se–Se–C–) is not linear but contains a torsion angle (dihedral angle) between the two Se atoms (Pauling, 1960; Kessler and Rundel, 1968).

The regularities seen in the structure/activity relationships of monoseleno-dicarboxylic acids (formula I) are also evident in studies with selena-carboxylic acids (formula III). The latter are fatty acids which contain a single Se atom in lieu of a $-CH_2-$ group in the C chain (Schwarz and Fredga, 1969b).

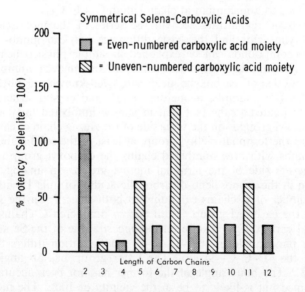

FIG. 3. Effect of the length of the carbon chains on the potency of selena-carboxylic acids containing equal numbers of carbon atoms in the alkyl and acid moieties of the molecule, $CH_3-(CH_2)_m-Se-(CH_2)_n-COOH$, m = n (Schwarz and Fredga, 1969b).

Selena-carboxylic acids (Fig. 3) containing straight chains with equal numbers of C atoms on both sides of the Se atom (m = n) are identical to the corresponding monoseleno-dicarboxylic acids (formula I) except that like the monoseleno-dicarboxylic acids they show very low activity at chain lengths of three and four C atoms. A large difference in potency appears between chain lengths C_4 and C_5. The alternating effect is seen between C_5 and C_{12}, with *even* numbered C chains showing *low* and *uneven* numbered C chains showing *high* activity. An optimum of activity is seen at chain length C_7.

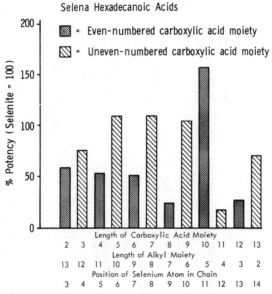

FIG. 4. Effect of the carboxylic acid moiety and the length of the alkyl moiety on the potency of selena-hexadecanoic acids in the prevention of dietary liver necrosis, $CH_3-(CH_2)_m-Se-(CH_2)_n-COOH$, m (from left to right) varying from 12 to 1, and n (from left to right) varying from 2 to 13 (Schwarz and Fredga, 1969b).

Analogous but more complex results were obtained with series of selena-pentadecanoic and hexadecanoic acids comprising all possible positions of the Se atom in the C chains; several other series of selena-carboxylic acids varying in chain lengths from 4 to 33 atoms were also tested. As an example, results with the selena-hexadecanoic acid series are shown here (Fig. 4). Two main phenomena can be distinguished:

209

Table II. *Effect of alkyl groups with chain lengths C_1 to C_6 on the potency of selena carboxylic acids* (Schwarz and Fredga, 1969b)

Series	Carboxylic Acid (Amide) Moiety	Alkyl Group					
		CH_3	C_2H_5	C_3H_7	C_4H_9	C_5H_{11}	C_6H_{13}
		Potency (% of potency of selenite)					
4-Selena-carboxylic acid amides	Propionic acid amide	138	96	27	20	116	122
Selena-capramides	Decreasing from C_8 to C_3	73	51	10	38	116	96
12-Selena-carboxylic acids	Undecanoic acid	96	65	24	17	137	69
12-Selena-carboxylic acid amides	Undecanoic acid amide	224	127	36	43	137	137
Selena-pentadecanoic acids	Decreasing from C_{13} to C_8	84	55	26	19	110	55
Selena-hexadecanoic acids	Decreasing from C_{14} to C_9	—	71	27	17	157	105
Means:		(123)	78	25	26	129	97

1. The carboxylic moiety of the molecule affects biological potency as long as the Se atom is located close to the carboxyl group. Up to a distance of 9 to 10 C atoms, the alternating effect of the carboxylic C chain is observed, *uneven* numbered chains showing *high* and *even* numbered chains showing *low* activity.

2. When the Se atom is further removed from the carboxyl group the nature of the alkyl moiety strongly affects biological potency. High activity is seen at the C_5 and very low activity at the C_4 and C_3 chain lengths of the alkyl residue. This finding is analogous to that exhibited by the corresponding monoseleno-dicarboxylic acids and the selena-carboxylic acids with equal numbers of C atoms on both sides.

The strong inhibitory effect of alkyl residues with C_3 and C_4 C chains and the activating effect of C_5 chains were observed in several other series of selena-carboxylic acids (Table II). A fully satisfactory explanation of the phenomenon is currently not available.

The compounds described in this paper include several which clearly exceed selenite-Se in biopotency. Substances of high potency have also been found in other, very different categories of organo-Se derivatives. The results presented here have led to a number of important questions. Among others, the problem arises whether the compounds are metabolically converted into a specific, cofactor-like Se derivative or whether they are effective as applied. Experiments to clarify this point have been carried out with some closely related substances differing greatly in potency, such as the C_4 and C_5 monoseleno-dicarboxylic acids presented above (Southwell-Keely and Schwarz, 1970). Thus we hope to gain new insight into the mode of action of Se.

Acknowledgement. This work was supported in part by U.S. Public Health Service Research Grant AM 08669.

REFERENCES

KESSLER, H. & RUNDEL, W. (1968). *Chem. Ber.* **101**, 3350.
PAULING, L. (1960). *The Nature of the Chemical Bond.* pp. 134–136. Ithaca, N.Y.: Cornell University Press.
SCHWARZ, K. (1951). *Proc. Soc. exp. Biol. Med.* **77**, 818.
SCHWARZ, K. (1961). *Fedn Proc. Fedn Am. Socs exp. Biol.* **20**, 666.
SCHWARZ, K. & FOLTZ, C. M. (1958). *J. biol. Chem.* **233**, 245.
SCHWARZ, K. & FREDGA, A. (1969a). *J. biol. Chem.* **244**, 2103.
SCHWARZ, K. & FREDGA, A. (1969b). Submitted for publication.
SOUTHWELL-KEELY, P. T. & SCHWARZ, K. (1970). To be published.

DISCUSSION

Diplock (London). How do you think α-tocopherol fits into this scheme?

Schwarz (Long Beach). I think α-tocopherol is converted into an active form, and that it is effective in the electron transfer scheme somewhere closely related to NADH or NAD$^+$. (Schwarz, K. and Baumgartner, W. 1970. *Harry Steenbock Symposium on the Fat Soluble Vitamins.* In press.) We have strong evidence that tocopherol at this site shifts the oxidation-reduction state and thus the ratio of NAD$^+$/NADH$^+$ and this in turn determines electron flow. We also believe that the effect of Se is close to this electron transfer site related to SH or vicinyl SH sites. We can produce respiratory decline artificially in vitamin E supplemented mitochondria by giving Cd or arsenite and we can show this to be preventable by vitamin E.

SELENIUM METABOLISM. MECHANISMS FOR THE CONVERSION OF INORGANIC SELENITE TO ORGANIC FORMS

H. E. GANTHER

Department of Biochemistry, School of Medicine,
University of Louisville, Louisville, Kentucky, U.S.A.

THE mechanisms for incorporating inorganic selenite into organic compounds containing C–Se or S–Se bonds have been investigated in this laboratory for a number of years. The biosynthesis of volatile dimethyl selenide is a major metabolic pathway for detoxifying selenite in the rat and proved to be a useful model system for studying reductive pathways of Se utilization. Studies with liver slices (Ganther, 1963) demonstrated that this process occurred directly in animal tissues at a rate commensurate with the rate *in vivo*, thus dispelling any lingering suspicion that the observed biosynthesis of organoselenium compounds in animals might be the work of intestinal microflora. Further studies (Ganther, 1966) with cell-free extracts provided additional evidence for a bio-synthetic pathway in liver involving one or more enzymes. A very significant finding with the cell-free system was an absolute, specific requirement for glutathione. The specific role of glutathione in the biosynthesis of dimethyl selenide is the main subject of this report.

The first step was to determine the fate of selenite in systems containing thiols. Painter (1941) had proposed a direct reaction between thiols and selenious acid as follows:

$$4 \text{ RSH} + \text{H}_2\text{SeO}_3 \longrightarrow \text{RSSeSR} + \text{RSSR} + 3\text{H}_2\text{O}$$

Besides having a possible bearing on the enzymic synthesis of dimethyl selenide, the reaction was worthy of study because it concerned the direct conversion of inorganic selenite to an organic form in which Se is bound to two S atoms. Studies with a variety of thiols established the validity of Painter's reaction (Ganther, 1968) and the compounds thus formed are referred to as seleno-trisulphides. Formation of selenotrisulphide linkages is clearly relevant to the non-enzymic binding of selenite by proteins containing sulphydryl groups, and selenotrisulphide formation has indeed been demonstrated in reduced RNase treated with selenious acid (Ganther and Corcoran, 1969).

Based on this information it seemed likely that a seleno-trisulphide derivative of glutathione, formed non-enzymically, might be the first intermediate in the biosynthesis of dimethyl selenide. Moreover, glutathione reductase might then catalyse an NADPH-linked reduction of the selenotrisulphide, forming a labile reduced selenol or selenopersulphide which would undergo rapid methylation in the presence of S-adenosyl methionine:

$$\text{H}_2\text{SeO}_3 \xrightarrow{\text{ GSH }} \text{GSSeSG} \xrightarrow[\substack{\text{glutathione} \\ \text{reductase}}]{\text{NADPH}} [\text{GSSeH}] \xrightarrow{\text{S–AM}} (\text{CH}_3)_2\text{Se}$$

Certain characteristics of the enzyme system (Ganther, 1966) provide circumstantial evidence in support of such a pathway: (1) a high specificity for glutathione; (2) the apparent involvement of NADPH-linked enzymes; (3) a marked sensitivity to arsenite, a potent inhibitor of dithiol enzymes such as glutathione reductase.

Some direct evidence for the above pathway has now been obtained. First, selenodiglutathione (GSSeSG) is readily converted to dimethyl selenide at a rate comparable to that for selenious acid, thus meeting one criterion for an intermediate. Although the conversion of GSSeSG to dimethyl selenide occurred to an appreciable extent when glutathione was omitted from the system, the requirement for glutathione for optimal activity persisted. Secondly, GSSeSG is in fact an excellent substrate for glutathione reductase. When the products of the reaction between glutathione and selenious acid (Ganther, 1968) at a concentration of 0·13 mM were incubated in a cuvette at 25°, pH 5·6, in the presence of 0·27 mM NADPH, oxidation of NADPH and formation of Se° occurred immediately after the addition of 6 μg. of yeast glutathione reductase. In the absence of enzyme no Se° was formed and only a very slow decrease in optical absorption at 340 nm occurred as a result of NADPH destruction in the slightly acidic medium. GSH at a concentration of 0·26 mM did not cause any decomposition of selenodiglutathione. It is concluded that glutathione reductase catalyses the NADPH-linked reduction of GSSeSG to an unstable intermediate such as GSSeH, which decomposes to Se°. In the presence of a methylating system the unstable product might be efficiently converted to dimethyl selenide; Se° itself is very poorly utilized. Although most of these observations are consistent with the pathway described it is only meant to serve as a working hypothesis to guide further experiments.

REFERENCES

GANTHER, H. E. (1963). Dissertation, University of Wisconsin.
GANTHER, H. E. (1966). *Biochemistry, N.Y.* **5,** 1089.
GANTHER, H. E. (1968). *Biochemistry, N.Y.* **7,** 2898.
GANTHER, H. E. & CORCORAN, C. (1969). *Biochemistry, N.Y.* **8,** 2557.
PAINTER, E. P. (1941). *Chem. Rev.* **28,** 179.

DISCUSSION

Diplock (London). You stated that α-tocopherol had no effect on your system. Did you merely study the effects *in vitro* or did you examine the vitamin E status of your animals?

Ganther (Louisville). At first we studied it *in vitro* as we hoped that by adding tocopherol we could abolish the need for anaerobic conditions, but this was not so. Later, animals fed normal diets but given high levels of vitamin E were compared with animals given no supplementary vitamin E; again there was no difference. Ascorbic acid also had no effect on the *in vitro* system but we have not yet tried the effect of vitamin E deficiency.

Diplock (London). I was wondering if there was a parallel between your experiments and mine and whether in fact I may be measuring as my acid-labile compounds some similar compound to one of your intermediates.

Ganther (Louisville). I believe you added mercaptoethanol to your homogenates and observed the formation of more reduced

214

species. This would be predictable if selenite was around and was converted to selenotrisulphide. If there is a large excess of thiol these selenotrisulphides decompose to other species and eventually to elemental Se so what would be formed is hard to say.

Schwarz (Long Beach). When Steekol first made the observations that selenite reacted with sulphydryl groups his assessment was that he had 4 SH groups reacting with 1 atom of Se. We have devised a method whereby you can make the 4– and the 2–SH compounds in parallel. Can you say if the reaction product you use in your enzyme reaction is truly the di-form or could there not be an intermediate that would make it easier to postulate a free radical type of reaction?

Ganther (Louisville). We can rule out tetra-glutathione as a reaction product. We showed by elemental analysis that what we had was selenodicysteine and presumably other compounds of this stoichiometry. At the end of the reaction we believe we have selenodicysteine and presumably, by analogy, seleno-diglutathione. If tetra-compounds were present you would certainly have a marked increase in the ultraviolet absorption spectrum and we see intermediates in spectrophotometric observations of the reaction which do have a high extinction and which decay to give the final reaction products.

EFFECT OF SELENIUM IN THE HAMSTER

D. M. HADJIMARKOS

Department of Preventive Dentistry,
University of Oregon Dental School, Portland, Oregon, U.S.A.

CHRONIC selenium toxicity in man resulting from the daily consumption of locally produced foodstuffs containing small amounts of Se constitutes an important public health problem which has remained virtually unexplored (Hadjimarkos, 1968; Hamilton and Beath, 1964; Rosenfeld and Beath, 1964).

It is well known that, among the common laboratory animals, rats are the most resistant to chronic selenosis. The present investigation was designed to study the response of hamsters to Se intake. No such data are presently available.

MATERIAL AND METHODS

Thirty weanling, male golden hamsters were equally divided into a control and two experimental groups and kept individually in cages with raised screen bottoms in an air-conditioned room. All animals consumed Purina chow. The water supply of the two experimental groups contained 3 p.p.m. of either selenite-Se or selenate-Se. Water intake was measured accurately as described previously (Hadjimarkos, 1966). Food intake was not measured.

RESULTS AND DISCUSSION

The findings in Table I demonstrate that hamsters possess an increased resistance to Se intake compared with rats. All animals survived the experimental period. Furthermore, the Se-treated animals gained as much weight as the controls, indicating that all animals consumed the same quantity of food. Water intake by hamsters on selenate-Se was reduced considerably.

Table I. *Effect of selenium intake in the golden hamster. (The experiment lasted for 4 weeks. The significance of the differences between the mean values was tested by using 'Student's' t test.)*

Variable	Control	Selenite-Se	Selenate-Se
No. of animals	10	10	10
No. of survivors	10	10	10
Mean initial weight (g.)	33·6 ± 0·8*	33·6 ± 0·9	33·9 ± 0·5
Mean final weight (g.)	92·7 ± 1·7	91·4 ± 1·7†	92·2 ± 2·1†
Mean water intake (ml.)	12·4 ± 0·7	10·9 ± 0·6†	9·9 ± 0·3‡
Selenium intake (mg./kg. body wt/day)		0·36	0·32

* Standard error. † Not statistically significant from the control, $P > 0.05$.
‡ Statistically significant from the control, $P < 0.01$.

In a previous experiment rats which drank water containing 3 p.p.m. selenite-Se consumed the same amount of Se/kg. of body weight/day as the hamsters in the present study, shown in Table I, but they developed typical symptoms of chronic selenosis (Hadjimarkos, 1966). These included significant ($P < 0.001$) reductions in weight gain and in food and water consumption; there was also a 13 per cent. mortality.

The superior tolerance of hamsters to Se intake may be utilized in studies which aim to determine the long-term effects of increased levels of Se in inducing liver tumours or producing other pathological changes. Such studies in the past have been hindered when rats were used because of numerous early deaths from Se toxicity (Tinsley *et al.*, 1967; Schroeder, 1967). Hamsters may also prove more useful than rats for studying the effect of Se on dental caries. Results from three epidemiological studies, conducted by independent investigators, among children in the states of Oregon, Wyoming, Montana, and South Dakota indicate that continuous consumption of small amounts of Se from locally produced food-stuffs during the period of tooth development increases the prevalence of caries (Hadjimarkos, 1965, 1968, 1969; Hadjimarkos and Bonhorst, 1958; Ludwig and Bibby, 1969; Tank and Storvik, 1960). Experiments with rats provided additional support to these findings (Buttner, 1963).

Se may increase caries by changing the chemical make-up of the protein components of enamel during the period of tooth development; Se is known to be incorporated readily into the protein fraction of many tissues. Experimental evidence has suggested that the initial attack in dental caries appears to involve the protein of the enamel (Darling, 1963).

REFERENCES

BUTTNER, W. (1963). *J. dent. Res.* **42**, 453.
DARLING, A. I. (1963). *J. dent. Res.* **42**, 488.
HADJIMARKOS, D. M. & BONHORST, C. W. (1958). *J. Pediat.* **52**, 274.
HADJIMARKOS, D. M. (1965). *Archs envir. Hlth*, **10**, 893.
HADJIMARKOS, D. M. (1966). *Experientia*, **22**, 117.
HADJIMARKOS, D. M. (1968). In *Advances in Oral Biology*, vol. 3, p. 253. Ed. Staple, P. H. New York: Academic Press.
HADJIMARKOS, D. M. (1969). *Caries Res.* **3**, 14.
HAMILTON, J. W. & BEATH, O. A. (1964). *J. agric. Fd Chem.* **12**, 371.
LUDWIG, T. G. & BIBBY, B. G. (1969). *Caries Res.* **3**, 32.
SCHROEDER, H. A. (1967). *J. Nutr.* **92**, 334.
ROSENFELD, I. & BEATH, O. A. (1964). In *Selenium*, p. 279. New York: Academic Press.
TANK, G. & STORVIK, C. A. (1960). *J. dent. Res.* **39**, 473.
TINSLEY, I. J., HARR, J. R., BONE, J. F., WESWIG, P. H. & YAMAMOTO, R. S. (1967). In *Selenium in Biomedicine*, p. 141. Ed. Muth, O. M. Westport, Connecticut: Avi Publishing.

DISCUSSION

Schwarz (Long Beach). I believe the incorporation of Se into the matrix protein of enamel is a logical explanation of these effects, but in my experience the amounts of Se needed to get into this situation, as with horn and hair, are always very close to the severely toxic dose level. I point this out because the levels of Se excretion shown in the human populations which initially stimulated your search for the effects of Se are not very unphysiological and are not the result of dose levels similar to those that you have applied to experimental animals. The amount excreted in the urine of your children never reached more than 0·08 p.p.m. In our experience of Se in urine in man this is within the physiological level. You may have been led to a theory that is fine in experimental animals by data from man which is not showing that Se toxicity is a true problem. Do you have any other evidence of toxicity in these children that gave rise to the development of the theory that there is an effect of Se on caries?

Hadjimarkos (Portland, Oregon). Nobody knows what set of symptoms are characteristic of chronic Se toxicity in children. In the late nineteen-thirties the U.S.. Public Health Service conducted studies among farm people populations in the seleniferous areas of South Dakota and Nebraska and they listed the most prominent symptom as being a high incidence of dental caries and this started my investigations. On the basis of present evidence we know that when the 24-hour urine specimen contains 0·1 p.p.m. Se and above, there is the indication that the individual has consumed dangerous amounts of Se. This has been published by Rosenfeld and Beath and also by Glover of Cardiff who stated that when the urine of workers in the selenium industry contained more than 0·1 p.p.m. Se they were withdrawn from the process causing exposure.

SELENIUM AND OESTROGENIC PASTURES

KENNETH O. GODWIN

Division of Nutritional Biochemistry, C.S.I.R.O.,
Kintore Avenue, Adelaide, South Australia

SUBTERRANEAN clovers were introduced into Australia about 1830; their use as a pasture species began about 100 years later, at first slowly, followed by a virtual explosion in 1950 to 1960. Today they are an almost indispensable source of feed over millions of acres of Australia. Early in the nineteen-forties there was the rather sudden, widespread appearance of infertility associated with flocks grazing such pastures; this led to the recognition of 'clover disease', a problem that continues to engage the attention of many Australian workers.

In 1946 Bennetts, Underwood and Shier suggested that clover

218

infertility might be due to oestrogen-like compounds in the plants; subsequently these compounds have been identified as the iso-flavones formononetin, biochanin A and genistein. Present evidence points to formononetin being the most significant oestrogen due to its relative solubility.

During investigations into Se metabolism in this laboratory it became apparent that in areas where Se-deficiency was found, as revealed by abnormal ECG patterns in grazing flocks, the dominant pastures were often subterranean clovers. Subsequent analyses showed that the Se status of both flocks and pastures in such areas was low. Clover pastures were in the range of 0·02–0·07 p.p.m. and whole blood Se gave values between 0·02–0·04; these values we consider to be at most one-fifth of normal.

The hypothesis that a relationship exists between Se and oestrogenic pastures was tested by setting up a field trial involving 400 maiden ewes. They comprised 2 x 100 from different 'non-clover' areas and 200 born to ewes on a clover-dominant property. Five group treatments were used:

A   Control
B   50 mg. Se once before mating
C   10 mg. Se every two weeks
D   100 i.u. Vit. E (intramuscular injection)
E   Treatments C and D combined.

A further division was made, the ewes being divided equally into mobs of 200 to run, throughout the experiment, on clover pasture ('oestrogenic', mainly Yarloop,—*Trifolium subterranean* L.) or grass ('non-oestrogenic').

Phyto-oestrogen levels in the clover-dominant paddock at the beginning, the mid-point and the end of the experiment were, formononetin 0·15, 0·28 and 0·24 per cent., genistein 0·32, 0·62 and 0·30 per cent., and biochanin A 0·048, 0·58 and 0·64 per cent.

The experiment ran for two years since oestrogenic effects do not usually show the first year.

Blood and milk Se levels were followed in ewes and lambs. Lamb weights were recorded through to the season after birth.

It was found that the single 50 mg. drench raised the level of blood Se for two to three months but the lamb derived no benefit; this was consistent with the absence of a rise in milk Se in this group. On the other hand, 10 mg. Se every two weeks led to the maintenance of 'normal' blood Se. Lambs born to these ewes had raised blood Se and were significantly heavier; these findings were consistent with the presence of a rise in milk Se in the corresponding ewes.

219

Vitamin E appeared not to influence Se levels in the tissues but it led to significantly better growth of lambs born to the treated ewes.

The most important finding was that the single 50 mg. drench of Se did influence oestrogenic infertility. During the second year the percentage fertilities for the five treatment groups (*vide supra*) were A = 34, B = 66, C = 59, D = 51 and E = 50. Whilst all the treatment groups appeared higher than the untreated (group A) the difference only showed at the significant level (P < 0·05) between A and B.

Between the two years a significant oestrogenic effect, causing infertility, developed in the mob running on the clover pasture. Overall fertility on both pastures for the first year (there was no difference between pastures) was 51·7 per cent.; for the grass pasture alone this rose to 73·1 per cent. (P < 0·01) the second year, whereas the mob on clover pasture the second year showed a 56·6 per cent. fertility. Comparing this with the grass pasture-fed ewes the second year it shows as a significant oestrogenic effect (P < 0·01). Treatment effects were absent from the ewes on grass pasture both years.

Examination of the performance of individual ewes suggested that the effect of Se was two-fold: (1) it allowed ewes to lamb the second year when they were barren the first, and (2) it prevented ewes from becoming infertile after the first year.

There appears to be no ready explanation for this effect of Se in ewes grazing clover dominant pastures. There may be some point in comparing the findings with those of Hartley (1963) in New Zealand, though there has never been any suggestion that Hartley was dealing with an oestrogenic problem.

Attempts are being made to obtain similar effects on oestrogenic infertility by supplying Se to the ewes in other ways.

REFERENCES

BENNETTS, H. W., UNDERWOOD, E. J. & SHIER, F. L. (1946). *Aust. vet. J.* **22**, 2.
HARTLEY, W. J. (1963). *Proc. N.Z. Soc. Anim. Prod.* **23**, 20.

THE ROLE OF NON-HAEM IRON IN LIPID PEROXIDE FORMATION AND DRUG OXIDATION IN MICROSOMES AND THE EFFECTS OF IRON OVERLOAD

E. D. WILLS

Department of Biochemistry, Medical College of St Bartholomew's Hospital, London, U.K.

SUSPENSIONS of microsomes prepared from livers of 4- to 6-month-old rats form lipid peroxide slowly when incubated at 37° but the rate of peroxide formation and oxygen uptake is speeded up markedly by the addition of NADPH or ascorbate in a low concentration (Wills, 1969a).

Lipid peroxide formation in presence of NADPH or ascorbate is strongly inhibited by addition of metal chelating agents such as EDTA, o-phenanthroline or desferrioxamine in concentrations of 0·2 mM or less. A rapid rate of peroxide formation may, however, be restored by addition of ferrous or ferric iron in a very low concentration (10^{-5}M). The effect of Fe is specific and no other metal can replace it adequately (Wills, 1969b).

Washing the microsomes free of chelating agents also restores the capacity to form peroxide. No measurable quantity of Fe is removed by treatment with chelating agent and these experiments indicate that a non-haem form of Fe, firmly bound in the preparations, possibly to protein or nucleic acid, is an essential component of the microsomal system catalysing lipid peroxide formation (Wills, 1969b). 'Non-haem' Fe forms approximately 30 per cent. of the total Fe determined in rat liver microsomes although it is unlikely that all the non-haem Fe is involved in the peroxidation process.

It is well established that the microsomal fraction of liver contains a large proportion of the total ferritin and to examine the possibility that lipid peroxide formation depends to a certain extent on stored Fe, groups of 8- to 10-week-old mice were injected with 5 mg. Fe per mouse (average weight 43 g.). At daily intervals microsomes were prepared from pooled groups of livers from three mice and determinations were made of the non-haem Fe, total Fe, protein, rates of lipid peroxide formation in presence of ascorbate and of NADPH. As it has been shown (Wills, 1969c) that lipid peroxide formation in the microsomal fraction leads to the loss of capacity of the microsomes to carry out hydroxylations,

221

the rates of oxidative demethylation of aminopyrine and *p*-chloromethylaniline were also measured.

Within 48 hours of Fe injection (5 mg. Fe as iron dextran) the non-haem Fe content was increased almost four times, from $6\cdot80 \pm 3\cdot59$ to $27\cdot48 \pm 7\cdot99$ whilst the total Fe increased by a similar factor, from $19\cdot78 \pm 7\cdot61$ to $73\cdot05 \pm 24\cdot27$, all figures recorded as mμmol. Fe/mg. microsomal protein. The Fe content did not change significantly over the duration of the experiment which was usually 12 days and the protein content of the microsomal fraction was not significantly altered by Fe injection. A small but significant increase, approximately 6 per cent., resulted in the rate of lipid peroxidation in presence of NADPH but a much larger increase of peroxidation rate occurred in presence of ascorbate which, averaged over all experiments, was $1\cdot36$ to $1\cdot62$ times that of the control group of animals. The rate depended on the concentration of ascorbate used. Rates of oxidative demethylation were reduced significantly in Fe injected animals by 6 to 11 per cent. as compared with controls. Changes in rate of peroxidation and oxidative demethylation occurred within 24 hours of Fe injection and were maintained without significant change for the 12-day duration of the experiments. Microsomes prepared from some mice kept for 96 days after injection showed little significant change as compared with the 12 day group. In a few experiments groups of mice were injected with 10, 15 and 20 mg. Fe. Although these injections caused further increases in the non-haem and total Fe content of the microsomes, rates of oxidative demethylation or of peroxidation in presence of NADPH were not altered significantly as compared with the groups of mice injected with 5 mg. Fe but peroxidation in presence of ascorbate was increased.

These experiments demonstrate that the non-haem Fe content of the liver microsome fraction is present in at least two forms, one a storage form and another a component which is active as part of an electron transport chain catalysing lipid peroxide formation in presence of NADPH. A small portion of the injected Fe is converted into this form which then causes a small increase in the rate of NADPH-induced peroxidation. Ascorbate, however, can utilize Fe in the normally stored form, ferritin, possibly by releasing it first, to an inorganic form to catalyse lipid peroxide formation.

It is therefore clear that in Fe-overloaded animals an increase in the rate of lipid peroxide formation can occur and this is accompanied by an increase in the rate of degradation of the membranes of the endoplasmic reticulum and, as a consequence,

222

a decrease in the capacity of the liver to oxidise drugs and carry out related detoxications.

REFERENCES

WILLS, E. D. (1969a). *Biochem. J.* **113,** 315.
WILLS, E. D. (1969b). *Biochem. J.* **113,** 325.
WILLS, E. D. (1969c). *Biochem. J.* **113,** 330.

DISCUSSION

Murray (Minneapolis). What is the effect of endogenous Fe overload on lipid peroxide formation? I wonder if there could be a self-perpetuating cycle of Fe overload from haemolysis causing more lipid peroxide formation. This could result in more haemolysis and the liberation of more Fe in situations like haemolytic anaemia.

Wills (London). The system we are discussing has a complex electron transport chain with non-haem Fe as a component. It may not be correct to assume that such a cycle could develop.

OBSERVATIONS ON EXPERIMENTALLY PRODUCED IRON-DEFICIENCY ANAEMIA IN PIGLETS

J. HANNAN

Department of Veterinary Medicine, University College, Dublin, Eire

EXPERIMENTAL

IN a series of six experiments, 40 seven-day-old pigs from five litters (three Large White and two Large White Lardrace cross) were divided randomly into two groups within litters. When the pigs were 10 days old they were weaned and put into individual Fe-free cages. The animals were fed a low-Fe food consisting of equal parts of spray-dried skim milk and spray-dried whole milk. Vitamins and trace minerals except Fe were added to this mixture at levels suggested by Beeson *et al.,* (1964), as being sufficient to meet the known requirements of the piglet. This food and de-ionized water were available to the pigs at all times.

Iron deficiency was prevented in one of the groups of pigs by the intramuscular administration of 200 mg. Fe (Imposil; Fisons Pharmaceuticals, U.K.) at three days and again at 28 days of age.

The piglets were weighed and blood samples were taken at weekly intervals. When the blood haemoglobin levels of the Fe-deprived pigs fell below 3 g./100 ml. they and their Fe-treated littermates were killed. The pigs were fasted for 15 hours and 45 to 60 minutes, before slaughter, histamine acid phosphate was injected subcutaneously at a dosage of 0·4 mg./10 kg. bodyweight in order to investigate the capacity of their gastric mucosae to secrete acid. Immediately after death the abdominal cavity was opened, the oesophageal and pyloric outlets of the stomach ligated and the stomach removed. The pH and total titratable acid in the gastric fluids were recorded. Pieces of the fundic area of the stomachs were fixed in formal saline and prepared for histological examination in the usual manner.

RESULTS AND DISCUSSION

Although the Fe-deprived pigs continued to increase in bodyweight throughout the experimental period, they grew at a slower rate than their Fe-treated littermates. The mean bodyweights in kg. and numbers of animals observed (in brackets) of the Fe-treated pigs at 13, 20, 27, 34 and 41 days of age were: $3·7 \pm ·19(15)$, $5·2 \pm ·13(20)$, $7·5 \pm ·17(19)$, $10·6 \pm ·21(19)$ and $13·5 \pm ·28(17)$ respectively. The corresponding values for their Fe-deprived littermates were: $3·5 \pm ·18(15)$, $4·4 \pm ·18(20)$, $4·7 \pm ·23(20)$, $5·8 \pm ·27(20)$ and $6·5 \pm ·27(18)$. The difference between the two experimental groups was significant ($P < ·001$) when the pigs were 20 days old and older.

There was a marked and linear drop in the blood haemoglobin levels of the Fe-deprived pigs as they grew older. At 13, 20, 27, 34 and 41 days of age the mean haemoglobin levels (g./100 ml.) in these pigs were $6·3 \pm ·19(16)$, $5·5 \pm ·22(19)$, $4·7 \pm 2(19)$, $3·8 \pm ·21$ (20) and $3·2 \pm ·19(12)$ respectively. The corresponding values for their Fe-treated littermates were $9·4 \pm ·39(16)$, $11·5 \pm ·3(18)$, $10·9 \pm ·31(17)$, $11·2 \pm ·31(18)$ and $11·3 \pm ·29(13)$. The difference between the groups was significant ($P < ·001$) at all these ages.

The amount of titratable acidity in the gastric fluid recovered from the Fe-treated pigs was seven times greater than in the gastric fluid from their Fe-deprived littermates. The mean value in μ mol./kg. bodyweight was $83 \pm 3·9(14)$ for the Fe-treated and $11·7 \pm 3·3$ (12) for the Fe-deprived group. The difference between the means was significant ($P < ·001$). The mean pH of the same fluid from the Fe-treated pigs was $2·3 \pm ·24(14)$ and that of the Fe-deprived pigs was $4·9 \pm ·39(14)$. The difference between these means was also significant ($P < ·001$). The gastric fluid had the consistency

224

of mucus in the Fe-deprived pigs and that of water in the Fe-treated pigs.

When the mucosa of the fundic zone of the stomachs of both groups of pigs were examined the following changes were consistently observed in those pigs that had been deprived of Fe: (1) a decrease in the height of the fundic mucosa, (2) a decrease in the number of fundic glands, (3) an increase in interglandular connective tissue, (4) a pronounced decrease in the number of parietal or acid secreting cells and (5) mucoid metaplasia of the cells comprising the lower third or more of the fundic glands (Figs 1 to 4).

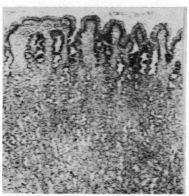

FIG. 1. Fundic mucosa from a 43-day-old Fe-treated piglet. The mucosa is relatively deep and is occupied almost exclusively by parenchymatous cells. (H & E x 50)

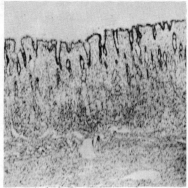

FIG. 2. Fundic mucosa from a 43-day-old Fe-deprived piglet. The mucosa is relatively shallow. It contains less parenchyma and more interglandular connective tissue than the same tissue from an Fe-treated littermate (Fig. 1). (H & E x 50)

225

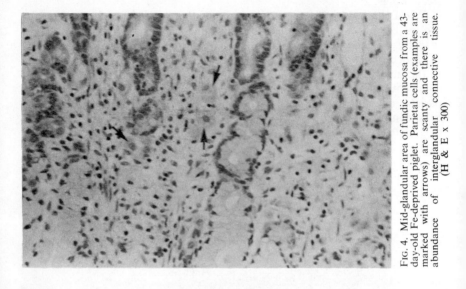

FIG. 4. Mid-glandular area of fundic mucosa from a 43-day-old Fe-deprived piglet. Parietal cells (examples are marked with arrows) are scanty and there is an abundance of interglandular connective tissue. (H & E x 300)

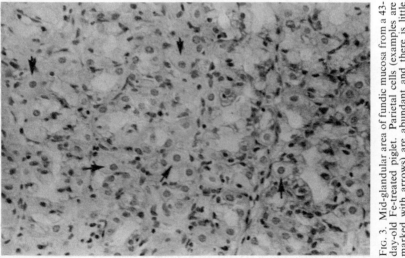

FIG. 3. Mid-glandular area of fundic mucosa from a 43-day-old Fe-treated piglet. Parietal cells (examples are marked with arrows) are abundant and there is little evidence of interglandular connective tissue. (H & E x 300)

Somewhat similar atrophic changes in the fundic mucosa together with a reduction in acid secretion by the stomach has been observed in Fe-deficiency in man but not in other species (Witts, 1966). It is suggested therefore that the piglet may be a useful experimental model for the study of Fe-deficiency anaemia and its associated gastric pathology in man.

Acknowledgement. The Irish Medical Research Council gave financial assistance for this project.

REFERENCES

BEESON, W. M., BECKER, D. E., CRAMPTON, E. W., CUNHA, T. J., ELLIS, N. R. & LUECKE, R. W. (1964). *Nutrient Requirements of Swine.* Washington, D.C.: National Academy of Sciences, National Research Council, Pub. 1137.
WITTS, L. J. (1966). *The Stomach and Anaemia.* London: Athlone Press.

DISCUSSION

Murray (Minneapolis). In this very fine study of the histological changes did you determine the Fe content of liver or other tissues? We have tried to produce similar lesions in rats but have failed, as have Wahlberg and Witz, and I am wondering whether this is a species difference or whether you succeeded in achieving a more severe depletion of tissue Fe? Our liver Fe concentrations were down to about 35 μg. per g. which may not be low enough.

Hannan (Dublin). There was a significant difference in serum Fe levels between groups. Our low limit of detection for liver Fe was about 5 μg. per g. and our livers contained less than this. We have attempted to produce the lesion in both mice and dogs and have failed and I feel it must be a species difference.

Murray (Minneapolis). Results are even inconsistent in human beings; lesions are present in some individuals without much anaemia so there may be variability within species.

Hansard (Knoxville). Would you consider blood haemoglobin level a dependable criterion for assessing body Fe status of the pig and below what level would you consider a pig to be anaemic?

Hannan (Dublin). I think haemoglobin level is the best criterion we have and I have the impression that when the level is below 6 per cent. there is a definite decrease in growth.

Horvath (Budapest). Have you examined the oxygen uptake of gastric mucosa in Fe-deficiency? About four to five years ago we found about a 50 per cent. decrease in oxygen consumption *in vitro* in the gastric mucosa of Fe-deficient as compared with control pigs.

Hannan (Dublin). No we have not done this.

SECTION 4

TISSUE DISTRIBUTION AND
STORAGE OF THE TRACE ELEMENTS

President: G. J. EVERSON

Vice President: J. QUARTERMAN

ZINC METABOLISM IN RUMINANTS

W. J. MILLER, D. M. BLACKMON AND F. M. PATE

*Department of Dairy Science and School of Veterinary Medicine,
University of Georgia, Athens, Georgia, U.S.A.*

To more adequately understand the role which zinc plays in animals, its metabolism was studied over a range of intakes from the deficient to levels approaching the toxic.

When young ruminants are fed a very Zn-deficient diet, the Zn content of some tissues declines, but in others there is little or no change. If dietary Zn is sufficiently low, plasma or serum Zn will decline sharply and immediately (Mills *et al.*, 1967). Feeding a Zn-deficient diet also results in some reduction in the Zn content of liver, pancreas, kidney, spleen, bone, rumen wall, and hair (Miller, 1969; Miller, Blackmon, Gentry *et al.*, 1966; Miller *et al.*, 1968; and unpublished data). Apparently, the effect of the Zn-deficient diet on tissue Zn has two components, one occurring soon after the low Zn diet is initiated and the other developing slowly over a period of time. In most tissues in which a Zn-deficient diet causes a reduced Zn content, the reduction is not large and there is considerable variation among similar animals given the same dietary treatments. The Zn content of some other tissues, among which are muscle and brain, is not affected by feeding a Zn-deficient diet.

Following the work of Feaster, Hansard, McCall, Skipper and Davis (1954), it was generally assumed that cattle could absorb only a very small and fairly fixed percentage of dietary Zn in the 3 to 10 per cent. range (Underwood, 1962). Calculations from our work relative to Zn requirements of Holstein bull calves with a 9 p.p.m. Zn diet (Miller *et al.*, 1963) indicated that either a much higher percentage was retained or the normal body Zn composition had declined considerably while the animals were growing normally.

Several experiments with [65]Zn have shown that the percentage of dietary Zn which is absorbed by young cattle and goats varies widely (Miller and Cragle, 1965; Miller, 1969; Miller, Blackmon, Gentry, Pitts and Powell, 1967; and Miller *et al.*, 1968). The most influential factor is the dietary Zn level. With a Zn-deficient diet, an early and very large increase in the percentage of Zn absorbed is observed. Continuation of the deficient diet until clinical Zn deficiency develops results in a further increase in [65]Zn absorption

(Miller, Blackmon, Gentry, Pitts and Powell, 1967). Net absorptions as high as 80 per cent. have been observed with deficient animals.

Faecal output is the major route of endogenous Zn excretion. Endogenous losses are decreased by a Zn-deficient diet and further reduced when the animals develop a clinical deficiency (Miller, Blackmon, Powell *et al.*, 1966).

Young calves absorb a much higher percentage of dietary Zn than older cattle (Miller and Cragle, 1965). When fed a diet containing 38 p.p.m. Zn, 2·5 month-old calves retained 51 per cent. of an oral dose of ^{65}Zn compared to 13 per cent. for 4·5-month-old animals (Miller *et al.*, 1968). However, with a Zn-deficient diet containing 2 p.p.m. Zn, the age differences disappeared. Thus, apparently, the age effect was an indirect one with the intestine of older animals able to absorb as much Zn as that of younger ones when the Zn intake was low.

The effects of varying dietary Zn levels on ^{65}Zn absorption and endogenous losses indicated that ruminants have a homeostatic control mechanism(s), which operates both through changes in Zn absorption and endogenous re-excretion into the gastrointestinal tract. However, since the Zn content of some tissues declines when the deficient diet is fed, the mechanism is obviously only partially effective. It can be hypothesized that it is probably sensitive to some change which is associated with a reduction in Zn content of one or more tissues. Early effects of Zn deficiency include reduced feed intake, growth rate and feed efficiency. It was reasoned that a reduction in growth rate and feed efficiency may be associated with a relatively greater decrease in tissue Zn deposition than of food intake. These changes should be reflected in a lower percentage of dietary Zn absorbed. To test this hypothesis an experiment was conducted in which a practical diet containing 33 p.p.m. Zn was fed in normal amounts or restricted to an estimated maintenance level. As predicted, there was a corresponding reduction in ^{65}Zn retention from 44 per cent. to 33 per cent. of the oral dose and an even greater decrease in estimated stable Zn absorption (unpublished data).

Feeding a Zn-deficient diet for seven days prior to a single oral ^{65}Zn dose caused a considerable increase in the affinity of the metabolically more active tissues (including liver, heart, lung, kidney and small intestine) for the absorbed Zn (Miller *et al.*, 1968). However, there was no marked change in the affinity for Zn of hair, bone and muscle.

In a number of experiments (Miller *et al.*, 1968; and unpublished data) ^{65}Zn distribution and turnover have been studied in several tissues of Zn-deficient and normal bull calves over periods up to 56 to 70 days following oral or intravenous dosing. After oral dosing peak levels of ^{65}Zn are attained in plasma within one to three days with a subsequent rapid, though decelerating, decline for three or four weeks, after which the decline is very slow. The ^{65}Zn content in liver follows a similar pattern to that of plasma.

The turnover rate of ^{65}Zn in many tissues is very slow. For example the levels in bone, muscle and red blood cells continue to increase for several weeks following a single oral or intravenous dose. Very soon after oral dosing the liver contains higher concentrations of ^{65}Zn than any other tissue which has been studied (Miller, Blackmon, Gentry, Pitts and Powell, 1967). Following a single dose there is, in time, a continual redistribution among body tissues with decreasing relative amounts in metabolically more active tissues such as liver, kidney and spleen, and increasing relative amounts in those that are less active metabolically such as muscle, red blood cells and bone. This results in a continually increasing biological half-life. The turnover rate is slower in Zn-deficient calves than in normal ones.

To adequately understand the factors and mechanisms which control Zn metabolism, it is essential to study Zn metabolism when very high levels of Zn are fed. Ott, Smith, Harrington and Beeson (1966) observed no adverse effects from feeding 500 p.p.m. of dietary Zn to cattle, but, at 900 p.p.m. Zn, a reduction in feed consumption and weight gain occurred. An experiment was conducted in our laboratory (unpublished data) with male Holstein calves to investigate the effects on Zn metabolism of adding relatively high, but non-toxic, levels of Zn to cattle diets. The experimental diets included practical diets which contained 33, 233 and 633 p.p.m. Zn. These were fed for seven days prior to a single oral dosing with ^{65}Zn. Fourteen days following ^{65}Zn dosing the calves were killed and tissues analysed for stable Zn and ^{65}Zn.

Increasing dietary Zn from 33 to 233 p.p.m. resulted in a substantial increase in stable Zn content of pancreas, liver and rumen wall, and a moderate increase in kidney, abomasum, small intestine and hair (Fig. 1A). When dietary Zn was elevated to 633 p.p.m. the Zn content of liver, pancreas, kidney and small intestine increased at a far faster rate than dietary Zn intake. Dietary Zn level did not materially affect the Zn content of round muscle, heart muscle or testes. The Zn levels in rib bone increased somewhat with the higher dietary Zn levels.

233

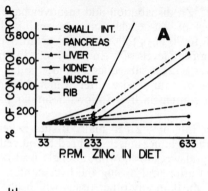

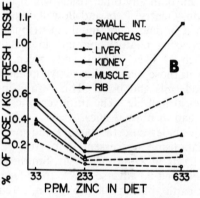

FIG. 1. Effect of level of dietary Zn on tissue composition in male Holstein calves: A, Stable Zn on dry matter basis with values expressed relative to that of controls (controls fed 33 p.p.m. dietary Zn) as 100 per cent. B. ^{65}Zn, 14 days after a single oral dose. Four animals per treatment.

The ^{65}Zn content of every tissue studied declined markedly when the dietary Zn level was increased from 33 to 233 p.p.m. (Fig. 1B). Apparently this effect was related to the lower ^{65}Zn absorption and indicates that the homeostatic control mechanisms which were evident with Zn-deficient diets continued to operate. Elevation of dietary Zn from 233 to 633 p.p.m. caused a further moderate reduction in ^{65}Zn content of testes, muscle, heart, abomasum, caecum and large intestine. However, there was a striking increase in ^{65}Zn concentration of pancreas, liver and kidney. Accompanying the increase to 633 p.p.m. Zn, smaller increases were evident in ^{65}Zn levels in the small intestine with little change in rib bone or hair samples.

234

Both the changes in stable Zn and ^{65}Zn concentrations in liver, pancreas and kidney when dietary Zn is increased from 233 to 633 p.p.m. indicate that some homeostatic control mechanism has been overcome and is no longer operative, or at least not to the same degree, in these tissues. Thus, it is evident that this homeostatic control on tissue Zn concentrations is much less effective against high Zn levels than against lower levels. The unaffected Zn levels in muscle and heart indicate that homeostatic control for these tissues is very effective both with low and high levels of dietary Zn. Viewed biochemically it appears that muscle and heart tissues probably have a given number of Zn binding sites and that these hold the Zn with great tenacity. The liver and pancreas probably have several different types of binding sites which hold the Zn with widely varying tenacity. Ott, Smith, Harrington, Stob *et al* (1966) also observed a greater than linear increase in liver, pancreas and kidney Zn levels over a portion of the range of high dietary levels.

In our earlier studies (Miller *et al.,* 1965) in which lactating cows were fed Zn levels from 44 to 1279 p.p.m., plasma Zn levels continued to increase with each increase in dietary Zn. However, increase in milk Zn content presented a curvilinear pattern with values just as high with 692 p.p.m. dietary Zn as at the highest level. Thus it appeared that the udder discriminates against higher levels of Zn with homeostatic control mechanism becoming increasingly more effective or possibly almost complete above certain levels.

Acknowledgement. Journal Series Paper no. 559, University of Georgia College of Agriculture Experiment Station, College Station, Athens, Georgia and Institute of Comparative Medicine Paper no. 743. Supported in part by USPHS Research Grant no. AM 07367–NTN.

REFERENCES

FEASTER, J. P., HANSARD, S. L., McCALL, J. T., SKIPPER, F. H. & DAVIS, G. K. (1954). *J. Anim. Sci.* **13,** 781.

MILLER, J. K. & CRAGLE, R. G. (1965). *J. Dairy Sci.* **48,** 370.

MILLER, W. J. (1969). *Am. J. clin. Nutr.* **22,** 1323.

MILLER, W. J., BLACKMON, D. M., GENTRY, R. P., PITTS, W. J. & POWELL, G. W. (1967). *J. Nutr.* **92,** 71.

MILLER, W. J., BLACKMON, D. M., GENTRY, R. P. & POWELL, G. W. (1967). *Proc. 7th Int. Congr. Nutr.* **5,** 749.

MILLER, W. J., BLACKMON, D. M., GENTRY, R. P., POWELL, G. W. & PERKINS, H. F. (1966). *J. Dairy Sci.* **49,** 1446.

MILLER, W. J., BLACKMON, D. M., POWELL, G. W., GENTRY, R. P. & HIERS, J. M. Jr. (1966). *J. Nutr.* **90,** 335.

MILLER, W. J., CLIFTON, C. M. & CAMERON, N. W. (1963). *J. Dairy Sci.* **46,** 715.

MILLER, W. J., CLIFTON, C. M., FOWLER, P. R. & PERKINS, H. F. (1965). *J. Dairy Sci.* **48,** 450.

MILLER, W. J., MARTIN, Y. G., GENTRY, R. P. & BLACKMON, D. M. (1968). *J. Nutr.* **94**, 391.
MILLS, C. F., DALGARNO, A. C., WILLIAMS, R. B. & QUARTERMAN, J. (1967). *Br. J. Nutr.* **21**, 751.
OTT, E. A., SMITH, W. H., HARRINGTON, R. B. & BEESON, W. M. (1966). *J. Anim. Sci.* **25**, 419.
OTT, E. A., SMITH, W. H., HARRINGTON, R. B., STOB, M., PARKER, H. E. & BEESON, W. M. (1966). *J. Anim. Sci.* **25**, 424.
UNDERWOOD, E. J. (1962). *Trace Elements in Human and Animal Nutrition*, 2nd ed. New York: Academic Press.

DISCUSSION

Reinhold (Beirut). Do you have any idea as to the nature of the homeostatic control mechanisms? I gather that you envisage two distinct sites of control namely at the gastrointestinal tract and within individual organs. As I see it the situation here is somewhat different than that for Fe in that here you have control and then suddenly an increase in uptake and retention as the oral Zn intake is increased.

Miller (Athens, Georgia). I think that it is probable that each individual organ exerts its own control of uptake of available supplies of Zn. The figures we obtained for pancreas and liver compared with muscle and milk would certainly support this idea. Increasing the Zn content of the diet from 33 to 633 p.p.m. caused an 11 per cent. increase in the Zn content of muscle but, in contrast, that of the pancreas increased by a factor of 18.

Miller (E. Lansing). Kidney, liver and pancreas are the main excretory organs for Zn. Do you think that a sudden increase in the content of these organs reflects an inability to excrete any more Zn?

Miller (Athens, Georgia). I am not able to comment on that possibility; I think you would know more about that point than I would.

Ward (Babraham). You mentioned, in passing, the effects of deficiency upon appetite and hunger; do you have any observations in ruminants comparable with those of the Rowett group? Is there for example the rapid increase in appetite within a matter of hours after treating deficient animals with Zn?

Miller (Athens, Georgia). We haven't measured the response within hours; their observations are much more detailed than ours. Certainly there is a response within one day and even when a very small amount of Zn is given there is a very rapid improvement of clinical condition and this is notable for example even when animals have been accidentally given a small marginal Zn supplement.

NEONATAL HEPATIC MITOCHONDROCUPREIN: THE NATURE, SUBMITOCHONDRIAL LOCALIZATION AND POSSIBLE FUNCTION OF THE COPPER ACCUMULATING PHYSIOLOGICALLY IN THE LIVER OF NEWBORN ANIMALS

H. PORTER

Department of Neurology, New England Medical Center Hospitals and Department of Medicine (Neurology), Tufts University School of Medicine, Boston, Massachusetts, U.S.A.

THE copper proteins in animal tissues can at present be divided into two groups: first, those Cu proteins which have known enzymatic activity but which account for a relatively small proportion of total tissue Cu, and second, those Cu proteins which account for major proportions of tissue Cu but which have no enzymatic function known at the present time. The group having known enzymatic activity includes cytochrome oxidase (Griffiths and Wharton, 1961) and tyrosinase (Brown and Ward, 1959), in both of which Cu participates directly in the enzymatic reaction. The group accounting for major proportions of tissue Cu includes the soluble Cu proteins hepatocuprein from adult liver (Mann and Keilin, 1939; Porter *et al.*, 1964b), cerebrocuprein I from adult brain (Porter and Folch, 1957b; Porter and Ainsworth, 1959) and haemocuprein or erythrocuprein from erythrocytes (Markowitz *et al.*, 1959). It also includes the insoluble Cu protein neonatal hepatic mitochondrocuprein from newborn liver (Porter *et al.*, 1962).

Neonatal hepatic mitochondrocuprein from newborn liver differs fundamentally from the soluble Cu proteins and known Cu-containing enzymes of adult tissues. That normal newborn liver contains much larger concentrations of Cu than other tissues has long been known (Cunningham, 1931, Lorenzen and Smith, 1947). We found the largest proportion of this physiologically increased Cu of newborn liver to be localized in the mitochondrial fraction (Porter *et al.*, 1961). From the mitochondrial fraction of newborn bovine liver, we were able to obtain a subfraction containing more than 4 per cent. Cu by employing successive differential centrifugations in deoxycholate, Tween 80, and dodecylsulphate to remove the contaminating detergent-soluble proteins (Porter *et al.*, 1962). The name neonatal hepatic mitochondrocuprein was suggested for the Cu protein of immature liver mitochondria represented by this subfraction. Similar material has been obtained from normal newborn human liver (Porter *et al.*, 1964a). In the normal animal neonatal hepatic mitochondrocuprein appears to be specific to the neonatal period. Thus the yield of Cu in the detergent-insoluble subfraction from newborn liver averaged more than 40 times that in the corresponding material from adult livers.

The Cu content of crude neonatal hepatic mitochondrocuprein, exceeding 4 per cent. is about 10 times greater than that of the soluble Cu proteins and Cu-containing enzymes previously described. The Cu bound to this protein and in the parent total mitochondrial fraction was non-dialyzable and was insoluble in water over a wide pH range, in detergents and denaturing agents, and in a variety of organic solvents but could be quantitatively released into soluble form by treatment with trypsin. It reacted directly with sodium diethyldithiocarbamate, although at an extremely slow rate.

Crude neonatal hepatic mitochondrocuprein also contains an extraordinarily large proportion of half-cystine (Porter, 1966), apparently amounting in our present improved preparations to about 25 per cent. half-cystine on a molar basis. No free-SH groups were demonstrated before or after the removal of Cu (Porter, 1966). More than 90 per cent. of the Cu and about 75 per cent. of the protein in the detergent insoluble subfraction could be solubilized by reduction with mercaptoethanol or by S-sulphonation of the cystine residues (Porter, 1968). These results suggest that the insolubility of neonatal hepatic mitochondrocuprein is at least in part related to its high cystine content.

METHODS AND MATERIAL

Precautions were taken to avoid contamination with extraneous Cu as in previous work (Porter and Folch, 1957a; Porter *et al.*, 1961). The general conditions of fractionation procedures and the methods used for Cu and amino acid analyses and for determination of cystine *plus* cysteine were identical with those previously employed (Porter *et al.*, 1962; Porter, 1968). The Cu rich, cystine rich, detergent insoluble subfraction was prepared from livers of calves less than 10 days old by the procedure previously described (Porter *et al.*, 1962). At each step in the present preparations

238

special attention was paid to thorough mechanical homogenization of the insoluble material to ensure optimum exposure to the detergent.

S-sulphonation of the detergent insoluble subfraction was carried out by the method of Bailey and Cole (1959) in 8 M urea at pH 9·0 to 9·2 by the addition of a total of 80 μmol of sodium sulphite and 80 μmol of sodium tetrathionate per g. fresh tissue represented. These quantities gave ratios of sulphite and of tetrathionate to half-cystine in the subfraction of about 150:1. Three successive portions of sulphite, each followed by an equal portion of tetrathionate, were added over a period of approximately two hours at 37° C, after which the reaction was allowed to continue with continuous magnetic stirring overnight at room temperature.

For the experiments on the submitochondrial localization of Cu in neonatal liver, the mitochondrial fraction was prepared from livers of calves less than seven days old by the method of Schneider (1964) employing 0·25 M sucrose brought to pH 7·6 with Na_2HPO_4 as the isolation medium. The time from death of the animal to completion of homogenization was about two hours. The mitochondria were osmotically lysed in ice-cold water (1·05 ml. per g. fresh tissue) by the method of Caplan and Greenawalt (1966). Inner and outer membrane fractions were prepared from the water-washed mitochondria by the discontinuous Ficoll gradient method of Schnaitman, Erwin and Greenawalt (1967). Protein was determined by the method of Lowry et al. (1951). Succinic dehydrogenase was determined spectrophotometrically with phenazine methosulphate and dichlorophenol-indophenol as described by King (1967). Samples were preincubated in the presence of phosphate and KCN at 37° C as described by Caplan and Greenawalt (1968). Cytochrome oxidase was assayed polarographically as described by Schnaitman, Erwin and Greenawalt (1967) with slight modifications. For electron microscopy pellets were prepared and fixed in 6·25 per cent. glutaraldehyde, post-fixed in 1 per cent. OsO_4, dehydrated and embedded in Epon 812, as described by Schnaitman et al. (1967). The pellets were sectioned with an LKB ultratome and stained with 1 per cent. uranyl acetate for 30 minutes and then with lead citrate for 20 minutes at room temperature. The sections were photographed in a Phillips EM 200 at plate magnifications of about 12,500.

RESULTS AND DISCUSSION

S-sulphonation of the Cu *protein and separation of soluble S-sulphonated peptide with very high half-cystine content.* In the

239

present preparations by the improved method, the half-cystine content of the dodecylsulphate-insoluble Cu protein has been increased to about 26 per cent. (Table I) compared to the average of 17 per cent. half-cystine found in preparations by the earlier method. The material solubilized by S-sulphonation of this detergent-insoluble subfraction contained more than 90 per cent. of the Cu and about 75 per cent. of the protein in the parent subfraction. This solubilized material was placed on a Sephadex G-25 column (5·0 x 82 cm. for material from 350 g. fresh tissue) equilibrated with 0·1 M-ammonium bicarbonate/8 M-urea brought to pH 9·0 with NH$_4$OH and eluted with the same medium. All of the protein detectable by the Lowry reaction or by absorbance at 280 nm. was found in the void volume. The tissue Cu was separated from the protein and was eluted in a later peak near the total column volume as a blue fraction of low molecular weight. The lyophilized protein was suspended in 8·9 M-urea to a volume providing a 1 per cent. protein concentration (4·5 ml.), one-ninth volume of 1·4 M-citric acid was added and the suspension centrifuged at 8000 g for 30 minutes. A small amount of material insoluble in urea at pH about 3·0 was sedimented. The soluble material was placed on a column of Dowex 50W-X2 (205 x 21 cm.), equilibrated with 0·14 M-citric acid/8 M-urea, pH 3·0, and the material not bound by the Dowex at this pH was eluted with the same medium. The yield of this material not bound by Dowex 50 at pH about 3·0 was about 80 per cent. of the protein placed on the column, suggesting that it represents the major component(s) of the material solubilized by S-sulphonation of the Cu protein.

The results of the preliminary amino acid analyses, carried out by Dr Lucien Cuprak, of the fractions obtained by this procedure after S-sulphonation of crude neonatal hepatic mitochondro-cuprein are shown in Table I. The material remaining insoluble after S-sulphonation, amounting to about 25 per cent. of the total protein, had a relatively low half-cystine content compared to the parent total detergent-insoluble subfraction and had an increased proportion of glycine, aspartic acid, leucine, isoleucine and phenyl-alanine. The material solubilized by S-sulphonation had an increased half-cystine content roughly appropriate to the amount of low-cystine insoluble material removed from the parent sub-fraction. The soluble material not bound by Dowex 50 at pH about 3·0 showed a further increase in half-cystine content to very high levels, in preliminary analyses apparently exceeding 33 per cent. half-cystine on a molar basis. It is also relatively rich in lysine and serine. It seems probable that this very high half-cystine

Table I. *Amino acid composition of fractions of S-sulphonated crude neonatal hepatic mitochondrocuprein*

Amino acids expressed as mol./100 mol. total amino acids recovered.

Amino acid*	Total detergent insoluble subfraction	Material insoluble after S-sulphonation	Material solubilized by S-sulphonation	Soluble material not bound by Dowex 50†
Lysine	6·2	3·7	9·1	11·1
Histidine	1·3	1·3	0·7	—
Arginine	3·6	4·2	2·7	1·9
Aspartic acid	5·1	7·4	3·1	1·5
Threonine	3·6	4·0	3·1	3·7
Serine	7·6	5·9	8·2	9·3
Glutamic acid	6·8	9·8	5·5	5·6
Proline	5·5	7·8	7·4	6·5
Glycine	11·5	15·6	11·2	8·4
Alanine	7·4	10·2	8·2	7·8
Half-cystine‡	25·9	4·8	32·5	39·4
Valine	4·8	7·2	3·9	3·5
Methionine	0·9	1·5	0·5	0·7
Isoleucine	2·6	3·7	1·2	—
Leucine	4·2	7·7	1·7	—
Tyrosine	1·2	1·9	0·5	—
Phenylalanine	1·8	3·5	0·7	—

* No determinations were made of tryptophan or amide nitrogen.

† Material not bound by Dowex 50W–X2 at pH 3·0 in 0·14 M-citric acid/8 M-urea.

‡ Determined as cysteic acid after performic acid oxidation.

content has some relation to the very high Cu binding capacity of neonatal hepatic mitochondrocuprein, but the nature of this relationship has not yet been established.

Submitochondrial localization of the Cu *in newborn liver.* Six preparations of mitochondria from newborn bovine liver have been fractionated by the discontinuous Ficoll gradient method. Fractions rich in inner membrane can be obtained from newborn liver as slaughterhouse material by this method, although the unlysed mitochondria appeared damaged and the yield of concentrated inner membrane was small. Electron microscopy, carried out by Dr John R. Hills, showed the Ficoll sediment fraction to consist predominantly of inner membrane from which most of the outer membrane and much of the matrix protein had been removed (Fig. 1). The specific activity of succinic dehydrogenase in this fraction was almost double that in unfractionated, unlysed mitochondria (Table II). In this bovine material it was demonstrated

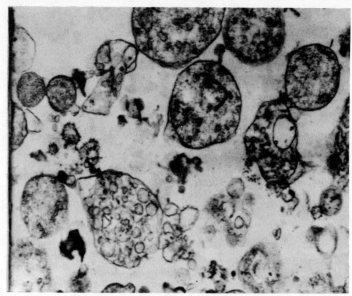

FIG. 1. Section of Ficoll sediment (inner membrane) fraction. Fixed with glutaraldehyde and OsO_4 and stained with uranyl acetate and lead citrate. Plate magnification 12,500. Print magnification 25,000.

Table II. *Distribution of copper and succinic dehydrogenase activity among submitochondrial fractions from newborn liver prepared by the discontinuous Ficoll gradient method*

Fraction	Protein* (mg.)	Cu Total* (μg.)	Cu Ratio (μg./mg.)	Succinic dehydrogenase Total* units	Succinic dehydrogenase Specific activity†
Mitochondria	19·7	34·2	1·7	944	47·9
Water-soluble I	6·3	0·9	0·1		
Water-soluble II	1·1	0·3	0·3		
Sucrose at top	1·8	0·6	0·3		
Interface (outer membrane)	1·3	0·9	0·7	46	35·4
Ficoll supernatant	5·7	4·5	0·8	301	52·8
Ficoll sediment (inner membrane)	2·4	23·5	9·8	223	93·0

* Protein, total Cu and total succinic dehydrogenase expressed as units per g. fresh tissue.

† Specific activity of succinic dehydrogenase expressed as n.mol. of indophenol reduced per min. per mg. protein.

that most of the loss of total succinic dehydrogenase activity occurred during the water lysis step.

In the six preparations more than 60 per cent. of the mitochondrial Cu was consistently found in the Ficoll sediment fraction representing concentrated inner membrane and the Cu concentration in this fraction was increased to more than five times that in the whole mitochondria (Table II). The proportion of total Cu in this fraction was greater than the proportion of total recovered succinic dehydrogenase activity, suggesting that mitochondria from newborn liver may possibly behave heterogeneously under these conditions and that the mitochondria of higher Cu content may have greater density.

The bulk of the Cu in the Ficoll sediment fraction from newborn liver could be separated from cytochrome oxidase Cu by extraction of the latter with sodium deoxycholate at a ratio of 3 mg. deoxycholate per mg. protein followed by dialysis. Thus the material solubilized by deoxycholate contained less than half of the total Cu but 90 per cent. or more of the total cytochrome oxidase activity (determined by Dr Joseph Warshaw).

The localization of neonatal hepatic mitochondrocuprein to the inner mitochondrial membrane, together with its extraordinarily high Cu content, suggests that neonatal hepatic mitochondrocuprein may have a storage function for Cu in the immature animal specifically as a reservoir for the formation of hepatic cytochrome oxidase during the neonatal period.

Acknowledgements. The author is much indebted to Dr John R. Hills for carrying out the electron microscopy, to Dr Lucien Cuprak for carrying out the amino acid analyses, to Dr Joseph Warshaw for carrying out the cytochrome oxidase determinations and to Miss Barbara Blaikie for technical assistance.

The previously unpublished investigations described in this paper were supported by research grant NB–01733–10, 11 from the National Institute of Neurological Diseases and Stroke, United States Public Health Service.

REFERENCES

BAILEY, J. L. & COLE, R. D. (1959). *J. biol. Chem.* **234**, 1733.
BROWN, F. C. & WARD, D. N. (1959). *Proc. Soc. exp. Med.* **100**, 701.
CAPLAN, A. I. & GREENAWALT, J. W. (1966). *J. cell Biol.* **31**, 455.
CAPLAN, A. I. & GREENAWALT, J. W. (1968). *J. Cell. Biol.* **36**, 15.
CUNNINGHAM, I. J. (1931). *Biochem. J.* **25**, 1267.
GRIFFITHS, D. E., & WHARTON, D. C. (1961). *J. biol. Chem.* **236**, 1850.
KING, T. E. (1967). *Meth. Enzym.* **10**, 322.
LORENZEN, E. J. & SMITH, S. E. (1947). *J. Nutr.* **33**, 143.
LOWRY, O. H., ROSEBROUGH, N. J., FARR, A. L. & RANDALL, R. J. (1951). *J. biol. Chem.* **193**, 265.
MANN, T. & KEILIN, D. (1939). *Proc. Roy. Soc.* **126**, 303.
MARKOWITZ, H., CARTWRIGHT, G. E. & WINTROBE, M. M. (1959). *J. biol. Chem.* **234**, 40.

PORTER, H. (1966). *The Biochemistry of Copper.* p. 159. Ed. by Peisach, J., Aisen, P. & Blumberg, W. E. New York: Academic Press.

PORTER, H. (1968). *Biochim. biophys. Acta,* **154,** 236.

PORTER, H. & AINSWORTH, S. (1959). *J. Neurochem.* **5,** 91.

PORTER, H. & FOLCH, J. (1957a). *Archs Neurol. Psychiat., Chicago,* **77,** 8.

PORTER, H. & FOLCH, J. (1957b). *J. Neurochem.* **1,** 260.

PORTER, H., JOHNSTON, J. & PORTER, E. M. (1962). *Biochim. biophys. Acta,* **65,** 66.

PORTER, H., SWEENEY, M. & PORTER, E. M. (1964a). *Archs Biochem. Biophys.* **104,** 97.

PORTER, H., SWEENEY, M. & PORTER, E. M. (1964b). *Archs Biochem. Biophys.* **105,** 319.

PORTER, H., WIENER, W. & BARKER, M. (1961). *Biochim. biophys. Acta,* **52,** 419.

SCHNAITMAN, C., ERWIN, V. G. & GREENAWALT, J. W. (1967). *J. cell Biol.* **32,** 719.

SCHNEIDER, W. C. (1964). *In Manometric Techniques,* p. 177. Ed. Umbreit, W. W., Burris, R. H. & Stauffer, J. F. Minneapolis: Burgess.

DISCUSSION

Ganther (Louisville). Is the insolubility of this protein due to polymerization by disulphide linkages to form large aggregates? If 25 per cent. to 40 per cent. of the amino acid residues are half-cystine residues there may be difficulty in forming intra-molecular disulphide linkages because of geometry restrictions.

Porter (Boston). I believe so in that if you break the S–S linkage by, for example, mercaptoethanol then the Cu comes off with the exception of a small residual component. It nevertheless seems to me that the Cu should remain bound into the liberated half-cystine residues, but even though we thought this should be true when we took all the Cu off we could still not detect any free SH groups.

Schwarz (Long Beach). Have you tried any other methods of solubilization than desoxycholate? What happens on sonication?

Porter (Boston). We tried a wide range of detergents, urea, small amounts of proteolytic enzymes and formamide. You cannot release the bulk of the Cu by sonication unless you treat it with trypsin. Treatment with only small amounts of trypsin liberates only a small part of the Cu; if you use enough trypsin to remove the greater part of the Cu you finish up with small fragments and the Cu falls out of the molecule at this stage to combine with lysine and you finish up with a blue Cu-lysine product.

Schwarz (Long Beach). I see there is a lot of lysine in the compound; do you feel that lysine may be involved in the binding of Cu?

Porter (Boston). If you treat the protein with trypsin and sonicate you do get blue compounds which have lysine as the major amino acid together with some pure Cu-lysinate. The problem is whether this is the way the Cu was bound in the original tissue or whether it has become released from its original site and has formed Cu-lysinate as an artefact. The original material is a muddy-green colour and has a high extinction at 280 nm. which is probably due to the Cu–N bond rather than to its amino acid composition as it has a very low content of tryptophan and phenylalanine.

Hoekstra (Madison). Is it possible that your Cu protein is not actually in the inner membrane fraction of mitochondria but happens to appear in that fraction during separation? Could it exist in some other subcellular particle? Also have you compared the apoprotein of your preparation with that of Vallee's metallothionein?

Porter (Boston). It is certainly possible that a protein is merely accompanying the inner membrane fraction of mitochondria but we don't consider this likely in view of electron micrograph studies. We are however considering this possibility further in work that is at present in progress. There are several differences between our apoprotein and metallothionein. Metallothionein has a very different amino acid composition with a high content of free SH groups. It is also a highly soluble protein whereas ours is not.

Hoekstra (Madison). It now seems reasonable to believe that cytochrome oxidase is synthesized outside the mitochondrion. How do you feel this fits with your postulate that mitochondrocuprein is a precursor store of Cu for the synthesis of cytochrome oxidase?

Porter (Boston). The hypothesis seems reasonable in view of the fact that the level of mitochondrocuprein falls rapidly during the first three weeks after birth and we know that the synthesis of cytochrome oxidase is proceeding rapidly at this time. Because of this I don't think that the problem of different localization greatly detracts from the postulate.

Sourkes (Montreal). Did you measure monoamine oxidase activity in your vesicular interfacial fraction? Also in your introduction you referred to molecular weight and other physical properties of the Mann and Keilin hepatocuprein preparation; has this work been published?

Porter (Boston). The monoamine oxidase activity of the

fraction is increased about three or four fold; this isn't as good as one would like but it does suggest that we are achieving separation. The physical data on hepatocuprein that I quoted were based on work we carried out in 1964 in which we isolated human adult hepatocuprein from soluble fractions of liver. This had a characteristic pale green colour and absorption spectrum. The question is however whether this preparation from human liver is the same as Mann and Keilin's; the same query applies to comparisons of Mann and Keilin's haemocuprein against erythrocuprein prepared by the Salt Lake City Group. I would suspect that these preparations are the same with possibly some minor species differences.

Matrone (Raleigh). We have some observations that are relevant to Porter's speculations on the fate of hepatic Cu in the young growing animal. The piglet is born with a very low level of caeruloplasmin and serum Cu and yet the liver contains quite a bit of Cu. In one experiment we tried to see whether this liver Cu is used for the synthesis of caeruloplasmin. In piglets fed a low Cu diet there is a slight increase up to seven days of age in caeruloplasmin level and then it does not rise further unless dietary Cu is given. This would tend to bear out your suggestion that your Cu protein may be used for cytochrome oxidase synthesis.

Porter (Boston). This is similar to the case in the human child where caeruloplasmin is low at birth and this for example makes it impossible to diagnose Wilson's disease on the basis of a low caeruloplasmin activity until after six months of age. In contrast the cytochrome oxidase in the liver is increasing rapidly during the first couple of weeks and it does seem reasonable to suggest that the time that the animal requires a lot of Cu rapidly is for early cytochrome oxidase production rather than for caeruloplasmin which rises much later.

Heaton (Lancaster). Is it possible that any of this mitochondrial Cu could arise by redistribution of Cu during cellular homogenization or fractionation?

Porter (Boston). I don't think so. These results we obtain are very consistent in animals of a given age and also the Cu is very firmly bound as is that of the soluble Cu proteins of the liver which do not yield up their Cu even with treatment with diethyldithiocarbamate. I feel that it is very unlikely that appreciable redistribution and incorporation into the mitochondrial fraction could occur from these soluble proteins.

Howell (Liverpool). Does your mitochondrial Cu protein disappear after two or three weeks of life in both human and bovine liver?

Porter (Boston). Yes; in both.

Macdonald (Aberdeen). Is the distribution of Cu within the whole liver of newborn bovine animals uniform throughout the lobes and does influencing the blood flow influence the distribution of that Cu?

Porter (Boston). I don't know the answer to that question.

FACTORS AFFECTING THE CONCENTRATION OF COPPER IN THE LIVER OF THE RAT

T. L. SOURKES

Laboratory of Chemical Neurobiology, Department of Psychiatry, McGill University, Montreal, Canada

BECAUSE of my interest in the chemistry of hepatolenticular degeneration (Wilson's disease), among other extrapyramidal disorders, and in the role of copper in dopamine-β-hydroxylase (Missala *et al.*, 1967) studies were undertaken in my laboratory a few years ago to develop Cu-deficient diets and to elaborate the dietary and constitutional factors affecting the uptake and utilization of Cu. Some of our results are summarized in this paper.

IRON-COPPER INTERRELATIONSHIPS

In 1932 Elvehjem and Sherman reported that Cu-deficient rats may have relatively more iron in their liver than control animals do. Although this increased storage may not occur in mild Cu deficiency (Houk *et al.*, 1946) in our laboratory (Sourkes *et al.*, 1968) we have had no difficulty demonstrating it (Table I). A similar relationship has been observed in two other species. Sheep grazing on Cu-deficient soils acquire elevated concentrations of Fe in the liver (Marston, 1952). Recently Lee, Nacht, Lukens and Cartwright (1968) have shown that after the oral administration of radioactive Fe to pigs there is more of the radioactive material in the mucosa of the small intestine of those animals that are Cu-deficient than in controls. Thus, Cu is essential for the utilization of dietary Fe but how it facilitates this utilization, indeed, which

247

particular processes of Fe metabolism it catalyses, has not yet been clarified. The difficulty in Cu deficiency seems to be in the movement of Fe from specific repository sites (liver, spleen, duodenal mucosa, reticuloendothelial system) to the region(s) of the cell where its biosynthetic incorporation into macromolecules such as haemoglobin, other haeme proteins, and Fe flavoproteins, takes place. An alternative possibility is that Cu is needed for the catalytic conversion of Fe from its storage form to the chemical form required in biosynthetic reactions. One might, then, expect to find a cuproprotein subserving this function. In fact some authors consider that this is the function of ceruloplasmin.

Cassidy and Eva (1958) found another type of nutritional relation between Fe and Cu. In pigs fattened on diets varying only in Cu concentrations hepatic Cu increased because of this increasing intake but the concentration of hepatic Fe progressively decreased. Thus consumption of Fe was the same for all groups but its storage was reduced by dietary supplements of Cu. This has been demonstrated in the rat by Bunn and Matrone (1966).

A few years ago we initiated some experiments that ultimately led to the finding of an inverse relationship between hepatic Fe and Cu in the rat (*see* Fig. 1 in Sourkes *et al.,* 1968). There was no reason for anticipating a role of Fe in the absorption of Cu or its utilization, or both, from the literature on the subject. In the past a serious drawback to the study of the Cu/Fe relationship has been the practice of preparing doubly-deficient animals by feeding them a milk diet to the point of anaemia and then re-alimenting with both metals to provide positive controls, or with Fe (usually) for the experimental group. There has been insufficient emphasis

Table I.* *Concentrations of* Fe *and* Cu *in the liver of rats consuming experimental deficiency diets*

Dietary group	Fe		Cu	
	no. of rats	Concentration (μg./g.)	no. of rats	Concentration (μg./g.)
Controls	14	57 ± 6·0†	10	4·6 ± 0·57
Fe-deficient	15	27 ± 2·0	14	14·7 ± 3·45
Cu-deficient	9	162 ± 19·5	11	3·6 ± 0·43
Doubly-deficient	13	30 ± 6·8	13	3·1 ± 0·47

* From Sourkes, Lloyd and Birnbaum (1968). Male Sprague-Dawley rats were housed in nickel stainless-steel cages and were killed at intervals during a period of 4 to 13 weeks. Livers were removed, perfused with 0·3 molar sucrose, and sampled for analysis of Fe and Cu.

† Mean ± standard error (moist weight basis).

248

on the development of chronic deficiency of each metal and the effect of this deficiency on the absorption, storage and utilization of the other. Our experiments, consisting of a 2 x 2 design (4 diets, $\pm$ Fe $\pm$ Cu), were meant to study this question. The basal diet consisted of milk powder and corn starch. The animals used, as in all our experiments (with one minor exception), were male Sprague-Dawley rats. The elevated hepatic Fe concentration in Cu-deficiency, already mentioned, is evident in the data of Table I. An unexpected finding was that at low Fe concentrations the hepatic Cu may rise considerably above control levels. Moreover, as the deficiency in the one metal progresses there are statistically significant increases in the concentration of the other. The regression equations relating concentration of the metal (μg./g. fresh weight of liver) to duration of the experiment (days) are for Fe: $Y = 55 \cdot 21 + (1 \cdot 94 \pm 0 \cdot 49) X$; for Cu: $Y = -2 \cdot 17 + (0 \cdot 34 \pm 0 \cdot 13) X$; ($b \pm SE_b$ in parentheses). With 11 degrees of freedom in each case the t-test indicates that $P_{slope} < 0 \cdot 005$ for Fe, and $< 0 \cdot 025$ for Cu.

It is interesting that the excess Cu accumulating in Fe-deficient rats is distributed within the cell very much in the same way as a parenteral load of Cu: there is a high proportion in the 'nuclear' and 'mitochondrial' fractions (Gregoriadis and Sourkes, 1967).

Certain amine oxidases contain Cu and, because this was suggested as a possibility for the mitochondrial enzyme also, we decided to measure monoamine oxidase (MAO) activity in homogenates and mitochondria of liver taken from Cu-deficient rats. However, even after prolonged experiments (up to 13 weeks) there was no alteration in the rate of oxidation of kynuramine and benzylamine (Youdim, 1966; Sourkes, 1968). This is in agreement with the very low concentrations of Cu in purified preparations of MAO (Youdim and Sourkes, 1966; Erwin and Hellerman, 1967; Yasunobu et al., 1968). We also measured the activity of MAO in the livers of rats in our 2×2 Fe–Cu experiments for we thought we might find an interaction of the two metals here. In these, and in subsequent experiments with Fe deficiency alone, we found a statistically significant reduction of enzymic activity, of the order of 18 to 31 per cent. in rats chronically deficient in Fe (Symes et al., 1970). One can postulate various roles of Fe: (1) participation in the action of the enzyme; (2) function in the biosynthesis of MAO; (3) binding of MAO in the external membrane of the mitochondrion. Whichever one may eventually be demonstrated this represents the first evidence for an effect of metal nutrition on the measured activity of mitochondrial MAO. There seems to be no

249

associative effect resulting from simultaneous Cu deficiency so that the formation of haemoglobin remains the only process, as Matrone (1960) has pointed out, for which there is clear evidence of an interaction between the two metals.

PROTEIN NUTRITION AND CU METABOLISM

The predilection of Cu for binding to proteins (Sass-Kortsak, 1965) led Gregoriadis to postulate a special importance of this process for the hepatic metabolism of the metal, e.g. in the maintenance of Cu balance in the adult animal. If this hypothesis is correct then interference with the synthesis of protein could be expected to result in an altered ability of the liver to retain or eliminate Cu. The hypothesis was tested in rats treated with various inhibitors of protein synthesis including actinomycin D, DL-ethionine and acetoxycycloheximide. The administration of these compounds in subacute experiments did not significantly affect the Cu concentration of the liver of otherwise normal rats but if the animals received a Cu load of up to 2·5 mg./kg. for three to four days (intraperitoneal injection) then the inhibitors of protein synthesis given either on the same days as the extra Cu or subsequent to the period of Cu loading, led to significantly elevated amounts, as well as concentrations, of Cu in the liver (Gregoriadis and Sourkes, 1968).

These results agree with the finding that more Cu accumulates in the livers of animals fed 7 per cent. dietary protein than 14 per cent. (Reinhold *et al.*, 1967). A related finding is that protein affords protection of swine (Wallace *et al.*, 1960) and sheep (MacPherson and Hemingway, 1965) against the toxic effects of excess dietary Cu. We have carried out two experiments on the dietary protein level. In the first we used diets containing 8 and 22 per cent. protein, respectively. Subgroups of rats at each level of protein received parenteral Cu daily for seven days in doses of 2, 1, 0·5 mg./kg.; other rats received only saline by injection. The relation between the concentration of hepatic Cu and the dosage of injected metal was the same for animals on 8 per cent. as on 22 per cent. protein, although there was some tendency for the 'low-protein' rats to have higher concentrations of Cu in the liver. In another experiment six groups of four rats each received increasing levels of protein (0 to 30 per cent., in six steps) in their diets which were fed for eight days; during the first seven days the rats received 1 mg. Cu/kg. body weight daily (intraperitoneally) and were killed 24 hours after the last dose for analysis of hepatic Cu. Rats on the 12 per cent. protein diet just maintained body weight which was initially very close to 100 g. Rats on the protein-free diet had a significantly higher concentration of hepatic Cu than all other groups, and those on the 6 and 12 per cent. levels, whose mean concentrations were almost identical, had significantly higher concentrations than rats receiving 30 per cent. protein ($P < 0.05$). There is a significant regression of hepatic Cu (μg./g.) on the protein level of the diet (a = 46·34, b = 0·90 $\pm$ 0·20). In other words, in Cu-loaded rats, increasing the protein content of the diet aids in maintaining lower levels of hepatic Cu. This does not necessarily imply a simple relation; the larger livers found in rats with adequate protein nutrition may be disproportionately effective in eliminating Cu. For example, the mechanism could involve an indirect nutritional effect of protein on some organelle of the hepatocyte which is concerned with the elimination of Cu.

PITUITARY GLAND

In chronic experiments hypophysectomized rats acquire a three-fold increase in hepatic Cu concentration (Cheek et al., 1966). Moreover, growth hormone prevents the rise in hepatic Cu (in microsomes and cytosol) when hypophysectomized rats are given injections of $CuSO_4$ (Hermann and Kun, 1961). The role of endocrine factors in Cu metabolism has been of interest to us and we decided to follow up these results. In one experiment we compared the levels of hepatic Cu in young and adult rats given various loads of Cu i.p. for a week. The results are shown in Table II and indicate that young rats accumulate more Cu in the liver, although the mechanism for limiting this accumulation in both age-groups can be overwhelmed by giving sufficient Cu parenterally.

Table II. *Effect of age on the accumulation of injected* Cu *in the liver*

Dose of Cu* mg./kg.	Mean concentration of hepatic Cu, μg./g.		SE of the mean difference	Probability
	Young	Adult		
0	4·83	3·87	0·28	< 0·01
0·5	7·11†	4·28	0·91	< 0·025
1	14·76	11·94	5·27	> 0·05
2	37·18	29·54	11·20	> 0·05

Mean final body weights were 72 g. and 242 g., respectively, for the two groups of animals.

* Given daily for 7 days. Rats were killed 24 hours after last dose, and livers were taken for analysis.

† After deducting the means for rats receiving no parenteral Cu the net increase for young rats was 2·28 $\pm$ 0·67 μg./g. (t = 3·39, P < 0·025), and for adults was 0·41 $\pm$ 0·67 (t = 0·61, P > 0·05).

In another experiment we compared the effect of various Cu loads on hypophysectomized and sham-operated rats beginning four days post-operatively. Weight gains during the eight test days for the two groups were $18 \pm 2\cdot5$ g. and $43 \pm 1\cdot6$ g., respectively. The regression of hepatic concentration of Cu (μg./g.) on the daily dose of Cu (mg./kg., i.p.) for hypophysectomized rats was: $Y = 7\cdot2 + 67\cdot1$ X; and for the controls was: $Y = 3\cdot3 + 24\cdot9$ X. A statistical comparison of the means for the three dosage groups (0, 0·5 and 1 mg./kg.) showed that the hypophysectomized rats had significantly higher concentrations of hepatic Cu in each case. For example, the mean concentrations ($\pm$ SE) in the saline-injected animals given no parenteral Cu, were (μg./g.): $8\cdot07 \pm 0\cdot41$ for hypophysectomized and $5\cdot31 \pm 0\cdot59$ for sham-operated ($P < 0\cdot01$). These results show that some factor in the pituitary is important in the elimination of Cu from the liver or in prevention of its uptake.

Preliminary data indicate that hypophysectomized rats receiving growth hormone (NIH–GH–B14–Bovine) subcutaneously, 0·1 mg. daily for seven days, have significantly less hepatic Cu than similar animals receiving saline injections ($P < 0\cdot01$). Growth hormone has no effect under these conditions in intact rats.

Hypophysectomy deprives the animals of many regulators besides somatotropic hormone and we are therefore seeking other endocrine effects. Some of these result from adrenalectomy. Thus, rats maintained for six weeks on a standard laboratory diet (but 0·9 per cent. NaCl to drink) are not only smaller than their sham-operated controls but have significantly elevated hepatic Cu and plasma caeruloplasmin concentrations (increases of 15 per cent. and 46 per cent. respectively); the renal Cu concentration is reduced (by 24 per cent.). In subacute experiments adrenalectomized rats have been given parenteral Cu (1·25 mg./kg. on three successive days). As a consequence they accumulate $63 \pm 5\cdot3$ μg. Cu/g. liver. Sham-operated controls under the same conditions have only $26 \pm 3\cdot8$ μg./g. This relationship holds even if the operations are performed after the course of Cu injections (Gregoriadis and Sourkes, 1970).

CONCLUSION

The interrelationship of Fe and Cu in nutrition has been examined with special reference to recent data. The need for new studies on this relationship at the cellular and molecular levels, and not solely the nutritional, is stressed.

It was suggested earlier on the basis of studies with inhibitors of protein synthesis that the significance of this process for the removal of hepatic Cu lies in the need for intracellular transport protein(s) that would carry Cu from the organelles which bind it to the parenchymal cell membrane; here Cu would be transferred to the bile-collecting ducts for excretion. Further studies implicating protein nutrition in Cu metabolism have been carried out. The effect of dietary protein in favouring lower hepatic Cu concentration under certain experimental conditions is probably related to the biosynthesis of specific proteins functioning in the elimination of Cu from the liver or to the formation of cellular organelles concerned with this process.

The effects of some constitutional factors such as age and hormones are briefly reported.

Acknowledgements. Research in the author's laboratory is supported by a grant of the Medical Research Council (Canada). The author thanks Miss Brenda A. Willey for expert technical assistance in some of the experiments described here. Growth hormone was donated by National Institutes of Health, Bethesda, Maryland.

REFERENCES

BUNN, C. R. & MATRONE, G. (1966). *J. Nutr.* **90**, 395.
CASSIDY, Y. J. & EVA, J. K. (1958). *Proc. Nutr. Soc.* **70**, xxxi.
CHEEK, D. B., POWELL, G. K., REBA, R. & FELDMAN, M. (1966). *Bull. Johns Hopkins Hosp.* **118**, 338.
ELVEHJEM, C. A. & SHERMAN, W. C. (1932). *J. biol. Chem.* **98**, 309.
ERWIN, V. G. & HELLERMAN, L. (1967). *J. biol. Chem.* **242**, 4230.
GREGORIADIS, G. & SOURKES, T. L. (1967). *Can. J. Biochem.* **45**, 1841.
GREGORIADIS, G. & SOURKES, T. L. (1968). *Nature, Lond.* **218**, 290.
GREGORIADIS, G. & SOURKES, T. L. (1970). *Can. J. Biochem.* **48**, 160.
HERMANN, G. E. & KUN, E. (1961). *Expl Cell Res.* **22**, 257.
HOUK, A. E. H., THOMAS, A. W. & SHERMAN, H. C. (1946). *J. Nutr.* **31**, 609.
LEE, G. R., NACHT, S., LUKENS, J. N. & CARTWRIGHT, G. E. (1968). *J. clin. Invest.* **47**, 2058.
MACPHERSON, A. & HEMINGWAY, R. G. (1965). *J. Sci. Fd Agric.* **16**, 220.
MARSTON, H. R. (1952). *Physiol. Rev.* **32**, 66.
MATRONE, G. (1960). *Fedn Proc. Fedn Am. Socs exp. Biol.* **19**, 659.
MISSALA, K., LLOYD, K., GREGORIADIS, G. & SOURKES, T. L. (1967). *Europ. J. Pharmac.* **1**, 6.
REINHOLD, J. G., KFOURY, G. A. & THOMAS, T. A. (1967). *J. Nutr.* **92**, 173.
SASS-KORTSAK, A. (1965). *Adv. clin. Chem.* **8**, 1.
SOURKES, T. L. (1968). *Adv. Pharmac.* **6A**, 61.
SOURKES, T. L., LLOYD, K. & BIRNBAUM, H. (1968). *Can. J. Biochem.* **46**, 267.
SYMES, A. L., SOURKES, T. L., YOUDIM, M. B. H., GREGORIADIS, G. & BIRNBAUM, H. (1970). *Can. J. Biochem.* **47**, 999.
WALLACE, H. D., McCALL, J. T., BASS, B. & COMBS, G. E. (1960). *J. Anim. Sci.* **19**, 1153.
YASUNOBU, K. T., IGAUE, I. & GOMES, B. (1968). *Adv. Pharmac.* **6A**, 43.
YOUDIM, M. B. H. (1966). Ph.D. Thesis: McGill University, Montreal.
YOUDIM, M. B. H. & SOURKES, T. L. (1966). *Can. J. Biochem.* **44**, 1397.

DISCUSSION

Porter (Boston). What do you think the organelles are that bind Cu in the acutely Cu-intoxicated rat? We found in one case of Wilson's disease that a lot of the liver Cu appeared to be in the mitochondrial fraction and we speculated that this might be similar to what we found in newborn liver. The people at the Albert Einstein however believe from electron microscope studies that the Cu in acute Cu intoxication is lysosomal rather than mitochondrial. Are you investigating this?

Sourkes (Montreal). We shall be doing this. Lindqvist found a lot of Cu in lysosomes after he had given Cu intravenously as Cu albuminate but this route of administration may however make a difference. Dr Lal has studied the effects of carbon tetrachloride and α-naphthylisothiocyanate on Cu accumulation and he finds much of the Cu accumulated is in both nuclear and mitochondrial fractions and he is loath to give up the idea that nuclei play an important role. Our working hypothesis is that some adaptive inducible process exists in liver which can hold on to Cu. Dr Miller's paper this morning made me think that this could quite well also happen with Zn.

Porter (Boston). Where do you think this process may take place?

Sourkes (Montreal). Gregoriadis and I feel that it may be in the cytosol. May I now ask you a question Dr Porter? You at one time reported that your green cuproprotein contained variable amounts of Fe. Do you think that this might be the type of protein which is involved in the Cu/Fe interrelationship?

Porter (Boston). The Fe in bovine preparations has been variable and in human preparations less variable. As preparative methods have improved the Fe content has become lower so that we now feel that the Fe in the original preparation probably arose from contamination with haem and nonhaem Fe from other mitochondrial elements rather than being a component of the protein.

Murray (Minneapolis). Where do you think the extra Fe comes from in Cu deficiency; from increased absorption or from red cell Fe?

Sourkes (Montreal). I had always assumed that it was dietary Fe that was retained in excess.

Murray (Minneapolis). There is a possibility that bone marrow hypoplasia reduces the need for Fe and this excess Fe is then deposited in the liver.

Sourkes (Montreal). We have only looked at the haemoglobin level and this falls rapidly but I suppose it is possible that Fe from this source reaches the reticulo-endothelial system and thence into the liver.

Ishmael (Liverpool). In what form do you give the Cu?

Sourkes (Montreal). Copper sulphate in saline solution.

Todd (Belfast). Can I ask a question about the composition of your rations? In work with sheep we found that increasing the protein content of the ration depressed the liver Cu level. The increased protein content was achieved by replacing barley with soya bean meal and in doing so we increased the Mo intake and this was presumably responsible for the effect. Have you noticed any similar effects?

Sourkes (Montreal). We have used vitamin-free casein as a protein source and have replaced this by sucrose so it is probable that the Mo content of the diet was not greatly affected.

Hoekstra (Madison). I wonder if either of the previous two speakers on Cu would care to comment on the probable metabolic causes of Wilson's disease?

Porter (Boston). With regard to the pathogenesis of the lesions I think it is reasonable to assume that this represents in effect a Cu intoxication in the tissues. I think this is shown by the fact that if you can pull the Cu out there is a recovery. I don't think anyone knows the answer to why the Cu accumulates in the tissues although possibly this is related to the increase in loosely bound Cu in the plasma associated with the low level of caeruloplasmin.

Hoekstra (Madison). Is it the idea then that these people may retain a more infantile pattern of Cu metabolism?

Porter (Boston). This may be true in two respects in that they retain the infantile low level of caeruloplasmin and they have a high liver Cu as in the infant. In the only case where we have had access to satisfactory autopsy material we have also found a high level of liver mitochondrocuprein.

Murray (Minneapolis). At what point in embryonic life is the increase in Cu detectable?

Porter (Boston). We have only measured this in the last trimester when we had two premature infant livers. The Cu appeared to increase as term approached.

THE CHANGES OF ^{65}Zn DISTRIBUTION IN THE GUINEA PIG

C. GARCIA-AMO, E. IRANZO, A. CHUECA AND A. SANTOS-RUIZ

Department of Biochemistry, Faculty of Pharmacy, University of Madrid, Spain

THE biological roles of trace elements (Schroeder *et al.*, 1968) and the existence of disorders due to dietary deficiencies of these elements (Prasad *et al.*, 1963; Prasad *et al.*, 1967) are well recognized today. Isotopic studies are valuable methods of investigating trace element function and we have made a study of changes with time of radioactive zinc (^{65}Zn) distribution in the guinea pig.

In the literature there are very divergent figures of ^{65}Zn uptake in both humans (Richmond *et al.*, 1962) and animals (Ballou and Thompson, 1961) and of its biological half-life.

After trying various ways of administration (Garcia-Amo and Ribas Ozonas, 1967; Iranzo *et al.*, 1968) we selected the intraperitoneal and oral routes for a comparative study. From the mean activity values that were obtained we calculated the respective exponential functions of the distribution in relation to time and then the biological half-lives as the best comparative term for understanding the action of ^{65}Zn.

In our tests we used seven lots of six animals. The ^{65}Zn was administered in one dose at the rate of 60 μCi./kg. body weight. The animals were sacrificed at regular intervals and the following organs were examined: carcass, skin plus hair, brain, eyes, nails, teeth, liver, pancreas, spleen, stomach, intestine, kidneys, testes, lung and heart. From the means of the results obtained from the samples the corresponding functions were obtained indicating that the tissues can be assigned to four main types.

Type 1. *Carcass.* The whole of the skeletal and muscular system represented a group characterized by slow assimilation and dissimilation.

When Zn was given intraperitoneally, the ^{65}Zn content decreased from the seventeenth day when the carcass contained 33 per cent. of the dose; we were able to distinguish two periods: firstly one of rapid decrease (20 days biological half-life, which

256

increased to 65 days) and secondly, a later phase in which there was a slow decrease up to the end of the experiment and where the decline in activity corresponded to the following equation:

$$y = 7 \cdot 9 \ e^{-0.039\,t}$$

and from which we calculated a biological half-life of 178 days.

In the case of an oral dose of Zn the concentration decreased from the first determination according to the equation:

$$y = 5 \cdot 83 \ e^{-0.023\,t}$$

from which we obtained a biological half life of 30 days.

Type 2. *Liver, viscera.* The pattern here was characterized by a quick assimilation and dissimilation and it was exhibited by nearly all the thoracic and abdominal viscera (Molina *et al.*, 1962) including the liver. The loss of ^{65}Zn activity from these tissues after both oral and i.p. administration was continuous. After dosing intraperitoneally the function describing this decline was:

$$y = 6 \cdot 9 \ e^{-0.5386\,t}$$

from the day 6 to day 80, from which we obtained 13 days for the biological half-life. From day 80 onwards the biological half-life was increased. Using the oral route, the decrease was rapid for 30 days and then from day 30 to day 140 it was slow, the exponential function describing it being:

$$y = 2 \cdot 53 \ e^{-0.2102\,t} + 0 \cdot 091 \ e^{-0.0041\,t}.$$

The biological half-lives that were calculated for the two periods were 30 and 169 days.

Type 3. *Central Nervous System.* After intraperitoneal administration of ^{65}Zn there was a progressive accumulation up to the twentieth day reaching 0·24 per cent. of the dose. From this date to day 80 a rapid decrease began and for this period we calculated a biological half-life of 19 days, from the function:

$$y_1 = 0 \cdot 49 \ e^{-0.362\,t}.$$

From day 80 there was a continuous decline in the ^{65}Zn content at the rate of 0·02 per cent. per day of the quantity injected as described by the following equation:

$$y_2 = 0 \cdot 04 \ e^{-0.0054\,t}$$

from which we calculated a biological half-life of 128 days.

After an oral dose there was a remarkable decrease from the fifth to the fifteenth day, from 0·05 to 0·02 per cent. of the administered dose; from day 15 to day 120, i.e. to the end of the experiment, the decrease was very slow and followed the equation:

$$y = 0 \cdot 032 \ e^{-0.0174\,t}.$$

Type 4. *Hair*. The hair represents the most outstanding tissue accumulating Zn (Iranzo *et al.*, 1969). On the day after an intra-peritoneal injection, we found 0·04 per cent. of the injected ^{65}Zn dose/g. hair. From this date to the sixth day, in which we found 0·22 per cent. of the dose/g., the increase in Zn content followed the equation:

$$y_1 = 0·03 \ e^{0.3425 \ t}.$$

The increase was slower until day 24 when it reached about 0·50 per cent.; the change during the period from day 6 to day 24 is represented by the equation:

$$y_2 = 0·14 e^{0.0669 \ t}.$$

The whole process of ^{65}Zn accumulation by the hair was represented by:

$$y = 0·14 \ e^{0.0669 \ t} - 0·13 \ e^{-0.1349}.$$

The day after an oral dose of the isotope the uptake of ^{65}Zn by hair reached 0·004 per cent. of the dose/g. and reached 0·023 per cent. by the sixth day, showing a rapid rate of increase. From this date onwards the increase was slower and we found 0·045 per cent. at the end of the experiment after 30 days.

The whole process was accumulative and the following equation was obtained:

$$y = 0·02 \ e^{0.0248 \ t} - 0·021 \ e^{-0.2201 \ t}.$$

REFERENCES

GARCIA-AMO, C. & RIBAS OZONAS, B. (1967). *An. R. Acad. Farm., Madr.,* **33**, 197.

IRANZO, E., CHUECA, A., GARCIA-AMO, C. & SANTOS RUIZ, A. (1968). *R. esp. Fisiol.* **24**, 109.

IRANZO, E., CHUECA, A., GARCIA-AMO, C. & SANTOS RUIZ, A. (1969). *R. esp. Fisiol.* **25**, 93.

MOLINA, G., RIBAS, B., DELSO, J. L., GALARZA, A., GARCIA-AMO, C. & SANTOS RUIZ, A. (1962). *R. esp. Fisiol.* **17**, 81.

PRASAD, A. S., MIALE, A., FARID, Z., SANDSTEAD, H. H. & SCHULERT, A. R. (1963). *J. Lab. clin. Med.* **61**, 537.

PRASAD, A. S., OBERLEAS, D., WOLF, P. & HORWITZ, J. P. (1967). *J. clin. Invest.* **46**, 549.

RICHMOND, C. R., FURCHNER, J. E., TRAFTON, G. A. & LANGHAM, W. H. (1962). *Hlth. Phys.,* **8**, 482.

SCHROEDER, H. A., NASON, A. P., TIPTON, I. H. & BALASSA, J. J. (1968). *J. chron. Dis.* **20**, 179.

INFLUENCE OF EDTA ON RETENTION AND BIOLOGICAL HALF-LIFE OF ^{54}Mn AND ^{65}Zn IN CHICKENS

K. LÖRCHER,* P. KOEPPE** AND M. AKKILIC*

* Institut für Tierzucht und Tierernährung der Freien Universität Berlin and
** Klinikum Steglitz der Freien Universität Berlin, Strahlenklinik und Institut, Abteilung für Ganzkörperzählung und Datenverarbeitung, Berlin, W. Germany

Suso and Edwards (1967, 1968) reported that EDTA added to a practical broiler diet at levels ranging from 0 to 0·24 per cent. did not increase ^{54}Mn absorption to a statistically significant extent. Similarly 0·19 per cent. EDTA in the diet had no significant effect on ^{65}Zn absorption in chickens. However, growth rate and feed utilization in broiler chicks are reduced by EDTA concentrations higher than 0·16 per cent. (Waldroup et al., 1968; Greene et al., 1965).

Since in earlier studies (Akkilic and Lörcher, 1970) we obtained significantly increased ^{54}Mn contents in liver and skeleton in three and six weeks old chickens which had 0·2 per cent. EDTA added to their diet continuously without any impairment of weight gains, another trial was conducted to determine if chicken performance, retention and biological half-life (BHL) of ^{54}Mn and ^{65}Zn could be influenced by addition of 0·2 per cent. EDTA to a corn-soybean meal broiler diet.

EXPERIMENT

The basal diet (for analysis, see Table I) composed of 57 per cent. yellow corn, 10 per cent. soyabean meal (44 per cent. protein), 10 per cent. milo corn, 8 per cent. fishmeal, 8 per cent. dried skimmed milk plus microingredient mix, 5 per cent. meatmeal, 1 per cent. soyabean oil, 0·7 per cent. dicalcium phosphate and 0·3 per cent. calcium carbonate provided more than sufficient of all nutrients, except Mn, to satisfy the estimate of requirements by the National Research Council (1966). By adding 0 (Ia and IIa) or 0·2 per cent. EDTA (Ib and IIb) and 15 or 45 p.p.m. Mn as manganese sulphate four different experimental diets were obtained containing 30 (Ia and Ib) and 60 p.p.m. Mn (IIa and IIb) respectively.

Table I. *Nutrient content of basal diet*

Protein (% N×6·25)	21·8	Ca (%)	0·98	Fe	(p.p.m.)	129
Ether Extract (%)	4·2	P (%)	0·76	Zn	(p.p.m.)	80
Crude Fibre (%)	2·5			Mn	(p.p.m.)	15
Ash (%)	5·1			Cu	(p.p.m.)	11

Twenty-four one-day-old broiler-type chicks per treatment, housed in raised wire-floored battery cages at optimal environmental conditions were supplied with food and water *ad libitum*. The birds and food were weighed at weekly intervals for six weeks.

At the age of six weeks nine chicks of each group were given orally a single dose (0·025 mCi) of ^{54}Mn and ^{65}Zn as chloride by means of a gelatine capsule (specific activity > 25 mCi ^{54}Mn/mg. Mn, 2 mCi ^{65}Zn/mg. Zn; NEN Chemicals Cat. No NEZ–040/–0111). One, 2, 4, 7, 9, 11 and 14 days after simultaneous dosing with both radioisotopes total body ^{54}Mn and ^{65}Zn content of chickens was determined using whole body counting techniques. Four 5″ × 4″ NaI-Tl crystals of a human whole body counter were arranged according to the volume of the birds which were immobilized in a PVC box during the counting procedure. Peak area integration was used to determine the activity of ^{65}Zn (1·11 MeV) and ^{54}Mn (0·84 MeV) discriminated by γ ray spectrometry in a multichannel analyser. Counts appearing in the ^{54}Mn channel due to the Compton region of ^{65}Zn were subtracted as a constant percentage of the ^{65}Zn counts to obtain the true ^{54}Mn count rate in double labelled samples. Also corrections were made for background, radioactive decay and selfabsorption.

Digital data processing equipment (IBM 1800) was used to evaluate single measurements as percentages of oral ^{54}Mn and ^{65}Zn dose. These were computed for each bird as well as for groups as exponential functions versus time by means of the method of least squares. The fractional rate of release (K) of incorporated ^{54}Mn and ^{65}Zn was transformed to BHL by the formula BHL $= \ln 2/K$ when the rate of isotope loss from the body approximated to a first order reaction.

RESULTS AND DISCUSSION

No significant differences were noted between the performance of chickens fed either EDTA supplemented or unsupplemented diets or fed different levels of Mn. Also the feed to weight gain ratio [1:1·84 (Ia); 1:1·87 (Ib); 1:1·89 (IIa) and 1:1·88 (IIb)] was unaffected by addition of 0·2 per cent. EDTA to the diet. This result does not fully correspond with one of those obtained by Waldroup *et al.* (1968). In an earlier experiment, however, we also observed impaired growth rate and feed utilization in chickens when the diet contained 0·2 per cent. EDTA and 120 p.p.m. Mn.

The 24 hours retention of ^{54}Mn and ^{65}Zn as a percentage of orally administered dose is summarized in Table II.

From this it can be seen that those birds fed rations containing

Table II. *Biological half-life (BHL) and 24 hours retention (as percentage of oral dose) of* ^{54}Mn *and* ^{65}Zn

9 chicks, 6 weeks of age per group	Experimental diet contains			24 hr. Retention (as % of oral dose)		Biological Half-life (days)	
	Zn (p.p.m.)	Mn (p.p.m.)	EDTA (%)	^{54}Mn	^{65}Zn	^{54}Mn	^{65}Zn
Ia	80	30	None	6·2 ± 1·6[a]	18·6 ± 8·6[a]	14·9 ± 3·1[a]	77·6 ± 117·7[a]
Ib	80	30	0·2	25·3 ± 12·1[b]	35·6 ± 13·4[b]	6·4 ± 0·8[b]	16·1 ± 4·2[b]
IIa	80	60	None	7·8 ± 2·7[a]	17·8 ± 4·7[a]	11·4 ± 1·7[a]	59·7 ± 49·9[a]
IIb	80	60	0·2	21·0 ± 10·0[b]	30·3 ± 11·4[b]	6·2 ± 0·8[b]	16·5 ± 3·1[b]

Within a column, means with different superscripts are significantly different (P < 0·01) according to Wilcoxon's range test.

0·2 per cent. EDTA retained significantly more ^{54}Mn and ^{65}Zn. This fact itself does not signify a change in the biological availability of the incorporated trace elements. Differences in ^{54}Mn retention due to variations in total Mn content of the feed usually observed (Akkilic and Lörcher, 1969; Mathers and Hill, 1967; Panić *et al.*, 1968) were not detected in this trial in which the Mn concentration of the diet was increased from 30 to 60 p.p.m. The 24-hour retention of ^{54}Mn, however, in birds not supplied with EDTA, in general corresponded with comparable data reported in the literature (Hennig *et al.*, 1966).

The discrepancy of ^{54}Mn and ^{65}Zn retention data given in Table I and the results published by Suso and Edwards (1968) are mainly due to different presentation. Contrary to Suso and Edwards whose data refer to the extrapolated values of the linear component of the calculated exponential curve, here we are dealing with the means of measured 24-hour retention of ^{54}Mn and ^{65}Zn. If we solve the computed exponential functions for 24-hour retention of ^{54}Mn and ^{65}Zn, thus including all measurements from the second day of the experiment, the following figures are obtained:

^{65}Zn retention: 17·8 ± 8·5 (Ia); 21·7 ± 9·1 (Ib); 14·7 ± 4·0 (IIa) and 18·8 ± 7·4 (IIb):

^{54}Mn retention: 4·7 ± 1·2 (Ia); 11·5 ± 8·0 (Ib); 4·4 ± 1·1 (IIa) and 9·5 ± 7·1 (IIb).

The differences observed are not significant except that between birds of group Ia and Ib with respect to ^{54}Mn retention.

We have as yet no explanation for the remarkable difference in data concerning the BHL of ^{54}Mn and ^{65}Zn between our experiments and those of Suso and Edwards (1968). An increase of ^{54}Mn and ^{65}Zn retention induced by EDTA appears at least partially compensated by an accelerated turnover rate of these elements. In special cases, as for instance after incorporation of radioactive Zn and Mn isotopes, a reduced BHL is of great value. For practical purposes, however, the use of EDTA as an additive to broiler feed seems to have little or no beneficial effects with respect to the metabolism of Zn and Mn. On the other hand additional findings of Suso and Edwards (1968) should be taken into account; viz. as the levels of chelating substance were increased from 0 to 0·24 per cent. the absorption of ^{60}Co and ^{59}Fe was significantly decreased.

Acknowledgement. The efficient technical assistance of Mrs I. Grosser and Mrs H. Kude is greatefully acknowledged.

REFERENCES

AKKILIC, M. & LÖRCHER, K. (1970). *Zenthl. VetMed.* **11,** 272.
GREENE, D. E., WHITE, C. L. & STEPHENSON, E. L. (1965). *Poult. Sci.* **44,** 1374.
HENNIG, A., ANKE, M., JEROCH, H., KALTWASSER, H., WIEDNER, W., HOFFMANN, G., DIETTRICH, M. & MARCY, H. (1966). *Arch. Tierernähr.* **16,** 545.
MATHERS, J. W. & HILL, R. (1967). *Br. J. Nutr.* **21,** 513.
NATIONAL RESEARCH COUNCIL (1966). *Nutrient Requirements of Poultry.* Publication No. 1345. Washington: National Acadm. of Sciences.
PANIĆ, B., HRISTIĆ, V., STOŠIĆ, D., LATINOVIĆ, E. & NEDEJKOV, N. (1968). Cited by Panić, B. & Stošić, D. (1968). *Proc. FAO/IAEA Panel.*
SUSO, F. A. & EDWARDS, H. M. Jr. (1968). *Poult. Sci.* **47,** 1417.
WALDROUP, P. W., BOWEN, T. E., MORRISON, H. L., HULL, S. J. & TOLLETT, V. E. (1968). *Poult. Sci.* **47,** 956.

DISCUSSION

Spencer (Hines, Ill.). Do you have any explanation for the increased absorption of ^{65}Zn when EDTA was given orally, inasmuch as the EDTA is unabsorbed and is excreted in the faeces as shown by ^{14}C–EDTA studies?

Lörcher (Berlin). There is also an appreciable absorption of EDTA as is shown by the presence of $^{14}CO_2$ in the expired air.

Forth (Homberg). The decrease in the biological half-life of Zn and Mn is mainly due to an increased urinary excretion in the presence of EDTA. I therefore believe that the EDTA has been absorbed to a considerable extent.

Lörcher (Berlin). I should perhaps add that an increase in retention does not necessarily characterize biological availability. I would very much welcome suggestions from the audience as to how to measure biological availability of incorporated trace metals.

Quarterman [Chairman] (Aberdeen). This is a very large question indeed and I am afraid we are behind time!

Kratzer (Davis). We have been interested for some time in the mechanisms by which EDTA functions and some years ago we investigated the effects of radioactive EDTA in colostomized hens. About 5 per cent. of the radioactivity was exhaled in CO_2 and 10 per cent. excreted in the urine so there is good evidence that it is absorbed. More recently we have fed EDTA with toxic levels of some of the trace elements and we can reduce their toxicity with EDTA. It appears that under certain conditions EDTA can have a buffering effect by increasing availability while at the same time decreasing the toxicity of some elements.

IMPROVEMENT IN THE COPPER STATUS OF EWES AND THEIR LAMBS RESULTING FROM THE USE OF INJECTABLE COPPER COMPOUNDS

R. G. HEMINGWAY, A. MACPHERSON* AND N. S. RITCHIE

Glasgow University Veterinary School, Bearsden, Glasgow, U.K.

SEPARATE trials involving the use of three injectable copper compounds (Cu glycine, CuCa EDTA and Cu methionate) were carried out in south-west Scotland on three farms where there was a previous history of swayback. The effectiveness of these preparations was assessed by their effect on (1) changes in ewe blood Cu concentrations between mid- and late pregnancy, (2) lamb blood Cu concentrations, (3) lamb liver Cu concentrations obtained from both dead and slaughtered lambs and (4) the control of clinical swayback. At each farm several hundred ewes were treated with the particular Cu injection. Twenty-five of these were used as the experimental treated group. A comparable group of 25 ewes were left untreated as a control group.

Injections of 45 mg. Cu (as Cu glycine) or of 50 mg. Cu (as CuCa EDTA) given to ewes in mid-pregnancy effected increases in mean ewe blood Cu concentration from pre-injection levels of 0·45 and 0·74 p.p.m. Cu respectively to 0·79 and 0·88 p.p.m. respectively by late pregnancy. Over the same period the blood Cu concentration of untreated control ewes fell from 0·44 and 0·57 p.p.m. respectively to 0·34 and 0·46 p.p.m. respectively. The greatest response to injection was in those ewes with initially low blood Cu concentrations (*ca.* 0·30 p.p.m.) while for the untreated ewes those with normal levels in mid-pregnancy (0·80 p.p.m.) showed the greatest reductions by late pregnancy. Blood samples were not obtained from those ewes given Cu methionate.

Parenteral injection of the ewe was also effective in raising lamb blood and liver Cu concentrations compared to lambs from untreated ewes. Mean liver Cu concentrations of lambs from treated ewes were 74·9 p.p.m. (Cu glycine) and 107·9 (CuCa EDTA) compared to 8·2 and 13·2 p.p.m. for lambs born to the respective control groups of ewes. Injection of Cu methionate (40 mg. Cu) also proved effective in raising mean lamb liver Cu concentrations from 8·4 to 49·3 p.p.m.

* Present address: Chemistry Department, The West of Scotland Agricultural College, Auchincruive, Ayr.

Table I. *The mean concentrations of Cu in the blood and liver dry matter (p.p.m. Cu ± S.E.) of ewes and their lambs on three farms as influenced by injection of the ewe with various Cu preparations in mid-pregnancy (25 ewes in each group)*

	Cu glycine		CuCa EDTA		Cu methionate	
	Treated	Control	Treated	Control	Treated	Control
Ewe blood						
Mid pregnancy	0·45 ± 0·03	0·44 ± 0·02	0·74 ± 0·06	0·57 ± 0·06	n.d.	0·33 ± 0·02
Late pregnancy	0·79 ± 0·20	0·34 ± 0·02	0·88 ± 0·04	0·46 ± 0·05	n.d.	0·29 ± 0·02
Sig. diff. late pregnancy	< 0·001		< 0·001		—	
Lamb liver						
No. of lambs	12	10	7	8	7	6
Cu conc. in D.M.	74·9 ± 15·0	8·2 ± 0·9	107·9 ± 27·7	13·2 ± 3·9	49·3 ± 10·8	8·4 ± 1·4
Sig. diff.	< 0·001		< 0·005		< 0·005	
Lamb blood						
No. of lambs	8	7	7	8	1	5
Cu conc.	0·62 ± 0·07	0·49 ± 0·04	0·82 ± 0·07	0·48 ± 0·06	0·44	0·33 ± 0·06
Sig. diff.	n.s.		< 0·005		—	
No. of swayback lambs	0	7	1	0	0	1

Copper glycine effectively prevented a severe outbreak of sway-back. Seven swayback lambs were born to the 25 untreated ewes. Only one of a total of some 600 treated ewes on this farm gave birth to a swayback lamb. On the farm where CuCa EDTA was used there were no cases of swayback in the untreated group. One of the 25 treated ewes however gave birth to a lamb with swayback. This particular ewe was the only one where the injection did not give a marked increase in ewe blood Cu concentration and this particular swayback lamb was the only one born to a total of some 200 treated ewes. In the experiment where Cu methionate was used one swayback lamb was born to an untreated ewe.

Five of a total of 26 livers examined from lambs born to the variously treated ewes contained less than 20 p.p.m. Cu in the dry matter. It is concluded that quite frequently either the absorption of Cu from the injection site is not uniformly good or that the actual injection technique may not be performed in a consistently effective manner.

Increases in lamb liver Cu concentrations resulting from Cu injections given to the ewe were generally more effective than oral treatment of the ewe with two doses each of 1.5 g. $CuSO_4.5H_2O$ in the second half of pregnancy. In one such trial the mean concentration of Cu in the liver of lambs born to 14 untreated control ewes was $7\cdot2 \pm 0\cdot9$ p.p.m. and the mean of those born to 12 dosed ewes was $28\cdot0 \pm 7\cdot8$ p.p.m.

DISCUSSION

Lewis (Weybridge). It is always nice to hear a paper that agrees with one's own findings and I wonder if you would also agree that, although we all know that when you have a swayback lamb you also have a low Cu status, you may also get lambs of low Cu status without having swayback. Would you think that your evidence also shows that, by giving these Cu preparations, although the Cu status of the lamb is not always raised it does appear that the lamb absorbs enough during gestation to drastically reduce the incidence of swayback?

Hemingway (Glasgow). I think we require far more figures than we have before we can comment reliably on this. For example, in earlier work Dr Allcroft only quoted the results for analysis of Cu in five lambs from Cu treated ewes, one of which had a liver Cu content of 7·6 p.p.m. and had clinical swayback.

If, in fact, you are suggesting that even though the injection is not very effective in raising the overall Cu status it will nevertheless protect against swayback, I am not certain. There could be many reasons for these incidental cases of swayback such as ineffective injections through accidental administration of too small a dose or the formation of abscesses due to dirt at the site of injection.

Howell (Liverpool). Miss Lewis referred a moment ago to the question of finding normal lambs with a low Cu status. I think the picture obtained depends upon when you do your analyses as the vast bulk of evidence now suggests that swayback is a Cu deficiency disease of development so that if animals are 'Cu-sufficient' during development and later come into a Cu-deficient environment a low liver Cu can result. I think if you look at the central nervous system this will give you a truer picture of the situation.

Uvarov (Greenford, Mddx.). Did you examine the sites of administration of the different Cu preparations you used and, if so, how long after injection? We have studied more than 80 different Cu compounds and have rejected most. The Cu methionine complex would not have passed my criteria of evaluation for local reactions.

Hemingway (Glasgow). We have not had much trouble at the injection site and when it has occurred it has been after the injection of the Cu glycine preparations. On one farm a proportion of the abscesses, about 10 per cent., persisted right up to shearing time and in work on growing lambs we have obtained a reaction following the injection of 45 mg. of Cu as the glycinate to animals of six months of age, these reactions persisting up to 13 weeks. In connection with this problem it is interesting that in many of the initial screening trials it was reported that a lot of the Cu was recoverable from the injection site and this may account for the occasional failure to protect lambs from swayback mentioned by Miss Lewis.

Ishmael (Liverpool). In my experience a reaction is usually obtained with Cu glycinate. Copper Ca EDTA gives little or no reaction in the sheep. We have done a little work on the guinea-pig and find again that the EDTA preparation gives no reaction whereas the Cu methionine complex gives a tissue reaction with necrosis.

LESIONS FOUND IN EWES WHICH HAVE DIED FOLLOWING THE ADMINISTRATION OF COPPER CALCIUM EDETATE FOR PREVENTION OF SWAYBACK

J. ISHMAEL

Department of Veterinary Pathology, University of Liverpool

P. J. TREEBY

Robert Young & Co. Ltd, Glasgow

AND

J. McC. HOWELL

Department of Veterinary Pathology, University of Liverpool, U.K.

THE administration of copper calcium edetate (CuCa EDTA) to sheep results in a rapid accumulation of Cu in the liver (Camargo *et al.*, 1962) and, when given by subcutaneous injection to ewes midway through pregnancy as a dose containing 50 mg. Cu, this compound has proved effective in preventing the development of swayback. However, Allcroft, Buntain and Rowlands (1965) recorded deaths in young lambs following subcutaneous injection of CuCa EDTA as an attempt to prevent the delayed form of swayback. We have found that the compound may kill ewes even when given at the recommended level (Ishmael *et al.*, 1969). The number of such deaths in ewes reported to us for the years 1967, 1968 and 1969 has been equivalent to 0·07, 0·05 and 0·09 per cent. of the doses of CuCa EDTA sold. However, the majority of users have not reported trouble and the deaths have occurred on approximately 3 per cent. of farms which have purchased the compound. Deaths have occurred on farms where Cu therapy was being used for the first time following losses from swayback in the previous year and also on farms where Cu had been used for several years without loss. On some farms, where the flock was divided into groups which were treated on separate occasions, losses were confined to one of the groups. Younger animals appeared to be more susceptible. Almost all the deaths have occurred within the first 72 hours and many within 24 hours of injection. Affected ewes observed prior to death have appeared depressed, dyspnoeic and have defaecated blood or blood-stained faeces with staining of the perineal region. Temperatures have been normal.

Post-mortem examination has consistently revealed the following lesions: subcutaneous haemorrhages and oedema at the site of injection; excess straw-coloured fluid in the peritoneal, pleural and pericardial cavities; epicardial and subendocardial haemorrhages, the latter being particularly prominent in the left ventricle; oedema of the lungs with froth in the trachea; congestion of the small intestine with haemorrhagic contents and blood in the lumen of the large intestine and rectum. In pregnant animals there were subcutaneous haemorrhages in the foetus and in a few instances haemorrhage into the uterus. The livers of affected animals were mottled and had a well marked lobular pattern. The cut surfaces showed areas of intense congestion surrounded by paler tissue which produced a striking mottled appearance. In some cases there were haemorrhages in the wall of the gall bladder which was oedematous and thickened. Jaundice and haemoglobinuria were not seen and the urinary system was macroscopically normal.

Histological examination revealed pronounced centrilobular congestion and haemorrhage in the livers. This was often so intense that the hepatic parenchymal cells around the centrilobular vein were completely obscured. Neutrophil polymorphonuclear leucocytes and necrotic liver cells were present at the edge of the congested area. The parenchymal cells in the mid-zonal region showed reduced staining affinity for eosin and were depleted of glycogen. Frozen sections stained by Oil Red O showed small fat droplets in many mid-zonal and peripheral cells. Sections of kidney revealed congestion.

Extensive bacteriological examination of dead animals and examination of intestinal contents for the presence of clostridial toxins were made. Toxins were never found and organisms were not isolated from the majority of animals. Small numbers of *Escherichia coli* and *Clostridium welchii* were recovered from intestine and *Clostridium welchii* and *Clostridium septique* were isolated from the viscera of a small number of animals that were examined several hours after death. These findings were not considered to be significant.

Most of the flocks investigated were of low Cu status and had had swayback prior to administering Cu. Liver Cu values in the majority of the dead animals were less than 500 p.p.m. on a dry matter basis. The concentration of Cu in the kidneys ranged from 2 to 153 p.p.m. D.M., and in most instances was less than 100 p.p.m. The Cu content of whole blood taken from sick animals prior to death ranged from 0·08 mg. to 0·37 mg. per 100 ml. with the majority of values falling between 0·15 and 0·25 mg. per 100 ml. These values are lower than those usually associated with chronic Cu poisoning (Todd, 1962).

REFERENCES

ALLCROFT, R., BUNTAIN, D. & ROWLANDS, W. T. (1965). *Vet. Rec.* **77**, 634.
CAMARGO, W. V. de A., LEE, H. J. & DEWEY, D. W. (1962). *Proc. Aust. Soc. Anim. Prod.* **4**, 12.
ISHMAEL, J., HOWELL, J. McC. & TREEBY, P. J. (1969). *Vet. Rec.* **85**, 205.
TODD, J. R. (1962). *Vet. Bull., Weybridge*, **32**, 573.

DISCUSSION

Hemingway (Glasgow). Have you obtained similar lesions by the use of the Cu complexes of either glycine or methionine? Is there a marked reaction at the site of injection and are you using any unusual injection sites in your work?

Ishmael (Liverpool). We have not experienced this effect with other preparations. One of the striking features is that there is often some subcutaneous oedema or haemorrhage at the site of injection but there is often no sign of the Cu. We have paid particular care to use the same injection site within each flock.

Murray (Minneapolis). Did the blood clot appear normal at autopsy of these animals or was there any possibility of defibrination?

Ishmael (Liverpool). There was haemorrhage into the small intestine and into the rectum. In a few cases where we were able to collect blood from the live animal there did possibly appear to be some interference with clotting and I did wonder whether this might have been associated with liver damage. We have however had insufficient cases to examine clotting time.

Uvarov (Greenford, Mddx.). In this investigation do you regard the preparation you used as precipitating death or as the primary cause of death? Can you give any information on the nature of the vehicle and the CuCa EDTA used? Although there are a number of preparations available we have not succeeded in producing this condition in animals of normal Cu status by giving either one or two doses. In the last three years following nearly 200,000 ewe doses of a preparation of CuCa EDTA we didn't encounter any such deaths. We require far more information on the actual cause of death and the type of preparations you are dealing with in relation to local reactions and so on. In general, the reaction to the EDTA and the vehicle is negligible but I don't know what vehicle you are using with this particular product.

Ishmael (Liverpool). This work has been done with one particular type of CuCa EDTA. We did feel that younger animals might be more susceptible and we succeeded in reproducing the lesions experimentally in 'Cu-sufficient' hogs reared indoors and given an increased dose. We did this with CuCa EDTA from more than one source.

Howell (Liverpool). Miss Uvarov questioned my colleague Dr Ishmael about the cause of death of animals receiving CuCa EDTA preparations. I should emphasise that in this work we are describing a syndrome of clinical signs and lesions which are associated with death and apparently associated with the use of this compound. She also raised the pertinent point of the sources and vehicle we are using in this investigation but I stress that we have produced a syndrome experimentally using more than one source and have also produced liver changes without death using CuCa EDTA from more than one source. At our field station they had deaths using CuCa EDTA from a source other than the one we used, and in the following year they produced deaths with injections providing only 25 mg. Cu rather than the 50 mg. recommended. At the same time we have no desire to throw out the baby with the bath water; this compound does prevent swayback and in the vast majority of animals it doesn't have any clinical effect. It does have an effect on a small proportion of farms and we are interested in this effect.

Lörcher (Berlin). I feel that these lesions are probably caused by a heavy metal poisoning and that they are due to the type of capillary damage that we always see in heavy metal poisoning. But the question is what heavy metal is the cause? There are probably differences between Cu poisoning and Cu EDTA poisoning since it is possible that free Cu would not reach the same regions as Cu EDTA and it is therefore probable that Cu could be the heavy metal which is causing the lesions in this case. However, the effect of other heavy metal EDTA complexes could be investigated to see if they produce similar lesions.

Howell (Liverpool). That is a most interesting comment and we were particularly interested to hear from Dr Todd that acute Cu poisoning produces a picture which is very similar to the one we have described here.

Macdonald (Aberdeen). The syndrome described is similar to one seen where dosing with certain anthelminthics has occurred and the pattern is that of a massive shock from histamine or other amine release. This corresponds to a similar action of heavy metal poisoning on mast cells and in the ruminant the lung appears to be the target organ. We have seen some cases of chronic Cu poisoning that are not of the type described by Todd but correspond to those that Ishmael has described here and we have found equally high Cu levels in both the liver and the kidney.

Uvarov (Greenford, Mddx.). In many years of drug testing we have reproduced this type of syndrome with a wide variety of materials including once, in a pig, with a virus. Hence I think when we are talking about a syndrome we have to be very careful to clearly describe what we mean. Hence my request for further information about the cause of death. I was interested to hear that it could be caused by anthelminthics and this we would confirm.

Ishmael (Liverpool). Can I ask Dr Uvarov to describe the lesions she has found in sheep following the administration of these other agents? Was there centrilobular necrosis of the liver and haemorrhage as in our syndrome?

Uvarov (Greenford, Mddx.). Unfortunately as these were merely screening trials the cases were not examined histologically but I am certain that there was haemorrhage.

Ishmael (Liverpool). We have investigated the effect of CuCa EDTA injection at therapeutic levels in hogs and have followed events by liver biopsy prior to injection and 48 hours after injection. There was centrilobular necrosis of liver even in sheep with no clinical signs after 48 hours but the lesion had completely resolved two weeks later.

SELENIUM DISTRIBUTION AND RADIOTOCOPHEROL METABOLISM IN THE PREGNANT EWE AND FOETAL LAMB

M. HIDIROGLOU, I. HOFFMAN AND K. J. JENKINS

Research Branch, Canada Department of Agriculture, Ottawa, Canada

SELENIUM concentrations were determined at various stages of gestation in the bodies and foetal tissues of 26 ewes fed a nutritional muscular dystrophy (NMD) producing hay for two years, of which eight were injected intramuscularly with 6 mg. Se 10 days before slaughter.

Table I. *Mean tissue* Se *concentrations* ($p.p.m. \times 10^{-3}$) *of maternal and foetal sheep tissues* (*fresh weight basis*)

Tissues	Maternal tissues		Foetal tissues	
	Untreated	Se-treated	Untreated	Se-treated
Liver	140[c]*	360[a]	119[c]	174[b]
Muscle	41[ab]	50[a]	27[c]	36[b]
Heart	55[b]	120[a]	52[b]	101[a]
Lung	95[b]	229[a]	76[b]	78*f*
Kidney	480[b]	650[a]	171[d]	214[c]
Stomach	—	—	63[b]	110[a]
Intestine	—	—	92[b]	182[a]
Spleen	164[b]	264[a]	146[b]	264[a]
Adrenal	218[b]	321[a]	183[c]	—
Placenta	67[b]	145[a]	—	—

* Values followed by the same letter in the same row are not significantly different at $P \leqslant \cdot05$.

Maternal tissues in general contained more Se than the corresponding foetal tissues (Table I). As might be expected the injection of Se enhanced tissue concentrations in both ewes and foetuses. The pattern of Se concentration in the various tissues was

Table II. *Distribution of radioactivity in various tissues of lactating ewes and their lambs* ($DPM\ 10^{-2}/g.\ dry\ matter$) *five days after a single oral dose of* ^3H *radiotocopherol to the ewes*

Tissues	Ewe C	Lamb C^*_1	Lamb C^*_2	Ewe D*	Lamb D*
Adrenal	243	79	193	327	54
Liver	242	107	118	164	65
Spleen	242	100	122	134	114
Lung	129	41	59	68	34
Heart	129	11	27	99	102
Abomasum	48	24	29	34	36
Duodenum	78	54	116	33	24
Kidney	74	38	38	50	30
Muscle	30	15	23	20	10
Vena cava	47	13	31	13	6
Thyroid	—	23	30	—	14
Testes	—	36	41	—	—
Pancreas	117	—	—	57	—
Mammary gland	68	—	—	187	—
Fat	43	—	—	14	—
Colostrum 1st day	1798†	—	—	1133	—
2nd day	—	—	—	1291	—
3rd day	—	—	—	1823	—
4th day	—	—	—	1418	—

* C and D lambs were born 96 hours and 24 hours respectively after the radiotocopherol administration to their dams.
† Specific activity (DPM/ml. colostrum).

similar in dams and foetuses, with kidneys containing the highest amounts. Selenium concentrations in the tissues of both ewes and foetuses did not appear to change with stage of gestation.

A single oral dose of radiotocopherol was administered to each of 10 pregnant ewes which had been fed an NMD inducing hay for two years. Animals were slaughtered at different time intervals over a period of 13 days. It was found that in the liver, with a high rate of uptake in 24 hours, radioactivity fell sharply with increase in time interval between administration and slaughter, while in heart, muscle, kidney and lung tissues, in which initial uptake was lower, the decrease with time was slower. The difference in specific activities between maternal and corresponding foetal tissues tended to decrease with time. The ewes excreted the bulk of radio-activity within four days, primarily via the faeces; urinary excretion was comparatively small.

A striking difference became apparent in the levels of radio-tocopherol transferred by the ewe to (1) the foetus and (2) the suckling lamb (Table II). This difference was attributed to the fact that colostrum is a rich source of tocopherol and thus the corresponding tissues of the lamb would show higher activities than those of the foetus.

DISCUSSION

Desai (Vancouver). In view of the existence of a placental barrier for both Se and tocopherol, has the attempt been made to administer Se and tocopherol simultaneously to see whether such lack of placental transfer could be overcome by the concerted mechanism which we have reported from absorption studies carried out on chicks?

Hidiroglou (Ottawa). Yes, we have attempted this but, due to technical difficulties with counting procedures in attempting to count the two isotopes simultaneously, no conclusive results were obtained.

Bell (Oak Ridge). Did you find any differences in the stable Se concentrations in twin foetuses compared with that in single foetuses similar to that found in our work with [75]Se?

Hidiroglou (Ottawa). No, we found no differences between singles and twins.

SECTION 5

TRACE ELEMENT ABSORPTION, TRANSPORT AND EXCRETION

Presidents: J. G. REINHOLD (*Session* 1)
A. SANTOS-RUIZ (*Session* 2)

Vice Presidents: R. HILL (*Session* 1)
J. K. THOMPSON (*Session* 2)

THE DYNAMICS OF COPPER ABSORPTION

M. KIRCHGESSNER AND E. GRASSMANN

*Institut für Tierernährung Technische Hochschule München,
Friesing-Weihenstephan, W. Germany*

APART from the absolute level at which they occur in the ration, the absorption of trace elements is dependent on a number of other factors. These interactions are based on the reciprocal effects occurring in the intestinal tract between trace elements and other constituent nutrients. The reasons for these effects are in many instances still not clear, but metal complex forming reactions must occupy a predominant position. In recent years, therefore, we have directed our attention towards the various problems associated with the dynamics of trace element absorption, using copper as an example. Some of the results of this research are outlined below.

In vitro experiments (Weser and Kirchgessner, 1965a, b, c) had shown that the dialysis of copper sulphate is inhibited by dietary constituents. These results can be explained by the fact that the rate of diffusion is diminished by the formation of complexes. The inhibition increased with the extent and stability of the complexes. Corresponding results were obtained under analogous conditions *in vivo* (Kirchgessner and Weser, 1965a). Fasting animals absorbed the Cu from copper sulphate considerably faster than from Cu complexes.

The position was exactly the opposite when food was involved. The high concentration of Cu-binding substances in the intestinal tract generally leads to the formation of macromolecular compounds with the soluble Cu present in the food, and its rate of diffusion is thus considerably reduced. Under these conditions Cu is better absorbed from small stable chelates because it cannot be attacked by macromolecular ligands (Kirchgessner and Weser, 1965a; Kirchgessner and Crossman, 1970).

There is no doubt that an important part in these processes is played by the proteins or by the breakdown products they form in the gastro-intestinal tract: this by virtue of their quantity as well as of their affinity for the Cu ion. With this in mind we devoted a series of experiments (Kirchgessner *et al.,* 1967a; Kirchgessner and Grassmann, 1969) to investigating the effect of amino acids and some 'derivatives' on Cu absorption.

The method employed was as follows. Rats were fed on a very

low Cu ration for three to four weeks. Thereafter Cu was fed for 14 days at a rate of 50 μmol. (3·18 mg.)/kg. feed. The Cu content of the liver is the best indicator for comparative measurements of absorption rates from different Cu compounds (Kirchgessner and Weser, 1965b). When Cu was added as an amino acid, peptide or polypeptide complex, the Cu content of the liver was considerably higher than in the case of copper sulphate (P < 0·05). The relevant data are contained in Table I ($\pm$ indicates the standard deviations

Table I. *Copper content of the rat liver after administration of supplements of different Cu-L-amino acid complexes (μg./total liver)*

	without Cu	4·4 ± 1·0	
	CuSO$_4$	17·5 ± 2·1	
Cu-(L-alanine)$_2$	25·5 ± 4·2	Cu-(L-leucine)$_2$	43·2 ± 32·0
Cu-(L-alanyl-L-alanine)	22·1 ± 4·5	Cu-(L-leucyl-L-leucine)	32·0 ± 7·0
Cu-(poly-L-alanine)	21·5 ± 3·6	Cu-(L-leucyl-L-leucyl-L-leucine)	27·4 ± 4·4

of the individual values). This increased storage of Cu from Cu-amino acid complexes as compared with copper sulphate supplements leads one to suppose that the amino acid complexes are transported undissociated at least to the point of absorption. The unstable aquo-complex, on the other hand, must have reacted with the various ligands in the ration in the intestinal tract, the resulting and certainly generally larger complexes inhibiting Cu absorption to some degree.

Corroboration of this is provided by the following results. As shown by Table I the Cu content of the liver diminishes with increasing polymerisation both in the presence of Cu-L-alanine and Cu-L-leucine complexes (P < 0·05). The Cu complexes of monomeric amino acids, therefore, are better absorbed than those of dimeric. The latter in turn are better absorbed than those of trimeric or polymeric. Whereas in the case of monomeric, dimeric and trimeric L-leucine, as in the case of monomeric and dimeric L-alanine, the reduction in Cu storage in the liver is clearly obvious when larger complexes are added; this is not the case with poly-L-alanine compared with L-alanyl-alanine. This may be connected with a great reduction in stability associated with the high degree of polymerisation of the amino acid facilitating displacement reactions on the part of the ligands in the ration. The conditions for these complexes are the same as for copper sulphate, and so analogous associates must be assumed quite apart from the intervention of functional groups in the binding of the Cu.

Table II. *Copper content of the liver after supplements of* Cu-*amino acid complexes of different configurations* ($\mu g./total$ *liver*)

Cu-(L-alanine)$_2$	25.5 ± 4.2	Cu-(L-leucine)$_2$	43.2 ± 32.0
Cu-(D-alanine)$_2$	19.6 ± 5.4	Cu-(DL-leucine)$_2$	28.4 ± 3.6
Cu-(poly-L-alanine)	21.5 ± 3.6	Cu-(L-leucyl-L-leucine)	32.0 ± 7.0
Cu-(poly-D-alanine)	24.6 ± 8.1	Cu-(DL-leucyl-DL-leucine)	25.6 ± 2.6

Besides stability and size, the rate of absorption is also influenced by the configuration of the amino acid (Table II). When Cu-D-amino acid complexes were added considerably less Cu was stored in the liver than when the corresponding L-compounds were administered ($P < 0.05$), but not than with the less stable Cu-poly-D-alanine. The reduced absorption in the presence of D-compounds must be connected with the fact that the L-form of amino acids is either preferred to, or is more rapidly absorbed than, the D-form. There is no question of Cu-L and Cu-D-amino acid chelates being the same. In addition to size, stability and configuration of the complexes, another influential factor is revealed by these experimental results, namely, dependence on the type of amino acid. Cu from complexes of the leucine series, for example, was better absorbed throughout than from the much smaller alanine complexes (Table I). These results indicate that the influence of molecule size on absorption is not always strictly valid. Lengthening the alkayl residue in an amino acid, therefore, cannot be taken to be the sole criterion of the rate of absorption of the corresponding Cu complex. These indications of a specific influence on the part of amino acids in Cu absorption were investigated in the case of 15 different L-amino acid complexes

Table III. *Copper content of the rat liver after administration of supplements of* Cu *(II)-L-amino acid complexes*

($\mu g./$total liver)
mean final value in depleted animals 9.2 ± 2.4

Supplement	Number of animals	Cu content	Supplement	Number of animals	Cu content
CuSO$_4$ + 5H$_2$O	7	22.9 ± 3.9	Cu-(L-Thr)$_2$	5	21.8 ± 2.3
Cu-(L-Glu)	7	21.6 ± 3.7	Cu-(L-Ala)$_2$	7	23.6 ± 4.5
Cu-(L-Asp)	7	19.7 ± 2.8	Cu-(L-Val)$_2$	6	29.1 ± 5.9
Cu-(L-Arg)$_2$	6	24.1 ± 4.7	Cu-(L-Leu)$_2$	5	27.7 ± 3.5
Cu-(L-Lys)$_2$	6	27.0 ± 5.6	Cu-(L-Ile)$_2$	5	28.8 ± 4.4
Cu-(L-Cys)	6	25.5 ± 4.3	Cu-(L-Try)$_2$	7	26.1 ± 3.7
Cu-(L-Met)$_2$	5	26.1 ± 3.2	Cu-(L-Phe)$_2$	6	29.5 ± 5.6
Cu-(L-Ser)$_2$	7	25.7 ± 5.9	Cu-(L-Tyr)$_2$	6	27.9 ± 4.0

279

(Kirchgessner and Grassmann, 1969). The results are summarized in Table III. In this experiment again there was a sharp increase in the Cu content of the liver as the result of supplementation in all groups. Compared with liver Cu storage in the group receiving copper sulphate ($= 100$), retention in the other groups was of the order of between 80 and 140, particularly high in the case of Cu-(L-Val)$_2$, Cu-(L-Phe)$_2$ and Cu-(L-Ile)$_2$ supplements ($P < 0.05$) and also in the case of Cu-(L-Tyr)$_2$ and Cu-(L-Leu)$_2$ ($P < 0.01$). The greatest amount of Cu storage in the liver was associated with supplements of complexes with essential amino acids ($P < 0.02$). Whereas Cu-(L-Tyr)$_2$ fits into this group, no doubt because of its close connection with Phe, the essential Cu-(L-Thr)$_2$ is an exception ($P < 0.01$). With regard to absorption rate, moreover, an obvious difference was ascertained between the Cu complexes of acid and basic amino acids investigated. On the average the Cu content of the liver in the case of basic amino acids was more than 20 per cent. higher ($P < 0.02$). Differences between individual complexes with neutral amino acids were established only in the case of alanine and phenylalanine or valine ($P < 0.05$). These results also show that, in the Cu complexes of most of the natural amino acids, there is no connection between liver storage of Cu and the stability constants of the chelates administered. Within the range of the stability constants of the amino acid complexes examined, specific effects of the ligands are no doubt of primary importance. The same may be deduced with regard to molecular size. Thus Cu retention was more or less of the same order with ligands of very different sizes, namely phenylalanine (mol. wt. 165) and valine (mol. wt. 117) and considerably higher compared with threonine (mol. wt. 119) and alanine (mol. wt. 89). Within certain limits, therefore, molecular size is less important than specific influence. This is further corroborated by the fact that absorption from the different complex types [Cu (Lig)$_2$ and Cu-(Lig-Lig)*] is different, despite more or less equal molecule sizes. To obtain further information, Cu storage in the liver was related to characteristics of the complexes. No correlation could be established either with complex stability (Rauen, 1964) or solubility (Gmelin, 1966).

Multiple correlations were established on the other hand between Cu storage in the liver and the Michaelis constants for uptake of ligands into the intestinal wall (Finch and Hird, 1960b) and their absorption (Delhumeau et al., 1962). The simple linear correlations are as follows:

Cu content (y) : Michaelis constants (x)

* Lig = amino acid ligand.

$y = 27{\cdot}0 - 0{\cdot}101\,x\,;\,r = 0{\cdot}76\,;\,B = 0{\cdot}58\,;\,P < 0{\cdot}01\,;\,n = 11\,;$
Cu content (y) : absorption rate of amino acids (x)
$y = 18{\cdot}4 + 0{\cdot}116\ x\,;\ r = 0{\cdot}76\,;\ B = 0{\cdot}58\,;\ P < 0{\cdot}01\,;\ n = 14\,;$ (see Fig. 1).

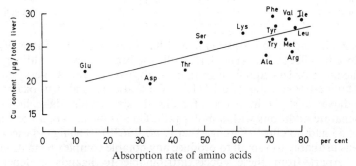

Fig. 1. Relationship between Cu storage in the liver and amino acid absorption.

These correlations indicate that the ligands have a specific effect on the Cu absorption rate. This also explains the difference in Cu absorption between essential and non-essential amino acid complexes. Most of the values of the Michaelis constants, as well as of the absorption rates of amino acids, reveal better absorption conditions for essential amino acids. To transport the amino acids through the intestinal wall three independent mechanisms are required: for neutral, acid and basic amino acids (Heinz, 1961). The obvious difference in Cu absorption from its compounds with acid and basic amino acids might be connected with this factor. It is possible, however, that only the differential uptake into the intestinal wall is responsible (Finch and Hird, 1960a, b). So far as neutral amino acids are concerned the differences in Cu absorption from the complexes are too small on the whole for any relationship between Cu absorption and the characteristics of the ligands to be strictly obvious. The high level of absorption throughout in the case of ligands with branched carbon chains and aromatic residues indicates a connection between the properties present in the C skeleton and uptake into the intestinal wall or the absorption process itself. In summary it may be said that, besides the stability and size of the Cu complexes, specific effects on the part of the ligands can play a decisive part in Cu absorption. So far as amino acid complexes are concerned, it may even be a dominant role.

Improved Cu absorption was found in Cu complexes with

Table IV. *Copper content of the rat liver after administration of supplements of different* Cu *complexes (µg./total liver)*

Without Cu	13·9 ± 1·4	Cu fumarate	37·8 ± 1·8
Cu sulphate	34·9 ± 5·5	Cu oxalate	39·1 ± 4·2
Cu citrate	34·7 ± 5·5	Cu EDTA	42·2 ± 6·1

organic acids also (Grassmann and Kirchgessner, 1969; Table IV). Specific effects, however, have still not been observed, although the more or less equally high rates of absorption from Cu-ethylene diamine-tetraacetate (Cu-EDTA), Cu-(L-Leu)$_2$ and Cu oxalate indicate a slight influence of molecule size within these limits. Separate additions with a molar ratio Cu : oxalic acid of 1 : 5·5 or 1 : 55 had no effect (Kirchgessner *et al.,* 1967b). The ligand excess was probably too small to produce any notable complex formation.

Apart from these effects attributable to ligands a dependence on calcium content in the ration of ruminants, already noted by Tompsett (1940), was quantitatively estimated (Kirchgessner, 1959) and clarified. As the Ca content of the ration increases, utilization of dietary Cu by the ruminant diminishes sharply. A graph illustrating this relationship is shown in Figure 2. It is clear

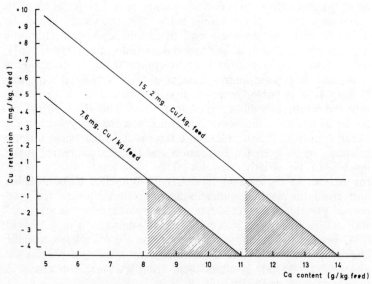

FIG. 2. Influence of the calcium content of the ration on the retention of Cu

that a given amount of Cu in the ration progressively less well utilized the higher the Ca content of the ration. For example, if a ration contains 7 to 8 mg. Cu/kg. dry matter, which is in keeping with the mean requirement of a cattle beast, 3 mg. Cu/kg. feed is retained where the Ca content of the ration is 6 g./kg.: i.e. more than 40 per cent. of the quantity administered. If the ration contains more than 8 g./kg. feed on the other hand, Cu retention is negative. A 0·2 per cent. increase in the Ca content of the ration, therefore, means that the normal Cu supply is no longer adequate. This is true even when the ration contains more Cu. Thus, double the normal supply of Cu is inadequate if the Ca content of the feed is increased to 1·1 per cent.

This position can be explained by the following investigations (Weser and Kirchgessner, 1965b). Since dietary Ca stems to a large extent from compounds with a basic reaction, these weaken the acidity of the intestinal content and thus increase its pH value. In our *in vitro* experiments, however, we found that dialysis of the Cu aquoion ($CuSO_4$) decreases very much above pH 5·5 because it is precipitated as hydroxide (Fig. 3). The pH of the fore-stomach

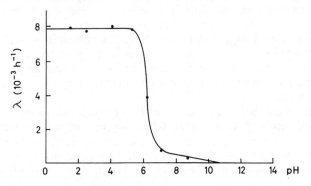

FIG. 3. Dependence of Cu dialysis constants (λ) on pH value.

of the cow is usually very high. Thus a relatively small amount of basic Ca compounds is sufficient to bring the pH within the precipitation range of soluble Cu. This means that the effect of Ca on Cu utilization may be attributable to a reduction in absorption capacity. The same position does not obtain in the case of pigs and chickens because the pH level in their stomachs is essentially lower (Kirchgessner, Munz and Oelschläger, 1960).

The reciprocal relationship existing between the Cu content of the ration and iron, zinc, manganese and cobalt retention could

283

likewise be explained as an effect on the absorption of these trace elements (Kirchgessner and Weser, 1963, 1965a). High levels of copper sulphate supplementation in pig rations produced greater retention of Fe, Zn, Mn and Co (Table V). To explain this influence

Table V. *Influence of copper supplements on the retention of trace elements in growing pigs*

| Group | daily retention | | | | |
	Cu mg.	Fe mg.	Zn mg.	Mn mg.	Co ug.
Without Cu	0·9 ± 0·3	0·3 ± 10·7	6·0 ± 1·2	1·3 ± 0·6	10 ± 6
With CuSO$_4$	29·7 ± 9·2	12·5 ± 5·2	8·1 ± 0·6	2·4 ± 1·7	38 ± 4

we carried out some dialysis experiments. Egg albumin as a macromolecular complexing ligand and physiological quantities of Fe, Zn, Mn and Co were suspended in aqueous KCl solution and the dialysis coefficients of these cations determined. When the experiment was repeated under similar circumstances, but with the addition of copper sulphate, the coefficients were higher. Since Cu belongs to the strongest complex-forming metals of the first transition group, it forces the more weakly bound metals out of the macromolecular protein complexes and thus improves absorption conditions.

In several balance experiments on growing pigs we investigated the influence of a chlortetracycline supplement on the retention of Cu and other trace elements (Kirchgessner, Oelschläger and Munz, 1960). Some of the results of these experiments are gathered together in Table VI. The daily retention of Cu was obviously

Table VI. *Influence of a chlortetracycline supplement on the daily retention of some trace elements in growing pigs*

Chlorte- tracycline	Cu mg.	Zn mg.	Co μg.	Fe mg.	Al mg.	Mo μg.
nil	0·3 ± 0·3	10·8 ± 1·7	5·1 ± 2·6	102 ± 29	129 ± 14	183 ± 35
33 mg. per day	1·0 ± 0·8	22·8 ± 9·6	12·8 ± 5·7	130 ± 21	138 ± 24	175 ± 36

increased in the antibiotic group, as was that of Co and Zn. Some other trace elements, however, exhibited no increase. But antibiotics only have an effect on the deposition of trace elements when a growth effect is present simultaneously: this could be proved particularly in the case of chicks (Kirchgessner and Friesecke, 1965). At all events, however, the greater trace element retention—and it may be increased several times over—is not proportional to either liveweight gain or nitrogen deposition. The effect on trace element deposition is probably to be sought rather in an alteration in the absorption conditions. Whether the chelate forming properties of chlortetracycline are responsible for the increased absorption of trace elements was investigated in experiments with rats (Kirchgessner and Weser, 1965c). These showed that the chelate forming properties of chlortetracycline are not responsible for the increased storage of Cu occurring in the liver. The positive effect on Cu absorption should no doubt be sought in a generally greater readiness to absorb.

REFERENCES

DELHUMEAU, G., PRATT, G. V. & GITLER, C. (1962). *J. Nutr.* **77**, 52.

FINCH, L. R. & HIRD, F. J. R. (1960a). *Biochim. biophys. Acta*, **43**, 268.

FINCH, L. R. & HIRD, F. J. R. (1960b). *Biochim. biophys. Acta*, **43**, 278.

GMELIN, G. (1966). *Handbuch der Anorgan. Chemie*, Syst. No. 60 (B) No. 4. Weinheim: Chemie.

GRASSMANN, E. & KIRCHGESSNER, M. (1969). *Z. Tierphysiol. Tierernähr. Futtermittelk.* **25**, 125.

HEINZ, E. (1961). *Colloquieum Ges. physiol. Chem.* **12**, 167. Berlin: Springer.

KIRCHGESSNER, M. (1959). *Z. Tierphysiol. Tierernähr. Futtermittelk.* **14**, 278.

KIRCHGESSNER, M. & FRIESECKE, H. (1965). *Arch. Geflügelk.* **29**, 67.

KIRCHGESSNER, M. & GRASSMANN, E. (1970). *Z. Tierphysiol. Tierernähr. Futtermittelk.* **26**, 3.

KIRCHGESSNER, M., MUNZ, W. & OELSCHLÄGER, W. (1960). *Arch. Tierernähr.* **10**, 1.

KIRCHGESSNER, M., OELSCHLÄGER, W., MUNZ, W. (1960). *Z. Tierphysiol. Tierernähr. Futtermittelk.* **15**, 321.

KIRCHGESSNER, M. & WESER, U. (1963). *Z. Tierphysiol. Tierernähr. Futtermittelk.* **18**, 181.

KIRCHGESSNER, M. & WESER, U. (1965a). *Z. Tierphysiol. Tierernähr. Futtermittelk.* **20**, 44.

KIRCHGESSNER, M. & WESER, U. (1965b). *Z. Tierphysiol. Tierernähr. Futtermittelk.* **20**, 261.

KIRCHGESSNER, M. & WESER, U. (1965c). *Z. Tierphysiol. Tierernähr. Futtermittelk.* **20**, 317.

KIRCHGESSNER, M., WESER, U. & MÜLLER, H. L. (1967a). *Z. Tierphysiol. Tierernähr. Futtermittelk.* **22**, 76.

KIRCHGESSNER, M., WESER, U. & MÜLLER, H. L. (1967b). *Z. Tierphysiol. Tierernähr. Futtermittelk.* **23**, 28.

RAUEN, H. M. (1964). *Biochemische Taschenbuch*, Vol. 2. Berlin: Springer.

TOMPSETT S. L. (1940). *Biochem. J.* **34**, 961.

WESER, U. & KIRCHGESSNER, M. (1965a). *Z. Tierphysiol. Tierernähr. Futtermittelk.* **20**, 34.

WESER, U. & KIRCHGESSNER, M. (1956b). *Z. Tierphysiol. Tierernähr. Futtermittelk.* **20**, 37.

WESER, U. & KIRCHGESSNER, M. (1965c). *Z. Tierphysiol. Tierernähr. Futtermittelk.* **20**, 41.

DISCUSSION

Ullrey (E. Lansing). What was the level of Cu supplementation in the rations of rats used in the studies in which you found an increased retention of Zn, Fe, Mn and Co?

Kirchgessner (Munich). The dietary concentration of Cu was 250 p.p.m. You need a concentration as high as this to displace other trace elements from complexes; with smaller amounts you do not get such an effect.

Ullrey (E. Lansing). Were you not surprised to find an increased retention of Zn when these high levels of Cu were fed? Some other workers have found a decline in liver Zn under these circumstances.

Kirchgessner (Munich). No, and this is because Cu has a higher affinity for complex formation than Zn. Different conclusions are sometimes reached on the nature of interactions between such metals depending upon whether one studies trace element balance in the whole animal or whether one restricts observations to measurements of storage in the liver.

Forth (Homburg/Saar). It is important to determine whether Cu administered as a chelate liberates Cu in the gut lumen or whether the Cu chelate is absorbed intact. Do you have any experimental evidence from *in vitro* studies that are related to this question?

Kirchgessner (Munich). We have work in progress to investigate whether Cu amino acid complexes go through the wall intact. We believe that monomeric amino acid complexes may go through but this work is still in progress.

Forth (Homburg/Saar). We have carried out some *in vitro* work with Cu glycine using Fisher-Parsons preparations of isolated intestine. There is an increase of penetration of our preparations but we cannot yet decide whether Cu is set free or whether the Cu complexes penetrate intact. We are hoping to be able to determine this in experiments with Cu glycinate in which both the Cu and the glycine are isotopically labelled.

Kirchgessner (Munich). It is difficult to determine such complexes in the blood and although you prefer the *in vitro* technique we feel that these effects have to be demonstrated *in vivo*.

Hoekstra (Madison). I believe you were adding these complexes to a semi-synthetic diet which contains protein. Would you comment on the possibility of the dissociation of the original complexes under the acid pH of the stomach? Will not all the complexes dissociate when they are subjected to such an acid environment with pH values down to 2 or 3?

Kirchgessner (Munich). Most are stable even down to as low as pH 2, but for example, poly-alanine is not stable and this is the reason why this complex degrades and the Cu combines with other ligands originating from the food and a different rate of Cu uptake is observed.

Topps (Aberdeen). How was the retention of trace elements measured in the young growing pig?

Kirchgessner (Munich). It was determined by balance trials.

COMPETITION BETWEEN COPPER AND ZINC DURING ABSORPTION

D. VAN CAMPEN

U.S. Plant, Soil and Nutrition Laboratory,
Soil and Water Conservation Research Division, Agricultural Research Service,
U.S. Department of Agriculture, Ithaca, N.Y., U.S.A.

THE biological antagonism between copper and zinc was recognized at least thirty years ago when Smith and Larson (1946) found that supplemental dietary Cu would alleviate certain symptoms of Zn toxicity in rats. Van Reen (1953) demonstrated a decreased activity of the Cu-dependent enzyme, cytochrome oxidase, in the liver of rats fed 500 to 700 mg. Zn/100 g. diet and found that supplemental dietary Cu increased the liver cytochrome oxidase activity in the rats. The reverse situation also holds true, i.e. Zn supplementation can alleviate certain Cu toxicity symptoms. Ritchie *et al.* (1963) observed symptoms of Cu toxicity in pigs fed a diet containing 250 p.p.m. Cu and found that addition of 100 p.p.m. Zn to this diet prevented the symptoms. Similarly, Suttle and Mills (1966) found that high levels of dietary Cu caused increased serum Cu and aspartate transaminase levels in pigs and addition of either 500 p.p.m. Zn or 750 p.p.m. Fe reduced serum Cu and transaminase to levels similar to those of the controls.

Large quantities of either Zn or Cu are generally required to produce a toxic response in animals receiving a normal diet; however, when animals are receiving a diet deficient in one of the elements, much less of the antagonistic ion is required to produce a detrimental response. R. M. Leach (personal communication) found that the addition of as little as 60 p.p.m. Zn to a diet containing about 1 p.p.m. Cu and 25 p.p.m. Zn increased four-week mortality of chicks from 30 per cent. to 95 per cent. Hill, Matrone, Payne and Barber (1963) also have reported detrimental responses to 100 p.p.m. Zn when it is added to the diet of Cu-deficient chicks.

Thus, at the time the work to be reported in this paper was begun, biological antagonism between Zn and Cu was well established; however neither the site nor the mechanism of this antagonism was known. These studies were initiated to determine if this antagonism was manifested during absorption of these elements from the intestine and, if so, to determine the specificity, site and mechanism of the antagonism.

MATERIALS AND METHODS

Male rats of the Sprague-Dawley strain were used in these experiments and were housed in stainless steel cages. They were fed a commercial diet* that contained, according to atomic absorption spectrophotometry (Perkin-Elmer Model 303, Norwalk, Conn.), an average of 10 p.p.m. Cu and 45 p.p.m. Zn.

An *in vivo* ligated segment technique was used in these experiments. Basically this technique involves injection of a test substance into a segment of intestine that has been tied off at each end. Absorption of the test substance can be estimated by measuring its disappearance from the ligated segment or its uptake by selected tissues. Some of our first experiments (Van Campen and Mitchell, 1965), indicated that both ^{64}Cu and ^{65}Zn were absorbed faster from the duodenum than from other parts of the small intestine; thus, duodenal segments were used in the rest of the studies on Cu/Zn antagonisms. Details of the procedure have been published previously (Van Campen and Mitchell, 1965; Van Campen, 1966).

^{64}Cu was received as the nitrate and ^{65}Zn was received as the chloride (Union Carbide Corpn. Tuxedo, N.Y.). Due to its short half-life (12·8 hours) the specific activity of ^{64}Cu changes quite rapidly; thus, each shipment was diluted to a constant Cu concentration and each rat received the same amount of Cu, although the number of counts varied from shipment to shipment. A similar

---

* Big Red Dog Chow, Agway Inc., Syracuse, N.Y. (Trade names and company names are included for the benefit of the reader and do not imply any endorsement or preferential treatment of the product listed by the U.S. Department of Agriculture.)

Table I. *Effect of zinc, cadmium, silver and mercury on tissue uptake and distribution of* ^{64}Cu

Cation administered	% of dose in sampled tissues[1,2,3]	Relative distribution[4]				
		Blood	Heart	Kidneys	Liver	Spleen
None	21·9[a]	24·5[a]	0·4[a]	17·1[a]	58·1[a]	0·4[a]
Zn	9·3[b]	20·6[a]	0·3[a]	19·7[a]	58·9[a]	0·3[a]
Cd	1·0[c]	33·2[b]	0·8[a]	16·5[a]	48·2[a]	0·9[b]
Ag	19·3[a]	11·5[c]	0·3[a]	15·6[a]	71·9[b]	0·5[a]
Hg	13·1[a, b]	18·7[a]	0·4[a]	36·4[b]	44·4[b]	0·5[a]

[1] Per cent. of dose recovered in blood, heart, kidneys, liver and spleen.
[2] Each value is the mean of five observations.
[3] Values in any column that are not followed by the same letter are significantly different.
[4] Relative distribution was calculated by dividing the c.p.m. recovered in a particular tissue by the total c.p.m. recovered in all five sampled tissues.

procedure was used with Zn and absorption and tissue uptake of the radioisotopes are expressed as a percentage of the administered dose. Additional references and pertinent details regarding procedures will be provided along with the results of the experiments to which they pertain.

RESULTS AND DISCUSSION

Some early experiments (Van Campen, 1966) were designed to determine if Zn did interfere with ^{64}Cu absorption and also to test the effects of certain other chemically similar cations. Rats were given, intraduodenally, a ^{64}Cu solution containing 0·01 μmol. Cu and either 0 or 6·0 μmol. of one of the metals being tested (Zn, Cd, Hg and Ag). The effects of these ions on tissue uptake of ^{64}Cu and on the distribution of ^{64}Cu among the sampled tissues are summarized in Table I.

Zinc and Cd depressed the uptake of ^{64}Cu by the sampled tissues but Ag and Hg did not. Cadmium, Ag and Hg all affected the distribution of ^{64}Cu among the sampled tissues; Cd increased the proportion found in blood; Ag decreased the proportion in blood, and increased that in liver, and Hg increased the proportion found in the kidneys. Zinc had relatively little effect on ^{64}Cu distribution in these experiments; however, in subsequent experiments (Van Campen, unpublished observations) intraduodenal administration of Zn has consistently increased the proportion of the absorbed ^{64}Cu in the kidney. Thus, Zn did depress the intestinal absorption of Cu and it would appear that this Zn-induced depression is specific, at least to the extent that the Zn effects on ^{64}Cu uptake and distribution are not duplicated by any of the other cations tested.

In experiments where ^{64}Cu and Zn are both put into a ligated segment, the Zn-induced depression in ^{64}Cu uptake could be due to the Zn effect of any of several different organs. The following diagram indicates some possibilities:

$$\begin{array}{c} \text{Kidney} \\ \uparrow \downarrow \\ \text{Intestinal} \longrightarrow \text{Intestinal} \longrightarrow \text{Serum} \longrightarrow \text{Liver} \\ \text{Lumen} \longleftarrow \text{Epithelium} \longleftarrow \quad \uparrow \downarrow \longleftarrow \\ \text{Other} \\ \text{Tissues} \end{array}$$

Accumulation of Zn in any of these tissues could interfere with Cu absorption. There could be a direct antagonism caused by Zn

290

accumulating in the intestinal epithelium and preventing normal transit of Cu across the epithelial cells. Alternatively Zn could accumulate in one or more of the non-intestinal tissues where it would prevent normal metabolism of Cu in that tissue and by 'feedback' inhibit further Cu absorption. When rats were given Zn via a ligated segment Zn levels of intestine, serum and liver were all higher than those of the controls; thus one could not distinguish which of these organs was primarily involved in the depression of Cu uptake. It was later found that intraperitoneal administration of Zn would increase Zn levels of serum, liver and kidney without significantly increasing the Zn concentration of intestinal tissue. Based on this result a series of experiments were designed to determine if Zn inhibited ^{64}Cu absorption directly by blocking its absorption at the intestinal level or indirectly by accumulating in non-intestinal tissue and, thus, interfering with ^{64}Cu uptake by these tissues (Van Campen and Scaife, 1967).

Rats were allocated to one of five treatments. A dose of ^{64}Cu containing 1 μg. Cu was put into a ligated duodenal segment of each rat and unlabelled Zn (1 mg./rat) was given either intra-duodenally or intraperitoneally. The treatment designations were: (1) control; (2) ID-0 (Zn given intraduodenally along with ^{64}Cu); (3) IP-0 (Zn given intraperitoneally at the same time as ^{64}Cu); (4) IP-2 (Zn given intraperitoneally two hours before ^{64}Cu); (5) IP-18 (Zn given intraperitoneally 18 hours before ^{64}Cu). Three hours after administration of ^{64}Cu, the rats were exsanguinated and tissues were taken for ^{64}Cu, total Cu and total Zn determinations. A summary of the results is given in Table II.

Intraduodenally-administered Zn depressed ^{64}Cu uptake by about 50 per cent. whereas intraperitoneal administration of Zn did not depress ^{64}Cu absorption. In considering the possibility that Zn first builds up in some non-intestinal tissue and subsequently interferes with Cu absorption, a comparison of the tissue Zn levels of rats that received Zn intraduodenally with those of rats that received Zn intraperitoneally is useful. Liver Zn levels were significantly higher in all of the intraperitoneally-dosed rats (IP-0, IP-2, IP-18) than in the intraduodenally-dosed rats (ID-0). Similarly, serum Zn levels in the rats that received Zn intra-duodenally (ID-0) were not significantly higher than those that received an intraperitoneal dose of Zn simultaneously with the ^{64}Cu (IP-0). Comparable results were obtained with the other non-intestinal tissues, i.e. tissues from the intraperitoneally dosed rats were as high or higher in Zn than those from the intra-duodenally dosed rats. These same tissues were analysed for total

Table II. *Effect of method of Zn administration on absorption of ^{64}Cu from ligated segments and on tissue Zn concentrations*[1]

Method of Zn administration[2]	Disappearance of ^{64}Cu from ligated segment[3]	Tissue Zn concentrations					
		Serum	Erythrocytes	Heart	Kidney	Liver	Segment and Contents[4]
	% of dose	µg./ml.			µg./g.[4]		µg.[4]
Control (no Zn)	50·6[a]	4·7[a, b]	14·2[a]	93[a]	144[a]	128[a]	41[a]
ID—0	31·5[b]	9·6[c]	14·6[a]	91[a]	123[a]	146[a, b]	930[b]
IP—0	45·9[a]	8·4[b, c]	14·5[a]	92[a]	148[a]	161[b]	113[a]
IP—2	55·1[a]	5·2[a, b]	17·0[a]	164[a]	144[a]	165[b]	58[a]
IP—18	53·0[a]	3·4[a]	14·1[a]	106[a]	149[a]	195[c]	77[a]

[1] Each value is the mean of nine observations; for key to routes of administration see text.
[2] ID = intraduodenal; IP = intraperitoneal; 0, 2, and 18 indicate Zn was administered simultaneously with, two hours prior to, or 18 hours prior to administration of ^{64}Cu.
[3] Entries in any column that are not followed by the same letter are significantly different.
[4] Dry-weight basis.
[5] Total Zn in ligated segment and its contents.

Table III. *Effect of method of Cu administration on absorption of ^{65}Zn from ligated duodenal segments and on tissue Cu levels*[1]

Method of Cu administration[2]	Disappearance of ^{65}Zn from ligated segment[3]	Tissue Cu concentrations					Segment and Contents[5]
	% of dose	Serum	Erythrocytes	Heart	Kidney	Liver	$\mu g.$[5]
		$\mu g./ml.$		$\mu g./g.$[4]			
Control (no Cu)	40·6[a]	1·1[a, b]	0·9[a]	25·4[a]	24·7[a]	18·9[a]	3·1[a]
ID—0	28·3[b]	1·2[a, b]	1·0[a]	25·0[a]	30·2[b]	27·5[a]	151·9[b]
IP—0	35·8[a, b]	1·5[b]	1·1[a]	24·7[a]	31·0[b]	49·3[b]	17·2[a]
IP—2	40·9[a]	1·4[a, b]	1·2[a]	23·8[a]	30·3[b]	50·6[b]	6·3[a]
IP—18	55·3[c]	1·4[a, b]	1·0[a]	24·2[a]	34·2[b]	61·0[b]	9·5[a]

[1] Each value is the mean of eight observations; for key to routes of administration see text.
[2] ID = intraduodenal; IP = intraperitoneal; 0, 2 and 18 indicate that Cu was administered simultaneously with, two hours or 18 hours prior to ^{65}Zn.
[3] Entries in any column that are not followed by the same letter are significantly different.
[4] Dry-weight basis.
[5] Total Cu in ligated segment and its contents.

293

Cu and there were no significant differences between treatments. Thus, if one considers the possibilities in the preceding Table in light of the fact that increasing the Zn concentrations of several non-intestinal tissues had no effect on ^{64}Cu absorption, then it seems that the most likely site for Zn interference is at the intestinal site with high levels of intraduodenally administered Zn preventing either the entry of ^{64}Cu into the epithelial cells or its release from those cells.

These effects of Zn on ^{64}Cu absorption are consistent with the idea that there is direct competition between Zn and Cu during absorption. If so one would expect that the reverse situation would also hold, i.e. Cu should interfere with the intestinal absorption of Zn. Experiments designed similarly to those preceding were conducted to test this possibility (Van Campen, 1969).

Again the ligated segment technique was used and rats were allocated to one of five treatments. A dose of ^{65}Zn containing 5 μg. Zn was put into a ligated segment in each rat and unlabelled Cu (200 μg./rat) was given either intraduodenally or intraperitoneally. The treatments were (1) control; (2) ID-0 (Cu given intraduodenally at the same time as ^{65}Zn); (3) IP-0 (Cu given intraperitoneally at the same time ^{65}Zn was given); (4) IP-2 (Cu given intraperitoneally two hours before ^{65}Zn); (5) IP-18 (Cu given intraperitoneally 18 hours before ^{65}Zn). Three hours after receiving ^{65}Zn rats were killed and tissue samples were taken for ^{65}Zn, total Zn and total Cu determinations. The results of these experiments are summarized in Table III.

When Cu was given intraduodenally along with ^{65}Zn it depressed subsequent uptake of the isotope. When given intraperitoneally Cu did not depress ^{65}Zn uptake. It is apparent from Table III that the Cu concentrations of the non-intestinal tissues from the intraperitoneally-dosed rats were as high or higher than those of intraduodenally-dosed rats. Thus increasing the Cu concentrations of non-intestinal tissues apparently does not depress ^{65}Zn absorption and in fact, the only treatment that did depress Zn absorption was that of putting Cu into the ligated segment along with the ^{65}Zn. This also caused ^{65}Zn to accumulate in the intestinal tissues indicating a block at the intestinal level. These results are consistent with the earlier ones and suggest that the Cu-induced depression in ^{65}Zn absorption is mediated at the intestinal level and is a result of direct competition between Cu and Zn.

DISCUSSION

Since the precise mechanisms for Zn and Cu absorption are not known the means by which competition between these two elements is mediated remains a matter of pure speculation. Possibilities include competition for a binding site in or on the mucosal cells, or competition for some 'carrier' molecule or molecules. A number of potential 'carrier' compounds have been investigated recently.

Sarkar and Kruck (1966) isolated amino acid-bound Cu from normal human serum and later work (Neumann and Sass-Kortsak, 1967; Harris and Sass-Kortsak, 1967) indicated that a number of the serum amino acids can compete effectively with albumin in the binding of Cu. Additionally Kirchgessner and others (1967) have reported that the oral administration of amino acid Cu complexes resulted in higher levels of liver Cu than did administration of aqueous Cu. Thus, amino acids present some possibilities as potential 'carriers'.

More recently attempts to isolate protein-bound Zn and Cu have been reported. Starcher (1969) reported that ^{64}Cu present in the duodenal mucosa of chicks was attached to protein with a molecular weight of about 10,000 and that Zn and Cd appear to act as Cu antagonists by binding to and displacing Cu from this protein. Suso and Edwards (1969) have reported on similar work with ^{65}Zn. They found ^{65}Zn bound to protein fractions of both serum and intestinal mucosal extracts. The ^{65}Zn in serum apparently was bound to the albumin fraction; however that in the mucosal extracts chromatographed differently and presumably was not bound to albumin.

In our laboratory (Van Campen, unpublished observations) we have been able to separate protein-bound ^{65}Zn from the soluble fraction of homogenates of intestinal mucosa from rats by chromatography on either DEAE cellulose or Sephadex G-100. The elution pattern from Sephadex G-100 is somewhat similar to that obtained by Starcher (1969), however, we also get a large radioactive peak coming off the column immediately after the void volume. Attempts to further purify the column eluates by starch and acrylamide gel electrophoresis resulted in an apparent dissociation of the ^{65}Zn from the protein during migration in an electric field.

The actual role of amino acids, proteins or any other potential carrier in Zn and Cu absorption and in the competition between the two remains to be determined. However, competition for a common carrier or carriers does provide an explanation for the

295

results reported here and is consistent with the idea that at least part of the biological antagonism between Cu and Zn is due to direct competition during the absorption process.

REFERENCES

HARRIS, D. I. M. & SASS-KORTSAK, A. (1967). *J. clin. Invest.* **46,** 659.

HILL, C. H., MATRONE, G., PAYNE, W. L. & BARBER, C. W. (1963). *J. Nutr.* **80,** 227.

KIRCHGESSNER, M., WESER, U. & MÜLLER, H. L. (1967). *Z. Tierphysiol. Tierernähr. Futtermittelk.* **22,** 76.

NEUMANN, P. Z. & SASS-KORTSAK, A. (1967). *J. clin. Invest.* **46,** 646.

RITCHIE, H. D., LEUCKE, R. W., BALTZER, B. V., MILLER, E. R., ULLREY, D. E. & HOEFER, J. A. (1963). *J. Nutr.* **79,** 117.

SARKAR, B. & KRUCK, T. A. P. (1966). In *The Biochemistry of Copper,* ed. Peisach, J., Aisen, P. & Blumberg, W. E., p. 183. New York: Academic Press.

SMITH, S. E. & LARSON, E. J. (1946). *J. biol. Chem.* **163,** 29.

STARCHER, B. C. (1969). *J. Nutr.* **97,** 321.

SUSO, F. A. & EDWARDS, H. A. (1969). *Fedn Proc. Fedn Am. Socs exp. Biol.* **28,** 761.

SUTTLE, N. F. & MILLS, C. F. (1966). *Br. J. Nutr.* **20,** 135.

VAN CAMPEN, D. (1966). *J. Nutr.* **88,** 125.

VAN CAMPEN, D. (1969). *J. Nutr.* **97,** 104.

VAN CAMPEN, D. & MITCHELL, E. A. (1965). *J. Nutr.* **86,** 120.

VAN CAMPEN, D. & SCAIFE, P. U. (1967). *J. Nutr.* **91,** 473.

VAN REEN, R. (1953). *Archs Biochem. Biophys.* **46,** 337.

DISCUSSION

Spencer (Hines, Ill.). Is the amount of Zn present in the duodenal loop important in this antagonism? You did not have the effect when you gave Zn intraperitoneally but when Zn is given intraperitoneally or intravenously it does circulate into the intestine and I am wondering whether the amount arriving there after i.p. injection was too small to be effective.

Van Campen (Ithaca). We determined Zn on these segments and the amount present after three hours was quite small even when given intraperitoneally; it was not significantly different from the amount present in control animals. There is no doubt that Zn is secreted into the intestine but the amount was insufficient to measure.

Hoekstra (Madison). There is a chance that local high concentrations of Zn or Cu might inhibit the cells of the intestinal mucosa. Do you have control studies to show that other absorptive processes (e.g. of amino acids or sugars) are unaffected by the local concentrations of Cu and Zn you have used?

Van Campen (Ithaca). We don't have direct evidence but we have taken segments at the end of the incubation period and found that they are histologically normal. The amounts of Zn we are adding are not excessive and they correspond approximately to the amount of Zn in one day's intake but we are of course giving it in solution in a small segment.

Hoekstra (Madison). But does this solution contain other natural materials such as peptides?

Van Campen (Ithaca). No, it is an aqueous solution merely adjusted to pH 5·5.

Forth (Homburg/Saar). We have tested the effect of several metals on water and sugar absorption in similar experiments to Dr Van Campen's. In many cases it was difficult to separate the effects of the acid pH needed to keep the metal in ionic form from the effects of the metal itself but in the case of Zn there was clear evidence that Zn had an inhibitory effect on water uptake and a small inhibitory effect on sugar uptake. Zinc had a 50 to 100 per cent. inhibitory effect on water absorption at concentrations of only 5 μmol./ml.

Van Campen (Ithaca). The experiments we did with Cd clearly showed that damage had occurred to the intestinal mucosa and sloughing of the epithelium was apparent at the end of the incubation period.

Mills (Aberdeen). Our work at the Rowett agrees very well with Dr Van Campen's findings regarding the antagonistic effects of Zn and Cu. In work with both rats and sheep we have found that an increased Zn intake depresses Cu storage in the liver. However, I think the point should be made that this interaction can probably also exist at sites other than the intestinal mucosa and this possibility may be the explanation of several apparently conflicting results. For example, in his work at the Rowett on Cu poisoning in the pig, Suttle found that high tissue Cu levels apparently affected Zn metabolism adversely, impaired its function and ultimately led to parakeratosis. This effect was, however, accompanied by an *increase* in liver Zn concentration. From all the published work on the Zn/Cu interaction it seems possible that under some circumstances a high Cu intake can adversely affect Zn absorption and lead to a depressed level of Zn storage while under other circumstances there is biological evidence for adverse effects of Cu on Zn metabolism with an accompanying increase in tissue Zn content. I think what this means is that competition exists at several sites and if the Zn doesn't get to

297

where it is supposed to go it may be excreted or may perhaps accumulate in the liver. These possibilities may explain some of the discrepancies between Dr Van Campen's work and Professor Kirchgessner's and may also underly the controversy regarding the effects of Cu on parakeratosis where some workers suggest that Cu may alleviate the condition and others suggest that Cu exacerbates it. There is now excellent evidence that Zn and Cu are competitors but the conclusions we reach regarding the mechanism of this competition may be different if we solely study the interaction by measuring tissue Cu and Zn contents or if we also take into account the fact that these metals can exist in tissues in forms which are not physiologically available.

Van Campen (Ithaca). I should perhaps stress that I didn't in reporting this work intend to exclude the possibility that the interaction could take place at other sites. Our work has solely been on absorption but we can't exclude the other possibilities you mention.

Hill (London). In some work with everted small intestine of the chick we have studied the uptake of Cu by mucosal cells from solutions which contained Cu, Zn and Mn at concentrations similar to those which would exist in the gut in birds fed a normal diet. Cu uptake appeared to be a fixed figure and this was not appreciably influenced by additions of Mn or Zn or both together.

ABSORPTION OF IRON AND CHEMICALLY RELATED METALS IN VITRO AND IN VIVO; THE SPECIFICITY OF AN IRON BINDING SYSTEM IN THE INTESTINAL MUCOSA OF THE RAT

W. Forth

Institut für Pharmakologie und Toxikologie der Universität des Saarlandes, Homburg/Saar, W. Germany

SOME of the results presented here have already been published (Forth, 1966; Forth *et al.*, 1966) and, since these will serve as an introduction to the topic, I will commence by summarizing the results of an experiment in which the penetration of iron through the gut wall and its uptake and binding in the mucosal tissue of normal rats is compared with that of Fe-deficient animals (see Table I).

Table I. *Penetration of iron through the gut wall and uptake and binding in the mucosal tissue of normal (n) and iron deficient (d) rats in·vitro*

Experimental conditions: isolated, blood-free jejunal segments of rats *in vitro* (Fisher and Parsons, 1949). Perfusion fluid: 50 ml. Tyrode's solution; time 2 hours; temperature 37°C. Means of 6 to 8 experiments ± s_x. Concentration of glucose in Tyrode's solution 15 μmol./ml. Serosal concentration of glucose/mucosal concentration: normal segments = 1·68; Fe deficient segments = 1·72.

Concentration of Fe added to the perfusion fluid nmol./ml.	Rat Fe status	absorbate ml.	Fe in the absorbate		Fe in the mucosal tissue	
			nmol./ml.	specific activity counts min^{-1}·ml^{-1}·nM^{-1}	nmol./100mg.	specific activity counts min^{-1}·ml^{-1}·nM^{-1}
—	n	1·7 ±0·14	8·6 ±0·9	—	37·4* ±10·8	—
—	d	1·9 ±0·09	3·6* ±0·2	—	12·5* ±7·2	—
250†	n	1·6 ±0·06	8·8 ±0·5	660 ±170	39·2 ±10·8	1220 ±280
250†	d	1·7 ±0·10	11·6* ±1·4	5100* ±400	41·0* ±5·9	3780* ±200

* P < 0·05 as compared to the normal controls.
† Specific activity of the perfusion fluid: 7650 counts · min^{-1} · ml.$^{-1}$ · nmol.$^{-1}$.

Rats were made Fe-deficient by repeated bleeding and by feeding an Fe-deficient diet, the Fe content of which amounted to 6×10^{-5} mol./kg. dry matter. In order to avoid a state of deficiency of the other metals tested we added 1.2×10^{-3} mol./kg. of cobalt, nickel and manganese and 2.5×10^{-5} mol./kg. of copper. The diet of normal animals contained 3×10^{-3} mol./kg. Fe (Förth and Andres, 1969).

In order to avoid any possible influence of factors controlling the process of Fe absorption, for instance the load of Fe depots, the Fe demand for erythropoiesis or the degree of saturation of transferrin with Fe (Bothwell et al., 1958; Charley et al., 1968; Laurell, 1947) the experiment was performed in vitro on jejunal segments without blood supply according to the method of Fisher and Parsons (1949). To remove any residues of blood from the isolated gut segments we perfused the upper mesenteric artery immediately before the experiment with ice-cold oxygen-saturated saline.

Gut segments treated in this manner from normal animals and from Fe-deficient rats were perfused on the mucosal side with Tyrode's solution to which iron sulphate was added together with ^{59}Fe in a final concentration of 2.5×10^{-4} mol./l. The chemical determination of Fe was carried out according to the method of Schade, Oyama, Reinhart and Miller (1954) with terpyridine as chelating agent.

Under these artificial conditions the gut segments of normal animals release Fe into the absorbed fluid even if no Fe has been added to the perfusion fluid. In Fe deficiency the concentration of Fe in the absorbed fluid is only one-third of that of the normal controls (Table I).

After having added Fe to the Tyrode solution perfusing normal segments, we were surprised to observe in another experiment that the Fe concentration did not increase appreciably; a similar result was obtained when we determined Fe in the mucosal tissue; here too, we did not observe a statistically significant increase in Fe.

In contrast to these findings, in Fe-deficient segments an impressive increase of the concentration of Fe in the absorbed fluid of more than 220 per cent. was measured as compared with the control experiment. The concentration of Fe is even significantly higher than in the absorbed fluid of normal segments. Uptake and binding of Fe in the mucosal tissue of Fe-deficient segments is also increased; the increase amounts to nearly 230 per cent. of the control. The uptake and binding of Fe by tissue is more than 10 times greater than the penetration of Fe into absorbed fluid.

300

As one could have expected, the specific activity in the absorbed fluid and in the mucosal tissue is lower than that of the perfusion fluid, because ^{59}Fe is diluted by inactive Fe during absorption and this is greater in the normal segments than in the Fe-deficient. The specific activity of Fe in the absorbate of Fe-deficient segments is eight times greater than that of the normal controls. In mucosal tissue of Fe-deficient segments the specific activity of Fe is only three times greater than that in the tissue of normal segments.

From the chemical determinations as well as from measurements of radioactivity, we may draw the conclusion that at least two steps are involved in the absorption of Fe; uptake and binding on one hand and penetration on the other (Forth and Rummel, 1965; Manis and Schachter, 1962). Most important for the critical evaluation of the following experiments is the fact that the increase in penetration and binding of Fe in Fe deficiency is not merely due to a simple tracer exchange. This increase is caused by an increase of penetration and binding of that Fe which has been offered at the mucosal side of the gut. This statement is important in so far that in the following experiments carried out with very low Fe concentrations we were unable, and this for simple technical reasons, to determine Fe chemically and therefore were limited to the measurement of radioactivity only.

These ideas arising from experiments with normal segments appear to be an improvement of Hahn's (Hahn *et al.,* 1939; Hahn *et al.,* 1943) and Granick's (1949, 1951) hypothesis of the so-called 'mucosal block' in Fe absorption; but the most important conclusion drawn from these results is that in Fe deficiency the mucosal epithelium takes up Fe apparently independently from the blood supply and moves it to the serosal side. A more detailed study of this phenomenon carried out in our institute during the last year led us to postulate the existence of an Fe-binding system in the mucosal cells which, according to the degree of saturation, takes up Fe. This system seems to be responsible for the absorption of Fe (Conrad and Crosby, 1963; Forth, 1966; Forth and Rummel, 1965, 1966, 1968; Forth *et al.,* 1966; Manis and Schachter, 1962; Ruliffson and Hopping, 1963) and for the regulation of uptake according to the Fe requirements of the organism (Forth, 1966; Forth and Rummel, 1966, 1968; Hahn *et al.,* 1939, 1943). If Fe is supplied as a chelate, the system competes with the intraluminal ligands for Fe (Forth *et al.,* 1963; Forth, Pfleger *et al.,* 1965; Forth and Rummel, 1966; Forth, Rummel and Pfleger, 1968; Forth, Rummel and Seifen, 1965; Forth and Seifen, 1961). The system is apparently located in the upper part of the jejunum and

301

Table II. *Penetration of metals through the gut wall and uptake and binding in the mucosal tissue of normal (n) and iron-deficient (d) rats in vitro*

Experimental conditions: everted jejunal sacs of rats *in vitro* (Wilson and Wiseman, 1954). Concentration of metals: 5×10^{-6} mol/l. corresponding to 50,000 counts; ml.$^{-1}$; min.$^{-1}$; time 2 hr.; temperature 37°C. Means $\pm s_x$.

metal	Normal segments (n)			Fe-deficient segments (d)			(d/n)†	
	conc. of metal in the serosal fluid; counts ml.$^{-1}$ min.$^{-1}$ $\times 10^3$	uptake of metal by mucosal tissue; counts · 100 mg.$^{-1}$ (dry) min.$^{-1}$ $\times 10^3$	N*	conc. of metal in the serosal fluid; counts ml.$^{-1}$ min.$^{-1}$ $\times 10^3$	uptake of metal by mucosal tissue; counts · 100 mg.$^{-1}$ (dry) min.$^{-1}$ $\times 10^3$	N*	serosal fluid	tissue
^{54}Mn as (MnCl$_2$)	3 ±0·8	55 ±11	8	9·3‡ ±3	143‡ ±47	4	3·1	2·6
^{59}Fe as (FeSO$_4$)	1·5 ±0·5	61 ±15	24	16·3‡ ±4·4	230‡ ±62	16	10·9	3·8
^{58}Co as (CoCl$_2$)	19 ±4·3	46 ±4	8	57‡ ±11	134‡ ±43	8	3·0	2·9
^{63}Ni as (NiSO$_4$)	10·4 ±3·7	6·7 ±2·3	14	42‡ ±13	16·5‡ ±3·7	10	4·0	2·5
^{64}Cu as (CuSO$_4$)	0·9 ±0·5	73 ±33	8	0·8 ±0·4	53 ±25	8	0·9	0·73
^{65}Zn as (ZnCl$_2$)	0·14 ±0·06	36 ±66	16	0·26‡ ±0·09	61‡ ±17	4	1·9	1·7

* Number of experiments.
† For calculation see text.
‡ $P < 0.05$ as compared to normal controls.

duodenum (Dowdle *et al.*, 1960; Duthie, 1964; Forth and Rummel, 1965, 1966; Laurell, 1947; Manis and Schachter, 1962); it depends on intact oxidative phosphorylation in the mucosal cells (Rummel and Forth, 1968).

One might enquire about the nature of the Fe-binding system but this question cannot yet be answered. It is obvious to suppose that the Fe-binding system is identical to apoferritin; however, because of the extremely long half-life of the Fe release of ferritin (about four days) this seems to be unlikely (Bielig and Bayer, 1955). One cannot exclude the possibility that apoferritin is a part of the Fe-binding system (Charlton *et al.*, 1965) though a rather unimportant one with respect to the rapid phase of absorption of Fe in Fe deficiency.

If we assume an Fe-binding system exists in the mucosal cell which is related to absorption, we become interested in the specificity of this system; I shall deal exclusively with this problem in the following part of this paper.

To test the specificity of the system we studied the absorption of Fe and chemically related metals *in vitro* and *in vivo* in normal and Fe-deficient rats. Metals of the eighth group of the periodic system were selected for this purpose; that is, Fe, Co and Ni; from the neighbouring group 7B:Mn, and for the sake of comparison with other metals, Cu and Zn from groups 1B and 2B respectively.

First we investigated the penetration and the uptake and binding of these metals with the aid of radioisotopes *in vitro*. For the sake of simplicity the experiments were carried out with, so-called, everted sacs according to the method of Wilson and Wiseman (1954). The metals were offered on both sides of the everted sac in a concentration of $5 \cdot 0 \times 10^{-6}$ mol./l. The penetration was measured by means of radioactivity added only on the mucosal side (Table II).

I cannot go into details about all the results presented in Table II but it should be mentioned here that under normal conditions the penetration of Co and Ni is greatest and it is much greater than that of Mn and Fe. The penetration of Cu and Zn is exceptionally small.

In Fe-deficient segments this sequence is changed because the penetration of Fe is greatly increased. The most important result of this experiment is that in Fe deficiency apparently not only the penetration of Fe is increased but also that of all the other metals apart from Cu.

Uptake and binding of the metals show some differences if

303

compared with penetration. It should be mentioned here that all metals for which an increased penetration has been found are also bound to a higher extent. The differences between the amount of Cu in the mucosa of normal and Fe-deficient segments (the latter contain less Cu) is not significant.

To determine the affinity of the system in the mucosal tissue for the metals tested, and its specificity for Fe, we calculated the ratio d/n. That is, the ratio of the amount of radioactive metals in the absorbed fluid of Fe-deficient (d) and normal (n) segments. A ratio of 1·0 means that, as in the case of Cu, the penetration of Fe deficient segments equals that of normal ones. The greater this ratio the greater the increase of penetration in Fe deficiency.

The ratio is greatest for Fe (Table II); in other words Fe is preferred as compared with the other metals or the system in the mucosa shows the highest degree of specificity for Fe. In order of the specificity, the chemically related metals of the group VIII follow, that is Co and Ni and thereafter Mn of neighbouring group VIIB. The specificity is less for Zn and with Cu the system does not seem to react at all. Calculating the ratio d/n from the amount of Fe taken up by the mucosal tissue we obtained the same sequence (Table II).

In principle, similar results were obtained when the radioactive metals were injected *in vivo* into tied loops of jejunum of rats *in situ*. In this series of experiments the absorbed amount of radioactive metals was measured after 1 hour, by means of a body counter. Previously the jejunal loops were removed. Excretion of radio-activity by urine was avoided by a urethral ligature. The metals were administered in an amount of 0·18 μmol. in 2 ml. Since there is no γ-emitting isotope of Ni with a reasonable half-life we had to omit this metal in the experiment.

I will limit my considerations to the ratio d/n which was calculated in this case on the amount of metals absorbed by Fe deficient (d) and normal (n) animals (Table III). We see in these experiments that the specificity of the system is highest for Fe, followed by Co, Zn and Mn. In these experiments the ratio for Cu is also 1·0; that means in Fe deficiency the absorption of Cu is, in contrast to the other metals, not increased. It should be added here that in ileum segments we get for Fe, Co and Zn a ratio d/n of 1·0 corresponding to the assumption that the Fe-binding system is located in the upper part of the gut.

Summing up the results presented so far, it is to be stated that Fe-deficient rats, as compared with normal animals, not only absorb more Fe but also more Co, Mn and Zn and probably also

304

Table III. *Absorption of metals in normal (n) and iron-deficient (d) rats in vitro*

Experimental conditions: tied jejunal loops of rats; amount of metals offered; 0·18 μmol. in 2 ml.; time 1 hr. The figures are means $\pm s_x$ and indicate the amount absorbed in per cent. of the dose administered.

Metal	Normal rats (n)				Fe deficient rats (d)				(d/n)†	
	Jejunal loops	N*	Ileal loops	N*	Jejunal loops	N*	Ileal loops	N*	Jejunum	Ileum
^{54}Mn as (MnCl$_2$)	5·7 ±3·5	5	—	—	9·5‡ ±1·4	—	—	—	1·7	—
^{59}Fe as (FeSO$_4$)	7·1 ±2·4	15	1·9 ±0·8	10	37·1‡ ±12·0	15	1·5 ±0·6	10	5·2	0·8
^{58}Co as (CoCl$_2$)	20·8 ±4·2	10	4·1 ±0·7	5	65·5‡ ±10·2	10	3·4 ±0·4	5	3·1	0·8
^{64}Cu as (CuSO$_4$)	9·3 ±2·4	10	—	—	11·4 ±3·0	10	—	—	1·2	—
^{65}Zn as (ZnCl$_2$)	7·7 ±1·3	10	2·4 ±0·8	5	16·5‡ ±3·7	10	2·5 ±0·8	5	2·1	1·0

* Number of experiments.
† For calculations see text.
‡ $P < 0.05$ as compared to normal controls.

Table IV. *Mutual inhibition of absorption of iron by cobalt, manganese and zinc and vice versa in Fe-deficient rats in vivo*

Experimental conditions: tied jejunal loops of rats. Amount of radioactive metals offered: 0·05 μmol./ml. The figures are means of 5 rats $\pm s_x$ indicating the amount absorbed in per cent. of the dose administered; time 1 hr.

Absorption of ^{59}Fe-(FeSO$_4$) in presence of:

	0	0·05	0·5	5 μmol./ml.
CoCl$_2$	38·6 ±9	30·8 ±10	11·7* ±4·5	7·2* ±1·2
MnCl$_2$	43·0 ±7			25* ±2·0
ZnCl$_2$	42 ±6			14·3* ±5·3

Absorption of ^{60}Co-(CoCl$_2$), ^{54}Mn-(MnCl$_2$), ^{65}Zn-(ZnCl$_2$) in presence of FeSO$_4$:

	0	0·05	0·5	5 μmol./ml.
^{60}Co-(CoCl$_2$)	60·6 ±10·6	43·0 ±20·4	28·9* ±10·3	11·5* ±2·8
^{54}Mn-(MnCl$_2$)	6·5 ±2·3			3·5* ±1·4
^{65}Zn-(ZnCl$_2$)	9·5 ±1·4			5·2* ±2·0

* $P < 0.05$ as compared to the control experiment.

Ni. The absorption of Cu remains unchanged. These results might be interpreted in terms of an Fe-binding system in the mucosa which shows the highest degree of specificity for Fe. It should also be added that these results find a parallel in the uptake of Fe by reticulocytes. We observed that reticulocytes not only took up Fe but the cells of a reticulocyte-rich suspension were also able to bind and incorporate Co, Mn and Zn to a higher degree than were the cells of normal suspensions. Again they did not incorporate more Cu. Furthermore a mutual inhibition of the uptake of Fe and Co was observed (Forth *et al.*, 1967; Forth, Rummel, Crüsemann and Simon, 1968). This correspondence suggests that there exists a similar mechanism for transcellular transport of Fe in both the intestinal mucosa and in reticulocytes.

If the hypothesis is valid that there exist binding sites for Fe in the mucosa which react also with other metals, although with less specificity, then we can expect that the metals compete one with the other in the process of absorption. This indeed is the case as shown here by the example of Fe and Co (Table IV).

In these experiments we used only Fe-deficient animals because it was expected that the Fe-binding system of these animals would be exceptionally active. The amount of metals together with their radioisotopes was decreased to 0.05 μmol. to keep the amount of competing non-active metals as low as possible. As had been expected, Co inhibited the absorption of Fe and *vice versa*, Fe that of Co. To inhibit the absorption of Fe and Co respectively to half that of the controls a tenfold excess of the competing metals was needed.

It should be added that for both Mn and Zn a mutual inhibitory effect upon Fe absorption could be shown. In these experiments a one hundredfold excess of the competing metal has been used (compare also Pollack *et al.*, 1965).

The increased absorption of Mn, Co and Zn (as well as that of Fe) could also be shown *in vivo* in Fe-deficient animals after administration of the metals by stomach tube (Table V). These experiments show an increased retention in Fe deficiency after 21 days for Fe only. Manganese, Co and Zn, which are initially absorbed to a higher degree in Fe deficiency, are excreted. The retention of metals by normal animals after intravenous administration equals that of Fe-deficient rats (Table VI) i.e. the higher retention of metals after oral administration is not caused by a decreased excretion of metals.

In summary I should like to repeat the two most important

307

Table V. *Retention of metals by normal (n) and Fe-deficient (d) rats after application by stomach tube*

Experimental conditions: amount of metals offered: 0·36 μmol. in 2 ml. The figures are means of six rats ± s_x indicating the amount retained in per cent. of the dose administered.

Metals		Days after oral administration					
		2	3	4	7	13	21
^{54}Mn as (MnCl$_2$)	n	20·0 ±8·4	11·2 ±5·5	7·0 ±1·8	4·4 ±1·2	2·3 ±0·2	1·4 ±0·2
	d	45·7* ±18·3	28·2* ±6·2	16·0* ±7·0	7·5* ±2·4	1·7 ±0·8	0·8 ±0·3
^{59}Fe as (FeSO$_4$)	n	21·4 ±9·0	19·2 ±7·7	16·5 ±5·7	15·2 ±4·9	15·5 ±4·5	15·0 ±4·2
	d	75* ±8·1	73* ±8·7	70* ±8·6	66* ±8·3	67* ±8	65* ±8
^{58}Co as (CoCl$_2$)	n	2·8 ±0·1	1·0 ±0·1	0·9 ±0·3	0·8 ±0·3	0·4 ±0·1	0·2 ±0·08
	d	3·9* ±0·4	2·1* ±0·3	1·7* ±0·3	1·3* ±0·3	1·0* ±0·2	0·2 ±0·1
^{65}Zn as (ZnCl$_2$)	n	35 ±4·3	31 ±3·1	29 ±4·5	27 ±4·5	19 ±1·3	18 ±0·8
	d	69* ±10·6	51* ±7·9	46* ±7·8	34* ±2·3	25·4* ±1·5	23·6* ±11

* P < 0·05 as compared to normal controls.

Table VI. *Retention of metals by normal (n) and* Fe-*deficient (d) rats after intravenous administration*

Experimental conditions: amount of metals offered: 0·18 μmol. in 1 ml. The figures are means of five rats $\pm$ s_x indicating the amount retained in per cent. of the dose administered.

Metals		Days after intravenous administration	
		2	6
^{54}Mn as (MnCl$_2$)	n	42	24
		± 4	± 2
	d	42	19
		± 3	± 3
^{59}Fe as (FeSO$_4$)	n	—	103
			± 6
	d	—	98
			± 5
^{58}Co as (CoCl$_2$)	n	10	4
		± 2	$\pm 0·6$
	n	8	3
		± 1	$\pm 0·5$
^{65}Zn as (ZnCl$_2$)	n	58	38
		± 4	± 3
	d	57	35
		± 3	± 3

facts of our investigations: first, in Fe deficiency, not only Fe but also other chemically related metals are absorbed to a higher extent, as for instance, Co, Mn and even Zn. Second, these metals are apparently competing with Fe in absorption. These results may be interpreted on the assumption of an Fe-binding system in the mucosal tissue which is responsible for the absorption of Fe. This system shows the highest specificity for Fe.

REFERENCES

BIELIG, H.-J. & BAYER, E. (1955). *Naturwissenschaften*, **42**, 466.
BOTHWELL, TH. H., PIRZIO-BIROLI, G. & FINCH, C. (1958). *J. Lab. clin. Med.* **51**, 24.
CHARLEY, P. J., STITT, C., SHORE, E. & SALTMAN, P. (1968). *J. Lab. clin. Med.* **61**, 397.
CHARLTON, R. W., JACOBS, P., TORRANCE, J. D. & BOTHWELL, T. H. (1965). *J. clin. Invest.* **44**, 542.
CONRAD, M. E. & CROSBY, W. H. (1963). *Blood*, **22**, 406.
DOWDLE, E. B., SCHACHTER, D. & SCHENKER, H. (1960). *Am. J. Physiol.* **198**, 609.
DUTHIE, H. L. (1964). *Br. J. Haemat.* **10**, 59.
FISHER, R. B. & PARSONS, D. S. (1949). *J. Physiol. Lond.*, **110**, 36.

309

FORTH, W. (1966). *Untersuchungen über die Resorption von Eisen und chemisch verwandten Schwermetallen an Därmen normaler und anämischer Ratten* in vivo *und* in vitro; *ein Beitrag zur Frage der Spezifität des eisenbindenden System in der Mucosa.* Homburg/Saar: Habil. Schrift.
FORTH, W. & ANDRES, H. (1969). *Arzneimittel-Forsch.* **19**, 363.
FORTH, W., LEOPOLD, G. & RUMMEL, W. (1968). *Naunyn-Schmiedebergs Arch. exp. Path. Pharmak.* **261**, 434.
FORTH, W., PFLEGER, K. & RUMMEL, W. (1963). *Naunyn-Schmiedebergs Arch. exp. Path. Pharmak.* **245**, 89.
FORTH, W., PFLEGER, K., RUMMEL, W., SEIFEN, E. & RICHMOND, Sp. J. (1965). *Naunyn-Schmiedebergs Arch. exp. Path. Pharmak.* **252**, 242.
FORTH, W. & RUMMEL, W. (1965). *Naunyn-Schmiedebergs Arch. exp. Path. Pharmak.* **252**, 205.
FORTH, W. & RUMMEL, W. (1966). *Med. Pharmacol. exp.* **14**, 289, 384.
FORTH, W. & RUMMEL, W. (1968). *Klin. Wschr.* **46**, 1003.
FORTH, W., RUMMEL, W. & BECKER, P. J. (1966). *Med. Pharmac. exp.* **15**, 179.
FORTH, W:, RUMMEL, W., CRÜSEMANN, D. & PFLEGER, K. (1967). *Naunyn-Schmiedebergs Arch. exp. Path. Pharmak.* **257**, 275.
FORTH, W., RUMMEL, W., CRÜSEMANN, D. & SIMON, J. (1968). *I. Intern. Symposium uber Stoffwechsel und Permeabilitat von Erythrocyten und Thrombocyten.* Ed. Deutsch, Gerlach & Moser. p. 444, Stuttgart: Thieme.
FORTH, W., RUMMEL, W. & PFLEGER, K. (1968). *Naunyn-Schmiedebergs Arch. exp. Path. Pharmak.* **261**, 225.
FORTH, W., RUMMEL, W. & SEIFEN, E. (1965). *Naunyn-Schmiedebergs Arch. exp. Path. Pharmak.* **252**, 224.
FORTH, W. & SEIFEN, E. (1961). *Naunyn-Schmiedebergs Arch. exp. Path. Pharmak.* **241**, 556.
GRANICK, S. (1949). *Bull. N.Y. Acad. Med.* **25**, 403.
GRANICK, S. (1951). *Physiol. Rev.* **31**, 489.
HAHN, P. F., BALE, W. F., LAWRENCE, E. O. & WHIPPLE, G. H. (1939). *J. exp. Med.* **69**, 739.
HAHN, P. F., BALE, W. P., ROSS, J. F., BALFOUR, W. M. & WHIPPLE, G. H. (1943). *J. exp. Med.* **78**, 169.
HOPPING, J. M. & RULIFFSON, W. S. (1963). *Am. J. Physiol.* **205**, 885.
JACOBI, H., PFLEGER, K. & RUMMEL, W. (1956). *Naunyn-Schmiedebergs Arch. exp. Path. Pharmak.* **229**, 198.
LAURELL, C. B. (1947). *Acta physiol. scand. Suppl.* **46**, 14.
MANIS, J. G. & SCHACHTER, D. (1962). *Am. J. Physiol.* **203**, 73, 81.
POLLACK, S., GEORGE, J. N., REBA, R. C., KAUFMAN, R. M. & CROSBY, W. H. (1965). *J. clin. Invest.* **44**, 1470.
RULIFFSON, W. S. & HOPPING, J. M. (1963). *Am. J. Physiol.* **204**, 171.
RUMMEL, W. & FORTH, W. (1968). *Naunyn-Schmiedebergs Arch. exp. Path. Pharmak.* **260**, 50.
SCHADE, A. L., OYAMA, J., REINHART, R. W. & MILLER, J. R. (1954). *Proc. Soc. exp. Biol. Med.* **87**, 443.
WILSON, T. H. & WISEMAN, G. (1954). *J. Physiol. Lond.*, **123**, 116.

DISCUSSION

Cuthbertson (Glasgow). I was very interested in your paper and in your use of the everted sac technique. Did you check histologically that the epithelium of the jejunum was intact? In past work we have found that it is very labile; within minutes or seconds of death, depending on the method of killing, there is often shedding. I don't think this will effect the relevance of your results but if the epithelium is shed it might affect the relative rates of absorption that you have observed. I would like to put in a word of warning against making the assumption that the everted sac represents physiological conditions unless there is good evidence suggesting that the epithelium has not been extensively damaged.

Forth (Homburg/Saar). We examined our preparations histologically and our mucosal preparations appeared to be good. Everted sacs do however swell during the experiment due to the incubation in saline. We have however carried out experiments using tissues prepared by the Fisher and Parsons method, because, by this method water absorption can be checked which of course gives a good indication of the integrity of the mucosa.

Topps (Aberdeen). Why does Cu behave so differently from other metals?

Forth (Homburg/Saar). Briefly—I have no idea.

Reinhold (Beirut). How does the affinity of transferrin for these metals compare with their rates of penetration?

Forth (Homburg/Saar). We know little about the relationship between penetration and binding in the mucosa. These processes behave differently in their response to metabolic poisons, for example, nitrogen perfusion has no effect on penetration and binding is only slightly suppressed whereas dinitrophenol suppresses both penetration and binding. If you inhibit uptake by adding ligands, for example adding Fe as a chelate, there is competition between mucosal binding sites and free ligands in the solution and there is no penetration. Penetration and binding are related but we can not say how. Transferrin must only have an indirect influence on this process in removing Fe from the mucosa.

Bremner (Aberdeen). In work we have done on trace metals in the digestive tract of the sheep we have found that the pH of the intestinal lumen markedly influences the properties of these metals. How closely have you compared the pH of your perfusion solutions with that of the jejunum of the rat?

Forth (Homburg/Saar). The perfusion solution has a pH of 6·9 to 7 and to 50 ml. of this we add 0·5 ml. of ferrous Fe at pH 2. A precipitate of ferric Fe is formed at the higher pH. We have compared Fe absorption from tied loops using perfusion solutions of different pH; absorption decreases sharply above pH 2·8 to 3.

Hoekstra (Madison). It is perhaps worth mentioning that Hopkins and Mertz have found that chromium and Fe share the

311

same transport site; the discrimination between Cr and Fe is thus probably very poor.

Hannan (Dublin). You mentioned the absorption of Fe by reticulocytes; do you feel this could be an additional transport mechanism?

Forth (Homburg/Saar). The uptake of Fe by reticulocyte-rich suspensions is higher than the uptake of normal blood suspensions. Reticulocytes also take up Co, Mn and Zn to a greater extent than does the red blood cell, but not Cu. The uptake of Cu is in fact decreased in reticulocyte-rich suspensions, but we do not know why. Dinitrophenol slightly reduces the uptake of these metals by reticulocytes but I feel that the uptake is probably a physiological process.

STUDIES OF ZINC METABOLISM IN MAN

HERTA SPENCER AND J. SAMACHSON

Metabolic Section, Veterans Administration Hospital, Hines, Illinois, U.S.A.

ONLY limited information has been obtained on the metabolism of zinc in man under controlled dietary conditions and on the influence of dietary factors on Zn absorption. In the present studies the effect of the dietary protein on Zn absorption and the interrelationship of calcium and Zn were investigated under controlled dietary conditions.

MATERIALS AND METHODS

Studies were performed in patients in a metabolic research ward during a low and high Ca intake during a low, normal and high protein intake and during total starvation. The low Ca intake averaged 250 mg., the high Ca intake 2000 mg./day, the normal protein intake was 1 g./kg., the low protein intake 0·5 g./kg. and the high protein intake 2 g./kg. Tracer doses of $^{65}ZnCl_2$ were given orally in each study phase and the plasma levels, urinary and faecal excretions of ^{65}Zn were determined. The effect of infusions of 500 mg. Ca on the urinary excretions of ^{65}Zn and stable Zn was studied. ^{65}Zn was counted in a well-type γ-counter, stable Zn was determined with an atomic absorption spectrophotometer (Willis, 1962).

RESULTS AND DISCUSSION

Following an oral dose of $^{65}ZnCl_2$ the ^{65}Zn plasma levels reached a peak at 4 hours in most cases and then decreased with time (Spencer et al., 1965). The major portion of the ingested ^{65}Zn passed with the stool, however, the faecal ^{65}Zn excretion was quite variable and ranged from 20 to 75 per cent. of the dose in 15 days, one-half of the patients excreting more than 50 per cent. in stools (Spencer et al., 1966). The average net absorption of ^{65}Zn was 50·8 per cent. Low ^{65}Zn plasma levels reflected a low absorption of ^{65}Zn determined from faecal ^{65}Zn excretions while high plasma levels reflected greater ^{65}Zn absorption. The correlation between the 4-hour plasma levels and the faecal ^{65}Zn excretions was highly significant, $P < 0.001$.

Previous studies have shown that raising the Ca intake from about 250 mg. to 2000 mg. per day did not significantly change the absorption of ^{65}Zn (Spencer et al., 1965). This is in contrast with the decreased utilization of Zn in animals during high Ca intake (Hoekstra et al., 1956; O'Dell et al., 1958; Hoekstra, 1964). The differences in the effect of the high Ca intake on Zn absorption in rats and man may be due to the much higher Ca intake in rats relative to the total body weight.

No correlation could be established between the urinary excretion of Ca, of ^{65}Zn or of stable Zn. Infusions of Ca increased the urinary Ca excretion markedly. At the same time, the urinary excretion of stable Zn increased by an average of 22 per cent. The mechanism for the increased excretion of stable Zn is not clear; the increase may be due to removal of Zn from soft tissues or from bone due to exchange of the infused Ca with bone Ca and concomitant removal of Zn from bone.

The absorption of ^{65}Zn differed during low and high protein intake as compared to the absorption on a normal protein intake of 1 g./kg. During a low protein intake of 0·5 gm./kg. the ^{65}Zn plasma levels were considerably higher and the faecal ^{65}Zn excretions were lower than during a normal protein intake indicating increased ^{65}Zn absorption. During high protein intake of 2 g./kg., the ^{65}Zn plasma levels were considerably lower and the faecal excretions were higher than during a normal protein intake, indicating decreased intestinal absorption of ^{65}Zn during high protein intake. These results are similar to those obtained with different protein levels in rats (Methfessel and Spencer, 1968).

The urinary excretion of stable Zn was low and ranged from 0·3 to 0·6 mg./day during a low or high intake of Zn. However,

313

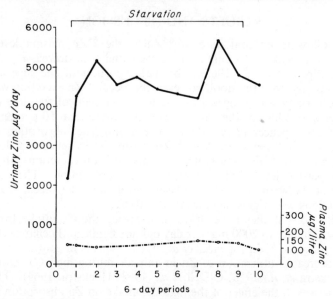

FIG. 1. Effect of starvation on urinary Zn and upon plasma Zn concentration.

during total starvation of several weeks' duration the urinary Zn excretion increased markedly and reached levels of 5 to 6 mg. per day. This high Zn excretion was not associated with a corresponding increase in the urinary Ca or magnesium excretion. Despite the marked increase in urinary Zn excretion the plasma level of Zn was not decreased during prolonged starvation (Fig. 1).

Acknowledgement. Supported by Contract AT (11–1)–1231–48 from the U.S. Atomic Energy Commission.

REFERENCES

HOEKSTRA, W. G. (1964). *Fedn Proc. Fedn Am. Socs exp. Biol.* **23**, 1068.
HOEKSTRA, W. G., LEWIS, P. K., PHILLIPS, P. H. & GRUMMER, R. H. (1956). *J. Anim. Sci.* **15**, 752.
METHFESSEL, A. H. & SPENCER, H. (1968). *Fedn Proc. Fedn Am. Socs exp. Biol.* **27**, 422.
O'DELL, B. L., NEWBERNE, P. M. & SAVAGE, J. E. (1958). *J. Nutr.* **65**, 503.
SPENCER, H., VANKINSCOTT, V., LEWIN, I. & SAMACHSON, J. (1965). *J. Nutr.* **86**, 169.
SPENCER, H., ROSOFF, B., LEWIN, I. & SAMACHSON, J. (1966). In *Zinc Metabolism*, ed. Prasad, A. S. p. 339. Springfield: Thomas.
WILLIS, J. B. (1962). *Analyt. Chem.* **34**, 614.

DISCUSSION

Lassiter (Athens, Ga.). If I remember correctly, work with swine has shown that increased dietary Ca levels increase Zn excretion in the urine. What do you think might be the cause of the difference between these observations and your own on man?

Spencer (Hines, Ill.). We expected that the urinary excretion of Zn would be increased as urinary Ca output increased but we did not find this correlation. I don't know why there is the difference between swine and man other than to suggest that it is a species difference.

Anke (Jena). We have found significant differences in the Zn concentration of liver, kidney and ribs of men as compared with women. Do you find sex differences in the absorption or excretion of Zn?

Spencer (Hines, Ill.). Most of our studies of Zn absorption have been carried out on men. We have, however, investigated the effect of oestrogens on Zn absorption and, if anything, ocstrogen slightly decreases the absorption of Zn.

Duncan (Aberdeen). Would Dr Spencer like to speculate on the origins of the large quantity of Zn excreted during starvation?

Spencer (Hines, Ill.). We were sometimes anxious that our patients might lose so much Zn that they ran into Zn deficiency. We would assume that this Zn is being withdrawn from body stores and our previous distribution studies have shown that most of the Zn is present in liver and spleen. The concentration of Zn in muscle is lower but of course the muscle mass is large and together with the Zn of bone these may be additional sources. I would assume however that most of it comes from the liver as there are large changes in liver mass during starvation.

Reinhold (Beirut). I take it that the plasma Zn concentration of these patients was within normal limits so presumably their Zn nutrition was adequate before the experiment. Was there a long period of total starvation?

Spencer (Hines, Ill.). The plasma Zn concentrations were normal before the experiment and the longest period of total starvation was 80 days. Zinc was continually excreted even when the excretion of all other elements had fallen to very low levels.

Reinhold (Beirut). Would you explain under what circumstances you were using ^{65}Zn in human subjects?

315

Spencer (Hines, Ill.). We use ^{65}Zn as the chloride and our dose was 0·1 μCi/kg. We are allowed to use it in patients over 50 years of age but not in younger patients.

Strain (Rochester). Can you comment on the forms of Zn present in the urine and how these change during starvation?

Spencer (Hines, Ill.). I do not know in which form it is excreted. We tried to correlate Zn excretion in urine with urinary nitrogen content but within the first 12 to 18 days of starvation the N excretion is very high but then falls off while Zn excretion remains high. We tried to correlate it with phosphorus but again P excretion decreases with time.

Elmes (Belfast). Is the Zn in the urine in starvation derived from breakdown of the cells of the small intestinal mucosa which at this time must be depending upon endogenous sources of N?

Spencer (Hines, Ill.). I suppose it could be but in this instance you would have to postulate that the Zn was reabsorbed into the blood stream before excretion in the urine.

Quarterman (Aberdeen). We have starved rats for three days and found similar decreases in the Zn content of several tissues including gut epithelium. In relation to Dr Elmes' question I should say that the decrease in the Zn content of gut epithelium was no greater than that of other tissues. I should like to ask Dr Spencer if there is any relation between the magnitude of urinary Zn excretion and the degree of illness or injury of hospitalized patients?

Spencer (Hines, Ill.). We have not tested this and I suppose that Dr Strain or Dr Pories could answer this question much better than I.

Pories (Rochester). We have found an increase in urinary Zn excretion following stress trauma and during cirrhosis. In fact, during cirrhosis, the zincuria is often massive and refractory to Zn medication; in some patients we found it difficult to raise the plasma Zn concentration above 0·60 to 0·65 μg./ml. Do you have any data regarding the faecal Zn excretion of your patients?

Spencer (Hines, Ill.). Only in those patients that are receiving food, as during prolonged starvation there is hardly any passage of faeces. Under normal conditions, with a normal food intake,

316

about 80 per cent. of the Zn is recovered in stools. Inasmuch as there is no production of stools during starvation there may perhaps be a shift of the pathway of Zn excretion from the intestine to the kidney.

THE INTERRELATIONS BETWEEN CADMIUM, ZINC, COPPER AND IRON IN METABOLISM OF HENS, RUMINANTS AND MAN

M. ANKE, A. HENNIG, H.-J. SCHNEIDER, H. LÜDKE, W. von GAGERN
AND H. SCHLEGEL

Department of Animal Production, University of Jena, G.D.R.

THE toxic effect of cadmium became generally known from the work of Parizek and Zahor (1956), however, up to now we have not been able to explain the complete mechanism of this toxicosis.

The most recent experiments organized in our institute examined the effect of Cd on female animals. Hens fed on 200 p.p.m. Cd daily stopped egg-production within six days and 50 and 100 p.p.m. reduced egg-production and decreased egg weight. When we stopped feeding Cd, the hens began to lay again after 10 days. The hen ovary changed very greatly under the influence of Cd nutrition; 100 and to a still larger extent 200 p.p.m. caused a complete atrophy. The gizzard showed typical signs of Zn deficiency. The epithelial structures began to degenerate when Cd was fed.

On the twenty-eighth day of the test the hens were killed and their bodies analysed. All the tissues examined of the hens fed on 200 p.p.m. Cd contained significantly more Cd than those of the control hens. The highest Cd concentration was found in the kidney (Table I).

Table I. *Cadmium and zinc concentrations (p.p.m.) found in different tissues and in the eggs of hens*

	Cd in tissue		Zn in tissue	
	Control	200 p.p.m. Cd	Control	200 p.p.m. Cd
Muscles	0·61	1·23 + +	125	77 + + +
Femur	5·07	6·42 +	244	149 + + +
Feathers	0·07	0·34 +	211	128 + + +
Kidneys	13·57	632　+ + +	160	166 −
Liver	3·20	245　+ + +	158	241 + + +
Eggs	0·46	0·37 −	60	68 −

− = P > 0·05, + = P < 0·05, + + = P < 0·01, + + + = P < 0·001.

Cadmium supplements caused a significant decrease of the Zn concentration in muscles, bones and feathers. The Zn-content of the kidneys remained, however, uninfluenced. The Zn removed from muscles, bones and feathers was concentrated in the liver. This also explains the Zn deficiency of the gizzard. There was no change in the Cd and Zn concentration of eggs laid on the sixth to seventh day of the trial.

In agreement with the results of Hill, Matrone, Payne and Barber (1963), Van Campen (1966) and Hennig and Anke (1964) in pigs we showed that high dietary Cd causes a largely decreased Cu concentration in the muscles, bones and feathers of hens. At the end of this 28 day experiment the Cu removed was concentrated in the kidneys and liver. The same was true for Fe. The egg

Table II. *Copper and iron concentrations (p.p.m.) found in different body parts and in the eggs of hens*

	Cu in tissue		Fe in tissue	
	Control	200 p.p.m. Cd	Control	200 p.p.m. Cd
Muscles	3·5	1·7 +	60	57 −
Femur	6·2	4·8 + +	106	83 +
Feathers	5·2	2·9 + + +	41	33 −
Kidneys	15·0	21·7 +	388	319 +
Liver	10·8	16·9 +	554	1051 + + +
Eggs	3·1	2·4 +	105	102 −

$- = P > 0·05$, $+ = P < 0·05$, $+ + = P < 0·01$, $+ + + = P < 0·001$.

analysis showed that the Cu concentration of the egg decreased under excess Cd nutrition. The Cd, Zn and Fe concentrations of the eggs remained practically uninfluenced. This fact is very important for theories about the effect of Cd on mammals.

For the studies with ruminants two-year-old goats were tested. These animals got a semisynthetic ration containing 75 p.p.m. Cd until death; the last of the animals died after 19 months. The Cd poisoned female goats came quite normally in to heat. They needed 1·2 inseminations to become pregnant while the control group needed only 1·0 inseminations and 50 per cent. of the high Cd goats aborted. None of the normally born kids was fit for life. We analysed the hair, kidneys and liver of both dams and kids. Cadmium was mainly concentrated in the kidneys and livers of the dams. On the other hand tissue Cd concentrations of their kids was not different from that of the control group, nor did the milk of the Cd goats contain more Cd. As in the experiment with hens, here also no Cd was transported from the dam to the new-

Table III. *Cadmium concentration (p.p.m.) in the hair, liver, kidneys and milk of both goats and kids fed on control and high-*Cd *rations*

	Dams		Kids	
	Control	Cd-group	Control	Cd-group
Hair	0·37	1·42 + + +	0·76	0·25 −
Kidneys	2·30	668 + + +	0·83	0·49 −
Liver	1·71	184 + +	0·99	0·58 +
Milk	0·70	0·69 −	—	—

− = P > 0·05, + = P < 0·05, + + = P < 0·01, + + + = P < 0·001.

born young, not even in the milk. As to Zn concentration, however, extra Cd nutrition to goats did influence the Zn metabolism of both dams and kids. While the Zn of the dam's body was highly

Table IV. *Zinc concentration (p.p.m.) found in the hair, liver, kidneys and milk of* Cd-*fed goats and their kids*

	Dams		Kids	
	Control	Cd-group	Control	Cd-group
Hair	179	190 −	143	145 −
Kidneys	87	330 + + +	101	86 −
Liver	158	421 + +	239	94 + + +
Milk	37	19 +	—	—

− = P > 0·05, + = P < 0·05, + + = P < 0·01, + + + = P < 0·001.

concentrated in liver and kidneys, the kids showed a lessened percentage of Zn in their livers and kidneys. Also the Zn excretion by the milk amounted to only 50 per cent. of the normal value. The greatest effect of extra Cd feeding was that on the Cu metabolism of goats and kids. Both dams and kids contained less Cu.

Table V. *Copper concentration (p.p.m.) found in the hair, liver, kidneys and milk of* Cd-*fed goats and their kids*

	Dams		Kids	
	Control	Cd-group	Control	Cd-group
Hair	8·9	2·7 +	8·3	9·4 −
Kidneys	9·8	8·3 −	19·0	5·4 −
Liver	11·3	4·5 +	63·3	5·4 +
Milk	2·7	1·4 +	—	—

− = P > 0·05, + = P < 0·05, + + = P < 0·01, + + + = P < 0·001.

The livers of kids from dams receiving Cd contained only 8 per cent. of the Cu of control kids. The milk contained significantly less Cu. The low life expectancy of the Cd-group kids was probably caused by an acute deficiency of Cu in conjunction with a shortage of Zn.

Summarizing we wish to say that Cd acts as an antagonist of Zn and Fe. Moreover, it influences the Cu concentration and for the next generations this influence can be very dangerous. Cadmium is not transferred to the next generation, not even by the milk; however it causes a drastic reduction of the Cu reserves in the foetus and the Cu concentration in the milk.

REFERENCES

HENNIG, A. & ANKE, M. (1964). *Arch. Tierernähr.* **14**, 55.
HILL, C. H., MATRONE, G., PAYNE, W. L. & BARBER, C. W. (1963). *J. Nutr.* **80**, 227.
PARIZEK, J. & ZAHOR, Z. (1956). *Nature, Lond.* **177**, 1036.
VAN CAMPEN, D. R. (1966). *J. Nutr.* **88**, 125.

DISCUSSION

Oberleas (Detroit). Did you determine the Cd content of brain tissue of any of your animals? I ask this because we have found that Cd does not cross the blood-brain barrier in the rat.

Anke (Jena). No we did not.

Hoekstra (Madison). Could the marked drop in human kidney Cd during the late stages of life and the increase in Zn, at least in the female, indicate that people high in Cd and low in Zn are those that die earlier? How do you interpret the sharp drop in Cd in man above the age of 70?

Anke (Jena). We have found a positive correlation between Cd and Zn concentration in liver, kidney and the ribs of man. We think it is possible that people who died at 65 years of age had a high Cd level and the others surviving to 70 had a lower Cd content. We have of course no way of proving this as we have no analysis at 65 years of age for those who survived to 70.

GASTRIC SECRETIONS AND IRON ABSORPTION IN RATS

J. MURRAY AND NELL STEIN

*Department of Medicine, University of Minnesota,
Minneapolis, Minnesota, U.S.A.*

THESE studies were designed to study the effect of gastric juice on assimilation of iron from the diet and to separate the effects of the non-acid from the acid portions of the juice.

Gastric atrophy was induced in 10, 23-day-old Sprague-Dawley rats by irradiation of the exposed mobilized stomach with 1750 rads of X-ray (Murray and Stein, 1970). They were fed laboratory chow. A control group of 14 untreated rats was fed a low-Fe diet and another untreated group of nine fed laboratory chow. At 168 days of life their haemoglobins, weights and gastric juice pH's (Shay *et al.*, 1954) were determined. They were killed and the livers removed for estimation of non-haem Fe as an indication of Fe stores. The mean data are recorded in Table I. It is evident that Fe deficiency is present in the irradiated group. To be sure that this was not due to gastro-intestinal bleeding we studied the fall-off in total body radioactivity in irradiated and control rats following parenteral injection of 0·25 μCi. ^{59}Fe. No differences between groups were observed. Thus assimilation of Fe appeared to be defective in rats with gastric atrophy.

In groups of 10 irradiated and 10 control rats we studied the effect of 1 ml. of the following factors on absorption of 0·25 μCi. ^{59}Fe as ferrous citrate: (1) H_2O, (2) 0·1 N–HCl, (3) neutralized rat gastric juice, (4) a medium containing protein, acid and Fe in concentration similar to gastric juice, (5) rat gastric juice and (6) human gastric juice. The effects of H_2O and HCl were similar and unremarkable in both groups. Neutralized gastric juice and synthetic medium increased absorption slightly in both groups. However, Fe stores as determined by liver non-haem Fe were reduced in the irradiated group so absorption should have been greater in the control group. This defect was corrected by rat or human gastric juice but not, as we have recently observed, by intrinsic factors or gastric juice from patients with pernicious anaemia. X-irradiation of single rat limbs with 1750 rads did not produce significant changes in haemoglobin, gastric juice pH or ^{59}Fe absorption.

If a factor in the stomach is necessary for optimal Fe absorption an antibody to it might inhibit its activity. Accordingly an anti-

Table I. *Data from dietary study*

Group and Diet	No. of Rats	Weight Gain g.	Haemoglobin Gain g.%	Gastric Juice pH	Liver Non-haem Iron µg./g.
1 Gastric Atrophy on Chow	10	+302	+1·5	7·3 ± 0·42	95 ± 33* P = < 0·001†
2 Normal on Low-Fe diet	14	+322	+2·3	1·61 ± 0·19	126 ± 35 P = < 0·001
3 Normal on Chow	9	+420	+3·8	1·28 ± 0·13	263 ± 41

* ± one standard error of the mean.
† P values (Student *t*) related to group 3.

body to rat gastric mucosa was prepared in rabbits. 1 ml. of the antiserum (Murray and Stein, 1969) was mixed with 0·25 μCi. ^{59}Fe. Absorption of this was measured in anaemic rats and in rats with gastric atrophy and compared with absorption when the ^{59}Fe was mixed with 1 ml. plain rabbit serum. In anaemic rats antibody produced a moderate depression of ^{59}Fe absorption but in rats with gastric atrophy absorption was almost completely inhibited.

The implication of these studies is that there is a factor in gastric juice necessary for optimal Fe absorption in rats faced with an increased demand for Fe.

REFERENCES

MURRAY, M. J. & STEIN, N. (1969a). *Proc. Soc. exp. Biol. Med.* **131,** 565.
MURRAY, M. J. & STEIN, N. (1970). *Prov. Soc. exp. Biol. Med.* In press.
SHAY, N., SUN, D. C. D. & GRUENSTEIN, M. (1954). *Gastroenterology,* **26,** 906.

DISCUSSION

Forth (Homburg/Saar). We have taken gastric juice from normal and Fe-deficient rats and added Fe. The juice from normal rats we put in isolated loops of intestine from deficient animals and vice versa. We could see no difference in Fe absorption resulting from any of these treatments.

Murray (Minneapolis). We have had the same experience with intestinal loops and we feel that the factor necessary is present in the stomach rather than in the intestinal loop.

Hannan (Dublin). Have you looked at the histology of the irradiated stomachs of your animals?

Murray (Minneapolis). Yes, there is absolutely total loss of mucosa. A few mucus cells are left and the only thing you find in these stomachs is a small amount of mucus.

Hannan (Dublin). Do you think your findings would also hold good for haemoglobin as a source of Fe?

Murray (Minneapolis). This is being investigated at the moment.

Panić (Zemun). Did you measure the affinity of gastric juice for Fe or did you attempt to isolate gastroferrin from the juice?

Murray (Minneapolis). No, but we have studied the effect of gastric atrophy on the rate of Fe uptake into the carcass. The factors we are talking about here are essential for the rapid transfer of Fe. If you give radioactive Fe then 80 per cent. is in the ferrous form in the carcass in two minutes. If gastric atrophy is present only 15 per cent. has been transported in two minutes. A gastric factor is essential for the rapid transfer of Fe through the mucosa but this need not necessarily be associated with binding. We are still working on this.

PLASMA IRON AND ITS TRANSPORT TO THE OVOCYTES OF LAYING HENS

B. R. PANIĆ

Institute for the Application of Nuclear Energy in Agriculture, Veterinary Medicine and Forestry, Zemun, Yugoslavia

THE onset of laying in the domestic fowl is accompanied by an increase in the concentration of plasma iron (Ramsay and Campbell, 1954). The increase of plasma Fe content can be induced also in immature pullets and cockerels by treatment with oestrogens (Ramsay and Campbell, 1956; Campbell, 1960).

The increase of Fe in the plasma of laying hens is closely connected with the excretion of relatively large quantities of Fe in the eggs. Ramsay and Campbell (1954) have found that a good layer may lose 150 to 200 mg. Fe in a year.

In the eggs the Fe is almost exclusively deposited in the egg yolk (Panić, 1969; unpublished data) where it is bound to a phosphoprotein, phosvitin (Greengard *et al.*, 1964). Although the egg white contains an Fe-binding protein, conalbumin, the amount of Fe in egg white is extremely low. This fact indicates that different mechanisms are involved in the transport of Fe to the egg yolk and egg white.

The purpose of this study was to elucidate the forms of Fe in plasma of laying hens and the mechanism of its transport to the ovocytes and egg yolks.

EXPERIMENTAL

The binding of Fe to the plasma proteins has been investigated both *in vitro* and *in vivo*. For *in vitro* investigations blood plasma of laying hens, normal and oestrogen-treated immature pullets (4 months old) and plasma of piglets were used. 4 μl. ^{59}FeCl$_3$

solution (0·1 μCi) was added to 0·5 to 1·0 ml. plasma and incubated for 15 min. at 37° C. The plasma proteins were pre-precipitated with trichloracetic acid (TCA) followed by extraction of Fe with 'colour reagent' according to the Fischl method (1960) for plasma Fe determination. This method was modified only by a three-fold extraction of Fe with colour reagent. After the extraction, the radioactivity of the protein precipitate and the total extract was measured using a 'well' type scintilation counter.

In *in vivo* experiments immature pullets of the same age as the above were divided into two groups consisting of five birds each. To the pullets of group 1, oestradiol propionate was injected intramuscularly for five days (2 mg. per day), while group 2 served as a control. The radioactivity of blood plasma was measured at intervals of 1, 2, 4, 24, 72 and 120 hours after the oral administration of $^{59}FeCl_3$ (50 μCi./kg. body weight).

Determination of Fe in plasma was carried out according to the method of Fischl (1960) with or without wet ashing of samples. Isolation of phosvitin from plasma of laying hens was performed by the method of Heald and McLachlan (1963).

RESULTS AND DISCUSSION

From the summarized results of *in vitro* studies (Table I) it can be seen that ^{59}Fe is more firmly bound to the plasma proteins in laying hens and in oestradiol treated immature pullets than in control pullets and piglets. By the precipitation of plasma proteins with TCA and by extraction of Fe with colour reagent it was possible to remove only one component of ^{59}Fe bound to plasma proteins (32·3 $\pm$ 2·0 per cent. in laying hens and 46·3 $\pm$ 5·2 per cent. in oestrogen-treated pullets); after this treatment the protein precipitate retained the greater part of the bound ^{59}Fe (67·0 $\pm$ 2·0 per cent. in laying hens and 53·7 $\pm$ 5·2 per cent. in oestrogen-treated pullets). However, in control pullets and piglets the same treatment of plasma removed almost all ^{59}Fe bound to plasma proteins. Radioactivity of protein precipitate after extraction by colour reagent averaged only 1·2 $\pm$ 0·5 per cent. in control pullets and 1·7 $\pm$ 0·2 per cent. in piglets, while radioactivity of the extract (^{59}Fe removed from proteins) amounted to 98·8 $\pm$ 0·5 and 98·3 $\pm$ 0·2 per cent. respectively. These data suggest that in plasma of laying hens and oestrogen-treated immature pullets some protein exists which binds Fe more tightly than transferrin (the Fe of transferrin is all released by the conditions of treatment used).

The results of our *in vivo* experiments support this assumption. Radioactivity of blood plasma in immature pullets treated with

325

Table I. Binding of ^{59}Fe to the plasma proteins and the concentration of stable Fe in plasma of laying hens, immature pullets and piglets

	Units	Laying hens	Immature pullets (4 months old)		Piglets (3 months old)
			Controls	Oestrogen-treated	
		(3)†	(3)	(4)	(4)
Initial radioactivity (0·5 or 1·0 ml. plasma + 4 µl. ^{59}FeCl$_3$	c.p.m.	53757 ± 764	43759 ± 427	43194 ± 827	54174 ± 590
TCA-protein precipitate after 3-fold extraction with 'Colour reagent'*	c.p.m.	32264 ± 587	491 ± 210	21974 ± 2399	859 ± 81
	% of recovered activity	67·7 ± 2·0	1·2 ± 0·5	53·7 ± 5·2	1·7 ± 0·2
Total extract (3 extraction with 4 ml. 'Colour reagent')	c.p.m.	15431 ± 1224	41053 ± 1376	18907 ± 1854	51163 ± 1713
	% of recovered activity	32·3 ± 2·0	98·8 ± 0·5	46·3 ± 5·2	98·3 ± 0·2
		(6)†	(8)	(4)	(6)
Total plasma Fe (after wet ashing of plasma samples)	µg./100 ml.	633 ± 150	127 ± 37	1204 ± 213	147‡
TCA-removable plasma Fe (Fischl method)	µg./100 ml.	173 ± 21	121 ± 21	210 ± 16	153‡

* Colour reagent: 30 g. of potassium thiocyanate is dissolved in 100 ml. of 4 per cent. acetone and mixed with 500 ml. of isobutanol.
† Number of animals.
‡ Pooled sample of serum from 6 piglets.

oestradiol propionate was several (10 to 80) times higher than in controls during 1 to 120 hours after oral administration of $^{59}FeCl^3$. About two thirds of plasma ^{59}Fe in oestrogen-treated pullets was tightly bound and could not be removed by TCA treatment, while, in controls, practically all protein-bound ^{59}Fe was removed by the same treatment.

The results of stable Fe determinations in plasma are in accordance with those obtained by the use of ^{59}Fe. The total content of Fe in the plasma of laying hens and oestrogen-treated pullets was much higher when plasma samples were ashed before estimation of Fe, than if Fe was determined without ashing. In control pullets and piglets the values of plasma Fe content obtained by these two methods did not show a significant difference (Table I).

The separation of proteins from the plasma of laying hens to which $^{59}FeCl_3$ was added, indicated that Fe is bound to phosphoproteins. When the separation of phosphoproteins on DEAE cellulose was performed according to Heald and McLachlan (1963), only the phosvitin fraction contained radioactivity. This finding is in accordance with the evidence that Fe in egg yolk is also bound to phosvitin (Greengard et al., 1964).

The increase of Fe content in plasma of laying hens and oestrogen-treated immature pullets can, therefore, be explained by the appearance of phosvitin to which is bound a considerable amount of the Fe present in plasma (phosvitin is absent from the plasma of non-laying hens and cockerels). The treatment of plasma with TCA (low pH) does not release stable Fe or *in vitro* bound radioactive Fe from phosvitin, as is the case with transferrin, because phosvitin binds Fe stronger than transferrin. It means that, contrary to case in mammals, plasma Fe in laying hens and oestrogen-treated immature pullets is bound to two proteins: to transferrin and to phosvitin. Phosvitin represents a specific plasma protein of laying birds which is responsible for the transport of Fe to the ovocytes.

REFERENCES

CAMPBELL, E. A. (1960). *Poult. Sci.* **39**, 140.
FISCHL, J. (1960). *Clin. chim. Acta,* **5,** 164.
GREENGARD, O., SENTENAC, A. & MENDELSOHN, N. (1964). *Biochim. biophys. Acta,* **90,** 406.
HEALD, P. J. & MCLACHLAN, P. M. (1963). *Biochem. J.* **87,** 571.
RAMSAY, W. N. M. & CAMPBELL, E. A. (1954). *Biochem. J.* **58,** 313.
RAMSAY, W. N. M. & CAMPBELL, E. A. (1956). *Biochem. J.* **62,** 227.

EFFECT OF ESCHERICHIA COLI ENDOTOXIN ON IRON METABOLISM OF PIGLETS

Z. HORVÁTH

University of Veterinary Science, Budapest, Hungary

THE so-called coli toxicosis of piglets (coli diarrhoea, oedema disease) often occurs simultaneously with Fe-deficient anaemia or not infrequently develops in consequence of the latter's resistance-decreasing effect. The coincidence of the two diseases initiated the present studies on the effect of *E. coli* endotoxin on Fe metabolism.

The experiments were undertaken to answer the following questions:

1. To what extent Fe deficiency increases the piglet's susceptibility to *E. coli* toxin.

2. How *E. coli* toxin affects the plasma Fe level and uptake of Fe by the blood plasma.

3. By what mechanism the effect induced by *E. coli* endotoxin develops.

MATERIALS, METHODS AND RESULTS

Suckling pigs 1 to 4 weeks old and older pigs 6 to 7 weeks old, were used. As an *E. coli* endotoxin we used the Westphal-type (0–89) lipopolysaccharide (LPS) extract. The piglets were treated with 150 mg. doses of Fe dextran either on one occasion on the third day of life or on two occasions on the third and tenth days. The control animals received no added Fe.

Experiment I. Susceptibility to *E. coli* endotoxin of piglets given Fe and of piglets with Fe deficiency was studied on 25 animals from three litters. They were divided into two groups on the basis of body weight and sex. One group received on the third postnatal day 150 mg. Fe dextran intramuscularly. One piglet from each litter received a similar dose of Fe by repeated injection at the age of 10 days. The control piglets received no additional Fe supply. Blood samples were taken at 23 days of age and were used for detailed haematological examinations. Erythrocyte count, haemoglobin and haematocrit reading were determined and also the diameters of the red blood cells were measured. The Fe level and Fe uptake of the blood plasma were determined and the saturation of the plasma with Fe was inferred. At 24 days of age, all piglets received 0·2 mg./kg. of *E. coli* endotoxin intraperitoneally. The shock reaction which had developed

Table I. *Blood characteristics of pigs in Experiment I*

Group	No. of pigs	Weight (kg.)	r.b.c. $\times 10^{-6}$	Hb (g. %)	Haema-tocrit	r.b.c. diameter (nm.)	Plasma Fe (μg. %)	Total Fe binding capacity (μg. %)	% Satn. Fe
I Control	12	$4\cdot10\pm0\cdot48$	$3\cdot96\pm0\cdot71$	$7\cdot70\pm2\cdot38$	$27\cdot0\pm\ 7\cdot0$	$5\cdot34\pm0\cdot17$	62 ± 43	1013 ± 148	$6\cdot6\pm\ 5\cdot2$
II 1×150 mg. Fe	10	$4\cdot50\pm1\cdot23$	$5\cdot75\pm0\cdot51$	$10\cdot42\pm1\cdot34$	$41\cdot0\pm\ 3\cdot8$	$6\cdot08\pm0\cdot52$	124 ± 71	$652\pm\ 36$	$20\cdot6\pm12\cdot2$
III 2×150 mg. Fe	3	$4\cdot97\pm0\cdot42$	$5\cdot62\pm0\cdot36$	$8\cdot76\pm3\cdot00$	$37\cdot0\pm13\cdot3$	$6\cdot20\pm0\cdot00$	81 ± 50	733 ± 226	$12\cdot8\pm10\cdot0$

to the toxin effect was checked initially every fifth hour, later every twelfth hour. The laboratory results are summarized in Table I.

As shown in the Table, the results of laboratory tests differed notably in the experimental and control group. There was also a negative correlation between the intensity of the endotoxin-induced shock and the haematological results. Three of the piglets with Fe deficiency died of endotoxin shock.

Experiment II. The second experiment was performed on three 6-week-old piglets. Our aim was to assess the Fe uptake and Fe level of the plasma after the injection of endotoxin. The piglets were given intraperitoneally a single dose of 0·3 mg./kg. of endotoxin. Plasma Fe level and Fe uptake were measured simultaneously with the injection and every twelfth hour afterwards. The average values are plotted out graphically in Figure 1. The diagram unequivocally shows that by the twelfth hour after endotoxin treatment the plasma Fe level fell notably by approximately 50 per cent., whereas the latent Fe binding capacity of the plasma tended to increase. The final result was a rise of the total Fe binding capacity of the plasma. According to our observations

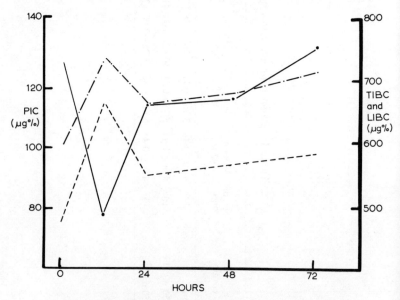

FIG. 1. The effect of *E. coli* endotoxin on plasma Fe content (PIC, •———•), total Fe-binding capacity (TIBC •—•—•) and latent Fe binding capacity (LIBC————) after a dose of 0·3 mg. coli-toxin/kg. body weight intraperitoneally (Experiment II).

the effect of a single endotoxin dose was of short duration, having lasted for 24 hours. Subsequently the plasma Fe values were close to normal, though slightly elevated.

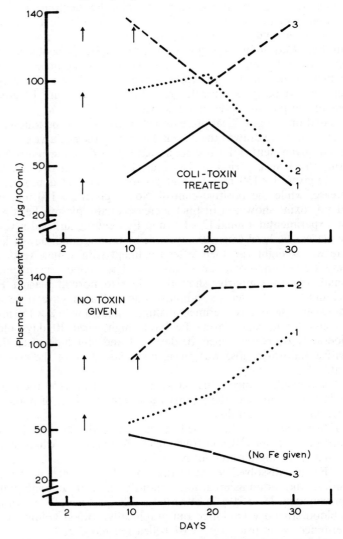

FIG. 2. The behaviour of plasma Fe concentration in coli-toxin-tolerant piglets, and in piglets given no toxin (Experiment III). 150 mg. Fe dextran was given intramuscularly as indicated by the arrows.

Experiment III. This experiment served to study the fluctuations of the plasma Fe level of six piglets exposed to long-term toxin effect, i.e. having developed tolerance to the toxin. Two animals received intramuscularly 150 mg. Fe dextran on two occasions when 3 and 10 days old respectively, and three animals received a single dose when 3 days old. One piglet was not treated with Fe. Endotoxin was given to three piglets subcutaneously every day in 0·1 mg./kg., 0·2 mg./kg. and 1·0 mg./kg doses during the first, second and third weeks, respectively. Three animals—negative and positive controls—received no endotoxin. Fluctuations of the plasma Fe level are shown in Figure 2.

Based on the graphical presentation of the results the following conclusions were drawn: the plasma Fe level of the negative control animal, given neither Fe nor toxin, tended to decrease uniformly during the 3-week period of the experiment. The positive control No. 1, given 1×150 mg. Fe and no toxin, showed a moderate increase, while the positive control No. 2, given 2×150 mg. Fe and no toxin, showed a distinct increase of the plasma Fe level. One experimental animal (2×150 mg. Fe + endotoxin) had a very low plasma Fe level when 10 days old; by the twentieth day of life there was a slight rise then, after treatment with a massive dose (1 mg./kg.) of endotoxin, an abrupt fall. The second experimental animal, treated similarly, showed a close to normal plasma Fe level until it fell after the administration of a massive dose of endotoxin. The third experimental animal, treated with 2×150 mg. Fe + endotoxin, had plasma Fe levels high when 10 days old, moderately decreased when 20 days old and still high after the massive endotoxin dose was given in the last stage of the experiment.

These results indicate that large doses of Fe (2×150 mg.) are capable of suppressing the plasma Fe decreasing effect of massive (1 mg./kg.) endotoxin doses.

Experiment IV. This aimed at examining the Fe kinetics by means of ^{59}Fe and ^{51}Cr in four piglets, 6 weeks old, which were exposed to a long-term endotoxin effect.

^{59}Fe was dissolved in ACD (anticoagulant, citrate, dextrose) solution and administered intravenously in a dose containing approximately 18 to 20 μCi of activity. The passage of ^{59}Fe from the blood stream was plotted out graphically. Blood volume was determined by infusion of ^{51}Cr-labelled red blood cells.

The release of ^{59}Fe from the blood stream is presented graphically (Fig. 3). The $T^{1/2}$ time of ^{59}Fe can be read from the diagram.

The release of Fe from the plasma of the two piglets not given

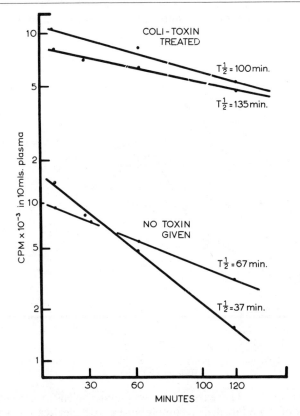

FIG. 3. Release of ^{59}Fe from plasma of piglets (Experiment IV).

endotoxin was fairly rapid ($T^{1/2}$ = 37 and 67 minutes). In contrast, in the piglets previously treated with endotoxin it slowed down ($T^{1/2}$ = 100 and 135 minutes). In this experiment, the Fe treatment given previously on one or two occasions had no notable influence on the release of ^{59}Fe from the blood stream.

Studies of Fe kinetics have shown that plasma Fe turnover rate (mg./kg./day) was nearly identical in the case of piglets treated and not treated with endotoxin (0·56 and 0·56; 0·87 and 0·50, respectively). Utilization of ^{59}Fe, that is the incorporation of Fe into red blood cells was, nevertheless, dissimilar. In the toxin-treated piglets the incorporation of ^{59}Fe tended to increase to 76 to 87 per cent. after the toxin effect had expired, as contrasted to controls where it was only 50·3 to 60·7 per cent. The dynamics

333

of the incorporation of ^{59}Fe into red blood cells are shown in Figure 4.

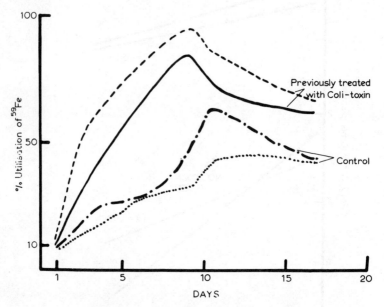

FIG. 4. Dynamics of incorporation of ^{59}Fe into haemoglobin (Experiment IV).

Experiment V. The experiment was undertaken to examine the release of ^{59}Fe-labelled haemoglobin-Fe in piglets exposed to long-term endotoxin effect. The incorporation of ^{59}Fe into the haemoglobin molecule was ensured by intravenous injection of 58 to 60 μCi of ^{59}Fe in saline into a pig weighing 13 kg. On the sixth day after, blood samples were taken. After centrifugation the red blood cells were washed three times with saline. The red cell sediment was suspended in saline and injected into the experimental animals. In this experiment 5 ml./kg. blood was withdrawn daily from two animals over a period of 14 days. They received in parallel by intraperitoneal route 0·1 mg./kg. endotoxin daily for eight days and 0·3 mg./kg. endotoxin daily for the subsequent seven days. Piglets 3 and 6 were given the latter dose of endotoxin uninterruptedly also during the isotope studies. The activities of red blood cells containing the labelled haemoglobin and of plasma Fe were measured.

Release of Fe from the red cells containing ^{59}Fe-labelled haemoglobin appeared to be slow. The activity of the red blood cell mass showed practically no change over the two hours following injection, as assessed from measurements performed at 15-minute intervals. During this time no measurable quantity of Fe had entered the plasma. But in the twenty-fourth hour after injection the activity of injected red blood cells decreased in the animals previously bled and treated with endotoxin, suggesting a deterioration of the labelled cells. The results are shown in Table II. Apparently, the deterioration of ^{59}Fe labelled erythrocytes occurred very slowly in the control group not treated with endotoxin, fairly rapidly in the group previously treated with endotoxin and very rapidly in the group still under the influence of endotoxin. In contrast, the plasma activity of ^{59}Fe was the highest in the control group, and the lowest in the group under coli toxin treatment.

Table II. *The effect of Coli endotoxin on the re-utilization of haemoglobin ^{59}Fe (Experiment V)*

	Previously treated with coli-toxin		Under coli-toxin effect		Control
No. of animals	1	4	3	6	2/3
r.b.c., c.p.m. in 10 ml.	540	510	370	440	730
plasma, c.p.m. in 10 ml.	170	160	10	20	310

(Total dose, 33,800 c.p.m. in r.b.c.).

DISCUSSION

The knowledge of the effect of the different toxins on Fe metabolism may be, apart from theoretical considerations, important in relation to the pathogenesis of the so-called infectious anaemias.

It is known that on intravenous administration the toxin of the attenuated *Mycobacterium tuberculosis* (BCG) strain induces an acute shock in rats and mice (Berri *et al.,* 1963; Suter, 1958, 1961). Also, the intravenously applied sonicated homogenate of *E. coli* bacteria produced an intensive shock in pigs with Fe deficiency (Coulter and Swenson, 1965; Osborne and Davis, 1968). Our findings show that pigs with Fe deficiency exhibit an increased shock-sensitivity also toward purified endotoxin.

In the development of shock induced by *E. coli* endotoxin hyposideraemia may also play an important role. Our observations indicate that the liability to convulsions manifested after the injection of *E. coli* endotoxin is partly due to the low plasma Fe

335

level. The plasma effect of *E. coli* endotoxin on plasma Fe was so great that it could only be overcome by a double dose of Fe dextran. Hyposideraemia very likely plays a role in the development of the so-called infectious anaemias. Release of Fe from the plasma brings about a tissular hypoxia partly through inhibiting the function of Fe-containing enzymes and partly by slowing down the synthesis of haemoglobin. Circulation insufficiency which is a natural sequel to the shock is further aggravated by these effects.

Our studies threw some light on the controversial problem of the mechanism by which the endotoxin-induced hyposideraemia develops. Though rat experiments have indicated a disturbance in the re-utilization of erythrocyte Fe (Kampschmidt and Upchurch, 1962), our experiments on piglets have unequivocally shown that *E. coli* endotoxin effects not only an increase of haemolysis but also inhibits the re-flow of the Fe released from the erythrocytes into the plasma.

In summary it may be stated that Fe deficiency is apt to increase the susceptibility of piglets to *E. coli* endotoxin. The endotoxin induces hyposideraemia. In piglets exposed to long-term endotoxin effect, the release of Fe from the plasma slowed down. After the expiration of endotoxin effect there was an increase in the rate of incorporation of Fe into the erythrocytes. The hyposideraemia consequent upon the injection of *E. coli* endotoxin is due to a decrease in the re-utilization of plasma Fe and it is suitable for developing an infectious anaemia.

REFERENCES

COULTER, D. B. & SWENSON, M. J. (1965). *Fedn Proc. Fedn Am. Socs exp. Biol.* **24,** 1820.
KAMPSCHMIDT, R. F. & UPCHURCH, H. F. (1962). *Proc. Soc. exp. Biol. Med.* **110,** 191.
OSBORNE, J. C. & DAVIS, J. W. (1969). *J. Am. vet. med. Ass.* **152,** No. 11.

INTRAVASCULAR TRANSPORT OF SELENIUM IN THE CHICK

K. J. JENKINS, R. C. DICKSON AND M. HIDIROGLOU

Animal Research Institute, Canada Department of Agriculture, Ottawa, Canada

ONE of the interesting aspects of selenium metabolism in animals is the binding of trace amounts of Se in various tissue proteins and that this binding occurs regardless of the chemical form of Se or method in which the element has been administered. Many

336

different chemical forms of Se also are at least partially active against the development of a number of the Se vitamin E deficiency conditions. In this light it appears to be a reasonable supposition that most Se compounds employed may be metabolized to a common active form of the element. Selenite and selenate are reasonably active and since they are simple compounds their comparative usage should facilitate an understanding of the formation of the active form or forms of Se. In the present study a comparison was made of the uptake of selenite and selenate by chick plasma proteins and red blood cells employing both *in vivo* and *in vitro* conditions.

The first information sought was the relative importance of the various plasma proteins for intravascular transport of selenite-Se in the chick. The chicks were dosed with labelled selenite by crop tube and the serum subjected to paper electrophoresis at various time intervals after dosing. The level of Se used was very small (0·2 μg. Se per chick). Within the first two hours after intubation with H_2 $^{75}SeO_3$, 33 to 44 per cent. and 20 to 24 per cent. of the serum protein radioactivity was located in the α_2- and α_3-globulins, respectively. The percentage of serum protein radioactivity bound to the γ-globulin increased at a rapid rate during the first 24 hours. During the subsequent 24 to 173 hour interval, 52 to 70 per cent. of the ^{75}Se was carried by the α_2- and γ-globulin fractions. The development of muscular dystrophy as the result of a concomitant dietary deficiency of Se, vitamin E and cystine had no effect on the time-distribution of ^{75}Se among the various serum protein fractions.

Elevation of the dose carrier level of Se from 2·1 μg. to 300 μg. caused a high proportion of the ^{75}Se to become bound to the albumin during the first 28 hours, after which the albumin activity dropped to that obtained for the low carrier level. It appears that at higher Se intakes the more active Se-binding sites in the serum globulins may become saturated, with the excess Se 'spilling over' to the less active sites in the albumin.

When the serum proteins were double-labelled with ^{75}Se and ^{14}C, the α_2- and α_3-globulins turned over ^{75}Se more rapidly than the ^{14}C label during the first 12 hours after dosage. The data indicate that initially Se is bound in a labile manner to the α_2- and α_3-globulins, as well as albumin if the Se dose level is high. Later, Se bound to the globulins is turned over at a slower rate than ^{14}C, probably because a higher proportion of a more stable complex of Se develops and also due to recycling of Se into the globulins.

In the following experiment the *in vivo* uptakes of selenite and selenate by plasma proteins and red blood cells were compared at a variety of Se dose levels. For both selenite and selenate most of the Se was plasma protein bound at the lower dose levels; at the higher levels more Se was located in the cells bound to the globin. At four hours after dosing none of the free Se in the plasma was found to occur as dimethyl selenide or as the trimethyl selenonium ion.

In an *in vitro* study, at low Se levels, selenite was preferentially bound to the plasma proteins and at higher levels occurred in a bound form in the cells as observed previously *in vivo*. Selenate was not taken up to any extent by the plasma proteins or cells, indicating that selenate must be converted to another form of Se by mechanisms not present in the blood before uptake by blood cells and proteins can occur. The data indicated that selenate may be converted to selenite before uptake occurs. Treatment of serum proteins from both selenite or selenate-dosed chicks with dilute alkali (pH 11·5) released 85 per cent. of the ^{75}Se of which 50 per cent. or more was selenite; no selenate was released.

In a further *in vitro* experiment, the effect of omitting the cells on Se uptake by the plasma proteins was studied. The results indicated that selenite may be taken up by the plasma proteins in at least two ways: by a rapid, direct reaction between selenite and the proteins and, secondly, by movement of selenite into the cells, probably with an alteration in the chemical forms of Se, one or more of which escape from the cells and complex with the serum proteins.

Previous studies have indicated that when selenite was intubated into chicks the bulk of Se in the plasma proteins existed in the seleno-trisulfide form. The fact that selenate has a similar plasma protein, the *in vivo* uptake as selenite and distribution pattern between the proteins, and the observation that selenite but not selenate is released on treatment of the plasma protein-selenium complexes of both selenite and selenate with dilute alkali all suggest that selenate may ultimately form the same seleno-trisulfide as selenite with the plasma proteins.

DISCUSSION

McConnell (Louisville). Have you done any study of the distribution of Se in plasma proteins at times less than one hour after administration? We did a similar study with the dog and in the first 10 minutes after feeding Se as selenite, the bulk of the Se was in the α^2- and β^1-albumin fractions. These components fell rapidly later.

Jenkins (Ottawa). No, we have not done this; it is very pertinent.

Underwood (Perth). What is the nature of this binding of Se to plasma proteins; is it a true incorporation, a displacement of sulphur in amino acids or what?

McConnell (Louisville). It is a true incorporation into the proteins in that it is a covalent bond between two sulphurs. Sulphur is required for Se incorporation and it is apparently held between these two sulphur atoms. It is interesting that in the nonruminant, S when ingested, goes through oxidation steps to sulphate whereas Se goes through a series of reduction steps going from plus 6 and plus 4 to minus 2 valency states, eventually, as Ganther and others have shown, being excreted as dimethyl-selenide. It seems that although Se is not replacing S the latter may be required for the incorporation of Se into proteins.

SELENIUM METABOLISM

K. P. McConnell, Dorothy R. Carpenter and J. L. Hoffmann

*Veterans Administration Hospital and University of Louisville
School of Medicine, Louisville, Kentucky, U.S.A.*

When evaluating selenium either as a dietary essential or carcinogenic risk, knowledge of the amount of administered Se retained by animals is important. It is well documented (Ewan *et al.*, 1963) that trace amounts of Se are retained for a long time, suggesting conservation of Se similar to that of body economy for Fe. A lactating dog with five one-day-old pups was injected subcutaneously with 7 μg. Se as $^{75}SeO_2^{2-}$ (McConnell and Roth, 1964). Milk samples collected at various intervals were analysed for ^{75}Se. The Se treated dog was bred again without further administration of the isotope, and ^{75}Se analysis of milk continued. ^{75}Se could be detected 278 days after injection of 7 μg. Se.

Incorporation or binding of trace amounts of Se in various proteins has drawn much attention (Jauregui-Adell, 1966). Apparently this occurs regardless of the form or manner of administration and is rapid, for within a few minutes after subcutaneous injection over 50 per cent. of the total serum ^{75}Se activity is protein-bound (McConnell et al., 1960). Many reports describe incorporation of Se into proteins of plants, microorganisms and mammals, including man (Shrift, 1967). Se has been observed in proteins of milk, in blood proteins, including globulin of haemoglobin, in liver, kidney, pancreas and in the various intracellular fractions of liver. Incorporation of Se into specific proteins includes: haemoproteins (haemoglobin, cytochrome-c, myoglobin) (McConnell and Cooper, 1950; McConnell and Dallam, 1962; McConnell, unpublished); enzymes (myosin, aldolase, urokinase, fibrinase) (McConnell and Roth, 1965; Celander et al., 1962); and nucleoproteins (McConnell and Roth, 1962).

In cell organelles that synthesize protein, Se is involved. Se participates in protein synthesis in both cytoplasmic and mitochondrial systems (McConnell and Roth, 1962). In a cell-free system incorporation of either inorganic or organic Se into ribosomes was dependent upon ATP, as well as cell sap (McConnell and Roth, 1968). Incorporation of Se into ribosomes could be accomplished enzymically or by an exchange reaction or a combination of both. With mitochondria incorporation of Se requires an oxidisable substrate and oxidative phosphorylation.

We know that excessive amounts of Se affect growth adversely (Harr et al., 1967) while trace amounts have been reported as essential for growth in plants and certain animals (Trelease and Trelease, 1939; Nesheim and Scott, 1958). Se is known to incorporate into rapidly growing tissues, especially at embryonic stages of development when the plans of many organ systems appear. After injection of trace amounts of ^{75}Se into the air sac of the egg, and assay of ^{75}Se in the various tissues of hatched chicks, a wide but varied distribution of Se was found in the tissues (McConnell and Wabnitz, 1964).

It is common knowledge that Se can pass the placental barrier (Rosenfeld and Beath, 1964; McConnell and Roth, 1964). If the maternal Se intake is high, abnormal growth and development follow in the offspring (Moxon, 1937). We have observed the passage of Se across the placenta in pups delivered by Caesarean section (McConnell and Roth, 1964).

Se also passes through the mammary glands. In the dog inorganic Se was converted into organoselenium that appeared in the milk. Nearly all the ^{75}Se remained in the proteins of the milk, distributed equally between casein and milk serum.

In specific cells such as the erythrocytes we found the apparent life span of Se in the dog red blood cells approximately that of the life span of dog red blood cells, i.e. 120 days (McConnell and Roth, 1968). Since trace amounts of Se seem to remain in the RBC throughout the life span of the cells perhaps this phenomenon could occur in other tissues and cells.

A discussion of Se at a cellular level should involve consideration of the process by which substances move across membranes and especially against concentration gradients. This process, by which nutrients enter the cell, requires energy and is called active transport. We know that L-selenomethionine, but not $^{75}SeO_3^{2-}$ and DL-selenocystine, is transported across cell membrane by an active energy-dependent process (McConnell and Cho, 1967). Selenomethionine and methionine apparently utilize the same transport system. Results from the establishment of sulphur-selenium antagonism could explain in part the qualitative aspect of the protein's protective action against excess Se exposure.

Since selenomethionine is found in proteins, by what process are seleno amino acids incorporated into proteins? One of the first steps in protein synthesis after the activation of amino acids and prior to the formation of polypeptides is the reaction of the activated amino acid with its specific t-RNA(s) (Novelli, 1967; Peterson, 1967). In the elaboration of the amino acid sequence of a protein, natural or unnatural amino acids usually are not incorporated in the place of other natural amino acids. Any amino acid analogue that can deceive the activating enzyme apparently will be incorporated into the protein in the place of the natural amino acid. We found that selenomethionine can deceive the methionine activating enzyme. *E. coli* methionyl-t-RNA synthetase aminoacylates methionine t-RNA with either methionine or selenomethionine (Hoffmann *et al.*, 1970). As with active transport there exists a competitive inhibition between methionine and selenomethionine. Aminoacylation and active transport studies support the concept that Se metabolism may take place at least in part via the S pathway.

REFERENCES

CELANDER, D. R., JACQUO, M. Jr. & NASCHKE, M. D. (1962). *Fedn Proc. Fedn Am. Socs exp. Biol.* **21**, 65.
EWAN, R. C., BAUMANN, C. A. & POPE, A. L. (1963). *J. Anim. Sci.* **22**, 1119.
HARR, J. R., BONE, J. F., TINSLEY, I. J., WESWIG, P. H. & YAMAMOTO, R. S. (1967). In *Symposium, Selenium in Biomedicine*, p. 153. Westport, Connecticut: Avi.
HOFFMAN, J. L., MCCONNELL, K. P. & CARPENTER, D. R. (1970). *Biochim. biophys. Acta*, **170**, 531.
JAUREGUI-ADELL, J. (1966). *Adv. Protein Chem.* **21**, 387.

341

McConnell, K. P & Cho, G. J. (1967). In *Symposium, Selenium in Biomedicine*, p. 329, Westport, Connecticut: Avi.
McConnell, K. P. & Cooper, B. J. (1950). *J. biol. Chem.* **183,** 459.
McConnell, K. P. & Dallam, R. D. (1962). *Nature, Lond.* **193,** 746.
McConnell, K. P. & Roth, D. M. (1962). *Biochim. biophys. Acta,* **62,** 503.
McConnell, K. P. & Roth, D. M. (1964). *J. Nutr.* **84,** 340.
McConnell, K. P. & Roth, D. M. (1965). *Proc. Soc. exp. Biol. Med.* **120,** 88.
McConnell, K. P. & Roth, D. M. (1968). *Archs Biochem. Biophys.* **125,** 29.
McConnell, K. P. & Wabnitz, C. H. (1964). *Poult. Sci.* **43,** 1959.
McConnell, K. P., Wabnitz, C. H. & Roth, D. M. (1960). *Tex. Rep. Biol. Med.* **18,** 438.
Moxon, A. L. (1937). *South Dakota Agr. Exp. Sta. Bull.* No. **311,** 1.
Nesheim, M. C. & Scott, M. L. (1958). *J. Nutr.* **65,** 601.
Novelli, G. D. (1967). *A. Rev. Biochem.* **36,** 449.
Peyerson, P. J. (1967). *Biol. Rev.* **42,** 552.
Rosenfeld, I. & Beath, O. A. (1964). In *Selenium,* p. 198. New York: Academic Press.
Shrift, A. (1967). In *Symposium, Selenium in Biomedicine,* p. 241. Westport, Connecticut: Avi.
Trelease, S. F. & Trelease, H. M. (1939). *Am. J. Bot.* **26,** 530.

DISCUSSION

Godwin (Adelaide). I believe you have noted an increase in the ^{75}Se in the milk of the bitch following its second pregnancy even though no additional ^{75}Se has been given. Did you measure the absolute amounts of Se in milk?

McConnell (Louisville). Yes we did, but we have no explanation for the rise that was observed.

Godwin (Adelaide). This raises an interesting species difference. When we gave large amounts of Se to ewes one month before mating there was no rise at all in milk Se content during lactation.

Schwarz (Long Beach). It is quite obvious that selenomethionine can be readily synthesized in micro-organisms and incorporated into their protein but, since the animal is unable to synthesize sulphur methionine, do you think there is any consistent evidence which suggests that selenomethionine can be produced in, say, the dog or other animals?

McConnell (Louisville). If I understand your question correctly, the incorporation of selenomethionine into mammalian proteins has been demonstrated at Harvard. The incorporation of inorganic Se into sulphur amino acids of plasma and other tissue proteins is a debatable one; it is certainly not an 'all or none' proposition.

Jenkins (Ottawa). We must agree that most monogastric animals will consume a range of Se compounds from plant sources, namely selenate, selenite and seleno amino acids or at least seleno-methionine—whether or not selenocystine exists in plants and organisms is a new point as well. This fact makes it important that we study the fate of a wide range of Se sources.

McConnell (Louisville). As Dr Ganther has shown there is good evidence that selenite is reduced in animal tissues. The important point is that there is a distinct possibility that the dimethylselenide formed could, by enzymic or exchange reactions, lead to the production of these seleno amino acids.

Schwarz (Long Beach). When large amounts of Se are given there is no doubt that selenomethionine and selenocystine can be found in plants, but I have never obtained any evidence that in the plant or in yeast grown under *normal conditions* Se is present in the form of these compounds. The Se compounds present under normal conditions appear to be different and their nature is unclarified. There are large metabolic differences between plants and micro-organisms which accumulate large amounts of Se and those which do not and it is probable that the latter may not perhaps use the pathway of S metabolism for Se assimilation.

McConnell (Louisville). In connection with this conflict of opinion I would like to emphasize that the Se trisulphide compounds that are formed initially are relatively unstable. When we find Se in animal tissues in a stable condition for several days or months we believe that it has changed to other forms. Paper chromatography and electrophoresis suggest to us that among these compounds may be traces of selenocystine and seleno-methionine. In work which has been done in which this idea is debated, or the finding refuted, there is always a trace of a protein fraction that has not been thoroughly investigated; we think that these compounds are in this fraction in stable forms.

SECTION 6

TRACE ELEMENT REQUIREMENT AND AVAILABILITY

President: V. BIENFET

Vice President: J. R. TODD

THE COMPLEXITY OF DIETARY FACTORS AFFECTING ZINC NUTRITION AND METABOLISM IN CHICKS AND SWINE

W. G. HOEKSTRA

*Department of Biochemistry and Department of Nutritional Sciences,
University of Wisconsin, Madison, Wisconsin, U.S.A.*

WHEN considering mineral nutrients for animals it is not un-common for numerous dietary factors other than the specific nutrient under consideration to have important effects, either favourable or unfavourable, on the utilization of the nutrient in question. Multiple factors affecting mineral elements such as calcium and copper are well documented. Since 1955 it has become apparent that the essential nutrient, zinc, is likewise affected by a complexity of dietary factors, including other mineral elements as well as numerous organic materials. Some of these have already received extensive documentation in the literature. Their effects are often so profound that naturally occurring Zn deficiency is often more dependent upon these 'secondary' factors than upon the absolute concentration of Zn in the diet. Among the important dietary factors known to affect Zn nutrition or metabolism of monogastric animals are calcium, phosphate, phytate, cadmium, copper, molybdenum, iron, protein source, chelating agents, vitamin D and method of feeding. It is not my purpose to review the extensive literature on these factors at this time.

In this symposium I will discuss some of our recent research on chicks and swine which demonstrates that a number of additional, previously unrecognized, dietary factors also have significant effects on the Zn deficiency syndrome. The primary gross signs of Zn deficiency in chicks are retarded growth, 'frizzled' feathers and a bone abnormality ('swollen hock' syndrome). In swine the main effects are retarded growth and a severe dermatitis (parakeratosis). The bone lesions of chicks and the dermatitis of swine are par-ticularly susceptible to modification or amelioration by dietary factors other than Zn and will receive the most attention in this paper. The effects of the dietary agents will be described and evidence as to their possible mechanisms of action will be discussed. Unfortunately such knowledge is still incomplete. The dietary factors to be discussed include amino acids (cysteine, histidine and arginine), histamine, anti-arthritic or anti-inflammatory agents and two mineral elements, magnesium and cobalt. Some of these

347

factors have been studied in both chicks and pigs, while others have been tested in one species only. It is hoped that knowledge of such factors will explain not only the highly irregular occurrence of Zn deficiency and the lack of correlation between Zn intake and deficiency, but will also shed light on the nature of the fundamental metabolic lesions in Zn-deficient animals.

AMINO ACID SOURCE AND THE ZN DEFICIENCY SYNDROME IN CHICKS

In the initial studies with chicks (Nielsen *et al.*, 1966a) our goal was to compare isolated soybean protein with acid-hydrolysed casein and dried egg white as possible amino acid sources to produce Zn deficiency for biochemical study. While experimental Zn deficiency could be readily produced by any of the three amino acid sources, we were surprised to find that the leg abnormality (characterized by swollen hocks, shortened and thickened long bones, stilted gait and sometimes twisting of the leg, but no substantial alteration in bone ash), which appeared in severe form in chicks fed soybean protein, was essentially absent or much less evident in chicks fed casein hydrolysate or dried egg white. In pursuing this observation we found that three amino acids have substantial effects on Zn deficiency. By adding amino acids to a soybean protein diet it was found that cysteine and histidine had effects on the Zn deficiency syndrome. Recently we found dietary arginine to be particularly important in relation to Zn deficiency in the chick. These amino acids will be discussed in turn.

Cysteine. In Zn-deficient chicks fed isolated soybean protein, a supplement of 0·5 per cent. cysteine alleviated all signs of Zn deficiency (Nielsen *et al.*, 1966b). It increased body weight (137 g. vs. 228 g. at 4 weeks of age), improved feathering, improved the leg score and length/width ratio of the femur and increased tibia Zn concentrations (32 vs. 45 p.p.m., fat-free, dry basis). In this respect cysteine alleviated Zn deficiency in much the same way as did several, but not all, synthetic chelating agents (e.g., EDTA) and was believed to act by improving Zn availability. Cystine, the oxidized analogue, did *not* have a similar effect. More work needs to be done with other sulphydryl compounds and other animal species to further delineate this effect.

Histidine. Histidine (0·5 to 2·0 per cent.) supplemented to a soybean protein diet also alleviated the leg abnormality of Zn-deficient chicks fed soybean protein, but unlike cysteine it did not

348

stimulate growth, consistently improve feathering or increase the Zn concentration in bone (Nielsen *et al.,* 1966b, 1967). It appeared to act in a manner other than by increasing Zn availability or Zn utilization by bone. We were particularly interested in following up this effect, as we hoped it might pin-point the metabolic cause of the leg abnormality. The histidine metabolite, histamine, produced a similar effect but at a substantially lower level in the diet (0·1 to 0·2 per cent.) (Nielsen *et al.,* 1967). Several other histidine analogues or metabolites were ineffective. Considerable but not unequivocal evidence indicates that histidine acts by partial conversion to histamine. Attempts to locate a defect in histamine metabolism in Zn-deficient chicks have been unsuccessful. Although it has been suggested that histamine is stored in mast cells as a Zn-histamine-heparin complex we could find no decrease in the histamine content of any of several tissues of Zn-deficient chicks. Histological studies of the epiphyseal plate of the tibiotarsus demonstrated a Zn deficiency defect which was oriented in relation to the vascular system (i.e., cells remote from blood vessels were abnormal, so that cross-sections through the plate showed a 'bulls eye' lesion about the blood vessels) (Westmoreland and Hoekstra, 1969*a, b*). The alkaline phosphatase staining of epiphyseal plate was also abnormal; only if cartilaginous cells were near a blood vessel did their alkaline phosphatase activity increase and then decrease normally during maturation and degeneration. Histamine did not correct these fundamental histological lesions caused by Zn deficiency. We have tentatively concluded that histamine alleviates the gross distortions in bone shape by some 'pharmacological' effect of excess histamine, probably on the vascular system or cartilaginous cells, but we have not yet pinpointed its action.

Because of the effects of histidine and histamine in the Zn-deficient chick we were also interested in testing their effects on the Zn-deficient pig and have experimented primarily with histidine. We have found the following effects of a supplement of 1 to 2 per cent. histidine to a semi-purified diet based on isolated soybean protein and fed to baby pigs: a marked alleviation, but not complete prevention, of parakeratosis, a lowered incidence of abnormal erythrocyte sedimentation rate and increases in histamine concentration in intestinal contents, intestine, whole blood, blood serum and possibly skin but not in liver. As in chicks, histidine had no effect on growth of Zn-deficient pigs or on the Zn content of blood serum, liver or bone. If anything, histidine decreased rather than increased the alkaline phosphatase activity of blood

349

serum. Similar effects of dietary histamine (0·2 per cent.) were indicated but experimentation has not been as extensive as for histidine. We have speculated that the cause of the skin lesions in Zn-deficient swine is biochemically similar to the cause of the bone lesion in Zn-deficient poultry and that histidine and histamine moderate each of these by an effect on the vascular system or connective tissues but do not correct the fundamental Zn deficiency lesion.

Arginine. The differing effects of various protein or amino acid sources, which were noted earlier, were not adequately explained by the above effects of cysteine and histidine. We therefore looked for other possible causes of the differences. One observation which led us to an important discovery was that in the blood serum of Zn-deficient chicks fed isolated soybean protein (chicks with severe leg deformities) there was about twice as much free arginine as in similar chicks fed dried egg white (chicks with mild leg deformities). We therefore tested the effects of adding arginine to the diets of chicks fed these protein sources with inadequate and adequate levels of Zn. A supplement of 2 per cent. arginine hydrochloride to the chicks fed adequate Zn had little or no effect. However, in the Zn-deficient chicks it markedly aggravated both the leg abnormalities and the feather defects and tended to depress growth. We then investigated the effects of various levels of dietary arginine in a casein-based diet. This was important because the arginine content of casein is low and O'Dell and Savage (1966) have shown the arginine requirement of chicks fed casein diets to be much higher than that of chicks fed other protein sources, presumably because of the high lysine content of casein. Total amounts of dietary arginine ranged from about 0·6 per cent. (basal) to nearly 4·0 per cent. At the lower levels of arginine, leg abnormalities were virtually absent, while at the higher levels they were severe. High arginine also aggravated the feather defect, but this was complicated since arginine deficiency, in itself, caused fraying of the feathers. In the proper range of arginine content marked effects on leg abnormalities were observed without differences in growth rate. In confirmation of previous experiments dietary histidine (1 per cent.) or histamine (0·2 per cent.) alleviated the leg abnormalities induced in Zn-deficient chicks by dietary arginine.

Of particular interest was the effect of dietary arginine on the Zn content of the tibia and feathers. For example, comparing groups which differed little in body weight but were fed 1·2 per cent. arginine or 4·0 per cent. arginine, the Zn content of bone of

350

the Zn-deficient chicks fed the former was 193 ± 13 (S.E.) p.p.m. (fat-free, dry basis) while that of chicks fed the latter was 95 ± 5 p.p.m. Feathers were affected to almost as great an extent. These effects of aginine on bone and feather Zn were also noted when 80 p.p.m. of supplemental Zn was added to the diet but the magnitude of the effect was not as great.

It is thus apparent that in the chick arginine is a potent antagonist of Zn in at least certain aspects of its metabolism. This appears to provide an adequate explanation for the differing effects of certain protein sources on the Zn-deficient chick noted earlier (Nielsen *et al.*, 1966a). Unfortunately these studies are in an early phase and we cannot yet further describe the specific sites and mechanisms of action of arginine on Zn metabolism. Other species have not yet been studied. The chick, however, is unusual in its arginine metabolism as there is virtually no synthesis *in vivo* so the effects observed in the chick may not extend to non-avian species.

Anti-arthritic and anti-inflammatory agents. Space does not permit an extensive discussion but the interesting observation should be noted that several anti-arthritic agents have effects on Zn-deficient chicks which are very similar to those described above for histidine and histamine; that is they rather specifically alleviate only the leg abnormalities (Nielsen *et al.*, 1968). Effective agents and their required concentrations in the diet were as follows: cortisone acetate (0·1 per cent.), phenylbutazone (0·2 per cent.), indomethacin (0·025 per cent.), chloroquin (0·05 per cent.) and aspirin (0·5 to 1·0 per cent.). Gold salts are the only anti-arthritic agents tested so far which do not benefit the leg abnormality of Zn-deficient chicks. The effective agents, like histamine, do not appear to correct the fundamental Zn deficiency lesion or to counteract an inflammation. They probably have some other effect on the vascular system or cartilaginous cells. These observations have caused us to speculate that there may be some relationship of Zn deficiency defects of chicks and swine, and possibly of histidine and arginine, to the 'connective tissue diseases' of man. This was the subject of a recent review (Hoekstra, 1969).

EFFECTS OF MG AND OF CO ON ZN-DEFICIENT SWINE

Because of the profound aggravation of Zn deficiency in swine caused by increased dietary Ca we initiated studies to assess the effects of the somewhat similar element, Mg. It became clear that Mg does not exert effects on Zn similar to those caused by Ca.

In fact high levels of Mg actually lessened some of the Zn deficiency symptoms. In two recent experiments with pigs we investigated the effects of high Mg levels (to 0.8 per cent. supplemental Mg supplied either in the form of MgO or $MgCO_3$) on pigs fed a high Ca practical diet which produced severe Zn deficiency unless supplemented with Zn. Although Mg did not stimulate growth of the Zn-deficient pigs, it delayed the appearance of parakeratosis and reduced its incidence and severity. Magnesium had no effect on thymus weight, serum alkaline phosphatase activity or Zn concentration in serum, bone or liver. However, high Mg did prevent, in part, the decrease in bone alkaline phosphatase caused by Zn deficiency and prevented the decrease in serum Mg caused by Zn deficiency. It did not affect bone or liver Mg concentration or skin or intestinal alkaline phosphatase activity. The mechanism of action of Mg in protecting against skin lesions is unknown.

Of particular interest are our recent preliminary observations on a possible Zn/Co interrelationship. We were led to study this possibility because Co has successfully replaced Zn *in vitro* in a number of Zn metalloenzymes. A single experiment to date showed that high levels of Co (50 and 100 p.p.m.) were nearly as effective as 100 p.p.m. of Zn in maintaining growth and appearance of the skin and hair in swine fed a high Ca practical diet. Growth virtually ceased and skin lesions were severe unless either Co or Zn was added as a supplement. It appears that Co at 50 p.p.m. was effective in this regard without increasing the Zn content of blood serum, bone, liver or hair. Cobalt had no effect on alkaline phosphatase activity of skin or intestine but tended to increase serum alkaline phosphatase activity and significantly increased bone alkaline phosphatase. The meaning of these observations is not clear and the preliminary nature of the work is stressed. The remarkable magnitude of effect of Co, however, caused me to relate it here. Studies on Zn-deficient chicks, fed a semi-purified diet with comparable levels of Co to those used in swine, have shown no sign of a sparing relationship between the two elements. Clearly, experimental variables such as species, diet, etc. appear to be important. Additional studies are required before definite statements can be made.

Acknowledgements. The author gratefully acknowledges the following co-investigators who were responsible for many of the observations reported in this paper: B. W. Coleman, E. J. Dahmer, E. C. Faltin, R. H. Grummer, C. W. Linn, F. H. Nielsen, E. M. Reimann, M. Somers and M. L. Sunde. We intend to publish separately more complete descriptions of some of the unpublished experiments and results discussed in this report.

REFERENCES

HOEKSTRA, W. G. (1969). *Am. J. clin. Nutr.* **22,** 1268.
NIELSEN, F. H., SUNDE, M. L. & HOEKSTRA, W. G. (1966a). *J. Nutr.* **89,** 24.
NIELSEN, F. H., SUNDE, M. L. & HOEKSTRA, W. G. (1966b). *J. Nutr.* **89,** 35.
NIELSEN, F. H., SUNDE, M. L. & HOEKSTRA, W. G. (1967). *Proc. Soc. exp. Biol. Med.* **124,** 1106.
NIELSEN, F. H., SUNDE, M. L. & HOEKSTRA, W. G. (1968). *J. Nutr.* **94,** 527.
O'DELL, B. L. & SAVAGE, J. E. (1966). *J. Nutr.* **90,** 364.
WESTMORELAND, N. & HOEKSTRA, W. G. (1969a). *J. Nutr.* **98,** 76.
WESTMORELAND, N. & HOEKSTRA, W. G. (1969b). *J. Nutr.* **98,** 83.

DISCUSSION

Mills (Aberdeen). Do you have any speculation on the mode of action of arginine?

Hoekstra (Madison). Not very good ones I'm afraid. We are checking whether it affects Zn absorption; it decreased the Zn content of tissues dramatically but it did not decrease growth rate very much so that its function may not be at that site. We are also interested in looking at some of the high arginine poly-cationic proteins of leucocytes, but at the moment we have no firm ideas on the possible mechanism of action of arginine.

Mills (Aberdeen). Has anyone ever looked at the metabolic fate of the guanidino-group of arginine in a Zn-deficient animal?

Hoekstra (Madison). I don't believe so.

Husain (Glasgow). What effect does Zn deficiency have on the hair of swine?

Hoekstra (Madison). The hair becomes brittle and breaks up. The regrowth of hair is quite different from the original coat and this is true also in the rat. We have studied the hair growth cycle in the rat and here the hair follicle goes through active and resting phases and these phases are accompanied by increases and decreases in alkaline phosphatase activity. From the limited amount of work we have done it seems that in the Zn-deficient rat the follicles remain in the resting phase.

STUDIES ON COPPER–MOLYBDENUM–SULPHATE INTERRELATIONSHIPS*

G. MATRONE

*Department of Biochemistry, North Carolina State University,
Raleigh, North Carolina, U.S.A.*

OVER 20 years ago, Ferguson, Lewis and Watson (1943) reported a scouring disease in cattle, correlated with the molybdenum content of the forage, which could be cured by feeding or drenching with copper sulphate. Later, Dick (1956) reported that inorganic sulphate under certain conditions intensified the harmful effects of Mo. Since the initial observations numerous studies have been reported (Miller and Engel, 1960; Underwood, 1962) about the Cu/Mo and/or sulphate interaction in a variety of species. An important consideration from these studies is that the effective toxic concentration of Mo in the diet of the ruminant is much lower (in the order of 100- to 200-fold less) than that of the non-ruminant (Mills, 1960). The data reported herein are from investigations (Dowdy and Matrone, 1968a, b; Gomez-Garcia and Matrone, 1969; Prentice and Matrone, 1969) carried out at North Carolina State University over the past several years in an attempt to gain some insight into the basic nature of the Cu/Mo/sulphate interaction. Our emphasis from the beginning has been to sort out, if possible, the interrelationships as manifested by the ruminant, since we think that the case for the non-ruminant is more complicated due to the high levels of Mo required to bring about toxicity. Accordingly our initial step was to carry out an experiment with lambs fed a purified, low Cu diet (Dowdy and Matrone, 1968a) containing varying levels of Mo and inorganic sulphate in order to study the biological manifestations of the interaction of $Cu/Mo/SO_4^=$ under defined dietary conditions. As shown in Figure 1, all animals exhibited decreasing plasma levels of Cu as the trial progressed. The rate of decline of plasma Cu was similar for all diets except the one containing 4 p.p.m. of Mo and 0·03 per cent. $SO_4^=$; animals fed this treatment showed a more rapid decline. A subsequent experiment confirmed these results and, in addition, showed that the caeruloplasmin activity in the serum followed a decline similar to serum Cu (Lee and

* Contribution from the Biochemistry Department, School of Agriculture and Life Sciences and School of Physical Sciences and Applied Mathematics. Paper No. 2922 of the Journal Series of the North Carolina State University Agricultural Experiment Station, Raleigh, North Carolina.

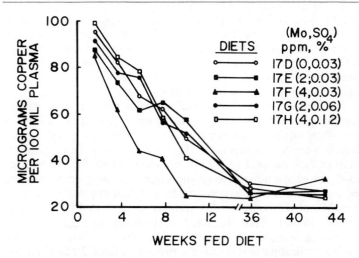

FIG. 1. Effect of diet on plasma copper levels of sheep. Mo added in the form of $MoO_4.2H_2O$; S in the form of Na_2SO_4 (Dowdy and Matrone, 1968a).

Matrone, 1968). The changes in haemoglobin values throughout the first experiment are shown in Figure 2. The greatest decline in haemoglobin was observed in animals fed the diet containing

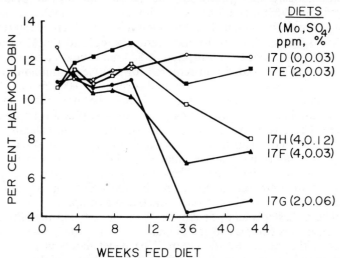

FIG. 2. Effect of diet on haemoglobin concentration of sheep. Mo added in the form of $MoO_4.2H_2O$; S in the form of Na_2SO_4 (Dowdy and Matrone, 1968a).

355

2 p.p.m. Mo and 0·06 per cent. $SO_4^=$. Animals fed 2 p.p.m. Mo and 0·03 per cent. $SO_4^=$, as well as those fed 0 p.p.m. Mo and 0·03 per cent. $SO_4^=$, maintained a normal leval of haemoglobin throughout the experiment. It is interesting to note that animals fed 4 p.p.m. Mo showed an intermediate decline in haemoglobin irrespective of the level of $SO_4^=$ in the diet.

Concurrently with the animal experiments chemical studies were being carried out with a precipitate which was observed to form when aqueous solutions of sodium molybdate and copper sulphate were mixed together. The studies using the continuous variation method of Job (1928), in which either the absorbance at 340 nm of the supernate or the weight of the precipitate were used as the measuring criteria, indicated that the molar ratio of Cu to Mo of the complex was approximately 4 to 3 (Dowdy and Matrone, 1968a). Tests for $SO_4^=$ in the precipitate carried out in our own laboratory and in an independent laboratory were negative, indicating that S was not present in the Cu/Mo complex.

Spectral scans from 190 to 850 nm of the supernate obtained from the Job's plot were carried out. The peak of Na_2MoO_4 absorption was approximately 208 nm, whereas for the copper sulphate two peaks were observed, one in the 205 nm region and the other at approximately 800 nm. Since the 800 nm region was unambiguously the spectra of the cupric ion in our system (Graddon, 1968) it could be used as a measure of complex formation. It could be reasoned that in our Job's plot, where we started with 0·0 Cu and 0·1 M/Mo and gradually replaced the Mo with 0·1 M/CuSO₄, that the absorption at 800 nm should be near zero until ionic Cu exceeded that required for complex formation. As is shown in Figure 3 an increase in absorption at 800 nm was not encountered until tube 6, substantiating the previous results indicating that the molar composition of the complex was approximately 4 to 3 (Cu : Mo). These series of observations established the formation of a Cu/Mo complex which formed at or near neutral pH. Preliminary data suggest that this complex is broken up at pH values of 3 and lower. These chemical data strengthen the notion that optimum conditions might well prevail in the rumen environment for the formation of the Cu/Mo complex.

The next step was to determine, if possible, the availability of the Cu in this complex to the animal. This was studied with two models: the piglet and the sheep. The piglet model was chosen because of previous work showing that, at birth, piglet serum shows a caeruloplasmin activity (CPA) one fifth less than that of an adult animal (Gomez-Garcia and Matrone, 1967). Moreover

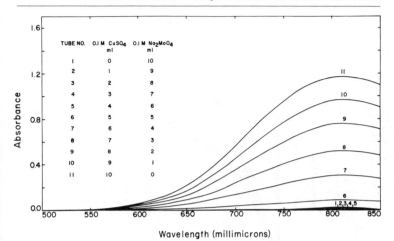

FIG. 3. Effect of molar variation of $CuSO_4.5H_2O$ and Na_2MoO_4 upon the spectral scans of the Cu/Mo complex in solution.

it was found that irrespective of the Cu content of the diet, CPA rises to about one third of normal in seven days, and thereafter, if the diet is deficient, the CPA levels off, whereas in the presence of adequate dietary Cu CPA continues to rise approaching adult levels by 14 days of age. A second consideration was that the gastric contents of the milk-fed piglet after a full feeding has a pH of 4 or more (Hartman *et al.,* 1961). It was reasoned, therefore, that the piglet could be used as a bioassay for the availability of Cu in the Cu/Mo complex. The details of the experiment are described elsewhere (Dowdy and Matrone, 1968b). A summary of the CPA results are shown in Figure 4. It is apparent from the CPA results that the Cu of the Cu/Mo complex was no more effective than Diet 1 containing no supplemental Cu indicating that it was unavailable. Copper and Mo data obtained from the liver, kidney, heart and brain (Dowdy and Matrone, 1968b) suggested firstly that the Cu/Mo complex was taken up and distributed as a unit, in part at least, in the body and secondly, that the Mo of the Cu/Mo complex was turned over less rapidly by the tissues since tissue Mo levels resulting from the Cu/Mo complex were higher than those resulting from an equal level of Mo, as sodium molybdate.

In the sheep experiment one animal was given an intravenous injection of [99]Mo via the jugular vein and the other was given a similar injection of the Cu/Mo complex made from ^{64}Cu and

357

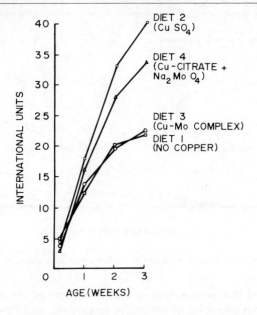

FIG. 4. Effect of diet on caeruloplasmin activity of piglets (Dowdy and Matrone, 1968b).

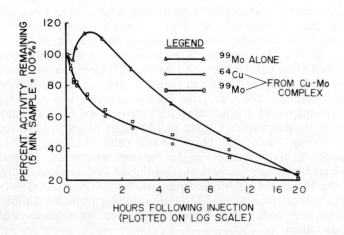

FIG. 5. Rate of isotope uptake from the blood of sheep (Dowdy & Matrone, 1968b).

^{99}Mo. The dose given to each animal had an equivalent level of Mo. The disappearance rate of these labelled compounds is shown in Figure 5. These data show that the Cu and the Mo from the Cu/Mo complex were removed from the blood at the same rate but the Mo was removed at a faster rate than when Mo was administered alone. Another difference noted in the disappearance curve of Mo alone was that it is initially removed from the blood into some pool and then re-enters the blood stream before its permanent removal. Data concerning the urinary excretion of Mo indicated that Mo of the injected dose of the Cu/Mo complex was excreted less rapidly than when Mo was injected alone (Table I). The results from the piglet experiment, suggesting that the Cu/Mo complex can exist *in vivo*, are supported by the results of the sheep study, showing that the rates of removal of Cu and Mo arising from the injection of the Cu/Mo complex were equal. The data from the sheep study, showing that the Mo from the Cu/Mo complex was excreted more slowly from the urine than when Mo alone was injected, support the results obtained from the piglet experiment, suggesting that the turnover rate of Mo was reduced when it was in the Cu/Mo complex. One further implication of the Cu/Mo complex data obtained *in vivo* is that the urinary excretion of Cu should be increased when animals are fed high Mo diets; this has been reported by various workers (Rys *et al.*, 1963; Marcilese *et al.*, 1967).

Table I. *Rate of* ^{99}Mo *excretion in the urine*

Time following injection	^{99}Mo from Cu/Mo complex	^{99}Mo alone
hr.	c.p.m.*	c.p.m.*
0 to 0·5	1097	1191
0·5 to 1·0	1307	3209
1·0 to 1·5	1533	3809
1·5 to 2·0	1518	4081
2·0 to 3·0	1345	2736
3·0 to 4·0	1257	2722
4·0 to 5·0	1176	2200
5·0 to 8·0	936	1270

* Values are expressed as counts per minute which were excreted per minute (as an average) between the time intervals indicated.

It seems reasonable to assume from these studies that the Cu/Mo complex is absorbed, transported and excreted as a unit. The role of sulphate, however, remains elusive. We have developed a working hypothesis to rationalize the Cu/Mo/SO$_4$$^=$ inter-

359

action in animals, particularly as observed in the ruminant. A basic assumption in this hypothesis is that the form of sulphate involved in the tri-metal interaction is not sulphate *per se* but an intermediate (X) in the bioreduction of sulphate to sulphide which occurs in the rumen. We have shown that the Cu of the Cu/Mo complex is unavailable. We propose that the Cu of the 'Cu/Mo/X', if formed, is also unavailable. An alternative to the formation of the latter complex is the formation of 'Cu/X' complex which would also be unavailable. It is postulated that at low levels of Mo, too low a level to inhibit reduction of $SO_4^=$ to X, X is formed and formation of 'Cu/Mo/X' is maximized. Under these conditions higher levels of $SO_4^=$ would enhance the toxic effects of Mo. At higher levels of Mo, the Mo inhibits the $SO_4^=$ reduction reaction, thereby reducing or completely eliminating formation of X. The consequence of this is that the effect of the sulphate level would be nullified and the effect of the toxicity of Mo is reduced, since an unavailable form of Cu could then be only mediated by $Cu^{++} + MoO_4^= \xrightarrow{\hspace{2cm}}$ 'Cu/Mo'. It may be interesting to note that Peck (1959) and Akagi and Campbell (1962) have shown that Mo inhibits sulphate reduction, utilizing pure strains of *Desulphovibrio*. In preliminary studies utilizing the rumen flora of sheep fed purified diets with urea as sole source of N and sulphate as sole source of sulphur, we have been able to completely inhibit sulphate reduction by these microorganisms with Mo (Prentice and Matrone, 1969). Currently studies are being carried out in our laboratory to test the hypothesis outlined above.

Acknowledgements. This work was supported in part by a grant from the Herman Frasch Foundation and Public Health Service Research Grant No. AM13055–01 from the National Institute of Arthritis and Metabolic Diseases.

REFERENCES

AKAGI, J. M. & CAMPBELL, L. L. (1962). *J. Bact.* **84,** 1194.

DICK, A. T. (1956). In *Inorganic Nitrogen Metabolism,* ed. McElroy, E. D. & Glass, B. p. 445. Baltimore, Md.: Johns Hopkins Press.

DOWDY, R. P. & MATRONE, G. (1968a). *J. Nutr.* **95,** 191.

DOWDY, R. P. & MATRONE, G. (1968b). *J. Nutr.* **95,** 197.

FERGUSON, W. S., LEWIS, A. H. & WATSON, S. J. (1943). *J. agric. Sci., Camb.* **33,** 44.

GOMEZ-GARCIA, G. G. & MATRONE, G. (1967). *J. Nutr.* **92,** 237.

GOMEZ-GARCIA, G. G. & MATRONE, G. (1969). Unpublished data.

GRADDON, D. P. (1968). In *An Introduction to Co-ordination Chemistry,* ed. Taube, H. & Maddock, A. G. p. 43. London: Pergamon Press.

HARTMAN, P. A., HAYS, V. W., BAKER, R. O., NEAGLE, L. H. & CATRON, D. V. (1961). *J. Anim. Sci.* **20,** 114.

JOB, P. (1928). *Annls Chim.* **10,** 9, 113.

LEE, D. D. Jr. & MATRONE, G. (1968). Unpublished data.

MARCILESE, N. A., AMMERMAN, C. A., VALESCCHI, R. M. & DAVIS, G. K. (1967). *Fedn Proc. Fedn Am. Socs exp. Biol.* **26**, 633.
MILLER, R. F. & ENGEL, R. W. (1960). *Fedn Proc. Fedn Am. Socs exp. Biol.* **19**, 666.
MILLS, C. F. (1960). *Proc. Nutr. Soc.* **19**, 162.
PECK, H. D. (1959). *Proc. natn. Acad. Sci., U.S.A.* **45**, 701.
PRENTICE, J. & MATRONE, G. (1969). Unpublished data.
RYS, R., KUKLEWICZ, M. & SOKOL, J. (1963). *Roczn. Naukro In.* **83b**, 145.
UNDERWOOD, E. J. (1962). In *Trace Elements in Human and Animal Nutrition.* New York: Academic Press.

DISCUSSION

Suttle (Edinburgh). In your *in vitro* studies of the formation of the Cu/Mo complex it is apparent that as you proceed away from the situation of equimolar concentrations of Cu and Mo the amount of precipitated complex formed falls drastically. Have you any information on the concentrations of Cu and Mo in the liquid phase of the digesta so that we can assess whether this complex can form *in vivo*?

Matrone (Raleigh). We have not tried to synthesise this complex in rumen fluid. It readily forms when the pH is near neutrality and we feel that in the adult monogastric animal this complex is less likely to occur because of the low pH; below pH 3 the complex begins to break up. One of our problems has been to find a quick way for detecting this decomposition and the absorption at 800 nm of the cupric ion is a good indicator of this.

Suttle (Edinburgh). We have tried to repeat your experiment by the intravenous administration of a Cu/Mo complex to sheep. We administered ^{64}Cu as a complex with nonradioactive Mo, as ionic Cu alone and as free Cu following the injection of an amount of Mo similar to that in the complex. We found no difference in plasma ^{64}Cu disappearance rates, no difference in ^{64}Cu distribution in the plasma and no difference in ^{64}Cu excretion in the urine. The reasons for this discrepancy may perhaps lie in the way we prepare our complex. We find we are unable to dissolve the complex in hydrochloric acid at pH 3 and have to go down to pH 2 before it dissolves. We are certain we are dealing with the complex because it has a strong absorption at 340 nm. I wonder if you have any comments on these points?

Matrone (Raleigh). We do get evidence of complex formation below pH 3. The slight difference in properties may be due to differences in the method of preparation; we start with the precipitate suspended in water and slowly add hydrochloric acid dropwise until solution takes place.

Smith (Edinburgh). Can you comment on the increase in the concentration of ^{99}Mo in blood immediately after injection which took place before the later decline in concentration?

Matrone (Raleigh). A general interpretation of that type of response curve is that immediately following the injection the dose goes into a separate pool and that it later comes out giving a 'hump' in the curve. I don't know what the separate pool could be in this case.

Horvath (Morgantown, W.Va.). In thinking about the fate of the Cu/Mo complex I'm not sure why we should attempt to draw a distinction between the ruminant and the monogastric animal. Won't the complex be subjected to roughly the same conditions of pH in the digestive tract in both groups of species?

Matrone (Raleigh). I think the important point is that before passage down the tract in the ruminant the conditions of pH in the rumen are very suitable for the formation of this complex and this may modify the influence of possible side reactions.

DIFFERENCES IN THE COPPER STATUS OF GRAZING AND HOUSED CATTLE AND THEIR BIOCHEMICAL BACKGROUNDS

J. HARTMANS AND MARIA S. M. BOSMAN

Institute for Biological and Chemical Research on Field Crops and Herbage, Wageningen, The Netherlands

THE literature data on field cases of copper deficiency in ruminants nearly all concerns grazing animals; this also applies to those areas where cattle are housed during part of the year. Some workers (Branion, 1960; Harvey *et al.*, 1961) have reported recovery from a low Cu status during housing or when feeding hay. The resulting difference in Cu status between spring and autumn has been recognized in the Netherlands for years and is considered as one of the most striking characteristics of Cu deficiency, especially in young growing cattle (Hartmans, 1960).

Ration analysis showed that the Cu supply indoors is not greater

Table I. *Effect of various treatments on the copper status of yearling cattle*

Expt	Treatment	Number of animals	Duration of expt. days	p.p.m. Cu in ration DM	p.p.m. Cu in liver DM		
					Initial	Final	Final as % of initial
1	Grazing	8	84	8·8	127	66	52
	stall feeding (same herbage)	6	84	8·8	124	58	47
2	Grazing	8	110	8·8	127	51	40
	hay (same growth stage)	6	110	8·7	142	86	61*
3	Young grass (8 to 10 cm.)	6	153	8·0	234	38	16
	Older grass (14 to 16 cm.)	6	153	6·7	221	72	33*

* Significant difference (t-test, $P < 0.05$) with the comparable group.

as a rule than at pasture. Except for a higher crude protein content in fresh herbage no distinct differences in mineral composition were found between fresh herbage and winter rations. It was observed that on farms where yearlings showed a good liver Cu status at the end of the housing period more hay was supplied and less silage than on the farms with a poor Cu status in spring.

In a series of experiments the differences between pasturing and stall feeding of hay were analysed into a number of factors and the effect of each of these on the Cu status of the ruminant was examined.

Investigations were made into the influence of:
(1) the environmental differences between house and pasture,
(2) differences arising from the feeding of fresh grass or hay and
(3) differences in the stage of growth of the herbage. The results of these experiments are presented in Table I. It was found that housing in itself does not affect the Cu status, but that the favourable effect of hay compared to fresh herbage was a result of the haying process as well as of the difference in growth stage normally present between pasture grass and hay.

These data further indicate that a low Cu status in grazing cattle is mainly caused by a poor availability of the mineral rather than by a low intake. Since horses grazing the same pastures are not Cu-deficient a relation between the rumen function and this poor availability is plausible. Earlier biochemical work on Cu-binding in fresh herbage and hay and in the rumen contents and faeces of cattle (Bosman, 1964, 1965, 1966) led to a study of the sulphide-forming capacity of the rumen contents in relation to the Cu status of cattle. A rapid decrease in the liver Cu status was accompanied by high sulphide concentrations in the rumen and *vice versa*. This suggests that sulphide formation in the rumen is an important mechanism in reducing the availability of Cu to ruminants.

Experiments with rumen liquor *in vitro*, as well as experiments with rumen-fistulated cows, revealed that in the rumen hydrogen sulphide was released very easily from R–S–H or R–S–S–R containing amino acids, but less easily from R–S–CH$_3$. Reduction of inorganic sulphate in considerable quantities takes place only after a period of adaptation. Molybdenum promotes the reduction of sulphur compounds to sulphide but also requires adaptation of the rumen flora. The capacity of the flora to form sulphide is increased by a relative protein excess in the rations (expressed in a low starch·equivalent/digestible crude protein ratio) and by a high digestibility of the rations causing a high rate of decomposition in the rumen. The conditions under which natural rations stimulate a high sulphide concentration in the rumen also result in a high urea content in the blood plasma.

In the light of these data many effects of diet on the Cu status of ruminants can be explained.

REFERENCES

BOSMAN, M. S. M. (1964). *Jaarb. Inst. biol. scheik. Onderz. LandbGewass.* 125.
BOSMAN, M. S. M. (1965). *Jaarb. Inst. biol. scheik. Onderz. LandGewass.* 97.
BOSMAN, M. S. M. (1966). *Jaarb. Inst. biol. scheik. Onderz. LandGewass.* 73.
BRANION, H. D. (1960). 8th *Int. Grassld Congr.* 564.
HARTMANS, J. (1960). *Jaarb. Inst. biol. scheik. Onderz. LandGewass.* 143.
HARVEY, J. M., RYLEY, J. W., BEAMES, R. M. & O'BRYAN, M. S. (1961). *Qd J. agric. Sci.* **18**, 85.

DISCUSSION

Mills (Aberdeen). How long does the rumen sulphide level take to reach equilibrium when sulphate is added to your diets? In work we carried out some years ago we found it took as long as one week to 10 days. Do you also find any relationship between the equilibrium level of sulphide and the Mo content of the diet?

Hartmans (Wageningen). We generally find that adaptation takes about two weeks. The continuous feeding of the sulphate supplements to give intakes which correspond to the levels found in herbage (approximately 0·2 per cent. S as sulphate) produced rather high concentrations of sulphide. Giving only 5 p.p.m. Mo produces no elevation of sulphide levels in the rumen after two weeks and the simultaneous addition of Mo and sulphate did not increase sulphide concentrations in the rumen above that from sulphate alone. However, when 20 or 50 p.p.m. Mo were fed increased sulphide concentrations were certainly found but only after a period of adaptation.

Mills (Aberdeen). I am interested to hear this as it agrees with what we found at the Rowett in some similar studies we carried out a few years ago. What puzzles me is how these findings we have both made fit in with what Professor Matrone has just described on the inhibitory effect of Mo on the reduction of sulphate to sulphide *in vitro*.

Matrone (Raleigh). I can't explain it either. The reduction of sulphate to sulphide has been demonstrated repeatedly in pure strains of bacteria and I can only suggest that there may be an adaptive system operating in the rumen which circumvents the system I have been looking at.

Hartmans (Wageningen). I would question whether your Mo/Cu compound would be stable under rumen conditions. Have you tried feeding it to ruminants?

Matrone (Raleigh). No, we have not yet done this.

Hartmans (Wageningen). I ask this because in the non-ruminant you would not expect sulphide formation; I wonder whether in the ruminant your compound would form in the presence of rumen sulphide.

THE NATURE OF TRACE ELEMENT BINDING IN HERBAGE AND GUT CONTENTS

I. BREMNER

Rowett Research Institute, Bucksburn, Aberdeen, U.K.

ALTHOUGH a considerable amount of information has now been collected on the influence of metal–metal interactions on the availability of trace elements to animals, not all instances of trace element deficiencies can be explained in these terms. Consequently, in an attempt to determine the possible importance of the dietary forms of the elements in the control of their absorption, an investigation has been carried out into the nature of the complexes of zinc, copper and manganese occurring in grass and in the alimentary tract of sheep.

On sequential treatment of ryegrass with 80 per cent. ethanol and water, approximately 60 per cent. of these metals were extracted. Although peptic digestion of the water-insoluble residue removed a further 20 per cent. of Zn (10 per cent. being due simply to the acid conditions used) tryptic digestion and extraction with phenol/water and sodium dodecyl sulphate were not effective in removing Zn, suggesting a limited association of Zn and protein. Treatment of the water-insoluble residue with a fungal cellulase preparation, however, liberated virtually all of the Zn and Mn and it would appear likely that these metals are associated in insoluble forms with the lignin-cellulose matrix in the plant.

It is suggested from the results of thin-layer chromatographic separations and of high-voltage continuous flow electrophoretic and gel filtration experiments that the Zn and Cu are present in the aqueous ethanolic extract of the grass in several anionic complexed forms of relatively low molecular weight (< 1500). The behaviour of these complexes, both in terms of their size and charge, was found to be very dependent on pH. Manganese was present in the extract in cationic form and it is possible that it existed in non-complexed form.

In rumen samples collected from sheep maintained on a dried grass ration, only 5 to 10 per cent. of the Zn and Mn and around 20 per cent. of the Cu were found to be in soluble form, despite the cellulolytic activity of the rumen organisms. Treatment of the insoluble residue with sodium dodecyl sulphate or by ultra-sonication liberated 77, 63 and 20 per cent. of the total rumen Cu, Zn and Mn respectively, in contrast to the negative results of similar treatment of the grass. It seems likely therefore that the insolubility of the Cu and Zn, and to a lesser extent of Mn, may result from association of the metals with microbial matter present in the rumen. This binding of the Cu seems to be unusually stable, as *in vitro* acidification of a rumen sample to a pH as low as 1·7 actually resulted in a slight decrease in the solubility of the Cu,

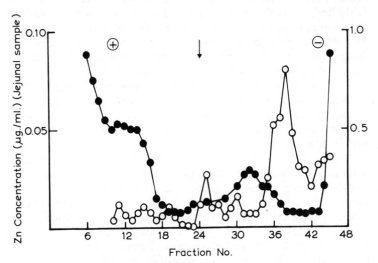

Fig. 1. Electrophoretic separation at pH 4·9 of Zn components of mid-jejunal sample (○) and of grass extract (●). The introduction point (↓), cathode (⊖) and anode (⊕) are shown.

although both Zn and Mn were completely soluble under these conditions.

Electrophoretic examination of the soluble fractions of the rumen sample at pH 6·5 revealed the presence of one anionic Zn complex, similar to the most anionic of the three dietary complexes, and also of a minor neutral complex. Several Mn complexes were present however, including the single cationic dietary complex as a minor component. Marked differences were noted in the separation pattern of Mn in samples collected before and after feeding, the main feature being the presence of a major neutral complex in the post-feeding sample only.

On passage of the digesta into the abomasum the solubility of the Zn and Mn was found to increase about 10-fold, approximately 50 and 80 per cent. of these metals now being soluble, but the solubility of the Cu decreased by about half. On detergent extraction of the insoluble residue practically all of the residual Zn and Mn were liberated but 40 per cent. of the total abomasal Cu was still insoluble. It appeared from gel filtration and electrophoretic separations that the soluble Zn and Mn in the abomasum were in non-complexed forms.

A gradual increase was noted in the solubility of Cu along the alimentary tract, about 30 per cent. of the total Cu in ileal samples being soluble. The solubilities of Zn and Mn, however, decreased fairly linearly as far as the lower jejunal region but then increased again on passage of the digesta into the ileal region. These changes in solubility appeared to be related at least in part to the pH of the sample and could be reproduced *in vitro* by pH adjustment of both rumen and abomasal samples. Dialysis experiments on the soluble fractions of samples collected along the alimentary tract revealed a decrease in diffusibility with increase in pH. At low pH around 95 per cent. of the Zn and Mn were diffusible but in lower jejunal samples (pH 7·5) only 50 per cent. of the Mn and less of the Zn was in diffusible form.

Gel filtration and electrophoretic experiments indicated that the soluble forms of Zn and Mn in the upper jejunum (pH 3·6) were in non-complexed forms. In mid-jejunal samples (pH 4·9), however, both cationic and neutral complexed forms of zinc were detected. None of these corresponded with the major Zn complexes present in a grass extract at this pH. The minor neutral Zn complex corresponded to the single complex detected in pancreatic juice and may therefore be carboxypeptidase. The major cationic complex was associated with a component with λ_{max} 270 nm. A small proportion of the Zn was excluded by Biogel P-2 and therefore had a molecular weight of > 2600. Two main fractions of lower molecular weight were separated on the gel. Manganese appeared to be present in non-complexed form in this jejunal sample.

Examination of samples collected from the lower jejunum and ileum revealed that both Zn and Mn were present in several anionic forms. Most of the Zn was excluded by Sephadex G-100 and must therefore be bound to macromolecules. One of the minor Zn complexes had an electrophoretic mobility similar to that of the Zn in the grass extract.

ACTION OF SOLANUM MALACOXYLON (S.M.) ON THE MINERAL BALANCE OF CALCIUM, PHOSPHORUS, MAGNESIUM AND COPPER IN SHEEP AND GUINEA-PIGS

H. R. CAMBEROS, G. K. DAVIS AND M. I. DJAFAR

University of Florida, Gainesville, Florida, U.S.A.

A DISEASE of cattle known as 'Enteque Seco' has been diagnosed for many years in the low land areas of Buenos Aires, Argentina. It is reported as the cause of death or slaughter of about 300,000 head of cattle each year. The cause of the disease is the consumption of leaves of a plant, *Solanum malacoxylon* (S.M.), a plant ubiquitous in the area. The symptoms are: loss of appetite, increase of blood calcium and inorganic phosphorus and stiffness with a characteristic calcification in the cardiovascular system. Previous studies have demonstrated that an aqueous extract of the leaves of S.M. *per os* reproduces the symptoms and lesions in cattle, sheep (Carrillo *et al.*, 1967; Camberos *et al.*, 1969) and guinea-pigs (Davis *et al.*, 1968).

We are reporting here the action of S.M. upon the mineral balance (Ca, P, Mg and Cu) in sheep and in guinea-pigs using chemical analysis and radionuclides ^{47}Ca and ^{64}Cu, administered orally, intravenously and intraperitoneally. In two experiments with sheep (28 animals) comparison was made of the effect of S.M. administration with the animals during a period previous to treatment and with control animals fed a limited amount of diet (low and normal intake).

The percentage composition of the basal diet used in sheep was: Bermuda grass hay ground 10; snapped corn ground 85;

13

Table I. *Apparent absorption of Ca, P and Cu by sheep fed basal ration with and without oral supplements of aqueous extracts of S. malacoxylon*(S.M.)*

Group/Time (days)	Daily feed intake (g.)	Pretreatment			1 to 7			59 to 66			112 to 116		
		Ca	P	Cu	Ca	P	Cu	Ca	P	Cu	Ca	P	Cu
Control	800	50	39	8·2	54	46	20·3	50	37	10·9	45	45	15·0
Low intake	250	51	45	8·6	—	—	—	58	79	0·5	48	52	33·0
S.M.†	465	53	51	6·3	62	62	-3·2	74	73	-10·7	73	77	-8·8
S.M.	83	52	40	10·0	60	58	7·5	-228	-140	-1·5	—	—	—

* Per cent. of intake.
† Equivalent to 5 g. of air dry S.M. leaves twice weekly.

soybean meal (50), 3; salt, trace mineralized (Carey Flow Mix), 1; vitamins A, D, and E, (4000 I.U. vit. A (palmitate), 540 I.U. vit. D2 and 10 mg. DL-alpha tocopherol/kg. of diet). The diet contains: Ca, 4·5 per cent.; P, 4 per cent.; Mg, 1·14 per cent.; Cu, 9·2 p.p.m. air dry basis.

The metabolic studies in young (1 year) wether sheep were carried out after a previous adjustment period. Balance studies were made during the pre-treatment period and after 7, 59 and 121 days of treatment with S.M. in Experiment 1 and after 7, 30, 60 and 120 days in Experiment 2. The S.M. treatment consisted of oral doses of water-extract of S.M. equivalent to 5 g. of air dry leaves (ADL) administered twice a week.

The mineral balance of young (2-month-old) guinea-pigs (Hartley strain) fed a commercial diet (Purina chow) was carried out over seven day periods during the first, fifth, sixth, eighth and eleventh weeks of a treatment with water extract of S.M. equivalent to 300 mg. of ADL. The metabolic balance of treated guinea-pigs was studied in comparison with a period previous to the trial and with animals pair-fed with the treated animals. There were three experiments using 50 guinea-pigs.

At the termination of the experiment all animals were sacrificed and plasma, bone, kidney and aorta were analysed for Ca, Mg and Cu by atomic absorption spectrophotometry and inorganic P by the method of Fiske and Subbarow (1925).

The oral doses of ^{47}Ca to each animal were 21 μCi in sheep and 1·5 μCi in guinea-pigs (as $CaCl_2$ in non-fat milk carrier). The intraperitoneal doses were 1 μCi of ^{47}Ca in guinea pigs. In sheep the intravenous doses were 18 μCi of ^{47}Ca in solution with calcium gluconate as carrier. Sheep received 5 mCi and guinea-pigs 200 μCi ^{64}Cu as copper nitrate given orally.

Whole body radioactivity was determined in guinea pigs in a whole body scintillation counter connected with a scintillation spectrometer.

Calcium. S.M. increased the apparent absorption of Ca in sheep (P < 0·01) and in guinea-pigs and obviously increased urinary Ca excretion (P < 0·01). In Table I are shown the results of the Ca absorption studies in sheep in the first experiment. The treated group was divided into two sub-groups because the intake of four of the animals was very low (below 100 g. daily). The use of ^{47}Ca (oral and intraperitoneal doses) confirmed our previous chemical balance in sheep and guinea-pigs and showed that the endogenous Ca decreased in the animals treated with S.M.

Table II compares the Ca balance of S.M. fed and pair-fed

Table II. *Calcium output and retention of guinea-pigs*
(% of orally administered ^{47}Ca)

	Carcass	Faeces	Urine
Pair-fed control	43	16	32
S.M. extract orally	50	4	26

control guinea-pigs. The Ca retention as ^{47}Ca activity in the carcass was higher in the treated animals but was not statistically significant.

There was a close relationship between increases of blood Ca and the increase in Ca absorption, in sheep as shown in Figure 1.

Phosphorus. The S.M. increased the absorption of P in guinea-pigs and sheep (Table I) and also increased urinary output of P. There were no statistically significant differences in P retention between treated and control animals.

Magnesium. S.M. increased the absorption of Mg and also produced a tremendous increase of Mg in urine in sheep and in guinea-pigs (Table III). The retention of Mg in the treated and low intake groups was lower than during the pre-treated period ($P < \cdot 01$).

Table III. *Magnesium balance in sheep given extracts of*
S. malacoxylon (Expt. 2)

	Urinary		
	Absorption	Excretion	Retention
Pre-treated (14)*	$43 \cdot 4 \pm 2 \cdot 2$	$14 \cdot 4 \pm 1 \cdot 5$	$29 \cdot 0 \pm 2 \cdot 4$
Low intake (4)	$44 \cdot 6 \pm 2 \cdot 6$	$34 \cdot 5 \pm 2 \cdot 1$	$10 \cdot 1 \pm 2 \cdot 1$
Treated S.M. (10)	$66 \cdot 0 \pm 3$†	$43 \cdot 9 \pm 2 \cdot 2$‡	$17 \cdot 1 \pm 2 \cdot 1$‡

* Number of animals.
† $P < \cdot 01$ between S.M. treated vs. Pre-treated and Low diet.
‡ $P < \cdot 01$ between S.M. treated and Low diet vs. Pre-treated.

Copper. The S.M. sometimes decreased Cu absorption in sheep and guinea-pigs in some periods as determined by a chemical balance. This circumstance is suggestive since with the natural Enteque Seco disease the blood and liver Cu values are frequently below the normal level. Table I shows the Cu balance in Experiment 1 with low and negative balance of Cu.

The studies with ^{64}Cu in sheep did not give clear results because the isotopes were found to be considerably contaminated; it will therefore be necessary to repeat these trials. In guinea-pigs the oral doses of ^{64}Cu did not affect absorption and excretion but the storage in liver and kidney in the treated guinea-pigs was lower than that in the control animals (Table IV). This may be a defect in Cu distribution, transport or uptake.

Table IV. *Distribution of orally administered* ^{64}Cu *in guinea-pigs* (% of administered dose)

	Faeces	Urine	Liver	Kidney
Pair-feeding	61	11	67	4·2
Treated S.M.	58	9·5	49	2·1

CONCLUSION

The S.M. produces similar and constant mineral metabolic changes in guinea-pigs and in sheep, viz: (1) increased absorption of Ca, P, and Mg; (2) a retention of Ca and P similar to that of control animals but a lower retention of Mg than in control animals; (3) an increased absorption of Ca accompanied by several related effects including decreased endogenous faeces losses, increased blood Ca, more rapid clearance of ^{47}Ca through the plasma and increased urinary Ca output; (4) an absorption of Cu that is irregular but often lower or similar to that of control animals; (5) a storage of Cu in liver and kidney that is always below that of control animals.

REFERENCES

CAMBEROS, H. (1969). Florida Academy of Sciences.
CARRILLO, B. (1967). *Rev. In. Agr. INTA* Series Pat. An.
DAVIS, G. K. (1968). Vol. IV, No. 2, FASEB.
FISKE, C. H. & SUBBAROW, Y. (1925). *J. biol. Chem.* **66**, 375.

DISCUSSION

Spencer (Hines, Ill.). Is the effect of this plant in producing hypercalcaemia and increased absorption of Ca due to a vitamin D-like substance and if so how soon after ingestion does the absorption of Ca increase?

Camberos (Gainesville). We do not know the nature of the active agent; it is perhaps a glucoside. We see no effects on bone so the action is not so similar to that of vitamin D. Calcium absorption increases 24 to 72 hours after an oral dose.

OBSERVATIONS ON THE ZINC METABOLISM OF CALVES

J. M. VAN LEEUWEN AND J. VAN DER GRIFT

Institute for Animal Feeding and Nutrition Research 'Hoorn', Keern, Hoorn, The Netherlands

THE zinc supply of cattle in Dutch herds is generally not low. Nevertheless Zn metabolism is a very interesting topic for research because of its therapeutic value for skin diseases and its possible importance for the economic production of white veal on an industrial scale. The experiments referred to below indicate the importance of Zn in these fields.

EXPERIMENTAL

All observations recorded here were carried out between 1965 and 1969 with black and white Dutch-Friesian cattle.

RESULTS AND DISCUSSION

Seriously ill calves from the region around Hoorn with symptoms of parakeratosis, as described by Miller and Miller (1960) and more recently by Mills, Dalgarno, Williams and Quarterman (1967) often showed decreased Zn values in blood plasma. Twenty animals, all within the age of about 3 months, had an average content of 0·87 mg. Zn per *l* plasma (the variation was 0·25 to 1·50 mg./*l*). In 75 per cent. of the cases the administration of a draught of 500 mg. $ZnSO_4.7H_2O$ per animal per day had a good result; in the other cases the Zn absorption via the digestive tract was clearly disturbed. This appeared from analyses of blood plasma and of liver samples taken by biopsy. In the latter cases the application of Zn ointment (pasta Lassar) on the sick skin had a better effect. However Zn absorption by the healthy and intact skin was very small. As shown in Figure 1 we could say that below a certain limit the quantity of absorbed Zn was better reflected by blood plasma than by liver; above that limit the opposite was true.

The Zn content in the dry matter of the ration, consisting of hay, concentrates and sometimes milk, was always more than 25 p.p.m. There was never an indication of vitamin A deficiency or of intoxication with high-chlorinated naphthalenes. Possibly there was a genetically increased need for Zn or, as Vikbladh (1950, 1951) has suggested for humans, the Zn absorption via the digestive tract was diminished by chronic infections such as broncho-

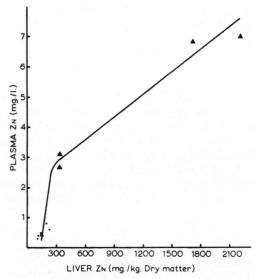

FIG. 1. The relation between plasma Zn and liver Zn in calves with
(●) and without (▲) parakeratosis. The latter animals had been
treated with 'pasta Lassar' (25 per cent. ZnO).

pneumonia or pyelonephritis. Our calves frequently had diarrhoea
or infections of the respiratory tract.

The inclusion of 10 per cent. toasted high quality soybean-oil
meal in milk replacers for veal calves decreased the Zn content
in the liver of the animals from 271 in the control group to 154
mg. Zn per kg. dry matter in the experimental group $(P < 0.001)$.
When 140 p.p.m. Zn as $ZnSO_4.7H_2O$ was added in a milk replacer
without soybean-oil meal the Zn content increased from 283 in
the control group to 1731 p.p.m. in the experimental group
$(P < 0.001)$. Judgement before slaughtering showed a significant
improvement of the meatiness of the hind quarters $(P < 0.05)$ and
after slaughtering there was a small increase in the paleness of the
veal $(P < 0.10)$. The total number of animals involved here was 60.
The Cu content of the liver decreased from 709 in the control
group to 355 p.p.m. in the Zn-supplemented group $(P < 0.001)$.
When 175 p.p.m. Zn was added in milk replacers with 15 per cent.
soybean-oil meal there was no change in either the Zn or the Cu
content of the liver. Probably the phytic acid content of the soybean
product caused Zn sequestration in these young calves without
any rumen flora (Smith et al., 1961). The Zn/Cu antagonism on

375

the pure milk replacer diet without soybean-oil meal was affected by the addition of soya. The same was true in the pasture when calves were given Cu-cake and trace element cake which contained Cu and Zn. We could show that there was no significant effect on Cu metabolism even if more than 450 mg. Zn was given per animal per day.

One day after calving, 12 cows had a little decrease in the Zn content of blood plasma (variation from 0·48 to 1·06 mg./*l*.). The newborn calf had an average content of 823 mg. Zn per kg. dry matter of liver. Normal values of Zn in liver of cattle varied between 100 and 200 mg./kg. dry matter. Normal values of Zn in blood plasma varied in this study between 90 and 150 mg./*l*. It seems therefore that many factors, both within and outside the animal, can influence Zn metabolism (van Leeuwen and van der Grift, 1969).

REFERENCES

MILLER, J. K. & MILLER, W. J. (1960). *J. Dairy Sci,* **43**, 1854.
MILLS, C. F., DALGARNO, A. C., WILLIAMS, R. B. & QUARTERMAN, J. (1967). *Br. J. Nutr.* **21**, 751.
SMITH, W. H., PLUMLEE, M. P. & BEESON, W. M. (1961). *J. Anim. Sci.* **20**, 128.
VAN LEEUWEN, J. M. & VAN DER GRIFT, J. (1969). *Versl. Landb. Onderz.* p. 731.
VIKBLADH, I. (1950). *Scand. J. clin. Lab. Invest.* **2**, 143.
VIKBLADH, I. (1951). *Scand. J. clin. Lab. Invest.* Suppl. **2**.

DISCUSSION

Spencer (Hines, Ill.). Do you have any idea of the cause of the increased salivation found in Zn deficiency?

Van Leeuwen (Hoorn). I am not able to explain it.

Mills (Aberdeen). We have seen this effect in our work on cattle and in sheep and, like Dr Van Leeuwen, we are not able to explain it. We are not sure whether it is excess salivation or the production of a more viscous saliva. We are interested in the possibility of the latter because this may be related to changes in the secretion of muco-substances that has been found in the intestine of the Zn-deficient rat as has been reported by Dr Quarterman.

SEX INFLUENCE ON ZINC REQUIREMENT OF SWINE

E. R. MILLER, D. O. LIPTRAP AND D. E. ULLREY

Animal Husbandry Department, Michigan State University, East Lansing, Michigan, U.S.A.

MANY dietary factors (Shanklin *et al.*, 1968) are known to influence the zinc requirement of swine. Serum Zn studies (Ullrey *et al.*, 1967) indicate that age and production practices may influence the Zn requirement of swine. Doubtless there are many environmental factors, as well as genetic factors, which indirectly influence this requirement. Studies by Strain and Pories (1966) in man and by Swenerton and Hurley (1968) in the rat indicate a sex influence on Zn requirement with a higher Zn requirement for the male.

In Zn deficiency studies with the baby pig (Miller *et al.*, 1968) the males have generally exhibited the deficiency symptoms earlier and more severely than the females. Studies with *ad libitum* or limited-fed growing-finishing swine (Hines, 1966) indicate that males gain more rapidly and efficiently than females or castrated males or females. Bruner, Cahill, Robison and Wilson (1958); Plank and Berg (1963); Baker, Jordan, Waitt and Gouwens (1967); Charette (1961) and Hines (1966) have shown that intact males and females have a higher percentage of lean tissue and a higher optimum protein requirement than male castrates.

These studies were undertaken to determine sex differences in the Zn requirement of infant and developing swine and to determine if an interaction exists between sex and dietary Zn requirement.

MATERIAL AND METHODS

In studies with the baby pig, animals were weaned from their mother at 3 or 4 days of age to a semi-purified diet (Miller *et al.*, 1968) containing isolated soybean protein and at one week of age were allotted to dietary Zn levels of 27, 36, 45 or 90 p.p.m. Pigs were individually reared in stainless steel cages. In studies with growing-finishing pigs, males, females and male castrates which were weaned at 5 weeks of age to a corn-soybean meal diet (average bodyweight about 15 kg.) were allotted to dietary Zn levels of 22 to 80 p.p.m. These pigs were group fed in concrete floored pens until groups receiving adequate Zn had exceeded an average bodyweight of 90 kg.

377

Table I. *Influence of sex upon serum zinc and alkaline phosphatase, gain and degree of parakeratosis*

Dietary Zn (p.p.m.)	Sex	Serum Zn (µg./100 ml.)	Serum alkaline phosphatase (Sigma units)	28-day gain (kg.)	Degree of Parakeratosis
27	Males	14	2·3	3·6	Severe
	Females	24	3·8	4·3	Moderate
36	Males	26	5·8	5·6	Moderate
	Females	38	7·8	5·3	Slight
45	Males	39	8·8	5·8	Slight
	Females	50	10·9	5·1	None
90	Males	93	14·0	7·6	None
	Females	84	13·5	6·7	None

RESULTS

Infant pigs. Results of the study with infant pigs are presented in Table I. The data on levels of serum Zn and alkaline phosphatase, gain and degree of parakeratosis from baby pigs receiving 45 p.p.m. or less of dietary Zn indicate that the Zn requirement of the male baby pig is greater than that of the female. This may be due to the somewhat greater growth and efficiency potential of the male baby pig.

Growing-finishing pigs. Results of two experiments involving 135 animals equally represented by males, females and male castrates indicate a lower dietary Zn requirement (in terms of concentration in the *ad libitum* diet) for the male castrates. Male castrates receiving corn-soybean meal diets with no supplemental Zn tended to gain more rapidly and efficiently than intact males and females. Furthermore, none of the male castrates developed parakeratosis, whereas parakeratotic lesions appeared in several of the intact males and females on the low Zn diet (22 p.p.m. of zinc). These lesions tended to be more severe in the males. Data on levels of serum Zn concentration and serum alkaline phosphatase activity support the contention that the basal corn-soybean meal diet is more Zn-limiting to the males and females than to the castrates. Since castrates consumed more of the low Zn diet daily than males or females their daily Zn intake was greater and was apparently sufficiently more to prevent parakeratosis and to support a more rapid and efficient gain.

REFERENCES

BAKER, D. H., JORDAN, C. E., WAITT, W. P. & GOUWENS, D. W. (1967). *J. Anim. Sci.* **26,** 1059.

BRUNER, W. H., CAHILL, V. R., ROBISON, W. L. & WILSON, R. F. (1958). *J. Anim. Sci.* **17,** 875.

CHARETTE, L. A. (1961). *Can. J. Anim. Sci.* **41,** 30.

HINES, R. H. (1966). Ph.D. Thesis. Michigan State University.

MILLER, E. R., LUECKE, R. W., ULLREY, D. E., BALTZER, B. V., BRADLEY, B. L. & HOEFER, J. A. (1968). *J. Nutr.* **95,** 278.

PLANK, R. N. & BERG, R. T. (1963). *Can. J. Anim. Sci.* **43,** 72.

SHANKLIN, S. H., MILLER, E. R., ULLREY, D. E., HOEFER, J. A. & LUECKE, R. W. (1968). *J. Nutr.* **96,** 101.

STRAIN, W. H. & PORIES, W. J. (1966). In *Zinc Metabolism.* Ed. Prasad, A. S. Springfield: Thomas.

SWENERTON, H. & HURLEY, L. S. (1968). *J. Nutr.* **95,** 8.

ULLREY, D. E., MILLER, E. R., BRENT, B. E., BRADLEY, B. L. & HOEFER, J. A. (1967). *J. Anim. Sci.* **26,** 1024.

THE MINERAL COMPOSITION OF LICHEN RELATED TO STUDIES OF TRACE ELEMENT METABOLISM IN REINDEER

G. N. HAVRE

Norges Veterinaerlogskole, Institutt for Biokjemi, Oslo, Norway

THE scope of the present work was originally to investigate the distribution of trace elements in lichen from various geographical and geological locations in Norway. Such information would be valuable as lichen is an important reindeer feed, particularly during the winter season. The first samples were collected from the northern districts during the summer of 1960 and were examined by a semiquantitative spectrographic procedure in order to get a broad survey of their trace element status.

This preliminary investigation gave interesting results. The ash content indicated a poor mineral content, 1 to 5 per cent. of ash, compared with 10 to 12 per cent. in grass ashed by the same procedure. The cobalt content seemed fairly high, 0·4 to 1·5 p.p.m. (D.M.), compared with a content of 0·1 p.p.m. in normal grass. It is difficult to state whether this is the real content in the plants or whether it is due to soil contamination. However, soil contamination may be most likely, especially when one considers the titanium figures. The Ti content was very high, above 70 p.p.m. in some samples, and this indicates soil contamination. The nickel content was also high (0·8 to 5·0 p.p.m.) compared with 1 to 2 p.p.m. which are usually found in Norwegian grass samples but this may also be due to soil contamination.

The content of lead is of some interest because there was found up to 11 p.p.m., which is much higher than what is normally found in hay and grass (1 to 3 p.p.m.). There is reason to believe that this is not solely due to soil contamination. The figures for the indicator elements Co and Ni are closely related, and also related to the ash content, but this is not true for Pb. High figures for Pb are found in samples low in ash and relatively low in Co and Ni. This seems to indicate a true accumulation of Pb, especially in the species *Cetraria nivalis*.

The elements mentioned above are all, with the exception of Co, substances which are not, with any certainty, known to cause deficiency symptoms in ruminants. As the high content probably is mainly due to soil contamination, and therefore is available only to a small extent to the animals, it seems unreasonable to expect poisoning symptoms to occur; possibly with the exception of Pb.

Far greater interest is attached to the elements copper, zinc, manganese and molybdenum. The preliminary investigations clearly indicated that the content of these elements in lichen was extremely low compared with what is normally found in grass and hay. An investigation series was therefore started in 1964 and during the following years several hundred lichen species were collected and analysed quantitatively for biologically important elements. The last samples are being collected this summer and, consequently, the results have not yet been treated statistically. A few words should be said about the results: the content of Zn and Cu is low, Cu extremely low, as found in the preliminary investigation. For Zn the mean values of six different lichen species are 28, 29, 42, 82, 25 and 32 p.p.m. respectively, and for Cu the same values are 1·7, 1·3, 1·4, 2·6, 1·4 and 2·5 p.p.m. These are samples collected in June. The same species collected in August/September had the following content: Zn: 35, 24, 60, 50, 40 and 40 p.p.m. and Cu: 1·8, 1·4, 1·9, 2·2, 1·5 and 2·7 p.p.m. Sheep and cattle fed grass or hay with such a low Zn and Cu content would inevitably develop symptoms of deficiency. However, it should be pointed out that the Mo content is extremely low as well and this may, to some extent, mean that the animals will need less Cu. It has been claimed, without exact references, that the mineral content of lichen is less available to the animals than minerals in grass, but this seems very unlikely and experiments carried out in the author's laboratory do not support this theory. However, these experiments are not yet finished.

We have also examined liver samples from reindeer before and after the winter grazing season to find out to what extent the trace element pool in the liver is depleted during the winter. It is necessary to repeat the examination for several winters consecutively, but the results obtained last winter seem to indicate that the trace element content of liver does not drop extremely during the season.

The work has, so far, only been to collect data, but the results give reason to suppose that studies of trace element metabolism in reindeer may give information of value also for a general understanding of these processes, and especially with respect to the influence of conditioning factors.

DISCUSSION

Oberleas (Detroit). You referred several times to the problem of soil contamination in interpreting the results of analyses on lichens. Is it possible to grow these in a greenhouse or other environment where this does not arise?

Havre (Oslo). Growing in water culture would be the ideal way of avoiding this but we have not tried it.

SECTION 7

SOIL/PLANT/ANIMAL RELATIONSHIPS IN THE AETIOLOGY OF DISORDERS ARISING FROM TRACE ELEMENT DEFICIENCY AND EXCESS

President: J. HARTMANS

Vice President: J. H. TOPPS

THE GEOCHEMICAL ECOLOGY OF ORGANISMS UNDER CONDITIONS OF VARYING CONTENTS OF TRACE ELEMENTS IN THE ENVIRONMENT

V. V. KOVALSKY*

Biogeochemical Laboratory, Vernadsky Institute of Geochemistry and Analytical Chemistry, U.S.S.R. Academy of Sciences, Moscow, U.S.S.R.

GEOCHEMICAL ecology is a division of ecology that deals with the influence of environmental geochemical factors on living organisms and their populations and investigates the mechanisms underlying the responses of organisms to the different levels of chemical elements (including trace elements) in the environment (Kovalsky, 1957, 1958, 1963a, 1964, 1968a).

The geochemical environment (parent rocks, soils, waters) has a mosaic character in relation to its content and relative concentrations of trace elements. These environmental differences give rise to certain changes in the biogenous movement of chemical elements in the biogeochemical nutritional chains (Fig. 1).

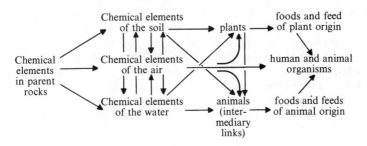

FIG. 1. Biogeochemical nutritional chains.

Reorganization of the links of the biogeochemical nutritional chains causes changes of the metabolic processes, changes in the synthesis of biologically active compounds and in the activity and other properties of enzymes (Kovalsky, 1963a, 1965a).

The lack or excess of trace elements in the environment may cause a corresponding deficiency or excess of elements in living organisms (soil micro-organisms, plants, human beings, animals) depending on the biological state and nature of the organisms.

Normal growth and development of organisms and normal synthesis of biologically active compounds occur only with certain

* In Professor Kovalsky's absence this paper was presented by Professor Rish.

concentrations of trace elements in the environment, the rations and tissues of the organisms.

A gradual rise of the concentration of trace elements in the environment and food is followed first by an increase and then by a stagnation of growth and development of animal organisms and also of the synthesis of biologically active compounds.

It has been shown, for example, that the growth of animals is retarded both by an excess and by a deficiency of Co, Cu or Zn in their rations.

In conditions of I deficiency (Kaluga district) supplementation of rabbits with increasing amounts of I causes first a loss of weight in the thyroid gland and an increase of thyroxine synthesis and then, with a further rise of I content of the ration, a gradual increase of the weight of the gland and a decrease of the synthesis of organic compounds of I (Kovalsky and Gustun, 1966).

A similar relationship exists in the synthesis of vitamin B_{12} by the micro-organisms of the digestive tract. The rate of synthesis of vitamin B_{12} is reflected by its concentration in the liver of animals. We have been able to demonstrate the following relationship between the environmental concentration of Co and the content of vitamin B_{12} in the liver of sheep: the amount of the vitamin diminished both in conditions of excess and of deficiency of Co (Kovalsky and Raetskaya, 1955, 1960).

Relationships of a similar kind exist between the synthesis of xanthine oxidase and the environmental concentration of Mo (Kovalsky and Yarovaya, 1966) and between the activity of certain oxidative enzymes, and the Cu content of the rations, etc.

The above mentioned findings and a number of similar ones establish a theoretical basis for care in the supply of trace elements used as supplements for the feeding of animals.

The adaptation of animals to factors of the geochemical environment influences the tissue concentration of trace elements, their absorption and excretion as well as the growth and development of the organisms and the synthesis of biologically active compounds.

Using soil micro-organisms as test objects we studied the problems of adaptation of living organisms to varying concentrations of trace elements, as well as some genetic aspects of adaptation and the possible role of mutations induced by extreme geochemical factors. The results of these investigations are partly presented at this meeting in the communication of Dr Letunova.

An ecological factor of major importance is the ratio of chemical elements in the environment. A well-known example is the interaction of Cu, Mo and SO_4^{2-} in inducing Cu deficiency and inhibiting or decreasing the synthesis of a number of oxidative enzymes. As a rule, pastures in the south of the USSR, where endemic ataxia of lambs occurs, contain rather normal amounts of Cu but a relative excess of Mo and SO_4^{2-} which disturbs the Cu metabolism of sheep. The ratio Cu : Mo : SO_4^{2-} in such pastures in Daghestan equals 1 : 0·6 : 330 (upper limit 1200) and in Uzbekistan 1 : 1 : 330 (upper limit 890). Under these conditions an inhibition of liver sulphide oxidase and plasma caeruloplasmin and benzylaminoxidase of Karakul sheep has been demonstrated (Rish and Egorov, 1962; Rish, 1964) as well as a 3- to 5-fold inhibition of brain and liver cytochrome oxidase activity.

The inhibition of a number of oxidative enzymes in the brain tissues of swayback lambs in Daghestan viz. cytochrome oxidase, succinate dehydrogenase, dopaoxidase, etc. was demonstrated by Kovalsky and co-workers by a histochemical technique as early as 1957 (Kovalsky, 1957, 1960). On 'healthy' pastures where no endemic ataxia is observed and the ratio of Cu:Mo:SO_4^{2-} equals 1:0·2:180, the activity of the above mentioned oxidative enzymes is not impaired.

The toxic effects of high B concentrations may be prevented by high Cu levels in the ration (Kovalsky and Shakhova, 1962).

Also of biological importance is the ratio of Ca : Sr in connection with the action of Sr on the chondral phosphatase and developing bone tissue of the epiphysis (Kovalsky, Blokhina et al., 1968) and in Sr-induced retardation of the growth of long bones (Kovalsky and Samarina, 1960). This ratio plays a major role in the aetiology of the chondrodystrophy of Urov-disease of humans and animals which is characterized by dwarfism and brachydactyly.

Simultaneous Co and I deficiency causes a more pronounced manifestation of endemic goitre and endemic enlargement of the thyroid gland than a simple I deficiency alone. This observation indicates that Co plays some essential role in I metabolism. The ratio Co : I in the non-chernozyem zone of the USSR with a high incidence of goitre comprises 1 : 0·77 and in the goitre-free chernozyem zone 1 : 2. Our experimental studies on this problem will be reported at this meeting by Dr Blokhina. They show that Co is essential for the synthesis of thyroid hormones (Kovalsky and Blokhina, 1963).

Of special interest is the biological function of Mo in humans and animals under conditions of relatively low Cu intake. There is a biogeochemical province in Armenia (Caucasus) where the

Table I. *Threshold concentrations of chemical elements in soils and possible responses of organisms (endemic diseases)*

Chemical element	Number of determinations	Deficiency (lower threshold concentrations)	Range of concentrations (% of air dry soil) Normal (range of normal regulatory functions)	Excess (higher threshold concentrations)
Co	2400	$< 2 - 7.10^{-4}$ Acobaltoses, anaemia, hypo- and avitaminosis B_{12}; aggravation of endemic goitre.	$7 - 30.10^{-4}$	$> 30.10^{-4}$ Possible inhibition of vitamin B_{12} synthesis.
Cu	3194	$< 6 - 15.10^{-4}$ Anaemia, bone deformities, endemic ataxia, in case of excess of Mo and SO_4^{2-}. Lodging of cereals, low yields of grain, dry tops of fruit trees.	$15 - 60.10^{-4}$	$> 60.10^{-4}$ Anaemia, endemic icterohaemoglobinuria, liver lesions. Chlorosis of plants.
Mn	1629	$< 4.10^{-2}$ Bone diseases, aggravation of goitre. Chlorosis and necrosis of plants, yellow specks on sugar beet leaves.	$7 - 30.10^{-2}$	$> 30.10^{-2}$ Bone diseases. Possible toxic effects on plants in acid soils.
Zn	1927	$< 3.10^{-3}$ Parakeratosis in swine. Chlorosis, 'little leaf' diseases in plants.	$3 - 7.10^{-3}$	$> 7.10^{-3}$ Possible anaemia, inhibition of oxidative processes.
Mo	1216	$< 1.5.10^{-4}$ Diseases of plants (clover).	$1.5 - 7.10^{-4}$	$> 7.10^{-4}$ Gout in humans, Mo toxicosis in animals.

Chemical element	Number of determinations	Deficiency (lower threshold concentrations)	Normal (range of normal regulatory functions)	Excess (higher threshold concentrations)
B	879	$< 3-6.10^{-4}$ Plant diseases, death of terminal buds of stem and roots. 'Heart rot' in sugar beet, browning of the cabbage flowers, and of the core of the turnip.	$6-30.10^{-4}$	$> 30.10^{-4}$ Boron enteritis in animals and humans. Plant abnormalities.
Sr	1269		up to 6.10^{-2}	$6-10.10^{-2}$ Chondro- and osteo-dystrophy, Urov disease, rickets. Brittleness of bones of animals.
I	491	$<2-5.10^{-4}$ Endemic goitre; aggravation of goitre in case of imbalance of I with Co, Mn, Cu.	$5-40.10^{-4}$	$> 40.10^{-4}$ Possible decrease of synthesis of I-compounds in the thyroid gland.

389

ratio of Cu : Mo equals 1 : 1 or even 1 : 1·4. This results in induction by Mo of an excessive synthesis of xanthine oxidase which in its turn increases the uric acid content of the organism.

Since humans are devoid of the enzyme urate oxidase such a rise of uric acid synthesis leads to a high incidence of gout among the local population (Kovalsky and Yarovaya, 1966). The paper presented at this meeting by Kovalsky and Vorotnitskaya deals with the regulatory processes of the organism under varying ratios of Cu : Mo.

Another important principle in geochemical ecology is the establishment of critical or threshold concentrations of trace elements in soils and rations in connection with the biological responses of organisms (Kovalsky, 1963a). Of vital importance are both the upper and the lower threshold concentrations of chemical elements beyond which the regulatory mechanisms of the organism fail.

In cases of extreme deficiency or excess of trace elements the failure of control mechanisms gives rise to disfunctions and pathological conditions (see Table I).

It is obvious that threshold concentrations cannot be expressed by exact values. They undergo certain changes under the influence of environmental and other factors, but the establishment of even such provisional threshold concentrations contributes to a better understanding of the following:

1. Probable conditions and regularities of intrapopulational biochemical variability of organisms,

2. The limits of trace element concentrations in the environment permitting a normal regulation of metabolic processes, of the synthesis of biologically active compounds and of normal growth and development of animals,

3. Alterations in the values of animal requirements for trace elements,

4. The conditions under which adaptation of the animal organism to environmental geochemical factors may occur.

It must be emphasised that the concentrations of trace elements which permit a normal regulation of metabolic processes vary greatly as a rule thus providing a relatively wide limit of requirements of animals for trace elements.

The establishment of threshold concentrations of trace elements, as well as of the laws which govern the variability of the biogeochemical nutritional chains in the biosphere and the occurrence of biological responses in organisms affords a basis for dividing the vast territory of the USSR into biogeochemical zones and provinces.

The biosphere which comprises the territory of the USSR may be divided into zonal regions called biogeochemical zones (Kovalsky, 1963b, 1964, 1965, 1968b). A biogeochemical zone is characterized by relatively uniform soil-forming processes, climatic conditions, uniform character of biogenous movement of chemical elements and biological responses of the organisms to geochemical and physical factors of the environment.

Environmental conditions exert their influence at all levels of organization of the biosphere: landscapes, biogeocenoses, populations, individual representatives of species, tissues, cells, subcellular particles, as well as at the molecular level, influencing the synthesis of specific enzymes (Kovalsky, 1965).

Studies at the molecular level provide a basis for comprehension of the different levels of organization of the biosphere.

Any of the environmental factors may acquire extreme values exceeding their upper or lower thresholds in regard to organisms of different systematic groups. This results in an increase of intrapopulational variability of organisms and in an intensification of natural selection (Kovalsky, 1968a).

The biogeochemical zones in their turn may be divided into subregions or biogeochemical provinces of two different kinds:

1. Zonal provinces which conform to the general zonal characteristics but differ between themselves with respect to the concentration and ratios of chemical elements.

2. Azonal provinces which show essential deviations from the general characteristics of the zone.

A schematic map of the biogeochemical zones and provinces of the USSR designed by Dr Kovalsky shows the regions where endemic diseases, intrapopulational variability and specific metabolic disorders in human and animal organisms due to geochemical influences may occur. It also shows the areas of intense natural selection due to excess or deficiency of trace elements (Kovalsky, 1968a).

A brief description of the biogeochemical zones and provinces of the USSR is now presented (Kovalsky, 1968b, 1965). The letters in square brackets refer to Figure 2.

Tayga and forest non-chernozyem zone [A]. The main environmental geochemical factors calling forth biological responses of organisms in this zone are the following: lack of Ca, P, K, Co

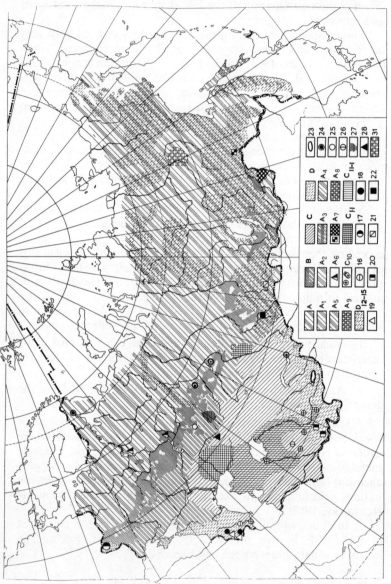

FIG. 2. Map showing the biogeochemical zones and provinces of the USSR

(73 per cent.)*, Cu (70 per cent.), I (80 per cent.), Mo (55 per cent.), B (50 per cent.), Zn (49 per cent.), adequacy of Mn (72 per cent.) and a relative excess of Sr (15 per cent.) particularly in river valleys.

Forest-steppe and steppe chernozyem zone including grey forest soils [B]. This zone is characterized by adequacy of Ca, Co (96;77 per cent.)†, Cu (72;76 per cent.)†, Mn (75;71 per cent.)† and a balanced ratio of I, Co, Zn, Mo in respect to each other and to macro-nutrients, frequent lack of P and sometimes lack of K, exchangeable Mn and, seldom, lack of B. As a rule, no adverse biological responses due to inadequate mineral nutrition, typical of other zones, are encountered.

Arid steppe, semi-desert and desert zone [C]. Nutritional problems in this zone are caused by excess of SO_4^{2-}, B (88 per cent.), Zn (76 per cent.), Sr (47 per cent.), Mo (40 per cent.), low content of I (80 per cent.), Cu (40 per cent.) and Co (52 per cent.).

Mountain zones [D]. These zones are characterized by a great variability of chemical composition of soils and ratios of trace elements and also by a diversity of biological responses depending on different parent rocks, soils and altitude belts of mountains.

In the tayga and forest non-chernozyem zone, Co deficiency results in reduction of microbial synthesis of vitamin B_{12} followed by hypo- and avitaminosis B_{12} in sheep and cattle but seldom in swine and horses [A_1].

In Cu-deficient provinces of this zone [A_2] 30 per cent. of pastures and hay contain less than 3.10^{-4} per cent. Cu (sometimes as low as $7·2.10^{-5}$ per cent.). The tissue Cu concentration of animals is usually low and coincides with an impaired activity of oxidative Cu- and Fe-containing enzymes. Haemosiderosis and endemic anaemia are encountered among livestock.

Lack of I in the soils of this zone calls forth an endemic enlargement in the thyroid gland and endemic goitre [A_3; D_{12}].

Under natural conditions lack of I does not necessarily correlate with incidence of endemic goitre, the latter more severe in areas of simultaneous I and Co deficiency as in the case of endemic goitre in sheep in some regions of the Yaroslav district [A_6].

In the Altay region the incidence of goitre correlates with a combined deficiency of I, Cu, and Co (Kolomiitseva, 1961).

Simultaneous lack of Cu and Co (predominantly in peat soils)

---

* In parentheses are given the percentages of soil samples (out of the total amount of analysed samples) which conform to the relevant characteristics.
† Figures in brackets refer to grey forest soils and chernozyem respectively.

results in endemic anaemia, acobaltosis, hypo- and avitaminosis B_{12} complicated by hypocuprosis [A_4].

Shortage of Ca and P [A_5] produces lesions in the osteo-articular system of growing animals.

In biogeochemical provinces with lack of Ca (Vinogradov, 1949) and relatively high concentrations of Sr (Kovalsky, 1957, 1958; Samarina, 1959; Khobotev, 1962) (Chita and Amur districts) [A_7] humans and animals suffer from the so-called Urov disease. Recently provinces with an elevated content of Sr [A_8] and a normal content of Cu and Co [A_9] have been discovered by our laboratory in Yakutia (Andrianova, 1967).

In the arid zone [C] provinces high in B and deficient in Cu are often encountered. The Cu deficiency is due to an excess of Mo and SO_4^{2-} and is manifested by depigmentation of wool, low productivity of livestock, endemic ataxia of lambs, calves and buffaloes [C_{10}] (Kovalsky, 1957, 1958; Kovalsky, Aliverdiev et al., 1968; Rish, 1964).

Excess of B manifested by endemic B enteritis [C_{11}] has been demonstrated in the north-western part of Kazakhstan, affecting humans, sheep and camels (Kovalsky, 1957, 1958; Kovalsky, Ananicher and Shakhova, 1965; Kovalsky and Shakhova, 1962) in the steppe of Koulunda (Plotnikov, 1962) and sporadically in steppes situated along the Volga river, affecting sheep only (Tertyshnyi, 1963).

It may be deduced that provinces high in B are wide spread in Kazakhstan and Central Asia [C_{11-1}].

Accumulation of B in the organs of animals impairs the excretory function of the kidney and partly inhibits the proteases and amylsae both of the pancreas and small intestine (Kovalsky, Ananicher and Shakhova, 1965).

Provinces low in I [D_{11}], Co [D_{13}], Cu [D_{14}], Ca [D_{15}] may be encountered in mountain zones.

Azonal provinces to be mentioned are the following: provinces high in Co [16]; low in I and Mn [Ivano Frankovsk district, see 17] with aggravation of endemic goitre (Antonov, 1965); provinces high in Pb [18] with myalgia, cephalalgia and other nervous symptoms in humans; provinces high in Mo [19] with high incidence of endemic gout in man and molybdenosis in animals [24]; provinces high in Sr and Ca [20] with brittleness of bones in animals and chondrodystrophy and rickets complicated by high Sr in man (Kovalsky, Blokhina et al., 1968); provinces high in Se [21] with deformity of hooves and alopecia in animals (Ermakov and Kovalsky, 1968); provinces with an imbalance of Cu, Mo and

Pb [22] that brings about disorders of the digestive tract in calves; provinces high in U [23] which accumulates in the tissues of plants and animals (Kovalsky and Shakhova, 1962); provinces of chronic Cu poisoning in sheep (Gololobov, 1952; Rish and Daminov, 1966) [25, 26]; provinces high in Ni, Mg, Sr, and low in Co and Mn [27] with endemic dystrophy of bone tissue (Kabish, 1967); provinces high in Ni [28] which causes lesions of epidermal tissue (Gololobov, 1952); provinces high in B on external frozen ground in Central Yakutia [31] (Andrianova, 1967).

Morphological changes in plants associated with accumulation of heavy metals in their tissues have been demonstrated in several provinces.

The biogeochemical zones and provinces mentioned above have been established as a result of 60 expeditions to various parts of the USSR. The present work is only a small part of what is yet to be done, but, even at this stage of research, biogeochemical classification may serve as a basis for investigations of the regions of the biosphere and further studies in geochemical ecology permitting a comprehensive approach to the elucidation of the laws of development and structure of ecological systems.

REFERENCES

ANDRIANOVA, G. A. (1967). Unpublished observations.
ANTONOV, YU. (1965). *Endimiya zoba i mikroelementy.* (Endemic goitre and trace elements.) Thesis: Moscow.
ERMAKOV, V. V. & KOVALSKY, V. V. (1968). *Trudy biogeokhim. Lab. Akad. Nauk. SSSR.* (12).
GOLOLOBOV, A. D. (1952). *Bulleten Moscov. o-va ispytatelei prirody, otd. biologii,* **57** (3).
KABISH, A. A. (1967). *Endemicheskaya osteodistrofiya.* Yu, Uralskoe Izd-vo.
KHOBOTEV, V. G. (1962). *Kaltsievo-strontsievaya provintsiya Vostochnogo Zabaikalya.* (*Ca-Sr zones of east Zabaikal.*) Thesis: Moscow.
KOLAMIITSEVA, M. T. (1961). *Soderzhanie i sootnoshenie nekotorykh mikroelementov (ioda, ftora, medi, kobalta) vo vneshnei srede i thanyakh cheloveka v raionakh zobnoi endemii.* (Contents and interrelations of some trace elements, I, F, Cu, Co, in the environment and tissues of man in areas of endemic goitre.) Thesis: Moscow.
KOVALSKY, V. V. (1957). *Novye napravleniya i zadachi biologicheskoi khimii selskozyaistvennykh zhivotnykh v svyazi s izucheniem biogeokhimicheshikh provintsii.* (New trends and tasks of the biochemistry of livestock in relation to the study of biogeochemical provinces.) Book: Moscow.
KOVALSKY, V. V. (1958). *Novye napravleniya i zadachi biologicheskoi khimii selskozyaistvennykh zhivotnykh v svyazi s izucheniem biogeokhimicheshikh provintsii.* (New trends and tasks of the biochemistry of livestock in relation to the study of biogeochemical provinces.) Book: New edition. Moscow.
KOVALSKY, V. V. (1960). *Trudy biogeokhim. Lab. Akad. Nauk. SSSR.* (11).
KOVALSKY, V. V. (1963a). *Izvestiya AN SSSR, ser. biol.* (6).
KOVALSKY, V. V. (1963b). *Voprosy khimizatsii zhivotnovodstva.* (*Chemical supplements in animal production.*) Book: Moscow.
KOVALSKY, V. V. (1964). *Geokhimicheskaya ekologiya. Priroda.* (3).

KOVALSKY, V. V. (1965a). *Funktsionalnaya evolyutsiya nervnoi systemy.* (*Function and evolution of the nervous system.*) Book: Moscow-Leningrad.

KOVALSKY, V. V. (1965b). *Doklady VASKhNIL,* (6).

KOVALSKY, V. V. (1968a). *Abiogenez i nachalnye stadii evolyutsii zhizni.* (*Abiogenesis in the study of the beginnings of evolution.*) Book: Moscow.

KOVALSKY, V. V. (1968b). *Biogeokhimiya. Veterinarnaya entsiklopediya, I.* (*Biogeochemistry. Veterinary encyclopaedia, I.*) Moscow.

KOVALSKY, V. V. (1969). *Trudy 5-go Vsesoyuznogo sovesch. Mikroelementi v selskom khozyaistve i meditsine.* (*Proceedings 5th All Union conference on trace elements in agriculture and medicine.*) Moscow.

KOVALSKY, V. V., ALIVERDIEV, A. A. & RISH, M. A. *et al.* (1968). *Doklady VASKhNIL,* (12).

KOVALSKY, V. V., ANANICHEV, A. V. & SHAKHOVA, I. K. (1965). *Agrokhimiya,* (11), 153.

KOVALSKY, V. V. & BLOKHINA, R. I. (1963). *Probl. endokrinologii i gormonoterapii.* (6).

KOVALSKY, V. V., BLOKHINA, R. N., ZASORINA, E. F. & NIKITINA, I. I. (1968). *Trudy biogeokhim. Lab. Akad. Nauk. SSSR,* (12).

KOVALSKY, V. V. & GUSTUN, M. I. (1966). *Doklady VASKhNIL,* (6), 26.

KOVALSKY, V. V. & RAETSKAYA, YU, I. (1955). *Dokl. Akad. Nauk. SSSR,* **100,** (6), 1131.

KOVALSKY, V. V. & RAETSKAYA, YU, I. (1960). *Trudy biogeokhim. Lab. Akad. Nauk. SSSR,* (11).

KOVALSKY, V. V. & SAMARINA, I. A. (1960). *Dokl. Akad. Nauk. SSSR,* **130,** (6), 1378.

KOVALSKY, V. V. & SHAKHOVA, I. K. (1962). *Dokl. Akad. Nauk. SSSR,* **146,** (4), 967.

KOVALSKY, V. V., VOROTNITSKAYA, I. E., LEKAREV, V. C. & NIKITINA, E. V. (1968). *Trudy biogeokhim. Lab. Akad. Nauk. SSSR,* (12).

KOVALSKY, V. V. & YAROVAYA, G. A. (1966). *Agrokhimiya,* (8).

PLOTNIKOV, K. I. (1962). *Letnie zheludochno-kishechnye i legochnye zabolevaniya yagnyat v Kulundinskoi stepi, terapiya i profilaktika ikh.* (*Summer gastrointestinal and pulmonary disorders of lambs in the Kulundin Steppe; treatment and prevention.*) Thesis: Novosibirsk.

RISH, M. A. (1964). *Biogeokhimicheskie provintsii Zapadnogo Uzbekistana.* (*Biogeochemical provinces in western Uzbekistan.*) Thesis: Samarkand.

RISH, M. A. & DAMINOV, R. A. (1966). *Voprosy fisiologii i biokhimii karakulskikh ovetz. Trudy Vsesoyuznogo in-ta karakulevodstva,* (16). Tashkent. (*Problems in the physiology and biochemistry of Karakul sheep.*)

RISH, M. A. & EGOROV, E. A. (1962). *Sb. Mikroelementi v zhivotnovodstve.* (*Trace elements and animal husbandry.*) Moscow.

RISH, M. A. & SHERBAKOVA, L. I. (1965). *Doklady VASKhNIL,* (2).

SAMARINA, I. A. (1959). *Issledovaniye mineralnogo obmena i prichiny ego naryshenii u molodnyaka krupnogo rogatogo skota v Zeiskom raione Amurskoi oblasti.* (*Mineral metabolism and the causes of disorders of mineral metabolism in young cattle.*) Thesis: Moscow.

TERTYSHNYI, V. T. (1963). *Vliyanie bora na azotistyi obmen u ovets.* (*Effect of B on nitrogen metabolism of sheep.*) Thesis: Belaya Tserkov.

VINOGRADOV, A. P. (1949). *Trudy biogeokhim. Lab. Akad. Nauk. SSSR,* (9).

DISCUSSION

Lewis (Weybridge). Can you tell us what the B content of pastures is in your high-boron regions?

Rish (Samarkand). We regard the threshold concentration as being more than 30 or 40 p.p.m. of the herbage dry matter.

Todd (Belfast). Have you seen ataxia due to Cu deficiency in cattle similar to that you have seen in lambs and, if so, how common is this?

Rish (Samarkand). We see it very rarely; we have seen it twice in Daghestan and twice in Uzbekistan but we have not investigated the condition.

Anke (Jena). Are you investigating the Cd content of your soil and feeding stuffs?

Rish (Samarkand). No, we have done little work as yet but more is starting in the immediate future.

GEOCHEMICAL RECONNAISSANCE AND THE DETECTION OF TRACE ELEMENT DISORDERS IN ANIMALS

I. THORNTON AND J. S. WEBB

Applied Geochemistry Research Group, Department of Geology, Imperial College of Science and Technology, London, U.K.

DISORDERS in livestock associated with dietary trace element excess and deficiency have been widely recognized for a number of years. Recently more intensive farming practice has resulted in an increasing awareness of these problems and has established the need for some method of mapping trace elements on a geographical basis. Over the past five years we have investigated the application of geochemical reconnaissance methods, initially developed for mineral exploration, to agriculture. Reconnaissance maps showing the regional distribution of trace elements have been shown both to delineate areas of recognized trace element disorders in livestock and in addition to indicate further suspect areas. The method used is based on stream sediment sampling at a density of from one to four samples per square mile. The minus 80-mesh fraction of the sample is analysed spectrographically for Ag, Bi, Co, Cr, Cu, Fe, Ga, Mn, Mo, Ni, Pb, Sn, Ti, V and Zn while colorimetric and atomic absorption procedures are used for analysis of selected samples for As, Se, Cu, Mn and Zn.

The trace element content of soils, and to a certain degree pasture, is influenced by the nature of the bedrock from which the soil parent material is derived. In general terms acid igneous and coarse sedimentary rocks contain lower concentrations of the trace elements associated with nutrition than do more basic igneous rocks and fine grained sediments. For example trace element deficiencies in livestock, crops and pasture are known to occur on granites, rhyolites and sandstones while metal toxicities have been reported on andesites and shales. Potential problem areas cannot be defined by a knowledge of the geology alone, however, as facies variations within any one rock type may give rise to considerable change in bedrock geochemistry.

By virtue of its origin the stream sediment approximates to a naturally derived composite sample of soil and rock upstream from the point of sampling. It has been shown that, to varying degrees, the trace element content of this active sediment reflects that of soils and rocks in the catchment as a whole.

RESULTS OF TRIAL SURVEYS

Much of the work has been carried out in areas where grassland farming predominates and in which it has been possible to compare geochemical data with the recorded occurrence of animal disease. Naturally the interpretation of stream sediment data in terms of animal disorders is by no means straightforward and is subject to a number of geological, pedological, environmental, chemical and physiological factors. The relationships between the metal content of stream sediment and soil, soil and plant, and plant and animal are in themselves all complex. Nonetheless an encouraging degree of correlation has been found between trace element distribution in the stream sediment on one hand and the occurrence and prevalence of recognized animal disorders related to trace element excess and deficiency on the other. The potentialities of this technique are illustrated by the following selection from the results of trial surveys carried out in Eire and the United Kingdom.

Cobalt. Reconnaissance in Co. Wicklow and Carlow, Eire, indicated a correlation between the Co content of stream sediment and the occurrence and severity of pine in sheep and cattle on soils derived from granite (Webb, 1964). More detailed studies in Devon showed patterns of low Co concentration ($<$ 10 p.p.m.) in stream sediments derived from granite on Dartmoor, reflecting soils of similarly low Co content on which pining in sheep has been recognized for a number of years (Fig. 1) (Webb, Thornton and Nichol, 1966; Patterson, 1938). Patterns of moderately low values (10–15 p.p.m. Co) on the Culm Measures* to the north

---

* The nomenclature of the Culm Measures has recently been revised by the Institute of Geological Sciences with the Upper Culm divided into Namurian and Westphalian as shown in Figure 1.

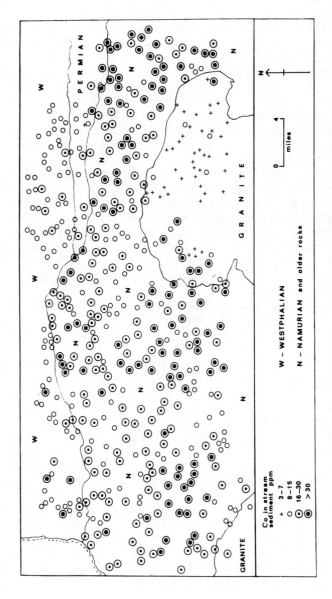

Fig. 1. Distribution of cobalt in stream sediment in parts of Devon and Cornwall.

and west of the granite are associated with areas in which pine has been more recently recognized and where the problem may have been present in a sub-clinical or latent form in the past.

The interpretation of geochemical data in this region is complicated by the leaching of Co in association with Mn from poorly drained soils and subsequent precipitation under a different pH–Eh regime in the stream bed (Nichol *et al.*, 1967). Thus Co-deficient soils, not reflected by low values in the stream sediment, give rise to pining in sheep in an area to the west of Dartmoor. When Mn is precipitated in the stream bed the sediment is usually seen to have a characteristic black staining. When such a stain is present it is necessary to carry out a systematic appraisal of soils for both Co and Mn content.

Moderately low contents of Co (10 to 15 p.p.m.) in stream sediments on Triasic drift in the Vale of Clwyd of Denbighshire are related to both soils and herbage of low Co content in an area in which unthriftiness and suspected pine are found in sheep. The problem is not found on neighbouring ground where the Co contents of sediments, soils and herbage are only a little higher. Stream sediments in drainage on the Bunter Sandstone in Derbyshire and North Staffordshire contain 10 to 15 p.p.m. Co while very low contents (< 5 p.p.m. Co) are found in both the sandy sediments and soils of the Bagshot Beds in Dorset (Thornton, 1968). Neither area is associated with clinical pine though very few sheep are in fact kept on the sandy heathland of Dorset.

Manganese. Mn and Co behave in a similar geochemical fashion and tend to occur in association with one another in rocks and soils. Investigations have in fact shown low patterns of Mn distribution coincident with those of Co in tributary drainage on the granite in Devon (< 300 p.p.m. Mn) and on the Bagshot Beds in Dorset (< 100 p.p.m. Mn). Although Mn availability to pasture is largely a feature of soil pH, and overliming may give rise to deficient pasture on almost any soil, it is also likely that deficient pasture will occur on soils of very low total Mn content. In Devon, low concentration of the element in stream sediments and soils correlates with the frequent occurrence of infertility problems in cattle attributed to Mn deficiency (Wilson, 1965). Similarly, moderately low patterns in drainage on the Vale of Clwyd (< 500 p.p.m. Mn) are associated with low levels in herbage (30 to 70 p.p.m. Mn in dry matter) and unthriftiness in livestock. In both Devon and Denbighshire the associated soils are also deficient in Co.

Secondary enrichment of Mn in the stream bed has already been mentioned. In this context deficient soils noted on high land on the Culm Measures in Devon and on the Denbigh Upland and Moorland have not been accompanied by low patterns of Mn in the drainage but rather by high metal contents and appreciable staining of the sediment due to leaching from the soil and re-precipitation in the surface drainage system.

Molybdenum. Drainage reconnaissance over part of Co. Limerick, Eire, outlined an area of some 30 square miles characterized by anomalies of Mo and Se related to an outcrop of marine black shale (Webb, 1964; Webb and Atkinson, 1965). Possible Mo-induced Cu deficiency in cattle had previously been recorded within the anomalous area (Fleming and Walsh, 1957). Detailed studies showed the sediment anomaly to be related to molybdeniferous soils and herbage while later investigations showed a highly significant correlation between the relative content of Mo in the stream sediment and blood Cu levels in grazing cattle (Thornton *et al.*, 1966).

In 1963 preliminary reconnaissance of 350 square miles centred on Tavistock in Devon disclosed a belt of molybdeniferous sediments on the Culm Measures (Webb, 1964). This was confirmed and extended as a result of a larger survey of the south west in 1965 when the pattern was related both to molybdeniferous soils and herbage and to the limited incidence of Mo-induced bovine hypocuprosis (Webb, Thornton and Nichol, 1966). The source of the Mo was traced to a black shale facies of the Lower Culm. Recent observations by the National Agricultural Advisory Service have shown widespread bovine infertility and general unthriftiness over part of this anomalous area. They are now seeking to establish whether these problems are linked with Cu deficiency (personal communications N.A.A.S., Exeter, Devon).

Geochemical reconnaissance in the southern Pennines has indicated Mo anomalies extending to 60 square miles (Webb *et al.*, 1968). Clinical bovine hypocuprosis was previously recognized over some 15 square miles of the anomaly, though the geochemical results suggested that the problem might be more widespread. Analysis of blood from 350 cattle in 26 herds indicated that twice the number of animals within the stream sediment anomaly had low blood Cu levels (< 0.07 mg. Cu/ml. blood) compared to those in nearby control areas (64 per cent. compared with 37 per cent.; if stock specifically fed mineral supplements are excluded, the percentages are 77 and 37 per cent. respectively). In several herds the outward symptoms of Cu deficiency were absent despite low blood Cu values. Copper supplementation trials carried out over the following two years in collaboration with N.A.A.S. and the Veterinary Investigation Service showed mean responses to Cu of 10 to 70 per cent., representing actual mean gains in live weight in Cu injected compared with control animals of 30 to 70 lb over the six-month grazing period. With few exceptions animals in these trials, though responding to Cu therapy, did not show any clinical symptoms of deficiency (Thornton, Kershaw and Davies; in preparation).

Smaller patterns of molybdeniferous stream sediments have been recorded on black shales of Ordovician age in the Crafnant and Lleyn Peninsula regions of Caernarvonshire and on coastal alluvium near Harlech in North Wales (Thornton and Webb, 1967). Bovine hypocuprosis is recognized in the latter area.

Preliminary studies on the Lower Lias in areas of Somerset and Gloucestershire, other than the 'teart' pastures, indicated anomalous patterns of Mo in stream sediments and soils over part of the outcrop, with normal contents (< 3 p.p.m. Mo) on other parts of the Lower Lias and on neighbouring rock types (Thornton, 1968). Subsequently geochemical reconnaissance was carried out over the entire Lias outcrop from the Dorset coast in the south to Yorkshire in the north; anomalous patterns of Mo (> 3 p.p.m.) totalled over 350 square miles (Fig. 2) (Thornton et al., 1969). Molybdenosis has been recognized for some years on the 'teart' pastures of Somerset and also recorded in parts of Gloucestershire and Warwickshire (Gimingham, 1910), while hypocuprosis has previously been observed on the Lower Lias in other parts of Somerset and Gloucestershire, the Vale of Marshwood, Dorset and parts of Warwickshire (personal communication, Miss P. E. Farmer and G. F. Kershaw). The geochemical survey, while confirming the extent of the recognized 'teart' pastures, has also delineated a further 200,000 acres of the Lower Lias possibly enriched in Mo. Soil studies within the anomalous reconnaissance pattern from Warwickshire to the south coast have shown a good degree of correlation between Mo in stream sediment and soil; herbage analysis indicates pasture Mo contents of 2 to 25 p.p.m. Collation of information from veterinary surgeons whose practices are on the Lias has shown more widespread problems of bovine unthriftiness and infertility than previously recognized, frequently in association with low blood Cu values, in those areas characterized by Mo-anomalous stream sediments. In the light of the geochemical survey it seems likely that such hypocupraemia is in

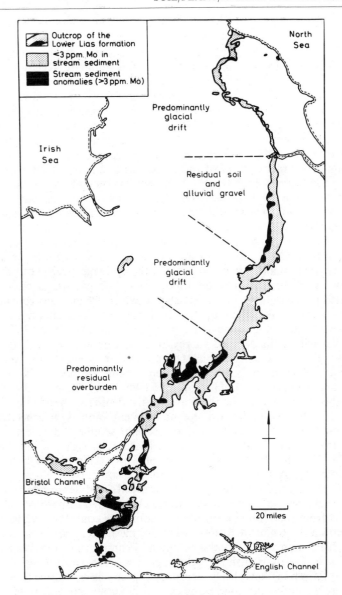

Fig. 2. Outcrop of the Lower Lias in England and Wales showing molybdenum anomalies in the stream sediment and variations in the nature of the overburden. (Reproduced by permission of the Editor of *Nature*).

fact Mo-induced and the possibility of more widespread sub-clinical deficiency must be noted.

Wherever geochemical reconnaissance has indicated anomalous patterns of Mo in stream sediment, the anomaly has usually been traced to a bedrock source of marine black shale. Such shale facies have been discovered in rocks of Cambrian, Ordovician, Carboniferous and Jurassic age. Current research has been directed at other areas of black shale where outcrops are of sufficient extent to be of potential economic agricultural significance. Of particular interest are widespread anomalies of Mo in drainage sediments on parts of the Oxford and Kimmeridge Clays (Thomson, in preparation). Although in general in the areas surveyed, bovine hypocuprosis is not clinically recognized, the results would suggest the possibility of deficiencies of a sub-clinical nature.

Selenium. As previously mentioned, stream sediment reconnaissance in Co. Limerick in the vicinity of known toxic Se areas indicated anomalous patterns of Se in the drainage. Subject to the influence of drift cover and topography, the pattern is closely related to the outcrop of marine shales (which are also molybdeniferous) and peak values up to 110 p.p.m. Se occur in drainage sediments near the shale (Fig. 3) (Webb and Atkinson, 1965). Studies within the detailed survey area indicated in Figure 3 have shown that while soils within the anomaly are seleniferous, toxic vegetation occurs only when seleniferous soils are poorly drained and organic and have a pH of over 5·5 (Webb and Atkinson, 1965). On the other hand in the same area molybdeniferous vegetation is found within the entire Mo stream sediment anomaly irrespective of soil type. Interpretation of the stream sediment data for Se in terms of the metal content of the pasture herbage can only be made with the detailed knowledge of soils. This illustrates the complementary nature of geochemical and soil surveys.

In the light of the association between Mo and Se found in Co. Limerick, Se was determined in selected molybdeniferous sediments from the United Kingdom. Anomalous contents have been found on the Culm Measures in Devon, the Lower Lias in Somerset, Namurian shales in the Southern Pennines and Ordovician shales in Caernarvonshire. Although peak concentrations of 9, 7 and 24 p.p.m. have been recorded respectively in sediment, soil and rock, under no conditions of soil environment encountered have toxic contents been found in pasture, possibly due to the acid nature of the soils (Webb, Thornton and Fletcher, 1966). Although geochemical reconnaissance has resulted in the first record of

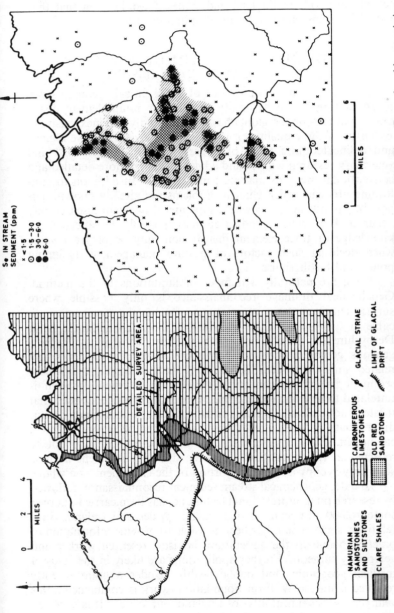

FIG. 3. Simplified geology and distribution of selenium in stream sediment in County Limerick, Eire. (Reproduced by permission of the Editor of *Nature*.)

seleniferous soils in England and Wales it would seem that they have little significance in terms of animal health.

ADVANTAGES AND LIMITATIONS OF GEOCHEMICAL RECONNAISSANCE

The fundamental importance of geochemical reconnaissance to agriculture lies in its ability to delineate multi-element distribution patterns on a regional basis, both rapidly and inexpensively. By virtue of these qualities it is possible to cover extensive regions and delineate those areas of interest to the agriculturalist and veterinary research worker and advisor wherein more detailed and conventional methods may be concentrated. In addition to confirming areas in which clinical problems are already known, it is possible to indicate areas where sub-clinical or latent diseases may occur and in which production may possibly be affected. A knowledge of trace element distribution may be of great value when deciding such factors of pasture management as liming policy and fertilizer use.

There are naturally a number of limitations to the method. Geochemical drainage reconnaissance is only possible where surface tributary drainage is adequate and is therefore not applicable in such areas as the outcrop of carboniferous limestone in Derbyshire and the chalk of Salisbury Plain. In regions of heterogeneous geology, where an admixture of small rock units and related soils may occur within any one catchment, the stream sediment presents a composite sample and its metal content is unrelated to any one specific soil. Finally, it must be stressed that the technique does not give a field-by-field evaluation nor does it differentiate between the different soil series occurring within a catchment. It is possible that toxic or deficient soils will not be reflected in the metal content of the drainage sediment if these soils only occupy a small proportion of the catchment as a whole.

To date, geochemical stream sediment reconnaissance, followed by research on interpretational technique, has been carried out over some 16,000 square miles of England, Wales and Ireland. In a relatively short time it has been possible to provide information of practical value to the agricultural advisor, research worker and veterinary surgeon. Further applications are likely in the fields of medical geography and public health. Under a grant recently received from the Wolfson Foundation, work is commencing this year on a geochemical atlas of England and Wales. It is expected that the atlas will be completed within a five-year period.

Trace element problems are recognized in most of the countries of the world. The application of geochemical techniques abroad, both in highly developed and emergent territories, would seem a valuable aid towards obtaining the increased levels of livestock production essential to maintain a rapidly rising population in a world of overall food shortage.

Acknowledgements. The authors wish to thank their students, W. J. Atkinson, K. Fletcher, R. N. B. Moon, and I. Thomson, who have contributed towards the the work. The National Agricultural Advisory Service, Veterinary Investigation Service and Irish Agricultural Institute have also given valuable assistance and advice. The research was originally financed by the Department of Scientific and Industrial Research and latterly by the Natural Environment Research Council.

REFERENCES

FLEMING, G. A. & WALSH, T. (1957). *Proc. R. Ir. Acad.* **58** *B*, 151.

GIMINGHAM, C. T. (1910). *J. Bd. Agric. Fish.* **17,** 529.

NICHOL, I., HORSNAIL, R. F. & WEBB, J. S. (1967). *Trans. Instn Min. Metall. B* **76,** 113.

PATTERSON, J. B. E. (1938). *Emp. J. exp. Agric.* **6,** 262.

THOMSON, I. *Regional Geochemical Reconnaissance of Black Shale Facies with Particular Reference to the Incidence of Trace Element Disorders in Crops and Animals.* Ph.D. Thesis, University of London. In preparation.

THORNTON, I. (1968). *The Application of Regional Geochemical Reconnaissance to Agricultural Problems.* Ph.D. Thesis, University of London.

THORNTON, I. & WEBB, J. S. (1967). *Welsh Soils Discussion Group Report* **No. 9,** 57.

THORNTON, I., MOON, R. N. B. & WEBB, J. S. (1969). *Nature, Lond.* **221,** 457.

THORNTON, I., ATKINSON, W. J., WEBB, J. S. & POOLE, D. B. R. (1966). *Ir. J. agric. Res.* **5,** 280.

WEBB, J. S. (1964). *New Scient.* **23,** 504.

WEBB, J. S. & ATKINSON, W. J. (1965). *Nature, Lond.* **208,** 1056.

WEBB, J. S., THORNTON, I. & FLETCHER, K. (1966). *Nature, Lond.* **211,** 327.

WEBB, J. S., THORNTON, I. & FLETCHER, K. (1968). *Nature, Lond.* **217,** 1010.

WEBB, J. S., THORNTON, I. & NICHOL, I. (1966). N.A.A.S. 'Open' Conference of Soil Scientists, London, 1966.

WILSON, J. G. (1965). *Vet. Rec.* **77,** 489.

DISCUSSION

Ullrey (East Lansing). What problems do you experience from artefacts attributable to industrial contamination when carrying out stream sediment analysis?

Thornton (London). This is an important feature in working in areas such as the U.K. when initial reconnaissance surveys are carried out and the presence of possible sources of contamination, e.g. old smelter workings, is noted. In Derbyshire, for example, lead enrichment has been found a considerable distance to windward of old workings and in S.W. England contamination due to mining and mine dumps has been taken into account during initial survey work.

MacPherson (Auchincruive). What were the herbage Mo and Cu levels in the Mo-anomalous areas where you obtained growth responses from the administration of Cu to cattle?

Thornton (London). In Derbyshire and North Staffordshire the concentration of Mo at the time we sampled was not very high and was in the range of 2 to 8 p.p.m. in grasses and slightly higher in clovers. The Cu levels of herbage were normal.

Hemphill (Columbia). In these areas where smelting has been previously carried out have you found any changes in the plant species as a result of contamination?

Thornton (London). Although this would be very interesting to investigate we have not yet done so.

Hill (London). You have concentrated on areas where there are known animal problems or areas near these. Results are largely positive, but do you have negative results to emphasise the reality of the positive ones?

Thornton (London). We most certainly have! For example we investigated 1000 square miles in North Wales where lambs commonly suffer from swayback but we found no relation to any abnormal metal distribution in stream sediments. In such widespread surveys we do however come across interesting features that may have agricultural implications as, for example, in the North Wales survey where we found a pocket of high Mo in Ordovician shales which had not been previously recognized.

Reith (Aberdeen). What advantages do you see in geochemical surveys compared with the normal soil surveys which provide similar data?

Thornton (London). This is a very important question. The main advantages are of course speed and cheapness. In 1965 we had two post-graduate students carry out a preliminary reconnaissance survey of 2800 square miles in the course of one summer field period. Reconnaissance surveys are relatively cheap and rapid whereas the soil survey takes considerably longer. Soil surveys and geochemical surveys are to some extent complementary and information from the one may help in the interpretation of the other. For example, the Evesham series of soils derived from the Lower Lias may or may not be molybdeniferous depending on the particular horizon from which the soil is derived. The geochemical survey will delineate the molybdeniferous areas whereas the soil survey alone will only map the distribution of the soil series.

Fleming (Wexford). To comment on what Dr Reith and Dr Thornton have just said I would like to point out that the stream sediment analysis only gives an indication of the total quantities of trace metals to be expected in a given area whereas in the normal soil survey analyses the extractability of trace metals may often be investigated. Geochemical surveys and stream sediment analyses by their very nature only delineate areas of inherently high or inherently low trace element content; they give no indication of availabilities of these elements. This difference is of course well known to soil people but may be not so well known to veterinarians and it is important to recognize that there can be at least three types of trace element deficiency, namely, inherent deficiencies in which the parent material is low in trace element content, acquired deficiencies in which the deficiency has arisen during soil development and lastly acquired deficiencies which result from the modification of soil conditions by cultural practices such as liming or draining soils.

Reith (Aberdeen). Dr Fleming is right in his remarks. It is only a proportion of the total trace metal content of a soil that is available to plants and ultimately to animals and this is why various arbitrary extraction procedures have been developed in soil analysis in the attempt to determine availability.

Tinsley (Aberdeen). Dr Thornton's results are based upon the analysis of stream sediment samples that have passed through an 80 mesh sieve. Since the gross chemical composition of sand particles generally differs considerably from that of fine clay the results could depend greatly on the particle size distribution in the fraction sampled. Could Dr Thornton comment on this?

Thornton (London). The metal content certainly changes with the size of the particle, for example the Cu content is commonly higher in the finer fractions. The fraction chosen is arbitrary and has been selected because it can be used under a wide variety of circumstances. It would undoubtedly be better in some areas to use finer fractions as these would probably reveal an increased number of anomalous patterns of metal distribution. The '–80' fraction has however been chosen as it covers a wide range of geological and environmental situations. It gives information that is of interest both in agriculture and in mineral exploration.

SOIL FACTORS INFLUENCING THE TRACE ELEMENT CONTENT OF HERBAGE

J. W. S. REITH

The Macaulay Institute for Soil Research, Aberdeen, Scotland, U.K.

SOIL factors, including geological nature of the parent material, texture, pedological drainage conditions, lime status and fertilizer treatment, can directly affect the trace element content of mixed herbage in temporary leys by influencing uptake by individual species In addition, in these leys containing ryegrass (*Lolium perenne*), cocksfoot (*Dactylis glomerata*), timothy (*Phleum pratense*), red clover (*Trifolium pratense*), and white clover (*Trifolium repens*), the proportions of the various grasses and clovers present can be altered by lime and fertilizer dressings, thereby producing indirect effects. Previous papers by Mitchell, Reith and Johnston (1956, 1957), Mitchell (1963) and Reith and Mitchell (1964) have given results showing the effects of these factors and this paper summarizes the main findings from field and laboratory work.

Soils derived from basic igneous rocks usually have higher readily soluble contents of the important trace elements than corresponding soils from acid igneous or metamorphic parent materials. Herbages grown on these different soil types normally show similar trends. For instance, on freely drained soils derived from basic igneous parent material the mean cobalt content of red clover, sampled in June just after flowering and averaged over about 10 sites, was 0·28 p.p.m. Co, compared with 0·11, 0·12, 0·11 and 0·08 on corresponding soils from Old Red Sandstone, acid igneous and slate tills, and fluvio-glacial sands and gravels respectively. A similar trend was shown by copper, the corresponding means for the five soil types being 7·8, 8·1, 6·8, 6·2 and 4·7 p.p.m. respectively.

The amounts of readily soluble trace elements are generally smaller in coarse-textured than fine-textured soils. For instance, the amount of Co extracted by 2·5 per cent. acetic acid from a granitic soil containing 8 per cent. clay was 0·14 p.p.m. Co compared with 0·39 p.p.m. in a similar granitic soil containing 24 per cent. clay.

The amounts of most trace elements in plants grown on soils with poor pedological drainage conditions, even when field drains are installed to remove excess water, are normally higher than in

410

plants grown on corresponding freely drained soils. Typical results, averaged over five pairs, for Co, Cu, Mn, Mo and Zn in mixed herbage are 0·14, 4·2, 76, 1·1 and 24 p.p.m. respectively from the freely drained soils and 0·86, 5·4, 124, 1·4 and 27 from the poorly drained areas. The effect of variable drainage conditions was very large in a field with a slightly acid soil high in Mo, the content in mixed herbage rising from 7 p.p.m. on the freely drained part to 31 p.p.m. Mo on the poorly drained area.

It is well established that lime dressings can reduce the Co content of herbage. Cu is frequently reduced slightly by liming. For example, clovers grown on plots with soil maintained at a pH (water) of 5·0 contained an average of 7·9 p.p.m. Cu while the corresponding content on plots with a pH of 6·5 was 6·9 p.p.m. The effect of lime on Zn is similar, the clovers containing 28 p.p.m. at pH 5·0 compared with 23 p.p.m. at pH values of 6·0 and 6·5. Ryegrass shows very similar effects to clover for both Cu and Zn. On plots maintained at pH values of 5·0, 5·5, 6·0, 6·5 and 7·0 the average Mo contents of clovers were 0·8, 1·3, 2·7, 3·9 and 6·6 p.p.m. respectively. For ryegrass the corresponding range was 0·6 to 4·6 p.p.m. Mo. On these plots the Mn content of the clovers were 55, 30, 22, 14 and 12 and of ryegrass 104, 68, 51, 23 and 13 p.p.m. respectively. In north-east Scotland the lime content and pH value of a soil can thus have a very large effect on the trace elements in herbage, particularly on Mo and Mn.

High rates of fertilizer N reduce or eliminate clovers from mixed swards and this can lower the contents of Co, Cu and Mo in the herbage, because the amounts of these three elements are usually higher in clovers than associated grasses. For instance on a soil deficient in both Co and Cu, 180 lb N per acre per annum applied in three equal dressings during the growing season reduced the contents of Co, Cu and Mo in mixed herbage from 0·08, 4·7 and 1·6 to 0·05, 3·6 and 1·4 p.p.m. respectively. The N treatment, however, had practically no effect on the contents of the three elements in the clovers separated from the mixed herbage. The accompanying ryegrass likewise showed no consistent reduction in Co content but the N dressings lowered its contents of both Cu and Mo. Following the application of 2 lb $CoSO_4.7H_2O$ and 20 lb $CuSO_4.5H_2O$ per acre to correct the deficiencies, the Co and Cu contents of the mixed herbage, ryegrass and clovers were appreciably higher and were not reduced by the N treatment. The Zn contents of mixed herbage, ryegrass and clovers have not shown any large or consistent effects of N dressings.

It appears that N applications are likely to have relatively small

411

effects on the Co, Cu and Zn contents in herbage, provided the soil is adequately supplied with these elements, but they have consistently reduced Mn and Mo.

The limited information available on the effects of P and K fertilizers used at normal rates suggest that these nutrients are unlikely to produce any large or consistent changes in the trace element contents of herbage.

REFERENCES

MITCHELL, R. L. (1963). *Jl R. agric. Soc.* **124,** 75.
MITCHELL, R. L., REITH, J. W. S. & JOHNSTON, I. M. (1956). *Analyse des Plantes et Problèmes des Fumures Minérales* (*2e Colloque*), p. 249, Paris: I.R.H.O.
MITCHELL, R. L., REITH, J. W. S. & JOHNSTON, I. M. (1957). *J. Sci. Fd Agric.* **8,** S51.
REITH, J. W. S. & MITCHELL, R. L. (1964). *Plant Analysis and Fertilizer Problems* (*4th Colloquium*). *Brussels,* p. 241. East Lansing: American Society of Horticultural Science.

DISCUSSION

Whitehead (Hurley). What form of fertilizer nitrogen was used in your experiments? Changes in soil pH can have a large effect on the uptake of trace elements such as Mo, Co and Mn and different effects on pH can arise from fertilizers such as nitro chalk and ammonium sulphate.

Reith (Aberdeen). The form used was nitro chalk; it had no effect on soil pH in these experiments.

VEGETATIONAL FACTORS AFFECTING THE TRACE ELEMENT CONTENT OF PLANTS

J. C. BURRIDGE

The Macaulay Institute for Soil Research, Aberdeen, Scotland, U.K.

ATTENTION is drawn to some variations of plant trace element content associated with differences between species, stage of growth and distribution within the plant. These factors are termed 'vegetational' to contrast them with those that are related more directly to soil conditions. The trace element content of pasture herbage is dynamically influenced by interactions between these three factors. Studies by Fleming (1965, 1968), Fleming and

412

Murphy (1968) and Davey (1957) contain much trace element information and extensive references to related work. Varietal differences of leaf: stem ratio in ryegrass (Hryncewicz, 1967), agronomic assessment of herbage (Miles, 1960) and aspects of pasture plant physiology (Langer, 1967) are also of general relevance.

Clover and grasses growing within the same sward often differ significantly in their trace element content and consequently botanical composition affects the trace element content of mixed herbage samples, as indicated by Reith (this volume, p. 410). A comparison has been made of the concentration in dry matter of clover (*Trifolium pratense* and *repens*) and of ryegrass (*Lolium perenne*) from temporary pastures at two local sites and Table I

Table I. *Comparison of concentration in dry matter of clover and ryegrass samples from two sites over several years*

	Species with the higher content	No. of samples					
		Co	Cu	Fe	Mn	Mo	Zn
Site A	Clover	8	3	12	0	5	5
	Ryegrass	1	9	0	12	7	7
Site B	Clover	19	9	22	1	12	18
	Ryegrass	3	13	0	21	10	4

shows the number of times each of these species had the higher content. Both sites are Co- and Cu-deficient; all samples were from plots without trace element additions. The relative contents of Fe and Mn form the most consistent pattern. Clover had the higher Fe content on every occasion, while Mn was higher in the ryegrass 33 times out of 34. The mean contents at the two sites were: for Fe, clover 64 and 56 p.p.m., ryegrass 43 and 37 p.p.m., for Mn, clover 44 and 33 p.p.m., ryegrass 81 and 83 p.p.m. The definite trend for Co to be higher in clover is well known. On the other hand, Cu concentration is lower in clover than in ryegrass, only on deficient soils (Mitchell *et al.*, 1957). When the levels of soil Cu, Mo and Zn are high, clover generally contains much more of these elements than does ryegrass since luxury uptake seems to occur more readily with the former species.

Plant trace element content varies considerably with stage of growth. This is illustrated in Table II for field-grown oats (*Avena sativa* var. Sun II); each sample, cut 2·5 cm. above ground level, contained about 600 tillers. The contents are expressed by weight

Table II. *Content of above-ground part of oat plants at different stages of growth; p.p.m. in oven dry matter and µg. per tiller*

Sampling Date	Growth Stage		Co	Cu	Fe	Mn	Mo	Zn
28.5.64	2 leaf	p.p.m.	0·07	6·4	170	53	1·3	41
		µg.	0·007	0·7	18	6	0·1	4
16.6.64	3–4 leaf	p.p.m.	0·003	2·9	51	48	0·79	24
		µg.	0·002	1·5	26	25	0·4	12
15.7.64	Headed	p.p.m.	0·007	1·7	32	43	0·52	15
		µg.	0·015	3·6	70	92	1·1	32
20.8.64	Grain milky	p.p.m.	0·008	1·8	40	39	0·32	15
		µg.	0·025	5·7	124	121	1·0	46
4.9.64	Grain ripe	p.p.m.	0·03	1·8	52	39	0·28	15
		µg.	0·092	5·5	161	121	0·9	47

per tiller as well as by concentration in dry matter to illustrate different aspects of the trace element changes. The dilution effect of rapid plant growth in the early stages is clearly seen for Cu between 28th May and 16th June. While Cu content more than doubled between these dates, the concurrent five-fold increase in tiller dry weight resulted in a concentration decrease from 6·4 to 2·9 p.p.m. Uptake of Mn, on the other hand, more closely followed dry matter production and concentration varied least for this element. The Co and Fe contents of the first sample may be affected by slight soil contamination.

The extent to which trace element content can vary between different parts of the same plant is clearly shown by Davey and Mitchell (1968). They reported the distribution of 24 major and trace elements in 10 parts of cocksfoot (*Dactylis glomerata*) tillers at flowering stage. Variability between these parts, expressed as the ratio of maximum : minimum content on a concentration basis was Co 2·9, Cu 2·8, Fe 25, Mn 2·7, Mo 5·8 and Zn 15. Leaf blades made a relatively small contribution to the total tiller content of trace elements, amounting to less than 20 per cent. for Co, Cu, Mn and Zn.

From the point of view of animal production, assessment of the nutritional value of trace elements in pasture herbage requires a knowledge not only of their amount and distribution, but also of their digestibility. Variations of digestibility possibly exist between plant parts comparable to those found, for example, between fresh herbage and hay for Mo and Cu (Ferguson *et al.*, 1943; Hartmans and Van der Grift, 1964). It is considered that the effects of the plant factors described above require detailed evaluation when the trace element metabolism of animals is studied under field conditions.

REFERENCES

DAVEY, B. G. (1957). Ph.D. Thesis, University of Aberdeen, Scotland.
DAVEY, B. G. & MITCHELL, R. L. (1968). *J. Sci. Fd Agric.* **19,** 425.
FERGUSON, W. S., LEWIS, A. H. & WATSON, S. J. (1943). *J. agric. Sci., Camb.* **33,** 44.
FLEMING, G. A. (1965). *Outl. Agric.* **4,** 270.
FLEMING, G. A. (1968). *Agri. Dig.* **14,** 28.
FLEMING, G. A. & MURPHY, W. E. (1968). *J. Br. Grassld Soc.* **23,** 174.
HARTMANS, J. & GRIFT, J. VAN DER (1964). *Jaarb. Inst. biol. scheik. Onderz. LandbGewass* 145.
HRYNCEWICZ, Z. (1967). *Rech. agron. Suisse,* **6,** 227.
LANGER, R. H. M. (1967). *Proc. N.Z. Soc. Anim. Prod.* **27,** 146.
MILES, D. G. (1960). *Proc. 8th Int. Grassld Congr.* **112.**
MITCHELL, R. L., REITH, J. W. S. & JOHNSTON, I. M. (1967). Second symposium. Analyse des plantes et problèmes des engrais minéraux. *6th Int. Congr. Soil Sci.* R249. Paris: I.R.H.O.

DISCUSSION

Hartmans (Wageningen). Did you investigate any correlations between the N content and trace element distribution in different parts of the plant? Trace elements usually have functions associated with enzymes and thus with protein complexes and such relationships would be expected.

Burridge (Aberdeen). Davey and Mitchell have looked at the distribution of 24 major and minor elements including N. As would be expected the N content was highest in the young developing parts of the plant and the patterns of N distribution were very similar to those of Zn. Also I would like to add that the possible relationships between the major elements and S and the minor elements Mo and Cu make it imperative not to consider the distribution of these elements in isolation.

THE MICROELEMENT CONTENTS OF PLANTS CONSUMED BY WILD MAMMALS, PARTICULARLY BY BIG GAME, IN DIFFERENT GAME MANAGEMENT REGIONS

Gy. Tölgyesi

University of Veterinary Medicine, Budapest

AND

L. Bencze

University of Forestry and Wood Industry, Sopron, Hungary

ALTHOUGH in Hungary many notable stags and roe-bucks are brought down every year, the habitats of big game are very different in the various regions and their value as trophies is also different. The reason for this is sought by the experts in regional game management, in soil conditions and, recently, in possible differences in the quantitative supply of microelements. The feeding of red deer (*Cervus elaphus*) was investigated from this aspect by the authors.

Firstly, the microelement contents of more than 500 wild growing plants which serve as feeding stuffs for big game (deer, roe mouflon) were established. The results of these investigations are shown in Table I. Of the herbaceous plants not listed in Table I the monocotyledons (particularly the families Cyperaceae and Juncaceae) contained more manganese, while the dicotyledons contained more copper and cobalt. Molybdenum accumulation occurs more frequently in Cruciferae and Papilionaceae. Tölgyesi (1965) pointed out that the taxonomic place of plants is very characteristic of their microelement content. So on the basis of analogies, conclusions may be drawn (even without chemical analyses) as to the possible microelement composition of game fodders not examined so far.

The effect of soil conditions was investigated by plant analysis on six soil types. On each site 30 to 80 plant species consumed by big game were analysed as the differences between the regions in the growth of game may be reflections of the different forages available. On fens and calcareous sands there are plants of low Cu content, while on alkali ('szik') soils and calcareous sand sites species of low Zn and Mn concentration are growing. In the vegetation of fens showing an alkaline reaction which exceeds pH 7 the Mo content is unfavourably high.

The microelement content of wild growing plants is affected by the soil properties in two ways. The influence manifests itself, on the one hand, in the dissimilar microelement uptake of the same wide-spread plant species. However, it is of still greater importance that in the various regions the botanical composition of the

Table I. *Average microelement content in the needles of trees belonging to the family of conifers and in the leaves of some deciduous genera, as well as the average microelement quantities in vegetation growing on some soil types listed below. (All data in p.p.m. of the dry matter.)*

	Fe	Mn	Zn	Cu	Mo
ABIETACEAE—Conifers	215	260	36	5·9	
Acer—maple	210	110	30	6·8	
Alnus—alder	632	208	26	11·0	
Carpinus—hornbeam	161	560	26	9·0	
Cornus—cornel	157	61	17	5·1	
Crataegus—hawthorn	179	36	23	6·5	
Euonymus—spindle-berry	187	64	28	6·2	
Fagus—beech	415	434	28	8·0	
Fraxinus—ash	172	64	17	5·2	
Populus—poplar	162	67	97	7·6	
Quercus—oak	154	520	22	8·6	
Robinia—black locust	169	49	29	7·9	
Salix—willow	234	236	103	8·8	
Tilia—linden	142	250	24	6·9	
VEGETATIONAL MEANS FOR	*Av. 3788 / 227*	*208*	*35.5*	*7.5*	
Acidic sand	200	210	46	5·6	0·12
Calcareous sand	185	60	19	5·0	0·21
Alkali 'szik' soil	305	40	21	6·1	2·05
Fen	140	75	27	4·3	5·20
Limestone	153	89	30	5·9	1·90
Gneiss	282	740	33	7·0	0·32
	Av 211	*202*	*30*	*5.6*	*0.90*

vegetation is also different. The data presented for the several soil types in Table I reflect the joint effect: they show the average elemental composition of the plant species to be found in a certain region.

The changes in the foodstuffs may be established by the chemical analysis of the deer faeces. Such investigations revealed that of the elements Fe, Mn, Zn, Cu and Mo only a small portion is incorporated into animal tissues in comparison to the quantities present in the fodder (Márkus and Tölgyesi, 1969). The amount voided with urine and milk is also unimportant. Therefore the microelement concentration of the faeces and particularly the mutual relations of the various elements reflect very well the

417

composition of the consumed fodder and, through this, that of the soils. According to the data of the authors the dry matter of the deer faeces averaged 920 (120 to 6200) p.p.m. Fe; 600 (42 to 1770) p.p.m. Mn; 120 (51 to 240) p.p.m. Zn and 0·28 (0·12 to 4·2) p.p.m. Mo. Tenfold differences in element content were sometimes found and this cannot be unimportant in the development of the animal. Biometrical calculations (with Spearman's rank correlation) revealed that the Mn, Zn and Mo contents of the vegetation and deer faeces were correlated at the probability level (P) of 5 to 10 per cent. A significant correlation was found between the Cu content of the fur and that of the vegetation whereas vegetation and faeces did not show a similar relationship.

For the investigation of regions in which there is intensive game management the chemical analysis of single widely distributed plant species may be applied as a convenient method. For example the microelement content in the needles of the Austrian pine (Pinus nigra) changes within a wide range under different soil conditions. For the establishment of elements present in small quantities only in plants and therefore hardly measurable, species of accumulative capacity can be used. The Mo content of cut-leaved mignonette (Reseda lutea) may be 50 times as high as that of the soil. Applying this species as model plant it renders the methods of investigation faster and more precise.

Stenotopic plants (having a restricted range of geographical distribution) are mostly site indicators too and may, therefore, give information on extreme soil conditions even solely by their abundant occurrence or entire absence. The connection existing between nitrophily and cuprophily or between hygrophily and Mn demand has already been pointed out in a previous paper by one of the authors (Tolgyesi, 1969).

The investigations reported here are of considerable importance in practice because they proved that in Hungarian regions of intensive game management, big game consume plants of very different microelement content. This fact may be one of the reasons causing considerable differences not only in the habitats of deer, but also in the trophy quality of stags.

REFERENCES

MARKUS, J. & TÖLGYESI, GY. (1969). Az ásványianyag-ellátottság megitélése a kiürülés vizsgálata alapján. (The evolution of mineral material supply according to investigations on their excretion.) In preparation.

TÖLGYESI, GY. (1965). Acta agron. hung. 13, 287.

TÖLGYESI, GY. (1969). A növények mikroelemtartalma és ennek, mezőgazdasági vonatkozásai. (The microelement content of plants and its importance for agriculture.) Budapest: Mezögazdasági Kiadó.

RESEARCH ON THE AETIOLOGY OF SECONDARY COPPER DEFICIENCY IN GRAZING CATTLE

H. BINOT, F. LOMBA AND V. BIENFET

Faculté de Médecine Vétérinaire, Cureghem, Brussels, Belgium

INTERESTED by the problem of the aetiology of secondary copper deficiency in grazing cattle, we undertook a statistical study in order to verify, in a part of Belgium, the data published on this subject.

For this study we had the results obtained in 22 farms of the province Hainaut. These results concerned the mineral composition of blood and hair in cattle and of grass and soil in pastures. Samples were taken during six consecutive years at different periods of the year and at least once a year from a significant number of animals and grazed pastures. The results were recorded in means per farm so that it was possible to study the relations of the mean values of Cu in blood and hair with the different minerals determined in grass and soil.

There was no clinical Cu deficiency in any of the 22 farms although in seven of them the mean blood Cu content remained lower than 60 μg./100 ml. of blood, and in only one of these was the Cu of both blood and grass below the required level. Between Cu in blood and in hair there was a correlation significant at the 5 per cent. level.

We were able to confirm the principal conclusions found in the literature about the aetiology of Cu deficiency. We found significant positive correlations between Cu in blood and Cu in grass, significant negative correlation between Cu in blood on the one hand and sulphate, lead, zinc, and calcium in grass and between sulphate, lead, zinc, calcium, molybdenum and pH of soil on the other. All the elements significantly correlated with Cu in blood, were also correlated between themselves and with the other elements we analysed. It was shown that there is a significant negative correlation between Cu in grass and exchangeable amounts of SO_4, Mn, Zn, Pb and Mo of soil as well as with soil pH.

Since similar correlations were found with Cu in the blood, it was necessary to search for the interrelations of these factors and we investigated partial correlations. With constant grass Cu, only the correlations between Cu in the blood and exchangeable Zn, Pb and Mo in the soil remained significant. The contents of

419

exchangeable Zn, Pb and Mo in soil or factors affecting these contents could thus affect Cu metabolism in the animal. This effect could be independent of Cu in grass. As far as exchangeable SO_4 in soil is concerned, it seems that in our country its effect is exerted only through an influence on the content of Cu in grass.

The following groups of positive correlations were found:

In grass: Pb/Zn/Fe

In soil: Zn/Pb/Mn/sulphate/phosphate
Zn/Pb/Mn/Mo/phosphate
Zn/Pb/Mo/phosphate/pH

Correlations between Zn, Pb and phosphate were found in the three soil groups examined and only phosphate is not correlated with copper in blood or with copper in hair.

It is seen from these data that Cu in blood of grazing cattle in this province is not influenced by a well-defined element but rather by many interactions, poorly understood until now, which could intervene either directly on animal Cu metabolism or indirectly on Cu in grass, or on both. It is perhaps possible that another element, not yet studied here, acts on the blood Cu content and could be correlated positively with each of the elements listed here above.

The same investigation was carried out previously in four farms located near metallurgic factories in Luxembourg province and four farms near Liège where cattle were suffering clinical Cu deficiency. It was possible to compare the mineral content of grass and soil in their pastures with the similar means of the province of Hainaut. It was demonstrated that all the elements negatively correlated with blood Cu in the province of Hainaut were found also in Luxembourg but with higher content in both grass and soil. In the province of Liège, only Zn, Pb and SO_4 in grass or Zn, Pb, Mn and SO_4 in soil were higher. When comparing both Liège and Luxembourg to Hainaut we obtained higher contents of Zn and Pb in grass and of exchangeable Zn, Pb, Mn and SO_4 in soil.

SUMMARY

In these studies we found associations between most of the factors usually or occasionally suspected in the aetiology of Cu deficiency and after reaching the above conclusions we tried to induce Cu deficiency experimentally in grazing cattle. On the basis of the results presented above we investigated the effects of the elements Fe, Zn and Pb in this experiment. A pasture was divided into three equal parts on each of which four growing bulls

Table I. Cu *concentrations of blood of bulls receiving no trace element supplement (I), or supplement in food (II) or supplement via spray on grass (III)*

Results expressed as μg.Cu/100 ml. plasma			
	I	II	III
Before start of experiment	92	91	95
After 1 month	84	71	71
After 2 months	73	53	49

were grazing. In part I, the four bulls were left untreated. In part II, we fed daily a concentrated food in such a manner that each animal received a supplement of 2 g. Fe, 0·4 g. Zn and 0·06 g. Pb. These amounts were calculated to give the same total daily intake as that of animals grazing near metallurgic factories. The three elements were given in the form of nitrates and were thus quite soluble. In part III, we regularly sprayed onto the grass a solution of Fe, Zn and Pb nitrate with polyvinylpyrrolidone which retains the ions on grass. The contents of Fe, Zn and Pb in grass were frequently determined and by spraying more or less we tried to reach the same intake by the bulls in parts II and III. Blood and hair were analysed monthly. The first analyses done gave the results shown in Table I. The differences between the initial mean of Cu content of blood and those recorded after one month are significant in parts II and III.

AMOUNTS OF SELENIUM IN SWEDISH FORAGES, SOILS, AND ANIMAL TISSUES

P. LINDBERG AND N. LANNEK

Department of Medicine, Royal Veterinary College, Stockholm, Sweden

MUSCULAR degeneration (MD) in calves, lambs, foals and pigs is widespread in Sweden. The disease can be effectively prevented by giving doses of selenium preparations to livestock. This practice is limited to prescriptions by veterinary surgeons; Se toxicity, spontaneous or accidental, is unknown.

The method for Se determination has been described (Lindberg, 1968). Samples of grain, collected from 10 areas extending from far south to far north of the country, ranged from 4 to 46 ng. Se/g. D.M., 66 out of 72 being below 21, and 30 out of 72 being below 11 ng./g. (Lindberg, 1968). Samples of hay from various parts of the middle area varied between 8 and 47 ng./g.

The Se content of forage plants and of the corresponding soil is shown in Table I. No correlation between plant and soil Se is apparent, indicating that availability to plants is a major factor. Thus the Örebro area, where MD is common, is characterized by low Se in grains (see also Lindberg, 1968) in spite of high Se in soil. Acid soil conditions predominate which may lead to formation of non-available Se compounds (Lakin, 1961). It is generally accepted that MD is more frequent after cold and rainy summers than after hot and dry ones. The correlation between summer temperature and Se in oats is demonstrated in Figure 1. It appears that Se and nitrogen contents will be higher during a warm vegetation period. High summer temperature probably improves

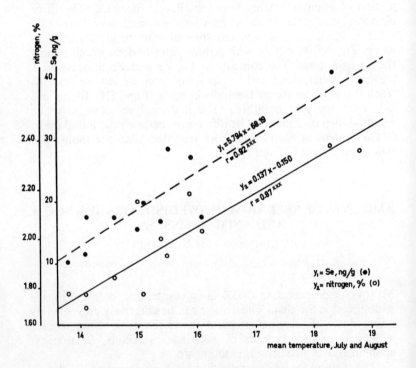

FIG. 1. Se and nitrogen content of oats as related to summer temperature. Each pair of dots represents one year, the sampling covering years 1953 to 1967. The samples were collected from one and the same area, measuring approximately 800 × 800 metres.

Table I. *Selenium (ng./g. D.M.) in forage plants and in corresponding soil (in 1968)*

		Svalöv (Skåne)		Ultana (Uppland)		Orebro (Närke)		Kalmar (Småland)		Linköping (Östergötland)		Skara (Västergötland)		Norsbron (Värmland)		Undrom (Västernorrland)	
		plant	soil	plant	soil	plant	soil	plant	soil	plant	soil	plant	soil	plant	soil	plant	soil
Barley	Ingrid	11	400	14	198	6	945	8	292	22	333	9	328	12	373	7	221*
	Hellas											9	297	11	400		
Oats	Sol II			9	198	11	945	14	205	33	307					9	221*
	Condor															8	198†
Timothy						11	976					11	357	29	450		
Red clover				18	199												
Cocksfoot				61	188												
Meadow-fescue						64	976										
Flax				6	165												
Alfalfa				40	199												

* Se content of subsoil 267 ng./g.
† Se content of subsoil 85 ng./g.

the formation of protein in oats (Persson and Bingefors, 1956). A great proportion of the Se in herbage of pasture plants under conditions of low Se nutrition is present as seleno-amino acids in protein (Peterson and Butler, 1962).

With low Se supply, as under 'normal' Swedish conditions, there is a rather close quantitative relationship between Se in the food and Se in animal tissues. Selenium concentrations of kidney cortex and skeletal muscle of pigs receiving 100 ng. Se/g. food are roughly five times higher than corresponding values for pigs receiving 20 ng. Se/g. food. At even higher Se intakes, though still in non-toxic amounts, the surplus is readily excreted and tissue levels are but little increased (Lindberg and Lannek, 1965).

Determination of blood Se has proved to be a valuable diagnostic tool. We conclude that MD is associated with < 25 ng. Se/g. food. Blood Se will then vary from hardly measurable to about 20 ng.ml. In a beef herd, where hay (8·2 ng. Se/g.) and silage (14·0 ng. Se/g.) were given, blood Se in the cows varied between 4·0 and 5·0 ng./ml., milk Se between 1·7 and 4·9 ng./ml., and blood Se in suckling calves between 5·0 and 8·0 ng./ml. Blood Se in healthy herbivores extends to 100 ng./ml. or slightly more. When higher values are obtained it usually turns out that Se preparations have been administered.

Taking the interrelationship of vitamin E and Se into account it ought to be mentioned that there is no evidence of lack of vitamin E in Swedish forages.

In carnivores, where Se-responsive diseases have so far not been convincingly demonstrated, blood Se seems to be high. The average for 28 Swedish dogs was $326·5 \pm 55·7$ ng./ml. (mean$\pm$s.d.).

Acknowledgement. The samples analysed in Table I were kindly supplied by the Swedish Seed Improvement Association.

REFERENCES

Lakin, H. W. (1961). Geochemistry of selenium in relation to agriculture in Selenium in Agriculture. In *Handbook 200*, ed. M. S. Anderson *et al.* Washington: U.S. Department of Agriculture.
Lindberg, P. (1968). *Acta vet. scand.* Suppl. 23.
Lindberg, P. & Lannek, N. (1965). *Acta vet. scand.* **6,** 217.
Persson, P. J. & Bingefors, S. (1956). *Sver. Utsädesför. Tidskr.* **3,** 174.
Peterson, P. J. & Butler, G. W. (1962). *Aust. J. biol. Sci.* **15,** 126.

DISCUSSION

Godwin (Adelaide). Am I right in saying that the α-tocopherol level is not low in these areas where muscular dystrophy is arising in association with a low level of Se?

Lannek (Stockholm). There has been no extensive survey of the tocopherol levels of plants in Sweden but some years ago Lindberg carried out a small survey of the tocopherol content of Swedish grains. The levels were roughly similar to those in other countries and we have no reason to suspect a deficiency of α-tocopherol. Tocopherol is often used as a therapeutic agent against muscular dystrophy and although it is not useless under our conditions its efficiency is significantly lower than that of Se.

Ullrey (East Lansing). Did you say that it is not permissible to add Se to feeding stuffs in Sweden?

Lannek (Stockholm). Selenium preparations can be purchased only by veterinary prescription but the vet. may prescribe powder preparations which the farmer can mix with food for his own stock. The factory preparation and sale of feeding stuffs supplemented with Se is not permitted.

Ullrey (East Lansing). What levels of supplementary Se are added and in what form?

Lannek (Stockholm). The dosage corresponds roughly to 60 μg. of Se in the form of sodium selenite per kg. of liveweight of animal to be given once or twice a month. This is sufficient for preventing the disease.

Godwin (Adelaide). Does infertility arise in these areas where muscular dystrophy is common and are these conditions associated with any particular pasture species?

Lannek (Stockholm). The possible existence of other Se-responsive diseases has been inadequately investigated so far in Sweden. We have found cases of hepatosis dietetica in the pig but this disease disappeared from Sweden about six or seven years ago and this may have been associated with the use of Se preparations which were first used about this time. Muscular degeneration is by far the most important condition we have associated with Se but ill-thrift and infertility in different species have so far not been convincingly associated with Se deficiency under our conditions. It is possible however that we may yet find such an association.

Walker (Aberdeen). To what extent do you think the low Se content of plants is due to the low soil pH or to a low Se content of the rocks of parent material? You mentioned that some soils had a pH as low as 5·0; was this measured in water or KCl?

425

Lannek (Stockholm). The soil investigations were carried out by the Agricultural College at Uppsala and I can't tell you what method they used. The lowest soil pH found was 5·2 in the Örebro area.

McConnell (Louisville). Have you any idea of the forms in which Se is present in the herbage of these areas?

Lannek (Stockholm). This has not been investigated.

GEOCHEMICAL ECOLOGY OF ENDEMIC GOITRE

R. I. BLOKHINA

Vernadsky Institute of Biochemistry and Analytical Chemistry, Moscow, U.S.S.R.

THE study of the influence of the chemical composition of the environment upon the incidence of endemic goitre is one of the problems of the new trend in ecology—the study of geochemical ecology which is being developed in the U.S.S.R. by Professor V. V. Kovalsky. In this report the results of our joint investigations are presented.

It is universally recognized that the main specific cause of endemic biogeochemical goitre is iodine deficiency in the environment. The critical I concentration at which endemic goitre develops may be determined by its content in soil and ranges from traces to approximately 0·0005 per cent. (Kovalsky, 1967). However, I deficiency alone can not explain why goitre never occurs universally in all the people inhabiting endemic areas; why I therapy in many cases only diminishes the frequency of the disease and does not completely eliminate it and, finally, why goitre may also be found in places provided with I. It is obvious that the sensitivity of people to I and, consequently, their reaction to its deficiency (an increase in endemic goitre) cannot be predicted from only the I content in the outer environment.

Searches for the causes of the inconsistencies between the low level of I in the environment and the spread of goitre have lead to the detection of a whole range of aetiological factors (neuro-humoral, sanitary-hygienic, social life conditions, climatic, toxico-infectious, food, strumogenic, genetic) which directly or indirectly may influence the function of the thyroid gland or its regulating system. However, the role of these factors seems to be secondary as no one of them taken separately explains the origin and geography of endemic goitre.

Besides the enumerated additional factors some chemical elements may influence the sensitivity of people to I since, in regions of endemic goitre, the biogeochemical food chains involving I exert their influence upon the people not separately but in common with the many macro- and microelements of the environment.

There is reason to assume the existence of secondary geochemical factors of goitre which through food chains may influence I metabolism and by this strengthen or weaken the action of the initial cause of goitre—the I deficiency. Generalisation of the large experimental and literary material on this problem shows that in various biogeochemical zones and provinces the spread of goitre correlates not only with I deficiency but also with the lack, excess or the imbalance in the environment of the following chemical elements: Co, Mn, Sr, Cu, Ca, Mo, Zn. At the same time in the chernozem zone goitre occurs as an exception although 77·6 per cent. of the investigated samples of its soils are as deficient in I as regions with high incidences of goitre. Apparently the action of I deficiency on the people is not shown here owing to the fact that in the environment of this zone I is balanced with respect to Co, Cu, Mn.

It has been shown that when the content of these elements in the environment is disturbed, a change in the morphological structure and chemical composition of the thyroid glands altered by goitre is observed. However, the establishment of a correlative bond between goitre and these elements, as well as the morphological and chemical disturbances associated with goitre, do not prove their participation in the aetiology and pathogenesis of this disease. Just as the highly important role of I in the origin of endemic goitre was definitively proved only after establishing its necessity for the synthesis of thyroid hormones, the significance of any other chemical element will also be considered as proved only when its participation and points of action in I metabolism have been established.

At present only for two elements (Mn and Co) has it been shown that their content in the diet influences the processes of hormonogenesis in the thyroid gland. It has been established that optimum synthesis of thyroid hormones occurs within a definite range of Mn concentrations in the diet (0·63 to 1·33 μg./g.); but Mn doses higher or lower than this optimum range impede the biosynthesis of hormones.

We have studied the role of Co as a geochemical factor of goitre in the Yaroslavskaya province where the distribution of endemic goitre, as shown by investigations, correlates with the low I and Co level in the environment (Kovalsky, 1957; Kovalsky and Blokhina, 1963). A similar pattern of I and Co intake was produced in an experiment with white rats. It was shown that the thyroid glands of rats, which for 11 months had been given food with low I and Co contents, were characterized by a high absolute (28 mg.) and

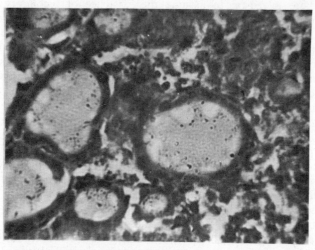

I and Co deficiency

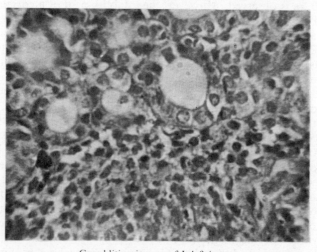

Co addition in case of I deficiency

Fig. 1. Microphotographs of t

relative (16) weight. In the microstructure of these glands small and middle-size follicles (average diameter 44·1 μ) prevailed, the epithelium was in the main cubic (average height 5·1 μ), the clear spaces of follicles were filled by vacuolised colloid and the inter-follicular tissue was developed (Fig. 1). Radio-autochromato-graphic analysis, used for the estimation of the thyroid gland

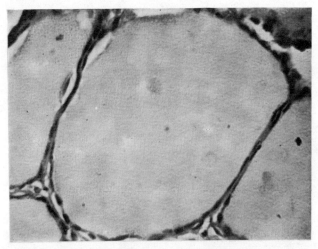

I addition in case of Co deficiency

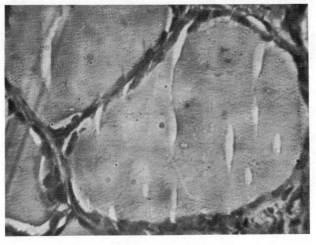

I and Co addition

of rats (1320 fold magnification).

function showed these glands to contain a high content of free I compounds which is a direct criterion of their hormonal activity (Fig. 2).

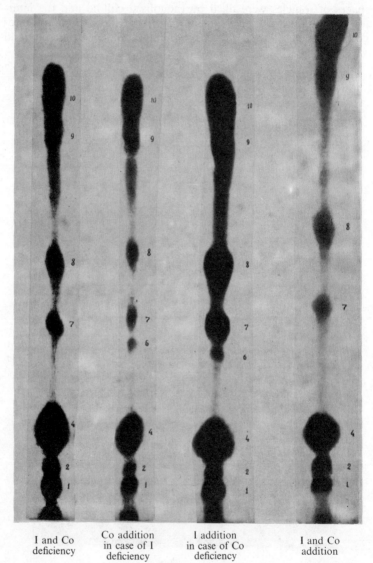

| I and Co deficiency | Co addition in case of I deficiency | I addition in case of Co deficiency | I and Co addition |

FIG. 2. Radiochromatograms of thyroid gland extracts of rats.

The addition of the physiological doses of Co to the diet which was not naturally high in I or Co, did not change the weight of the gland (30 mg. absolute weight; 15 relative weight) but caused definite histological changes; the size of follicles diminished from 44·1 to 33·1 μ and the height of the epithelial cells increased from 5·1 to 7·8 μ. The inter-follicular tissue grew strongly and the degree of colloid vacuolisation rose (Fig. 1).

The biochemical processes in these thyroid glands, judging by the high content in them of free I compounds, were also strengthened under the influence of Co (Fig. 2). Thus, in cases of I deficiency, Co raised the activity of the gland without changing its weight. Co raised in the gland the level of free iodothyronines, iodotyrosines and iodides, but simultaneously lowered the colloid content in follicles, apparently causing by this a displacement of the equilibrium in the cyclic process of hormonogenesis towards the proteolytic splitting of thyroglobulin. One of the probable points of Co action may be the first stage of hormonogenesis—the capture of I by the gland as indicated by the increased fixation of ^{131}I when additional Co is given to the animals. The investigations carried out suggest that Co strengthens one of the compensatory mechanisms of the thyroid gland, namely its ability to concentrate I, in consequence of which the synthesis of thyroid hormones may become normalized even in cases of an insufficient supply of I to the person. However, the size of the gland remains increased.

Normalization of the I content in the same diet caused other changes in the thyroid gland: its weight decreased to nearly half, the size of follicles increased from 44·1 to 60·7 μ, the height of the epithelium was flattened from 5·1 to 2·9 μ, the clear space of follicles was filled by thick unvacuolised colloid frequently showing cracks and the inter-follicular tissue was almost lacking (Fig. 1). Simultaneously, the content of free I compounds in the gland decreased on average by 44 per cent. (Fig. 2). All these changes in the gland caused by the action of I additives bear witness to a lowering of its functional activity. To judge from the same tests, a simultaneous normalization of I and Co in the diet of rats lowers the functional activity of the gland in the same manner as I alone does but to a considerably lesser degree (Fig. 2).

The effects demonstrated permit the conclusion that the appearance of endemic disturbances of thyroid gland function in people inhabiting biogeochemical provinces with a low I and Co content depend not only on the level of I and Co but also on the ratio of these elements in the environment.

REFERENCES

KOVALSKY, V. V. (1967). *Dokl. Vses. Akad. Sel'skoklov. Nauk.* (11), 2.
KOVALSKY, V. V. (1957). *New trends and problems of the biological chemistry of farm animals in connection with the study of biogeochemical provinces.* Moscow.
KOVALSKY, V. V. & BLOKHINA, R. I. (1963). *Probl. Endokrinol. Gormonoterap.* **9**, (6), 42.

DISCUSSION

Oberleas (Detroit). Is the effect of cobalt on thyroid gland that you have reported an effect of elemental Co or Co associated with vitamin B_{12}?

Blokhina (Moscow). I regret that we cannot answer this question. We added Co to the diet as Co salts and not as vitamin B_{12}.

Ullrey (East Lansing). What species of animal was used in these experiments?

Blokhina (Moscow). The paper refers to work with rats but the same results have been obtained with sheep.

Lassiter (Athens, Ga.). You mentioned that the optimum level of dietary Mn for thyroid hormone synthesis lies between 0·63 and 1·33 p.p.m. How big a depression in thyroid hormone synthesis do you find if higher levels of Mn are fed? I ask because we have fed considerably higher concentrations of Mn in our diets than the levels you find to be optimal.

Blokhina (Moscow). The optimal range is one that we have found under our local conditions. It does not necessarily apply to different environmental and different geochemical conditions or areas.

GEOCHEMICAL ECOLOGY OF SOIL MICRO-ORGANISMS

S. V. LETUNOVA

Biogeochemical Laboratory, V.I. Vernadsky Institute of Geochemistry and Analytical Chemistry, U.S.S.R. Academy of Sciences, Moscow, U.S.S.R.

MICRO-ORGANISMS are of special interest for investigations in the field of geochemical ecology owing to their great variability under the influence of external conditions and their rapid rate of reproduction.

V. V. Kovalsky and I (1964) have studied the geochemical ecology of micro-organisms inhabiting soils and mud deposits enriched in cobalt (Azerbaijan S.S.R.), selenium (Tuva ASSR), boron (Kazakhstan), uranium (Lake Issyk-Kul), molybdenum, vanadium and copper (Uzbek and Armenian S.S.R.). For comparison micro-organisms living in soils and muds poor in these elements were taken (Moscow, Kostroma and Yaroslav provinces). All together over 1,000 strains of micro-organisms belonging to various systematic groups were studied. These included spore-forming and sporeless bacteria, mycobacteria, actinomycetes and fungi. Investigations were carried out in laboratory conditions using nutrient media to which were added different concentrations of trace elements chosen with regard for their content in enriched and impoverished soils and muds. The effects of adding soil extracts which contained natural concentrations and ratios of trace elements were also investigated.

It was shown that micro-organisms adapt to different contents and ratios of the micro-elements studied. The adaptation is expressed by the following ecological reactions of micro-organisms. In strains isolated from soils and muds low in trace elements the maximum accumulation of biomass and the optimum action of various biochemical functions specifically depending on metals (synthesis of the Co-containing vitamin B_{12}; fixation

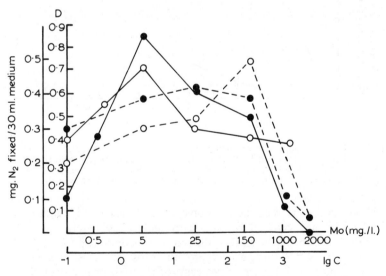

FIG. 1. Adaptation of A. chroococcum to molybdenum content of natural environment. ————, Moscow strain; ————, Uzbek strain; ○, growth; ●, N_2 fixation.

of atmospheric nitrogen connected with Mo, V and Cu; formation of pigments depending on B) are observed at lower concentrations of these elements in comparison to strains isolated from natural substrates enriched in the elements being studied (Kovalsky and Letunova, 1964, 1966; Letunova *et al.*, 1968).

In Figure 1 the growth of two strains of *Azotobacter chroococcum* and the fixation of atmospheric nitrogen by them at different Mo concentrations in the medium are shown. Strain 7 was isolated from a soil from the environs of Moscow poor in Mo (2.0×10^{-4} per cent.). Strain 23 was isolated from Uzbek soil enriched in Mo (4.3×10^{-3} per cent.). According to this the growth and nitrogen fixation optima of the *Az. chroococcum* strain from Moscow environs lie at a lower Mo concentration (5 mg./*l*.) in comparison with Uzbek strain (25 to 150 mg./*l*.).

The adaptation of micro-organisms to natural B concentrations in soils of the north-western Kazakhstan is shown in Figure 2.

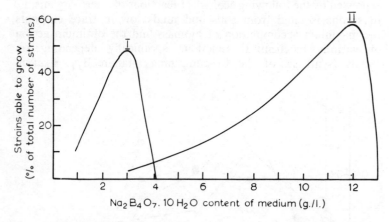

Fig. 2. Adaptation of Actinomycetes to differing contents of soil boron as illustrated by tolerance to boron concentration in growth media. Curve I, strains isolated from soils with 1.5×10^{-3} per cent. B. Curve II, strains isolated from soils with 2.5×10^{-2} per cent. B.

From this it is seen that strains isolated from soil containing 1.5×10^{-3} per cent. of B could grow only at relatively low concentrations of this element in the nutrient medium (up to 3 g./*l*. of borax). At 4 g./*l*. there was no growth. Most strains isolated from soil containing 2.5×10^{-2} per cent. of B (16·6 times more) grow well at 12 g. of borax/*l*. These organisms may be considered as ecological forms that are stable to B excess in a natural habitat.

It must be taken into consideration that under one and the same geochemical condition of physiological inhomogeneity of microbic population is observed. Thus, among strains inhabiting soils rich in B, 12·6 per cent. are able to grow only with a low B concentration in the medium (3 to 4 g./*l.* of borax). Apparently unequal degrees of adaptation to excess or deficiency of trace elements in the habitat serves as a basis for natural selection and evolution of micro-organisms.

We have shown that under laboratory conditions it is possible for micro-organisms to adapt themselves to deficiency or excess of micro-elements. By means of multiple passages on artificial nutrient media with different Se concentrations (0·1 and 5 μg./100 ml.) some strains of *Bacillus megaterium* adaptated to these concentrations. An exception was strain 8, the reseedings of which on a medium without Se did not lead to a displacement of the growth optimum towards lower concentrations of this element.

Using Se as an example a study was made of the biochemical processes of adaptation to a definite content of this element in the environment. Micro-organisms have the ability to reduce soluble compounds of Se to an insoluble elemental state. This was investigated with cellular suspensions and non-cellular extracts of strains of *B. megaterium* which are characterized by different degrees of resistance to Se. Figure 3 shows that *B. megaterium* strain 8 which was resistant to high concentrations of Se, reduces

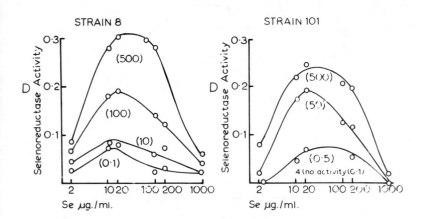

FIG. 3. Influence of various selenite concentrations in the incubation medium on selenite reduction by *B. megaterium* suspensions. Figures in parentheses indicate selenium concentration (μg./100 ml.) under which organism originally grown.

selenite when incubated with it after being grown on a substrate devoid of Se. The reducing ability increases with Se content in the nutrient medium. Thus, selenoreductase of strain 8 is constantly found, irrespective of the presence or absence of Se in the nutrient medium. Obviously selenoreductase is a constitutive enzyme in this organism. This is clearly explained by the fact that strain 8 inhabits soil rich in Se. The organism has adapted itself to excess of the element by reduction of soluble Se to the elemental state.

B. megaterium strain 101, which lives under low-Se conditions, has no need to protect itself against an excess of this element. Consequently selenoreductase is formed only when the organism is grown on a medium with added Se, and is to be regarded in this case as an induced adaptive enzyme.

In strain 101 isolated from soil poor in Se, the formation of selenoreductase on a medium devoid of Se might be caused by genetic transformation. To study this, DNA of strain 8 (which is stable to Se excess in the medium and has a constitutive selenoreductase) was added to a suspension of competent cells of strain 101. In Figure 4 it is seen that the cells of the recipient (strain 101) grown on a medium devoid of Se, do not possess selenoreductase activity while cells of the donor (strain 8) under these conditions

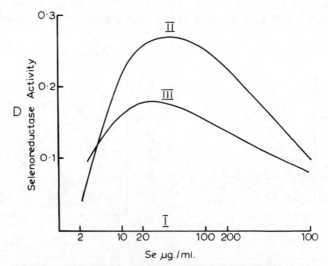

FIG. 4. Transformation in *B. megaterium*. I, recipient (straing 101, no selenoreductase activity; Curve II, donor (strain 8); Curve III, transformant (strain J41).

form a selenoreductase. The transformant obtained by including DNA of strain 8 into the cell of strain 101 possesses seleno-reductase activity when growing on a medium devoid of Se.

REFERENCES

KOVALSKY, V. V. (1963). *Izv. Akad. Nauk. SSSR, Ser. biol.* **28,** (6), 830.
KOVALSKY, V. V. & LETUNOVA, S. V. (1964). *Usp. sovrem. Biol.* **57,** (1), 71.
KOVALSKY, V. V. & LETUNOVA, S. V. (1966). *Agrokhimia,* (7), 73.
LETUNOVA, S. V., KOVALSKY, V. V. & ERMAKOV, V. V. (1968). *Trudy biogeokhim. Lab. Akad. Nauk. SSSR,* (12), 238.

DISCUSSION

Hartmans (Wageningen). How far are the differences you have shown caused by genetic factors or by environmental changes such as those of the trace element content of the growth medium?

Letunova (Moscow). This is a difficult question to answer but our transformation experiments suggest that a genetic rather than an adaptive change has occurred.

SECTION 8

PROBLEMS IN THE DETECTION OF TRACE ELEMENT DEFICIENCY AND EXCESS: AN EVALUATION OF SURVEY TECHNIQUES

President: G. N. HAVRE

Vice President: G. A. HALL

THE DETECTION OF COPPER DEFICIENCY AND OTHER TRACE ELEMENT DEFICIENCIES UNDER FIELD CONDITIONS

J. Hartmans

Institute for Biological and Chemical Research on Field Crops and Herbage, Wageningen, The Netherlands

In surveying the geographical distribution of certain trace element deficiencies in ruminants diverse methods can be applied. The method used ultimately, usually depends on many factors.

CHOICE OF A SURVEY METHOD

In the first place the objective of the survey should be known because this determines the minimum degree of accuracy and detail required. Sometimes methods are unsuitable for application merely because the specific knowledge about the element concerned, e.g. a chemical index in the animal, is still missing. In the next place the practicability should be considered, not only in the financial sphere but rather more important are the facilities for chemical analysis and the availability of a skilled and expert staff, etc.

When all these points have been considered the question arises whether the results to be expected and their practical use are justified in terms of the investment and trouble. In addition the limitations of the various methods should be known.

EVALUATION OF THE METHODS

When few data are available about the element to be investigated and one would be satisfied with general introductory information over a wide area, some idea can be obtained by examining the nature of the geological formation. Young and alkaline geological formations are more abundant in most trace elements than the older, more acid and the coarse, sandy, formations. In this way an impression is gained about the total soil supply of a trace element. Usually the relationship of total supply to availability to the plant is positive. For some trace elements a distinct negative correlation is found between the soil pH value and the quantity available to the plant; this applies for example to manganese and to a lesser extent to zinc and iron, whereas the relation between the pH value and molybdenum is positive. When the correlation between availability and pH value is less specific, availability of a trace element can be better assessed by a survey based on chemical analysis of the soil (extract) from the root zone.

441

The next move is a direct analysis of the trace element content in the plant. This avoids the inaccuracy resulting from the imperfect correlation between the content in the soil and that in the different plant species. The content in the plant is not only dependent on the available soil supply but sometimes also on other competitive elements, on the growth rate and growth stage of the crops and on the season. By analysing samples of the rations, or with grazing animals of the pasture grass, the trace element intake by the animal can be much more accurately determined than by analysing soil samples. It is essential, however, that the herbage samples should be free from soil particles. Mitchell (1963) indicates that soil contains 20 to 1000 times the Co and Fe content found in pasture grass growing on this soil. Even the smallest contamination, such as rain-spattered soil particles, gives a falsely enhanced measure of the actual content in the herbage. In several countries the determination of the Co content in the soil is therefore preferred to that in the herbage. For the other trace elements the misrepresentation due to contamination with soil particles will be less and crop analysis will be more reliable than soil testing.

With crop analysis one does not know exactly whether the animal actually takes in the material sampled or whether it grazes selectively; other uncertainties are the quantity eaten and especially how well or how poorly the mineral intake is utilised by the animal. Because the apparent availability of most trace elements is very low a small absolute change in availability may have a considerable effect on the total requirement for dietary trace elements. Therefore the trace element content in the ration is usually a very imperfect criterion for the supply status of the animal. It should only be used as an indicator of a possible deficiency. A ' normal ' content in the ration does not guarantee a sufficient supply to the animal.

For years ways have been studied to assess the supply status of the animal with regard to certain minerals, for example by observation of clinical signs or by applying a chemical criterion. It would be ideal if the mobilisable body reserves, thought to be present in many cases in the animal, were known and could be determined, as, for example, the Cu, Co and Fe contents of the liver. Analysis of the following body fluids also provides suitable indices to reflect the body reserves or the supply status: blood, which usually only indicates when the supply is insufficient; urine, which within a wide range is a reasonable indicator for iodine, fluorine, Mo and probably also for selenium and lastly, milk which is another suitable criterion for assessment of the I status.

When knowledge of the metabolism of a trace element is insufficient but it is known that such a deficiency will induce certain clinical signs, it is reasonable to make surveys based on these signs. These types of investigations are much easier to carry out than surveys based on chemical analysis and at first sight are more appealing to practice. Yet the overall picture obtained in this way is less detailed than that based on a chemical criterion in the animal. Distinct clinical signs and especially those specific for a trace element only develop, as a rule, when the supply is already clearly inadequate. However, in cattle farming at a high production level it is increasingly necessary to locate the cases bordering on sufficiency or deficiency because in such borderline cases unspecific signs such as a somewhat lower production and fertility level grow more and more important.

Comparison of Methods in a Field Investigation

In an investigation concerning the occurrence of Cu deficiency in grazing cattle and its relation to various clinical signs four methods have been applied simultaneously. The experimental area, the province of Friesland in the north-western part of the Netherlands, is about 2000 sq. km. and the south-eastern part consists of Pleistocene sandy soil, the northern and western parts consisting of diluvial marine clay. Midway between these soil types are low peat areas and many transitions.

On 40 farms distributed at random in the area blood samples were taken and analysed for Cu from at least five yearling cattle per farm at the beginning and at the end of the grazing period. Simultaneously on 10 of these farms liver biopsy samples were taken for Cu analysis. The animals were inspected clinically three times while at pasture. Each farm was marked for every criterion on a scale from 0 (clinical effects not present) to 6 (serious clinical effects in many animals). The pastures were sampled two to three times for chemical analysis of the herbage. The soil of the root zone was sampled and analysed for the pH value, organic matter content and extractable ('plant-available') Cu content. Because a relation was suspected between the moisture status in the fields and the Cu status in the animals, the profile structure and the moisture status were determined in all the fields up to a depth of 1·20 m. The farms were arranged in an order from 1 to 40 in accordance with the extent of water excess in the top soil.

On the basis of the blood plasma Cu contents in autumn, the farms were divided into three groups: 10 with the highest average values (normal or almost normal, *viz.* 0·76 to 0·48 mg./*l.*), 10 with the lowest values (0·20 to 0·05 mg./*l.*) and an intermediate group of 20 farms. The results of soil testing, herbage analysis and clinical observations have been compared to the blood plasma Cu contents in autumn. Though in general the liver Cu level is considered as the most reliable criterion to assess the Cu status of the animal (Van der Grift, 1955; Hartmans, 1960) in this case the plasma levels in autumn also give a good reflection of the loss of Cu by the animals during the grazing period since the average liver Cu levels in spring were not different between groups. The results of comparing the ultimate groups are shown in Table I.

Neither the plant-available Cu content of the soil nor the Cu content in the herbage shows any positive relationship with the Cu status of the animal; the former content is even negatively correlated. This seemingly unlikely situation can be explained by a great number of the poor farms being situated on the heavier soil which naturally has a higher Cu content. This does not result in a higher Cu content in the herbage. This finding is in agreement with the investigation of Van Luit and Henkens (1967) according to whom only when the HNO_3-extractable Cu in the soil is below 5 mg. per kg. are the Cu contents in soil and herbage related. Normal and even high soil and herbage Cu contents do not in any way guarantee a better Cu supply status in the animal compared to low soil and herbage Cu contents. The absence of any relation between the Cu status of the animal and the soil and herbage Cu content is mainly caused by the very low availability of dietary Cu. A small absolute difference in availability has a relatively great effect on the dietary Cu requirement. In general, for trace elements with a low availability a survey based on the contents in the rations or in the soil will hardly provide any information about the supply status of the animal.

With the exception of hair depigmentation, the clinical signs shown from previous investigations to be causally related to the Cu status of the animal (Hartmans, 1962) were also found to occur, though less frequently, at normal or almost normal plasma Cu levels. Furthermore, it was found that the signs, including the typical depigmentation, occur in by no means all cases of very low Cu status. In fact, such latent cases of Cu deficiency without clinical signs may very rapidly manifest themselves when other adverse factors are introduced such as wet and cold weather, gastro-intestinal parasites and decreased feed intake due to wet or unpalatable herbage. Thus, in a survey based upon clinical signs alone there is a great risk of missing even serious cases of deficiency.

The contents of Mo, total sulphur and inorganic sulphate do

...or low Cu status of yearling cattle at the end of the grazing period

Property	Normal Cu status		Low Cu status		Significance of difference
	average	variation	average	variation	
*soil analysis**					
Cu (HNO₃-extractable) mg./kg.	5·4	3·8– 9·8	7·5	3·7–12·6	0·10 < P < 0·20
pH-KCl	—	5·0– 6·4	—	4·5– 6·6	
organic matter %	12·4	8·4–24·0	23·2	9·2–34·3	P < 0·01
water excess in top soil‡	6·9	1–18	29·7	20–40	P < 0·001
*herbage analysis (D.M. basis)**					
crude protein %	19·2	13·9–24·1	20·1	12·4–26·4	
Cu mg./kg.	10·0	6·6–14·0	10·5	7·4–15·0	
Mo** mg./kg.	2·57	1·87–3·85	3·34	2·15–5·93	
total S %	0·30	0·22–0·37	0·34	0·24–0·39	
inorganic S %	0·115	0·02–0·20	0·127	0·06–0·21	
Ca %	0·57	0·52–0·80	0·55	0·42–0·75	
P %	0·44	0·38–0·53	0·44	0·33–0·56	
Ca–S–P§ meq./kg.	(−)321	(−)194–(−)483	(−)362	(−)241–(−)478	0·01 < P < 0·05
Mn mg./kg.	178	70– 370	259	90– 470	0·01 < P < 0·05
clinical signs in cattle†	total score‡		total score‡		
grey depigmentation of black hair¶	0		17		P < 0·01
other hair discolourations (e.g. brown)	6		12		
staring coat on withers¶	9		20		0·05 < P < 0·10
dull coat	7		15		
scouring (chronic diarrhoea)¶	10		28		0·05 < P < 0·10
thickening of epiphysis¶	4		11		0·10 < P < 0·20
coarse fetlock	11		19		
cow hock (X legs)	12		5		
white scour in calves	1		8		0·10 < P < 0·20

* P values calculated according to Wilcoxon's test.
† P values calculated according to χ² test.
‡ See explanation in text.
§ After Deijs *et al.* (1956).
¶ Causal relation with copper status experimentally demonstrated.
** Only referring to 4 farms per group.

445

not show a distinct relation to the Cu status. The Mn content and 'Ca-S-P', a factor introduced by Deijs, Bosch and Wind (1956) however, show a negative and a positive relation, respectively. Nevertheless the values of both quantities in the two groups overlap to such an extent that they can hardly be applied in field surveys. (It is possible that the correlation with the Mn content is indirect as is suggested from the very close correlation found between the Cu status of the animals and the extent of water excess: under reducing conditions in the soil Mn is much more available to the plant.)

Differences between the two groups of farms in the extent of water excess are highly significant and the individual values do not overlap. Water excess is the result of complex situations and occurs especially on heavy soils with a dense impermeable top soil. It is also promoted by a high ground water level. Many signs of reducing conditions in the soil, for example rust concretions and mainly grey instead of brown colours, are found in the root zone. Water excess occurs least on not too finely grained well permeable soils which are adequately drained. Differences in soil organic matter content are also significant but some overlapping values were found in the two groups.

FURTHER DEVELOPMENTS

The criterion of water excess was tested by us and by others (Bool, 1961) in other parts of the Netherlands; it is found to be efficient in assessing the occurrence of Cu deficiency in ruminants in autumn. The causal relationship, however, is not yet understood.

In the meantime others have also found additional factors which may be correlated with the Cu status of animals. Various authors mention a very close correlation between the oxidase activity of blood or other tissues and the Cu status of the animal or the occurrence of clinical signs. Several Animal Health Services in the Netherlands nowadays apply the oxidase activity of the blood plasma as a simplified chemical method to assess the Cu status of ruminants (Bosman, 1961). Similar developments have taken place in Great Britain and Ireland, where Mills, Williams and Poole (1963) and Poole (1963) stated that measurements of tissue cyto-chrome oxidase activity provide an early and sensitive indicator of Cu deficiency. The value of other enzymic indicators of deficiency was also studied by them and to quote Mills (1967): 'simplified procedures for their assay are being developed wherever possible to facilitate their application in field survey investigations. These techniques are particularly of great value in borderline cases, where clinical signs are absent or unspecific'. With the ever-increasing production level in cattle farming serious deficiency signs will occur rather seldom but the detection of borderline cases with, as the only signs, a somewhat reduced production and fertility level— sometimes accompanied by general signs of ill-thrift—will become more and more important. It is therefore essential that every effort should go into continuing the development of these techniques and their adaptation for application in field investigations.

REFERENCES

BOOL, C. H. (1961). *Landbouwvoorlichting* **12,** 776.
BOSMAN, M. S. M. (1961). *Jaarb. Inst. biol. scheik. Onderz. LandbGewass.* p. 83.
DEIJS, W. B., BOSCH, S. & WIND, J. (1956). *Versl. cent. Inst. landbouwk. Onderz.* 88.
HARTMANS, J. (1960). *Jaarb. Inst. biol. scheik. Onderz. LandbGewass.* p. 143.
HARTMANS, J. (1962). *Jaarb. Inst. biol. scheik. Onderz. LandbGewass.* p. 157.
MILLS, C. F. (1967). *Feed Forum* **2,** 1.
MILLS, C. F., WILLIAMS, R. B. & POOLE, D. B. R. (1963). *Biochem. J.* **87,** 10 P.
MITCHELL, R. L. (1963). *J. R. agric. Soc.* **124,** 75.
POOLE, D. B. R. (1963). Thesis: University of Dublin (cited by Mills, 1967).
VAN DER GRIFT, J. (1955). Thesis: University of Utrecht.
VAN LUIT, B. & HENKENS, C. H. (1967). *Versl. landbouwk. Onderz. Ned.* No. 695.

DISCUSSION

Reith (Aberdeen). Did you find any increase in the Mo content of herbage and also any relationship between Mo content and water excess in the soil?

Hartmans (Wageningen). The Mo content of herbage increases as the season proceeds; the lowest values are found in May and June. The rate of increase is greater than the rate of increase in nitrogen content as the season proceeds. We did not find a relationship between Mo content and water excess.

Underwood (Perth). The Mo contents of the herbage found in your survey work ranging from 2 to 5 and sometimes up to 7 p.p.m. are sufficient under Australian and New Zealand conditions to precipitate signs of clinical Cu deficiency in cattle where the Cu intakes are otherwise marginal. I think Dr Hartmans' work serves to underline the point that such surveys can only be effective if a number of elements are estimated at the same time and the conditions are adequately described. In Australian areas where chronic Cu poisoning has occurred Mo contents may be as low as 0·01 or 0·001 p.p.m. in the herbage. I feel that Dr Hartmans' figures may be quite significant in relation to the development of a Cu deficiency in cattle.

Hartmans (Wageningen). I have described only one survey. In others again we have found no significant correlation between the Mo content of herbage and Cu deficiency in cattle. As I said earlier in our experiments on sulphide formation in the rumen we could not increase sulphide levels by feeding 5 p.p.m. Mo and we doubted therefore whether this would have any effect on the Cu metabolism of the animal. I would however agree that Dick has suggested other possible mechanisms for the action of Mo on Cu.

A SURVEY OF THE COPPER STATUS OF CATTLE USING COPPER OXIDASE (CAERULOPLASMIN) ACTIVITY OF BLOOD SERUM

J. R. TODD

Veterinary Research Laboratories, Stormont, Belfast, U.K.

CAERULOPLASMIN is a protein, occuring in blood plasma, which contains copper as an integral part of the molecule (8 atoms). It has enzymic properties and acts as an oxidase towards polyamines and polyphenols. No definite physiological function has been ascribed to it although it has been postulated to control Cu balance. The case for this is not entirely proven although it explains Wilson's disease in the human which on this basis would be explained by low plasma caeruloplasmin levels favouring the pathological accumulation of Cu in tissues (Scheinberg, 1966).

Caeruloplasmin is almost synonymous with the 'indirect-reacting' Cu of blood plasma and constitutes a large proportion of the total plasma Cu (probably about 80 per cent.) (Gubler *et al.*, 1953; McCosker, 1961a and b; Suttle and Field, 1968). It is not surprising therefore that highly significant correlations have been found between caeruloplasmin and various blood Cu fractions such as plasma Cu, serum Cu and total blood Cu. This has been shown to hold for various species (McCosker, 1961a; Bosman, 1961; Tyburczyk, 1964). Correlation coefficients of 0·80 to 0·94 have been obtained between whole blood Cu and serum caeruloplasmin of cattle. Typical relationships obtained during our own work are illustrated in Figure 1.

ADVANTAGES OF CAERULOPLASMIN ESTIMATION OVER BLOOD COPPER FOR THE DETECTION OF COPPER DEFICIENCY

Low contamination risk. Trace element standards of cleanliness are not required either in collecting samples or in the laboratory.

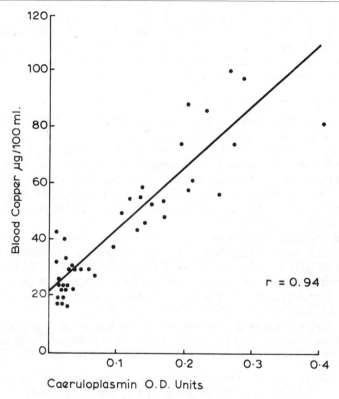

FIG. 1. Blood copper and Caeruloplasmin Cattle.

This is important if large numbers of samples are being collected. Being a fairly specific enzyme reaction, contamination is unlikely and contamination with metals, particularly Cu, is taken into account in the analysis. The control reading measures non-enzymic oxidation and the difference between test and control, which represents the caeruloplasmin, is reasonably constant up to 20 μg. of added Cu/ml. serum.

Stability. Serum left standing for five days at room temperature shows no loss of activity. Transport of samples to laboratory therefore presents no problem. Varley (1964) states that serum may be stored for at least two weeks at 4° C.

Technically convenient analysis. A small sample (0·1 ml.) is required (as opposed to 1 ml. or more for Cu estimation). The method simply involves the addition of buffer and substrate and

449

the incubation of the mixture. The reaction is stopped with sodium azide and a second sample, similarly treated, is treated with Na azide before incubation to give the control reading for non-enzymic oxidation. The method is therefore suitable for batch operation (up to 90 per batch in our laboratory).

SURVEY TECHNIQUE AND RESULTS

Caeruloplasmin estimations are performed by Ravin's method as described by Varley (1964) and blood Cu estimations by the method of Brown and Hemingway (1962). Copper analyses are performed at intervals and regressions calculated in order to establish the relationship between caeruloplasmin and blood Cu. For survey purposes about 100 caeruloplasmin estimations are performed per day on samples obtained from various parts of the country. Results are expressed in terms of equivalent whole blood Cu and distribution expressed in terms of the number of animals in each herd falling into the following groups: (1) more than 70 μg./100 ml.; (2) 60 to 69 μg./100 ml.; (3) 50 to 59 μg./100 ml.; (4) less than 50 μg/100 ml. Suspected Cu deficiency as revealed by caeruloplasmin estimation is followed up by blood Cu analyses and clinical examination of the stock.

Table I shows the distribution of the results on a number of farms. As represented by farms A to E the majority of the animals in most parts of the country are normal or about the lower limit

Table I. *Distribution of blood copper levels in cattle on farms* (*Blood* Cu *calculated from caeruloplasmin regression*)

	No. of animals with Blood Cu			
	> 70 μg./100 ml.	60–69 μg./100 ml.	50–59 μg./100 ml.	< 50 μg./100 ml.
Farm A	38	1	0	1
B	12	4	1	0
C	11	1	1	0
D	5	0	0	0
E	6	1	0	0
F	16	2	2	1
G	5	4	5	3
H	1	0	1	16

of the normal range (i.e. columns 1 and 2). Several farms in one area, represented by farms F and G, have individual animals in all four categories but although blood Cu analyses confirmed hypo-cupraemia no clinical effects are evident in the stock at present. On the other hand farm H showed an extremely deficient pattern and blood samples taken from 17 cows showed that 16 had blood

Cu levels of below 50 μg./100 ml., four were below 20 μg./100 ml. and the normal animal was one recently introduced into the herd. This was a beef suckler herd and in fact the calves were showing definite signs of Cu deficiency with abnormal coat colour, swollen fetlocks and unthrifty appearance although the farmer accepted this as normal. This revealed an area where Cu deficiency was not previously suspected.

These results confirm, therefore, that caeruloplasmin estimation may be used as a rapid screening method for detecting Cu deficiency.

REFERENCES

BOSMAN, M. S. M. (1961). *Jaarb. Inst. biol. scheik. Onderz. LandbGewass.* p. 83.
BROWN, N. & HEMINGWAY, R. G. (1962). *Res. vet. Sci.* **3**, 345.
GUBLER, C. J., LAHEY, M. E., CARTWRIGHT, G. E. & WINTROBE, M. M. (1953). *J. clin. Invest.* **32**, 405.
MCCOSKER, P. J. (1961a). *Nature, Lond.* **190**, 887.
MCCOSKER, P. J. (1961b). *Clin. chim. Acta,* **6**, 889.
SCHEINBERG, I. H. (1966). In *The Biochemistry of Copper.* Ed. Peisach & Blumburg. p. 513. New York: Academic Press.
SUTTLE, N. F. & FIELD, A. C. (1968). *J. comp. Path. Therap.* **78**, 351.
TYBURCZYK, M. (1964). *Annls Univ. Marie Curie—Sklodowska,* Sect. DD. **19**, 35.
VARLEY, H. (1964). *Practical Clinical Biochemistry,* 3rd ed. London: Heinemann.

DISCUSSION

Rish (Samarkand). From your diagram illustrating the relationship between caeruloplasmin activity and whole blood Cu content I see that the regression line does not go through the origin. We have frequently observed this and in some cases have obtained a caeruloplasmin colour yield in the absence of Cu. Can you comment on these points?

Todd (Belfast). I think there are two possible causes for such effects. Firstly, contamination can arise during blood sampling from the use of hypodermic needles made of brass coated with nickel or some other metal which will lead to the introduction of small traces of Cu and, secondly, I think that colour yield varies with the batch of para-phenylenediamine in use.

Hartmans (Wageningen). Further to Professor Rish's remarks I think we should remember the work of the Utah Group (Gubler *et al.*) showing that we have to account for 'direct reacting' Cu with no oxidase activity and indirect reacting Cu in caeruloplasmin. I feel that changes in the proportions of these types of Cu are likely to account for these differences.

Todd (Belfast). We are of course determining whole-blood Cu in our studies.

THE GEOCHEMICAL ECOLOGY OF ORGANISMS IN DEFICIENCY AND EXCESS OF COPPER

M. A. Rish

Samarkand State University, Samarkand, U.S.S.R.

As has been pointed out in V. V. Kovalsky's paper, the mechanism of function of trace elements in living organisms is one of the main concerns of geochemical ecology. There is no doubt that the chemical composition of parent rocks, soil and herbage exerts its influence on the health and productivity of livestock. This influence, however, must not be over-estimated since only a few breeds of farm animals depend on pastures for their diet, while most of them are provided with feeds manufactured on an industrial scale and supplemented with vitamins, mineral additives, etc.

A breed that is ideally suited for studies of soil/plant/animal interrelationships is the Karakul sheep, which is kept on desert pastures the whole year round and receives additional feeds only in case of drought and other emergencies.

Among the manifold nutritional problems experienced with this breed, Cu feeding plays an important role. Karakul sheep are affected by diseases related both to deficiency and excess of Cu.

Copper deficiency is brought about by an imbalance of Cu, Mo and sulphate in the diet of sheep and is manifested by endemic ataxia, depigmentation of wool and a general impairment of productivity including fertility, yields of wool, etc.

Of special interest for Karakul sheep breeders is the influence Cu deficiency exerts on the quality of Karakul fleeces which may lose their lustre and pigmentation.

We have been able to demonstrate that Cu deficiency in Karakuls is accompanied by a marked inhibition of a number of enzymes: cytochrome oxidase of brain and liver, benzylamine oxidase of blood and liver mitochondria and sulphide oxidase of liver. The decrease of the activity of the latter is accompanied by a significant rise in the concentration of sulphides in liver and brain. The sulphides may act as a toxic agent which causes damage to the liver of sheep.

It has been demonstrated that apparently healthy Karakul lambs killed for their fleeces in Cu-deficient areas of Uzbekistan show a parenchymic hepatitis of the same kind as in endemic ataxia, but to a lesser degree. This gives reason to consider liver disease as a primary development preceding the dystrophy of

452

brain tissue in delayed cases of endemic ataxia. Since no sulphides could be detected in the blood stream of the Karakuls they must be of metabolic origin and formed by catabolism of cysteine and other S-containing amino acids in the liver.

Indirect evidence shows that under conditions of Cu deficiency in Karakul sheep there must be some essential changes, not only in the absorption and excretion of Cu but also in its chemical forms.

It has been demonstrated that supplementation of sheep with Cu in Cu-deficient areas of Uzbekistan leads to a relatively fast repletion of Cu in the liver which may exceed normal values, but the concentration of Cu in brain increases very slowly, almost never reaching values characteristic for sheep on 'healthy' pastures.

One may speculate that the 'direct-reacting' plasma Cu which is absorbed by tissues is transformed by liver sulphides into less accessible compounds of this element, which do not penetrate the histo-haematic barriers of the organism. From this point of view brain lesions would be, as already stated, a secondary event connected with a primary impairment of liver function.

Since clinical symptoms in Cu deficiency seldom develop and the principal economic losses are brought about by a drastic decrease of productivity of sheep, an early diagnosis of Cu deficiency in sheep is of vital importance.

This can be achieved by a study of the response of sheep to Cu supplementation. Such trials being decisive, they are at the same time very time-consuming. In this connection we turned to the chemical analysis of readily accessible tissues of the sheep, that is blood and wool.

Whole blood Cu values do not always reflect the real Cu status of the animal, since it takes a long time for them to fall beneath a normal level. Conversely, we have been able to show that caeruloplasmin levels reflect minor changes in Cu metabolism, decreasing even at liver Cu concentrations of 30 to 40 p.p.m. w/w, which are considered to be within the normal range. As caeruloplasmin in sheep is four to five times less active than in man and almost 10 times less active than in pigs, its amount cannot be directly related to its activity using coefficients developed for humans.

We adopted as a normal level of caeruloplasmin the optical density value of 0·2 which we found in sheep on 'healthy' pastures. In Cu deficiency states the values were three to four times less dependent on the age and state of depletion of the animals.

Assay of caeruloplasmin levels alone is not sufficient, however, to determine the Cu status of the animal, since we observed that caeruloplasmin activity decreases not only in Cu deficiency but also in cases of hepatogenous Cu poisoning of sheep. It is low in animals which accumulate Cu in their livers without showing any clinical signs of Cu toxicity.

Consequently we have used as another test of the Cu status of Karakul sheep the content of trace elements in their wool. Quite unexpectedly we did not find a low Cu content in wool of Cu-deficient lambs. On the contrary, the amount of Cu in the wool was slightly higher compared to normal values (10 and 8 p.p.m. respectively) but this difference was of no statistical significance.

There was, however, a highly significant difference in the content of Zn and Mo and some other metals in the wool of new-born lambs. The amount of Zn, for instance, increased almost two-fold compared with normal values (250 and 120 p.p.m. respectively). I should mention that high Zn values in the wool of sheep in Cu deficiency have been also demonstrated by Healy and co-workers in New Zealand, who found values up to 400 p.p.m. D.M. This finding may be explained on the assumption that the wool is one of the routes of excretion of trace metals which in cases of conditioned Cu deficiency appear to be more rapidly excreted from the organism.

Concluding my short report, I should say that a simultaneous analysis of blood caeruloplasmin levels and of trace metal content of wool provide a basis for a relatively accurate estimation of the Cu status of sheep.

DISCUSSION

Thornton (London). Are any of these Cu deficiency disorders you have reported associated with excess Mo in the herbage and what range of Mo levels are you finding?

Rish (Samarkand). In Uzbekistan such pasture contains 5 p.p.m. Cu and 4 p.p.m. Mo. Especially in summer when the sheep are drinking brackish water, the sulphate intake may amount to 20 g. per head per day but it is usually 5 to 10 g. per head. We thus consider this condition to be induced by Mo and sulphate. Recently we have however doubted whether Mo is as important as sulphate. In Daghestan we have areas where the Mo is low (1 p.p.m.) where there is a more severe type of Cu deficiency. In my opinion Mo is not always the operative agent. It appears to me that sulphate is the main agent provoking this disease.

Suttle (Edinburgh). Are the levels of 'direct-reacting' Cu in plasma elevated in your induced cases of Cu deficiency as they are in Cu deficiency induced experimentally by supplementary Mo? Could I also ask are there differences in the syndrome between the areas high or low in lead particularly with reference to hepatitis?

Rish (Samarkand). We didn't find the method of Cartwright and his co-workers for measuring 'direct-reacting' Cu sufficiently satisfactory to carry out much work.

Suttle (Edinburgh). You referred in your paper to the development of low caeruloplasmin levels during Cu poisoning in sheep. At what stage during the development of poisoning do these low values develop?

Rish (Samarkand). The cases of Cu poisoning we have are due to ingestion of the plant *Heliotropeum dasycarpum* and are similar to Australian cases resulting from *H. europeum*. Low caeruloplasmin levels, sometimes as low as 50 per cent. of normal, have been found before and after the haemolytic crisis. We are thus of the opinion that in hepatogenous Cu poisoning low caeruloplasmin levels can be found for several months before clinical signs of Cu poisoning occur and levels may be down to those associated with Cu-deficient animals.

Anke (Jena). You have described Cu deficiency in sheep in these areas but is there also Cu deficiency in cows and in goats?

Rish (Samarkand). Copper deficiency also arises in goats and cattle. Goats die early of Cu deficiency and thus very few goats are kept in these areas and it has not been possible to do much experimental work. Cattle depend much on processed concentrates which prevent the development of such dramatic signs of Cu deficiency as those seen in sheep, but nevertheless judging by blood and liver Cu values they are also of low Cu status.

Ishmael (Liverpool). Did you only find low caeruloplasmin in Cu poisoning arising from *H. dasycarpum* or also in that arising from the excessive ingestion of Cu? You also mentioned the release of enzymes into the blood of sheep suffering chronic Cu poisoning. Which enzymes were affected and how long before the haemolytic crisis could the changes in activity of blood enzymes be detected?

Rish (Samarkand). Copper poisoning due to a high content of Cu in the soil and pasture was detected in south-east Bashkiria

Province by Kovalsky and his colleagues 10 years ago. At that time no work on caeruloplasmin levels was done but I know from the literature that chronic or acute Cu poisoning caused by the administration of Cu causes a lowering of caeruloplasmin level. A rise to normal caeruloplasmin levels occurs after the animal regains health. We tried unsuccessfully to detect the early stages of Cu poisoning by assay of serum transaminases, aldolase and phosphatase but no rise was detectable one week to two days before the crisis. These enzymes rose simultaneously with the development of the haemolytic crisis but they were of no help in an early diagnosis.

Mills (Aberdeen). Have you any experience with experimental Cu poisoning of sheep using diets containing urea? We have had great difficulty in producing Cu poisoning on such diets even when the rations provided 60 p.p.m. Cu. I am puzzled by this and I would be glad to hear if others had met this situation?

Rish (Samarkand). I have carried out no experiments of this type, but perhaps we may infer that here Cu is chelated in some abnormal way and this may prevent poisoning. We have loaded Karakul sheep with Cu in diets not containing urea and six months was needed to kill after giving 1 g. of copper sulphate per day and three months after giving copper carbonate to provide the same amount of Cu. However, in regions where hepatogenous Cu poisoning occurs, only one month elapsed before Cu poisoning appeared using these levels of Cu salts.

Todd (Belfast). Is the Karakul sheep similar to the Merino in that it survives the haemolytic crisis, whereas British breeds generally die?

Rish (Samarkand). About 10 to 15 per cent. generally survive.

AN EVALUATION OF TISSUE CYTOCHROME OXIDASE ACTIVITY AS AN INDICATOR OF COPPER STATUS

C. F. MILLS AND A. C. DALGARNO

Rowett Research Institute, Bucksburn, Aberdeen, Scotland, U.K.

MANY outbreaks of copper deficiency in farm livestock have been successfully detected by the use of survey techniques based upon the determination of blood and liver Cu content of animals. When experience is gained using these techniques in particular areas there are few problems in the interpretation of results once standards for 'normal' and 'deficient' animals have been derived. It cannot be generally assumed, however, that such values are uniformly applicable in different circumstances. The work of Hill, Thambyah, Wan and Shanta (1962) provides an excellent example of the problem of establishing such values in areas that have not been previously studied; reference to this problem is also contained in the papers by Hartmans and by Poole in this volume.

Such problems will remain until we have more extensive knowledge of the metabolic roles of the different forms of Cu found in blood and liver and their relationship to the clinical syndrome of deficiency. In the attempt to overcome these limitations our approach to the problem of developing a diagnostic method for detecting deficiency is based upon the assay of known Cu-containing enzymes in tissues and in the study of the relationship of enzyme to clinical conditions. Such techniques should have the advantage that a direct assessment can be made of whether sufficient Cu is available to meet a known physiological function and should overcome the problems that led Hill *et al.* (1962) to conclude that 'a more reliable index of copper deficiency than liver values is required, particularly in adult stock'.

Some of our early studies of the relationship of liver cytochrome oxidase activity in cattle to the existence of clinical signs of deficiency have been reported earlier (Mills *et al.,* 1963). Other work has been reported by Poole (1963). Our more recent work has been devoted firstly, to the development of a simple spectrophotometric assay for the determination of cytochrome oxidase activity which avoids the technical complications of the conventional manometric assay, and, secondly, to investigate the relationship of muscle cytochrome oxidase activity to clinical condition. The problems encountered by inexperienced personnel during the collection of liver biopsy samples make the routine investigation of liver enzyme activity a difficult task; in contrast, muscle biopsy under local anaesthesia is a simpler technique.

DETERMINATION OF TISSUE CYTOCHROME OXIDASE ACTIVITY

The assay is based upon the spectrophotometric determination of the rate of oxidation of reduced cytochrome C by cytochrome oxidase by noting the rate of decline of the 550 nm. absorption peak of reduced cytochrome c after adding crude preparations of liver or muscle mitochondria. Cytochrome c (20 mg. in 10 ml. water) is reduced by the addition of solid potassium borohydride

457

(7·5 mg.). After allowing a 15-minute period for reduction, excess borohydride is decomposed by the addition of a cation exchange resin (H^+ form) (approximately 150 mg.). The evolution of hydrogen is aided by intermittent stirring and after about 15 to 30 minutes the preparation is ready for use. Good preparations have an optical density ratio 550:565 nm. that exceeds 7.

A 0·5 per cent. (w/v) homogenate of muscle or liver in cold 0·25 M-sucrose solution is prepared in a Potter-Elvehjem glass homogeniser and the homogenate is centrifuged for not more than 1,000 'g. min.' to remove cell debris and nuclei. The following components are added to a cuvette with a 1 cm. light path:

    1·0 ml. reduced cytochrome c preparation

    Sodium phosphate buffer (0·05 M, pH 7·2) to give 3 ml. final volume

    0·05 to 0·2 ml. mitochondria supernatant.

The rate of decline of optical density at 550 nm. is determined; the quantity of mitochondria preparation added should be such as to give a linear rate of reaction during at least the first four minutes. Using the above system a fall in OD^{550} of 1·0 units corresponds to the oxidation of 0·166 μmol. cytochrome c; units of activity are based upon the quantity of substrate oxidised/min./mg. protein as determined by the Folin method or by determination of the OD at 280 nm.

In using this method care should be taken to ensure that the cation exchange resin (H^+ form) is washed with distilled water just before use to remove free acid; failure to do this results in a poor yield of reduced cytochrome c. Good commercial preparations of oxidised cytochrome c have a brick red colour; samples having a brownish colour should be avoided as they frequently contain a component which partly inhibits the reaction—suitable material has been obtained from Seravac Laboratories, Holyport, Berks., England. Assays are carried out on a Hilger-Gilford reaction kinetics spectrophotometer (Rank Precision Industries Ltd., London); to use instruments not having the same facility for readings at high optical densities, instrument balance should be attained at a scale reading of zero when using a solution having an OD^{550} of about 0·8 as 'blank' rather than water.

RESULTS

Table I illustrates that clinical Cu deficiency in the rat is accompanied by a greater fall in the cytochrome oxidase activity of semitendinosus muscle than of liver. Studies by one of our colleagues (Paul, 1968) suggested that semitendinosus muscle provided a suitable sampling site as it is relatively free from areas of 'red' muscle which have a high activity and are difficult to sample uniformly. His work also illustrated that a small but significant decline in semitendinosus muscle activity occurred in normal animals 8 to 10 weeks after weaning.

Table I. *Cytochrome oxidase activity, liver copper and blood haemoglobin in normal and clinically* Cu-*deficient rats*

	Cytochrome Oxidase Activity*	
	Semitendinosus Muscle	Liver
+ Cu	0·339 ± ·029	0·222 ± ·021
− Cu	0·054 ± ·004†	0·048 ± ·005†
	Haemoglobin (g./100 ml.)	Liver Cu (p.p.m. DM.)
+ Cu	14·9 ± ·4	18·9 ± 1·0
− Cu	8·6 ± ·7†	3·0 ± ·2†
	(10 rats/treatment)	

* μmol. cytochrome c oxidised/min./mg. protein
† $P < 0.01$.

Liver and muscle samples were obtained from clinically normal cattle and sheep with both a normal and low Cu status as judged by blood Cu analysis. Samples were also obtained from clinically deficient animals of low blood Cu status. Approximately 100 mg. (fresh weight) samples of muscle were obtained by biopsy under local anaesthesia from the semitendinosus muscle of cattle and the semimembranosus muscle of sheep. Approximately 50 mg. of muscle was taken for each assay. The mean cytochrome oxidase activity of semitendinosus muscle samples taken from 17 clinically normal cattle drawn from a wide variety of sources was $0·280 \pm 0·21$ units (μmol. cytochrome c oxidised/min./mg. protein). The activity of liver from the same animals was $0·071 \pm ·004$ units. Calves undergoing experimental Cu depletion had a semitendinosus muscle activity of $0·141 \pm ·017$ units in contrast to a mean activity of $0·200 \pm ·009$ units in animals fed the same diet supplemented to provide 7·5 p.p.m. Cu. It should be noted that at the time of sampling no clinical signs of Cu deficiency were evident even though the blood Cu levels of 'deficient' and control animals were $0·25 \pm ·05$ and $0·96 \pm ·06$ μg./ml. respectively. Semitendinosus muscle samples from cattle suffering a suspected field outbreak of Cu deficiency in which poor growth of young stock was observed had a cytochrome oxidase activity of 0·044 units (range 0·011 to 0·071). Muscle cytochrome oxidase activity rose to a mean level of 0·097 units (range 0·055 to 0·164) in animals injected with Cu EDTA while in untreated

459

animals which underwent a spontaneous recovery from the clinical condition the mean activity was 0·103 units (range 0·082 to 0·124).

Studies have also been carried out on semimembranosus muscle of sheep undergoing experimental Cu depletion on a diet providing less than 1 p.p.m. Cu and from these studies combined with those on calves and rats we may draw the following conclusions:

1. Changes in muscle cytochrome oxidase activity in response to Cu depletion of the ruminant are not as marked as those in rat muscle and probably do not occur at as early a stage of depletion.

2. In the rat, the changes in muscle cytochrome oxidase activity in response to depletion are greater than the changes in the activity of this enzyme in liver. Changes in muscle cytochrome oxidase activity in response to Cu depletion of the ruminant appear to be smaller than those found in liver tissue judging by comparison of our own findings with muscle and those of other workers (Poole, this volume, p. 465; Mills *et al.*, 1963) using liver.

3. In the experimentally depleted ruminant a very significant decline in blood caeruloplasmin activity and whole blood Cu content may precede the onset of clinical symptoms by periods of up to several months; the decline in muscle cytochrome oxidase activity occurs at a later stage.

4. Losses of cytochrome oxidase activity in rat muscle during storage at—20° C for a period of one month are small; in contrast, losses of activity in deep frozen ruminant muscle may be as high as 30 to 40 per cent. in 24 hours and it has been found preferable to store samples at +1°C.

We thus conclude that despite the advantage gained by the simple technique of muscle biopsy the limitations to this procedure probably make it less suitable for the detection of Cu deficiency than assay of liver cytochrome oxidase activity. Our results do however suggest that the determination of tissue cytochrome oxidase activity provides a more satisfactory index of clinical Cu status than the determination of plasma monoamine oxidase activity that was previously investigated by us (Mills *et al.*, 1966).

Acknowledgement. We are grateful to Mr A. K. Paul for his participation in the early stages of this work.

REFERENCES

HILL, R., THAMBYAH, R., WAN, S. P. & SHANTA, C. S. (1962). *J. agric. Sci., Camb.* **59**, 409.

MILLS, C. F., DALGARNO, A. C. & WILLIAMS, R. B. (1966). *Biochem. biophys. Res. Commun.* **24**, 537.

MILLS, C. F., WILLIAMS, R. B. & POOLE, D. B. R. (1963). *Biochem. J.* **87**, 10P.

POOLE, D. B. R. (1963). *Copper deficiency in calves.* M.Sc. Thesis: University of Dublin.
PAUL, A. K. (1968). Tissue cytochrome oxidase activity as an indicator of copper deficiency in rats, sheep and cattle. M.Sc. Thesis: University of Aberdeen.

DISCUSSION

Sourkes (Montreal). Are you screening amine oxidase in normal and Cu-deficient ruminants and, if so, what do you think the function of this enzyme is in ruminant serum?

Mills (Aberdeen). We were at one time interested in mono-amine oxidase as a possible indicator of Cu deficiency and we have carried out some survey work on clinically normal sheep. Rather to our disappointment we found there was an extremely close correlation between whole blood Cu concentration and amine oxidase activity and the relationship was so close that there appeared to be no advantage in determining oxidase activity rather than measuring blood Cu content. We had hoped that the relationships between blood Cu and oxidase activity would be different in clinically normal animals with a low blood Cu content than in clinically deficient animals. This was not the case and amine oxidase activity gave no better indication of Cu status than did measurement of blood Cu.

COPPER STATUS AND MILK YIELD OF DAIRY COWS

D. B. R. POOLE AND M. J. WALSHE

Agricultural Institute, Dunsinea, Castleknock, Co. Dublin, Eire

THE data for this paper has been collected at the Dairy Research Station of the Agricultural Institute in Fermoy, using cows which were on a grazing management experiment. Two comparable herds were involved, one being of 39 cows rotationally grazed over paddocks at the rate of 1·08 acres per cow and the other herd being of 35 cows 'set stocked' on a single area of grass at 1·2 acres per cow. In both cases the winter feed was silage which was cut from the grazing area; no concentrate rations were fed. In the second year the total number of cows was reduced to 44 and they were combined as a single herd on a rotational system of grazing.

The grazing was a grass/clover reseeded pasture of about three years' standing, receiving annual dressings of nitrogen, phosphate

461

and potash at the rate of 23 lb, 27 lb and 56 lb per acre respectively; in addition the silage areas received 46 lb of nitrogen per acre before closing up. This farm is on an area of Old Red Sandstone.

Pasture samples taken during the first season showed Cu levels varying from 6 to 9 p.p.m. in grass and from 8 to 14 p.p.m. in clover; pasture molybdenum levels did not exceed 2 p.p.m. (average 1·4). Major elements were present at normal levels (Ca 0·7 per cent. in grass and 1·5 per cent. in clover, Mg 0·16 per cent. in grass and 0·26 per cent. in clover, K 3·5 per cent., Na 0·35 per cent. and P 0·45 per cent.). The average milk yields per lactation for the cows in the first year were 4,900 lb for the set stocked area and 5,700 lb for the rotationally grazed. In the second year the average yield was 6,000 lb of milk.

It had previously been observed that the Cu status of some of these cows was low although the activity of liver cytochrome oxidase appeared to be within the normal range. A Cu supplement was given to half of the cows in each herd, parenterally as CuEDTA ('Coprin', Glaxo Laboratories). This was first given in May and was repeated in July and November of the first year and in March, May and July of the second year. The dose on each occasion was 100 mg. Cu, with the exception of the second dose which was 200 mg.

Liver samples for Cu assay were collected on two occasions in the first year and on three occasions in the second year; blood samples were collected on three occasions in the first year and on four occasions in the second year. The results are given in Table I.

During the first year changes in blood Cu reflected changes in liver Cu levels. It was not possible to obtain liver samples before the start of the experiment but samples taken in July suggest an effect of the grazing system on liver Cu levels. Both in the treated and in the control cows liver Cu was higher on the rotationally grazed area than in similar cows maintained under 'set stocked' conditions.

During the second year blood Cu levels in the control cows were higher than in the previous year but the level in the treated animals remained normal. Liver Cu values remained low in the control cows; the Cu-treated cows maintained normal levels and were above 35 to 40 p.p.m. in almost every case.

Using a regression analysis the effect of additional Cu on milk yield and butter fat yield was assessed together with the relationship between milk yield and liver and blood Cu. Cu supplementation had no significant effect in either year or on either herd on total milk yield or on butter fat yield.

Table I. Blood and liver copper of cows under different conditions of grazing management with and without parenteral CuEDTA

Management	Cu treatment	1st year						2nd year					
		Blood Cu*			Liver Cu†			Blood Cu*			Liver Cu†		
		May	July	Oct.	July	Sept.	Mar.	May	July	Sept.	May	July	Sept.
Rotational grazing	CuEDTA	0·05‡	0·06	0·10	41	50	0·11	0·11	0·09	0·11	75	70	79
Set stocked	CuEDTA	0·05‡	0·06	0·10	12(3)§	46	0·07	0·08	0·08	0·09	7(22)	12(14)	10(12)
Rotational grazing	nil	0·05	0·05	0·07	12(6)	6(1)							
Set stocked	nil	0·05	0·04	0·05	5(14)	8							

* mg. per 100 ml.
† p.p.m. on dry matter.
‡ Before parenteral CuEDTA.
§ Number of individual values less than 5 p.p.m.

463

In the first year the control cows (those not receiving supplementary Cu) showed a negative relationship which was significant at the 1 per cent. level between milk yield and liver Cu; this amounted to a depression of 135 lb of milk (per lactation) for every unit increase in liver Cu. The trend was the same for blood Cu but was not statistically significant. In the second year this effect was not seen. For the Cu-supplemented cows there was no relationship in either year between Cu status and milk yield.

Although the breeding records of these herds show a poor conception rate (48 per cent. holding to the first service in the first year and 41 per cent. in the second year) Cu supplementation had no beneficial effect in either year in improving the conception rate, nor did it reduce the calving to service interval. It is clear from these results that Cu supplementation did not increase milk yield or butter fat yield, even when given to cows of low Cu status. The negative relationship of liver Cu to milk yield in the first year could, I think, be misleading as it occurred only in the one year. It must be pointed out that the total yields of these cows by international standards are low but are usual for Irish conditions. It would not be possible to extrapolate these findings to cows of a higher milk yield without additional information, nor to cows on different pastures where Mo levels might be higher or where other nutritional factors might come into play. It seems, however, that on an all-pasture and silage system such as this cows can show a considerable reduction in Cu status and may yet remain healthy and fully productive.

Acknowledgements. The copper analyses were undertaken by the Service Section, Animal Nutrition and Biochemistry Department, Agricultural Institute. The Coprin was supplied by Glaxo Laboratories Ltd.

DISCUSSION

Gartner (Yeerongpilly). I would like to support Mr Poole's findings by mentioning that trials conducted in cases of uncomplicated Cu deficiency in dairy cattle also giving relatively low milk yields grazing on the alluvial planes of south-east Queensland showed no production response to Cu therapy despite low hepatic and low whole-blood levels of Cu. I would like to ask whether Mr Poole has found liver Cu to be a repeatable estimate, that is when sampling from a population at different periods do animals maintain their ranking within a herd?

Poole (Dublin). Yes, they do. We have the impression that each animal has its own normal Cu level in liver which it tries to maintain and this can only be upset by fairly drastic treatment such as the injection of Cu. Under the conditions of silage feeding that I have described we don't see a seasonal variation in Cu values as has been described from the Netherlands.

CYTOCHROME OXIDASE IN INDUCED HYPOCUPROSIS

D. B. R. POOLE

Agricultural Institute, Dunsinea, Castlenock, Co. Dublin, Eire

THERE are now a number of published reports on the effect of copper deficiency on the activity of cytochrome oxidase, particularly in enzootic ataxia in sheep and in Cu deficiency in rats. Mills, Williams and Poole (1963) showed that Cu-deficient calves had lower cytochrome oxidase activities than did their Cu-supplemented companions. During the past two years we have used cytochrome oxidase assay as a confirmatory test in suspected cases of induced hypocuprosis in the bovine. The occasional incidence of low Cu status in apparently normal cattle necessitates some confirmatory test before diagnosing Cu deficiency on the basis of liver or blood Cu analysis.

An example of the use of cytochrome oxidase assay is given in a case which involved 40, 2-year-old, in-calf, Hereford heifers, which were grazed on a field the herbage of which was subsequently found to contain 5 to 15 p.p.m. molybdenum. Pasture Cu levels were normal, varying from 6 to 15 p.p.m. and sulphate-S levels averaged about 0·1 per cent. These heifers, during the latter part of the summer, showed ill-thrift with poor coat texture and a tendency to lose coat colour. Occasional scouring was observed. Blood and liver biopsy samples were collected and the animals were treated with 100 mg. Cu subcutaneously (as CuEDTA, Glaxo Laboratories Ltd.). There was a marked clinical response, animals appearing to thrive within a few days following treatment. Further samples were collected from the same animals 14 days later; these showed pretreatment average blood levels of 0·03 mg./ 100 ml. (for 20 samples) and liver Cu concentrations of < 5 p.p.m. in each case for 12 animals. Following treatment these values increased to 0·06 and 17 respectively on average. Cytochrome oxidase (manometric estimation) varied from Qo_2 0 to 55 before treatment (average 28) and from 57 to 160 after treatment (average 78).

Further work was necessary to elucidate more fully the seasonal variation in cytochrome oxidase activity and the response to treatment or to change of diet. During 1968 it was possible to follow Cu and enzyme levels in $1\frac{1}{2}$-year-old Friesian bullocks grazing cut-over peat land pasture where Mo values ranged from 5 to 25 and Cu values 5 to 15 p.p.m. There were 10 animals on each of the three pasture stocking rates, and five animals on each stocking rate were given 200 mg. Cu as (CuEDTA) subcutaneously.

Cattle were introduced to the pasture at the end of April and on the 8th June the liver and blood samples were collected. Subsequently, liver samples were taken on four occasions. From Table I it can be seen that the average Cu value was quite low by the beginning of June (15 animals had values < 10 p.p.m. in the liver). The response of liver Cu to therapy was obvious, the values increasing from 8 to 70 p.p.m.; and remaining about 15 p.p.m. throughout the remainder of the season, although the residual effect may not have been high enough to give optimum growth rate. Moreover the levels in the control animals (2 to 5 p.p.m. on average) were probably not low enough to expect serious clinical symptoms. Nonetheless an effect on cytochrome oxidase (colorimetric assay) was seen, treated cattle having levels of about 14·0 μmol./min./g. wet tissue. The levels before treatment 9·4 mol./min./g. wet tissue) were not as low as we normally encounter in clinical Cu deficiency cases and even by the end of the grazing season the activity in untreated animals had not fallen much further.

The average weight of the cattle in June was 415 kg. The average weight gain of Cu-treated cattle was 105 kg., that of control animals 95 kg. At the highest stocking rate the effect of Cu was more clear; 84 kg. increase for the treated animals and 64 for the control animals. In this group the difference in cytochrome oxidase activity between treated and control animals was also more obvious.

Subsequent to the 8th November six cattle from the control groups were stalled and fed a ration of hay and barley meal. This feed contained low levels of Mo (hay 2·9 p.p.m. and barley 1·2 p.p.m.). Three animals were given parenteral Cu, the other three remained untreated.

Cattle were subjected to liver biopsy on eight occasions subsequent to the 8th November—the last being on 10th January. Liver Cu values increased rapidly after treatment from 4 p.p.m. to 80 p.p.m. and maintained these values during the 63 day observation period; the control animals' liver Cu values did not

Table I. *Liver copper and cytochrome oxidase activity values*
(means of 5 animals)

| | High Stocking Rate | | | | Medium Stocking Rate | | | | Low Stocking Rate | | | |
| | Copper Treated | | Control | | Copper Treated | | Control | | Copper Treated | | Control | |
	Liver copper	C. oxidase activity	Liver copper	C. oxidas activity	Liver copper	C. oxidase activity	Liver copper	C. oxidase activity	Liver copper	C. oxidase activity	Liver copper	C. oxidase activity
June 8th*	9	9·29	11	7·73	8	7·66	14	11·52	9	9·99	14	10·09
July 5th	79	13·65	5	8·72	88	11·99	8	9·76	73	12·42	6	8·56
Sept. 4th	13	13·95	3	6·39	18	18·48	2	11·72	16	18·15	2	10·82
Oct. 4th	17	15·45	4	8·49	16	16·42	5	12·29	21	18·25	5	8·92
Nov. 8th	11	13·99	4	7·99	12	10·79	6	9·76	15	10·02	5	7·66

Liver copper units: p.p.m. dry matter.
Cytochrome oxidase activity units: μmol. cyto. c oxidised/min./g. wet tissue.
* Levels on 8th June are pre-treatment levels.

Table II. *Liver copper and cytochrome oxidase activity values*
(means of 3 animals)

Nov. 8th Pretreatment	Copper treated		Control	
	Liver Copper	Cytochrome oxidase Activity	Liver Copper	Cytochrome oxidase Activity
Day 1	4	7·06	4	6·46
Day 4	81	11·02	2	7·03
Day 7	80*	12·29*	2	6·69
Day 13	78	15·58	1	10·07
Day 18	55	15·61	1	8·82
Day 22	95	13·62	1	7·33
Day 29	94†	14·79	5	11·29
Day 40	79	19·78	7	19·25
Day 63	101	18·38	34	17·08

Liver copper units: p.p.m. dry matter.
Cytochrome oxidase activity units: μmol. cyto. c oxidised/min./g. wet tissue.
* Only one animal sampled.
† Mean of two animals.

show any increase for 30 days and marked increase did not occur until 60 days after housing. The cytochrome oxidase activity showed an immediate increase following Cu treatment with a subsidiary increase later. The untreated animals did not show any marked increase in cytochrome oxidase activity until about 40 days after housing, although there had been a slight increase at about 20 days (See Table II).

The overall weight gain for the animals during their indoor period was 0·77 kg. per day for treated animals and 0·39 kg. per day for control animals.

From these results it can be seen that there is under field conditions in cattle a close relationship between Cu status and liver cytochrome activity. Normal values for cytochrome oxidase, it is suggested, are in excess of 7·0 μmol./min./g. wet tissue; but the interpretation of values below this is not clear. Cytochrome oxidase activity in fully healthy cattle appears to be in excess of 14·0 μmol. The clear difference between cytochrome oxidase values in the treated and control animals in this experiment was not reflected in a statistical difference in weight gain, although the trend was in favour of the Cu-supplemented cattle. Under the conditions of increased stress in the high stocking rate, the effect of Cu on weight gain was much more clear. Clinical observations on these cattle suggested a better coat texture and a healthier appearance in the treated animals, but again this was neither clear nor consistent. There was at no time any evidence of anaemia. It is suggested that under conditions of favourable environment animals can remain healthy with levels of cytochrome oxidase below 7·0 μmol. for restricted periods, but under prolonged conditions of Cu depletion, or under stressful conditions, these animals are likely to suffer ill-effects attributable to Cu deficiency. The slow recovery of both liver Cu and of cytochrome oxidase on the change to normal diet suggests the need for Cu supplementation in addition to a change of diet. This is confirmed by the difference between the weight gains of these animals.

Acknowledgements. The author is grateful to Mr E. P. Hilliard for skilled technical assistance in enzyme estimation; the service section of the Animal Nutrition and Biochemistry Dept. for mineral analyses, and to Glaxo Laboratories Ltd for supplying Coprin.

REFERENCE

MILLS, C. F., WILLIAMS, R. B. & POOLE, D. B. R. (1963). *Biochem. J.* **87**, 10P.

DISCUSSION

Mills (Aberdeen). One of the primary objectives in arranging this morning's session was to review field conditions of Cu deficiency and to examine the problems that exist in attempting to detect and explain these disorders. In arranging this session we were hoping that those of us who are working on experimentally induced Cu deficiency and the importance of interacting factors in the production of deficiency would get some guide from the experience of field workers as to whether field Cu deficiency can be fully explained by the situations of straightforward inadequacy in the diet or alternatively by postulating the existence of a Cu/Mo/sulphate interrelationship. My question is, are field workers of the opinion that an appreciable number of Cu deficiency conditions occur in situations where Mo can not be incriminated and, secondly, how important is the relationship between Cu intake and the intake of sulphate or total sulphur in producing clinical Cu deficiency in the field? A lot of research effort is being put into the study of those situations which suggest, superficially at least, that our understanding of the factors which control Cu intake, storage and utilization is far from complete. In this context it is perhaps worth mentioning that on semi-purified diets we find that we have to reduce the Cu content to less than 0·5 p.p.m. in order to produce Cu deficiency whereas, in the field, situations have been reported where 5 p.p.m. has proved inadequate even where there is no evidence of elevated Mo or sulphate concentrations in herbage. This suggests that there is a very big difference indeed between this type of diet and practical field diets and yet we have no idea what this difference is. The evidence from Dutch field work reported by Dr Hartmans clearly suggests that Mo is not the only important factor and other work suggests that the total S intake may be just as important. I think we would welcome an expression of opinion from field workers on how far their deficiency conditions can be explained on the basis of inadequacy of Cu content of the herbage, the existence of a high Mo level or the existence of a high S level.

Todd (Belfast). Some of our own experiences in work on hypocuprosis in cattle in Northern Ireland and adjacent counties of Southern Ireland are relevant to this question. In one area we have clinical Cu deficiency in cattle where the herbage Cu is usually between 7 and 10 p.p.m., Mo 5 to 6 p.p.m. and sulphate 0·3 to 0·5 per cent. In another area we have very similar Cu, Mo and sulphate levels but no clinical signs of Cu deficiency and, even though there is hypocuprosis, there is no clinical response to Cu dosing. I feel we can not explain the existence of many cases of clinical or nonclinical hypocuprosis on the basis solely of an interaction between Cu, Mo and sulphate levels.

Lewis (Weybridge). I think we have to define our conditions very closely. From our experience at Weybridge we feel that the conditions leading to Cu deficiency in sheep can be quite different from those leading to deficiency in cattle. We also have to be rather careful in our terminology, for example we have always used 'hypocuprosis' to indicate clinical Cu deficiency and 'hypocupraemia' to denote low blood Cu. We do not see any clear association between hypocuprosis in cattle and herbage sulphate content and we are left with the Cu/Mo relationship. Here we have the impression that in cattle lower levels of herbage Mo are associated with hypocupraemia than we have previously thought possible and thus the work of Matrone is of particular interest. As far as sheep are concerned we have no evidence that high herbage Mo levels are associated with Cu deficiency conditions in the field.

THE ZINC CONTENT OF BLOOD SERUM AND BONE AS INDICES OF DIETARY ZINC ADEQUACY IN THE RAT

R. W. LUECKE, BRUNA E. RUKSAN AND BETTY V. BALTZER

*Department of Biochemistry, Michigan State University,
East Lansing, Michigan, U.S.A.*

IN the determination of the requirement of various species of experimental animals for dietary zinc, gain in body weight has been the most frequently used criterion. This is undoubtedly due to the fact that attempts to relate tissue Zn concentrations to alterations in the intake of this metal have frequently given uncertain results. However, Dreosti, Tao and Hurley (1968) have found plasma Zn to be quite sensitive to alterations in dietary intake. With this in mind it was decided to initiate studies with the rat in an effort to determine whether blood serum and bone Zn levels would adequately reflect the dietary intake of this element. Accordingly, an experiment with weanling, 21-day-old male rats was started using a Zn-low (0·8 mg./kg.) basal diet with dried egg white as the protein source. The composition of the basal diet, care and feeding

471

of the animals was similar to our previously reported work (Luecke *et al.*, 1968). A total of seven diets were used each containing supplementary Zn in the following amounts (in mg./kg.): 0, 5, 7·5, 10, 12·5, 15 and 20. Eight individually fed rats were used per dietary treatment and the length of the feeding period was 21 days. At the end of the experimental period the rats were placed under light anaesthesia with ether and killed by removing as much blood as possible by heart puncture. The blood was centrifuged and the serum used for Zn determinations. The liver as well as the femur from the left hind leg were removed and frozen until the Zn analyses could be performed. The Zn and copper content of the tissues, as well as all of the diets, were determined by atomic absorption spectrophotometry.

The results of the growth study as well as the Zn and Cu tissue analyses are shown in Table I. Although the Zn content of the liver was determined the results indicated no significant changes due to dietary treatment and thus are not reported. Reinhold, Kfoury and Thomas (1967) were also unable to find any increase in liver Zn in rats due to dietary Zn supplementation.

Table I. *Effect of dietary Zn level on various parameters measured in the rat*

There were eight male rats per group with an average initial weight of 59·4 g. The feeding period was 21 days and the values expressed are means with their standard errors.

Supplementary Zn level	Total gain	Diet intake	Serum Zn	Femur Zn*	Liver Cu†
(mg./kg.)	(g.)	(g.)	(μg./100 ml.)	(μg./g.)	(μg./g.)
0	16 ± 2	108 ± 3	38 ± 4	71 ± 4	15·2 ± 1·7[d]
5	75 ± 6[a]	201 ± 8[a]	58 ± 5[a]	88 ± 3[a]	9·7 ± 0·5[c]
7·5	112 ± 3[b]	252 ± 4[b]	90 ± 3[b]	126 ± 5[b]	—
10	133 ± 4[c]	303 ± 8[c]	134 ± 7[c]	186 ± 4[c]	5·6 ± 0·9
12·5	130 ± 4[c]	292 ± 6[c]	148 ± 3[c]	228 ± 5[d]	—
15	136 ± 6[c]	292 ± 10[c]	146 ± 5[c]	241 ± 6[d]	6·9 ± 0·6
20	133 ± 5[c]	283 ± 10[c]	145 ± 5[c]	257 ± 4[e]	5·4 ± 0·5

* Values expressed on dried fat-free femurs.
† Values based on dry weight of liver.
[a] Significantly greater than least mean, [b] least 2 means, [c] least 3 means, [d] least 4 means and [e] least 5 means (P < 0·01).

An inspection of the mean total gain as well as diet intake (Table I) indicates that a maximum value was reached at the 10 mg. level of supplementary Zn (11 mg./kg. Zn by analysis). This value is in very good agreement with the requirement figure of 12 mg./kg.

for the growing rat as reported earlier by Forbes and Yohe (1960) who also used a diet containing dried egg white.

Blood serum Zn appears to be quite sensitive as an index of the Zn status of the rat. Statistically significant increases in the concentration of this element were found with each increment of dietary Zn until a level approximating the requirement was reached; beyond that point no additional significant increases were found. A word of caution should perhaps be inserted at this point to the effect that the avoidance of haemolysis of the erythrocytes into the serum is a necessity if reliable results are to be obtained. The liberation of Zn from the haemolyzed erythrocytes will give erroneously high values.

The Zn content of the femur increased with each incremental increase in dietary Zn. However, unlike the results obtained with serum Zn, no observable plateau in concentration was reached with the dietary levels fed.

A reduced level of liver Cu was found in the rats fed suboptimal levels of Zn with the highest concentrations found in the unsupplemented group. There have been a number of reports to the effect that high dietary levels of Zn will cause a depression in Cu absorption (Van Campen and Scaife, 1967). However, it is not likely that the relatively low levels of Zn used in this study were sufficient to cause any alterations in Cu absorption. Rather, it seems more likely that the higher Cu levels found in the two groups fed suboptimum amounts of Zn was a reflection of the elevated Cu storage normally found in the livers of the newborn and very young rat which, due to the very poor growth, was not utilized.

Based on the results of this study it is concluded that blood serum Zn values may prove to be valuable in the assessment of the nutritional status of the animal with respect to this element.

REFERENCES

DREOSTI, I. E., TAO, S.-H. & HURLEY, LUCILLE S. (1968). *Proc. Soc. exp. Biol. Med.* **128**, 169.
FORBES, R. M. & YOHE, M. (1960). *J. Nutr.* **70**, 53.
LUECKE, R. W., OLMAN, M. E. & BALTZER, B. V. (1968). *J. Nutr.* **94**, 344.
REINHOLD, J. G., KFOURY, G. A. & THOMAS, T. A. (1967). *J. Nutr.* **92**, 173.
VAN CAMPEN, D. R. & SCAIFE, P. U. (1967). *J. Nutr.* **91**, 473.

NUTRITIONAL INFERTILITY IN CATTLE AT PASTURE

V. Bienfet, H. Binot and F. Lomba

*Department of Medical Pathology, Faculty of Veterinary Medicine,
Brussels, Belgium*

Nutritional infertility is still an undefinable clinical condition in our countries. Many factors such as insufficient intake of energy, protein, P, Mn, I, Cu, Co, Se and vitamin A and excess intake of oestrogens have been suspected as possible causes (Bienfet, Hennaux *et al.*, 1965). Undoubtedly in some conditions each of these factors can have an effect on fertility but in clinical cases it is rarely possible to show which are the aetiological factors.

On the other hand it seems certain that many cases of infertility cannot be related to any infection or genital defect of the cow or to sterility of the bull. The generally accepted view that nutritional infertility does exist is supported by the increased incidence of cases of infertility when cows are turned out to pasture and vice versa. It seems to be more prevalent when milk production is intensified and when the levels of pasture fertilisation are high.

Our investigations in this subject were made at the request of the artificial insemination centres, which have been greatly concerned at the abnormally high number of returns in some herds. Because of our lack of experience in this field we concentrated initially on the accumulation of data, especially on P, Cu and Mn. We encountered some cases of Cu deficiency (Bienfet, Lomba *et al.*, 1965; Binot *et al.*, 1969) and were faced with the problem of the diagnosis of Mn deficiency (Binot *et al.*, 1968).

However, in spite of our interest in the metabolism of Cu, Mn and the other trace elements, we became increasingly aware that an explanation of the occurrence of clinical cases of infertility could not be obtained by a straightforward consideration of these metals. In this paper the approach we have adopted to the problem of nutritional infertility in cattle will be described.

As example, experiments were conducted on farm 'Fr' of 12 hectares in the sandy-silty region of Belgium, with 20 milk cows with a yearly production of 900 gallons of milk and five to six heifers. From 1965 onwards the fertility of the cows and heifers decreased. When any medical cause of infertility was established the case was referred to us.

In winter the lactating cows received hay, fodders or turnips, grass silage and concentrates, containing 18 to 24 per cent. protein.

No supplement was fed when the cows were grazing. Pasture was traditionally fertilized in spring with 600 kg. slag (15 to 16 per cent. P) and 120 U of K and five or six times during the season with 150 kg. ammonium nitrate. The pasture had not been limed for seven to eight years but a supplement of $CuSO_4$ had been applied in 1966.

Investigations were started in spring 1967. In the period May to October of that year only 13 pregnancies resulted from 41 inseminations, giving a fecundity index of 3·15. When it had been established that Mn deficiency was not responsible for the infertility, 5 g. $MnSO_4$ was given to each cow during the first year to appease the owner.

In Table I the analytical results obtained from pasture where infertility was recorded are compared with those from normal neighbouring pasture. Large differences can be seen in soil pH with a parallel decrease in exchangeable Ca, K, Na, Mn, Pb and Fe. Although Cu levels were slightly higher this was probably a consequence of the $CuSO_4$ application in 1966. These differences were less marked in the grass where lower contents of only Ca, P, K and Na were recorded. The low P content in grass is not thought to be significant as the amounts fall within the normal I.R.S.I.A. range (Table II).

In Table III the changes in fertilization procedure in farm 'Fr', and the resulting changes in fecundity are shown. The changes in soil and grass composition are noted in Table IV. It can be seen that the soil pH has approached that of the neighbouring pasture and that similar increases have occurred in the levels of Ca, K and Na but not of the trace elements. The level of Fe has decreased.

Similar increases were noted in the levels of K, Na, P, Zn, Cu and Pb in grass. Only slight increases were noted in Ca levels whereas the levels of Se and Mn decreased.

The analytical results obtained from 47 samples of soil and grass from five other farms in the same region are given in Table V. They give some idea of the variations encountered in the concentrations of the different elements and also illustrate the problems in obtaining satisfactory reference data. The improvement noted in fertility appears to be independent of the levels of Cu and Mn.

In 1968 we analysed for several elements hair samples collected from animals on the two neighbouring farms. No significant differences were noted but unfortunately, as no results were obtained in 1967, it is unknown whether the changes in fertilisation procedure have had any effect on the hair concentrations.

However, in spite of the limited data available we consider these

475

Table I. *Comparison of soil and pasture composition of farm 'Fr' (poor fertility) and an adjacent farm (normal fertility) in 1967*

GRASS

	mEq./100 g.						p.p.m.									
	SO_4	PO_4	K	Ca	Mg	Na	Zn	Al	B	Cu	Mn	Pb	Fe	Cr	Co	Se
Fr. Farm Annual mean	23·8	39·3	85·2	25·5	13·5	3·6	46·5	78	11·5	10·7	309	6·4	142	2·7	0·95	0·032
Farm in the vicinity Annual mean	24·3	45·1	108·7	29·3	13·3	5	39·2	67	14·3	9·1	250	5·0	137	2·9	—	0·035
Level of significance of the difference between the means	—	+	+	+	—	+++	—	—	—	—	—	—	—	—	—	—

SOIL

	pH		mEq./100 g.				mg./100g.		in exchangeable amounts p.p.m.							
	H_2O	KCl	Ca	Mg	K	Na	P_2O_5	Zn	Al	Mo	Cu	Co	Ni	Mn	Pb	Fe
Fr. Farm Annual mean	5·84	5·28	5·5	0·77	0·53	0·24	10·3	27·2	1328	1·4	5·4	1·6	2·5	112	17·5	460
Farm in the vicinity Annual mean	6·16	5·73	10	0·71	0·68	0·33	9·9	29·0	1121	1·2	4·5	2·0	2·0	317	23·0	792
Level of significance of the difference between the means	+	+	+++	—	++++	+++++	—	—	—	—	+	—	—	++	++	+

− not significant, + $P > 0.05$, ++ $P > 0.02$, +++ $P > 0.01$

The Ni and Co contents of the grass are lower than 1 p.p.m.

Table II. *Mean results of grass and soil analyses for which the differences between the two farms are significant*

	Fr. Farm mean of 3 cuttings	Farm in the vicinity mean of 3 cuttings	I.R.S.I.A. data mean of 3 cuttings in the same region
In grass	mEq./100 g.	mEq./100g.	mEq./100 g.
PO_4	41·7	47·1	41·4
K	82·2	99·5	89·4
Ca	23·3	33·4	37·4
Na	3·75	5·65	7·1
In soil			
pH H_2O	5·97	6·11	
pH KCl	5·43	5·73	
	mEq./100 g.	mEq./100 g.	
Ca	6·15	10·0	
K	0·56	0·68	
Na	0·21	0·33	
Cu	6·16	4·5	
Mn	118	377	
Pb	19	23	
Fe	486	792	

Table III. *Fertility in 1968*

Pasture fertilisers (per Ha)

in 1967	in 1968
600 kg. slag (15−16%P)	1500 kg. kalk (60%)
120 U.K (600 kg. kainite)	2 × 30 U.K (60 kg. KCl in spring and in June)
6 × 150 kg. NH_4NO_3	3 × 200 kg. $NaNO_3$

Fertility at pasture (from May till October)

in 1967	in 1968
$\frac{43 \text{ inseminations}}{13 \text{ pregnancies}} = 3·15$	$\frac{20 \text{ inseminations}}{14 \text{ pregnancies}} = 1·42$

findings to be sufficiently hopeful for us to adopt as a routine method the analyses of soil, grass and animals for all the elements included in the appropriate Tables. We are aware that this approach to the problem of nutritional infertility is limited in so far as we are concerned mainly with changes in pasture. On the other hand we have no proof in every case that there is a correlation between the amounts of the elements in grass and in hair.

Table IVa. *Comparison of soil contents between 1967 and 1968 in farm 'Fr' and an adjacent farm*

| | pH | | mEq./100 g. | | | | mg./100 g. | in exchangeable amounts p.p.m. | | | | | | | | |
	H_2O	KCl	Ca	Mg	K	Na	P_2O_5	Zn	Al	Mo	Cu	Co	Ni	Mn	Pb	Fe
'Fr' Farm																
Annual means in 1967	5·84	5·28	5·5	0·77	0·53	0·24	10·3	27·2	1328	1·4	5·4	1·6	2·5	112	17·5	460
in 1968	6·46	5·60	9·4	0·92	0·98	0·33	8·5	31·7	991	1·2	5·2	1·6	1·5	85	15·9	307
Level of significance of the difference between the means	++++	+	++	—	++	+	—	—	—	—	—	—	—	—	—	++
Farm in the vicinity																
Annual means in 1967	6·16	5·73	10·0	0·71	0·68	0·33	9·9	29·0	1121	1·2	4·5	2·0	2·0	317	23·0	792
in 1968	6·40	5·75	10·4	0·94	0·85	0·20	17·1	34·0	932	1·5	4·1	1·8	3·0	236	19·1	666
Level of significance of the difference between the means	—	—	—	—	—	+	++	—	—	—	—	—	—	—	—	—

— not significant, + P > 0·1, ++ P > 0·05, +++ P > 0·02, ++++ P > 0·01.

Table IVb. *Comparison of grass contents between 1967 and 1968 in farm 'Fr' and neighbouring farms*

	mEq./100 g.						p.p.m.									
	SO$_4$	PO$_4$	K	Ca	Mg	Na	Zn	Al	B	Cu	Mn	Pb	Fe	Cr	Co	Se
'Fr' Farm Annual means																
in 1967	23·8	39·3	85·2	24·5	13·5	3·6	46·5	78	11·5	10·7	309	6·4	142	2·7	0·95	0·032
in 1968	25·0	43·7	100·6	25·9	13·3	8·4	81·5	148	12·5	12·7	165	12·1	212	4·5	1·6	0·021
Level of significance of the difference between the means	—	++++	++++	—	—	++++	++++++	—	—	—	++++	++	—	++	—	++
Farms in the vicinity Annual means																
in 1967	24·3	45·1	108·7	29·3	13·3	5·0	39·2	67	14·3	9·1	250	5·0	137	2·9	—	0·035
in 1968	26·5	49·0	102·0	29·3	13·4	3·9	58·0	128	11·7	13·9	286	7·1	122	4·6	—	0·036
Level of significance of the difference between the means	—	—	—	—	—	—	+	—	—	—	—	—	—	++	—	—

— not significant, + P > 0·1, ++ P > 0·05, +++ P > 0·02, ++++ P > 0·01.

The Ni and Mo contents in the grass are lower than 1 p.p.m.

Table V. *Comparison between the regional mean contents of each element and the mean contents recorded in farm 'Fr' and in the adjacent one in 1968*

GRASS

	mEq./100 g.						p.p.m.									
	SO_4	PO_4	K	Ca	Mg	Na	Zn	Al	B	Cu	Mn	Pb	Fe	Cr	Co	Se
'Fr' Farm	25·0	43·7	100·6	25·9	13·3	8·4	81·5	148	12·5	12·7	165	12·1	212	4·5	1·6	0·021
Farm in the vicinity	26·5	49·0	102·0	29·3	13·4	3·9	58·0	128	11·7	13·9	286	7·1	122	4·6	—	0·036
Regional mean	26·1	46·6	98	26·5	14·7	5·4	71·5	118	11·4	12·5	214	11·0	378	4·7	2·1	0·025
Standard deviations of the regional means	4·4	5·9	15	6·9	2·9	4·7	35·3	148	10·0	7·0	106	9·5	118	1·4	3·6	0·020

SOIL

	pH		mEq./100 g.				mg./100g.	in exchangeable amounts p.p.m.								
	H_2O	KCl	Ca	Mg	K	Na	P_2O_5	Zn	Al	Mo	Cu	Co	Ni	Mn	Pb	Fe
'Fr' Farm	6·46	5·60	9·4	0·92	0·98	0·33	8·5	31·7	991	1·2	5·2	1·6	1·5	85	15·9	307
Farm in the vicinity	6·40	5·75	10·4	0·94	0·85	0·20	17·1	34·0	932	1·5	4·1	1·8	3·0	236	19·1	666
Regional mean	6·48	5·76	7·8	1·00	0·75	0·23	10·8	27·0	817	1·3	3·6	1·5	1·7	123	15·5	440
Standard deviations of the regional means	0·24	0·34	4·2	0·41	0·34	0·18	6·3	14·3	333	1·0	2·4	1·3	1·5	98	6·1	253

All the data from each farm with infertility are compared with the same data from normal neighbouring pastures and the differences examined. A range of favourable results such as this one would enable us to find the significant factors.

Acknowledgements. Supported by 'I.R.S.I.A.' 6 rue de Crayer, Brussels 6. We thank Professor Van de Plasche and Dr De Bruyne who referred the cases of infertility to our attention.

REFERENCES

BIENFET, V., HENNAUX, A., VANDEN HENDE, A., COTTENIE, A., LOMBA, F., CHAUVAUX, G. &. BINOT, H. (1965). *Annls Méd. vét.* **109**, 448.

BIENFET, V., LOMBA, F., VANDEN HENDE, A., COTTENIE, A., CHAUVAUX, G., BINOT, H. & HENNAUX, L. (1965b). *Annls Méd. vét.* **109**, 313.

BINOT, H., LOMBA, F., CHAUVAUX, G. & BIENFET, V. (1968). *Annls Méd. vét.* **112**, 666.

BINOT, H., LOMBA, F., CHAUVAUX, G. & BIENFET, V. (1969). *Annls Méd. vét.* **113**, 101.

DISCUSSION

Hartmans (Wageningen). When studying such nonspecific conditions as infertility it is often difficult to rule out effects due to poor management conditions, the effects if infestation with internal parasites and other complicating factors which may act directly or indirectly. Can I ask what steps you took to study these possibilities?

Bienfet (Brussels). The biggest problem is to choose the area in which to carry out the study and if there is any suspicion of infectious disease, adverse genetic effects on fertility or management problems the area is not selected. Only when such possibilities are ruled out by intensive study, and this may take a year of work, are trace element investigations begun. Even then there are disappointments and it is not unknown for a spontaneous improvement in fertility to occur after the first year of a two or three year trace element investigation. Such research is difficult, but we feel that there is no other way to deal with this increasing problem resulting from intensified production.

Hartmans (Wageningen). Did you carry out tissue analyses to determine the trace element status of your animals?

Bienfet (Brussels). We have started to look for correlations between infertility in cows and the Cu and Mn contents of hair but so far we have found no significant differences.

SOME OBSERVATIONS ON THE RELATIONSHIPS BETWEEN THE FLUORINE CONTENT OF SOIL, FODDER AND BONES AND THE EFFECTS ON HEALTH AND PERFORMANCE OF DAIRY COWS

H. HUBER AND A. SCHÜRCH

Department of Animal Nutrition, Swiss Federal Institute of Technology, Zurich, Switzerland

IN the vicinity of fluorine-emitting industrial plants it is often difficult to decide if any impairment of the health and performance of farm animals, mainly ruminants, is due to F or to other causes. A more accurate assessment of the factors responsible for damage in a region with higher than normal F content of forages is possible only if the various steps between emission, deposition and effect of F in the body are better understood. The results quoted in this paper have been derived principally from long-term observations on 38 farms at different distances from an aluminium reduction plant and also from a 3-year feeding experiment with 12 dairy cows (Huber, 1966).

The analysis of grass, silage and hay samples from the 38 farms revealed average F contents of 20 to 50 p.p.m. whereas the grass and hay fed to the experimental cows in the 3-year experiment contained an average of 44 p.p.m. Higher values were usually found in autumn, with a maximum in October. These values coincided in most cases with a high contamination of the fodder plants with soil. At first we considered such contamination as non-absorbable and therefore harmless. However balance experiments by Gisiger (1967) in Switzerland and by Wöhlbier (1967) in Germany with sheep and cattle showed that the apparent digestibility and the retention of F from soil cannot be neglected (Table I).

Table I. *Apparent digestibility and retention of F from soil and sodium fluoride in ruminants*

Source of F	Apparent digestibility (%)	Retention (% of intake)
F from soil:		
Gisiger (sheep)	17–24	20
Wöhlbier (cattle)	37	32
Sodium fluoride:	81–85	53–58

The differences between the results of the two experiments with soil shown in Table I are probably due to variations in the amounts of F-containing dust deposited and to varying F-binding capacity of the soils. These experiments show that F from soil contamination can be used with an efficiency 40 to 55 per cent. of that of sodium fluoride and is therefore a factor which has to be accounted for when the possibility of a F damage is considered.

In Figure 1 the F intake of the 12 experimental cows during a 3-year period is shown.

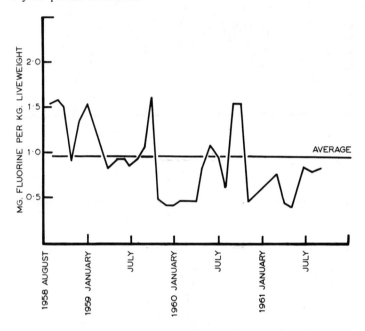

FIG. 1. Average fluorine intake of experimental cows.

The variations over the year shown in Figure 1 are partly due to soil contamination in autumn, to the changeover from winter to summer and from summer to winter feeding and to differences in the stage of lactation. In this experiment the average F intake amounted to only 0·9 mg. per kg. liveweight. Figure 2 shows the F content of faeces and urine compared to that of the feed.

It can be seen from Figure 2 that both curves for the excreta do not follow the curve for the F in the feed. This divergence could be due to two factors. Firstly, the F in the faeces represents

483

mainly naturally-occurring F from plants and soil and not the absorbable part of the F emission which affects mainly the urine, and secondly the F excretion in the urine does not depend only on

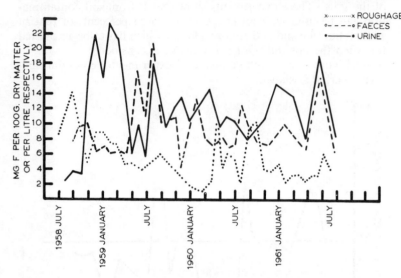

FIG. 2. Fluorine content of roughage, faeces and urine of the experimental cows.

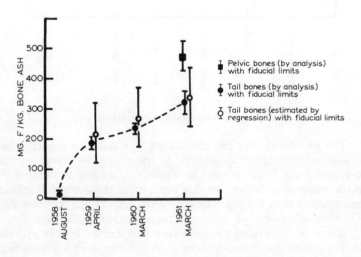

FIG. 3. Fluorine content of bones of experimental cows.

the intake with the feed but also on the F status of the bones. The F contents of faeces and of urine are not reliable criteria for judging intake of emitted F by the animals.

Figure 3 shows the increase in the F content of the bone ash of tail bones sampled by biopsy four times during the experiment.

Due to a higher F content of the feed at the beginning of the experiment and probably also due to a higher capacity for F uptake of the not yet fully mature bones, the F content of the tail bones increased more at the start of the experiment than later. After 2·5 years with an average daily intake of 0·9 mg. F per kg. liveweight, the bone ash reached an average of 3160 p.p.m. in tail bones which about equals the amount in the fat-free dry matter of the pelvic bones.

A statistical analysis of F values in pelvic bones as related to the time the animals spent in the contaminated region and to the distance from the F source, i.e. the F content of the fodder, yielded the relationships shown in Figure 4. The animals were assessed in four groups, those kept less than 3 km. (curve 1), between 3 and 5 km. (curve 2), over 5 km. in the main wind direction from the emission source (curve 3) and finally those kept in a side valley (curve 4) (in this protected valley the animals showed almost normal F values in the bone ash).

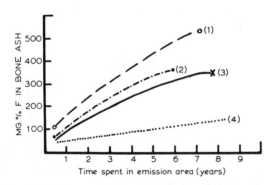

Fig. 4. Fluorine content of pelvic bones in relation to time spent in contaminated region and distance from emission source.

From the results shown in Figure 4 the following highly significant multiple regression equation has been derived (Huber, 1961):

$$Y = (5·51 + 0·09\ X_1 + 2·1\ X_2)^2$$

Y = mg. F in 100 g. bone ash; X_1 = duration of stay of the animals in the emission area in years; X_2 = F content of the ration in mg. per 100 g. This equation shows that the F content of the bones reflects the integrated F intake of the animals more accurately than the F excretion. In addition to the mentioned measurements, observations have been made concerning the health of the experimental animals. At the start of the three-year experiment the animals had between one and three pairs of incisors. At the end of the experiment some of the animals showed slight changes of the I_3 and I_4, characteristic of mild dental fluorosis such as yellow stain, chalkiness, hypoplasia of the enamel and pit. Other symptoms of fluorosis were not detected. Body weights and lactation curves were normal and the offspring, which were also fed the same F-containing forage as the cows, grew at a normal rate.

In agreement with other authors we concluded from these results that F contents of roughage up to 50 p.p.m. daily intakes of F lower than 1 mg. per kg. liveweight and F values in the bone ash around 3000 p.p.m. in 3- to 4-year-old animals can be considered as marginal and do not lead to economical losses.

REFERENCES

GISIGER, L. (1967). *Schweiz. landw. Mh.* **44,** 221.
HUBER, H. (1961). *Z. Tierphysiol. Tierernähr. Futtermittelk.* **16,** 322.
HUBER, H. (1966). Thesis ETH: Zürich.
WÖHLBIER, W. (1967). Alusuisse, Neuhausen.

DISCUSSION

Suttie (Madison). Can you comment on your fluoride accumulation curves for bone and upon your equation relating time of exposure to fluoride to bone fluorine content? Your data show a retention/accumulation curve which is much flatter than that reported from studies in which sodium fluoride has been fed to animals and we have also noted from our work that in field cases the accumulation of fluoride is not as extensive as would be expected from experimental studies.

Schürch (Zurich). During the three years of our experimental study the nearby aluminium factory installed F absorption equipment. The F content of the feed dropped and this may play a part in our results. But I think there is another factor which is of importance. As the F content of bone increases I think that the capacity to absorb further F decreases, possibly in a logarithmic manner.

Suttie (Madison). I agree that this can occur but I still feel that the F levels encountered in field cases are less than one would expect from experimental results. Can I ask whether in your experiments there was monitoring of ambient fluoride levels over a number of years? Can you say what atmospheric fluoride levels were associated with the accumulation of 40 to 50 p.p.m. fluoride in forage.

Schürch (Zurich). Atmospheric fluoride was measured but I cannot quote you absolute values.

FLUORINE IN BONES OF GRAZING ANIMALS IN NON-INDUSTRIAL AREAS

M. K. LLOYD

Central Veterinary Laboratory, New Haw, Weybridge, Surrey, U.K.

TAIL bones were collected from cattle and sheep at knackeries and slaughter houses in the area served by the Ministry of Agriculture, Fisheries and Food, Veterinary Investigation Centre at Bangor, North Wales, in collaboration with W. T. L. Rowlands.

In this area the possibility of aerial deposits containing fluorine from industry is slight. The grazing animals of the area include dairy and beef cattle and sheep.

Fluorine levels in cattle and sheep bones in the United Kingdom of 500 to 1,000 p.p.m. in bone ash were regarded as normal by Blakemore, Bosworth and Green (1948) and Burns and Allcroft (1964) give 100 to 1,500 p.p.m. as a common normal range with an average of about 800 p.p.m.

The sources of F in these bones have been attributed to the 'natural' farm source, such as herbage and other home-grown food, which arises from the soil, to ingestion of the soil itself and to drinking water. Adventitious sources are also recognized, such as F-containing phosphates used in mineral supplements, hay and other feeds contaminated by industrial atmospheres or other sources of contamination.

In considering so-called normal levels it seems reasonable, therefore, to separate the natural sources, due to the soil-plant-animal complex, from the artificial sources where the F arises as a contaminant brought into the farm or deposited on herbage.

487

Figure 1 gives an indication of this division of sources. Sheep feed largely on herbage and home-produced food, and get small amounts of purchased food compared to cattle, particularly dairy cattle. The 59 samples from sheep show a closer grouping in the

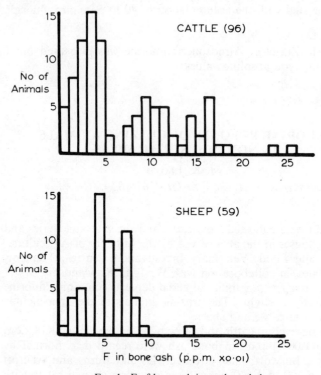

Fig. 1. F of bone ash in cattle and sheep.

0 to 1,000 p.p.m. range than the 96 cattle bones which extend up to 2,000 p.p.m. Over 10 per cent. of the cattle samples exceed the range quoted by Burns and Allcroft (1964).

None of the bones approaches levels at which damage from fluorosis would be expected. Some do approach levels at which tooth staining might be present provided exposure occurred at the right age.

Further enquiries were made at nine farms where the higher levels were found. Ten of the 11 samples from these farms were from animals over 5-years-old (average age 9 years). Age is an important factor in interpreting these results since F accumulation in bone can continue throughout life. The survey is of animals going for slaughter or dying and may not be representative of the whole population. Nine of these 11 animals were milk cows, one was a 13-year-old bull and the last a yearling. They are thus a group more likely to have been fed on purchased and mineral-supplemented food.

All but one was born on the premises or nearby. This is an important point in interpretation since animals reared in industrial fluorosis areas could be brought to the farms bringing their F with them. On three of the nine farms it was the practice to use a mineral supplement in the ration rather than depend on the minerals present in a purchased ready-compounded ration.

Further samples were collected from two of these farms in an attempt to identify sources. On one farm, calf nuts containing 28 p.p.m. of F in the dry matter and fattening nuts containing 16 p.p.m. were found. These would help to account for the bone levels. The mineral supplement contained 220 p.p.m. and used at 3 per cent. in a ration would not make a very significant contribution. On the other farm a cattle nut sample was found to contain 20 p.p.m. and a hay sample 22 p.p.m. This hay was bought in from outside the area. Again these sources would help to explain the higher bone levels. The home produced hay from both farms contained 2 to 4 p.p.m. Pond and stream samples had less than 0·15 p.p.m. These samples indicate that the 'natural' sources of F on these farms are low; they would not be expected to result in bone levels as high as those observed.

It is interesting that on one of the farms investigated in more detail, F from two separate sources, hay and nuts, was present. Although none of the feeds examined would be likely to be a hazard by itself, it is clear that occasionally a combination of factors, each safe in itself, might lead to toxicity.

REFERENCES

BLAKEMORE, F., BOSWORTH, T. J. & GREEN, H. H. (1948). *J. comp. Path. Ther.* **58,** 267.

BURNS, K. N. & ALLCROFT, R. (1964). *M.A.F.F. Animal Disease Surveys Report,* No. 2, part I. London: Her Majesty's Stationery Office.

DISCUSSION

Suttie (Madison). I would like to add a point to Dr Lloyd's comment on sources of fluoride in rations other than those arising from industrial contamination. We have a regulation in the USA that feeds sold shall not exceed 90 p.p.m. in fluoride content. Of 200 samples of commercial dairy feeds we have examined, between 8 and 10 per cent. of these exceeded this figure and some contained up to 250 p.p.m. fluoride. Thus, despite the regulation, some materials high in F do find their way on to the market.

Lloyd (Weybridge). We have the same situation in this country and, although we have no statutory regulations governing fluoride content, feeding stuffs compounders work to a self-imposed limit. We have recently been investigating a case involving pedal bone fractures in six cows in a herd of 100 animals where the mineral supplement, fed at a level of 3 per cent. of the ration, contained over 5,000 p.p.m. fluoride. Like Professor Suttie I suspect that we do not monitor feedingstuff fluoride levels sufficiently well.

METHODS OF ASSESSING THE FLUOROSIS HAZARD TO FORAGE-FED LIVESTOCK

K. N. BURNS

Agricultural Research Council, London, U.K.

INFORMATION obtained during the course of a survey of industrial fluorosis covering 832 farms in 21 industrial areas of England and Wales (Burns and Allcroft, 1964) and during experimental work at one particular farm (Allcroft *et al.*, 1965) provides some basis for monitoring fluorine intake and illustrates some of the variables affecting it.

The F levels in herbage varied greatly at different times on the same farm or even on the same field. For example, on one field of the farm studied in detail the lowest value (as p.p.m. F on the dry matter of the herbage) was 25 and the highest 292. In spite of the variability, however, a seasonal trend was evident, levels being higher in winter and lower in summer. In addition to variation in time there was variation between different types of forage. The F values were highest in kale, lowest in hay, with intermediate levels in pasture and silage.

An inverse relationship between the herbage F levels and rainfall was discernable. It seems likely that rain reduces deposition of F on the herbage and also that, as rainfall in the districts investigated tends to be higher in the summer, the faster rate of growth of the grass at this season has a diluting effect on its F content.

Data over several years showed a fairly close relationship between the F level of the pasture and the mean urine F level of a herd of cows which grazed it (Fig. 1). There were marked fluctuations between different periods but the fluctuations occurred broadly together. Both herbage and urine F tended to be low in summer and higher in the winter. It was notable, however, that

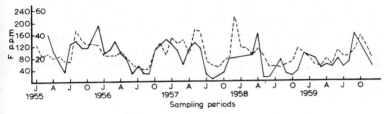

FIG. 1. Relationship between mean fluorine values of monthly a.m. samples of urine from cows and samples of pasture from fields in which they grazed. — — — —, urine; —————, pasture.

in the autumn the rise in urine F levels tended to be greater than the rise in pasture F levels. It is likely that the reason for this was that kale was fed in the autumn and the F level of this was higher than that of the pasture. This emphasizes the point that the herbage/urine relationship can be disturbed by factors such as an intake by the animals of feed (additional to the herbage being sampled) which is either particularly high or particularly low in F.

In fluorosis areas, where economically damaging fluorosis has occurred, the range of herbage F values tends to be from about 60 up to about 200. These figures suggest a threshold level of somewhere below 60. A threshold level of 40 might be suggested as a long-term average as it is consistent with field observations, is supported by experimental results which show that at 40 some symptoms can be observed in some animals, and it is in the middle of the range 30 to 50 regarded as borderline by the National Research Council (Phillips et al., 1960). However, in young cattle and sheep living entirely off pasture at a time when permanent teeth are developing, short peak levels of contamination within a long-term average of 40 might result in dental fluorosis.

Urine F levels rise within a few days of the F intake going up and urine is thus a rapidly responding indicator. Although urine levels show great individual variation, nevertheless, when samples were taken during the survey from a large number of herds a relationship could be seen between urine F levels and the severity

491

of lameness due to fluorosis. The self-contained herds which had dental fluorosis but were not affected by lameness had a mean urine F level of about 10 p.p.m. (corrected to a urine specific gravity of 1·030); this would appear a suitable figure to use as a threshold level.

Bone F levels associated with fluorosis lameness were in the range 4,000 to 10,000 p.p.m. F on bone ash. On a group basis, bone samples are useful as an indication that the animals are at risk from fluorosis lameness but have the disadvantage that the information about F intake is retrospective. Dental lesions in teeth are a very sensitive indicator of a raised F intake but like bone have the disadvantage that they are retrospective indicators.

REFERENCES

ALLCROFT, R., BURNS, K. N. & HEBERT, C. N. (1965). *Animal Disease Surveys Report* No. 2, part II. London: Her Majesty's Stationery Office.

BURNS, K. N. & ALLCROFT, R. (1964). *Animal Disease Surveys Report* No. 2, part I. London: Her Majesty's Stationery Office.

PHILLIPS, P. H., GREENWOOD, D. A., HOBBS, C. S., HUFFMAN, C. F. & SPENCER, G. R. (1960). *The fluorosis problem in livestock production. A report of the Committee on Animal Nutrition.* National Research Council Publication No. 824. Washington: National Academy of Sciences.

DISCUSSION

Fleming (Wexford). You suggested that the increase in F content of pasture during the winter months was possibly due to soil contamination. While this may well be the case it may not necessarily be so. Lead is known to accumulate in plants over the winter period in conditions where soil contamination is absent and I wonder whether in your case you made any measurements of aluminium or titanium which could give evidence of soil contamination?

Burns (London). I think that Professor Schürch has more to say about soil contamination than ourselves; we have tended to ascribe the high winter F contents to slower growth coupled with greater deposition because of weather conditions. It is generally believed that this F arising from contamination lies mainly on the surface of the grass and is not absorbed through the soil and the root. I was very interested in the importance Professor Schürch attaches to soil contamination and I wonder whether he has any criteria by which he assesses this?

Schürch (Zurich). Soil contamination has a great effect on the validity of results for F analysis of herbage and we assessed contamination by the sedimentation method. Usually there is a good correlation between F content and soil contamination but there are exceptions that we can not explain.

Suttle (Edinburgh). Aluminium smelting is about to begin in Scotland in an area where there is already evidence of cobalt deficiency. Can you say whether the toxicity of F is materially affected by the presence of other trace element deficiencies?

Burns (London). There is hypocupraemia in cattle in many of the industrial areas where we have investigated fluorosis. On many of the farms hypocupraemia existed along with mild fluorosis, the animals remained healthy and production was not affected. Where 'ill-thrift' existed this was undoubtedly associated with defects of management, these often not being directly the fault of the farmer. In these areas it is often difficult to achieve good grass-land management because of the poor growth of grass in an industrial area and because units are small. These are all important contributory factors to the development of 'ill-thrift' in areas of industrial fluorosis.

SECTION 9

AN APPRAISAL OF ANALYTICAL TECHNIQUES FOR THE DETERMINATION OF THE TRACE ELEMENTS

President: R. L. MITCHELL

Vice President: C. F. MILLS

PROBLEMS IN TRACE ELEMENT ANALYSIS

R. O. Scott

*Department of Spectrochemistry, The Macaulay Institute for Soil Research,
Aberdeen, Scotland, U.K.*

During this symposium the influence of many elements, including Zn, Cu, Mo, Ni, Co, W, Mn, F and Se, on animal metabolism has been discussed. These are mainly, but not exclusively, metallic elements, and the concentration levels involved are from about 0·001 p.p.m. upwards.

Two aspects of trace element analysis will be considered: the often expensive analytical determination itself, and the even more important problem of contamination of the sample before and during the analysis. Our experience has been largely with spectrochemical techniques. The determination of most trace elements individually is relatively simple and is mainly a question of cost, both of instruments and labour. This cost, and the other efforts involved, can only be justified if the sample reaching the analyst has been controlled throughout the experimental, sampling and packaging procedures.

Choice of Method

The choice of analytical method depends on whether only one or two elements have to be determined in the sample or if multi-element determinations are required. Very few elements at present require to be determined by a specific, single-element method of analysis. Generally, several are, or could be, determined together and numerous instrumental methods have been developed for this purpose. The following enumeration of methods is intended only to indicate some of the analytical techniques available, from the single-element analytical methods to those which are, or could be, employed for multi-element determinations: these involve spectrophotometry, spectrofluorimetry, atomic absorption, specific ion electrodes, flame photometry, flame fluorescence, neutron activation, spectrography, direct-reading emission spectrophotometry, X-ray fluorescence (including micro-probe), spark-source mass spectrometry, etc. When several elements have to be determined in a sample to the lowest possible limits a combination of techniques may often be required.

At the Macaulay Institute multi-element spectrochemical methods are generally employed, but there are two exceptions where very large numbers of samples require to be analysed for Mg or Co.

The determination of Mg in solutions prepared and submitted by other Institute departments is carried out using a laboratory-built direct-reading spectrometer employing porous-cup solution-spark excitation (Scott and Ure, 1958). Magnesium contents in the 0·1 to 6 p.p.m. range are determined, little interference being caused by variations in the Ca, Na, K, Al or P contents of the samples. The other single-element determination is for Co in soil extracts by atomic absorption, using a butane-air flame. This estimates the availability of soil Co to plants and hence to the animals consuming the plant (Ure and Mitchell, 1967).

Flame photometry and atomic fluorescence are usually regarded as single element methods. At the Macaulay Institute two three-channel instruments have however been built for the simultaneous acetylene-air flame photometric determination of Ca, Na and K in the same solutions as those used for the determination of Mg. Although such instruments are not commercially available they could readily be produced in a laboratory workshop. Low limits of determination of other elements are now obtainable by flame methods, using different gas mixtures such as those including nitrous oxide, and by separated flames (Ure, 1969).

Multi-element analysis can be accomplished by many instrumental techniques, the choice largely depending on the limits of determination and the reproducibility required. At the Macaulay Institute such analyses are carried out by emission spectrochemical methods, such as porous-cup solution-spark methods employing a Hilger medium direct reading spectrometer (E750/E498) and direct-current arc-excitation of powder samples, employing either photographic or direct reading techniques. For the latter a large multi-element direct reader has been installed (Hilger and Watts Polychromator, E789) with which some 40 elements can be determined. Sixty-three electronic outputs are available for the 49 analysis channels, and internal standard, background and inter-element corrections, as well as range expansion above the normal concentrations, can be made (Scott et al., 1969). By such spectrochemical methods, with preliminary chemical concentration where necessary, the lower limits of determination are from 10 p.p.m. down to 0·001 p.p.m.

CONTAMINATION

Contamination, probably the most difficult problem in trace analysis, is well known to the analytical chemist but the implications are often not fully appreciated by the plant and animal physiologist. The sources, especially in the plant and animal

498

nutritional field, can be broadly separated into three phases: (1) plant or animal growth experiments; (2) sampling and packaging and (3) analytical procedure. These will be dealt with in more detail later.

It should be emphasized that if a sample has become contaminated during the first two phases the subsequent analysis is not justified and the sample should be rejected.

Plant or animal growth experiments. Some constructional environmental materials must be employed and for strength and rigidity these are often inorganic: metals or alloys, brick, stone, concrete, cement, plaster or glass. Organic materials such as plastics or wood may be preferable for certain studies if they have adequate rigidity and the required corrosion and heat resistance. All materials should be chosen to provide the minimum introduction, as a result of disintegration or corrosion processes, of the elements it is desired to determine and should be checked for undesirable metal content prior to use. Thus, for trace element metabolism experiments, some metallic contamination may have to be accepted; when metals are necessary, the two least objectionable are probably Al and mild or carbon steel. Even these should be carefully chosen as some Al alloys contain up to 4 per cent. copper whilst certain free-cutting mild steels contain lead and occasionally selenium. Copper, brass and bronzes, which contain Cu, Zn and other elements, are usually undesirable, whilst plated materials can introduce Cr, Ni, Cu, Zn or Cd contamination. High-alloy steels, such as austenitic rust-resistant steels should be employed with caution as these contain Cr (8 to 30 per cent.), Ni (8 to 25 per cent.) and Mo and Mn up to 5 and 3 per cent. respectively. Tool and high temperature steels contain other undesirable elements such as Co (10 per cent.), V (2 per cent.) and W (18 per cent.) in addition.

Building materials such as stone, brick and concrete, with the associated cement and plaster, only pose problems if their dust is allowed to contaminate the experiment. The sealing of such surfaces is usually achieved by painting but again a suitable paint should be carefully chosen, Zn, Pb, Al or Ti oxides being common pigments, with Co or other heavy metal complexes as hardeners. Deterioration of such paint surfaces must be avoided.

Natural materials such as wood and rubber are relatively free from most trace metals but manufactured rubber often has a high Zn content. Synthetic plastics should always be tested prior to use since many contain heavy metal catalysts which have been incorporated during the manufacturing process and these may be released under certain conditions, particularly if animals can lick or gnaw them.

Table I. *Some elements present in the ash of various synthetic plastic materials, the contents being shown as high (probably often unacceptable), medium, and low (possibly acceptable)*

	Element content		
	high	medium	low
Polythene			
high pressure: natural*		Si, Mg	Cr, Cu
high pressure: natural*		Mg	
high density: yellow	Ti, Ba, Zn, Cd	Fe	
high density: black		Ti, Fe, Ca	
high density: white	Ti	Fe, Si, Mg	Cr, Cd
expanded foam: white		Si, Mg	Cr, Cu
expanded foam: black		Si, Mg	Cr, Cu, Mn
Polypropylene			
tube: natural	Ti	Fe, Si, Mg	Cr, Mn, Ni, Cu
sheet: natural		Fe, Si, Mg, Ti	Cu
Polyvinylchloride (PVC)			
sheet: grey	Ti, Zn, Na	Fe, Si, Mg	Cd
tube: clear†	Cd	Sn, Mg	
tube: natural‡		Sn	
tape: white	Ti	Zn, Mg	
Methylmethacrylate (Perspex)			
clear		Si, Mg	Cu
white	Ti	Si, Mg, Fe	Cd
black	Cr, Cu	Si, Mg	Ba, Sn, Zr, Pb
Polystyrene			
clear		Zn, Mg	
expanded foam: white	Zn	Si, Mg, K, Na	Cu, Cr, Sn, Pb
expanded foam: yellow		Si, Mg, Na	Cu, Pb, Mo
Polyamide (Nylon)			
rod: natural		Cr	Cu, Sn
Polytetrafluoroethylene (Fluon, Teflon, PTFE)			
rod: natural		Cu, Mg	
aerosol spray	Ti		
Phenolic resin (Bakelite, Tufnol, Paxalin, etc.)			
black	Ti, Ba, Mn, Zn	Cr, Ca, Fe, Mg	Sr, Cd
paper based: brown		Mn, Zn, Cu, Mg	Ba, Sr, Pb
asbestos based: green	Mg, Si	Cr, Ni	Mn, Cu
Silicone rubber			
tube: natural	Si		
Adhesive tapes			
cellulose based: clear	Ba, Cd, Mg	Zn, Ti, Sr	Ni, Cr, Mn, Cu
embossing tape: red	Cr, Mo, Pb	Ba, Na	Sr, Cu, Cd, Sn
embossing tape: green	Cr, Cu, Pb	Ba, Na	Cd, Sn
embossing tape: blue	Ti, Ba, Cu	Mn, Na	Sr

* Different suppliers.
† Cd and Sn water soluble.
‡ Sn water soluble.

Table I indicates some of the elements present in some typical synthetic plastic materials. The same products from different manufacturers can be quite different, as many of the biologically important metals are suitable catalysts in the plasticizing process. In Table I three levels of contents are given: high (probably often unacceptable, greater than 1 per cent. in the ash), medium and low (possibly acceptable, less than 100 p.p.m.). All the phenolic-resin plastics contain many elements, only a few of which are listed.

For trace element experiments, polyethylene, polypropylene, nylon, perspex, fluon and silicone rubber are possibly the most acceptable plastics, but, as mentioned previously, all such materials should be analysed prior to use; for example, one grade of nylon (not listed in Table I) employed for instrument bearings contained MoS_2 as a lubricant. A proportion of some elements in certain plastics is water soluble, for example the Sn and Cd in polyvinyl-chloride tubing.

Elements occurring in greenhouse dust have been reported by Mitchell (1960) and Table II lists these together with an indication

Table II. *Some elements present in greenhouse dust, indicating the possible source from which these may have been derived*

(mainly from Mitchell, 1960)

Elements present	Content	Possible source
Si	major amounts	soil
Al	major amounts	soil
Ca	major amounts	soil
Na	major amounts	soil
K	major amounts	soil
Ba	1500 p.p.m.	paint
Pb	5000 p.p.m.	paint
Ti	4000 p.p.m.	paint, soil
Zn	1200 p.p.m.	paint
Sb	400 p.p.m.	paint
Co	25 p.p.m.	paint
Zr	700 p.p.m.	soil
Sr	700 p.p.m.	paint, soil
Cu	200 p.p.m.	paint
Mn	600 p.p.m.	
Cr	150 p.p.m.	
Ni	100 p.p.m.	metals, paint, fuel
Sn	100 p.p.m.	ash, soil
V	150 p.p.m.	
Y	70 p.p.m.	
La	50 p.p.m.	

of the possible sources. Of these, soil, paint dust and metal corrosion products appear to be the chief sources of the contaminating elements.

Sampling and packaging. After the experimental phase the sample must be collected by an appropriate technique and packaged for submission to the laboratory. Sampling of plant material, for example, should take account of the plant species, stage of growth and the plant part, as mentioned by Burridge (this vol., p. 412), whilst the sampling of biological materials such as blood, livers and kidneys, raises other problems.

All samples must be representative of the experimental material and must be collected and packaged so that no contamination is introduced. Few publications give advice on sampling and still fewer on the problems of the packaging and the transport of samples to the laboratory (Mitchell, 1960, 1963; Winsor, 1957).

The sample should preferably be stored in polythene bags or boxes or in all-glass bottles, and never in glass bottles or containers with metallic screw-tops. As shown in Table I, the black phenolic-resin employed for plastic screw-on covers contains many elements of biological importance. The method of labelling the containers or identifying the samples can also cause contamination, since the red and green ink in glass fibre pens contains Cu and Na and that in black felt pens contains, in addition, Ti, Zn and traces of Mn, Cr, Co, Sn and Pb. Embossing tapes (see Table I) contain many possible contaminants such as Cr, Mo, Pb and Cu. No label should therefore ever be put inside a container in contact with samples.

Table III. *Some elements present in paper storage containers, the contents being shown as high (probably often unacceptable), medium, and low (possibly acceptable)*

(mainly from Mitchell, 1960)

Container	Element content		
	high	medium	low
Brown paper bag	Si, Mg, Ca, K, B*	Cr, Cu, Mn, Ni, Pb, Zn	Ag, Be, Co, Mo, Sn, Sr, Ga, V, Y, Zr
Brown paper bag: lined greaseproof paper	Si, Mg, Ca, K, Ti, B*	Cr, Cu, Mn, Ni, Pb, Zn	Ag, Be, Co, Mo, Sn, Sr, Ga, V, Y, Zr
Brown paper bag: lined bitumen impregnated paper	Si, Mg, Ca, K, V, B*	Cr, Cu, Mn, Ni, Pb, Zn	Ag, Be, Co, Mo, Sn, Sr, Ga, Y, Zr

* Winsor, 1957; Mitchell, 1963 and text.

ANALYTICAL TECHNIQUES

The packaging and storing of samples in paper bags lined with greaseproof paper or composed of waterproof bitumen-coated paper can seldom be justified where certain trace element determinations are required. Table III indicates the possible contaminants which could be introduced from these. Mitchell (1963) showed that a plant sample originally containing 3·5 p.p.m. B rose to 31·0 p.p.m. B after storage for 15 weeks in a greaseproof paper-lined brown paper bag. The B present in paper has probably been added as a fire-retardant or as a roller lubricant, and is present in a relatively volatile form.

Analytical procedure. The preparation of the sample for analysis includes drying and grinding. The drying of a sample is most conveniently carried out in an Al-lined oven at about 80°. Thereafter it is ground either in a steel hammer mill or in some type of agate mortar or ball mill. If the determination of Si or Fe is contemplated, mortars of boron carbide or sapphire can be used. Tungsten carbide, employed for grinding vials and cutting tools, contains Co as a binder and a brazing alloy with Cu, Zn and Sn may also be present. Tungsten carbide mills should therefore generally be avoided and contamination from lubricant-additives containing Mo, W, etc., guarded against.

Contamination arising in the laboratory can usually be controlled. It can consist of dust from deteriorating paint and plaster or the corrosion products from metals. The materials of construction, both for laboratory fittings and for apparatus, should be chosen to provide the minimum possibility of introduction into the sample of the elements it is desired to determine. Many of the contamination problems which can arise during the laboratory procedure have been described by Mitchell (1960), whilst Thiers (1957) has drawn attention to another problem, the possible loss of trace elements by absorption on the surface of glass or plastic vessels. The choice or purification of reagents intended for the determination of trace elements has also been discussed by Mitchell (1964).

REFERENCES

MITCHELL, R. L. (1960). *J. Sci. Fd Agric.* **11,** 553.
MITCHELL, R. L. (1963). In *Analytical Chemistry. Proceedings Feigl Anniversary Symposium, Birmingham 1962,* p. 314. Amsterdam: Elsevier.
MITCHELL, R. L. (1964). *Tech. Commun. Commonw. Bur. Soils,* **44A.**
SCOTT, R. O. & URE, A. M. (1958). *Analyst,* **83,** 561.
SCOTT, R. O., BURRIDGE, J. C. & MITCHELL, R. L. (1969). *Boln Geol. Minero,* **80,** 446.
THIERS, R. E. (1957). *Meth. biochem. Analysis,* **5,** 273.

URE, A. M. & MITCHELL, R. L. (1967). *Spectrochim. Acta,* **23B,** 79.
URE, A. M. (1969). *Proceedings of the International Conference on Atomic Absorption Spectroscopy,* Paper B7.
WINSOR, H. W. (1957). *Soil Sci.* **84,** 389.

DISCUSSION

Mills (Aberdeen). I think this paper has given us all a salutory warning in that what we have often regarded as being a relatively trace metal-free material which we can use for the construction of an environment for experimental animals in fact proves to be far from this. It is obviously fortunate that the trace metals that form a component of so many plastics used in the construction of accommodation for small animals are in such forms that their availability to those animals is limited. At least this is what we assume but I wonder if differences in the trace metal content of plastics used for this purpose might not underly some of the contradictory statements that exist regarding trace metal requirements. Dr Scott's observations will certainly help in the selection of suitable materials for this work.

THE APPLICABILITY OF ELECTRON PROBE X-RAY MICROANALYSIS TO TRACE ELEMENT STUDIES

T. A. HALL

Cavendish Laboratory, Cambridge, U.K.

THE purpose of this paper is to describe the capability of electron probe X-ray microanalysis, especially for applications which may interest workers in the field of trace element metabolism. I shall first review physical fundamentals, discuss the features which are salient for the analyst, then describe a few typical biological studies and finally indicate how the method is used quantitatively.

It must be stressed at the outset that the electron probe is incapable of trace analysis. The instrument provides microanalyses of very small amounts of chemical elements within microvolumes of a specimen, *in situ.* Nevertheless electron probe analysis can contribute to the study of the biological roles of trace elements since there may be local concentrations of a trace element above the limit of detectability, which is of the order of 100 p.p.m., even when the bulk concentration in a specimen is far below this level.

PHYSICAL FUNDAMENTALS

An electron beam is focused into a small spot, diameter usually 1 μm. or less, at the surface of the specimen (Fig. 1). The X-rays characteristic of the constituent elements are excited within the

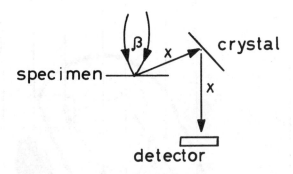

FIG. 1. The fundamentals of electron probe X-ray microanalysis.

microvolume reached by the electrons, which may be restricted to a few μm.^{3} or less. By rotating a diffracting crystal to the correct angle one can reflect the radiation from the chosen element onto the detector (a gas-filled or solid-state counter) while discriminating quite effectively against the characteristic radiations of all other elements.

Most of the basic components of the apparatus are indicated in Figure 2, but this does not show how one places the beam at the desired point in the specimen. The specimen can be moved about by a fine mechanical stage and the beam may be displaced laterally through approximately 1 mm. by scanning coils or plates. To see the point of impact of the beam most modern probes are equipped with optical microscopes with magnifications up to approximately × 600. Alternatively the beam can be scanned over a rectangular area and a varying electron signal (electrons scattered back from, knocked out of, or retained in the specimen) can be used to regulate the brightness on the persistent screen of a synchronously scanned cathode ray display tube, giving an electron image just as in the scanning electron microscope. The beam can then be stopped and positioned with reference to this image.

SALIENT FEATURES OF THE METHOD

1. Specimen preparation can be simple. For example, one can quickly freeze a block of fresh tissue, cut a section in a cryostat,

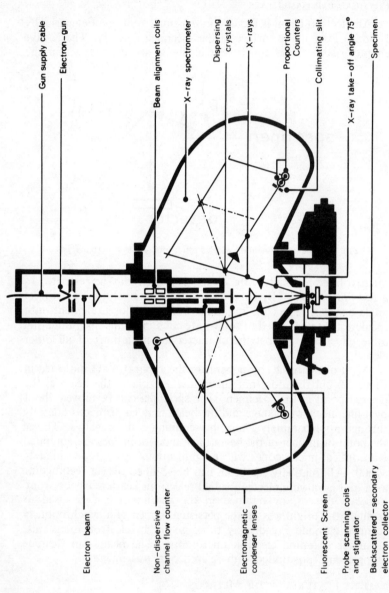

FIG. 2. The main components of the instrumentation (*courtesy of the Cambridge Instrument Company*).

mount the section frozen on a very thin plastic supporting film (collodion, Formvar or nylon) and dry it in a vacuum. At this stage the preparation looks like Figure 3 and the only step remaining before probe analysis is to evaporate a thin coating of carbon or aluminium onto the surface in vacuum in order to conduct away electrical charge and heat. The struggle against contamination is

Fig. 3. A 5-μm. tissue section mounted for probe analysis on a very thin film of nylon (thickness approx. 2,000 Å) stretched over an aluminium tube, diameter 1 cm.

helped by the simplicity of preparation and also by the fact that one analyses microvolumes which can be inspected by optical microscopy or in the scanning electron image.

2. There is no need for chemical pre-treatment and for the sake of the analysis itself there is no need for sections to be stained. (However, it may be necessary to resort to stains in some cases in order to see the specimen well enough to put the probe in the desired place.)

3. The X-ray line spectra of the elements, which depend in an orderly way on atomic number, are simple and virtually indepen-

dent of chemical binding. Consequently there is virtually no interference between lines in X-ray microanalysis and one analyses for elements as such without regard to chemical state. (However, slight 'chemical shifts' are observable at the long-wave-length end of the X-ray spectrum.)

4. The method is non-destructive in the sense that usually no changes are seen microscopically during analysis and the X-ray signals are steady, indicating no loss of constituent elements from the specimen.

5. Spatial resolution is a few μm. or better. For all elements above atomic number 8 the minimum detectable amount of element is of the order of 10^{-16} g. and the minimum analysable local weight-fractions are in the range 10 to 1,000 p.p.m., usually near 100 p.p.m. The last value refers to the specimen as presented to the probe; hence it is a dry-weight value for frozen-dried un-embedded specimens, but the value for the tissue proper is not so good where embedding material is present. (The detectability at very low weight-fractions is limited by the background of con-tinuum X-radiation which is excited by the probe in all elements in addition to the line spectra.) For atomic numbers 6, 7 and 8 the sensitivity is somewhat poorer for a variety of technical reasons. X-ray spectroscopy of elements below atomic number 6 is not prac-tical at present in biological tissues, although very specialised tech-niques are available in a few laboratories.

7. The method is quantitative, as discussed below.

The reader who wants more information about electron probe analysis and its biological applications may consult the extensive review by Andersen (1967) or the book by Hall *et al.* (In press).

EXAMPLES OF BIOLOGICAL STUDIES

Zinc in mammalian sperm cells. There is a surprisingly high con-centration of zinc (1 to 2 mg./g. of dried cells) in the sperm cells of several mammalian species. The localisation of the element within rat sperm cells has been studied by Hall (1966). Epididymal fluid containing the cells was diluted, deposited directly onto thin films like the one shown in Figure 1, and dried. Isolated sperm cells were observed in the scanning electron image and Zn X-rays were monitored with the probe placed at different points along the cells. Especially high count rates were recorded near the junction of the head and the midpiece of the cell. The microvolumes with the highest concentration of Zn contained about 10^{-15} g. of the element.

Still smaller amounts of element are often measured in the combination electron microscope-microanalyser (EMMA) developed from the prototype of Duncumb (1966) and now available commercially. In this instrument the X-ray spectroscopes are attached to the column of an electron microscope and one can analyse microvolumes within ordinary EM sections by looking at the ordinary EM image and then focussing the electron illumination into a microprobe falling on the selected micro-area. Instrumentation of this type was used for the two studies to be described now.

The accumulation of calcium in pre-stages of mineralization. In order to learn about the way in which calcium is first accumulated in tissues which are about to mineralize, Höhling *et al.* (1968) have measured Ca and P concentrations in the cell-free matrix located between the odontoblasts and the mineral dentine in alcohol-fixed embryonic rat incisors. The cell-free matrix is a band approx. 1 to 10 μm. wide. Microprobe assays within this band gave Ca weight-fractions around 3 mg./g. while the P fraction was around 0·6 mg./g., proving that most of the Ca accumulated at this stage was not bound to phosphate.

Calcium in striated muscle. There is evidence that Ca plays a role in triggering muscular contraction and that it is stored in pouches at the 'Z' bands at the ends of individual sarcomeres (Costantin *et al.,* 1965). Microprobe assays have confirmed directly that the electron-dense deposits seen in the pouches in electron micrographs are indeed rich in Ca (Podolsky, Hall and Hatchett, 1970). In this study the tissue sections were 1 to 2,000 Å thick and the probe was confined to a diameter of 0·3 μm. or less, so that the analysed volumes were around 10^{-14} ml. The minimum measured weight-fraction of Ca was approx. 0·7 mg./g. and the minimum measured amount of Ca was approx. 10^{-17} g.

QUANTITATION

In thick specimens the weight-fraction of an element is measured by comparing the intensities of the characteristic X-radiation from the assayed spot and from a standard of known composition run under the same conditions. In first approximation, which is often quite accurate, the weight-fraction is simply the ratio of the intensities from the specimen and from a pure-element standard. In some cases, for quantitative analysis one must employ a complicated but well-established theory of corrections to the first

509

approximation (cf. Andersen, 1967) but the act of measurement still consists simply of recording the X-ray intensities.

In thin specimens, a characteristic intensity is a measure of the local mass per unit area of the corresponding element. To determine weight-fraction one must divide such a datum by a measure of the total mass per unit area. The latter may be obtained by monitoring the *continuum* X-radiation with a counter receiving radiation directly from the specimen (the so-called 'non-dispersive' counter in Figure 2). The theory of such measurements and the means of calibration have been described by Hall and Höhling (1969).

I should conclude with an unfortunate practical note. Microprobe analysis is a hybrid of two complicated techniques, electron microscopy and X-ray spectroscopy. The instruments are therefore extremely elaborate (Fig. 4) and cost £30,000 to £40,000

FIG. 4. A microprobe shown with its electronic components (*courtesy of the Cambridge Instrument Company*).

each. As yet, on a world scale, there is not much probe time available for biology. In addition, it follows from the high spatial resolution of the technique that the volume of material studied per unit time is very small. For these reasons the microprobe should not be used for survey studies but only for carefully formulated research problems. However, I shall be glad to discuss the feasibility of particular studies and the availability of probe time with any interested persons.

ANALYTICAL TECHNIQUES

REFERENCES

ANDERSEN, C. A. (1967). In *Methods of Biochemical Analysis*, ed. Glick, D. p. 147. New York: Interscience.
COSTANTIN, L. L., FRANZINI-ARMSTRONG, C. & PODOLSKY, R. J. (1965). *Science, N.Y.* **147,** 158.
DUNCUMB, P. (1966). In *The Electron Microprobe,* ed. McKinley, T. D., Heinrich, K. J. F. & Wittry, D. B. p. 490. New York: Wiley.
HALL, T. A. (1966). In *X-ray Optics and Microanalysis,* ed. Castaing, Descamps & Philibert, p. 679. Paris: Hermann.
HALL, T. A., RÖCKERT, H. & SAUNDERS, R. L. de C. H. *X-ray Microscopy in Clinical and Experimental Medicine.* Springfield, Illinois: Thomas. In press.
HALL, T. A. & HOHLING, H. J. (1969). In *5th International Congress on X-ray Optics and Microanalysis,* ed. Molkustedt & Gauhler, p. 582. Berlin: Springer.
HÖHLING, H. J., HALL, T. A., BOYDE, A. & VON ROSENSTIEL, A. P. (1968). *Calcified Tissue Research,* **2,** Supplement Paper 5.
PODOLSKY, R. J., HALL, T. A. & HATCHETT, S. L. (1970). *J. Cell Biol.* **44,** 699.

DISCUSSION

Mitchell (Aberdeen). Can you comment on a comparison between the electron probe microanalyser and the laser probe?

Hall (Cambridge). The laser microprobe is much more destructive and spatial resolutions as good as those attainable with the electron microprobe have not been claimed. With great care resolutions down to 15 or 10 microns can be obtained with the laser. The electron microprobe is not destructive and this does enable you to take time to select your appropriate field, and the fact that it gives you a 1 micron resolution is very important if you are trying to investigate cytological structure or if you are interested in narrow bands or areas as we were with dentine.

Schwarz (Long Beach). Am I correct in saying that the differentiation between elements is excellent? How well can you differentiate for example between Ca and Sr or S and Se?

Hall (Cambridge). Ease of differentiation is a feature of difference in atomic number. The differentiation between Ca and Sr is excellent. The use of a diffracting crystal permits the X-ray separation of elements of adjacent atomic number; the only difficulty with separation lies where there is an overlap between the K line of one element and the L X-ray line of another element arising from first and second order diffraction. The greatest sensitivity is for elements having an atomic number between 20 and 40, but other than this the sensitivity is pretty uniform throughout the periodic table.

Hoekstra (Madison). Is the sensitivity limited by physical factors or is there the possibility that sensitivity can be improved in the future?

Hall (Cambridge). The sensitivity is limited by the 'weight fraction' and this is not so amenable to improvement. The 'weight fraction' governs the signal to background ratio and if you go to too low a concentration the ratio becomes hopeless; I doubt if we will ever be able to achieve a better sensitivity than 10 p.p.m. There are good prospects that spatial resolution can soon be improved down to about 0·1 micron as brighter guns become available as these will mean we can put more current into smaller spots. The total *amount* of element determinable in these smaller volumes will be proportionately less.

DETERMINATION OF TRACE ELEMENTS IN BIOLOGICAL MATERIAL BY NEUTRON ACTIVATION ANALYSIS

H. SMITH

Department of Forensic Medicine, The University of Glasgow, Glasgow, U.K.

INTRODUCTION

Neutron activation analysis (Smith and Lenihan, 1964) is a technique which can be applied to the analysis of any material for the total content of one or more of the elements. The method makes use of the properties of induced radioactivity and, as a result, the extremely sensitive detection systems available for estimating nuclear radiation can be applied. The most widely used method of inducing radioactivity is that in which the material under investigation is placed in an environment where there is a large number of free neutrons moving with very low velocity. These conditions are found, for example, in nuclear reactors where there may be as many as 10^{12} to 10^{14} neutrons crossing through an area of 1 cm.^{2} in every second (neutron flux). The majority of these neutrons are usually in the thermal range (low velocity). A few of the atoms of the exposed elements undergo nuclear reactions. The products of these reactions are usually radioactive species of the original element. These radio isotopes then decay to stable

512

forms with the emission of various radiations which can be detected and measured.

The technique is especially applicable to tissue and organic material because the matrix materials (H, C, O, N) do not become radioactive and this reduces greatly the separations required and the possibility of overexposure to radiation.

METHOD AND DISCUSSION

Samples and preparation. All biological materials are suitable for activation analysis. They should be obtained with great care (Smith, 1965) as the high sensitivity makes significant contamination from instruments (scissors and blades) and containers very easy. Generally tissue should be vacuum dried and packed for irradiation in polyethylene or aluminium foil as irradiation conditions allow. If the sample must be irradiated wet, or if very high neutron fluxes $(n/cm.^2/sec.)$ are used, then packing in heat sealed silica ampoules is necessary. As the method is comparative, a known amount of the element under investigation must be packed with each batch of samples.

Irradiation. The choice of conditions depends on the element under investigation, the other major sources of radiation likely to be present and the method of separation, if any, to be used before the final estimation of the radiation. For single element analysis a good general guide is irradiation for one half-life (the time taken for half of the radioactivity from the isotope to decay) or one week, whichever is the shorter. One week is chosen because most reactors base charges on a 1 week unit.

Processing. On return of the material after irradiation there are two techniques available. The first depends on instrumental analysis and the second on chemical separation.

Instrumental analysis makes use of a γ-spectrometer. Most isotopes give off γ-rays of different energy. Basically these can be resolved on a γ-spectrometer and the radiation in one energy band due to a particular element can be estimated and hence the amount of that element present. This technique allows multi-element analysis but at a lower sensitivity than the second technique.

When chemical separation is used in trace element analysis the radioactive samples are destroyed, normally by a wet oxidation technique, in the presence of known amounts of inactive carrier element. This allows chemistry to be carried out on the very small samples (10^{-6} to 10^{-12} g.) of radioactive trace element without much loss. If the carrier is not present and the trace element is below the μg. range then severe if not complete loss on, for example, glass surfaces may be the result. The carrier also allows minor losses in the chemical process to be allowed for when the carrier recovery is found. This method allows the maximum sensitivity to be attained, even with relatively simple apparatus. The sensitivity is often 100 to 1000 times better than that obtained using other methods. Table I shows the sensitivities available at ordinary neutron fluxes. At the moment facilities are available to increase these sensitivities by up to 100 times, using more powerful nuclear reactors. However, the increase in cost is large.

Table I. *Approximate sensitivity by neutron activation analysis*
(10^{12}n/cm.^{2}/sec. *for* 1 *week or to saturation, whichever is the shortest*)

Sensitivity Range (μg.)	Element									
9–1	Ca Fe Pb S									
0·9–0·1	Bi Cr Mg P	Pt Sn Tl Zr								
0·09–0·01	Ag Ba Cd Cs Ce Cl Gd Hf Mo Nd Ni									
	Os Ru Se Si Te Tm Ti Zn									
0·009–0·001	Au Br Co Er Ga Ge Hg I K Na Nb									
	Pd Rh Rb Sb Sc Sr Ta Tb U W Y Yb									
0·0009–0·0001	Al As Cu Ho Ir La Pr Re Sm V									
0·00009–0·00001	In Lu Mn									
0·000009–0·000001	Dy Eu									

Estimation. The radiation and hence the element content of the sample or separated product is detected using either a scintillation counter (γ-rays) or a Geiger counter (β-rays). Geiger-counting is to be preferred as the background count rate is much lower and therefore the sensitivity is greater. The disadvantage is that this can be used successfully for samples containing only one isotope whereas with γ-spectrometry many elements may be analysed at the same time. Once the activity has been found the value may be corrected, if any processing has taken place, by correcting for carrier losses. Thereafter the sample and standard weights and activities are compared to give the final result. If required the absolute identity of the element may be established by examining the physical properties of the radiation. The result can therefore be given with the assurance that no interfering element is being included.

APPLICATIONS

In dealing with problems in general medical, veterinary or agricultural research, where the level of trace elements is important, one of the basic requirements is a technique capable of accurate analysis at all levels. The technique of activation analysis has for the first time made it possible accurately to analyse a complete range of samples. Though γ-spectrometry can be used with great ease and rapidity, where the highest sensitivity is not required the following selection of applications was chosen to demonstrate the use of very simple and inexpensive single element analysis, using Geiger counter detection and ordinary chemical laboratory facilities. Even so the samples may be analysed with surprising rapidity and no loss of accuracy. As an example the values quoted in the first application below were dealt with at a rate of 40 to 50 per day, excluding sample preparation, weighing and irradiation. As a further point of interest it should be noted that all the samples in this example were irradiated at a distance of 400 miles from the laboratory in which they were processed.

The following examples illustrate some of the applications of the technique in research on biological material.

Survey of trace element levels. The basic requirement of any research on trace elements in tissue is an accurate set of normal concentrations. These are often not available or are expressed as less than the limit of detection or vary widely from source to source. As examples of activation analysis applied to trace element studies of large numbers of samples Tables II and III show the levels of copper and arsenic in dry normal human tissue. About 10 mg. of dry tissue was required for each analysis. The tissue was taken from subjects who died by violence and who had no history of any disease. Results of this type are used as reference points for further studies in trace element level changes due to disease or environment. Closer examination of the results show that the distribution pattern for Cu in any tissue is normal and for As in tissue, log-normal. Further work (Liebscher and Smith 1968) has suggested that all essential trace elements have normal distributions and all non-essential trace elements have log-normal distributions.

Microanalysis. Due to the small sample weights required studies of environment and metabolism are easily carried out. The result of trace element deposition and accumulation in different tissues or even in many different areas of the same tissue can be studied. Molokhia and Smith (1967) describe the deposition of several elements in human lung from the environment by way of food and

515

Table II. *Copper in Dry Tissue* ($\mu g./g.$)

Tissue	No. of Samples	Maximum	Minimum	Median	Arithmetic Mean	Arithmetic σ ($\pm$)	Geometric Mean	Geometric σ ($\times \div$)
Adrenal	18	28·9	1·14	5·34	7·36	6·94	5·35	2·24
Aorta	25	21·9	2·44	6·30	6·69	3·93	5·93	1·62
Blood (whole)	5	15·6	4·10	—	9·46	—	—	—
Bone	18	11·8	0·85	2·94	4·24	3·43	3·18	2·19
Brain	21	39·4	13·1	23·2	23·9	6·36	23·1	1·30
Breast	3	8·36	1·35	—	4·55	—	—	—
Hair	29	54·5	7·64	19·1	23·1	11·7	20·6	1·61
Heart	24	22·9	10·1	16·3	16·5	3·68	16·7	1·26
Kidney	23	35·7	5·10	13·2	14·9	6·89	13·7	1·50
Liver	24	46·8	9·21	25·2	25·5	11·5	22·9	1·64
Lung	28	15·9	4·23	10·1	10·5	3·39	9·92	1·43
Muscle (pectoral)	22	13·8	1·95	4·93	5·43	2·82	4·89	1·58
Nail	33	58·2	3·18	14·9	18·1	12·1	14·7	1·97
Ovary	11	16·5	3·08	7·00	8·12	4·17	7·24	1·65
Pancreas	29	20·0	2·37	5·79	7·38	4·65	6·22	1·80
Prostate	9	11·0	1·76	6·58	6·48	2·80	5·80	1·73
Skin	10	5·39	0·29	1·76	1·98	1·69	1·30	2·87
Spleen	24	16·1	3·13	6·03	6·83	2·85	6·38	1·44
Stomach	20	36·6	4·50	11·0	12·6	7·69	10·8	1·72
Teeth	103	39·7	1·59	7·88	10·1	7·84	7·62	2·20
Thymus	3	11·5	3·25	—	6·66	—	—	—
Thyroid	24	17·5	1·63	5·37	6·05	3·22	5·40	1·63
Uterus	13	25·2	3·47	7·05	8·44	6·02	7·15	1·75

σ —Standard Deviation

Table III. *Arsenic in Dry Tissue (µg./g.)*

Tissue	No. of Samples	Maximum	Minimum	Median	Arithmetic Mean	Arithmetic σ (±)	Geometric Mean	Geometric σ (×÷)
Adrenal	22	0·293	0·002	0·029	0·061	0·077	0·029	3·90
Aorta	29	0·570	0·003	0·031	0·063	0·105	0·035	2·85
Blood (whole)	12	0·920	0·001	0·038	0·147	0·270	0·036	7·04
Bone	20	0·240	0·010	0·057	0·080	0·068	0·053	2·74
Brain	19	0·036	0·001	0·013	0·016	0·010	0·012	2·30
Breast	3	0·221	0·030	—	0·095	—	—	—
Hair	1250	8·17	0·020	0·460	0·650	0·698	0·460	2·28
Heart	23	0·078	0·002	0·024	0·027	0·023	0·021	2·69
Kidney	25	0·363	0·002	0·033	0·050	0·075	0·026	3·45
Liver	27	0·246	0·005	0·028	0·057	0·059	0·034	2·84
Lung	56	0·514	0·006	0·082	0·113	0·101	0·078	2·50
Muscle (pectoral)	24	0·431	0·012	0·063	0·091	0·098	0·062	2·38
Nail	124	2·90	0·020	0·300	0·362	0·313	0·283	2·04
Ovary	13	0·260	0·013	0·037	0·071	0·071	0·048	2·48
Pancreas	30	0·410	0·005	0·045	0·088	0·111	0·047	3·16
Prostate	10	0·090	0·010	0·046	0·045	0·022	0·039	1·85
Skin	76	0·590	0·009	0·090	0·124	0·119	0·080	2·77
Spleen	23	0·132	0·001	0·020	0·032	0·035	0·017	3·62
Stomach	21	0·104	0·003	0·037	0·037	0·034	0·022	3·28
Teeth	75	0·635	0·003	0·050	0·070	0·084	0·049	2·31
Thymus	11	0·332	0·003	0·015	0·047	0·095	0·019	3·52
Thyroid	22	0·314	0·001	0·042	0·079	0·085	0·042	3·88
Uterus	23	0·188	0·010	0·031	0·058	0·057	0·037	2·67

σ—Standard Deviation

airborne dust. They also show the interrelationship of the concentration of trace elements in different regions of the same lung (see Table IV) and have made comparisons of healthy lung tissue with neoplasms.

Table IV. *Segmental Analysis of a Lung Pair for Antimony, Arsenic and Copper (μg./g., wet weight)*

Lung Segment	Antimony	Arsenic	Copper
Right upper lobe			
Apical	0·0078	0·018	1·392
Anterior	0·0102	0·018	1·456
Posterior	0·0038	0·010	1·750
Right middle lobe			
Lateral	0·0068	0·022	2·200
Medial	0·0076	0·008	1·770
Right lower lobe			
Superior	0·0080	0·010	1·182
Medial basal	0·0120	0·006	1·730
Anterior basal	0·0058	0·010	1·348
Lateral basal	0·0062	0·012	2·520
Posterior basal	0·0056	0·012	1·276
Left upper lobe			
Apical posterior	0·0108	0·014	1·200
Anterior	0·0098	0·028	1·384
Superior lingular	0·0074	0·022	1·348
Inferior lingular	0·0036	0·016	1·460
Left lower lobe			
Superior	0·0102	0·024	1·160
Anteromedial	0·0068	0·026	1·554
Lateral basal	0·0099	0·038	1·076
Posterior basal	0·0046	0·008	1·780
Mean	0·0074	0·016	1·430

Metabolism of the elements in relatively small animals such as mice (Molokhia and Smith, 1969a) where individual organ analysis is difficult by other techniques, can be studied. It is also possible (Molokhia and Smith, 1969b) to take repeated blood samples from the tails of mice over a long period of time without causing them any discomfort. The sample size is in the region of a few microlitres but this is enough for many studies. An example is shown in Table V where the distribution of antimony between cells and plasma was studied over a period of 16 hours. The average volume of blood removed for each sample was 5 μl.

Submicrogram analysis. The extreme sensitivity is useful when only very small samples are available. Many elements may be measured in tissue samples of 1 to 10 mg. and concentrations in the

518

normal range. Occasionally when the sample size is very small it becomes necessary to push the method near to its working limit.

Table V. *Antimony in plasma and red blood cells ($\mu g./g.$ wet weight) of a mouse taken in repeated 5 $\mu l.$ samples over 16 hours after a single dose (20 mg./kg.) of tartar emetic*

Time	Plasma	Red blood cells
15 minutes	2·35	5·88
1 hour	0·75	2·31
2 hour	0·82	1·29
4 hour	0·61	1·16
8 hour	0·32	0·57
16 hour	0·35	0·33

A recent study of the metabolism of antimony in parasite worms (*Schistosoma mansoni*) by Molokhia and Smith (1968) illustrates this. The dry weight of the parasites is about 60 $\mu g.$ and the parts analysed were in the 1 $\mu g.$ range. The results showed Sb to be present in a concentration of about 1 $\mu g./g.$, i.e. a total sensitivity for Sb of better than 10^{-12} g.

Though the analysis technique is capable of dealing with this work the problem of sample handling is difficult. A balance with a sensitivity of better than 10^{-8} g. is necessary but, more important, is a suitable technique of microdissection. The best method found involved teasing the wet tissues apart on polyethylene sheet under a microscope using very fine silica capillaries through which gentle suction could be applied. By this means contamination is reduced to the very minimum and the wet tissue can be transferred with little difficulty to polyethylene films for drying and subsequent weighing and packing. As dry tissue samples in the $\mu g.$ range are almost invisible to the naked eye and very difficult to handle, this wet handling is essential.

SUMMARY

Neutron activation analysis is a powerful analytical tool which as yet has been applied only to a limited extent in the investigation of trace element in tissue. This is unfortunate because biological materials are the substances which can be analysed most easily by this technique. The equipment required need not be expensive and most applications can be handled in a normal chemical laboratory as the working is simple and the radiation level usually very low.

Added to this is the advantage of great sensitivity and the certainty of identity which is often a problem in other techniques.

REFERENCES

LIEBSCHER, K. & SMITH, H. (1968). *Archs envir. Hlth,* **17,** 881.
MOLOKHIA, M. M. & SMITH, H. (1967). *Archs envir. Hlth,* **15,** 745.
MOLOKHIA, M. M. & SMITH, H. (1968). *Ann. trop. Med. Parasit.* **62,** 158.
MOLOKHIA, M. M. & SMITH, H. (1969a). *Bull. Wld Hlth Org.* **40,** 123.
MOLOKHIA, M. M. & SMITH, H. (1969b). *J. trop. Med. Hyg.* **72,** 222.
SMITH, H. (1965). In *Activation Analysis,* ed. Lenihan, J. M. A. & Thomson, S. S. p. 135. New York: Academic Press.
SMITH, H. & LENIHAN, J. M. A. (1964). In *Methods of Forensic Science,* Vol. III, ed. Curry, A. A. p. 69. New York: Interscience.

DISCUSSION

Smith (Edinburgh). Can you give me an idea of the costs per irradiation?

Smith (Glasgow). The irradiation of a container of dimensions 3 in. by 1 in. for 1 week costs about £15 with an additional handling charge of £15. Using 10 mg. samples 50 to 100 samples can be put into such a container.

Underwood (Perth, W. Australia). Have you used activation analysis for determining Cr in blood? I have recently had to survey published work on the Cr content of fractions of human blood. These results were obtained by a variety of methods and the range is unbelievably wide. Cr is an element that is exciting considerable attention in this field and existing analytical techniques leave much to be desired.

Smith (Glasgow). I have used activation analysis for the determination of Cr in several tissues but the method has the disadvantage that sensitivity is low and the half-life of Cr is long so that unless you use a very powerful reactor the technique is not particularly suitable.

Schwarz (Long Beach). I agree with Dr Smith's comments and I would add that there are other methods that are much more sensitive. Sensitivity varies greatly with the element and for example sensitivity for V exceeds that for Cr by a factor of 10,000 to 1.

Smith (Glasgow). Even with V there are problems which arise from the fact that there the half-life is only about 2·8 minutes and the best chemistry we have been able to achieve in work with V has taken four minutes, so that a lot of sensitivity is lost before you get round to detecting the element. Gamma spectrometry is probably a more suitable technique for determination of V.

Hoekstra (Madison). You suggested in your paper that all non-essential trace elements may have a log-normal distribution and all essential elements a normal distribution and that this might provide a basis for distinction between these categories. Can you say which elements you have investigated and grouped into these categories?

Smith (Glasgow). So far we have done arsenic, antimony, mercury, cadmium, manganese, zinc and copper. The selection of these elements is based upon forensic grounds rather than therapeutic considerations.

Sourkes (Montreal). What techniques do you recommend for the dissection of samples?

Smith (Glasgow). The most critical dissections are carried out using silica chips. Stainless steel instruments, if used at all, should be used once and then thrown away. It is extremely easy to carry contamination from one sample to another by using the same knife and extreme precaution should be taken here.

CONCLUDING PLENARY SESSION

President: SIR DAVID CUTHBERTSON

GENERAL DISCUSSION

Reporter: C. F. MILLS

THE general discussion was opened by Sir David Cuthbertson who invited contributions relating to the work of previous sessions of the Symposium.

VARIATIONS IN BIOLOGICAL RESPONSE DURING TRACE ELEMENT INVESTIGATIONS

Dr Wiener opened the discussion by referring to the many instances during the week in which variability in response had been reported within species in investigations of trace element function and in studies of interactions between the trace elements and other nutrients. He pointed to evidence from his own work with sheep which showed that the critical minimum level for blood Cu below which degenerative changes in the nervous tissue of the offspring arose is apparently under genetic control. He suggested that between-animal variation encountered in trace element experimentation may not always be ascribed to error variation as there undoubtedly existed a component of variation which was due to differences in genetic homeostasis. Dr Mills, supporting this comment, pointed out that Dr Sourkes had demonstrated some years ago that genetic differences existed in the subcellular distribution of Cu in the liver of different strains of rats, some of these differences being extremely large, particularly with respect to the proportion of the total Cu present in the cytosol. Professor Schwarz, supporting Dr Wiener's comments, described work which illustrated that large genetic differences existed between different strains of rat in the quantities of Se required for 50 per cent protection against dietary liver necrosis.

In response to an enquiry from Sir David Cuthbertson regarding the importance of environmental temperature as a component influencing biological response, Professor Schwarz briefly described early work on dietary liver necrosis in the rat, carried out by himself at Heidelberg and by Dr Naftalin at the Rowett Institute, which clearly indicated that both in the rat and the pig there was an optimum temperature range for the development of this lesion. Above or below this temperature range of composition of the diet had less influence on the development of liver necrosis.

Turning to a further aspect of individual animal variability, Professor Kay emphasized that in ruminants it was not uncommon

525

to find large differences in the nature of the population of rumen micro-organisms in animals that were otherwise apparently identical. He suggested that if these extended to differences in the proportions or total numbers of organisms responsible for producing sulphide, this might have profound effects on the metabolism of several trace elements and in particular might account for between-animal differences in the apparent availability and utilization of Cu. The response of rumen micro-organisms to changes in the composition of the diet of the host animal was by no means uniform and this point should not be overlooked in studies of trace element availability.

COBALT/ZINC INTERACTIONS

Dr Forth enquired of Professor Hoekstra whether in his view his studies on the beneficial effects of Co supplementation in Zn-deficient pigs was due to a true replacement of Zn by Co and whether he had any evidence of interactions between Co and the utilization of dietary amino acids. In reply Professor Hoekstra stressed that these observations were only of a preliminary nature. They were carried out on weanling pigs aged six to eight weeks and fed a high calcium maize/soya bean diet. Unless Co or Zn was given growth ceased after four weeks and Co or Zn supplements administered after this stimulated growth, led to a disappearance of skin lesions and to an improvement in the structure of the hair coat. He suggested it was possible, but certainly not proven, that Co may have replaced Zn for some functions, but he stressed that similar experiments carried out with chicks did not demonstrate any effect of Co in the Zn-deficient bird. This difference could be attributed to species differences, to age or to differences in diet and certainly much more work was required before this interaction in the pig could be clearly understood. He had no evidence to suggest that amino acid utilization was in any way affected and there was no evidence that Co supplementation influenced the absorption of Zn at the dietary concentrations used in these studies with the pig.

COPPER/MOLYBDENUM/SULPHUR RELATIONSHIPS

Several participants referred to the discussions that took place in the session on 'Problems in the Detection of Trace Element Deficiency and Excess' regarding the explanation of many outbreaks of Cu deficiency that could not be accounted for either by a low Cu content of the diet or by the presence in the diet of excessive amounts of Mb or sulphate and the question was raised whether or not the search should continue for other possible antagonists to Cu utilisation of either an inorganic or organic nature. Professor Underwood expressed concern lest the assumption should be made that such antagonists would automatically be other major or trace elements and he emphasized the need for a closer investigation of organic components which could have adverse effects upon trace element utilization. He cited as extreme examples the effects of hepatotoxic alkaloids and their influence on Cu poisoning and the profound effects upon mineral metabolism, and particularly upon the metabolism of Cu and Fe, resulting in cases of lupinosis. He expressed the view that far more consideration should be given to such possible interactions in future studies.

SOURCES OF DIETARY COMPONENTS FOR TRACE ELEMENT INVESTIGATIONS

Professor Schwarz described the difficulties that were sometimes encountered in the search for suitable sources of supply of purified components for inclusion in trace element deficient diets and he suggested that the greater part of this problem could be overcome if the bodies responsible for the organization of future symposia of this nature could be induced to compile an index of the sources of such suitable materials. These should if possible include sources of amino acids, carbohydrate components and components for inorganic salt mixtures. A useful purpose would be served if this body could also undertake to hold standard materials for comparative trace element analyses in different laboratories. In reply Sir David Cuthbertson agreed that such action would be highly desirable and suggested that the present organizing and parent committees should make preliminary investigation of the possibilities and submit a report to the International Union of Nutritional Sciences who may be prepared to act as a clearing house for such information.

The Symposium President, Sir David Cuthbertson, then invited Professor E. J. Underwood to present his concluding lecture.

CONCLUDING LECTURE

E. J. UNDERWOOD

University of Western Australia, Perth, Australia

You will notice that the programme does not commit me to a summary of the Symposium; it merely says 'Concluding Lecture'. This is just as well, because about halfway through the proceedings I began to feel like a certain garage operator who was attempting to fill one of those very large automobiles with petrol. After some time he put his head in the window and said to the driver: 'Turn the engine off, mate, it's gaining on me.' This is what happened to me by about Thursday afternoon—the papers began to gain on me.

Perhaps this doesn't matter so much as none of you want to hear merely a rehash of the proceedings—a sort of *Readers' Digest* version of a great book. Rather I imagine you would prefer some comments on the extent to which the objectives of the Symposium have been met and on the most worthwhile impressions which can be taken back for the improvement and furtherance of our own future contribution to trace element research and its applications to animal health and nutrition or human preventive medicine.

Let me, therefore, remind you what the objectives of the Symposium were. They were, firstly, 'to provide a forum in which recent progress in studies of the metabolism and functional roles of the trace elements can be discussed'. And secondly, 'to provide the opportunity for an interchange of ideas between workers investigating these fundamental aspects of the biological function of the trace elements and those whose task is to apply their findings in the fields of nutrition and preventive medicine, both of man and domesticated animals'.

These are, indeed, worthy objectives and I doubt if there is anyone present who would not agree that substantial progress towards their achievement has been made over the last five days. Furthermore, this progress has been made over an exceedingly wide front. Over 160 individuals with widely varying backgrounds and primary areas of interest and expertise, from 23 countries, have come together to listen to and to comment upon 86 papers covering virtually the whole spectrum of research activity with the trace elements. A surprising and disappointing feature of the Symposium from the international point of view was the very limited presentation of papers from Australia and New Zealand, especially in the light of the importance of trace elements to those countries and the considerable contributions they have made.

Equally disappointing, but perhaps not so surprising, was the absence of participation from the developing countries of Asia and Africa. This probably reflects the apparent unimportance of trace elements to the animal industries at their present stage of development and with the other serious limitations to animal health and nutrition which still exist. As these limitations are steadily identified and overcome and as the workers in those countries become more aware of the vastly improved diagnostic, preventive and therapeutic procedures for the detection and control of trace element deficiency and toxicity states now available, we can expect much greater interest and participation from the developing countries in Symposia such as the one now concluding. In this connection it is appropriate to mention that several papers in this Symposium dealt with analytical, diagnostic and control procedures which could already find wide and useful applications in environments well beyond those in which the observations were made. This, of course, is part of the internationalism of science which is one of its most cherished aspects.

The distribution of papers among the different elements is of some interest. Of the total of 86 no less than 20 dealt directly with copper, 17 with zinc and 13 with selenium. The extent of interest and progress with these elements is even more apparent when it is realised that they also formed a part of many of the remaining papers with a wider coverage.

By contrast, only one paper was concerned with iodine and only three with cobalt, if we include the intriguing work of Dr Blokhina of the USSR on the effect of cobalt on thyroid hormonogenesis and the remarkable preliminary work of Dr Hoekstra of the USA, pointing to a synergism between cobalt and zinc in porcine nutrition. Strangely enough, chromium, the most recent of the essential trace elements, was hardly considered at all, except in the introductory lecture and indirectly by Dr Schwarz in relation to his special environmental control 'isolator' techniques for trace element studies. It is clear that these techniques will become increasingly necessary as the search for new essential elements proceeds. In fact it is already being used for this purpose as was evident from Dr Schwarz' paper and from the courageous attempt to demonstrate an essential function for nickel presented by Dr Ullrey.

It is always invidious to select particular papers for special commendation but I don't think anyone will quarrel with me if I mention at this point the very revealing paper of Drs Wiener and Field on genetic variation in copper metabolism in sheep. We have long accepted species differences in nutritional studies. As someone once said 'all men are not guinea-pigs and only a few are rats'. What we have now to appreciate, nutritionally speaking, is that all sheep are not sheep, or at least not sufficiently so to allow confident extrapolation from one genetic group to another. It is to be hoped that this work with copper will be extended to other elements and will be followed by further studies designed to identify the actual physiological mechanisms which are genetically controlled. In any case we must now consider the possibilities of genetic variations in animal populations as factors in some of the inexplicable 'area' differences in the incidence of trace element deficiencies and excesses known to exist and considered by several speakers in this Symposium.

A great service was done to us all by Dr Mills and Dr Suttie in their papers drawing attention to the profound importance of food consumption patterns in metabolic studies with trace elements and to the erroneous conclusions that can be drawn from reliance upon the simple, paired-feeding technique. I have the feeling that Dr Suttie will be receiving numerous enquiries for the details of his ingenious automatic feed dispenser and the 'little black box' that goes with it.

May I also comment upon the paper by Drs Thornton and Webb on 'Geochemical Reconnaissance and the Detection of Trace Element Disorders in Animals'. I found this particularly stimulating and encouraging partly because it lies so far outside the scope and knowledge of most of us and partly because of the reported correlation of the results of the examination of stream sediments with the incidence of clinical evidence of trace element disorders in animals. This is remarkable considering the many variables interposed between the sediments and the grazing animal. It suggests that we have here the beginnings of a technique with predictive possibilities which could become of great value in many other parts of the world.

A further area of particular importance to the future is that concerned with trace element requirements and availability. Several speakers made it abundantly clear that studies of trace element deficiencies and toxicities based on the gross intakes of a single element can be seriously misleading, both because of the host of other elements and other organic complexes that can affect absorption and utilisation and because the chemical combination in which the element in question exists within feeds, or in which it is presented to animals, also greatly influences absorption and utilisation. This was apparent from the papers presented by Drs Hoekstra, Kirchgessner, Van Campen and Matrone and from those by Drs Bremner and Hartmans. In my view this is one of the most significant areas for future trace element research. The precise nature of the biochemical and physiological mechanisms involved in such trace element interactions, and of the chemical combinations in which they exist in foods in relation to availability, present some of the most challenging and potentially rewarding aspects of trace element research.

These odd speculations should not minimize or obscure an overall impression of satisfactory, even striking, progress over a wide front. This was equally evident in the many fine papers concerned with the basic biochemical mechanisms at the cellular or tissue level and in those dealing with more practical clinical applications under field conditions. Participation in this Symposium should ensure that such progress will continue at an enhanced and more informed level, both as an outcome of the formal papers and discussions and from the more informal discussions and contacts made and from the many old friendships which have been cemented and the new ones that have been made. We have had the opportunity to meet and hear colleagues from a wide variety of disciplines working with trace elements in rocks and soils and plants to animals and man, from geochemistry and genetics to enzymology, applied nutrition and clinical medicine. For most of us this combination of breadth and depth has been a unique experience from which we must surely emerge more competent to tackle our own immediate problems and more aware of the variety of approaches that can be be made and are being made towards the achievement of our common goal. This goal may not be as spectacular as that of some of our colleagues in the physical sciences as a result of whose efforts three brave men are now speeding to the moon, but it can hardly be more worthy, since we are concerned with the improvement of the nutrition of man and his physical and mental well-being upon this earth.

I feel that I would be doing less than my duty if I did not express on your behalf our deep appreciation to Dr Mills and his colleagues on the Organizing Committee of their enterprise, efficiency and friendliness in making this first International Symposium possible and in ensuring that it has run smoothly and successfully. It has been said that the only resolution ever carried unanimously at any International Conference is one affirming the need for another one in the near future. I hope that this Symposium will be no exception. All those in favour of a second International Symposium on Trace Element Metabolism in Animals say 'Aye'.

Carried unanimously.   531

BUSINESS MEETING

At the conclusion of Professor Underwood's address a short business meeting was held to consider the possibility of organizing future symposia. The following proposals from participants were considered:

1. That future symposia on the topic of trace element metabolism in animals should be held.

2. The interval between meetings should be from three and a half to four years.

3. That participation in future symposia should continue to be by invitations issued to workers actively concerned with the topics under discussion to maintain the present character of the meeting.

4. That an International Guiding Committee should be constituted to select locations for future meetings and to advise the local organizing committee formed in each host country.

5. That the International Council of Scientific Unions should be advised of forthcoming symposia and that sponsorship of each symposium should be sought from the National Academy of Science of each host country.

These proposals were unanimously approved.

There being no further business the President closed the Symposium with a vote of thanks to participants and to the Local Organizing Committee.

INDEXES

INDEX OF AUTHORS AND DISCUSSION PARTICIPANTS

Figures in bold type refer to contributed papers

SUBJECT INDEX

539

Tocopherol, metabolism, in sheep and foetus, 272
    relations with selenium and nonhaem iron proteins, 196
    role in metabolism of organic selenium, *in vitro*, 212
Trace elements, deficiency, detection in field, 441
      experimental problems, 39
    effect on copper absorption, 290
    effect on dental caries, 90
    estimation, contaminants, diet, 28, 36
      contamination, 497
      electron probe, 504
      laser probe, 511
      methods and conditions, 7, 25
      neutron activation analysis, 512
      problems, 497
      sterile unit, 26
    imbalance in aetiology of endemic goitre, 427
    in browse for wild mammals, 416
    in hair, in infertility, cattle, 474
    in herbage, and soil, 410
      effect of species and maturity, 412
      relation to copper deficiency, cattle, 444
      relation to infertility, cattle, 474
    in lichens, importance to reindeer, 380
    in soil, disorders in livestock, geochemical detection, 385, 397
      effect on organisms and food chain, 385
      geology for assessment, 397
      relation to copper deficiency, cattle, 444
    in wool, effect of copper deficiency, sheep, 454
    interactions in absorption, 283, 317
    metabolism, absorption, and retention, effect of age and sex, rat, 80
      effect of chlortetracycline, pig and poultry, 284
      effect of environmental temperature, cattle, 50
      interactions of cadmium, zinc, copper and iron, man, laying hen and ruminants, 317
    mode of action, 15
    problems in health and nutrition, man, 9
    requirements, unidentified, 25, 38
    role in enzyme activity, rat, 17
    role in nucleic acids, rat, 18
    studies, biological variations, 525
      diets, 527
    unidentified factor G in metabolism, 38
Tungsten, distribution in tissues, pig and sheep, 71
    metabolism, excretion, effect of route of administration and diet, pig and sheep, 70
    pig and sheep, 70

Unidentified factor G in trace element investigations, 38
Urate oxidase, in liver and kidney, effect of copper and molybdenum, rat, 176
Uronic acid, in egg-shell, effect of manganese and phosphorus in diet, laying hen, 138

SUBJECT INDEX

Zinc, metabolism (cont.)
    role of pancreas, dog, 78
    ruminants, 232, 374
  requirement, sex difference, pig, 377
  role in protein synthesis, man, 84
  role in wound healing, 75, 81, 84
  status, contents in blood serum and bone, rat, 471